MARINES AND MILITARY LAW IN VIETNAM: TRIAL BY FIRE

by
Lieutenant Colonel Gary D. Solis
U.S. Marine Corps

HISTORY AND MUSEUMS DIVISION
HEADQUARTERS, U.S. MARINE CORPS
WASHINGTON, D.C.

1989

Volumes in the Marine Corps Vietnam Series

Operational Histories Series

U.S. Marines in Vietnam, 1954-1964, The Advisory and Combat Assistance Era, 1977

U.S. Marines in Vietnam, 1965, The Landing and the Buildup, 1978

U.S. Marines in Vietnam, 1966, An Expanding War, 1982

U.S. Marines in Vietnam, 1967, Fighting the North Vietnamese, 1984

U.S. Marines in Vietnam, 1969, High Mobility and Standdown, 1988

U.S. Marines in Vietnam, 1970-1971, Vietnamization and Redeployment, 1986

In Preparation

U.S. Marines in Vietnam, 1968

U.S. Marines in Vietnam, 1971-1973

U.S. Marines in Vietnam, 1973-1975

Functional Histories Series

Chaplains with Marines in Vietnam, 1962-1971, 1985

Anthology and Bibliography

The Marines in Vietnam, 1954-1973, An Anthology and Annotated Bibliography, 1974, reprinted 1983; revised second edition, 1985

Library of Congress Card No. 77-604776
PCN 190 003105 00

For sale by the Superintendent of Documents, U.S. Government Printing Office
Washington, D.C. 20402

Foreword

This is the second of a series of functional volumes on the Marine Corps' participation in the Vietnam War, which will complement the nine-volume operational and chronological series also underway. This particular history examines the Marine Corps lawyer's role in Vietnam and how that role evolved. Also considered is the effectiveness of the Uniform Code of Military Justice in a combat environment.

Military law functioned in Vietnam, but was it acceptably efficient and effective? There were several thousand courts-martial tried by the 400 Marine Corps lawyers who served in Vietnam. Those trials stand as testament to the Marines, officer and enlisted, who made the justice system yield results through their work, dedication, and refusal to allow the circumstances of Vietnam to deter them.

Did the military justice system really work? The reader can be the judge, for both successes and failures are depicted here. This book presents a straightforward and unflinching examination of painful subjects. Marine lawyers in Vietnam came to legal grips with drug use, racism, fragging, and the murder of noncombatants, along with the variety of offenses more usually encountered. The Marine Corps can take pride in the commanders and the judge advocates who ensured that whenever those crimes were discovered they were exposed and vigorously prosecuted. There were no cover-ups; no impediments to the judge advocates who conscientiously represented the accused or the United States.

To study the military lawyer is to examine the military criminal. Reprehensible acts and unsavory individuals are described here. The outcomes of some cases are shocking and dismaying. But while verdicts cannot be ordered, the cases were always brought to trial.

The author, Lieutenant Colonel Gary D. Solis, was first in Vietnam in 1964 as an amphibian tractor platoon commander. He returned there in 1966-67, when he commanded Headquarters and Service Company, and then Company A, 3d Amphibian Tractor Battalion. He later received his law degree from the University of California at Davis and a master of laws degree in criminal law from George Washington University. He was chief trial counsel of the 3d Marine Division on Okinawa in 1974, then of the 1st Marine Division at Camp Pendleton in 1975-76. Later, he was the staff judge advocate of Headquarters Fleet Marine Force, Atlantic, and head of the Military Law Branch, Judge Advocate Division. He served two tours as a general court-martial judge and is a member of the bar of three states and the District of Columbia. He is a past secretary of the Marine Corps Historical Foundation and a member of the Supreme Court Historical Society. He served with the History and Museums Division from August 1986 to June 1989, when he retired from active duty.

E. H. SIMMONS
Brigadier General, U.S. Marine Corps (Retired)
Director of Marine Corps History and Museums

Introduction

The war in Vietnam has long since passed from the headlines to the history books, yet the many issues it raised have only slightly receded, and the controversy barely at all.

The functioning of the military justice system in that war—the practice of criminal law on the battlefield—is one of those issues, and the controversy sparked by it is far from being extinguished. To the contrary, that system's increasing "civilianization" by statutory and appellate law keeps the ember alive, potentially to flame anew to bedevil our commanders in the next war.

But, as with so many such issues, the debate is conducted with little fact intruding on the rhetoric. This volume goes a long way toward remedying that omission. In it are assembled the recollections, reflections, and accumulated wisdom of those charged with making that system—a relatively primitive version of today's—work in Vietnam.

What a curious group it was: The senior leadership of Marine Corps lawyers (they would not be titled "judge advocates" until well past halfway in the war) was predominantly combat officers, who had served in World War II and Korea in "line" billets, and who had later come into the legal field. The "worker bees," the trial and defense counsel, were almost exclusively first-tour Reservists, many only recently removed from the hotbeds of antiwar activism which their college campuses had become. A surprisingly thin cushion of mid-career lawyers filled the interface.

Yet differences of background and of such temperament and philosophy as existed were submerged, for in its essential construct, the law is the great unifier of peoples and societies. And thus it was too for our lawyers in Vietnam: the single focus of this diverse group and of their common effort was to make the system "work." We each must draw our own conclusion concerning their success or failure.

However, to read this volume only to resolve such weighty questions is to overlook much of its worth. It also tells an interesting story—as well it should. For writing history is much like preparing a difficult and complicated case for trial. One must conduct thorough research, interview many witnesses, visit the scene of the crime, develop a theory of the case, marshal the facts persuasively to support it, and finally, present the results of all this effort in a manner that will hold the listener's attention.

Accordingly, when we conceived the idea of an official history of the activities of Marine Corps judge advocates in Vietnam, we looked for an officer who excelled as a trial advocate and who had fought in Vietnam. We found one in the author, Lieutenant Colonel Gary D. Solis.

As this volume attests, we made a good choice. Because he has been both a combat officer and a judge advocate, Lieutenant Colonel Solis brought to this effort a unique perspective. He also brought to it a talent for research and writing, which I think has resulted in not only an outstanding piece of scholarship, but also a compelling and unusual piece of literature.

MICHAEL E. RICH
Brigadier General, U.S. Marine Corps
Director, Judge Advocate Division

Preface

"In the Armed Forces, as everywhere else, there are good men and rascals, courageous men and cowards, honest men and cheats."

Ball et al. v. United States
366 U.S. 393, 401 (1961)

Of the 448,000 Marines who served in Vietnam, only a small percentage came into contact with the military justice system. By far the greater number served honorably and never committed illegal or improper acts. But in a book about lawyers and military law—a criminal justice system—the focus is necessarily upon criminals as well as lawyers.

In this volume a number of cases are recounted in which the accused escaped punishment or even trial, despite clear indications of guilt. Military law, like civilian criminal law, demands proof of guilt beyond a reasonable doubt for a conviction. When the government falls short of that high standard, for whatever reason, the accused must go free. Occasionally that results in a seeming miscarriage of justice. Recounting such cases may illustrate the workings of the system and make for interesting reading, but they were not the norm. The reader should not be misled into thinking that most Marines were criminals, nor that most, or even many, courts-martial ended in acquittal.

This book relates events that occurred in Vietnam, with only that description of incidents in the U.S. and elsewhere as necessary to explain the evolution of the Marine Corps' Judge Advocate Division and to describe a few wartime cases tried in the U.S. There is little mention of the significant support provided Vietnam lawyers by judge advocates on Okinawa, in Japan, and in the United States. Nor is distinction made between Reserve and regular officers; such distinctions were ignored in the combat zone. The grades used in the body of the text are those held by individuals at the time they are mentioned.

Court-martial cases are described to the exclusion of nonjudicial punishment. Although NJP was the commander's most immediate and most frequently employed disciplinary tool, it does not usually involve lawyers, it is reserved for minor offenses, and no detailed records of its employment are kept.

Not all participants will agree with everything I have written. The voice of memory is single and uncontested and tends to rigidify with time. History, on the other hand, allows many voices, is open to debate and calls for revision. Still, all history is an interpretation, and I have doubtless made mistakes. I alone am responsible for the text and any errors found there.

The history of Marine Corps lawyers in Vietnam is based on more than official records, books, records of trial, journals, and newspapers. Hundreds of letters to and from the lawyers who served in Vietnam have resulted, I believe, in a uniquely personal view of the events of that period which no official source can impart. I thank those who contributed so much through their responses to repeated inquiries, notably Colonels Clarke Barnes, Pete Kress, Charlie Larouche, Mike McCollum, and former Captains Tone Grant and Chuck Kall. Also, Mr. Denzil D. Garrison was unfailingly helpful. Almost a hundred reviewers, most of whom served in Vietnam, read a draft of the manuscript. Their comments were indispensable and where applicable are incorporated into the text.

Thanks are due Mrs. Pat Amenson and her predecessor, Mrs. Ellen Burkett, of the

Promulgation Section, Office of the Judge Advocate General of the Navy. They lent vital support in locating obscure records of trial.

No history volume has a single author. Colonel W. Hays Parks began this project some 10 years ago. The questionnaire he developed and the letters he collected were critical foundations for my research. Major Leonard A. Blaisol's perceptive critiques of draft chapters were invaluable. Mr. Jack Shulimson, Histories Section head, and Mr. Henry I. Shaw, Jr., Chief Historian of the History and Museums Division, were patient mentors who willingly imparted their experience and expertise.

Thanks to Brigadier General Michael E. Rich, Director of the Judge Advocate Division and friend of many years, who conceived the idea for this book. He was my harshest critic, strongest support, and most perceptive editor.

Finally, this volume is dedicated to Mrs. Carolyn Faye W. Marshall, personal secretary to every director of the Judge Advocate Division since its formation in 1968, and secretary to the Head, Discipline Branch, before that. Besides her encyclopedic memory, good humor, and always willing assistance, her long and dedicated service to the Marine Corps and its lawyers are without parallel. She is a wonderful person and we are proud to know her.

GARY D. SOLIS
Lieutenant Colonel
U.S. Marine Corps

Table of Contents

Foreword iii
Introduction v
Preface vii
Table of Contents ix

PART I FROM GENESIS TO VIETNAM 1

Chapter 1 Origins of Military Law and Marine Corps Lawyers 2
   Ancient Roots 2
   Beginnings: Army Courts, Naval Boards 3
   World War II and Beyond: Military Justice is to Justice
      as Military Music is to Music 4
   The Uniform Code of Military Justice, 1950: Old Ills Redressed 5
   Continuing Tension: Justice Versus Discipline 7
   The Death Penalty in the Armed Forces: Yes But No 7
   Marine Corps Lawyers: From The Line to Discipline Branch 8
   In Support: Navy Lawyers 11
   In Support: Headquarters Marine Corps 13
   The Pentalateral Agreement: Diplomatic Riflemen 14
   Military Law Comes to Vietnam 15
   A Beginning 17
Chapter 2 1965: 3d Marine Division and 9th MEB Open Shop 18
   From a Lawyer's Case File: One Homicide, Two Victims 23
   Trying Cases 24
   III MAF: Headquarters Without Lawyers 27
   1st Marine Aircraft Wing: Touching Down 28
   Legal Duty in a Combat Zone: Problems 29
   From a Lawyer's Case File: The Marine Corps' First War Crime
      Conviction in Vietnam 32
   Perspective 34
Chapter 3 1966: Building on Sand 35
   Trying Cases: Using 'The Red Book' 35
   From a Lawyer's Case File: Pilot to Copilot to Brig 37
   The Other Prisoners: North Vietnamese POWs 39
   The 1st Marine Division Arrives: More Lawyers, More Cases 40
   Force Logistic Command: New Guy on the Block 42
   Trying Cases 45
   Courtroom Personnel: Just Passin' Through 51
   Homicide on Patrol: Men, Women, and Children 53
   3d Marine Division: On The Road Again 54
   III MAF: Double-Hatting The Lawyer 55
   Perspective 56

PART II BUILD UP AND CONSOLIDATION 58

Chapter 4 1967: Trying Times.. 59
  III MAF: Double-Hatted Twice.. 60
  1st Marine Division: Rising Caseloads, More Lawyers........................ 63
  3d Marine Division: More Combat, Fewer Courts.............................. 65
  Force Logistic Command: Continue to March.................................. 68
  1st Marine Aircraft Wing: Much Like Home................................... 69
  From a Lawyer's Case File: Psychiatry and Appellate Review................. 70
  Project 100,000: Prelude to Problems....................................... 73
  Drugs: Recognizing the Problem... 74
  Transportation: Hitchhiking to Court....................................... 75
  Trying Cases... 76
  Marine Corps Lawyers in Combat: They Also Serve............................ 82
  The First Lawyer General Officer: No Immediate Change...................... 83
  Perspective.. 84
Chapter 5 1968: High Tide... 88
  1st Marine Division: Lawyers in the Storm's Eye............................ 89
  3d Marine Division: Every Marine a Rifleman................................ 91
  1st Marine Aircraft Wing/Force Logistic Command: Doing Time at Da Nang.. 96
  From a Lawyer's Case File: Civilian Court-martial.......................... 99
  Drugs: 'High' Tide...103
  Trying Cases...104
  Trial Under Fire: Khe Sanh Court...106
  Legal Assistance, Claims, Reviews: Someone Has To Do It....................109
  Fragging: Friendly Fire With Malice..110
  Homicide on Patrol: Nothing Hidden...111
  III MAF Brig Riot: Prisoner's Kangaroo Courts..............................114
  Perspective..119

PART III WINDING DOWN...123

Chapter 6 1969 Preamble: Discipline in Disarray...............................124
  The Military Justice Act of 1968: Evolutionary Fine-Tuning.................124
  Marijuana: Persons of Ill Repute...126
  Racial Conflict: Black, White, and Green...................................127
  Administrative Discharge: The Right Fix....................................131
  Fragging: Killers In Our Midst...133
  From A Lawyer's Case File: Murder of a Company Commander...................134
  Real or Imagined: The 'Mere Gook' Rule.....................................138
  Perspective..140
Chapter 7 1969: Military Justice Tested.......................................142
  III MAF: No Longer Two Hats..142
  1st Marine Division: The Law Center Concept................................142
  3d Marine Division: More Combat, Fewer Courts..............................147
  From a Lawyer's Case File: Murder on Stage.................................148
  1st Marine Aircraft Wing: Looking For Action...............................151
  Force Logistic Command: Approaching Breakdown..............................156
  Trying Cases...159
  Exits: Marine Corps Draw Downs...162
  Perspective..164
Chapter 8 1970-71 Preamble: Discipline in Disarray............................167
  Civilians at Courts-martial: Latney Reversed...............................167

 Fragging: Killers in Our Midst..168
 From a Lawyer's Case File: Criminal-Criminologist........................169
 Drugs: Marijuana and More..170
 Racial Conflict: High Tension..171
 Administrative Discharge: The Marines Clean House.....................171
 From a Lawyer's Case File: Homicide on Patrol...........................174
Chapter 9 1970-71: Redeployment...191
 Force Logistic Command: Playing Catch-Up................................191
 From a Lawyer's Case File: The Defense Wins Four.......................193
 1st Marine Aircraft Wing: Prepared for Takeoff.............................196
 1st Marine Division: New Broom..196
 Trying Cases..202
 Last Call for Combat..208
 Closing Cases Versus Best Defense...208
 The Last Marine Lawyer Out...212
 Perspective...216

PART IV AFTERMATH AND ECHOES...217

Chapter 10 Prisoners of War, and Others...218
 Prisoner Misconduct: Charges...218
 From a Lawyer's Case File: Wartime Acts, Post-War Trial.................221
 Deserters in the Hands of the Enemy..223
 White VC?: Robert R. Garwood...223
Chapter 11 Mopping Up..231
 Drugs, Race, Dissent: Same Problems, New Venues.......................231
 Vietnam Finale: Bien Hoa and the Rose Garden...........................232
 Perspective...240
 The Uniform Code of Military Justice: Did It Work in Vietnam?.........241
 Summation...244

NOTES..245

APPENDICES
 A. Marine Corps Lawyers, Navy Law Specialists, and Naval Service
  Judge Advocates who Served as Lawyers in Vietnam..................269
 B. Staff Legal Officers/Staff Judge Advocates in Vietnam..................274
 C. U.S. Medals Awarded Marine Corps Lawyers
  and Judge Advocates for Vietnam Service.............................275
 D. Cases Cited..278
 E. Review of Confinement Adjudged in Cases of Marines Convicted
  of the Murder of Vietnamese Noncombatants, 1965-71...............280
 F. Confinement Actually Served in Selected Cases of Marines Convicted
  of the Murder of Vietnamese Noncombatants, 1965-71...............282
 G. Senior Marine Corps Lawyers, 1950 to 1966.............................283
 H. Heads of Discipline Branch and Directors of the
  Judge Advocate Division, 1950 to 1988................................284
 I. List of Reviewers...286

INDEX..288

PART I
FROM GENESIS TO VIETNAM

CHAPTER 1
Origins of Military Law and Marine Corps Lawyers

*Ancient Roots—Beginnings: Army Courts, Naval Boards—World War II and Beyond:
Military Justice is to Justice as Military Music is to Music—The Uniform Code of Military Justice, 1950:
Old Ills Redressed—Continuing Tension: Justice Versus Discipline—The Death Penalty in the Armed Forces:
Yes But No—Marine Corps Lawyers: From The Line to Discipline Branch—In Support: Navy Lawyers
In Support: Headquarters Marine Corps—The Pentalateral Agreement: Diplomatic Riflemen
Military Law Comes to Vietnam—A Beginning*

Captain Peter N. Kress arrived in Vietnam a little after noon on 8 March 1965. He carried a seabag, a *Manual for Courts-Martial*, a JAG Manual, and a yellow legal pad.* He was the first Marine Corps lawyer assigned legal duty in Vietnam. Three hours earlier that day, at 0903, elements of the 9th Marines were the first ashore in a major escalation of the war. At the same time, Air Force C-130s carrying portions of the 1st Battalion, 3d Marines began landing at Da Nang, arriving from Futema, Okinawa.[1] Captain Kress was in the initial contingent that arrived by air. At the end of a second tour of duty in Vietnam six years later, Lieutenant Colonel Kress would be one of the last Marine Corps lawyers to leave Vietnam.

The units that landed in Da Nang were part of the 9th Marine Expeditionary Brigade (MEB), from Okinawa. The senior lawyer on Okinawa was Colonel Olin W. Jones, the staff legal officer (SLO) of the 3d Marine Division. Several days before the landings he had conferred with the Commanding General, 9th MEB, Brigadier General Frederick J. Karch. They decided to detail a legal/civil affairs officer to the MEB, which was then afloat in the South China Sea preparing for the imminent Vietnam landings.[2] They selected Captain Kress.

As Captain Pete Kress recalled his arrival, Da Nang was even more humid and hot than Okinawa. But this was not his first time in uncomfortable operational circumstances. He had been a Marine for nearly 11 years, formerly a company commander and, just two years previously, a weapons instructor at The Basic School. While stationed at Quantico, Virginia, he had attended Georgetown University's law school at night, graduating in 1962. He transferred to Quantico's staff legal office and in December 1964 proceeded to Okinawa for duty.

After landing, Captain Kress and the other members of the MEB staff trudged to the nearby French-built compound that lay just west of the Da Nang Airbase runways. They moved into an unpainted concrete, one-story, L-shaped building, reputedly a former French Foreign Legion barracks. Field desks were set up throughout the short side of the L and the MEB staff began operating ashore. The small rooms that ran down the long arm of the L served as the officers' billeting spaces.

Because his work would involve occasional confidential discussions with Marines needing legal assistance, as well as those involved with some aspect of courts-martial, Captain Kress was given permission to locate his "office" in his quarters, away from the distractions of the MEB staff. He set up a field desk in his room, penned "Staff Legal Office" on a piece of yellow legal paper, and taped it to the door. The Marines' first legal office in Vietnam was open for business.[3] Captain Kress was beginning the newest chapter in a story of military law and Marine Corps lawyers that had begun long before.

Ancient Roots

Military law is virtually as old as military force. Until recently, there were two distinct bodies of military law: that of the sea, and that of land armies. A body of sea-law took form under the Phoenicians, eventually inherited and shaped to the modern world by the English, who, in 1649, during the era of Cromwell, adopted rules for governing the fleet. These were the precursors of modern American naval law.

The law governing armies arose under the Romans and their legion tribunes, who administered the *Magistri Militum*. Later, the Franks produced the first known written code of military law, and William the Conqueror introduced his version of military justice to England in 1066. In 1640 Parliament passed the landmark Ordinances of Armies, and later the American colonies followed the British pattern.

In 1775 the Continental Congress adopted the first American code, based on the British Articles of War. On the naval side, Rules for the Regulation of the Navy

---

*Usually referred to as "the JAG Manual," its correct title was *Manual of the Judge Advocate General of the Navy*. It contained legal administrative matters and material supplementing the *Manual for Courts-Martial*.

Photo courtesy of Col Peter N. Kress, USMC (Ret.)

Peter N. Kress is promoted to the grade of captain by LtGen Frederick L. Wiesman, Commanding General of Marine Corps Schools, Quantico, Virginia. Fourteen months later Capt Kress landed at Da Nang, the first Marine lawyer assigned legal duty in Vietnam.

of the United Colonies were enacted in 1776. During this period, Marines were governed by the Army's Articles of War when serving ashore, and by the Rules for the Regulation of the Navy when serving afloat.[4] Over the next 87 years Congress made six changes to naval law and, in 1862, passed the Articles for the Government of the Navy (25 in number), commonly referred to as "Rocks and Shoals."* With several amendments, Rocks and Shoals remained in effect until 1951. Army law, meanwhile, underwent significant revisions in 1786, 1806, 1874, and 1917.[5]

In 1865 the United States established the position of Solicitor and Naval Judge Advocate General, but Congress abolished the office after the death of the incumbent.[6] Several years later, in 1878, Marine Corps Captain William B. Remey served as Acting Judge Advocate General, until 1880, when Congress passed legislation creating the office of the Judge Advocate General of the Navy.[7] President Rutherford B. Hayes appointed Captain Remey the Navy's first Judge Advocate General, to serve with the grade of colonel while in that billet. Colonel Remey held the billet for the next 12 years.**

Beginnings: Army Courts, Naval Boards

By the end of World War I a three-tiered court-martial system was well-established. In the naval service the lowest level court was the deck court (called a summary court-martial in the Army), a one-officer proceeding, limited to punishment of confinement or solitary confinement for up to 20 days. Bread and water for a similar period was authorized. The inter-

---

*The term derives from Article XIX, Rules and Regulations for the Government of the Navy, 1862: "If any officer . . . shall, through inattention . . . suffer any vessel of the navy to be stranded, or run upon rocks or shoals . . . he shall suffer such punishment as a court martial shall adjudge." The term came to be applied to those Articles for the Government of the Navy, enumerated in *Naval Courts and Boards*, that were required to be read periodically to ships' crews.

**Colonel Remey's final years found him mentally infirm. He died in a Massachusetts institution in 1894. (Biographical files, RefSec, MCHC).

Col William B. Remy, U.S. Marine Corps, was appointed the first Judge Advocate General of the Navy.

mediate level court was the summary court-martial (called a special court-martial in the Army), composed of at least three officers. It could impose punishments of a bad conduct discharge, bread and water, and up to 30 days confinement or solitary confinement. The general court-martial in both the Navy and Army was reserved for offenses that, in the convening officer's opinion, were of the most serious nature, meriting more significant punishment. The general court-martial was composed of no fewer than five officers and could impose sentences up to and including death.[8]

The period following World War I brought pressure for change in the military's justice system and set the stage for reforms bringing both streams of military justice, sea and land, into the modern era.[9] During that time convening authorities sometimes appointed members (jurors) to suit their own ends, trial-level reviews were sometimes less than impartial, and lawyers were a rarity in courts-martial. There were no judges, disinterested or otherwise. Meaningful review was virtually nonexistent. Convening authorities could order reconsideration sessions and, indeed, during World War I fully one-third of all Army court-martial acquittals were "revised" to findings of guilty in such reconsideration sessions.[10] Until 1920 a court-martial conviction need only be approved by the officer who convened the court, except in officer dismissal and death cases.

The administration of military justice in the Navy and Marine Corps entailed similar inequities under *Naval Courts and Boards*, the Navy legal manual of the day, and Rocks and Shoals. During this period no lawyers or judge advocates acted as such in the Marine Corps. Neither did the Navy place a particularly high premium on uniformed lawyers. The World War I Navy Judge Advocate General's Office boasted that there was not a single lawyer on its staff.[11] In fact, the Judge Advocate General of the Navy was not required to be a lawyer until 1950.[12]

Akin to the Army's reconsideration session, *Naval Courts and Boards* provided the specific format for the order directing members of a court-martial to reexamine their results with a view to stiffening a sentence:

> 1. The record of proceedings . . . is returned herewith to the court.
> 2. The [Navy] department, after careful consideration, is of the opinion that the sentence adjudged by the court is not adequate to the offense found proved . . . .
> 3. The court will reconvene for the purpose of reconsidering its sentence.[13]

Such direction made clear what was expected.

Public pressure grew for reform of the Army's justice system. The result was the 1920 Articles of War, the first major legislative revision of Army law since the Revolutionary War, and the guide under which the Army conducted its courts-martial until the Korean War. Although the Navy and Marine Corps' Articles for the Government of the Navy were not similarly amended, a military-wide pattern for change was discernible for the first time.

World War II and Beyond: Military Justice is to Justice as Military Music is to Music

During World War II millions of Americans joined the ranks of the Armed Forces and, in far greater numbers than in World War I, the citizen-soldier again came into contact with military justice. There were about 1,700,000 convictions by courts-martial during the war.[14] Sentences were often harsh and inconsistent with inexplicable verdicts and, too often, overbearing command influence. This reflected, in part, the inexperience of the personnel who comprised the courts and the harsh views of some commanders as to the purpose of military justice. As one antimilitary partisan phrased it:

> No one blushed in admitting that the court-martial was not a trial, that the commander used it to enforce his disciplinary policies and inculcate military values in his men,

that it was administered by officers alone, that there was no right to review, and that the sentences were calculated to set an example and not to provide justice.[15]

It became apparent that what had worked well enough for the small prewar Armed Services could not bear the stress of major wartime expansion in the modern day. The Marine Corps, for example, was manned at 65,881 on the eve of the war and reached a peak strength of 484,631, an increase of almost 750 percent.[16] Although official Marine Corps records of the number of courts-martial tried were not kept during World War II (nor were they kept until the late-1960s), most were tried without lawyer participation, suggesting the uneven quality of justice that sometimes prevailed during those years.

During World War II the few regular Marine Corps officers with law degrees were assigned to Atlantic or Pacific fleet headquarters or to Headquarters Marine Corps. For the remaining reservist-lawyers on active duty, a law degree was simply an item of passing interest in his field record, like having been to barber's school. Not until mid-1942 was a staff legal advisor first provided for: a captain's billet on the staff of each Marine division.[17] (An Army division, in contrast, was authorized a three-officer judge advocate section of lieutenant colonel, captain, and warrant officer, plus two enlisted clerks.) Otherwise, a law degree only made one assignable to each general court-martial tried in one's battalion; not necessarily viewed as a blessing. Rather than looking to lawyers, commanders divined their legal counsel from hard-won experience and *Naval Courts and Boards*. Of course, having a billet for a staff legal advisor required neither that the billet be filled nor that the incumbent, if any, be a lawyer. Indeed, he usually was not, because lawyer-Marines with career aspirations believed that being sidetracked from a normal career path onto the dead-end legal road (no major's billet for a legal advisor existed) was not the route to either command or promotion. Nevertheless, during the late war years the Marine Corps recognized the utility of lawyers and employed Reserve officers, primarily, to fill its headquarters commands' legal billets. At war's end, by Marine Corps bulletin, officer volunteers were again sought for postgraduate training in law, recognizing the need for more senior, regular officers who could lead the reservist lawyers.[18] The Marine Corps had periodically sought officer-lawyer candidates in that way since after World War I.[19]

With the end of the war unification of the Services was in the air, and pressure again mounted for reexamination of the military system of justice.[20] The American Legion, other veteran's groups, and state bar associations all pressed for change. Studies were initiated and boards convened, all with reform as their goal.

Movement toward change was slow, but legislation moved forward. In 1948 the U.S. Army's Judge Advocate General's Corps was formed despite strong opposition by the Army Chief of Staff, General Dwight D. Eisenhower.* He viewed the divorce of lawyers from the rest of the officer corps as contrary to Service harmony. Since 1862 the Army had assigned "judge advocates" to the headquarters of every field army. Until 1948, however, any commissioned officer could be designated a "judge advocate."[21] In addition to a JAG Corps, the Army's Articles of War were again modernized in 1948. The Navy sought to introduce a companion bill to the Army's, but was unsuccessful. The Navy had waited to see the outcome of the Army's bill and the congressional session ended before action could be taken on the Navy bill. So the Navy and Marine Corps continued to operate under essentially the same Articles for the Government of the Navy, which they had followed for two hundred years.

It was unclear if the 1948 Army modifications applied to the newly established Air Force, formerly a part of the Army. Nevertheless, the Air Force quickly published its own blue-covered *Manual for Courts-Martial* and proceeded to trial. In fact, no military appellate court ever decided whether or not the Air Force properly claimed jurisdiction for itself. The soon-enacted uniform code subsumed the Air Force manual, making it a moot point.

The Uniform Code of Military Justice, 1950: Old Ills Redressed

On 26 July 1947 legislation abolished the War Department and created the Department of the Army and the Department of the Air Force. Those two departments, along with the already existing Department of the Navy, were bunched under the newly

---

*Although the Army's modern JAG Corps was formed in 1948, the first Judge Advocate of the Army was appointed during the Revolutionary War, on 29 July 1775. In July 1862 the Congress provided for an Army corps of judge advocates. The Army's Bureau of Military Justice, established in 1864, became the Judge Advocate General's Department in 1884, and, on 24 June 1948, became the Judge Advocate General's Corps. (*Military Laws of the United States—1949* [Washington: Government Printing Office, 1950] Sec.62, p. 71-74.)

formed National Defense Establishment, which was redesignated the Department of Defense in 1949.[22] The first Secretary of Defense, James V. Forrestal, took office in September of 1947. He recognized that the recent legislation reforming the Army's court-martial system would soon become law and that it was contrary to Armed Services unification. Secretary Forrestal acted to supersede the one-Service reform and to produce a justice system applicable to all the Services.

He formed another committee, with a particularly ambitious and demanding mandate. He directed the committee to integrate the Army's (and the Air Force's) Articles of War, the Navy and Marine Corps' Articles for the Government of the Navy, and the Disciplinary Laws of the Coast Guard.* Additionally, the committee was to write a modern code "with a view to protecting the rights of those subject to the code and increasing public confidence in military justice, without impairing the performance of military functions."[23] Secretary Forrestal had set them a formidable task.

Headed by Edmund M. Morgan, the members were Assistant General Counsel of the Department of Defense Felix E. Larkin and the Under-Secretaries of the Army, Navy, and Air Force. Morgan was a highly respected Harvard law professor and, along with Larkin, proved to be the driving force of the committee and its team of supporting lawyers.

In January 1949 the Morgan Committee reported to Secretary Forrestal that it had completed the writing of a uniform code of 140 articles. Three issues remained upon which they could not agree. It fell to the Secretary to make the decision, over Army objection, to adopt a military appellate "Judicial Council" (or Court of Military Appeals, as it was finally designated) of three civilians. The Secretary also approved, despite Navy objection, the seating of enlisted personnel as court-martial members, if requested by an enlisted accused. Finally, a "law officer," who was required to be a lawyer, gained approval, again over the Navy's objection. Although the Army had been employing a "law member" in general courts-martial since 1920, there had been no requirement that he be a lawyer until their short-lived 1948 modifications.

The modern trilogy of summary, special, and general courts-martial was now in place for all Services. For the first time law officers—less than judges but more than senior members—were required to be lawyers. Also, lawyer defense counsel and trial counsel (prosecutors) were permitted at all levels of court-martial, although they were required only at general courts. In addition, any time the trial counsel was a lawyer, the code required that the defense counsel be similarly qualified.

Safeguards against improper command influence, a major concern of the drafters, were woven throughout the new code. Although no system could be made totally immune from misuse, the Morgan Committee, which was well aware of the public's concern regarding past problems, sought "to draw a line between the commander's duty to enforce military law and his power to influence its administration."[24] They acted to preclude future abuses by, among other things, including two new articles making improper command influence a military crime.[25] The capstone of the effort was establishment of the Judicial Council, or Court of Military Appeals, the specialized civilian tribunal empowered to entertain appellate review.[26] Finally, Article 36 of the new Code opened the way for the last aspect of this major overhaul, a new *Manual for Courts-Martial*.

The first Uniform Code of Military Justice was a landmark achievement which brought the military court-martial into the mainstream of contemporary law. The United States Court of Military Appeals, the military's highest court, later said:

> Members of the legal profession within the military establishment are made primarily responsible for the elimination of the abuses formerly affecting military justice, and are relied upon for the establishment of a court-martial system truly judicial in viewpoint, and administered in accordance with established American concepts of jurisprudence.[27]

The Code became law on 5 May 1950.[28] President Truman ordered the 1951 *Manual for Courts-Martial*, which implemented it, into effect on 31 May 1951, repealing the Articles for the Government of the Navy, the Articles of War, and the Disciplinary Laws of the Coast Guard.**[29] The *Manual* specified that from that

---

*The United States Coast Guard, a separate military service since January 1915, first employed the Disciplinary Rules for the Revenue Cutter Service as its disciplinary tool, later adopting the Disciplinary Laws of the Coast Guard. In November 1941 it began operating as part of the U.S. Navy for the war's duration, and came under the Articles for the Government of the Navy. At the war's conclusion it again utilized its Disciplinary Laws until the 1950 UCMJ became effective. (50 CMR ix, 1975.)

**In 1955 the first JAG Manual, then known as the *Naval Supplement to the Manual for Courts-Martial, United States, 1951*, was published for the use of Navy law specialists and Marine Corps lawyers. It was six by nine inches in size and cost ten cents.

date Army and Air Force lawyers could be appointed "judge advocates." Navy and Coast Guard lawyers, it said, were to be "law specialists." Marine Corps lawyers, however, went unmentioned in the new manual.[30] This, presumably, was because the drafters assumed the Navy would provide Marines their legal counsel, as it did their chaplains and doctors. The failure to appreciate and provide for the fact that the Corps would want its lawyers to come from its own ranks was to have considerable effect. Over the next 10 years, until Marine Corps lawyers were given their own career pattern, it affected the promotions and careers of Marine Corps lawyers, senior and junior, who would find themselves in Vietnam courtrooms. But in 1951, named in the Code or not, lawyers became a fact of everyday Marine Corps life.

Continuing Tension: Justice Versus Discipline

Despite the barbs of critics, the phrase "military justice" was no longer a contradiction in terms. Still, until the modest amendments of 1920 and the major reform of 1950, discipline had prevailed while justice stood in shadow. As a 1945 editorial in the *Chicago Tribune* read:

> Martial law was drafted in different times, for a different kind of soldier to the one who wears the United States uniform today. The professional soldier of a century or more ago was recruited, as often as not, from the dregs of society. When a weapon was placed in his hand the most savage discipline was required to insure that he did not turn it against those whom he was enlisted to protect. Such a code is neither necessary nor desirable to govern civilians in uniform defending a free country of which they are free citizens.[31]

The reforms of 1950 reflected the continuing question of the purpose of military law: is it to enforce discipline or to insure justice? Or both? Can both ends be simultaneously served? If so, in what order?

Until 1950 the commander had great influence over courts-martial. Trial procedure was simple, requiring no legal training or experience to employ it. Review procedures lent themselves to quick confirmation of verdict and sentence. In this way discipline was enforced by demonstrating to all the swift punishment of infractions. The influence of the commander was not lightly surrendered, nor the military lawyer eagerly received. General William Tecumseh Sherman, himself a lawyer, earlier stated from the commander's perspective:

> It will be a grave error if by negligence we permit the military law to become emasculated by allowing lawyers to inject into it the principles derived from their practice in the civil courts, which belong to a totally different system of jurisdiction.[32]

Marine Corps Colonel Olin W. Jones recalled "the enmity of virtually all Marine Corps commanders to the new system. This was the first time they had to be told they could not do many things they had done in the past . . . . This transition period was difficult for many of us."[33]

In the 1950 UCMJ the balance between discipline and justice was apparent. The commander would appoint counsel, members, and law officer, and have first review of the case. Lawyers would conduct the pretrial investigation and guard against baseless charges. The law officer would ensure a trial according to law. His performance and the record of trial, as a whole, would be subject to review not only by the commander, but by a military appellate panel. A second, final appellate review would be in the hands of the all-civilian Court of Military Appeals. Apropos of the court-martial which the new Code ushered in, trial attorney F. Lee Bailey, himself a former Marine Corps legal officer, wrote: "The [civilian jury] system simply can't be counted on. In my opinion, despite all the criticism leveled at the military, the odds are that a military court will produce a more accurate verdict in a disputed issue of fact than a civilian jury."[34]

The Death Penalty in the Armed Forces: Yes But No

In 1817 William Boyington, U.S. Marine Corps, was executed by a firing squad, the last Marine to be put to death pursuant to the sentence of a court-martial. His offense goes unrecorded, but during that period the death penalty was reserved for mutiny, desertion, and murder. According to the sketchy and incomplete records of the era, three other Marines were certainly executed before Boyington, and another three probably were.

There has not been an execution in the U.S. Navy since 1849 when two seamen were hanged from a ship's yardarm as a result of a mutiny on a smallboat from the U.S. Survey Schooner *Ewing*. (Their conviction followed a spirited defense by a prominent civilian defense attorney, paid for by the Navy.) Prior to the *Ewing* hangings, five other sailors were certainly executed and another three probably were. Among the five known to have been executed, three were alleged mutineers of the brig-of-war *Somers*, hanged from the yardarm after a summary proceeding in 1842. One of the three was Midshipman Philip Spencer, son of a former Secretary of War, which led to the "*Somers* Incident" becoming a *cause celebre*. As a result of the executions the captain of the *Somers*, like the commodore who authorized hanging the *Ewing* mutineers, was himself tried by a court of inquiry. The commodore was suspended from duty for five years; the *Somer's* captain was exonerated. Since those nineteenth century executions, a number of sailors and Marines have been condemned to death whose sentences were commuted to a lesser punishment.[35]

In the U.S. Army 270 soldiers were executed prior to World War I. During World War I 35 more were executed, and during World War II 146 death sentences were carried out. (Two soldiers of that number were executed after the war as a result of sentences imposed during the war.) Since implementation of the Uniform Code of Military Justice in 1950, the Army has executed 10 soldiers, the last in 1961 for the rape of an Austrian child.[36] The U.S. Air Force executed three men in 1948 and another two in 1954.[37] There has not been a death sentence carried out by the U.S. Coast Guard.

The stark difference in the number of executed death sentences in the Army and the naval service was due to dissimilar procedures for approving them in the naval services' Articles for the Government of the Navy and the Army's Articles of War. Under the Articles of War commanding generals of armies in the field in time of war were empowered to order death sentences carried out. The Articles for the Government of the Navy, on the other hand, required approval by the President of the United States of any sentence to death, except in very limited situations. With enactment of the UCMJ in 1950, approval procedures were made uniform, and Presidential approval is now required before a death sentence can be carried out in any armed service.

Since the last military execution in 1961 there have been numerous court-martial sentences to death, but as of this writing, all such sentences that have been ruled upon have either been mitigated to lesser punishments or reversed by military appellate courts. Since 1986 the Army's prescribed method of execution, although never put to use, has been lethal injection. The naval service has not prescribed a method of execution.*

Before a court-martial may sentence a convicted serviceman or woman to death, the *Manual for Courts-Martial* must authorize death as a penalty for the offense, the officer referring the case to trial must specifically authorize the court to consider death as a possible punishment, and the members must unanimously sentence the convicted individual to death. Other procedural steps complying with current U.S. Supreme Court opinions are mandated by Court of Military Appeals decisions.

Marine Corps Lawyers:
From The Line to Discipline Branch

Under the late Articles for the Government of the Navy there was no requirement for lawyers in a Marine Corps general court-martial. The commander simply could detail an officer to be the judge advocate (prosecutor), a "suitable officer" to be defense counsel, and five members and try the accused.[38] Until 1920 (in the Army), a conviction only needed approval of the officer who convened the court for the sentence to be executed, except in cases of officer dismissal or a death sentence. But in 1950, the Marine Corps and the other services realized that the new UCMJ would require a great many lawyers to meet its requirements. Now the Marines had to survey those within its ranks who were law-trained but laboring in other orchards, as well as locating regular officers who wanted to become lawyers. In the next few years the Marine Corps found exemplary officers to meet the new challenge.

Colonel Hamilton M. Hoyler, for example, was an infantry and artillery officer, as well as a Harvard Law School graduate. In World War II he saw action on Tulagi and earned the Silver Star Medal on Guam, where he commanded a battalion. He was awarded the Purple Heart for wounds received on Bougainville while a member of the 3d Raider Battalion. During the Korean War he commanded the 5th Marines and, before heading the Marine Corps' Discipline Branch in 1961, served as chief of staff of the 3d Marine Division.[39]

Major James F. Lawrence, Jr., had been an infantry platoon commander on Guadalcanal and Cape Gloucester. In Korea he was awarded the Navy Cross for his leadership of an infantry battalion during the breakout from the Chosin reservoir. He gained his law degree in 1953 and later became the first officer promoted to the grade of brigadier general as a lawyer.

Major Duane L. Faw held two Air Medals, earned as a dive-bomber pilot in combat over Guadalcanal, Munda, Rabaul, and other World War II Pacific islands. He later was the first brigadier general Director of the Judge Advocate Division.

Major Joseph R. Motelewski held a law degree when he was commissioned in 1942. As a motor transport

---

*Rule for Court-Martial 1113(d)(1): "A sentence to death which has been finally ordered executed shall be carried out in the manner prescribed by the Secretary concerned."

officer he saw combat on Guadalcanal and Peleliu. In Korea he briefly commanded the 1st Battalion, 7th Marines. In Vietnam he would be the chief of staff of the 3d Marine Division.

These men, and others, exemplified the Marine Corps tenet that every Marine is a rifleman. Commandants and commanders wanted their newly highlighted legal officers to be regular, as opposed to Reserve, officers with line experience and preferably with command experience. Such a background provided an advocate with insight into the problems of both the commander and the enlisted Marine. But it proved difficult and, finally, impossible to meet the desire for lawyers with such qualifications.

Since the end of World War I the Marine Corps had detailed a few officers each year to duty as law students, ordering them to civilian law schools. During the 1920s and 30s it was Harvard University's School of Law from which Marine Corps officers often graduated.[40] During World War II the program languished, but thereafter several majors were sent each year to law school with full pay. The post-war program, which placed officers at George Washington, Georgetown, or Catholic Universities, all in Washington, D.C., was in full force in 1950 in anticipation of the UCMJ's requirements for lawyers.[41] Marine Corps law students were required to purchase their own books and to assume duties in the office of the Judge Advocate General of the Navy during school breaks and vacations. Army, Air Force, and Coast Guard law students had no similar requirements. Major Earl E. Anderson, a student at George Washington University's law school from 1949 to 1952, recalled that "many of us had full-time [military] jobs.... For example, for over a year, I was the Foreign Claims Officer for JAG, handling all foreign claims."[42] After 1952, largely due to Major Anderson's petitioning the Judge Advocate General of the Navy on the matter, naval service law students were no longer required to simultaneously mix law study and military duty, or to spend school breaks in the office of the Navy JAG. During the 1950s the graduating officer received a secondary military occupational specialty (MOS) designator of 0185, trial/defense counsel, upon passing a state bar examination.

The assignment of a secondary, rather than a primary MOS, after three years of specialized and expensive civilian schooling, was significant. It reflected a philosophy that legal work was the graduate's secondary job, his primary duty remaining infantry

Department of Defense Photo (USMC) 311245
Gen Clifton B. Cates, 19th Commandant of the Marine Corps, was a second lieutenant in France during World War I, a year after graduating from law school.

command, or flying, or whatever his pre-law school specialty had been. Every Marine a rifleman. It also put the lawyer who was a regular officer in a difficult position.

In the years between World War II and Vietnam, a law degree, combined with command experience, was recognized as a positive factor in gaining promotion—not necessarily to employ as one's primary duty, but as an indication of drive, ambition, and ability. Indeed, until 1967 when James Lawrence was promoted to brigadier general, only three of the eight serving or future general officers who had law degrees—Cates, Anderson, Wensinger, Twining, Axtell, Beckington, Kier, and Snedeker—ever practiced law in the Marine Corps, or anywhere else.* Yet in the 1950s, the Marine Corps fostered an approach of specialization without application by creating lawyers on the one hand, while branding their specialty as secondary on the other. The Marine Corps lawyer with career ambitions recognized that he should try to remain in his former nonlegal specialty and, more importantly, obtain command of a unit.** That outlook squared with Headquarters Marine Corps' view that legal expertise was needed, but only as a specialized skill for the commander to call upon when necessary.*** The Marine Corps looked for a solution to the issue of traditions versus specialization. Is every Marine, including the lawyer, a rifleman? The Marine Corps found the answer in Vietnam.

During the 1950s and 60s the legal community was also securing its position in the command structure of the Marine Corps. After World War II, lawyer assignments were not tracked or controlled in any formal way, there being no reason to be concerned with attorneys. With the advent of the UCMJ and its mandate for lawyers, concern became a necessity.

Gen Holland M. Smith, seen in 1919 as a major in France, graduated from law school in 1903 and practiced in Alabama before being commissioned in 1905.
Department of Defense Photo (USMC) 515291

---

*General Clifton B. Cates, 19th Commandant of the Marine Corps, was a 1916 University of Tennessee law school graduate. He retired from the Marine Corps in 1953. General Earl E. Anderson was a lieutenant colonel when he graduated from George Washington University's school of law (as law review editor-in-chief) in 1952. For the next 12 years he mixed legal and aviation duties then, until his retirement in 1975, was an aviator and a senior staff officer. Lieutenant General Walter W. Wensinger was a 1917 University of Michigan law school graduate before joining the Marine Corps and, other than duty in the Office of the Navy JAG for three years, was a career infantry officer. General Merrill B. Twining, a 1932 graduate of George Washington University's law school, was a career infantry officer. Lieutenant General George C. Axtell was a career aviator who graduated from George Washington University's law school as a major in 1952. Lieutenant General Herbert L. Beckington, an artillery and infantry officer, graduated from Catholic University law school in 1953, as a major. Major General Avery R. Kier was a 1927 graduate of Kansas City School of Law, but was a career aviator. Brigadier General James Snedeker, an infantry officer, was a 1940 law school graduate who represented the Marine Corps and the naval service on numerous boards and committees relating to military law, and was the first Marine to hold the billet of Deputy Judge Advocate General of the Navy. In an earlier era, General Holland M. Smith, who retired in 1946, was a graduate of the University of Alabama's law school, and practiced, briefly, before entering the Marine Corps. (RefSec; and Gen Anderson ltr to author, dtd 22Feb89; Anderson folder, Marines and Military Law in Vietnam file, MCHC).

**After World War II, when the postgraduate law program was curtailed for several years, Congress became concerned over the number of new lawyers who were returning to their pre-law school military specialties without practicing that which had been paid for with public funds. Additionally, General Earl E. Anderson recalls that Navy law specialists lobbied Congress for an end to Marine Corps participation in the law program because of dissatisfaction that their JAG and deputy JAGs remained line officers, rather than members of a JAG corps. (Gen Anderson ltr to author, dtd 22Feb89, Anderson folder, Marines and Military Law in Vietnam file, MCHC).

***As late as 1964, the Commandant of the Marine Corps, General Wallace M. Greene, Jr., expressed that view when he said, "We want Marine lawyers to vary their legal duties with command and staff assignments because we feel they make better military lawyers as a result." (*The Army, Navy, and Air Force Journal and Register*, 4Jan64, p. 13.)

Legal matters were conducted by Discipline Branch (usually referred to by its Headquarters designation, "Code DK"), a part of the Personnel Department of Headquarters Marine Corps. Although Discipline Branch had existed during World War II, not until the Uniform Code of Military Justice became effective was Discipline Branch headed by a lawyer.* The first attorney to be designated head of Discipline Branch was Colonel James C. Bigler, who had been assigned to the branch since 1949. Successive branch heads were Colonels St.Julien R. Marshall in 1952, Paul D. Sherman in 1954, and John S. Twitchell in 1956. As lawyer identification, assignment and utilization became routine, Discipline Branch, or Code DK, evolved into a branch concerned solely with legal matters.

In the late 1950s the Commandant found it difficult to meet the requirements for junior officer-lawyers. The Marine Corps had 129 officer-lawyer billets, filled primarily by Reserve officers augmented by a few senior, regular officer-lawyers who alternated between legal and nonlegal assignments. Lawyer shortages were a continuing problem. To resolve that problem, in 1959 the Commandant proposed establishing a new, primary MOS for lawyers who desired to perform only legal duties. He also proposed safeguards against promotion discrimination and sought more reservists to meet the expanding requirement for lawyers. He hoped to avoid a separate legal corps, such as the Navy was proposing.[43] By Marine Corps order Reserve lawyers were soon being recruited as candidates for regular commissions.[44] Within two years 0185 (trial/defense counsel), and 0195 (law officer), became primary MOSs, assigned upon graduation from law school and the passing of a state bar examination, and lawyers were assured equality of promotion opportunity.**[45]

That was the situation on the eve of the Marine landings at Da Nang in March 1965. The U.S. Army's JAG Corps had existed since 1948. The Air Force employed a de facto JAG Corps while claiming opposition to a separate category of lawyer-officer. The Navy was seeking legislation providing for its own JAG Corps, but the Marines opposed it because the intended legislation precluded a Marine from again becoming the Judge Advocate General of the Navy, no matter how remote such a possibility was.[46] (The Navy had to wait until 8 December 1967 for its lawyer-officers to become a JAG Corps.)[47] The Marines, while complaining that one of their own could not be Navy JAG, insisted that a Marine Corps JAG corps was neither needed nor desired.

In Support: Navy Lawyers

In 1942 the Naval Courts and Boards Training Course was established at the Advance Base Receiving Barracks, Port Hueneme, California. It was the naval services' first legal school attended by both Navy and Marine Corps personnel. In April 1946 a seven-week training course for Navy yeomen and Marine legal clerks was added to the curriculum, and in February 1950 the school, now redesignated the U.S. Naval School (Naval Justice), was relocated to the Naval Base, Newport, Rhode Island. It was again redesignated in May 1961, this time as the Naval Justice School.

In 1965 Navy lawyers were properly referred to as "law specialists." Confusingly, law specialists could also be staff judge advocates, if assigned that specific billet on the special staff of a commander. The title "staff judge advocate" was a carryover from the period before the UCMJ, when the senior officer in a legal billet on the commander's staff was referred to as the "staff judge advocate," whether he was a lawyer or a layman. Marine Corps lawyers remained unmentioned and untitled in the UCMJ. Nevertheless, as with their Navy counterparts, if they served in a legal billet, they were commonly, if inaccurately, called "judge advocates."

The UCMJ's omission of the Marine Corps lawyer had an effect on a more substantive level. Records of court-martial proceedings must be reviewed for legal sufficiency and correctness. Cases involving significant punishment, as defined in the Uniform Code, required review by appellate courts. The 1950 UCMJ specified that the records of some lower-level courts, summaries and specials that did not include a bad conduct discharge as a part of the sentence, need not go to the appellate level. They did, however, require review for legal sufficiency and correctness by a law specialist or judge advocate. Marine Corps lawyers, not being classified as either, were in the position of prosecuting significant numbers of courts-martial while lacking the authority to review many of them. The solution was for the Navy to assign a law

---

*Before 1941, legal issues arising in the field, few as they were, were an aspect of the personnel officer's duties. Courts-martial and legal matters were first mentioned in Headquarters Marine Corps' organization in 1941 when the Personnel Department formed a Courts and Boards Branch. Courts and Boards evolved into Discipline Section, then Discipline Division, and finally, Discipline Branch, which continued in existence until the Judge Advocate Division came into being on 17 April 1968. (RefSec, MCHC).

**In 1964 the 4405 MOS designator was first assigned Marine Corps lawyers. (LtCol Brian B. Kent ltr to author, dtd 28Feb89, Comment folder, Marines and Military Law in Vietnam file, MCHC).

The staff of the Naval School of Justice, Port Hueneme, California, March 1948. 1stLt Robert C. Lehnert, second from right, was the school's first Marine Corps instructor though not yet a lawyer. In 1967 he became Staff Legal Officer of the 1st Marine Aircraft Wing in Da Nang, Vietnam. His relief at the School of Justice was Capt William A. Murphy, USMC, second from left. Navy Lt (later Capt) Wyman N. Jackson, third from right, was a law officer in Vietnam during 1966 and 1967. The school's commanding officer, Cdr (later RAdm) Frederick Albrink, center, later was Assistant Judge Advocate General of the Navy.

specialists, who were authorized to conduct the required review, to all major Marine commands that convened courts-martial. The Navy was glad to accommodate the Marines, because such assignments offered Navy lawyers a broader exposure to military justice practice. In exchange, Marine Corps lawyers in roughly equal number were assigned to Navy legal offices and the appellate sections in the Office of the Judge Advocate General of the Navy.[48]

The Navy sought legislation, with Marine Corps concurrence, to amend the UCMJ to permit review of all court-martial records by "any qualified officer lawyer of the Navy or the Marine Corps, whether or not he is designated as a law specialist."[49] But in March of 1965, when the Vietnam landings occurred, passage of that amendment was several years away and the Marine Corps relied on Navy lawyers to help man its legal offices. At the same time, Headquarters Marine Corps continued to hold that Marine Corps lawyers remained unrestricted officers who could serve in any billet. By fiat, every Marine was still a rifleman.*

In Washington disagreement continued between the Marine Corps and the Navy's Judge Advocate General's office over the establishment of a Navy JAG corps. The Marines still opposed legislation offered by the Navy that would create a Navy JAG corps, now because the Navy would not include provision for a Marine Corps Assistant Judge Advocate General of the Navy, a rear admiral/brigadier general billet.[50] (The

---

*During this period, acceptance of a primary legal MOS was still optional for regular officers. Lawyers commissioned prior to 1961 had primary MOSs other than legal. Another Marine Corps order decreed that "when there is a sufficient number of lawyers to meet the needs of the Marine Corps, those officers not assigned a primary legal MOS will be detailed to assignments other than legal . . . in accordance with the requirements of the Marine Corps." (Headquarters, U.S. Marine Corps, Division of Information, Service Information Release, Release No. RWJ-67-63, 29Mar63; and MCO 1040.21, dtd 26Dec62, Subj: Marine Corps Lawyers; policy concerning, Para 3.b(3); 4400 MOS Establishment folder, Marines and Military Law in Vietnam file, MCHC).

Marines had given up their insistence that language be included in the legislation to provide for the possibility of a Marine in the top billet, Judge Advocate General of the Navy.) This conflict, though without impact on Marine Corps lawyers in Vietnam, raised basic issues. For example, in the Navy legal community it was suggested that there should only be one "law firm," and it should wear a blue suit; that is, be composed entirely of Navy personnel.[51] Eventually, the Marine Corps itself was to ask if that might not be the wiser course.[52]

In Support: Headquarters Marine Corps

Critical to Marine Corps lawyers in Vietnam was the support of those in charge of legal matters at Headquarters Marine Corps. Since the UCMJ had gone into effect, the number of Marine Corps lawyers had grown significantly. Headquarters' Discipline Branch continued its evolution within the Personnel Department. In the branch's Navy Annex offices plans were formulated for eventually moving from Personnel and making "legal" a separate division. Colonel John S. Twitchell and his successors, Colonels Hamilton M. Hoyler, Robert A. Scherr, and Robert B. Neville, laid the groundwork for the future Judge Advocate Division during their tenures in Discipline Branch, from 1956 to 1966.[53]

The problems they faced were daunting. Should lawyers be assigned only legal duty? If so, that would reduce the number of lawyers required and probably ensure "green suit" (Marine), rather than "blue suit" (Navy) lawyers. Legislation to this effect was proposed in 1958, but then withdrawn for fear of establishing a single-skill, JAG-type corps in the Marines. Instead, in 1962, a Marine Corps order established the compromise policy that regular officers would not have to perform solely legal duties if they did not wish to, but could if they wanted; on the other hand, Reserve lawyers (usually captains and lieutenants) could serve only in legal billets. A later modification established the policy that lieutenant and captain lawyers would serve one tour of duty out of three in a nonlegal billet. Presumably, this would ensure that every Marine would continue to be a rifleman.[54] Another issue was the lawyers' continuing concern that they might not receive consideration by promotion boards equal to that of line officers.* In 1964 that, too, was addressed by Marine Corps order.[55] Further, to be on a par with the other services, Marine Corps lawyers sought credit for the time spent in law school preparing for the specialized duty they performed. Such "constructive service" would be significant when promotion eligibility was considered, because the practical effect would be that lawyers would be promoted to captain with less time on active duty than nonlawyer officers.

Without constructive service, not only was there a lack of recognition for the effort and time spent preparing to become a service lawyer, but disparities in grade could arise between lawyers. Captain W. Hays Parks, for example, initiated his service while still a college undergraduate. He arrived in Vietnam seven years later, a captain with seven years time in service. Although he had not been on active duty, he had been advanced in grade throughout the seven years he had been in college and law school. His law school classmate, Jerald D. Crow, was commissioned upon graduation from law school, and arrived in Vietnam at about the same time as Captain Parks. Without constructive service, and because of his later commissioning date, Crow was a second lieutenant receiving little more than half the pay that Captain Parks did.[56] Constructive service would have put the two officers, who had equal time actually in uniform, on a par, rather than essentially rewarding Parks for merely having signed his service contract earlier. Legislation was proposed to meet the constructive service issue, but it remained unresolved for several more years.

The number of lawyers being commissioned in the Marine Corps was not sufficient to meet the needs of a Service expanding to meet the Vietnam War. Nor did the pressure of the draft entirely close the lawyer manpower gap. A solution came in 1961, when a traditional source of officer accessions, the Platoon Leaders' Class (PLC), was expanded to embrace law student candidates as well as undergraduates who intended to pursue a law degree following graduation.[57] The PLC (Law) program allowed prospective officers between college graduation and law school to be commissioned as second lieutenants. Previously this route had been open only to graduating college seniors who could immediately begin Marine officer training. The PLC (Law) program, by committing lawyers to Marine Corps service before law school, addressed the shortage of lieutenants and captains. However, the continuing paucity of midlevel lawyers, majors and lieutenant colonels, was a retention problem which was to burden the Marine Corps for the entire war.

---

*A "line officer" is an officer assigned to the combat arms of the service involved. In the case of the Marine Corps those are infantry, artillery, armor, and engineer officers; as opposed to staff, service, and specialist officers.

Solutions to the problems were hammered out. Lawyers soon were assigned legal duty almost exclusively; the Commandant directed parity in promotions; and law school graduates were to receive constructive service. Those resolutions and their implementation were the result of long planning, intense effort, and inspired staff work. The officers in Discipline Branch in the late 1950s and early 1960s made the UCMJ a practical and workable system of military justice in the Marine Corps.

Among those matters upon which they advised the Commandant was the legal status of those Marines who were to land in Vietnam: invaders or invitees?

The Pentalateral Agreement: Diplomatic Riflemen

Few Marine riflemen in Vietnam knew that in terms of legal jurisdiction they were considered to be diplomatic mission clerks.

A basic tenet of international law is that the courts of a country have jurisdiction to try all cases arising out of wrongful acts committed in that country. With Vietnam's permission the United States could, in Vietnam, try U.S. citizens for wrongful acts committed in Vietnam, or lacking permission, the trial could be held elsewhere. But generally, a sovereign state has primary jurisdiction over all persons within its territory. This includes the military personnel of another nation, unless the host state consents to surrender its jurisdiction.[58]

The United States, naturally, desired to retain the greatest possible measure of jurisdiction over its own forces in Vietnam. In time of peace jurisdiction is a matter for negotiation with a host country, formalized in a status of forces agreement, or SOFA.*

Usually a SOFA is not concluded when one nation is engaged in a war on the soil of another nation. Moreover, in Vietnam government courts were still functioning and, according to international law, those courts retained primary jurisdiction over American troops in Vietnam. Clearly, an accord regarding jurisdiction was needed.

The Agreement for Mutual Defense Assistance in Indochina, commonly referred to as the Pentalateral Agreement, was concluded long before the 1965 landings, and resolved the issue of jurisdiction. That document, governing the legal status, rights, and obligations of American personnel in Vietnam, was signed in Saigon by the United States, France, Cambodia, Laos, and Vietnam on 23 December 1950. Although similar to mutual defense assistance agreements the United States had concluded with other allies, the Pentalateral Agreement was brief (less than six pages long), and its terms were broad and general, leaving many legal questions to be settled on a case-by-case basis.

The agreement provided that all American forces entering Indochina were to be considered members of the U.S. diplomatic mission with the same legal status as actual members of the U.S. mission of corresponding grade. American military personnel were divided into three categories: senior military members of the U.S. mission with full diplomatic status; a lesser, undefined category which, significantly, excluded its membership from the civil and criminal jurisdiction of Vietnam; and the third category, whose membership was again undefined, but with the legal status of clerical personnel of the diplomatic mission. In 1958, the United States advised the Vietnamese government that it would consider top U.S. military commanders to be in the first category, officers and warrant officers to be in the second, and enlisted men to be in the third category. So, in diplomatic terms, Marine riflemen were considered diplomatic mission clerks. Major General George S. Prugh, Judge Advocate General of the Army, wrote:

> When the pentalateral agreement was signed in 1950, the signatory parties obviously meant the agreement to apply to the activities of the small U.S. Military Advisory Assistance Group staffs operating at the time in Cambodia, Laos, and Vietnam. During the early 1950s, there were 200 to 300 of these military advisors . . . . It is unlikely that the diplomats ever imagined that its simple provisions would govern the legal status and activities of almost 600,000 Americans in Vietnam. Yet . . . no more detailed agreement was ever negotiated.[59]

As Major General Prugh pointed out, once large numbers of American forces were in the country, they were immediately engaged in combat, and a status of forces agreement, a peacetime document, never became necessary. The Pentalateral Agreement provided a minimal but adequate framework, and the generality of its provisions allowed a flexibility that proved valuable in meeting the many legal complications that were to arise.[60]

The legal status of American civilians in Vietnam, other than the actual diplomatic mission, was not ad-

---

*The concept of a SOFA first arose in 1941, when the United States leased bases in Great Britain in exchange for destroyers. The concept was "perfected" in the North Atlantic Treaty SOFA of 1951. (Burdick H. Brittin, *International Law For Seagoing Officers* (Annapolis: Naval Institute Press, 4th ed., 1981), pp. 187-193.

LtCol Paul J. Durbin was Deputy Staff Judge Advocate, U.S. Army, Pacific, when selected for temporary duty in Saigon in June 1959, the first Armed Service lawyer to be assigned legal duty in Vietnam.

dressed when the Pentalateral Agreement was reached. Eventually, 10,100 civilians would be in Vietnam, committing their share of criminal offenses, so their legal status and amenability to trial was no small issue. In 1965 military dependents, contractor employees, merchant seamen, reporters, and businessmen, were not considered by the American military legal system in Vietnam. Marine Corps lawyers would later be closely involved in the question of whether American civilians were subject to court-martial jurisdiction.

Military Law Comes to Vietnam

President Truman ordered the establishment of a U.S. Military Assistance Advisory Group (MAAG) in French Indochina, to provide materiel support to the French Expeditionary Corps fighting there. Lieutenant Colonel Victor J. Croizat, the first Marine Corps advisor to serve in Vietnam, arrived in August 1954.[61] Five years later, in June 1959, Lieutenant Colonel Paul J. Durbin, U.S. Army, was the first military lawyer assigned to Vietnam. He and five successor Army lawyers served on the staff of the U.S. Army Element, MAAG, in Saigon before Captain Pete Kress, the first Marine assigned exclusively for legal duty in Vietnam, arrived in March 1965.[62]

Beginning in May of 1961, volunteers from the 3d Marine Division, on Okinawa, and the 1st Marine Aircraft Wing, at Iwakuni, Japan, went to Vietnam as advisors for 30-day periods. In April 1962 a Marine helicopter squadron deployed from Okinawa to an old Japanese-built landing strip near Soc Trang. It supported forces of the Government of Vietnam battling Communist guerrillas. The squadron and its supporting establishment, known by the codename Shufly, moved from Soc Trang to Da Nang five months later. The French had rebuilt Da Nang's civilian airfield as a military base following World War II. The airbase, surrounded by the city itself, was relatively modern and was occupied by Vietnamese and U.S. Air Force units. It served the city as a commercial airport, as well as a military airbase.[63]

Marine Corps lawyers stationed in Japan and Okinawa noted that units were deployed in combat and considered how they also might get to where the action was. First Lieutenant Robert J. Blum, on temporary additional duty with Marine Aircraft Group 11 at P'ing-Tung, Formosa, convinced his commanding officer that the Marines at Da Nang were in need of legal assistance. (Legal assistance is the military term for counsel on virtually any legal matter other than military justice, e.g., indebtedness, divorce, taxes, adoption, to name but a few.) On 18 April 1963, Lieu-

The Da Nang Airbase was closely surrounded by the city of Da Nang. 9th MEB Headquarters and Capt Kress' office lay just to the left of the runways.

Courtesy of Col Robert J. Blum, USMC (Ret.)
1stLt Robert J. Blum was in Da Nang on 18 April 1963 to provide legal assistance for Shufly Marines almost a year before the 9th Marine Expeditionary Brigade landed.

tenant Bob Blum became the first Marine to reach Vietnam as a lawyer, and provided legal assistance for three days to the Shufly Marines. Although he did provide a service to the aviation unit, in truth, he said, he wrangled his way in-country "mostly just to see what was going on." Three months later he was again directed to Da Nang, this time to conduct a pretrial investigation.[64]

Two months after Lieutenant Blum's Vietnam visit, in June 1963, Colonel Earl E. Anderson arrived at MAAG Headquarters in Saigon to assume duties as chief of staff of the MAAG. Since attainment of his law degree in 1952, Colonel Anderson had been the staff legal officer of the 3d Marine Aircraft Wing, in addition to commanding several aviation units.* In Vietnam, Colonel Anderson served as chief of staff of the MAAG for the next year, while also flying more than 40 combat missions.[65]

A few other Marine Corps lawyers were in Vietnam

---

*Colonel Anderson had no further assignments in the legal field. After billets including Commanding General, Fleet Marine Force, Atlantic, and Assistant Commandant of the Marine Corps, he retired in 1975 as a general.

before the 9th MEB landed in March 1965. Major Brian B. Kent went ashore at Da Nang in September or October 1964 as counsel to an investigation conducted by the 1st Marine Aircraft Wing inspector. There had been reports that helicopter extractions had been negligently delayed, resulting in casualties to the South Vietnamese and their U.S. Marine Corps advisors. Major Kent remained in Vietnam for a week. The investigation determined that the delays had resulted from an insufficient number of available aircraft.[66] Major Paul F. Henderson, Jr., accompanied other members of the 9th MEB staff to Shufly headquarters for a week-long period in August 1964.[67] A few weeks before the Marine landings the staff legal officer of the 3d Marine Division, Colonel Olin W. Jones, accompanied the division commanding general on a liaison visit to Da Nang and Hue, as well.[68]

On the day of the initial 1965 Marine Corps landings, when Captain Pete Kress arrived for duty, Navy law specialist Lieutenant Hugh D. Campbell was already ashore at Da Nang. He was on temporary duty from the 3d Marine Division and provided income tax legal assistance to Shufly personnel.[69] The Navy and Marine Corps joint legal support for Vietnam Marines represented by Captain Kress and Lieutenant Campbell was to continue throughout the war and beyond.

A Beginning

On 8 March 1965 when Captain Kress stepped from the C-130 that had brought him to Da Nang, there were 168 lawyers in the Marine Corps.* Only 83 of them were regular officers. Forty-five percent of them were majors or above — an inordinately high percentage of supervisory officers. But the stage was set for trials in a combat zone.

---

*Of this number 19 were colonels, 34 lieutenant colonels (including the sole woman lawyer in the Marine Corps, LtCol Lily H. Gridley, a non-deployable reservist who was the long-time legal assistance officer at Headquarters Marine Corps in Washington), 25 majors, 20 captains, 60 first lieutenants, 9 second lieutenants, and a CWO-2 who had first enlisted in 1935. Two colonels and a major were lawyers but did not practice law in the Marine Corps. (HQMC, Code AI, Directory of Marine Officer Lawyers, dtd 1May65; Directories folder, Marines and Military Law in Vietnam file, MCHC).

Gen Earl E. Anderson, here a colonel, received the Legion of Merit with Combat "V" on 15 October 1964 for service with the MAAG in Saigon. In 1952 he was editor-in-chief of the George Washington University law review and graduated with highest honors.

CHAPTER 2

1965: 3d Marine Division and 9th MEB Open Shop

From a Lawyer's Case File: One Homicide, Two Victims — Trying Cases — III MAF: Headquarters Without Lawyers 1st Marine Aircraft Wing: Touching Down — Legal Duty in a Combat Zone: Problems — From a Lawyer's Case File: The Marine Corps' First War Crime Conviction in Vietnam — Perspective

---

Captain Peter N. Kress, acting Staff Legal Officer (SLO) of the newly arrived 9th Marine Expeditionary Brigade (MEB), discovered that he was less than overworked. In fact, his earliest employment of any significance was as the civil affairs officer, his secondary assignment.

Rats infested the old French compound that was now the MEB headquarters and billeting area. The question put to the legal-cum-civic action officer was how best to end this situation; traps or poison? Presumably Captain Kress fell heir to the problem because of the potential impact that poisoned rats might have upon the surrounding Vietnamese community. On occasion, the rodents found their way into the local diet. The consequences of civilian illness or death caused by American poison would be tragic. Sagely, Captain Kress recommended traps, which were subsequently requisitioned from Okinawa, delivered, and put to use. The value of a legal officer was thus demonstrated on another Marine Corps field of conflict.

In early May the MEB was redesignated III Marine Amphibious Force (III MAF), reflecting the Marines' increased strength and role in Vietnam. The change in designation had no effect on the legal section, which continued to service III MAF Headquarters, the 3d Marine Division, and until late May, the 1st Marine Aircraft Wing, as well.

Until 9th MEB's arrival in Vietnam, Shufly's few cases requiring trial by special or general court-martial had been disposed of by sending the accused and the essential witnesses back to Okinawa or to Atsugi, Japan, for trial. With so many Marines now in Vietnam, that course was less practical.

The first potential general court-martial case arose in March 1965, when a returning Marine patrol was mistakenly fired upon by other Marines, resulting in the death of two, and the wounding of two others. Captain Kress requested legal support from Colonel Olin W. Jones, the 3d Marine Division SLO on Okinawa, who dispatched First Lieutenants Frederick C. Woodruff and Donald W. Harris from Okinawa to act as defense counsels in the investigation of the incident. They joined Captain Kress and the two enlisted clerks who made up the MEB legal office. They were soon joined by Navy law specialist Lieutenant (junior grade) Keith G. O'Brian.

Eventually an Article 32 investigation, akin to a civilian court's preliminary hearing, was held in the airbase chapel, to the distress of the Navy chaplain. (In time, Vietnam courts-martial were routinely tried in messhalls, officers' clubs, staff offices, chapels — any place with sufficient seating space.) An unnoticed electrical outage stopped the recording of the proceeding before its conclusion and made the required verbatim transcript impossible. The partial record, though, was sufficient to allow the 9th MEB commanding general and convening authority, Brigadier General Frederick J. Karch, to determine that a court-martial was not warranted. The difficulty with electrical power, however, was a portent of generator failures, power drops, surges, and outages that would plague courts-martial as long as the Marines remained in Vietnam.

In April 1965 civil affairs and legal matters increased as the number of Marines in Vietnam increased. Two of the 3d Marine Division lawyers who had augmented Captain Kress' office for the shooting investigation, Lieutenant Harris and Navy Lieutenant O'Brian, remained in Da Nang, Lieutenant Harris as III MAF's first civil affairs officer.[1] Lieutenant Harris' initial assignment was to write a handbook on civil affairs, a subject about which he knew little. Undaunted, he visited a U.S. Army Special Forces unit in Da Nang and borrowed its Army civil affairs field manual. He copied most of it in longhand, making appropriate changes to conform to Marine Corps terminology, and forwarded "his" handbook to the commanding general. It was returned with the notation, "outstanding job, lieutenant." Lieutenant Harris' nonlegal assignment was secure.[2] His later Navy Achievement Medal recognized his more substantive achievement in the Vietnamese pacification program.[3]

Sometime later the commanding general directed Captain Kress to confer with Colonel George S. Prugh, the U.S. Army's Staff Judge Advocate at the U.S. Military Advisory Command, Vietnam (MACV), in Saigon. Colonel Prugh, a future Judge Advocate General of the Army, and Captain Kress coordinated commu-

Commanding General BGen Frederick J. Karch, sits fifth from right, and Capt Peter N. Kress, acting staff legal officer, and 1stLt Donald W. Harris, civil affairs officer, stand, center row, seventh and fourth from right, in this photo of 9th MEB staff in May 1965.

nication procedures between their respective legal offices, methods of handling foreign claims (over which the Army had cognizance), and other routine administrative matters.[4] That was the second of many meetings between Army judge advocates in Saigon and Marine Corps lawyers in III MAF. The first had been on 18 March 1965, when Colonel Prugh, along with his Vietnamese counterpart, Colonel Nguyen Mong Bich, and the MACV Chief of Claims, had flown to Da Nang to meet Captain Kress, discuss claims matters, and tour Marine Corps positions. Colonel Prugh said, "I think we enjoyed excellent relationships between MACV and Marine lawyers."

Through mid-1965 the 3d Marine Division (Rear), on Okinawa, continued to provide legal support for the 9th MEB/III MAF. Before the level of the division's eventual involvement in Vietnam became apparent, Colonel Jones, the Division SLO, planned to rotate the MAF's legal officer every few months. Accordingly, in May 1965, Major James P. King deployed from Okinawa to Da Nang to replace Captain Kress, who returned to Okinawa. On 1 July Lieutenant Colonel Thomas B. Sparkman, in turn, replaced Major King. On 1 August Lieutenant Colonel Sparkman was succeeded by Lieutenant Colonel Charles B. Sevier, who assumed the billet of Staff Legal Officer, the first in Vietnam to hold the title as well as the billet.[6] Lieutenant Colonel Tom Sparkman remained as Lieutenant Colonel Sevier's deputy.

The SLOs' increase in grade, from captain to lieutenant colonel in a period of five months, reflected the accelerating pace of Marine Corps deployments to Vietnam. In April two battalion landing teams and a regimental landing team headquarters arrived, followed by three squadrons of the 1st Marine Aircraft Wing. Those additions brought Marine Corps strength in Vietnam to 8,878. The future requirements for increased legal support, however, were not yet recognized, either on Okinawa or at Headquarters Marine Corps in Washington.

In May 1965 airbase construction began at Chu Lai, a barren stretch of coastline 57 miles southeast of Da Nang, where previously there had been no permanent American military presence. Three more battalion landing teams arrived there, and the 1st Marine Aircraft Wing established a forward headquarters at Chu Lai, as well.

By mid-June another 9,000 Marines were ashore in the three enclaves, now established at Da Nang, Chu Lai, and Phu Bai. In July Okinawa's 3d Marine Division (Rear) joined 3d Marine Division (Forward), uniting the division in Vietnam. In August the new commanding general of both III MAF and the 3d Marine Division, Major General Lewis W. Walt, split the division staff by establishing another headquarters, Task Force X-Ray, at Chu Lai.[7] As the build-up proceeded, the lawyers' caseloads increased as well. The III MAF SLO's small section was still servicing both the MAF headquarters and the 3d Marine Division, both of which had grown in size dramatically, as well as units of the 1st Marine Aircraft Wing.

The SLO, Lieutenant Colonel Charlie Sevier, had already been selected for promotion to colonel when he arrived in Vietnam. He had been an enlisted Marine in World War II, eventually becoming a lieutenant and a tank platoon commander. He had seen combat on Saipan, Tinian, and Okinawa and after the war earned his law degree and returned to active duty and the Korean War. In 1956 he was the prosecutor in the widely reported McKeon case, in which a Parris Island drill instructor was convicted of negligent homicide in the drowning deaths of six recruits at Ribbon Creek.[8]

Now in his third war, Lieutenant Colonel Sevier noted that, at first, the division moved support personnel, including lawyers, from Okinawa to Vietnam only with reluctance. An example was demonstrated by Major King, a 3d Division lawyer trained in civil affairs. Major King, having been relieved as the III MAF legal officer by Lieutenant Colonel Sparkman, wished to remain in Vietnam. Although there were no vacant legal billets, Major King prevailed upon the SLO on Okinawa to offer him to III MAF as the civil affairs officer, replacing Lieutenant Harris. Not long after Major King's arrival in Da Nang the commanding general spotted him and, recognizing him as a lawyer, growled, "What the hell are you doing here?"[9] Nevertheless, for the first time since the Korean War, Marine Corps lawyers were in the field with combat elements. As support personnel, they had no direct role in combat operations, but answered the commander's need for specialized advice and support.

Photo courtesy of BGen James P. King, USMC (Ret.)
Maj James P. King, III MAF Civil Affairs Officer, center, looks on as an officer is questioned by LtGen Victor H. Krulak, the Commanding General, Fleet Marine Force, Pacific, at Chu Lai in May 1965.

For a year after the initial landings the Staff Legal Office for III MAF headquarters and the 3d Marine Division remained a single office. Major General Walt commanded both units. Lieutenant Colonel Sevier recalled, "Walt had two hats. We talked to him in whichever office we happened to catch him, about either [unit]."[10] Although this duality of command often led to confused staff work, it was not a problem for the SLO, because the few court-martial cases presented no difficulty.[11] A general court-martial was not held in Vietnam for four months after the landings.[12] Initially, the Marines were too busy to fall prey to disciplinary problems. Lieutenant Colonel Sevier said, "when we first got down there, they were not let stray too much . . . . It's a combat situation that's new to them, so initially you don't get a lot of trouble. It's only when they've been in country a while and they've got their confidence built up."

Lieutenant Colonel Sevier's new deputy, Major Fred Grabowski, proved adept at the location and procurement of materiel useful to the legal office, often without disturbing usual supply channels. Shortly after his arrival, in July 1965, Major Grabowski acquired four highly valued general purpose tents. One of these he gave to new-found acquaintances in a nearby wing engineer unit. They, in return, constructed wooden framing and flooring for the remaining three tents, which were erected near the rear of MAF/Division Headquarters. The tents allowed the small legal staff to move from a partitioned corner of the messhall where they had previously been located. One of the tents was employed as the work space for the SLO, his deputy, and the enlisted legal chief, Master Sergeant Harold L. Tetrick; another was for the defense counsels, legal assistance, and claims lawyers; the third was for trial counsels. Later, a fourth tent was added and used as a "courtroom," to the relief of the chaplain, as well as the mess chief, whose messhall had also been pressed into service as a hearing room.[14]

The tents' sides could be rolled up in hot weather, but that provided little relief. The dank, heavy odor of a hot tent was not soon forgotten. The tentage found in Vietnam was old. Rain created problems of leakage, damage to documents, and drainage. Still, the lawyers knew they were better off than the many Marines who lacked even a tent.

Through 1965 the number of cases assigned to each counsel — the caseload — remained low. Recollections of the actual number of cases assigned varied from two or three cases to nine or ten.[15] In any event, the number was fluid and not very high. In September the surrounding city of Da Nang was put off limits to all Marines, except for purposes of official duty or business, two broad exceptions.[16] The commission of minor offenses and crimes was reduced by the off-limits order. Unlike later arriving units, the first Marines that landed in Da Nang were integral, cohesive units. That, too, contributed to the initially low offense rate. Second Lieutenant John E. Gillmor, Jr., recalled: "During that period we sent half the legal department to China Beach to go swimming . . . . Boredom was our biggest real enemy."[17]

Of the three levels of court-martial under the 1951 *Manual for Courts-Martial*, which was still in effect,

Maj Fred Grabowski, Deputy Staff Legal Officer, III MAF/3d Marine Division, works in a section of the messhall before legal personnel were assigned their own work space.
Photo courtesy of Col Daniel F. McConnell, USMC (Ret.)

Photo courtesy of Col Charles B. Sevier, USMC (Ret.)
In September 1965, LtCol Charles B. Sevier, III MAF/3d Marine Division Staff Legal Officer, stands before his recently erected "office" in the rear of the III MAF compound.

the most serious offenses were tried at a general court-martial, which required lawyer counsel. The intermediate-level special court-martial was employed for the majority of cases. Lawyers were not a requirement in special courts, although they were sometimes assigned. Summary courts-martial were one-officer hearings which disposed of minor offenses, as the term suggests, in a summary, greatly simplified proceeding. The maximum permissible punishment a summary court-martial could impose was much less than that of a special or general court-martial. The officer hearing the summary court-martial case did not have to be a lawyer, and rarely was. The accused could refuse trial by a summary court, in which case the officer with authority to convene the court-martial could, and usually did, upgrade the case to a special court-martial, which could not be refused.[18]

In many cases the non-lawyer officer assigned to conduct a summary court-martial would advise the accused, before trial, to confer with a lawyer. That could result in the lawyer advising the Marine to refuse a summary and request a special court, if a lawyer would then be assigned to represent him. Sometimes such an agreement could be struck with a convening authority. In that way the accused would have attorney representation, although he also risked greater punishment if found guilty at a special court-martial. However, most often, Marine Corps lawyers participated in special courts-martial only when the offense appeared to warrant a bad conduct discharge.[19]

Lieutenant Colonel Daniel F. McConnell, later a deputy SLO in Vietnam, noted that he regularly made the more capable junior lawyers available to act as summary courts-martial, as well. "The convening authority was generally pleased," McConnell recalled. "The accused felt more secure, and justice was served."[20] But within a few years, Marine Corps lawyers would be too occupied with more serious cases to allow such a luxury.

General and special courts-martial were decided by members. The 1951 *Manual for Courts-Martial* did not provide for a case to be heard solely by a judge. Indeed, there were no judges, as such. A law officer, similar to a judge, presided at general courts-martial. Occasionally, a law officer was made available to act as the senior member of a special court, which had no provision for a law officer and was otherwise directed by a nonlawyer officer.[21]

Most of those cases that reached Marine Corps lawyers in Da Nang were serious. For example, a high number of negligent homicide cases were tried.[22] Many of those were referred to as "quick draw" cases in which

Marines mishandled their weapons, often .45 caliber pistols, with tragic consequences.

A typical caseload was that of First Lieutenant Robert A. "Tony" Godwin. After spending five and a half months on Okinawa, he arrived in Da Nang in August 1965. In the seven and a half months he remained, he was defense counsel in ten general and five special courts-martial. The general courts-martial included two homicides, a vehicular homicide, two rapes, and two robberies. Among the special courts-martial was a "quick draw" assault with a deadly weapon, two assaults of officers, and sleeping on post. Seven of the 15 courts-martial were pleas of guilty, several with pretrial agreements which limited punishment to agreed upon limits. Of the eight cases that went to trial as not-guilty pleas, Lieutenant Godwin gained acquittals in three, conviction of a lesser offense in one, and mixed findings (guilty of some offenses, not guilty of others) in three. Only one resulted in a straight guilty finding.[23]

Homicide, rape, robbery—serious offenses were being tried in Vietnam, even at that early point. At the same time, 15 cases in seven and a half months is a very light caseload, even with the other duties all counsels carried out.

Those other duties included legal assistance counselling (always of significant volume overseas); boards of investigation which occasionally involved lawyer participation; administrative discharge boards; occasional informal, one-officer ("JAG Manual") investigations; and the usual legal advice to the command.*

1stLt Robert A. Godwin, starched and pressed, poses at Camp Courtney, Okinawa, shortly before his departure for Da Nang and duty as a defense counsel.
Photo courtesy of Col Robert A. Godwin, USMCR

From a Lawyer's Case File: One Homicide, Two Victims

Private First Class Kenneth Wheeler was 18 years old when he killed his best friend.[24] Before coming to Vietnam he and the victim, Private First Class Richard E. "Rick" Cronk, had been close, going on liberty together and living in the same squadbay. Wheeler had dated Cronk's sister. On 23 August 1965, with Company E, 2d Battalion, 9th Marines, they had been in combat, and later, were relaxing with their unit. As his friend, Cronk, floated on an air mattress in a shallow stream, Wheeler, thinking it unloaded, pointed his M-14 rifle at Cronk in jest. Cronk died almost instantly from a bullet that pierced his throat. Wheeler arrived at the battalion aid station in shock, unaware of his surroundings or those who carried him there. He could neither walk nor speak.

Forty-seven days later, before a general court-martial, he pleaded guilty to culpably negligent homicide. He offered neither defense nor excuse and made no plea for mercy. His defense counsel, First Lieutenant Tony Godwin, offered a letter in mitigation from the mother of the victim. She wrote:

> I was stunned and heartsick to hear that my son's friend K. Wheeler is being tried for his death . . . but we did know in our hearts it was a tragic accident . . . . All of these men were tired, dirty and probably tensed up from four days out on duty.
> Rick leaves a family who loved him dearly and he was so much a part of all our lives, but to know that Wheeler . . . must pay for his death won't make it any less hard to bear. In fact, we feel it will serve no purpose for this boy

---

*Boards of investigation, relating to non-judicial punishment, were provided for in the 1951 *Manual for Courts-Martial*. They expired with the implementation of the 1969 *Manual for Courts-Martial*.

Drinks were inexpensive but ambience was in short supply, at the Chu Lai officers' club.

to be punished any more than he is already. He is in his own private hell which is enough!

I hope, on our behalf, you can enter a plea for complete acquittal . . . . He needs his friends now.

The court-martial took only two hours and thirty-five minutes from opening to sentencing: confinement at hard labor for 12 months, forfeiture of all pay and allowances for a year, and reduction to private. Neither a dishonorable discharge nor a bad conduct discharge was a part of the sentence.

In his review of the trial the SLO, Colonel Sevier, wrote: "Under the circumstances of this case, confinement would be of no benefit to the United States or to the accused." The court-martial convening authority, General Walt, agreed and reduced the sentence to forfeitures of $60 a month for six months and reduction to private.

Within two weeks of the court-martial PFC Wheeler required psychiatric care, and on 18 November, suffering from severe depression, he was admitted to the psychiatric ward of the U.S. Naval Hospital in Yokosuka, Japan. After six months' hospitalization he was administratively discharged from the Marine Corps.[25]

Trying Cases

The lawyers of the combined 3d Marine Division/III MAF legal office prepared to split into two separate offices in early 1966. Meanwhile, that part of the airbase's former French Foreign Legionnaires' barracks that now housed Marine Corps officers was known as the bachelor officer quarters, or BOQ. Each room was assigned a Vietnamese housemaid, usually referred to as a "house mouse," who washed the occupants' clothes, kept the room reasonably clean, and shined boots to a high luster. The cost for these services was 500 piasters, or about $4.50, per month. The cost of rations was automatically deducted from each officer's pay. An officer's club which served 15-cent beer and 20-cent mixed drinks and employed Vietnamese waitresses, was available.[26]

The tent working spaces of the lawyers were not on a par with those of the staff in the permanent French buildings, but they were satisfactory. The four legal tents allowed for more space than the indoor staff enjoyed and a greater degree of privacy, which was necessary for interviewing witnesses and those accused.

Photo courtesy of LtCol John L. Zorack, USMC (Ret.)

Vietnamese interpreters were not assigned to legal sections. LtCol John L. Zorack, Task Force X-Ray's Staff Legal Officer in 1967, sits with an interpreter he hired, 13-year-old Binh Nguyen. With LtCol Zorack's assistance, Binh later emigrated to the United States.

Mud, rain, and dust were endured by everyone. The monsoon rains penetrated tents and rain gear. At times blowing almost parallel to the ground, the rain left puddles on cots, desks, and plywood floors. Mildew quickly formed on virtually any stationary object. In summer's heat the dust was ankle-deep in places, billowing in the air with each footfall. Passing vehicles left dust clouds hanging in their wake which deposited gritty coatings on exposed skin, papers, and court-recording equipment.

In Da Nang that important legal tool, the law library, was at best limited. The "standard issue" law library was not yet implemented. In 1965 and 1966 advance sheets did not reach Vietnam.* The Da Nang "law library" contained only bound volumes of past military appellate opinions, the *Martindale-Hubbell Law Directory* (a digest of state laws and a guide to attorneys in the U.S.), and the 1951 *Manual for Courts-Martial*. Volumes of the *United States Supreme Court Reports*, other Federal reports, form books, model jury instructions, legal treatises, and similar references were not among the combat materiel shipped to Vietnam.[27] In lieu of a law library the counsels relied on their notes from Naval Justice School and cited authority with which they hoped the law officer was familiar. Lieutenant (jg) John F. Erickson, a Navy law specialist, was once reduced to citing as authority a case he had read about in a recent edition of the *Stars and Stripes* newspaper, a lawyer's field expedient.[28]

Numerous Marines school-trained in the Vietnamese language were assigned to Vietnam as translators, usually to interrogator-translator teams and intelligence units. None served with the legal offices that often dealt with Vietnamese witnesses, victims, and claimants. For courtroom use the Marines hired translators from the local Vietnamese population, some of whom spoke excellent French and English.

---

*Advance sheets are copies of appellate court opinions, mailed to legal commands and offices as they are announced. Periodically the accumulated advance sheets appear as bound volumes. They are important to lawyers because they are the latest word on the appellate court's interpretation and application of the law.

At Chu Lai's Task Force X-Ray Lieutenant Colonel John L. Zorack's first interpreter was a 13-year-old boy. Of course, the Vietnamese were not trained as courtroom translators and their skills varied widely. In general, the standard was not high. "The problems in trying a case with an interpreter," Lieutenant Hugh Campbell recalled, "were just impossible . . . . [They] made it almost impossible to cross-examine witnesses."[29] Second Lieutenant John E. Gillmor, a 3d Marine Division defense counsel, added:

> Da Nang was on a border area for local dialects, and it was difficult to get a translator who could communicate with the [witnesses]. In addition, there was a cultural gap which made me suspect that the witnesses were trying to tell us what they thought we wanted to hear . . . . I was very much afraid that if we had a contested trial, my case would collapse over the translation issue.[30]

Although their function was explained and although the interpreter acknowledged understanding, counsel often realized in the midst of examination that the witness and the interpreter were having their own parallel conversation. The responses to questions often were suspected to be an amalgam of the witness' and translator's view of what constituted an appropriate answer. Sometimes a lengthy, obviously complex response by the witness would be translated by the interpreter as, "yes." But no case was reversed at the appellate level for inadequacy of translation, perhaps in recognition of the fact that all parties labored under the same burden.

As challenging as accurate translations were, locating and interviewing of witnesses, both military and Vietnamese, was equally difficult. The problems in locating a Marine witness, for example, were several. If he was an infantryman, he was probably in the field. But where was his company—if his company could be determined? Was the Marine unavailable because he was on patrol? Assigned to an outpost? Sent out of country on R & R? Had he been killed or wounded since the offense was reported? Had he already rotated back to the U.S. because his 13-month tour of duty in Vietnam was completed? Had he been sent home on emergency leave? Was he in an unauthorized absence status?

Although the same problems arose in non-combat areas, they were heightened in Vietnam by tactical considerations and inadequate communications and transportation. For lawyers accustomed to instant telephonic access, Vietnam was a new experience. Telephoning anyplace outside the vicinity reached by the unit's switchboard was a significant chore. Static, poor and broken connections, and interruption for higher priority calls were the rule. Captain William B. Draper, Jr., recalled his attempts to go from one codenamed switchboard to another via a military telephone, called a "double-E-eight," for its military designation, EE-8. As he recalled:

> It is doubtful if everyone doesn't have several hair raising tales of . . . frustration. Who can forget hollering "Isherwood, give me Grasshopper!" into a seemingly dead double-E-eight for hours on end, only to finally get the connection and have it pre-empted immediately. Occasionally communication foul-ups resulted in something more than jangled nerves: . . . walls with your fist imprint in them.[31]

As difficult as it was to locate a Marine, finding a Vietnamese was even more challenging. Phone books and subpoenas were not an option. To an American, Vietnamese names were similar and confusing. There simply was no practical way to summon a Vietnamese to a court-martial. All one could do, if the statement of a Vietnamese witness or victim was required, was to go to them.

Twenty-seven Navy lawyers served in Marine Corps legal offices in Vietnam during the war. The first was Lt (later RAdm) Hugh D. Campbell, shown at Da Nang in 1965. He was III MAF/3d Marine Division chief defense counsel. In November 1986 he assumed the duties of the Judge Advocate General of the Navy and Commander, Naval Legal Service Command.
Photo courtesy of RAdm Hugh D. Campbell, JAGC, USN (Ret.)

Colonel Sevier recalled when he first became aware that his lawyers were taking the initiative in the witness location process:

> I walked out of the legal tent and I saw this [military] truck, and it had about four of my lawyers and two of my NCOs on it, and they were all holding goddamn rifles! .... I turned to this Navy lieutenant [Campbell]: "What in the hell are you people doing?" "We're going out there in bandit country, and pick up the Vietnamese witnesses." Well, I looked, and then I said [to myself], I'm going to let them go and they'll hang me. But I said, "Okay." A Navy lieutenant! A helluva nice kid.[32]

Lieutenant Campbell, who became the Judge Advocate General of the Navy 21 years later, was on one of the earliest forays to find witnesses in contested territory. In the next six years countless similar missions to locate essential trial participants were carried out. It was a novel but necessary trial preparation method in Vietnam. As Colonel Sevier noted:

> It worked because of the people we had .... Lieutenants who'd gone through OCS and the Basic School. They had some background in the infantry and could get around. They were capable of leaving the C.P. and going to a regiment, or a battalion and doing their investigation, running a pretrial [investigation], going out in the bush with a patrol. They'd interview witnesses through an interpreter. They had that capability.[33]

When not locating witnesses or preparing for court, the lawyers often looked for other constructive activity to occupy free time. Civic action, for example, was not only the concern of the staff officers assigned to that section. The 3d Marine Division's command chronology for the period noted: "At this stage ... Division Civic Action units are stressing maximum contact with the local Vietnamese population."[34] Although attorneys had no formal connection with civic action, First Lieutenant Tony Godwin and other lawyers from the 3d Division/III MAF staff taught English in a local Vietnamese high school, using Vietnamese-English textbooks. The Marine Corps teachers concealed their sidearms under their utility uniform shirts.[35] Throughout the war Marine Corps lawyers took an active role in the civic action program.

III MAF: Headquarters Without Lawyers

After an enemy attack on the Da Nang Airbase in July 1965 General Walt, concerned with security, ordered the 3d Marine Division command post moved from the airbase to a location three miles to the west on the northern slope of Hill 327.

From 11 to 15 November in heavy monsoon rains the 3d Division Headquarters, including the Staff Legal Office, relocated to Hill 327.[36] The 1st Marine Aircraft Wing, including its legal personnel, and III MAF headquarters, remained at the airbase.

Colonel Vernon A. "Vap" Peltzer was the first Staff Legal Officer assigned to III MAF Headquarters. (Although Colonel Sevier had been overseeing III MAF Headquarters' legal affairs, he was actually assigned to the 3d Marine Division.) As a matter of fact, Colonel Peltzer was the headquarters's only legal officer at the time. Several other attorneys were on the MAF staff, but they were acting in other capacities.

In retrospect, the assignment of a colonel as SLO of III MAF was notable. Those making assignments at Headquarters Marine Corps could not have anticipated that, when the headquarters of III MAF and the 3d Marine Division became geographically separated, III MAF would not be designated a court-martial convening authority. The commanding general of the 3d Division had always had such authority. The command having only recently been formed in Vietnam, III MAF's commanding general did not have such authority. Without this authority (a simple administrative act by the Secretary of the Navy confers it) the MAF commanding general could not order a court-martial convened. Lacking that power, and having relatively few Marines assigned to it, the MAF had little need for lawyers, so the lawyers all moved to Hill 327 with the command that conducted trials, the 3d Division. It was not surprising that the SLO for the 1st Marine Aircraft Wing wrote the legal officer for Fleet Marine Force, Pacific that "although I do not know if III MAF has requested a lawyer, I earnestly do not feel that they need one. Any legal work that they have can be accomplished by the lawyers presently on hand as an additional duty."[37] The 3d Marine Division SLO, Colonel Sevier, was more laconic when he said about the III MAF legal office, "there wasn't much to do, down there."[38]

If Colonel Peltzer found himself without a great deal of work, the fault was not his. He shared an office with the III MAF surgeon, had no law library, did no legal assistance, and had no subordinates. What were the responsibilities of the III MAF SLO? "Just to keep General Walt informed as to what was going on," Colonel Peltzer recalled with frustration.[39] He also reviewed cases tried at other commands, convened a number of investigations, and acted as counsel for the growing Da Nang port facility.

The other attorneys on the MAF staff were assigned nonlegal duties. Colonel Olin W. Jones, SLO of the 3d Marine Division, had served with General Walt in

Department of Defense Photo (USMC) A-413090
Marine Corps lawyers served in numerous roles in Vietnam. In 1966 Maj Charles J. Keever became the III MAF Assistant Chief of Staff, G-5 and Special Assistant to the Commanding General (Civic Action).

Korea. Shortly after assuming command in June 1965, General Walt sent to Okinawa for Colonel Jones, who then acted as General Walt's Deputy Chief of Staff for Administration, Logistics and Area Coordination Matters. That novel billet continued for two months and made Colonel Jones available for legal consultation along with the MAF's assigned SLO.[40]

Major Charles J. "Chuck" Keever, recently of the Staff Legal Office on Okinawa, was the Assistant Chief of Staff, G-5 and Special Assistant to the Commanding General (Civic Action). General Walt believed that civic action was more than benevolence. He thought that it could be used as a weapon to sever the populace from Viet Cong control. Major Keever, without prior training in civic action, was directed to draft a policy that would give overall direction to the civic action program and focus the good-will efforts of individual Marines. He wrote the first MAF order for civic action and, upon its acceptance, saw to its implementation.

He later received the Legion of Merit for his work.[41]

Captain William T. Warren was assigned to the III MAF G-4 office. Like Major Keever, he had been a lawyer serving on Okinawa and had asked to be sent to Vietnam, even if in a non-legal capacity. In June he found himself the III MAF Real Estate Officer, another billet not found in the table of organization but closely related to the tactical security of the Da Nang Airbase. After the July 1965 Viet Cong raid on the airbase destroyed a number of Air Force planes, Captain Warren was tasked with clearing a 300-yard wide security zone around the entire perimeter of the airbase. That effort eventually involved the relocation of 826 Vietnamese houses, approximately 5,000 Vietnamese, and (a delicate matter) 6,000 graves. Working with Le Chi Cuong, the mayor of Da Nang, the relocation effort took three and a half months to dismantle and move houses, shrines, shops, and temples to new locations. Work crews, with the approval of the owners, simply demolished some structures, and III MAF compensated the Vietnamese. Each family received a 30,000 piaster (about $270) relocation allowance in addition to compensation, if their house was demolished. Captain Warren was surprised to find that the Vietnamese, although concerned, did not appear to be at all hostile.[42] His work was one of the few instances in 1965 when a lawyer had opportunity to directly support the commander's tactical mission.

Another lawyer on the staff of III MAF was Major Benjamin B. Ferrell, the Assistant G-1/Civil Affairs Officer. The citation for his Bronze Star Medal summarized his duties and performance:

> [His] area of responsibility covered approximately 7,000 square miles . . . . During the day he traveled throughout the area meeting the Vietnamese leaders of towns and hamlets, discussing their problems and ascertaining their needs. At night Major Ferrell prepared the detailed orders and reports required to implement a meaningful civil affairs program and to procure needed . . . supplies and equipment.[43]

The III MAF lawyers remained at the Da Nang Airbase while the 3d Marine Division Headquarters moved to Hill 327 into newly erected strongback tents.

1st Marine Aircraft Wing: Touching Down

Until 31 August the elements of the 1st Marine Aircraft Wing (1st MAW) in Vietnam were designated 1st MAW (Advance). Parts of the MAW headquarters remained at Iwakuni, Japan, until early in 1966, while most of the wing deployed to Da Nang in increments throughout 1965.[44]

The MAW's first SLO, Major Paul A. A. St.Amour,

arrived in Vietnam shortly after the wing commanding general moved his flag to Da Nang on 11 May. Major St.Amour's overseas tour ended a month and a half later and Colonel Harry S. Popper replaced him.

Colonel Popper, like most of the senior legal officers of the period, had served in World War II. He had commanded a light antiaircraft group and in 1956 was the commanding officer of the 3d Battalion, 2d Marines.[45] As the wing SLO in 1965, he supervised four lawyers, a gunnery sergeant as legal chief, five other enlisted legal clerks, and the wing's sole Marine Corps criminal investigator.

Like the 3d Marine Division, the 1st MAW had few cases with which to contend. Through the first eight months in Vietnam the Wing's lawyers tried no general courts-martial.[46] A variety of special courts similar to those in the 3d Division were conducted in addition to routine legal matters.

Legal Duty in a Combat Zone: Problems

The supporting elements that made the trials possible were of great importance to the accomplishment of the lawyers' mission in Vietnam. The enlisted legal clerks and legal chiefs met the daily challenges of administrative and clerical support under difficult conditions. Their dedication and ability to improvise were indispensable in bringing military justice to the combat zone.

More prosaic, but also important, was court recording equipment. Article 19 of the 1951 UCMJ specified that a bad conduct discharge could not be imposed unless "a complete record of the proceedings and testimony" had been made. Because a bad conduct discharge was a possibility in virtually all special and general courts-martial, almost every court required a verbatim record. The court reporter accomplished that by using an electrically powered recorder employing either a belt or reel-to-reel tape in conjunction with a closed-mask microphone — a mask/microphone fitting flush against the face, into which the reporter repeated everything said by the court-martial participants. The reporter's voice, contained by the mask, was inaudible to others in the courtroom. A "backup" recording was made on a second machine with an open microphone. After the court concluded, the reporter replayed the tape, either employing a speaker or, more often, earphones, and typed a word-for-word record on a manual typewriter, making four carbon copies. Dictaphone was the prevalent brand of recording equipment early in the war, but there were others, as well.[47]

Photo courtesy of Col Harry S. Popper, USMC (Ret.)
1st Marine Aircraft Wing (Forward) working spaces were no better than those of III MAF/3d Marine Division, early in the war. Here Col Harry S. Popper, Jr., Wing Staff Legal Officer, stands beside his "office."

The variety of recorder brands and models made repair and resupply a significant problem and created confusion when equipment familiarization was necessary. The expeditionary setting of Vietnam, where personnel were frequently transferred and resupply problems were greater, magnified the difficulties. Lieutenant Colonel Verne L. "Bubs" Oliver, a Yokosuka-based law officer in 1965, noted: "Each command would end up with two or three different makes, with no single agency or facility to service them. I do not care what make of machine you are employing, you must have a service and repair facility to help keep them on line."[48]

Lance Corporal Gene E. White was a legal clerk assigned to Headquarters Battalion, 12th Marines. His experience with the equipment of that period was typical. He recalled:

> A lot of trouble was experienced with my recorder/transcriber. I was using the old plastic belt, electric Dictaphone machine . . . . Sand/dust was also a big problem with my machine. The "floor" of our tent was ankle-deep sand. This sand filled the foot pedal on my machine and

Lawyers of the 1st Marine Aircraft Wing (Forward) legal office posed at Da Nang, Vietnam, June 1965. From left: 1stLt Bruce A. Hoffman; 1stLt John W. Clark; Col Harry S. Popper, Jr., Staff Legal Officer; LtCol Frederick H. Campbell; Lt Edward A. Arianna, USN.

got into the the Dictaphone itself. Only luck and a lot of cleaning kept them going.[49]

A number of court reporters used their personal tape recorders at trial in an effort to overcome balky government-issued equipment.[50] That usually precluded the professionally embarrassing exchanges found in a number of appellate opinions of that period, such as the case of *United States v. Private First Class Gary O. Harrison*, a general court-martial for murder. The opinion read:

> At the pre-sentencing stage the defense counsel offered an eyewitness . . . . After the testimony was given, it was discovered that the recording machine had failed and did not pick up [the witness'] testimony. The following stipulation of testimony was then entered: "DC: Due to a mechanical failure of the recording machine the machine did not pick up the testimony of [the witness], so trial counsel, with the express consent of the accused will enter into a stipulation with the defense concerning the sworn testimony of [the witness]."[51]

But what if the accused was not as agreeable as in this case, and would not stipulate? Was the witness still available to again testify? What effect would inevitable minor inconsistencies in the two testimonies have on the court? How might the opposing counsel attack the testimony, given a second "bite of the apple?" The potential pitfalls were several.

The U.S. Army, subject to the same reporting requirements and difficulties, took action to end the equipment problem. In October 1965, the senior Army judge advocate sponsored an interservice conference at MACV headquarters in Saigon. Colonels Popper, Sevier, Peltzer and Blackburn attended. Colonel Popper noted in a letter to Headquarters Marine Corps:

> One item of particular interest was the announcement that, after extensive investigation the Army has adopted the Gray Audiograph equipment; both the regular office model and the portable power pack model. I have not seen either of them, but we are particularly interested . . . . One advantage in regard to the Gray is that it can be serviced out of Saigon. I wonder if anyone in Headquarters Marine Corps has checked out . . . this equipment?[52]

Benefitting from the Army's research, the Marine Corps purchased Gray Audiograph recorders and the smaller, portable Gray Keynoters for issue to legal offices in Vietnam. But what looked promising at the outset became a serious problem. The machines proved unreliable in the extreme heat and dust, and, worse, repairs were unavailable in Saigon, contrary to initial assurances. Whether any recorder employing the technology of the 1960s could have overcome the harsh operating conditions that defeated the Grays is ques-

USO Entertainer Martha Raye visits Da Nang, 13 November 1965. She is flanked by 3d Marine Division lawyers Capt Fred R. Files, left, and Lt Hugh D. Campbell, USN.

Photo courtesy of RAdm Hugh D. Campbell, JAGC, USN (Ret.)

tionable. Those machines, combined with the undependable power sources upon which the reporters had to rely, vexed the legal system as long as the Marines remained in Vietnam and led to the reversal of several cases for lack of the required verbatim record.[53]

Another problem was the lack of a brig in the III MAF area, through 1966. At first, convicted Marines were confined at their unit in a tent, with a chaser (an armed Marine guard) posted at the "door."[54] That was satisfactory only so long as the sentence was not lengthy and the number of confined Marines remained very small. As the frequency of courts-martial rose with the number of Marines deployed to Vietnam, and sentences escalated in severity, another solution was required.

While the 3d Division and III MAF were still collocated, the provost marshal improvised a confinement "facility," which was simply a hole in the ground, quite deep, covered by barbed wire. Convicted prisoners with long-term sentences were to be kept there for the several days it took for transportation to be arranged to a brig on Okinawa or in Japan.[55] Colonel Peltzer, the III MAF SLO, was alerted to this procedure, which was contrary to military law and the Department of the Navy *Corrections Manual*. He immediately acted to ensure that the division did not use the "facility." His forceful discussion of the issue with General Walt's

The Martha Raye USO show pick-up band of Marine Corps musicians included lawyer-cum-civil affairs officer Maj James P. King, left, a trombone player of professional caliber, in Da Nang, 14 November 1965.

Photo courtesy of Mr. Donald W. Harris

Brig-in-a-tent without the tent. The week-long pretrial confinement of a Marine in this open-air enclosure at Phu Bai resulted in the dismissal of charges.

chief of staff led to a reexamination of the prisoner holding policy. The use of aircraft for ferrying prisoners to Okinawa could not continue indefinitely, because tactical missions required more and more aircraft, which left few to carry prisoners. Plans were initiated for a brig to be built in Vietnam, but construction was not completed until late 1966.[56] Until then the brig-in-a-tent system continued for short-term prisoners, while those with more substantial sentences were flown to Okinawa or Japan for confinement.

Offenses new to Marine Corps lawyers, if not to Marines, began to appear on court-martial charge sheets. The profits to be had from currency manipulation and black marketeering attracted the few who were willing to accept the risk of trial and punishment. Currency violations became common. Until 1 September 1965 U.S. dollars were an authorized medium of exchange in Vietnam. After that date U.S. currency was withdrawn from the economy and military payment certificates (MPC) substituted. The Vietnamese piaster remained in circulation in the civilian community. All service personnel entering the country had to exchange their "green" for MPC and were paid in MPC while they remained in-country. All U.S. facilities, such as PXs, clubs, and post offices, accepted only MPC. The purpose of withdrawing U.S. dollars from circulation was to keep U.S. and Vietnamese monetary systems separate and to deter black market operations and currency manipulation. This dampened the country's severe inflation which had lured some Americans to play the exchange rate of the piaster against that of the U.S. dollar, pocketing the difference as illegal profit.[57]

Illegal currency transactions often involved black market sales of items stolen from the PX system. Exchange pilferage losses in Vietnam for 1965, alone, amounted to $2.25 million. Besides the dollar loss, black marketeering weakened the already fragile Vietnamese economy.[58]

Black market activities were common among soldiers and Marines who were absent without leave (AWOL) from their units. They often found refuge in Da Nang and other large cities in South Vietnam, frequently with prostitutes. Captain Robert W. Wachsmuth, a Force Logistic Command trial counsel, recalled:

> AWOL Marines were afforded safe haven with Vietnamese prostitutes. They were told they could have all of the women, beer and food they wanted . . . in exchange for their making one trip to the exchange in Da Nang. Vietnamese prostitutes had collected considerable MPC in consideration of their favors, but were prohibited from possessing or spending MPC. Consequently, MPC would be given to the AWOL Marine who was instructed to purchase television sets at the exchange. When the television sets were handed over to the pimps or heads of the operation, the sets would be transported to Saigon where, upon resale, they often brought five to ten times their original purchase price.[59]

It was another, newer variety of crime that Marine Corps lawyers prosecuted throughout the war.

From a Lawyer's Case File: The Marine Corps' First War Crime Conviction in Vietnam

"War crime" is the legal expression for a violation of the law of war by any person, military or civilian.[60] Directive Number 20-4 of the Military Assistance Command, Vietnam, defined a war crime simply as, "every violation of the law of war." It referred to a willful killing (other than in combat) as a "Grave Breach."[61]

No Marine was charged with the commission of a war crime, as such, in Vietnam. Rather, any "violation of the law of war" committed by a Marine against a Vietnamese was charged as a violation of the UCMJ. For example, the murder of a civilian noncombatant was charged as a violation of Article 118, murder, rather than as a war crime in violation of the Geneva or Hague conventions. Technically, the killing of a South Vietnamese could not be a war crime. The victim was a citizen of an allied nation, protected by the laws of Vietnam, rather than an enemy protected by the Geneva Conventions.[62]

Other than homicides, the Marine Corps did not maintain records of offenses committed against Vietnamese.[63] Ninety-five U.S. Army personnel were convicted by court-martial of the murder or manslaughter of Vietnamese. Twenty-seven Marines were found guilty of the same offenses.[64] Lance Corporal Marion McGhee was the first Marine to be convicted of the murder of a Vietnamese noncombatant.

On 12 August 1965 Lance Corporal McGhee was a fireteam leader in Company M, 3d Battalion, 3d Marines, located on the Chu Lai perimeter. He had no record of prior disciplinary violations. Several of his buddies noted on the 12th that his behavior seemed unusual. Drunk, some testified; "strange," but not drunk, others testified.

Around 2100 that night Lance Corporal McGhee walked through Marine lines, past the defensive barbed wire and toward a nearby village. In answer to a Marine sentry's shouted question, he responded that he was going after a VC. Two Marines were dispatched to retrieve McGhee. As they approached the village they heard a shot and a woman's scream and then saw McGhee walking toward them from the village. Calmly, he said he had just killed a VC and other VC were following him. The other two Marines saw nothing. McGhee then exclaimed that he was going to get the other VC and strode back toward the village, despite efforts to stop him. Within a few minutes he returned to Marine lines a second time, now with a "wild look," according to a defense witness.

At trial Vietnamese prosecution witnesses testified that McGhee had kicked through the wall of the hut where their family slept. He seized a 14-year-old girl and pulled her toward the door. When her father interceded, McGhee shot and killed him. Once outside the house the girl escaped McGhee with the help of her grandmother. McGhee stood by his assertion that he had been pursuing someone he suspected to be a VC and, in a pleading encountered many times over the next few years, raised the defense of insanity.

After lengthy testimony by two psychiatrists the

LtCol Charles B. Sevier, right, with law officer Capt James E. Keys, USN, in 1965 stands behind the 3d Marine Division command post. Four years later Capt Keys represented Navy Cdr Lloyd M. Bucher, captain of the ill-fated Pueblo *(AKL 44), at his court of inquiry.*

Photo courtesy of Col Charles B. Sevier, USMC (Ret.)

court concluded that the government had met the burden of proving Lance Corporal McGhee's mental capacity; that beyond a reasonable doubt, he was free from mental defect, disease, or derangement and was able to distinguish right from wrong and adhere to the right. The court found him guilty of unpremeditated murder and sentenced him to reduction to private, loss of all pay and allowances, confinement at hard labor for ten years, and a dishonorable discharge. At the appellate level McGhee's confinement was reduced to seven years.[65] He actually served six years and one month.[66]

Perspective

In March 1965 the single Marine Corps lawyer assigned legal duties in Vietnam taped a hand-written sign to the door of his room: "Staff Legal Officer." By the end of the year three staff legal officers, all colonels, and more than 30 other Marine Corps lawyers and Navy law specialists were involved in trying courts-martial in Vietnam. Official totals of the number of cases tried in Vietnam in 1965 were not kept, but according to the Navy's Judge Advocate General, the number was proportionally lower than in other locations where Marines were based.[67]

High-level concern regarding the treatment of Vietnamese prisoners of war was already evident. In September the Commanding General, Fleet Marine Force, Pacific, Lieutenant General Victor H. Krulak, contacted Major General Walt, saying, "I am anxious that all of our people are made fully aware of their obligations, under the Geneva Convention, as to the treatment of prisoners. This point acquires particular importance now that the flow of replacements will bring you a large group of new and uninitiated people each month."[68] General Krulak emphasized the same point two months later, in another message to General Walt: "Ensure that every officer in the chain of command knows the rules, the reasons for the rules, and the penalties for their violation, and then accept no compromise at all."[69] Despite the concern for the proper treatment of prisoners, throughout the war Marine Corps lawyers would try Marines charged with the very acts feared by General Krulak.

But for the moment, while the war increased in intensity and the number of Marines in Vietnam continued to rise, crime remained a minor problem. Except for isolated instances, drugs were not yet a concern. "Fragging," the murder of officers and noncommissioned officers by their own men, was unknown. Civilian lawyers were not yet regular arrivals at the Da Nang Airbase. Racial conflict had not spread to the Marine Corps in any significant way.

For Marine Corps lawyers, 1965 was the first test of the *Manual for Courts-Martial* under expeditionary circumstances. Still, as staff officers, lawyers played no part in the commander's operational scheme. Lieutenant Colonel John L. Zorack, who led the 1st Marine Division's legal office at Chu Lai, recalled, "we were just 'there,' to be frank with you. When they [the Marine commanders] had a problem, they called on us."[70]

In Washington Colonel Robert B. Neville continued in charge of Discipline Branch, which remained a part of Personnel Department. The Marine Corps tried 204 general, and 4,620 special, courts-martial, world-wide, during the year.[71] So far, no special programs or requirements were identified that would assure an increase in the number of lawyers on active duty to keep pace with the 40 percent increase in Marine Corps strength.[72] The Corps did, however, increase recruitment levels in the Platoon Leaders' Class (Law). By 1965 there were 75 entrants, as opposed to only one officer in 1961, the program's first year.[73]

Personnel Department and Discipline Branch were concerned with the serious lack of senior lawyers who carried a primary legal MOS. To meet the need for these experienced majors, lieutenant colonels, and colonels, Colonel Neville and his seniors decided that the Marine Corps would have to rely on those with secondary legal MOSs—those officers who had been commissioned in fields other than legal then gained law degrees along the way, some on their own, and some with Marine Corps assistance. For the next decade, said the planners at Headquarters Marine Corps, they would have to serve solely in legal billets.[74] The choices earlier given riflemen-lawyers were narrowing with the drift toward lawyer specialization.

CHAPTER 3

1966: Building on Sand

*Trying Cases: Using 'The Red Book'—From a Lawyer's Case File: Pilot to Copilot to Brig
The Other Prisoners: North Vietnamese POWs—The 1st Marine Division Arrives: More Lawyers, More Cases
Force Logistic Command: New Guy on the Block—Trying Cases—Courtroom Personnel: Just Passin' Through
Homicide on Patrol: Men, Women, and Children—3d Marine Division: On The Road Again
III MAF: Double-Hatting The Lawyer—Perspective*

By January 1966 Major General Lewis W. Walt, Commanding General of III MAF and the 3d Marine Division, had more than 41,000 men under his command. The United States' recent decision to double U.S. forces in Vietnam meant that the 1st Marine Division, lately moved from Camp Pendleton, California, to Okinawa, would be moving again, this time to the combat zone.

The Marines in Vietnam were located in I Corps Tactical Zone, the northernmost of South Vietnam's four military regions. I Corps was bordered on the north by the Demilitarized Zone; to the south, by the Army's II Corps Tactical Zone; to the east, by the South China Sea; and to the west by Laos. The Marines operated from three tactical areas of responsibility (TAORs), and virtually all courts-martial arose from events that occurred within those TAORs. The Da Nang TAOR covered 530 square miles and contained over a quarter of a million South Vietnamese. The headquarters of III MAF, the 3d Marine Division, and the 1st Marine Aircraft Wing were located there. Three infantry regiments, an artillery regiment, and two aircraft groups were based in the Da Nang TAOR as well.

Fifty-seven miles to the south the Chu Lai TAOR contained over 100,000 civilians in 205 square miles. Chu Lai was home to two Marine Corps infantry regiments, an artillery group, and three aircraft groups. Units of the 1st Marine Division arrived during the first three months of 1966 and assumed tactical responsibility for the Chu Lai TAOR.[1]

The Phu Bai TAOR, 35 miles northwest of Da Nang, covered 76 square miles and held 36,000 South Vietnamese. Two infantry battalions, an artillery battalion, and one aircraft group were based there.

As the new year began Colonel Vernon A. Peltzer's Force Legal Office remained with the III MAF Headquarters staff at the Da Nang Airbase. Colonel Charles B. Sevier's 3d Marine Division legal office had moved from the airbase to the northern slope of Hill 327, southwest of Da Nang, along with the rest of the division staff. Colonel Harry S. Popper, Jr., and his 1st MAW legal office remained at the airbase with the 1st Marine Aircraft Wing staff.

Trying Cases: Using 'The Red Book'

Most of the courts-martial convened in Vietnam were being tried by officers who had never opened a law book. Their reference was the *Manual for Courts-Martial, 1951*, known to lawyers and nonlawyers alike as "the Red Book" for the color of its cover. (It was actually a distinctly maroon color.) Appendix 2 of the Red Book reprinted the Uniform Code of Military Justice (UCMJ), usually referred to simply as, "the Code." Article 27(b) of the Code read: "Any person who is appointed as trial counsel or defense counsel in the case of a *general* court-martial (1) shall be a judge advocate of the Army or the Air Force, or a law specialist of the Navy or Coast Guard." (Emphasis supplied.)

The prosecutor and defense counsels at special courts-martial most often were not lawyers, because lawyers were required only in general courts. (Lawyers had never been a part of summary courts-martial.) So most special courts were tried "in house" by the officers of the battalion to which the accused Marine belonged. The nonlawyer trial counsel and nonlawyer defense counsel, usually lieutenants and captains, were the work horses of the system represented by the Red Book. As a convenience, the staff legal officer (SLO) usually made a lawyer defense counsel available to a unit, either for advice or for an actual trial, in cases where the facts were unusually complex, or where potentially difficult legal issues were present. A questionable search, a shaky confession, or a circumstantial case, might lead to a request for lawyer assistance. But nearly every junior officer eventually acted as a trial or defense counsel in a special court-martial, and as a member (juror). Every Marine lawyer a rifleman, and every Marine officer a court-martial counsel.

In 1966 First Lieutenant John T. Fischbach was an artillery officer who had not been to law school, but who enjoyed participating in the military justice system. As he recalled:

35

Department of Defense Photo (USMC) A186827

1stLt Anthony P. Tokarz, without helmet, later a judge advocate, was an infantry platoon commander in Company L, 3d Battalion, 7th Marines, in March 1966. He was seriously wounded and earned the Silver Star Medal the day after this photograph was taken.

I travelled between battalions in the 12th Marines . . . as a wandering trial counsel. Since I liked to try courts-martial and most other non-lawyers didn't, the battalion adjutant, 1st Lieutenant Pete Van Ryzin, put me on most appointing orders when I was not out on operations . . . . I recall one trial interrupted by sniper fire and two interrupted by fire missions which required members of the court, witnesses, and the accused to man their posts. It was interesting to try cases where most parties, including the accused, were armed. Some cases were tried outdoors, with members sitting behind tables made of ammo boxes and everyone sitting either on camp stools or empty ammo boxes.

It was my experience trying cases as a non-lawyer counsel . . . that caused me to leave active duty to go to law school . . . . Practicing law under combat conditions gave me the opportunity to distinguish between the essentials of the law and the trappings.[2]

Lieutenant Fischbach's experiences were similar to those of other nonlawyer counsels who "practiced" under the Red Book.

Each battalion was assigned a legal clerk to monitor the companies' unit punishment books, track battalion disciplinary matters, and execute court-martial documents such as the charge sheet, convening authority's action, and Article 32 investigating officer's report. The legal clerk was also responsible for "taking" the court—recording the proceedings via the closed-microphone recording system. Finally, he typed the record of trial as well.

Usually, the legal clerk was also assigned other administrative duties within the battalion office, such as unit diary clerk, R & R clerk, or files clerk; whatever clerical work the battalion required. This approach to assignments inevitably had a negative effect on the performance of the legal clerk's specialized and demanding duties. Battalion adjutants, responsible for all of the many administrative matters within the command, often did not have the luxury of choice when it came to assignment of clerical personnel. Nevertheless, in an area as detailed as the law there was no room for part-time legal clerks. Court-martial processing errors were too often made because field commands could not afford to assign exclusively legal duties to their legal clerks.

What did the Marine infantry commander think about lawyers? Lieutenant Colonel Paul X. Kelley, later the 28th Commandant of the Marine Corps, commanded the 2d Battalion, 4th Marines, during part of 1966. Asked if lawyers had played any part in his exercise of command, he replied: "They really didn't, and there was a very good reason for that .... We had very little opportunity to have what I would consider the rear area problems; you don't have problems, normally, in the field .... So, as a battalion commander, I had very little requirement for lawyers." He went on to say that, until he had a court-martial case that required a lawyer, he simply gave lawyers no thought. So long as they were there when you needed them, lawyers were properly supporting the commander.[3]

Several nonlawyer trial and defense counsels in Vietnam later attended law school and returned to duty as judge advocates. The experience they gained in operational matters and in the command of Marines in combat would serve them well, and serve the Marine Corps well, in future years.

Among the future lawyers was Captain Kenneth T. "K.T." Taylor. In 1966 he was awarded the Silver Star Medal for heroism while an advisor to a Vietnamese army battalion.[4] In future years, as a colonel, he was the staff judge advocate of several major commands.

Corporal Philip A. Seymour, an infantryman, was awarded the Bronze Star Medal, the Navy Commendation Medal, the Vietnamese Cross of Gallantry, and the Purple Heart. He later gained college and law degrees and became a Marine Corps judge advocate.[5]

First Lieutenant Anthony P. "Tony" Tokarz was an infantry platoon commander. In March 1966, in a series of search and destroy missions during which he was seriously wounded, he earned the Silver Star Medal.[6] He later became a lawyer and attained the grade of colonel.

Captain James S. May, the combat cargo officer on board the *Calvert* (APA 32), was also the ship's legal officer.[7] As a colonel he was a staff judge advocate as well as a judge on the Navy-Marine Corps Court of Military Review. While in the latter billet he was to write the opinion upholding the conviction of turncoat Private First Class Robert R. Garwood.*

Captain Wallace L. "Wally" Campbell was an RF-4 Phantom reconnaissance systems operator in 1966. The Commandant of the Marine Corps presented him a Silver Star Medal for heroism in a series of reconnaissance missions over North Vietnam.[8] He, too, would become a colonel and the staff judge advocate of several Marine Corps commands.

Although not the only Marines to move from line billets to the courtroom, they belonged to that category of post-Vietnam lawyer who knew the military courtroom from the perspective of both commander and jurist. Like their World War II and Korean War predecessors, they were to lead a new generation of Marine Corps lawyers. Unlike their predecessors, they would have to deal with the disciplinary problems spawned by a nationally divisive war.

Along with other nonlawyer counsels and officer-lawyers, they also filled the need for court-martial personnel in Vietnam. The modest disciplinary rate of 1965 continued into 1966. According to the 1st Marine Division's command chronology:

> The current low disciplinary rate within the Division is indicative of the high state of morale. During the months of April through June 1966, the Division had 116 courts-martial [including summaries]. During a like period in 1965 when the Division was stationed at Camp Pendleton, there were 266.[9]

Although those circumstances would worsen dramatically within two years, light caseloads continued to prevail in Vietnam.

From a Lawyer's Case File: Pilot to Copilot to Brig

In 1966 the review was completed in the general courts-martial of the *United States v. Privates First Class Robert L. Bright and Lucien J. Gonzales*. In retrospect their cases may seem humorous footnotes, but they did not amuse those involved. A record of trial does not reveal the fear, anger, uncertainty, and violence involved in dealing with drunken, belligerent individuals in the prime of physical strength and aggressiveness. Potential tragedy was never far away in the less-than-grave events that transpired in the Bright and Gonzales cases.

At about 2030 on a July night Bright and Gonzales were returning to their unit, the 3d Engineer Battalion, after an evening of drinking. They were quite

---

*See Chapter 10.

Department of Defense Photo (USMC) A188367

Capt Kenneth T. Taylor, later a judge advocate, received the Silver Star Medal from MajGen Wood B. Kyle while sporting the black beret of the Black Panther Company, 1st ARVN Division, to which he was an advisor. Capt Taylor said, "General Kyle was less than enthusiastic about my rather unorthodox cover and facial hair. While he made no comment . . . . We did not spend any time in light conversation."

Infantry squad leader Cpl Philip A. Seymour, later a judge advocate, received the Bronze Star and Navy Commendation Medals and the Purple Heart, as well as the Vietnamese Cross of Gallantry, for combat actions in Vietnam with the 1st Battalion, 1st Marines.

Photo courtesy of Maj Philip A. Seymour, USMC

Marine Corps Historical Collection

Col James S. May, shown in a 1988 photograph. In 1965, as a captain, he was the combat cargo officer and also the legal officer on board the Calvert (APA 32) off Vietnam. He later became a judge advocate.

Capt Wallace L. Campbell, later a judge advocate, was an RF-4 reconnaissance systems operator with VMCS-1 when he was awarded the Silver Star Medal by Gen Leonard F. Chapman, Jr., Commandant of the Marine Corps, for a series of classified combat missions.

Photo courtesy of Col Wallace L. Campbell, USMC

drunk. Their route took them across the Da Nang Airbase and, as luck would have it, past the U.S. Air Force flight line where two B-57 bombers sat on 15-minute alert. Each bomber was armed with four 500-pound bombs, a number of smaller fragmentation bombs, and a machine gun. The bombers' jet engines could be started from the cockpit without an external power source, and the bombs, which were armed, could be dropped with the push of a button, even if the bomber was not airborne.

Recognizing their opportunity, a plan began to form. As Gonzales later testified, "me and my best friend wanted to do something more about the war . . . . We decided to try and fly one, to kill all the V.C. we could . . . . Bright, he is a pretty smart guy, he was going to drive the plane." Bright added: "I would fly out there on a bombing run and bomb the V.C. This is my fourth time down here [at Da Nang] and I know the land real well. I always wanted to fly, anyway." Minutes later, as a night-shift mechanic walked past the bombers, he heard someone calling, "Sir! Sir!" Looking up he saw Bright in the pilot's cockpit and Gonzales behind him in the navigator's cockpit. They had dropped a helmet and wanted the mechanic to pass it back up to them.

Within moments Bright and Gonzales were surrounded by numerous Air Force personnel who, recognizing the dangers of the armed munitions, tried to talk the Marines from the cockpit. Bright and Gonzales, however, only wanted help in starting the engines. As Bright worked the plane's controls, Gonzales yelled, "Leave the pilot alone. Co-pilot to pilot, let's get this thing off the ground!"

Frustrated by the lack of cooperation, Gonzales explained his next actions, saying, "if I couldn't fly it . . . nobody else was going to fly my plane, so I broke it." He pulled wiring loose, smashed indicator lights, and broke control mechanisms. "It seemed to me," he later testified, "every time you turned a knob, everything would fall off. It was fascinating." As he broke off each fascinating piece of equipment, he tossed it to the tarmac.

Eventually, Gonzales was induced to climb from the cockpit. Bright, however, remained determined to go "up to twenty thousand feet" and bomb VC. "Some people tried to get me to leave the plane. When I asked them for advice on how to start it, they pulled me out, without my consent." Indeed, Bright finally had to be lifted from the cockpit by the straps of the parachute he was almost wearing.

At trial, defense counsel for Gonzales, First Lieutenant Donald W. Harris, raised a spirited defense to the charges presented by First Lieutenant Frederick C. Woodruff, the trial counsel. But little could be done, given the accused's apprehension while engaged in the acts charged and surrounded by officers and air police. In his separate trial Bright was found not guilty of attempted wrongful appropriation of the bomber, but like Gonzales, he was convicted of willfully damaging it and of being drunk and disorderly. The court found Gonzales guilty of the attempted wrongful appropriation of the aircraft. On initial review the commanding general reduced their sentences to confinement at hard labor for twelve months, minor forfeitures for a year, and reductions to private. On appeal, after seven months of confinement had been served, the sentences were further reduced to five months' confinement and forfeitures.[10] Privates Bright and Gonzales both returned to duty, as engineers.

The Other Prisoners: North Vietnamese POWs

On 1 July 1966 U.S. Navy ships in the Gulf of Tonkin were attacked by three North Vietnamese PT boats. All three PT boats were sunk. Nineteen survivors were recovered and held on board the *Cavalier* (APA 37) as prisoners of war (POWs). At MACV's instruction, III MAF engineers completed construction of a POW screening facility near Da Nang on 5 September. It eventually included an adjacent, permanent brig facility for Marine prisoners in pretrial and post-trial confinement. Finally, the practice of holding Marine prisoners in a tent, or flying them to Okinawa, could be discontinued.

The 19 POWs were later transferred to the compound, where they were "screened" for the next four years. MACV considered them potentially valuable for exchange purposes and, just as importantly, they were said to be providing valuable information about North Vietnamese naval capabilities. For those reasons, the 19 never joined the other POWs that U.S. forces routinely turned over to the South Vietnamese.[11]

Because the POWs were held in the Da Nang TAOR, the SLO of the 3d Marine Division was responsible for ensuring that the conditions of the POW screening camp (which never held anyone other than the 19 PT boat crewmen) were in accord with the Geneva Convention. Later, III MAF assumed responsibility for the POWs. The 19 North Vietnamese were finally repatriated to North Vietnam in 1970.[12]

Aside from this nominal contact, Marine lawyers were never involved with enemy long-term prisoners

A U.S. Air Force B-57A Canberra bomber, shown here in a single-seat version, was the subject of wrongful appropriation charges against Marine PFCs Bright and Gonzales.

Department of Defense Photo (USAF) DF-SN-83-07782

of war, or with the five POW camps jointly manned by the South Vietnamese and the U.S. Army.[13]

The 1st Marine Division Arrives: More Lawyers, More Cases

On 27 March 1966 the 1st Marine Division's forward headquarters moved from Camp Courtney, Okinawa, to Chu Lai, South Vietnam. Initially, the senior lawyer with the advance party at Chu Lai was Navy law specialist Commander William E. Clemmons, accompanied by the legal chief, Master Sergeant Len E. Pierce, and a few lawyers and enlisted personnel. The Division's SLO, Colonel George P. Blackburn, Jr., along with his acting legal chief, Gunnery Sergeant Wesley Crow, and the remainder of the lawyers, remained at Camp Courtney until June, as did other support sections of the division staff not directly associated with combat operations. But by July they, too, had deployed to Chu Lai.

Colonel Blackburn had been an infantry platoon commander and artillery battery commander during World War II. After that war he commanded the 2d Battalion, 3d Marines, as well as the 1st Amphibian Tractor Battalion. In 1950 he attended law school on Marine Corps orders. In 1966, soon after accompanying his 12 lawyer-officers and 18 enlisted legal clerks to Vietnam his overseas tour of duty ended and in early August Lieutenant Colonel Tom P. Casey, the deputy SLO since January, assumed the SLO's duties.[14]

As were most of the senior lawyers in Vietnam, Lieutenant Colonel Casey was serving in his third war. He joined the Marine Corps as an enlisted man in December 1942. Commissioned shortly after boot camp, he received the Bronze Star Medal and the Purple Heart as an artilleryman on Saipan, Tinian, and Okinawa. After the war, on inactive duty, he earned his law degree and was recalled to active duty during the Korean War.

Now at Chu Lai, he and the other legal personnel moved into a partially completed camp near the beach. While awaiting conclusion of camp construction, the legal office was located in two widely separated areas, but within a month their offices were consolidated. As Lieutenant Colonel Casey remembered, "Except for some minor inconveniences such as crowded office spaces and an occasional generator failure, it was business as usual."[15]

Four Southeast Asia huts (SEAhuts) constituted the legal section offices. These were raised plywood build-

LtCol Thomas P. Casey, the Staff Legal Officer, 1st Marine Division, seen outside his office at Da Nang.
Photo courtesy of LtCol William B. Draper, Jr., USMC (Ret.)

GySgt William S. Kirkpatrick was promoted to the grade of second lieutenant by Maj-Gen Lewis J. Fields, left, Commanding General, 1st Marine Division, at Chu Lai on 15 July 1966, assisted by the Division Staff Legal Officer, Col George P. Blackburn.

ings roughly the same size as a general purpose tent, with plywood sidewalls, screened from the corrugated tin roofs halfway to the flooring. Eventually, the screens were augmented with canvas or green, translucent plastic sheeting which could be raised or lowered and served as protection from the frequent heavy rains. The staff conference room of division headquarters (in another nearby SEAhut) served as the general court-martial courtroom.[16] All in all, these were fairly comfortable accommodations for a combat zone.

As with the other major commands in Vietnam, the caseload was at first notably light in the 1st Division. "We had a low level of disciplinary problems during my entire tour as Division legal officer," Colonel Blackburn recalled. "We conducted intense schooling on the UCMJ prior to entering Vietnam, and believed it contributed a great deal to the low level of disciplinary problems."[17]

Inevitably, as more of the division's personnel deployed to Vietnam, the number of offenses grew. As in the other units, a disproportionate number of serious crimes were committed. In September, for example, 24 criminal investigations were initiated, of which three were rapes and eight were homicides.[18]

More than the caseload was changing. As at the beginning of World War II, Vietnam brought change in the fabric of the Marine Corps. Wartime expansion created a demand for many more Marines: more recruits, more officers, a shortened boot camp, and accelerated promotions. While the overall quality of the Marine recruit remained high, recruiters in all the Armed Services enlisted individuals who in peacetime would not have been accepted. The Armed Forces reflect the society from which they are drawn, and troubling aspects of civilian societal conflicts began to appear with the Marines arriving in Vietnam in 1966, although the signs remained muted.

To meet the need for experienced leadership, Marine noncommissioned officers were given temporary commissions to the grades of second lieutenant and warrant officer. In the past such "mustang" officers had proven their value in numerous campaigns and wars, and they were to do so again in Vietnam.

Gunnery Sergeant William S. Kirkpatrick was the administrative law and foreign claims chief in the 1st Marine Division's legal office when, on 15 July 1966, he became the first enlisted legal noncommissioned officer (NCO) to be commissioned a second lieutenant. Lieutenant Kirkpatrick had enlisted in the Marine Corps in December 1950 and had been a machine gunner in Korea. Selected for the legal field in 1958, his performance as an NCO was superior. In Vietnam, for example, his SLO noted: "His drive, enthusiasm, perseverance, and professionalism resulted in [the 1st] Division being termed by . . . MACV as having the most outstandingly effective foreign claims section in the entire Republic of Vietnam."[19] After receiving his commission, Second Lieutenant Kirkpatrick was transferred to the 7th Marines to serve as the regimental legal officer.[20]

Two weeks after Lieutenant Kirkpatrick's promotion, Gunnery Sergeant Kenneth W. Jones, chief court reporter of the 1st Marine Division's legal office, was similarly commissioned a second lieutenant and became the assistant foreign claims officer. A month before, on 30 June, the legal chief, Master Sergeant Len E. Pierce, had been appointed a warrant officer, and like Lieutenant Kirkpatrick, was promptly transferred, and became the adjutant of the 1st Battalion, 7th Marines.[21]

In October 3d Marine Division Headquarters moved from Da Nang to Phu Bai. The 1st Division's Headquarters, in turn, moved from Chu Lai to the vacated 3d Division headquarters area at Da Nang. Four Marine infantry battalions and their supporting units, designated Task Force X-Ray, remained at Chu Lai under the command of the 1st Division's assistant commander.[22] Lieutenant Colonel Casey and most of the 1st Division legal personnel left their recently occupied SEAhuts at Chu Lai and moved north with the division headquarters.

Lieutenant Colonel Casey's deputy, Lieutenant Colonel John L. Zorack, and a few lawyers and clerks remained at Chu Lai. Lieutenant Colonel Zorack, formerly an infantry company commander in Korea, had enlisted in the Marine Corps in World War II and was commissioned a second lieutenant in 1945. While Task Force X-Ray remained at Chu Lai from October 1966 to March 1967, Lieutenant Colonel Zorack's three lawyers, Captains Francis T. Coleman, Paul R. Constantino, and Daniel M. Hanlon, tried 26 general courts-martial, 16 of which involved capital offenses. It was an extremely taxing period, even though the Chu Lai lawyers were temporarily augmented by five lawyers from Colonel Casey's Da Nang office during the height of the trials.[23]

Force Logistic Command: New Guy on the Block

The procurement, distribution, and replacement of materiel is a major wartime challenge. In 1965 the Marines looked to the Force Logistic Support Group (FLSG), based in Da Nang, for logistic support. During that year, as the Marine presence escalated, FLSG grew from 700 personnel to more than 3,000 officers and men. To accommodate the increased size, function, and importance of the Vietnam logistic effort, a new unit, Force Logistic Command (FLC), was established on 15 March 1966 to provide sustained support to III MAF organizations.[24] Initially located near Da Nang, adjacent to a Vietnamese settlement fondly referred to as Dogpatch, in July FLC moved to Camp Books, Red Beach, eight miles northwest of Da Nang, where it would remain until the Marines left Vietnam. FLC's first commanding officer was Colonel George C. Axtell, Jr., an aviator and 1952 law school graduate who did not practice law while in the Marine Corps. Within 75 days of its formation, FLC grew to a strength of over 5,300.[25] Among the new personnel was Lieutenant Colonel Charles R. Larouche, FLC's first staff legal officer and, for several weeks, its only lawyer.

Lieutenant Colonel Larouche joined the Marine Corps in 1942, and was an enlisted scout on Guadalcanal. On Tarawa, Larouche received the Purple Heart. He saw further combat on Saipan and Tinian. Commissioned in 1945, he left active duty, completed college, and returned to the Marine Corps in 1950 with a law degree, after having briefly practiced law in Boston, Massachusetts. But FLC was a new experience:

> My reception at FLC was far from enthusiastic. . . . No one, other than the C.O., Colonel George Axtell, could even imagine why a lawyer was needed there. I was told to find myself a bunk, preferably unoccupied at the moment, since this new command was short of everything, especially bunks. This I did, for several nights, lying down on freshly vacated sacks. . . . While this was unpleasant, it was better than some of the infantry units. . . . I moved into at least a dozen different huts/tents while in VN. This was due to the constantly growing FLC.
> My working facilities were only slightly better: I was told there was no space then available for a legal office, but I could occupy a small corner of the messhall. I scrounged a large packing box for a desk and a small one for a chair, and a few pencils. . . . My library consisted of my own Manual for Courts-Martial and JAG Manual . . . . I had no clerk—I was the "legal office."[26]

Because the command was new it did not yet have any courts-martial pending, but a number of accidental death investigations awaited Lieutenant Colonel Larouche's review.

The command's sole attorney, Lieutenant Colonel Larouche sat upon his packing box writing reviews in longhand without clerk, references, or typewriter. An equitable borrowing of lawyers from the other nearby commands was initiated, and supplies were acquired. In June Major James R. Ziemann arrived, and other enlisted and officer personnel soon followed.

Major Ziemann located a tin shed, which allowed

"Dogpatch" was the cluster of Vietnamese small business establishments on the heavily travelled highway between the 1st Marine Division and Force Logistic Command headquarters. Many offenses that were tried by Marine Corps lawyers had their genesis here.

the office to move from its corner in the messhall. That the shed had formerly been a pig sty did not deter the lawyers. FLC's caseload was expanding with its population, and a permanent office was required, regardless of its past history.

Legal clerks were a constant problem. They were too few, and those who arrived in Vietnam were often inadequately trained. In 1967 Naval Justice School, at Newport, Rhode Island, would initiate a five-week legal clerk/court reporting course, but in 1966, Marine Corps legal clerks were receiving on-the-job training. Battalions and squadrons routinely dragooned Marines into legal clerk billets, even though the Marines might lack legal training or basic administrative skills. Usually, the units soon recognized that the legal arena was unsuited for OJT. Colonel Larouche devised a solution:

> It was painfully obvious that my Office needed more clerks . . . our subordinate units needed more legal clerks, and the two Divisions and the Wing needed more legal clerks. Rather than wait for clerks that would never come, or come too late, I decided to run a legal clerk school to train clerks for all the major commands in III MAF. The school would run for two weeks . . . . All major commands would pro-

LtCol Charles R. Larouche, shown in a 1968 photograph as a colonel, was Force Logistic Command's first staff legal officer and, for a while, its only lawyer.

Maj James R. Ziemann, left, and LtCol Charles R. Larouche stand in front of the former pig sty that was Force Logistic Command's first legal office location.

vide a few instructors each, and I would coordinate the whole thing.[27]

Colonel Larouche was well-qualified to form the class, having previously been the Marine Corps instructor on the staff of the Naval Justice School for three years. On 29 August the first class convened and graduated 30 newly trained legal clerks two weeks later.[28] The graduates were addressed by the III MAF Assistant Chief of Staff, attorney Colonel Robert B. Neville, now assigned to Vietnam after guiding Discipline Branch at Headquarters Marine Corps. Over the course of the next year, Lieutenant Colonel Larouche conducted several more legal clerk schools, temporarily solving the clerk problem.

Although the legal pace was quickening, duty was not onerous at the "Funny Little Circus," as FLC was dubbed by its less respectful Marines.[29] The SEAhuts were an improvement over tents, even if monsoon rains blew through them and summer heat made their interiors unbearably hot, much as the tents. One hundred and three Vietnamese women, usually called "hoochmaids," were hired to keep the officers' tents and clothing clean.[30]

Legal assistance services were a staple in the three-lawyer office. (Captain Franklin P. "Skip" Glenn reported on board in July.) The lawyers regularly visited FLC units at Chu Lai, Phu Bai, and Dong Ha to meet their legal assistance needs.[31] Domestic relations problems predominated, typically involving a wife back home seeking a divorce. In such instances, steps were taken to protect the Marine's interests and carry out his desires.

Besides their primary duty as litigators in the criminal forum, Marine Corps lawyers handled the usual problems faced by any attorney in civilian practice, such as powers of attorney, indebtedness, taxes, wills, naturalization, adoptions, contracts, name changes, and passports.

The issues involved in marrying a Vietnamese arose on a regular basis.[32] A proxy marriage between a regimental executive officer and a prospective bride in Georgia was unsuccessfully attempted, as well.[33] Some of the issues the lawyers solved would have challenged the most experienced counsel.

Vietnamese claims for compensation were similarly time consuming. Most often claims were submitted for relatively minor damage or compensation: a motor scooter hit by a Marine Corps truck, a rice paddy damaged by a tank, or a defaced burial mound. Usually, the claims presented were for legitimate and appropriate recompense for injury or damage done by Marine Corps activities or personnel. But not always. For example, Colonel Neville said:

> I recall one incident where Vietnamese villagers were claiming the standard payments for deaths and wounds of several villagers, saying one of our patrols had inflicted the damages.... The emphasis on prompt reporting made first reports very sketchy and generally unreliable. I stopped the report [for further investigation] .... The medical officer's examination of the wounds raised many doubts and a few hours later the basically friendly villagers told us the VC had inflicted the wounds and sent the villagers to collect the payment which was, of course, to be turned over to the VC.[34]

Soon FLC and the other commands would encounter similar claims which regrettably would prove legitimate.

At Camp Books, the new FLC camp at Red Beach, the general court-martial caseload was rising. During the same time the legal chief, Staff Sergeant Jerome E. Riser, was commissioned a second lieutenant and promptly transferred, hobbling office productivity.[35]

The SLO's offices had come a long way from the original partitioned corner of the messhall. Now they consisted of two Quonset huts, one of which was office space for the SLO, counsels, and clerks. Lieutenant Colonel Larouche directed Major Ziemann to arrange the other hut as a courtroom, which was to conform as closely as possible to civilian standards. Major Ziemann scrounged materials to produce a hearing room featuring a jury box and a judge's bench with a hand-carved figure of justice on its front. On the ceiling were 140 egg carton separators, each hand-dipped in white paint, their function purely decorative. Within months an enemy rocket would badly damage the courtroom, egg separators and all.

Trying Cases

In February 1966 Colonel Earl H. Johnson summoned the SLOs from III MAF Headquarters, the 1st and 3d Marine Divisions, and the 1st Marine Aircraft Wing to Camp Smith, Hawaii, headquarters of Fleet Marine Force, Pacific (FMFPac). Force Logistic Command was not formed until the next month, so was not represented. That first Staff Legal Officers' Conference was held from 15 to 17 February. Such conferences were to be an annual event until the war's end.

Numerous problem areas that had come to light over the 11 months since the Marines had landed in Vietnam needed resolution. Agenda items included such questions as: Were too many lawyer colonels assigned to Vietnam? What was a fair distribution among the legal offices of lieutenants and captains, given caseloads and trials? Would any electronic recording gear work in the hostile climate of Vietnam, and if so, how could the SLOs get that gear? How could the Marine Corps best retain the first-term lieutenants and captains who, for the most part, were returning to civilian law practice as soon as their obligated service was completed?[36]

A lawyer's quarters are rain-soaked at Camp Books, Red Beach, the morning of 31 August 1966. Rain is puddled on the plywood flooring, having blown in through the screening.

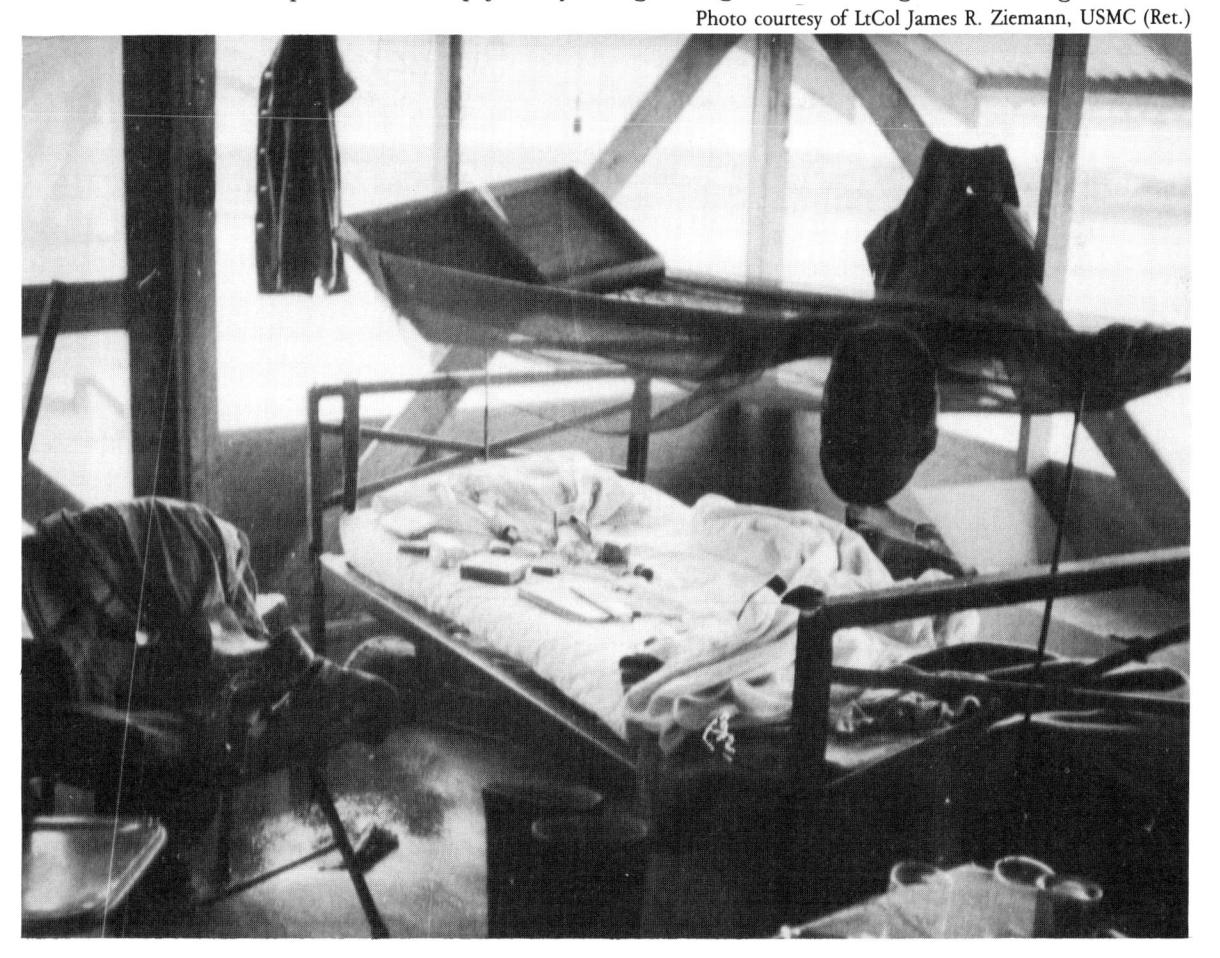

Photo courtesy of LtCol James R. Ziemann, USMC (Ret.)

Force Logistic Command's first general court-martial convened in the Red Beach officers' club. Trial counsel, Maj James R. Ziemann stands at left. Defense counsel, Lt John S. Szymanski, USN, a 1st Marine Aircraft Wing defense counsel, awaits the accused.

Photo courtesy of LtCol James R. Ziemann, USMC (Ret.)

Force Logistic Command's Quonset hut courtroom had a judge's bench; members' seating, right; counsel tables, left; and 140 hand-dipped egg carton separators overhead.

Photo courtesy of Col Charles R. Larouche, USMC (Ret.)

Photo courtesy of Col Daniel F. McConnell, USMC (Ret.)
The I Corps Bar Association's initial social event was held at Camp Books, Red Beach, 17 September 1966. At the head table, from left, unidentified officer; 1st Marine Aircraft Wing SLO, LtCol Ralph Culver; law officer LtCol William Wander; FLC Commanding Officer and lawyer, Col George C. Axtell, hidden; FLC's SLO, LtCol Charles R. Larouche; 3d Marine Division SLO, Col Charles H. Beale, Jr., standing; 1st Marine Division SLO, LtCol Thomas P. Casey, hidden; and two unidentified officers. Fly paper hangs from the rafters.

At such conferences, both in formal sessions and in casual conversation at the officers' club, common issues were raised and policies were informally hammered out. In Vietnam the lawyers had the I Corps Bar Association, a loose amalgam of lawyers primarily from the Marine Corps but with representation from all the Armed Services. The sole requirement for membership was presence at an association social event, really the principal purpose of the association. The I Corps Bar Association (originally called the Red Beach Bar Association) was, probably, the idea of FLC's Lieutenant Colonel Larouche. He hosted the first social event on 17 September 1966 at Red Beach, attended by most of the lawyers in I Corps, including four Navy law specialists from the nearby Naval Support Activity and four Army judge advocates attached to III MAF Headquarters as foreign claims specialists. "Jim Ziemann and his legal chief, Gunnery Sergeant [Bill] Dedic," Major William B. Draper, Jr. recalled, "did a substantial amount of scrounging, borrowing, and midnight requisitioning to supply steaks, a cocktail bar, wine, rolls, etc."[37] (Colonel Beale, the 3d Marine Division's SLO, referred to Major Ziemann as "possibly the greatest liberator since Lincoln," out of respect for Ziemann's skill as a scrounger.)[38] FLC's commanding officer, Colonel George C. Axtell, was the party's guest of honor. In Lieutenant Colonel Larouche's words: "The event seemed to generate ideas for a better future legal clerk's school, to develop ideas for greater mutual help and cooperation among all major commands in I Corps area."[39] In other words, there was plenty to drink, and everyone had a good time.

On a more serious level, lawyers continued to take part in the Marine Corps' people-to-people program. Lieutenant John F. Erickson, a Navy law specialist loaned to FLC by the Naval Support Activity, coordinated a program, supported by his home county in Kansas, which provided clothing and toys for a Vietnamese orphanage.[40] A thank-you letter from the commander of the 51st ARVN Regiment read, "The children of our orphanage, that is, the sons and daughters of men of our Regiment who has given their lives for our country's freedom, will be the recipients of your donations . . . . Words do not hold enough meaning to rightfully express our feelings."[41] Lieutenant Erickson later received a Navy Achievement Medal, in part for his civic action work.

Major Draper, a 1st Marine Division defense counsel, wrote to the *Daily Dartmouth*, the newspaper of his alma mater, suggesting that shirts would be appreciated by the local Vietnamese children. The Marine on the Dartmouth Navy ROTC staff, Major Orlo K. Steele, organized a major clothing collection effort on campus and at nearby Hanover, New Hampshire, based on Major Draper's letter. Soon, Major Draper found himself before the 1st Division's public affairs officer, explaining where 4,000 tee-shirts had come from (most emblazoned with "Dartmouth" across the chest) and why the public affairs office had not been consulted beforehand. That bureaucratic detail satisfied, Major Draper soon passed out the shirts to appreciative children in the Da Nang area.[42]

The Marine Corps had little direct involvement in Revolutionary Development, which was essentially civic action on a higher political level. An exception was Lieutenant Colonel Charles J. "Chuck" Keever. Formerly a 3d Marine Division lawyer on Okinawa, he came to Vietnam as a major on the III MAF staff. His subsequent expert direction of I Corps' civic action effort was noticed by U.S. State Department representatives in Saigon. In December 1966 Lieutenant General Walt advised the Commandant of the Marine Corps, General Wallace M. Greene, Jr., that:

> LtCol Keever has been offered high level policy making job on national level in Office Civil Operations (OCO), the new organization to control all civil agencies in revolutionary development in RVN . . . . Keever wants the job and I believe he could do us a lot of good in that position. Ambassador Porter recognizes Keever as an expert in civic action who can get things done and he needs that kind of man, especially now. Request guidance as to your desires in this matter. Very respectfully, Lew.[43]

A week later, the Commandant indicated his approval of the unusual arrangement and Lieutenant Colonel Keever was soon in civilian clothes, reporting to the Office of Civil Operations in Saigon, where he was to earn the Legion of Merit for his work.[44]

In Marine Corps courtrooms, meanwhile, lawyers were beginning to recognize that problems with witnesses were going to be difficult, if not impossible, to solve. While a criminal trial and the cross-examination of witnesses may be a great engine for the discovery of truth, unusual courtroom difficulties arose in Vietnam's expeditionary circumstances. The

Maj William B. Draper, Jr., a 1st Marine Division defense counsel, hands out tee-shirts featuring his alma mater's name, Dartmouth, to eager children of the Da Nang area.

Department of Defense Photo (USMC) 02-0465-67

Maj Curtis W. Olson conducts an investigation in a Vietnamese schoolhouse. "We rapidly found out that going to the people with investigative hearings was not the way to go."

trial process was foreign and disquieting to the Vietnamese witness. First the alleged offense was investigated, usually by an officer from the accused's unit. Next, witnesses were interviewed by the trial counsel and then the defense counsel, seldom on the same day. Then, if a general court-martial was anticipated, the lawyers conducted an Article 32 investigation. Finally, the Vietnamese witnesses were summoned to relate their testimony at the court-martial, and then cross-examined. Captain Francis T. Coleman recalled:

> Long patient hours must be expended in eliciting even the most simple narrative from these frail, bewildered, awestruck onlookers. Questions must be methodically worded and reworded . . . . Even the most diligent pretrial preparation of a witness often leaves the attorney shaking his head at the trial. Successful cross-examination is practically negated by the language barrier.[45]

South Vietnamese witnesses, like Marine Corps witnesses, were sometimes killed or wounded. They often were moved to new villages or resettlement camps. Frequently, not even the Vietnamese National Police could locate Vietnamese witnesses. Major Curtis W. Olson, a 1st Marine Division lawyer, recalled that "Vietnamese witnesses never fully understood why they had to appear again and again to repeat the same story over again."[46]

Occasionally, as Major Olson noted, the Marines would attempt to take the hearing to the witnesses:

> The theory was that we would take the investigations to the people, and thus get better cooperation from them, as it would be less of an interruption in their lives. It didn't work for a number of reasons. First, our portable recording equipment was not that good. Second, the Vietnamese did not have a very good appearance record at these hearings. They seemed to respond better if we sent a vehicle out to round them up . . . . [That] seemed more officially important to them than just showing up at the local schoolhouse . . . . We rapidly found out that going to the people with investigative hearings was not the way to go.[47]

Another factor influencing Vietnamese witnesses was that they were not paid a witness fee if the proceeding was taken to them. To be paid, they had to appear at a hearing held in a Marine compound. Colonel Charles H. Beale, SLO of the 3d Marine Division, recalled that "the witnesses were brought in by helicopter, and we paid them at the end of each day. They would immediately go on shopping trips and bought everything in sight."[48]

Even when Marines brought a Vietnamese witness to court things could go awry. Once, a general court-martial was in progress when the trial counsel called the rape victim to the witness stand. He began his direct examination, but encountered difficulty from the start. As the trial counsel questioned the woman, through the interpreter, he could not even establish her identity, as basic as that should have been. Finally the prosecutor discovered that, yes, she had been the victim of a rape, and yes, she was to testify at a Marine's court-martial, but, no, this accused was not her attacker. The wrong rape victim had been brought to court.[49]

Two FLC cases involving two Marines who were separately charged with committing the same offense, reflected the difficulty in securing Vietnamese witnesses for trial. The trial counsel, Captain Franklin P. Glenn, caught a ride to the Da Nang Airbase where he was able to get manifested on a C-130 departing at 0630 for Dong Ha. At Dong Ha he transferred to the unlikely-named "African Queen II," a 4-knot per hour LCM (landing craft) that took him down the Cua Viet River to the Gulf of Tonkin. There he crossed sand dunes, waded a stream, and traversed marshlands, finally reaching the small fishing village of Phoi Hoi, located in an area of heavy enemy activity. He found the witnesses and escorted them back to Da Nang. They testified, then departed for Phoi Hoi via a helicopter, arranged for by Captain Glenn. He accompanied them on the helicopter to persuade them of the need for them to later journey to Da Nang, again, for the trial of the second accused. At Phoi Hoi the trial counsel inadvertently was left behind by the helicopter pilot. After a tense night beyond friendly lines Captain Glenn caught an LCM and began his journey back to Red Beach.[50] The Vietnamese witnesses would not return for the second trial, and the case had to be dropped for lack of proof.

In Vietnam, not only Vietnamese witnesses presented difficulty. The memories of Marine Corps witnesses could become hazy, as the date of their return to "the world" approached. Advised that their testimony might require that they be kept in Vietnam on "legal hold," they sometimes developed signs of pronounced amnesia in an effort to avoid remaining in Vietnam any longer than necessary.[51]

In the courtroom problems with reliable electrical power and recording equipment persisted. Generator failure in the midst of trial was common; court adjourned until power was restored. Often, the generators would run, but their output was so reduced that the reporter's tape would barely turn. Other times power surges resulted in a recording on which all voices sounded like cartoon characters.[52] At the 1966 General Officers Symposium at Headquarters Marine Corps Major General Avery R. Kier noted that "generators have been another recurring problem. The expeditionary type generators do not stand up under continuous usage. The garrison type generators . . . are not supported by adequate spare parts. There is an insatiable demand for power."[53] In the 3d Marine Division

Two 1st Marine Division lawyers conduct interviews far from the Division Headquarters. "Vietnamese witnesses never fully understood why they had to appear again and again."

Photo courtesy of RAdm Hugh D. Campbell, JAGC, USN (Ret).

the Staff Legal Officer cured his power problem by purchasing portable Honda generators; expensive but effective.[54] Nor was efficient power the only courtroom problem. "The most frustrating aspect," recalled Colonel Benjamin B. Ferrell, "was the continual breakdown of recording equipment. No system we tried could be relied on to function for long in the dusty or rainy weather of Vietnam."[55] Recording equipment and power sources remained unsolved issues for the war's duration.

Courtroom Personnel: Just Passin' Through

In Vietnam, with the Uniform Code of Military Justice of 1950 and the 1951 *Manual for Courts-Martial*, military law was maturing with wartime application, despite the staggered changing of personnel every 13 months (the length of a Marine's tour of duty in Vietnam).

The judicial process began with the commander, who had the power to send, or refer, Marines in his command to a court-martial that convened at his direction. Colonel Robert B. Neville was an infantry officer in World War II, who saw combat on Guadalcanal, New Guinea, and New Britain, before he became the III MAF Deputy Chief of Staff and Headquarters SLO.[56] He said of convening authorities:

> In all honesty, I never met a convening authority who was disposed to violate or disregard the law. I have seen more subjective, arbitrary decisions and conduct by judges, justices of the peace, and prosecuting attorneys in civilian life than I have even heard about in the military . . . . I found convening authorities who were not lawyers to be more compassionate and understanding of human frailty than those who had formal legal training.[57]

Once referred to trial, if lawyer counsel was appointed, lieutenants and captains still tried most cases. Numerous attorneys were in Vietnam now, but experienced trial lawyers were few.[58] Lawyers who had not tried a case until arriving in Vietnam were often assigned to prosecute or defend the most serious of offenses after the briefest apprenticeship. Despite their lack of legal experience, most of the young lawyers thrived on the challenges, which they viewed as opportunities. When he was Judge Advocate General of the Navy, Rear Admiral Hugh D. Campbell recalled: "My experience in Vietnam [as a Navy lieutenant] is probably what caused me to augment into the Navy . . . . I was amazed at the responsibility I had in the trial arena—the types of cases . . . . I've never had challenges any greater than the challenges we had there."[59] "The dedication of the lawyers," added Navy Lieutenant John F. Erickson, "thrown together in a semi-combat situation, was remarkable . . . . I often thought, while I was at my second duty station in Hawaii, that the cases were tried better and faster in Vietnam."[60]

All general courts-martial were presided over by law officers, all of whom were lawyers. Under the Red Book, the law officer advised the members of their duties, directed the progress of the trial, ruled on motions and objections, and instructed the members. Like a judge he had broad discretion, and by virtue of his position and senior grade, was a figure of some authority in the courtroom. They were appointed law officers by the Navy's Judge Advocate General, the departmental judge advocate for the Marine Corps. Consideration for appointment came only after long seasoning as a trial-level defense counsel and trial counsel. The maxim that there is no test of character like authority fully applied to law officers. A law officer with a tyrannical or petty streak could make life very unpleasant for counsel. Most valued were those law officers who were firm, yet fair; who remained undisturbed by the inexperienced lawyer who might perform poorly in trial. Not every law officer possessed the wisdom and character to be a good jurist, but Vietnam lawyers were fortunate in that most were both highly respected and able.[61]

Colonel Beale, 3d Marine Division SLO, wrote: "I would be completely remiss if I did not mention the magnificent performances of the various military judges [law officers] during my tenure. I recall, in particular Colonel William Wander, Colonel Verne L. Oliver, Colonel Don Holben, and Captain [Wyman] Jackson, U.S. Navy."[62]

During 1965 and 1966 law officers were stationed in Yokosuka, Japan, and on Okinawa. In May 1966 a Navy-Marine Corps Judiciary Activity branch office was established in Da Nang.[63] When the SLO of a particular command believed that enough general courts were ready for trial to justify requesting a law officer, he did so and specified the anticipated period the law officer would be required. After arrival, if the general court-martial docket permitted, law officers also served as senior members of special courts-martial, sort of a super-juror. The canny wisdom of these senior lawyers was reflected in Major Draper's recollection of "the travelling law officer, Colonel Wander, who displayed his in-depth knowledge of lengthy supply lines and the inconveniences inflicted thereby, when he showed up in Chu Lai with his own olives and his own toilet paper."[64]

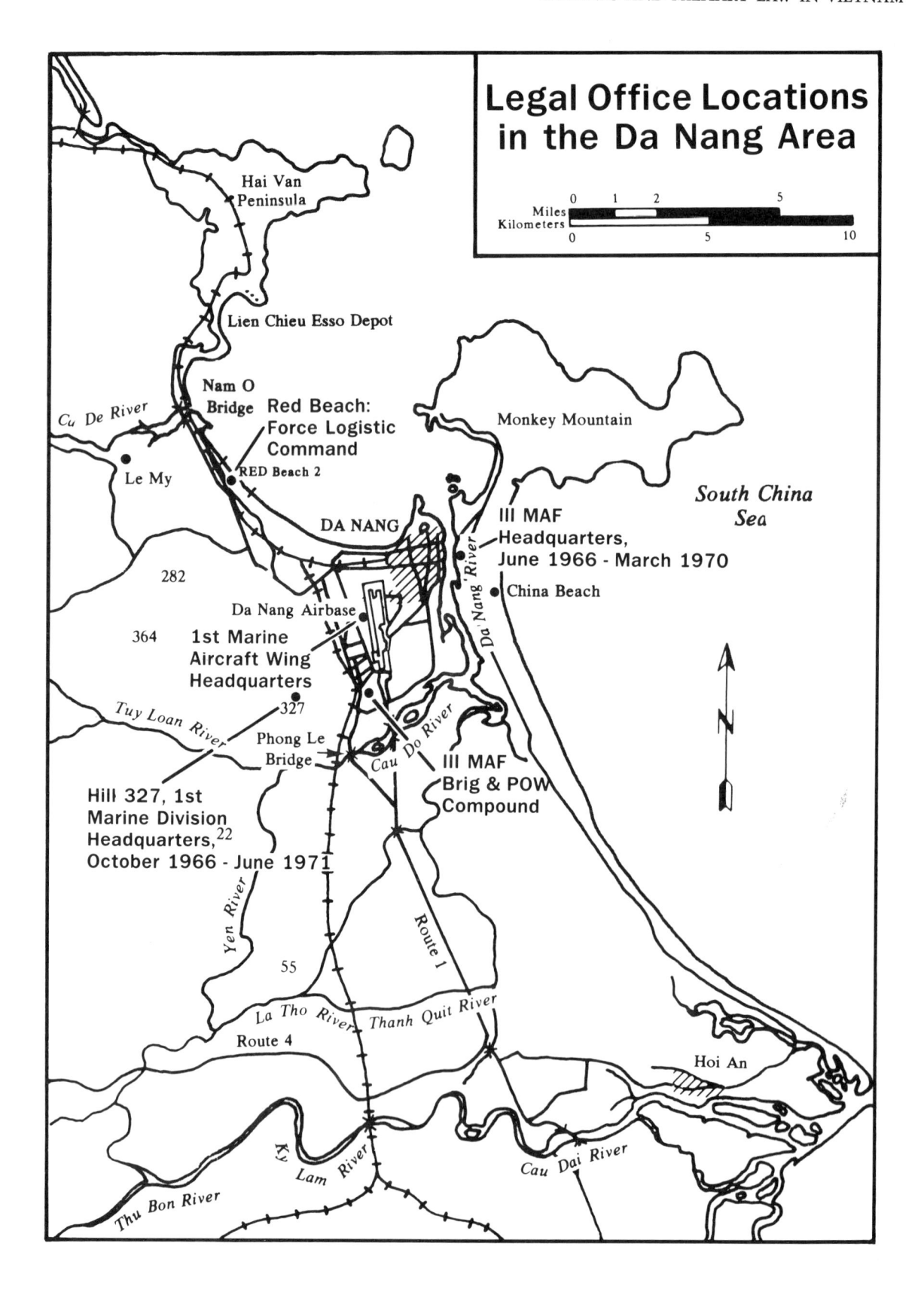

Legal Office Locations in the Da Nang Area

1966: BUILDING ON SAND

The enlisted Marines of every staff legal office were critical to the system's operation. Although legal chiefs were not found in the courtroom (they had already served their time in court, usually as reporters), they supervised and scheduled the work of the clerks and reporters. They assured the correct preparation of the numerous documents necessary to courts-martial, including the verbatim record of trial. Regarding his enlisted Marines, Colonel Beale recalled:

> I was blessed with two of the best—Master Sergeant Harold L. Tetrick and, later, Gunnery Sergeant Bill Dedic. And the court reporters were the most dedicated people I have ever known. We had so much trouble with our recording equipment that many of them used their own personal tape recorders (Akai or Sony) as back-up [to the closed-microphone recording system]. I always marveled at their efficiency; most of the time they typed up the record with a headset that had music from recording tapes going in one ear, and the court record playing into the other ear. The performance by these court reporters was absolutely superior. It goes without saying that the legal chiefs were outstanding leaders. They solved all difficulties.[65]

The caseload, meanwhile, continued to rise modestly, while remaining generally low. In FLC only about six general courts-martial per month were docketed.[66] The pace was even slower in the 1st Marine Aircraft Wing, where each lawyer's caseload averaged two or three cases at any time.[67]

Although the numbers were low, the caseload did not always tell the whole story. Sometimes a few cases could be overwhelming in terms of effort. In September 1966, 18 months before the killings at My Lai, a series of such difficult cases fell to the lawyers of the 1st Marine Division.

Homicide on Patrol: Men, Women, and Children

Lieutenant General Leo J. Dulacki was a colonel in 1966. He said:

> I remember sitting in General Walt's office—I was chief of staff at that time . . . discussing the case with him at length. Let me say, he had deep problems in trying to accept the results of the investigation. He couldn't believe that a Marine, any Marine, would do something like this . . . . This had to be someone other than Marines, because Marines just wouldn't do something like this . . . . We had to do this [refer the cases to general courts-martial] because the evidence was such that it indicated that these people were involved. Whether they were eventually acquitted, or not, we had no alternative . . . . We would not tolerate such action, they would be punished, and we didn't cover it up.[68]

At 1900 on 23 September a nine-man ambush patrol from the 1st Battalion, 5th Marines, left Hill 22, northwest of Chu Lai. Private First Class John D. Potter, Jr., an aggressive, combat-experienced 20-year old, effectively took control of the patrol, supplanting the nominal leader, Sergeant Ronald L. Vogel. Unusual as that was, the other Marines followed Potter rather than Vogel, whom they viewed as ineffective. The patrol's Navy corpsman, Hospitalman Jon R. Bretag, later testified:

> He [Potter] said that this would be a raid instead of an ambush . . . . We are to beat up the people, tear up the hooches, and kill, if necessary . . . . He told us to roll down our sleeves, take our insignias off, make sure our covers are on [and] assigned us numbers. He said if you want to get somebody, don't mention his name, call him by number . . . . The entire squad moved out.[69]

They entered the hamlet of Xuan Ngoc (2). They seized Dao Quang Thinh, whom they accused of being a Viet Cong, and dragged him from his hut. While they beat him, other patrol members forced his wife, Bui Thi Huong, from their hut. They pulled her three-year-old child from her arms. Then four of them raped her.

A few minutes later three other patrol members shot her husband, her child, her sister-in-law, and her sister-in-law's child, with automatic and semi-automatic rifle fire. Hearing the sister-in-law moan, Potter exclaimed, "Damn, she's still alive!" He fired another burst of automatic fire into her at point blank range. Potter then tossed a hand grenade near the bodies in an attempt to cover the patrols' atrocities and "to make it look good." Next, they shot the rape victim, Bui Thi Huong, and left her for dead. She lived to testify at their courts-martial.

Upon returning to the battalion command post, the company commander sought details of the reported "enemy contact." Suspicious, he ordered their new platoon leader, Second Lieutenant Stephen J. Talty, to go back to the scene of the "contact" with the patrol. Once there, Talty realized what had happened and directed efforts to disguise what had occurred. As they were doing so, one of the previously wounded children was discovered still alive. Potter raised his rifle over the child, saying, "someone count for me." Vogel counted to three as Potter repeatedly slammed his rifle butt into the child's head, killing him.[70]

The morning after the killings, the rape victim, Huong, was carried by her villagers to the Marine base for treatment of her gunshot wounds. The Navy doctor immediately reported her wounding and rape. When confronted by his company commander, Lieutenant Talty, a Marine for only ten months, admitted all.

Potter was convicted of five specifications of

premeditated murder, of rape, and the attempted rape of a second Vietnamese. He was sentenced to confinement at hard labor for life, reduction to private, loss of all pay and allowances, and a dishonorable discharge. The conviction and sentence were approved through the appellate levels. Potter was released in February 1978, after having served twelve years and one month. His was the longest period of confinement served by any prisoner convicted by Marine Corps court-martial of murdering a Vietnamese noncombatant.[71]

Hospitalman Bretag testified against Potter, hoping to gain favorable consideration regarding his six-month sentence for his own part in the rape of Huong. Another patrol member, Private First Class James H. Boyd, Jr., pleaded guilty to murder and was sentenced to four years confinement at hard labor and a dishonorable discharge. He, too, testified against Potter, as did Vogel. Vogel, convicted as a principal in the murder of one of the children and in Huong's rape, was sentenced to 50 years confinement at hard labor and a dishonorable discharge.* On appeal, his confinement was reduced to 10 years. After he had served more than nine years, the Secretary of the Navy further reduced confinement to eight years, and Vogel was released.[72]

Two patrol members were acquitted of major charges, but were convicted of a relatively minor assault with intent to commit rape. After final review each one's approved sentence included six months confinement. Three others were acquitted of all charges.

Lieutenant Talty was found not guilty of being an accessory to murder, but was convicted of the innocuous charge of making a false report. He was sentenced to dismissal from the Marine Corps, forfeitures of $500, and a loss of numbers on the promotion lineal list. Two years later, the dismissal was set aside upon appellate review.[73]

How could young Marines and a sailor, all with good prior records, commit such crimes? Potter did not speak in his own defense, but the words of the Navy psychiatrist, who found him to be sane, shed light on the actions of Potter and other Marines who committed war crimes:

> War in Vietnam is one where the enemy is usually unseen until he chooses to make himself known, while the Marines are forced to repeatedly expose themselves to attack and ambush. Civilians often shelter and aid the enemy and give rise to very strong resentment from the Marine troops, especially when it is clear that the civilians can prevent the death of numerous Marines by providing information about the presence of enemy troops and the location of booby traps and mines. This is a situation that caused PFC Potter to feel appropriately angry and frustrated and to look forward to raiding a village . . . . Potter's state of emotional turmoil against the Vietnamese people probably accounts for his [acts].

Captain James P. Shannon received the Navy Commendation Medal, in part for his energetic, tenacious, but ultimately fruitless, defense of Potter.[74]

These were not the last murders of Vietnamese noncombatants by Marines, though they were among the most heinous. If anything positive is to be found in these cases, it was the Marine Corps' approach to such cases. As Major William B. Draper pointed out, "we did not close our eyes or our ears to the allegations that a crime may have been committed in the name of combat . . . . Nothing was swept under the rug in hopes that it would go away."[75]

3d Marine Division: On The Road Again

The Marines' Vietnam command structure underwent major alteration in 1966, as Marine leadership was adjusted to best meet the tactical situation in I Corps. The year began with Colonel Sevier as the Division SLO, located at the division command post (CP) on Hill 327. In mid-March General Walt relinquished command of the 3d Division to Major General Wood B. Kyle in order to devote more time to his duties as III MAF Commanding General.

In June Colonel Sevier returned to Headquarters Marine Corps in Washington, D.C. His replacement as 3d Division SLO was Colonel Beale, another World War II combat veteran.

Then, in October, the division CP moved to Phu Bai, while 3d Marine Division (Forward) was established at Dong Ha.[76] When the division CP moved, several serious felonies were pending trial. The brig, with the lawyers' "clients," was at Da Nang. Phu Bai had no space for a legal office, nor could the base be expanded until the rainy season was over. So Colonel Beale's office remained temporarily at Hill 327, with the 1st Marine Division CP, which had moved into the area the 3d Division had vacated. Colonel Beale recalled:

> The physical plant changed so many times that it is difficult to recall. Originally [on Hill 327] the office was located in four strong-back tents. One of these was used as a courtroom. Then we moved the offices into a double Quonset hut, and still used the tent for a courtroom, [then, after moving north, we] used the officers' club for courts-martial.[77]

---

*A principal is one who does not actually commit an offense, but "aids, abets, counsels, commands, or procures its commission." (Art. 77, UCMJ, 1969.)

Photo courtesy of Col Daniel F. McConnell, USMC (Ret.)

Col Charles B. Sevier, center, stands with his relief as 3d Marine Division SLO, Col Charles H. Beale, Jr., second from right, with Navy law specialist Lt Bruce C. Murphy, left; Division Legal Chief, MSgt Harold L. Tetrick, second from left; and deputy SLO, LtCol Fred Grabowski, right, in front of one of the Division legal Quonset hut offices on Hill 327.

The 3d Marine Division SLO's office was on Hill 327, near Da Nang, in June 1966. "The [3d Marine Division's] physical plant changed so many times that it is difficult to recall."

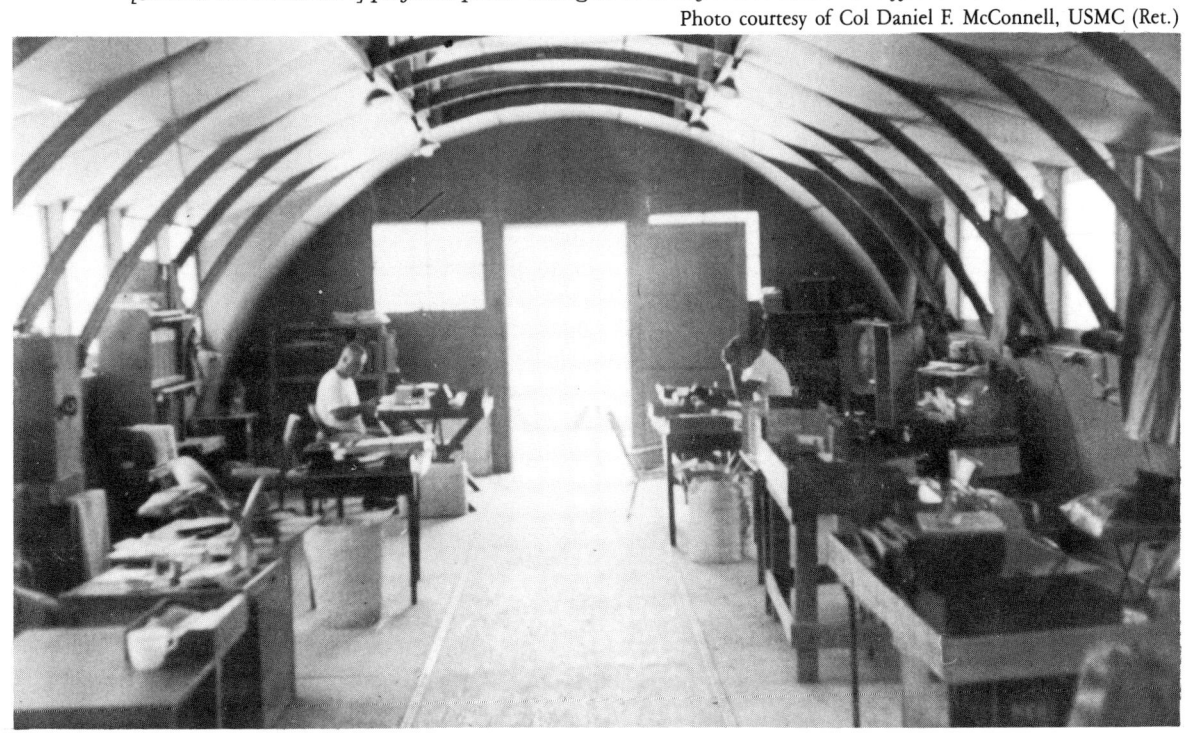

Photo courtesy of Col Daniel F. McConnell, USMC (Ret.)

Photo courtesy of Col Daniel F. McConnell, USMC (Ret.)

The III MAF Staff Legal Officer, Col Vernon A. Peltzer, left, in Da Nang with 3d Marine Division lawyer Maj Robert J. Chadwick (gesturing), and 1st Marine Division Staff Legal Officer, LtCol Thomas P. Casey (sunglasses). An unidentified officer stands at right.

Transportation was a major difficulty. The SLO and the lawyers were required to travel continually between Da Nang and Phu Bai to confer with the commanding general and other convening authorities, interview witnesses, and meet with accused Marines.

Finally, on 27 November 1966, more than a month after the 3d Division's CP had moved, the legal office followed. At Phu Bai they again had tents for office and courtroom, but as Colonel Beale noted, "I had a few uncomfortable nights, but the sack was always dry . . . and I always had clean, dry clothes."[78]

III MAF: Double-Hatting the Lawyer

On 26 June 1966, as Colonel Peltzer's tenure as III MAF SLO was ending, General Walt's Headquarters moved from the Da Nang Airbase, across the Han (Da Nang) river, opposite east Da Nang.[79] Shortly thereafter, Colonel Peltzer was relieved by Colonel Robert B. Neville.

Colonel Neville had served under General Walt as an infantry company commander in World War II and as an instructor at Marine Corps Schools, at Quantico, Virginia. Later, he and General Walt had also served together at Headquarters Marine Corps. When General Walt assigned Colonel Neville as his assistant chief of staff, as well as the Staff Legal Officer, Colonel Neville gladly accepted such double duty.[80] He was of the school that still considered nonlegal field assignments as necessary for promotion, and it was rumored that a general officer's legal billet might soon be authorized.

As under-utilized as his predecessor had been, Colonel Neville now found himself very busy. The III MAF chief of staff was a brigadier general, and the day-to-day direction of the MAF staff was largely left to his assistant, Colonel Neville. To relieve the pressure on him, General Walt asked the Commanding General of FMFPac, Lieutenant General Krulak, to assign in-coming Captain William B. Draper, Jr., to his staff. When General Krulak refused the request for Captain Draper or any other lawyer, General Walt persisted:

> [I] feel constrained to request you reconsider . . . . I need all the talent I can get . . . . If I assign Col. Neville primary duties as legal officer I am wasting his effectiveness. On the other hand if I continue him as deputy chief of staff with additional duties as force legal officer I am . . . subjecting him to an unacceptably excessive workload . . . . He has competed for selection [for promotion] as infantry officer, not as primary MOS lawyer . . . . He desires to complete his career in the same way . . . . It is again requested that Capt. W. B. Draper be assigned to III MAF.[81]

General Krulak relented: "[I] will provide a second lawyer to your staff immediately . . . . You are there

LtGen Lewis W. Walt poses with the III MAF staff in November 1966. LtGen Walt is seated, center. To his right sits his Assistant Chief of Staff, lawyer Col Robert B. Neville.

and know better than anyone else the nature of your staff needs.... The commander on the spot deserves the maximum support that his superiors can give him."[82] (Although General Walt got a second lawyer, he did not get Captain Draper.)

Perspective

By the end of 1966 Marine Corps strength stood at 278,000 men and women, the highest total since World War II. Two hundred and twenty-three of that number were lawyers—only one of whom was a woman.*[83] Throughout the Marine Corps, 213 general and 4,728 special courts-martial were tried in 1966.[84] No records survive that detail the number of courts-martial tried that year in Vietnam, but the total clearly was escalating. Drugs, fraggings, and racial conflicts were not yet on court-martial dockets in significant numbers. Reassuringly, the Uniform Code of Military Justice and the 1951 *Manual for Courts-Martial* appeared to be workable tools for pursuing justice in a predominantly static combat environment.

In Washington a Navy Commendation Medal was awarded and forwarded to Colonel Neville for the work he had done before going to Vietnam. His citation read, in part: "Fruition of his project recommendations for the combination of the Discipline and Legal Branches of the Personnel Department brought about significant economy of personnel and effort."[85] Despite the inference of the citation, however, there was still no separate legal branch at Headquarters Marine Corps. So Colonel Neville's successor at Headquarters, Colonel Charles B. Sevier, continued to bend Code DK, Discipline Branch, away from the Personnel Division and toward a separate legal section within Headquarters Marine Corps.

---

*First Lieutenant Patricia A. Murphy, first commissioned in June 1963, was the Marine Corps' second woman lawyer. The first, Lieutenant Colonel Lily H. Gridley, was commissioned in February 1943 and retired in 1965.

PART II
BUILD UP AND CONSOLIDATION

CHAPTER 4
1967: Trying Times

*III MAF: Double-Hatted Twice—1st Marine Division: Rising Caseloads, More Lawyers
3d Marine Division: More Combat, Fewer Courts—Force Logistic Command: Continue to March
1st Marine Aircraft Wing: Much Like Home—From a Lawyer's Case File: Psychiatry and Appellate Review
Project 100,000: Prelude to Problems—Drugs: Recognizing the Problem
Transportation: Hitchhiking to Court—Trying Cases—Marine Corps Lawyers in Combat: They Also Serve
The First Lawyer General Officer: No Immediate Change—Perspective*

As 1966 ended, the Marines of III MAF were fighting essentially two separate, interrelated wars. The 3d Marine Division fought a conventional war along the DMZ against North Vietnamese Army formations. At the same time, the 1st Marine Division continued a combination of large-unit and counterguerrilla operations south of Hai Van Pass, which stood a few miles north of Da Nang.

At the beginning of 1967 18 Marine infantry battalions and 21 aircraft squadrons occupied bases throughout I Corps. Those units and their supporting organizations totaled more than 70,000 Marines and sailors.[1]

On the legal front four general court-martial (GCM) commands were based in I Corps.* The 1st Marine Division was still headquartered at Da Nang with a detached brigade-sized force, Task Force X-Ray, at Chu Lai. Lieutenant Colonel Tom P. Casey remained the staff legal officer (SLO) at Da Nang (sharing space with the 3d Division legal office during the first part of the year), while his deputy, Lieutenant Colonel John L. Zorack, was in charge at Chu Lai. The 3d Marine Division (Forward) command post was at Dong Ha with the main command post at Phu Bai. The 3d Division's office moved from Da Nang to the main command post during April and May 1967. The 1st Marine Aircraft Wing (MAW), meanwhile, remained at the Da Nang Airbase. Its legal staff was now led by Lieutenant Colonel Ralph K. Culver. Force Logistic Command (FLC) was at Camp Books, Red Beach, near Da Nang with Lieutenant Colonel Charles R. Larouche still SLO. The fourth SLO was Colonel Robert B. Neville, who continued as III MAF's assistant chief of staff with collateral responsibility for MAF Headquarters legal matters.

In 1967 the Marines' missions were to counter the threat of enemy incursion across the I Corps border, to destroy Viet Cong/North Vietnamese Army units entering III MAF's tactical area of responsibility, and to ensure the security of allied base areas and lines of communication. In a change of strategy, South Vietnamese forces assumed primary responsibility for pacification of the civilian populace. Marine efforts in that regard nevertheless continued. The tempo of guerrilla warfare had substantially increased, and III MAF Headquarters anticipated large-scale attacks along the DMZ by enemy regular forces.[2]

Concern increased over the potential for legally significant incidents occurring in combat situations. The Commandant of the Marine Corps, General Wallace M. Greene, Jr., in a bulletin to all commanding officers, noted:

> I am extremely concerned in regard to recent incidents of wanton disregard for the personal lives and property of the civilian populace of the Republic of Vietnam.... I charge all Commanding Officers with the responsibility to insure that all personnel receive instruction in regard to the standards of conduct expected of the U.S. Marine.[3]

Equally concerned, General Krulak, Commanding General, FMFPac, wrote:

> The nature of the conflict in Vietnam has placed an unusual requirement on low ranking leaders to carry out sensitive combat operations, often in an environment where large numbers of civilians are present.... Determination of right and wrong ... has to be made on the spot, and often in the heat of battle.... The weight of this decision often falls on the shoulders of the small unit leader—platoon leader, squad leader, patrol leader ... individuals who, because of their relative youth and short time in service, are least able to exercise mature, deliberate judgement under the pressure of combat.... Nevertheless, [they] must be fully aware of their responsibilities for their conduct, and the conduct of their subordinates.... Moreover, every Marine must be made to understand that deviation from these standards is a grave offense and not to be tolerated.[4]

The SLOs continued to support the execution of their command's mission by prosecuting offenses, providing general legal advice to the commander, and furnishing technical support, such as legal assistance, claims service, and administrative discharge processing.

---

*A general court-martial command is one that is empowered to convene GCMs. The fact that a general officer commands a unit is not determinative of GCM jurisdiction. For example, III MAF, commanded by a lieutenant general, did not have GCM convening authority. In contrast, units commanded by colonels sometimes did have such authority.

By 1967 Marine Corps colonels and lieutenant colonels designated to be SLOs in Vietnam attended the Army's Judge Advocate General's School, in Charlottesville, Virginia, for a five-day indoctrination course.[5] Only then did they proceed to Vietnam.

More lieutenant—and captain—lawyers were in Vietnam now, but a high number of senior lawyers were also assigned there. Colonel Eugene B. "Doc" Fallon, slated to become the 3d Marine Division's SLO, believed that "[Headquarters Marine Corps] sent too many colonels to Vietnam." He noted that at one time in 1967, in the 1st Marine Division alone, there were four lawyer colonels, making turnaround time for colonels too brief.* He suggested that only three lawyer-colonels were required in Vietnam: one each for the 1st Division, 3d Division, and FLC. Neither III MAF Headquarters, nor 1st MAW, in his opinion, had enough work to justify a colonel as SLO.[6] Headquarters Marine Corps accepted the recommendation as to totals, if not distribution, and in later years the number of colonel lawyers in Vietnam dropped.

Headquarters III MAF, 1st Division, 1st MAW, and FLC, all benefitted from their common location in Da Nang. With the passage of time their facilities became more comfortable and settled, although subject to rocket and infrequent sapper attacks.

Numerous amenities were available in and around Da Nang. Twenty-four post exchanges and 43 snack bars were in American base areas there.[7] Large fans, small refrigerators, television sets, high-quality cameras, and a wide variety of other goods were routinely available. The 1st Division's incoming SLO, Lieutenant Colonel William T. Westmoreland, Jr., noted, "we were in pretty much of a base camp tactical situation during the time I was there, and any minor difficulties [were cured] by the fact that we had about 12 hours a day, 7 days a week to overcome them. A moving situation, of course, would have been different indeed."**[8]

The first woman Marine arrived for duty in Vietnam in March 1967 and served with MACV in Saigon.[9] Numerous female Navy nurses, Red Cross workers, and civilian news personnel were in the III MAF area, but no woman Marine lawyer was ever assigned to Vietnam.***

III MAF: Double-Hatted Twice

Across the Han River at III MAF Headquarters, on 1 June, Lieutenant General Robert E. Cushman, Jr., relieved Lieutenant General Walt as commanding general. In Saigon MACV directed III MAF to plan for construction of a strongpoint obstacle system south of the DMZ.[10] The incoming SLO would be heavily involved in that planning. Colonel Robert B. Neville, who was still "double hatted" as assistant chief of staff and MAF Headquarters SLO, was relieved on 30 July by Colonel Duane L. Faw.

Like his predecessor, Colonel Faw had seen extensive World War II combat. After Pearl Harbor he had enlisted as a Navy seaman and then become a Naval Aviation Cadet. Commissioned a Marine second lieutenant, he later piloted dive bombers in aerial combat over Guadalcanal, Munda, the Russells, and Rabaul. On inactive duty after the war, he earned his law degree and then returned to active duty during the Korean War. After that war he commanded the 2d Battalion, 6th Marines and led its deployment to Guantanamo during the 1961 Cuban Crisis. Later, for a brief period, he commanded the 6th Marines.**** Colonel Faw, a self-taught Vietnamese linguist, had sought the III MAF billet. "It was," he later said, "where the action was, with respect to the war, but there was practically no legal work." When Colonel Faw reported on board, Brigadier General Robert C. Owens, Jr., the MAF chief of staff, was about to go on R & R. He told Colonel Faw that in his absence, Colonel Neville, who was not returning to the United States for several days, would be the acting chief of staff. Could Colonel Faw act as the assistant chief of staff for that period of a few days? "Thirteen months later, I was still there," Colonel Faw recalled.

Although Colonel Faw was both assistant chief of staff and MAF Headquarters legal officer, the deputy legal officer, Major Ronald J. Kaye, handled day-to-day operations of the legal office. These included mak-

---

*Turnaround time was the period between Vietnam assignments. Those of the same grade and military occupational specialty with the longest time since their last overseas/unaccompanied tour of duty (usually Vietnam) became next scheduled for such duty. The fewer lawyer-colonels in the queue, the sooner each lawyer-colonel was sent to Vietnam; similarly, the more who were sent to Vietnam during any given period, the faster the queue moved and the faster one's turn came again.

**Colonel Westmoreland was not related to Army General William C. Westmoreland.

***In 1967 the sole woman Marine lawyer on active duty continued to be 1st Lieutenant Patricia A. Murphy.

****After leaving Vietnam Colonel Faw became one of the original 12 Navy Court of Military Review appellate judges. He then became the third Director of the Judge Advocate Division and the first to hold general officer grade, advanced to brigadier general on 7 August 1969.

Col Duane L. Faw, left, was III MAF Assistant Chief of Staff and Headquarters Staff Legal Officer, as was his predecessor, Col Robert B. Neville. Here, Col Faw discusses a III MAF case with civilian lawyer, Mr. Melvin Belli, who was visiting III MAF headquarters.

ing arrangements for the return from the United States of witnesses required in courts-martial and coordinating legal holds for all of III MAF.* Few disciplinary problems arose in III MAF Headquarters, and seldom were there more than one or two active cases at a time.[11] The few serious cases that arose in the headquarters were convened by other commands that, unlike III MAF, had general court-martial convening authority.

One of Colonel Faw's duties was to maintain liaison with the civilian mayor of Da Nang, Le Chi Cuong.** At one of their meetings the two realized that, between Marine intelligence sources and the mayor's less organized, but nearly as effective information sources, a fair guess could be made as to when VC rocket attacks on Da Nang would occur. Besides warning their respective countrymen, both were concerned about the safety of the *Helgoland*, a German hospital ship which had recently docked on the Han River near III MAF Headquarters. Colonel Faw and Mayor Cuong visited the *Helgoland's* captain and offered to warn him of impending attacks so that he might move to safety in nearby Da Nang harbor. The captain haughtily declined, saying that his ship's medical staff treated all Vietnamese, including VC, and no VC rocket would be fired that might endanger his ship.

Nevertheless, a few days later, Colonel Faw warned the *Helgoland's* captain that a rocket attack was anticipated that night. The warning was ignored. Late that night there was indeed a heavy rocket attack, in which two rockets bracketed the hospital ship, one hitting a ship moored just outboard of the *Helgoland*. After that warnings were welcomed and heeded by the

---

*Legal hold was an administrative action that held a Marine in Vietnam until an ongoing legal proceeding was concluded, or until the legal hold was lifted. Since it often resulted in keeping an individual in Vietnam beyond his scheduled departure date, legal holds were very unpopular with Marines.

**Eventually, Brigadier General Faw sponsored the American citizenship of Le Chi Cuong, his wife, two sons, and three daughters, all of whom escaped, separately, from Vietnam as it fell to the North Vietnamese. Their eventual reunion in California is an amazing story. In all, General Faw sponsored the citizenship of 13 South Vietnamese. (Faw intvw.)

1966 NSA Cruise Book

The German Red Cross hospital ship Helgoland *steams in Da Nang Bay. "People around there got to know that when the* Helgoland *left, we were likely to get a rocket attack."*

1st Marine Division lawyers seen at officers' call in the club. From left, Maj Winn M. Thurman; LtCol William T. Westmoreland, Jr.; 1stLt Donald E. Wittig; Capt Harry D. Sabine; Capt Ross T. Roberts; unidentified motor transport officer; Maj William B. Draper, Jr.; unidentified nonlawyer; Capt Paul R. Constantino; and Capt James P. Shannon.

Photo courtesy of Col Donald Higginbotham, USMCR

Photo courtesy of LtCol William B. Draper, USMC (Ret.)
Capt Donald Higginbotham was a 1st Marine Division lawyer and CO of Headquarters Battalion Reaction Company. At a Sunday steak fry, he is teased by officers' club employee, Mai Lee. Hill 327's cantilevered SEAhut living quarters are in the background.

Helgoland, and she would move into the harbor to escape the anticipated rockets. Colonel Faw recalled, "People around there got to know that when the *Helgoland* left, we were likely to get a rocket attack, so when it pulled out everybody buttoned up."[17]

The *Helgoland*, soon referred to as the "Chicken of the Sea," otherwise remained at its customary dockside position near III MAF Headquarters for almost three years. The ship, with its complement of nurses, hosted several I Corps Bar Association parties and dances over that period.[13]

1st Marine Division: Rising Caseloads, More Lawyers

In February Colonel Casey was relieved as SLO by Lieutenant Colonel William T. Westmoreland, Jr., who during World War II had commanded the Marine detachment on board the *Savannah* (CL 42). After World War II he commanded the 3d Battalion, 9th Marines and later the 1st Infantry Training Battalion. Remembering that promotions for senior lawyers had in the past required command of line units, he hoped for an infantry billet in Vietnam and was a staff legal officer only over his own objection.

After less than a year the 1st Division SLO's office had grown from 13 officers and 18 enlisted men to 24 officers and only 14 enlisted Marines. This included one lawyer assigned to process claims and a full-time legal assistance officer. As Lieutenant Colonel Westmoreland noted:

> I don't recall the caseload, but we had too many lawyers. I encouraged those hard-chargers who wished to, to seek duty with [combat] troops. As I recall, [Major] Winn Thurman was a battalion XO in the 7th Marines, for a while; [Captain Paul R.] Constantino had a rifle company; and [Captain Bernard A.] Bernie Allen had a platoon. [Captain Donald] Higginbotham was C.O. of the Headquarters Battalion Reaction Company. In addition, other personnel, both officer and enlisted, made inserts . . . with patrols from reconnaissance battalion.* [Navy Lieutenant John J.] Martens, the law specialist, was particularly enthusiastic about recon patrols.[14]

Until late March 1967 three 1st Division lawyers and several enlisted legal clerks remained at Chu Lai under the deputy SLO, Lieutenant Colonel John L. Zorack. By this time Chu Lai's tents had been replaced by SEAhuts, but living conditions remained more austere than those at the Da Nang Airbase. The SEAhuts were always damp and unheated. (Vietnam was surprisingly cold during the monsoon seasons.) Cold water showers were available.[15] Finally, on 26 April 1967 Task Force X-Ray was deactivated, and the U.S. Army's Task Force Oregon took over its responsibilities and facilities. After the other 1st Division lawyers left to join the rest of the office in the Da Nang area, Lieutenant Colonel Zorack remained at Chu Lai as the "Chief of Staff, Chu Lai Installation Coordinator," until completion of his tour of duty three months later.[16]

The location of a U.S. Army command in the I Corps TAOR was recognition by MACV of III MAF's difficulty in countering enemy incursions across the DMZ while also keeping base areas secure. During this time, III MAF had launched Operations De Soto and Cochise with units from Chu Lai. Further north 1st Division units had initiated Operations Stone and Lafayette in the first two months of the year. By deactivating Task Force X-Ray, the 1st Marine Division could move men northward and more easily meet the enemy threat to the 3d Marine Division on the DMZ. For the division's lawyers Task Force X-Ray's deactivation meant the SLO's office was once again consolidated, this time at Hill 327, near Da Nang.

The number of cases increased, but because a greater number of lawyers was available to try them, on an individual basis the caseload remained low: around four or five general and eight to 10 special courts-martial per counsel. Most special court-martial cases were still being tried by nonlawyers at the battalion

---

*The patrol inserts involved legal personnel accompanying the helicopter insertions of patrols. Lawyers did not participate in the patrols. More than one helicopter engaged in inserts or extractions was shot down, although never when a lawyer was on board.

Photos courtesy of author (top) and LtCol John L. Zorack, USMC (Ret.)

General purpose tents served as living quarters at Chu Lai until mid-1967. Plastic is nailed to the top frame to minimize rain leaks. The tents' sides were rolled up, weather permitting. Lower photograph shows the two Task Force X-Ray legal SEAhuts, with a four-holer, right.

Saturday night poker is played in the 1st Marine Division legal office. From left, 1stLt James Ehlers; Capt Harry D. Sabine; Maj William B. Draper, Jr.; and 1stLt James E. Barnett.

level, and some cases referred to trial with lawyer counsel were disposed of without trial. So the number of cases actually tried was less than the caseload indicated.* For example, during one year and two weeks in Vietnam, Captain Donald Higginbotham tried only six general and 12 special courts. (Although, like most counsels, a portion of his tour was spent in duties other than trial or defense counsel, reducing the time he was assigned to try cases.)[17] In August Colonel John J. Ostby relieved Lieutenant Colonel Westmoreland as SLO of the 1st Marine Division.

Meanwhile, the 1st Marine Division continued to conduct operations throughout the TAOR. Operations Union II and Medina were particularly hard-fought battles in III MAF's plan to destroy enemy bases previously left alone because of the lack of forces.[18]

3d Marine Division: More Combat, Fewer Courts

North of Da Nang the 3d Marine Division (Forward) command post remained at Dong Ha, not far from the coast and the South China Sea.** To the west of Dong Ha the 3d Division held Cam Lo, Camp J.J. Carroll, the Rockpile, and Khe Sanh, the latter only a few miles from the Laotian border. Just south of the DMZ, Con Thien and Gio Linh were being established as strongpoints and enemy contact was routine. Operations Prairie II, III, and IV continued throughout the year, with continuous, heavy combat. The first battle of Khe Sanh began early in the year.

A civilian-conducted study had proposed a barrier system across infiltration routes into South Vietnam. Secretary of Defense Robert S. McNamara, over Navy and Marine Corps objections, directed that a portion of the system be made operational by 1 November 1967. Construction of the strongpoint obstacle system, or "McNamara Wall," as it was often referred to, began in May.[19]

From Phu Bai, 3d Division lawyers served Marines throughout the TAOR, visiting each camp and out-

---

*A case could be dropped for lack of evidence, or it could be taken back by the accused's commanding officer and be dropped, or referred to a summary court-martial or an administrative discharge board. Essential witnesses may have been unavailable due to inability to locate them, if Vietnamese, or due to death or being wounded, if Marine.

**During 1967, Major Walter J. Donovan, serving near Dong Ha, was the operations officer of the 1st Amphibian Tractor Battalion, and later, of Task Force Hotel. He was awarded the Legion of Merit for his performance of duties in Vietnam. Returning to the United States, he attended law school at night, gaining his law degree in 1973. Later, he was a Distinguished Graduate of the Naval War College. In April 1983 he was promoted to the grade of brigadier general and became the ninth Director of the Judge Advocate Division.

Photo courtesy of BGen Walter J. Donovan, USMC (Ret.)
Maj Walter J. Donovan was operations officer of the 1st Amphibian Tractor Battalion. The future Director of the Judge Advocate Division is shown in October 1967 at Cua Viet with his trademark two wristwatches.

post as needed. The division SLO was Colonel Charles H. Beale, Jr. In World War II he was a radar officer on Guadalcanal and later participated in the invasions of Munda, Rendova, and Guam. After the war he earned his law degree and returned to active duty in the Korean War as commanding officer of a signal company. His duties after Korea were a mix of communications and legal assignments. After becoming SLO, Colonel Beale supervised the legal office's move from Da Nang to Phu Bai, conducted in stages from 28 March to 5 June.[20] The SLO's work spaces were the usual SEAhuts. By midyear, three of them housed all of "legal," one of the huts being the courtroom with not one, but two, air conditioning wall units.[21]

Familiar problems persisted through 1967. Lawyers arrived in Vietnam with no legal experience. Of the several captain-lawyers in the 3d Division, all but one had come directly from Naval Justice School. The young lawyers were only too aware of their lack of seasoning. Captain Charles E. Patterson's first general court-martial was a six-day murder trial with lengthy psychiatric testimony. As he recalled: "There were many times during the course of that trial that I wished that I had considerably more experience in the courtroom than I'd had at the time."[22]

The junior enlisted personnel constituted "a gross injustice," foisted upon field commands as trained le-

gal clerks, in Colonel Fallon's opinion as the incoming SLO. Five had been assigned their administration MOSs after only two weeks of legal school and then sent directly to Vietnam. Two of the five could not type, nor record a court-martial.

Telephones remained a test of patience. To get through to Da Nang from Quang Tri took hours, if one was fortunate. It sometimes took as long as two days. Captain Francis T. Coleman (a 1st Division lawyer), wrote: "The switchboard network . . . is more reminiscent of a backyard walkie-talkie than a serious vehicle of communication."[23]

The III MAF brig posed difficulties for the 3d Division lawyers, because it took defense counsels two to three days to visit an accused Marine incarcerated there. The SLO's suggestion of a detention facility, a brig extension at Quang Tri, was rejected by division headquarters as being unnecessary.[24]

In June Colonel Beale was briefly relieved by Lieutenant Colonel Norris C. "Sweeper" Broome. Lieutenant Colonel Broome became the deputy SLO less than a month later, when Colonel Eugene B. "Doc" Fallon arrived.

Colonel Fallon was a 1944 Naval Academy graduate who had been an infantry platoon commander in

Senior lawyers pose at Phu Bai, north of Da Nang. From left: 3d Marine Division Staff Legal Officer, Col Eugene B. "Doc" Fallon; his deputy, LtCol Norris C. Broome; and law officer, LtCol Donald E. Holben.
Photo courtesy of Col Paul F. Henderson, USMC (Ret.)

1967: TRYING TIMES

the battle for Okinawa. One of those few officers sent to law school by the Marine Corps in the early 1950s, he described his tenure as SLO as "the most challenging tour I've ever experienced as an officer lawyer, the most frustrating . . . and the most rewarding."[25]

He found that the several moves the office had experienced had been hard on recording equipment and typewriters. He also found that electrical power, essential to the office, was shut off for several hours every day. He turned to portable generators as a solution. Two newly arrived electric typewriters came with one power pack and no means by which to recharge it. Given the increasing number of trial records to be typed, Colonel Fallon instituted a 24-hour-shift system for court reporters.

Like the 1st Marine Division, the lawyer strength of the 3d Division had grown, but unlike the 1st Division, greater numbers were needed. Combat units were so heavily committed they could not muster enough officers to prosecute, defend, and make up members panels for their own special courts-martial. Colonel Fallon's solution was to provide them with trial

Photo courtesy of Col Paul F. Henderson, USMC (Ret.)
3d Marine Division Deputy Staff Legal Officer, LtCol Paul F. Henderson works in his Phu Bai office. Trial counsels worked on the other side of the partition.

Force Logistic Command's legal personnel, seen at Camp Books, Red Beach, early 1967. From left, Cpl Eckes; Sgt Harms; Capt Franklin P. "Skip" Glenn; Cpl Grover; SLO, LtCol Charles R. Larouche; Capt Charles J. Kall; Deputy SLO, LtCol Richard E. Wray; Cpl Hayes; Capt Larry J. Miner; Cpl Carr; unidentified driver; and office Legal Chief, GySgt Lyon.

Photo courtesy of Mr. Charles J. Kall

teams whenever possible: a trial and defense counsel and a senior member—all lawyers—and a court reporter.[26] Throughout the division, in any special court where a bad conduct discharge might be imposed, a trial team was detailed to the unit.[27]

The 3d Marine Division SLO's office was to move yet again. In December 1967 the commanding general ordered establishment of a new forward command post at Dong Ha and the actual movement of division support elements from Phu Bai to Quang Tri.[28]

Force Logistic Command: Continue to March

Logistical support of the Marines of III MAF continued to be the mission of the 5,500 officers and men of FLC. Although redesignated Headquarters, 1st Force Service Regiment/Force Logistic Command on 16 February 1967, it still was referred to as "FLC", or "Flick." The command grew to a strength of 9,551 by the end of the year.

Colonel Larouche and his lawyers supported FLC units located at the Da Nang headquarters, as well as Support Unit 1 at Dong Ha, Force Logistic Support Group (FLSG) Alpha at Phu Bai, and FLSG Bravo at Chu Lai.[29] Simultaneously they conducted their third legal clerk school for the five legal offices in Vietnam.[30]

On 1 June Colonel Larouche was relieved by Lieutenant Colonel Verne L. "Bubs" Oliver, who had already served in Vietnam in his previous billet as a law officer, based in Yokosuka, Japan. Lieutenant Colonel Oliver found that, besides a rising caseload (three general and 26 special courts-martial were tried during June, alone), the number of foreign claims and legal assistance cases increased. Most claims by Vietnamese involved motor vehicle accidents. Combat-associated claims were not considered, as they were under the cognizance of the Military Civic Action Program, handled by the Government of Vietnam.[31]

FLC's legal assistance docket for a typical month numbered 127 cases. Included were 32 domestic relations cases, 25 powers of attorney, 10 letters of indebtedness, 8 wills, 4 tax problems, and 3 naturalizations.[32] By late 1967 legal assistance attorneys in Da Nang could, with patience, occasionally complete telephone calls to the United States. This involved making the call through the division's communications section via one or more radio patches. Success depended upon good weather in the China Sea/Pacific area, after taking into account the international date line and a minimum of an eight-hour time zone difference. When successful, the lawyers often heard a disbelieving state tax clerk respond to a phone call from Vietnam.[33]

FLC's school for legal clerks fell by the wayside. Colonel Oliver noted that "various commands, for one reason or another, did not want to lose the services of their people for two weeks."[34] But, on a much reduced scale, Colonel Oliver continued training new clerks from the local FLC units

Marijuana offenses were being noticed for the first time. Judging from the charge sheets, replacement personnel in 1967 had more drug and disciplinary in-

Basic legal clerks shown at their graduation. LtCols Larouche and Wray stand, center. The third basic legal clerk's class graduated at FLC's Camp Books in April 1967.

Marine Corps Historical Collection

cidents than their predecessors. In rear area units, like FLC, the most severe disciplinary problems were to occur in coming months.

1st Marine Aircraft Wing: Much Like Home

Throughout 1967 fixed-wing aircraft squadrons rotated between the Da Nang Airbase and Iwakuni, Japan, where they underwent aircraft rehabilitation. Three squadrons returned to the United States and another to Japan and were replaced by squadrons from those locales.[35]

Living and working conditions at the airbase remained comfortable, despite the threat of rocket attacks. Captain Charles H. Mitchell recalled his arrival in Vietnam for duty with 1st MAW:

> I flew in to Da Nang airport on a Continental Airliner, replete with stewardesses . . . . I sort of expected there to be things like security, and people to be running around with guns, and . . . all I saw, looking out the window, were all the accouterments of U.S. garrison existence . . . . Then you got off the aircraft and . . . have the impression that you should be looking for a foxhole, or something . . . and when they finally get you inprocessed to the command you're going to, somebody comes by in a jeep, picks you up and drives you over to a compound which is stucco buildings and tile roofs and a good deal of air conditioning . . . . It was pretty comfortable. The culture shock in going to war, for me, was not one of deprivation, but shock at the opulence . . . . As time went on, I found out that, with the exception of the combat units . . . there wasn't any war going on at all, except an occasional rocket attack.[36]

The Wing SLO was Lieutenant Colonel Ralph K. Culver, another World War II veteran. His deputy was Lieutenant Colonel Charles E. "Chuck" Spence, described by a later director of the Judge Advocate Division as "one of the greats in this business."[37] In August, Lieutenant Colonel Culver was relieved by Colonel Robert C. "Curly" Lehnert, and the following month, Major William H. J. Tiernan became the deputy SLO, relieving Lieutenant Colonel Spence.*

Before becoming a lawyer, Colonel Lehnert had been a Marine fighter pilot during World War II and Korea and had been awarded a Distinguished Flying Cross in each conflict. Since the Korean war he had

---

*Brigadier General Tiernan became the eighth Director of the Judge Advocate Division in April 1980. As a captain he was an infantry company commander during the 1961 Cuban Crisis, and deployed to Guantanamo Bay. He served in the Office of the Judge Advocate General of the Navy, and was editor the JAG Journal. After Vietnam he served in a variety of legal billets, was a distinguished graduate of the Naval War College, SJA of five major commands, and chief of staff of the 1st Marine Division. (Biographical Files RefSec, MCHC).

Photo courtesy of Col Charles H. Mitchell, USMC
Capt Charles H. Mitchell, 1st Marine Aircraft Wing lawyer, waits in the Wing legal office to join a Rough Rider resupply convoy from Da Nang to Dong Ha.

alternated between flight duty and legal duty and recently had been squadron commander of VMF-312.[38] Now in another combat zone he took every opportunity to return to the cockpit. The Wing was willing to employ qualified, experienced pilots, and Colonel Lehnert flew with Marine Aircraft Group 12 out of Chu Lai, logging combat missions in A-4 aircraft. As Major Tiernan later recalled, "the figure that sticks in my mind is 85 combat missions . . . . He rarely missed a week."[39] And as Captain Mitchell remembered, "Major Tiernan ran the office, really, and Colonel Lehnert fought the war."[40] In his third war, Colonel Lehnert won a third Distinguished Flying Cross.

In an effort to better manage the wing's general court-martial caseload, Colonel Lehnert initiated a special court-martial "task force," and assigned a lawyer to be counsel for each wing unit, responsible for the special, as well as the general court-martial cases that arose in his group or squadron. Often, trial teams would be in the field several days a week and typically traveled to a squadron, prepared the cases for trial the first day, tried them the next, and returned to Da

Department of Defense Photo (USMC) 88583
1stLt Robert C. Lehnert stands beside his F4U Corsair in the Marshall Islands during World War II. He earned his third Distinguished Flying Cross as a colonel, while SLO of the 1st Marine Aircraft Wing in 1967-68.

Nang the third. General courts were usually tried at the wing headquarters at Da Nang.[41]

Despite these efforts to be responsive to the legal needs of the Wing commands and the relatively light caseload, problems of transportation, communications, equipment, and personnel made it impossible to satisfy everyone. Later, Major Tiernan recalled: "[There were] group commanders who were constantly complaining about the system being inadequate, and of course it was. It was a question of trying to get the work done with the resources we had . . . . Inadequate resources . . . . Too much work and not enough resources."[42]

Colonel Lehnert noted that commanders often were dissatisfied with delays in trying simple marijuana possession cases. But, as Colonel Lehnert pointed out:

> In the absence of a stipulation [that the substance was marijuana], which eager defense counsel rarely advised, the substance had to be transported out-of-country to Japan for laboratory analysis . . . . There were always the evidentiary problems relating to chain of custody, lack of cross-examination [of the analyst], coupled with the attendant delays.[43]

On the bright side, electrical power for courtroom recording equipment was seldom a problem at 1st MAW "legal." Additionally, its law library had improved, and publications like *Law Week* and the *Criminal Law Reporter* were promptly received.[44] On a more substantive level, Colonel Lehnert noted that, "the wing [legal office] was blessed with one sergeant/reporter who was skilled in the use of a stenotype machine—he was worth his weight in gold.* That equipment needed no power, was very portable, and could set up in field in an instant.[45] Reporters with stenotype proficiency, unfortunately, were rare in the Vietnam war.

From a Lawyer's Case File: Psychiatry and Appellate Review

The general court-martial of Private First Class Edward P. Boltik illustrates the roles of appellate review and psychiatry in the court-martial process.[46] Although both psychiatry and appellate practice figured in courts-martial convened under the old *Naval Courts and Boards*, under the "Red Book" they played an even more important part.

While Private First Class Boltik was standing sentry duty, a young Vietnamese boy grabbed a bottle of soda from him and ran. Private First Class Boltik raised his rifle and killed the boy with a single shot. At a general court-martial convened by the commanding general of the 3d Marine Division, Private First Class Boltik was charged with murder. He was defended by Captain Mark L. Haiman, the third lawyer assigned to represent him. The first assigned defense counsel, Captain James W. Jones, withdrew after he was physically beaten by Boltik, when Jones visited him in his cell. The second defense counsel, Captain Paul S. Zonderman, only participated in pretrial proceedings.

Prior to trial Boltik underwent psychiatric examinations in Vietnam, Japan, and Philadelphia, Pennsylvania.** At the Da Nang trial the law officer was Lieutenant Colonel Donald E. Holben; the trial counsel was Captain Charles E. Patterson. Psychiatric testimony raised questions as to Boltik's mental responsibility at the time of the shooting, but the members, nevertheless, found him guilty of unpremeditated murder. He was sentenced to a dis-

---

*Beginning in the late 1970s closed microphone court reporting of special and general courts-martial gave way to reporters using stenotype machines. Stenotype reporting, despite its advantages, was not considered practical for Vietnam employment because skilled reporters took several years to train, and were prohibitively expensive to school in the required numbers.

**The records of the case do not explain how Boltik came to be examined in Pennsylvania, an unusual occurrence in light of the numerous uniformed psychiatrists available in Vietnam and the western Pacific area.

All photos on this page courtesy of Col Charles H. Mitchell, USMC

LtCol Ralph K. Culver, the Wing SLO, was about to return to the United States after completing his tour of duty in July 1967. From left, Legal Chief, MSgt Evoy; Deputy SLO, LtCol Charles E. Spence, Jr.; LtCol Culver; Sgt Morgan; 1stLt Macauley Carter, Jr.; and Capt David B. King. Hidden behind King are GySgt Russell and Cpl Mitchell.

Left, the 1st Marine Aircraft Wing legal office, seen in 1967. One of the numerous post-World War II French-built buildings adjacent to the Da Nang Airbase runways. Below left, the deputy SLO, LtCol Charles E. Spence, Jr., right, at work in the 1st Marine Aircraft Wing legal office. Below, electrical power was seldom a problem at the 1st Marine Aircraft Wing. Wing defense counsel Capt Donald R. Pritchard rests in his bachelor officers' quarters room beside his reel-to-reel tape deck, fan, Tensor light, and radio.

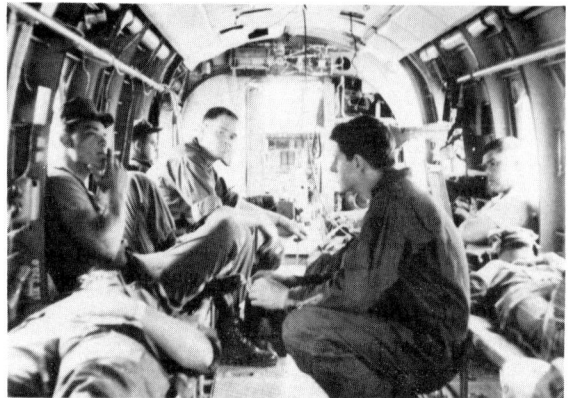

Photo courtesy of Col Rufus C. Young, USMC (Ret.)
A 1st Marine Aircraft Wing trial team shown in transit. Capt Donald R. Pritchard looks toward Capt Rufus C. Young's camera as the two lawyers fly from Da Nang to an outlying Marine unit in a CH-46 helicopter.

honorable discharge, confinement at hard labor for 30 years, forfeiture of all pay and allowances, and reduction to private. The convening authority approved the findings and sentence. The case then went to the Navy Board of Review in Washington, where military appellate counsels entered an appeal on Boltik's behalf.

At the Navy Board of Review in Washington, a panel of three senior judges heard oral argument and considered government and defense briefs. Boltik was not present, nor did the appellate panel ever see him. The panel was composed of Colonel George P. Blackburn, who had been the SLO of the 1st Marine Division in Vietnam; Colonel Ralph K. Culver, formerly the SLO of the 1st Marine Aircraft Wing in Vietnam; and K. B. Hamilton, a civilian judge serving on the Navy Board of Review.

On 5 September 1968 the Court issued a unanimous opinion finding Boltik insane. They observed that during the trial a Navy psychologist, when asked whether Boltik was responsible for his actions at the time of the shooting, answered no. He felt that Boltik was psychotic at the time, and gave his reasons for thinking so. Another Navy psychiatrist also testified that Boltik was indeed unable to distinguish right from wrong and that Boltik was not responsible for his actions. Next, the Chief of Psychiatry of the Navy Hospital, Yokosuka, a Navy captain with 17 years experience as a psychiatrist, testified similarly. A third Navy psychiatrist who also examined Boltik, however, testified that he believed him to be antisocial, but able to distinguish right from wrong. Yet another Navy psychiatrist testified and agreed with the third psychiatrist—Boltik could distinguish right from wrong.

The appellate court, in its opinion pointed out the greater experience of the Navy captain psychiatrist (the third expert witness who found Boltik unable to distinguish right from wrong), noting that he was neither selected nor paid by the accused, and repeated the psychiatrist's testimony from the record of trial:

> It has been my experience that psychiatrists in the Navy . . . are very conservative in the area of this "knew right from wrong" and "adhere to the right" and so on; that a person has to be quite sick, ill, mentally disturbed, before we will say this about him. And I think, personally, that I am probably more conservative than most of the psychiatrists within my acquaintance.

Placing the burden of proof where required by the 1951 *Manual for Courts-Martial*, the appellate court concluded:

> This Board is clearly convinced that the prosecution failed to prove . . . beyond reasonable doubt that the accused was so far free from mental defect, disease, or derangement as to be able . . . to distinguish right from wrong and to adhere to the right . . . . Accordingly, the findings and sentence are set aside and the charge and specification . . . are ordered dismissed.

Private First Class Boltik was tried in a combat zone and defended by a Marine lawyer, whom he did not meet until the lawyer was assigned his case. At his counsel's request, he received psychiatric examinations in hospitals in Vietnam, Japan, and the United States from a psychologist and four psychiatrists. Upon conviction his case was appealed on the basis of the stan-

Accused murderer PFC Edward P. Boltik, right, is shown with his defense counsel, Capt Mark L. Haiman, in the 3d Marine Division's legal office.
Photo courtesy of Col Mark L. Haiman, USMC

A panel of the Navy Court of Military Review similar to this one dismissed Boltik's conviction and sentence, finding that the government had failed to prove him sane. Shown in this 1972 photograph are, front, from left: Judge John L. Ostby, Col, USMC; Senior Judge Charles Timblin, Capt, JAGC, USN (Ret.); Chief Judge Gale E. Krouse, Capt, JAGC, USN; Judge J. Fielding Jones (a civilian jurist); Judge Robert C. Lehnert, Col, USMC. Rear, from left: Senior Judge Horace H. Morgan, Capt, JAGC, USN; Judge Louis L. Milano, Capt, JAGC, USN; Judge Paul F. Henderson, Jr., Col, USMC; Judge Thomas P. Smith, Jr., Capt, JAGC, USN; and Judge Raymond W. Glasgow, Cdr, JAGC, USN (Ret.).

Photo courtesy of Navy-Marine Corps Court of Military Review

dard one-paragraph, written request of his trial defense lawyer. An appellate defense counsel who never met Boltik represented him before a panel of experienced lawyers, two of whom had combat backgrounds and Vietnam service. They reversed his conviction within eleven months of his court-martial, all without financial cost to Boltik. That was the military justice system, as experienced by a Marine private first class in 1967 and 1968.

Project 100,000: Prelude to Problems

In 1964 the Federal Task Force on Manpower found that the military services rejected about 600,000 men each year who failed to meet intelligence standards. The task force, chaired by Daniel Patrick Moynihan, suggested that some of those individuals were suitable for military duty. The Department of Defense established a program which required the Armed Services to accept some of those previously rejected men. Secretary of Defense McNamara called the program "Project 100,000."[47]

The Armed Forces Qualification Test is administered to all prospective Armed Service volunteers and draftees. It classifies them in one of five intelligence categories according to their test scores. Those scoring in categories I, II, and III are automatically acceptable for enlistment or induction; those in category V are automatically rejected.[48] Since 1952 recruiters had accepted a small number of individuals scoring in category IV, but now all Services were required to significantly lower their standards to accept many more "Cat IVs," as they were termed by Marine Corps lawyers. In October 1966, the Secretary of Defense directed that 40,000 category IVs be accepted by the Services during 1967 and 100,000 each year thereafter.

After the first year the Marine Corps was required to accept 18 percent (18,000) of the 100,000 category IV individuals each year. As Brigadier General Jonas M. Platt told the 1967 General Officers Symposium: "Unfortunately it has been necessary to turn away many high quality applicants in order to meet the mandatory quotas of individuals of lower mental caliber. The Marine Corps is on record as opposing this requirement."[49]

The influx of category IV Marines had an immediate negative effect on discipline and on Marine lawyers. Major General Rathvon McC. Tompkins, commanding general of the 3d Marine Division in late 1967, said "that [Project 100,000] was a very grave problem . . . . [Category] IV was a guy who could see lightning and hear thunder, maybe . . . . It's a great waste of the taxpayer's money and every other damned thing . . . . Great waste of effort, great waste of time, and a very dangerous thing."[50] Captain W. Hays Parks, the 1st Marine Division's chief trial counsel, complained that "in the midst of the war the military—through Project 100,000—became a uniformed Job Corps . . . . The idea worked much like that of tossing water on a drowning man."[51] Army General William C. Westmoreland put it more bluntly:

> Category IV is a dummy . . . . Give him menial jobs and he is not a troublemaker. But it is awfully difficult to utilize that many category IVs . . . . That is important when you start reflecting on the drug syndrome, the fragging . . . . That introduced a weak-minded, criminal, untrained element . . . . When those people came to Vietnam . . . that's when disciplinary problems began on the battlefield.[52]

Statistics for the life of the program that compare the disciplinary rate of category IV Marines with other Marines have not been discovered, but category IV Army enlistees were initially found to have disciplinary problems and court-martial convictions at about double the rate of other soldiers.[53]

Disciplinary incidents associated with the "Cat IV" Marine did not end with the Vietnam War. Until the enlistments of the "Cat IVs" were completed in the mid 1970s, they remained disciplinary problems for commanders and cases for lawyers.

Drugs: Recognizing the Problem

Drugs and marijuana became a major concern in Vietnam only in 1967.* This coincided with the dramatic rise in their use in America. First noticed in 1966, military commanders only became aware of the depth of the drug and marijuana problem in the following year. III MAF's commanding general, Lieutenant General Cushman, Jr., shared his concern with Lieutenant General Krulak, Commanding General, FMFPac, in a September 1967 message:

> [I] am sure you have noticed that the use of marijuana is mentioned in far too many administrative and disciplinary reports originating in Marine units in Vietnam . . . . There has been a substantial increase in marijuana traffic in I Corps, this year . . . . It is sold locally both in bulk and in machine-rolled cigarettes. Major CID [Criminal Investigation Division] effort has been devoted to locating the source. It is clearly a Vietnamese operation . . . . Street vendors are usually women and children. Appetites are teased by tossing cigarettes on passing trucks carrying troops. Vendors are found at almost every place where American servicemen can be contacted. Prices have increased from 10 to 50 piastres per cigarette, over the past few months . . . . In spite of the seriousness of the problem, there is no epidemic of marijuana use in III MAF . . . . With the promised support and cooperation of the Mayor [of Da Nang, Le Chi Cuong,] and Vietnamese law enforcement agencies, the problem should be greatly reduced.[54]

But the U.S. command found drug abuse difficult to deal with in Vietnam: Vietnamese drug laws were ill-defined, no central Vietnamese narcotics enforcement agency existed, and enforcement of existing laws was lax. By 1967 opium sold for $1.00 per injection, and morphine was $5.00 per vial. Heroin had not yet appeared on the market.[55]

It seemed that all at once marijuana use was common. Da Nang and the Army's Long Binh-Bien Hoa areas were major problem areas.[56] A Congressional inquiry revealed that between 1 June and 3 October marijuana had been discovered in the III MAF brig on 16 occasions. In all 16 instances the source was said to have been Vietnamese who passed it to prisoners on working parties, often throwing it into passing trucks in which prisoners were being transported.[57]

General Krulak was concerned. He sent a confidential message to General Cushman: "The existence of the problem is apparent . . . . In order to acquire a full picture of the problem, I am sending LtCol W. C. Jaeck from this HQ on 24 November to confer with you, your staff, and anyone else who can help put the matter in perspective."[58]

Lieutenant Colonel William C. Jaeck was the assistant Force Legal Officer at General Krulak's Hawaii headquarters. His investigative mandate included only marijuana, because, as he noted, "in those days we were hardly conversant with anything stronger."[59]

Lieutenant Colonel Jaeck's subsequent report highlighted many of the problems associated with the prosecution of marijuana cases. He confirmed its ready

---

*Marijuana is a drug, according to Schedule I of the Controlled Substances Act (21 USC 812). A distinction is made in this volume because of the usual dichotomy between the two in the view of commanders and, usually, lawyers. The specification for charging a marijuana offense differs from that of other drug offenses, in both the 1951 and 1969 *Manual for Courts-Martial*. In the 1969 *Manual*, the maximum confinement for a marijuana offense is half that of other drugs, further illustrating the distinction.

Department of Defense Photo (USMC) A229525
LtGen Victor H. Krulak was Commanding General, Fleet Marine Force, Pacific. To gain a view of the burgeoning marijuana problem he sent LtCol William C. Jaeck, of the FMFPac legal office, to Vietnam.

availability and the difficulty in determining with any accuracy the extent of its use. He also noted the disparity in disciplinary approaches in the several commands: In FLC, marijuana possession or use was virtually an automatic general court-martial; in other commands it could go to a special or even a summary court. "The difficulty," Lieutenant Colonel Jaeck wrote, "is to determine the appropriate action to be taken against one who has had one [marijuana] cigarette while not in a specific duty status, who is no more impaired than the man who has had his daily ration of two beers."

The lack of a crime laboratory in Vietnam, he reported, was a major handicap to prosecutions. The only laboratory in the Far East was at Camp Zama, Japan, and test results could take as long as 45 days to be returned to Vietnam. He noted that "Dogpatch," a collection of Vietnamese shops astride the major Da Nang roadway, was a particularly troublesome area. It was a traffic chokepoint that allowed easy access by marijuana street vendors to Marines in slow-moving vehicles. Vietnamese authorities, he noted, were not overly concerned with the problem. His report concluded that "disciplinary measures are having little apparent effect in deterring the use of marijuana." Lieutenant General Krulak, in a handwritten addendum to the report, approved Lieutenant Colonel Jaeck's recommendation that Vietnam commands submit a monthly report to FMFPac on disciplinary and administrative actions taken in regard to marijuana, and he noted the need for uniformity in disciplinary action.[60] As accurate as his report was, Lieutenant Colonel Jaeck could hardly foresee the impact that marijuana and other drugs were to have on the Marine Corps in Vietnam and beyond.

Transportation: Hitchhiking to Court

Captain Donald Higginbotham, a lawyer in the 1st Marine Division SLO's office at Hill 327, said of transportation:

> Travel in RVN was purely on a "catch as catch can" basis. While there was assigned one Mighty Mite for some 20-plus personnel the damn thing was always broken down.... I have travelled in DC-3s which were used, at the same time, to bring the dead from staging areas; ridden helicopters, both Marine and Army; travelled on "rough rider" convoys where my temporary duties . . . were to man an M-60 machine gun; and became a past master at hitchhiking .... Transportation was a simple matter of going to a helipad or convoy staging area and begging or intimidating a ride to one's destination, limited only by one's ability and initiative as a con artist.... Travel for lawyers was normally based upon very low priorities.
>
> [Once], while returning by vehicle from the 3/1 area near Marble Mountain, three lawyers and the driver received sniper fire from a tree line.... We all departed the vehicle, with haste, into a ditch. Unfortunately, the ditch and the sniper were on the same side of the road. We never knew whether the sniper ran out of ammunition or simply could not draw another bead due to laughter.[61]

Despite the many vehicles usually in a Marine-controlled area, it was seldom easy to get to the scene of an offense, meet with witnesses, or report to a convening authority in the field. In rainy weather roads became virtually impassable; in some areas no roads existed. In hot weather, helicopters could muster only enough lift to carry essential passengers, which usually did not include lawyers. Helicopters were subject to abrupt and unannounced diversions from scheduled destinations.[62] Captain Robert A. Godwin recalled that this led "to uncomfortable situations, such as being left in remote areas at dusk when no Marines or ARVN troops were in the area. This happened to me on several occasions."[63] Regardless of the mode of travel, the waiting was often lengthy. Travelling counsels had no special priority.

Traffic between 1st MAW and the 1st Marine Division on Hill 327, or going to the III MAF brig, had to pass through "Dogpatch," a center of marijuana sales and prostitution.[64] Danger could be found there, as well. A hand grenade was tossed into a jeep in which Lieutenant Colonel Daniel F. McConnell, the 3d Marine Division's deputy SLO, was riding. Luckily, the grenade was a dud.[65] Captain Mark L. Haiman, a 3d Marine Division lawyer, when asked about transportation difficulties, replied, "no air, no trucks, no roads, no shit."[66]

Trying Cases

Securing witnesses for trial in the combat zone never became routine. Obtaining them often depended on the tenacity of the individual lawyer. The 3d Marine Division's SLO said: "I recall Major [Robert J.] Chadwick . . . going with a patrol on the day before he was scheduled to leave Vietnam, to locate some Vietnamese witnesses. The patrol was involved in a firefight, but Major Chadwick got his witnesses—and without them, there could have been no trial."*[67]

Finding the witnesses, Vietnamese and American, could be only the beginning. Captain Higginbotham recalled:

> Vietnamese witnesses were particularly difficult, since they seldom had any concept of dates or time . . . and could not understand why they were not allowed to testify as to what they had been told by others within their village . . . . On one occasion . . . before the matter [a rape charge] could go to trial, one of the defendants was killed in combat and the other was medically evacuated from RVN with a broken leg . . . . On still another occasion . . . I discovered, just as I was about to conclude my opening argument, that my witness had been sent home two days prior to trial, forcing me to grudgingly join with the defense in a motion to dismiss the charges.[68]

Vietnamese witnesses, most of whom did not own watches, described time in terms of cigarettes; they testified that an event took two cigarettes, or half a cigarette, to transpire.[69] Marine lawyers also found that

---

*On 2 March 1976, Robert J. Chadwick was promoted to the grade of brigadier general and four months later became the sixth director of the Judge Advocate Division. Commissioned a second lieutenant in June 1951, he was an infantry platoon commander in combat in Korea and, later, a reconnaissance platoon commander. After serving at the American Embassy in Paris, France, he earned a law degree and master of laws degree, eventually becoming SJA of several major commands, an appellate judge on the Navy Court of Military Review, and an Assistant Judge Advocate General of the Navy. (RefSec, MCHC).

Photo courtesy of Col Mark L. Haiman, USMC
Ground transportation was as difficult to secure as air transportation. Capt Mark L. Haiman, 3d Marine Division lawyer, sits behind the wheel of a Mighty Mite.

the Vietnamese seldom referred to their villages by the same names shown on American maps, which made direct and cross-examination confusing. Equally troublesome, Vietnamese witnesses often were unable to identify an accused because, as one record of trial read, "all Marines look alike to them."[70]

Sometimes it was not possible to examine a crime scene, or to go to a village in search of witnesses, because the place in question was in an unsecured area. The attorney could, however, request to accompany a Marine patrol to the desired location, or request that a patrol be designated to escort him to that location.

Captain James L. Williams commanded Company H, 2d Battalion, 4th Marines, in late 1967. He was assigned to take a party of Marine lawyers and witnesses, participants in an Article 32 investigation, to a village in contested territory. The charges involved the murder of Vietnamese. At first light Captain Williams led his entire company, with legal party, from Quang Tri. With one platoon forward, two back, and lawyers in the middle they proceeded about 10 kilometers through "Indian country" to the village. Upon arrival the area was cordoned off and the lawyers and witnesses entered to conduct their business. For several hours the infantry company remained immobile, and

Photo courtesy of Col Donald Higginbotham, USMCR

Maj Winn M. Thurman presides at an investigation in the NCO club of the 2d Battalion, 1st Marines, in July 1967. The reporter, Cpl Michael J. Partyka, uses the closed microphone system to record the testimony of the Vietnamese witness, as repeated by the translator. Other participants are Capts Ross T. Roberts and Eugene A. Steffen, at left.

On Thanksgiving Day 1967, near Quang Tri, Capt Ross T. Roberts uses a EE-8 telephone to search for witnesses. In the background, Capt Donald E. Wittig heats C-rations.

Photo courtesy of Col Donald Higginbotham, USMCR

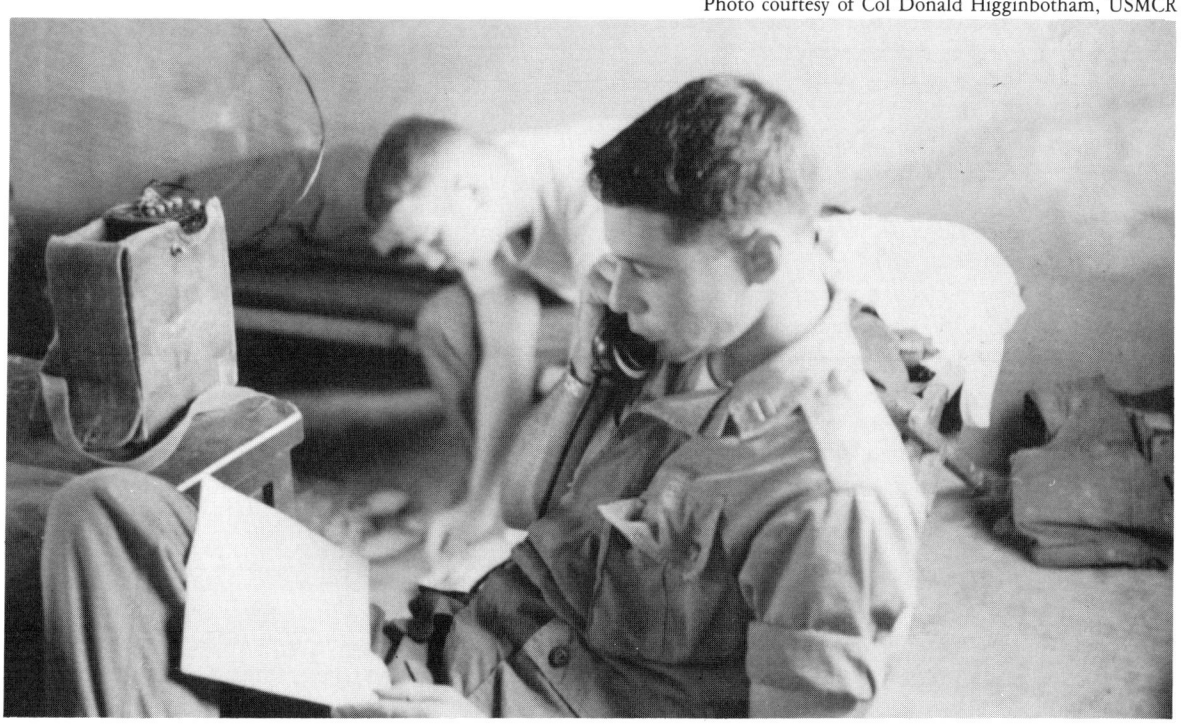

Photo courtesy of Mr. Victor J. Haydel

A lineup, with counsel present. From left, Capts Victor J. Haydel, Harvey J. Gleason, and Robert W. Wachsmuth; 1stLt Jerry G. Cunningham; Capts H. Edward Moore, Jr. and Dennis H. Siems, Force Logistic Command lawyers, at their Camp Books office.

subject to periodic sniper fire. No casualties resulted. Finally, mission accomplished, Captain Williams led his company and attached court personnel back to Quang Tri, arriving as darkness fell.[71]

Technology continued to bedevil courts-martial in Vietnam. By 1967 both the 1st and 3d Marine Division's SLOs countered electrical power losses with portable generators.[72] Recording machines remained inadequate to their tasks. Colonel "Doc" Fallon angrily pointed out that, on the average, three of his ten Grey Keynoters were in repair each week, and at one point, eight of 10 were under repair by FLC (whose personnel were not trained to repair Grey equipment) and it took up to six months to complete the work. He recommended they be written off and replaced with equipment manufactured by IBM, which was said to have in-country repair facilities.[73] Even when the machines were functioning, the heat of Vietnam could melt recording machine discs.[74] Perspiration fell on records of trial as they were reviewed, sometimes making them illegible.[75] "The systems," Captain Mitchell pointed out, "were put together with patchwork cables. You could find yourself in a situation where you had a combination of machines and cables which wouldn't allow you to use anything, even though you had two or three machines up."[76]

A solution, of sorts, to the inability to repair the Grey Keynoters and Audiographs was eventually found. If repairs were not available in Vietnam, take the machines where repair facilities were available: Okinawa or Japan. Sending a Marine, often an enlisted legal clerk or reporter, to Japan to wait several days while repairs were made had the added advantage of effectively gaining an R & R quota. As Major Michael Patrick Murray viewed it, that was "just a little bit of the usual Marine ingenuity."[77]

The Uniform Code of Military Justice specifically allowed an accused to be represented by a civilian lawyer in the court-martial process, and a surprising number of civilians made appearances in the combat zone on behalf of accused Marines.[78] Although fee arrangements were between lawyer and client, most often fees and expenses were paid by the accused or his family who frequently were distrustful of the quality of military representation. Often the civilian attorney appeared *pro bono*—that is, without fee, sometimes even paying his own expenses, such as transportation. Civilian lawyers ate in unit messhalls, used officers'

Photo courtesy of LtCol William B. Draper, Jr., USMC (Ret.)

Court is adjourned. 1st Marine Division lawyers relax at Chu Lai in October 1966, shortly before moving to Hill 327. From left, Lt Walter J. Landon, USN, back to camera; unidentified; 1stLt Michael J. Naughton; Capt Francis T. Coleman; and Capt Daniel M. Hanlon.

and enlisted men's clubs, and were billeted in officers' quarters. Lieutenant Colonel William T. Westmoreland, Jr., former SLO of the 1st Marine Division, noted that "everything—the head, the messhall, the showers, the courtroom—was either up or down hill. And it was raining and it was slippery. I felt we were very lucky not to have any civilian heart attacks or broken legs."[79]

Civilian representation at courts-martial can be a two-edged sword. The civilian usually brought a degree of experience and practiced skills outweighing those of the Marine trial counsel. On the other hand, they sometimes were unable to develop the rapport with Marine Corps members that was important to courtroom persuasion. They seldom knew how to deal effectively with a convening authority when seeking withdrawal or downgrading of charges or bargaining for a pretrial agreement. They did not know how to locate military witnesses or secure their presence, once located.

The accused's assigned military defense counsel normally continues in that capacity, even if a civilian lawyer is retained. The civilian lawyer usually enlists his military counterpart to carry out those functions relating to the military aspects of the trial, such as dealing with the convening authority, securing witnesses, and marshalling evidence of a military nature. Among military defense counsels so employed there sometimes is a feeling that they have done the most onerous preparation for trial, while the civilian is paid as if he alone had prepared and tried the case. But for the most part, a mutual respect existed between civilian and military lawyers in Vietnam.

On 18 January 1967, two West Virginians hired by an accused's family were among the first civilian lawyers to arrive in Vietnam, escorted by Lieutenant Colonel Frederick M. Haden.* Twelve days earlier Private First Class Charles W. Keenan, a sophomore at Wake Forest University before joining the Marine Corps, had been convicted of two specifications (counts) of murder and had been sentenced to hard

---

*Early in the war civilian lawyers were escorted from Hawaii to Vietnam by a Marine lawyer from FMFPac's legal office. That proved unnecessary and was soon discontinued.

labor for life, loss of all pay and allowances, reduction to private, and a dishonorable discharge.[80] His two civilian lawyers now wanted to review the record of trial, visit their client in the III MAF brig, and form their own opinion as to the fairness of the conviction. "They showed up quite aggressive; you might even say hostile," Lieutenant Colonel Westmoreland remembered.[81] The records were reviewed, the client visited, and the military defense counsel interviewed. As the SLO, Lieutenant Colonel Casey, recalled:

> They requested to see the scene of the incident. The request was granted, so an armed [patrol] was obtained, the attorneys were outfitted in . . . helmets, flak jackets, etc., and were asked to sign a waiver of liability in the event of death or injury, and had it explained to them that we did not have this area under control. At this point they reached the conclusion that a view of the scene was not necessary.[82]

In a message to the Commandant, General Walt wrote that "[the two lawyers] stated they would not want to risk having a Marine hurt on such a mission, and that official photographs taken at the scene . . . would serve their needs."[83]

Before they returned to West Virginia, the civilian lawyers were interviewed by an Associated Press reporter, Mr. Robert Ohman. They told him they had been shown everything they had asked to see, were "very satisfied" with the military defense counsel, Major Curtis W. Olson, and, demonstrating their basic ignorance of the military legal system, noted that they were surprised to learn Major Olson was a lawyer. Their client, they acknowledged, "got as fair a trial as he would have gotten in any civilian court."[84]

The Keenan case also generated correspondence illustrating the regard for military law held by at least one elected official. A West Virginia member of the U.S. House of Representatives, in a nine-page letter to the Secretary of Defense, protested the conviction of Keenan, his constituent, and berated the military justice system:

> Throughout the court-martial . . . there was always an underlying but unprovable suspicion that he was being prosecuted primarily at the urging of persons . . . who wished to curry favor . . . in the Saigon Government . . . . It was completely impossible to explain to anyone how a Marine

The government rests. In February 1967 LtCol John L. Zorack, right, officer-in-charge of the Task Force X-Ray legal office at Chu Lai, celebrates the conclusion of nine courts-martial, all involving charges of murdering noncombatants. One of those charged was PFC Charles W. Keenan. LtCol Zorack hosted a dinner, complete with wine, for defense and prosecution lawyers, including several sent from Da Nang to augment his staff for the nine cases. From left: Capt James P. Shannon; 1stLt Daniel M. Hanlon; unidentified partially hidden officer; Maj Curtis W. Olson; and Capt Francis T. Coleman.

Photo courtesy of LtCol John L. Zorack, USMC (Ret.)

could be charged with premeditated murder while on patrol and following orders . . . . That preposterous charge . . . . The monstrous damage which has been done to him almost defies a suggestion of proper restitution.[85]

The House member detailed his dissatisfaction with Keenan's conviction of murder by firing automatic rifle fire at point-blank range into an unarmed, elderly Vietnamese woman, and an unarmed Vietnamese man.* Then he suggested how amends might be made to Keenan:

> Only one course of action is possible . . . . I do request and require that you take action . . . to restore and make whole the life, career and reputation of P.F.C. Keenan immediately. Specifically, the following actions seem appropriate as a bare minimum:
>
> 5. A letter to P.F.C. Keenan from the Commandant of the Marine Corps complimenting him on his courage and his willingness to maintain the faith and the discipline of the Corps . . . . This letter should be widely publicized.
>
> 6. An official statement by the Department admitting that an error was committed and summarizing the actions being taken to restore and make whole the name and reputation of P.F.C. Keenan.
>
> There is no specific total dollar value which can be placed upon a man's good name. I must therefore reserve the right to consider alternative or supplementary courses of action. I would regret exceedingly the necessity to place this matter formally before a Congressional Committee . . . . I have seldom written an official of Cabinet level and then released the contents of my letter to the press prior to the time that I received his response. I believe it is an undignified procedure and I deplore the practice. In this case, however. . . .[86]

Secretary of Defense Clark M. Clifford, in a brief reply to the representative, noted that the case was still under review and that "it would be inappropriate for me to intervene." He closed, "your continued interest in matters relating to our national security is appreciated."[87]

Another case involved civilian attorney Grant B. Cooper. In June 1967 he arrived in Da Nang to defend a Marine lance corporal charged with the murder of one elderly Vietnamese man and the assault of another. Mr. Cooper was a prominent Los Angeles trial attorney, who had been defense counsel in a number of widely reported cases and was the author of several respected legal texts. He later defended Sirhan B. Sirhan, the murderer of Robert Kennedy.

The lance corporal represented by Mr. Cooper, according to the charges, had been riding in the canvas-covered bed of a Marine "six-by," a two-and-a-half-ton, multi-purpose cargo truck. He was intoxicated. As the truck passed through the village of An Khe, the lance corporal had indiscriminately fired several rounds from his M14 rifle. Allegedly, one of the rounds had gone through the truck's canvas covering, pierced the thatched wall of a dwelling, killed the victim, and continued on to wound the second victim in the shoulder. Several other Marines had been riding in the back of the truck, and there was evidence that more than one Marine had been firing his weapon.

At trial, in addition to Mr. Cooper, the lance corporal was defended by his assigned defense counsel, Captain Harry D. Sabine. Captain James P. Shannon was the prosecutor. Because of Mr. Cooper's presence, interest in the case was high, and several 1st Division lawyers observed the court-martial.

No defense motions were raised; both sides moved directly to the allegations. In two days the government called 14 witnesses, then rested. Mr. Cooper opened the defense of the lance corporal. He made no opening statement, but during the third day of trial, and part of a fourth, called nine defense witnesses and rested. The members had heard complex testimony from a ballistics expert, accident investigators, and a blood expert, as well as several conflicting accounts of the incident.

Normally, the trial counsel next makes an opening argument to the members, in which he summarizes the evidence, as viewed by the government, and argues the accused's guilt. The defense counsel then makes his closing argument, countering the government, and offers the defense view of the case. The trial counsel then makes a final argument, in which he may answer the defense's closing argument.

Major Bill Draper recalled the events of the trial:

> [Jim Shannon] had presented a good case, including several incriminating admissions from the accused during cross-exam. His major concern was how to keep Cooper from destroying him with his years of experience in closing argument. Jim decided that the best course was to cause a role reversal by waiving [giving up] opening argument. Then he would be able to poke holes in Cooper's argument. It was a well-conceived plan and would have no doubt been successful, had Cooper been as gullible . . . as Jim thought. Shannon

---

*After an initial mistrial, Keenan was convicted at a rehearing of the murder of the two Vietnamese. His resulting life sentence was reduced by the convening authority to 25 years confinement. Upon appellate review, the conviction of the woman's murder was dismissed, and Keenan's confinement was reduced to five years. Later clemency action further reduced his confinement to two years and nine months. A co-accused, Corporal Stanley J. Luczko, was also retried after his initial conviction for the two murders was set aside. The law officer at Luczko's Quantico, Virginia, rehearing was Colonel Jack E. Hanthorn, soon to be the SJA of the 1st Marine Division in Vietnam. Found guilty of voluntary manslaughter, Luczko was sentenced to a bad conduct discharge, forfeiture of all pay and allowances, reduction to private, and confinement for three years.

"The overall philosophy [was] that we were Marine officers first and attorneys second." Capt Donald Higginbotham was awarded a Legion of Merit for a combination of his combat actions and legal work.

Photo courtesy of Col Donald Higginbotham, USMCR

waived opening and Cooper promptly followed suit. Thus a complex case was submitted to the members without benefit of argument.[88]

After 35 minutes of deliberation the members found the lance corporal not guilty of all charges.[89] In the officers' club that night, the Marine lawyers and other officers accepted Mr. Cooper's offer of a celebratory round of drinks for the house.[90]

Marine Corps Lawyers in Combat: They Also Serve

Unlike the other Armed Forces, in which judge advocates or law specialists received military training in only their specialty, the Marine Corps lawyer had attended The Basic School, where all newly commissioned Marines are taught the skills that lead to qualification as an unrestricted officer. Every Marine was still a potential rifleman, every lieutenant and captain a potential platoon or company commander. With such training, several lawyers achieved recognition in Vietnam as Marine Corps small-unit leaders.

When he first arrived in the office of the 1st Marine Division's SLO in March 1967, Captain Donald Higginbotham was a defense counsel. He took every opportunity to be involved in combat operations. "The overall philosophy [was] that we were Marine officers first and attorneys second," he said. Practicing that belief, he once accompanied a four-tank reaction force sent to assist a heavily engaged platoon and for four days remained in combat. After that he was given command of a reaction company based near Hill 327.* Captain Higginbotham conducted numerous cordon and search operations and molded his reaction company into an effective combat unit.

When the North Vietnamese Tet Offensive began on 30 January 1968, enemy sappers mortared and overran a ridgeline above the division's command post on Hill 327, killing seven Marines. As the enemy was about to reach the division command post, Captain Higginbotham deployed his men and led a counterattack that threw back the enemy and secured a vital hill, where he established a defensive perimeter. His company continued in action through the next day with telling effect. For his actions, Captain Higginbotham received the Legion of Merit and the Vietnamese Cross of Gallantry.[91]

Second Lieutenant Michael I. Neil had just gained his law degree, when he came on active duty. Despite efforts to classify him as a Marine lawyer, Lieutenant Neil was adamant in his desire to be an infantry officer. (Although lawyers were permitted to request non-legal duties during their initial tours of active duty, at that time no lawyer lieutenant had done so.)[92] Lieutenant Neil prevailed, and in June 1967 he commanded the 1st Platoon, Company D, 1st Battalion, 7th Marines.

On the night of 20-21 December Lieutenant Neil, after having been on patrol for three days, was lead-

---

*A reaction company was a unit, often composed of Marines from various headquarters sections, which "reacted" to enemy incursions. It was a demanding assignment, compared to the usual rear area duty, since it was in addition to one's normal duties. Reaction forces usually assembled at night, were subject to frequent false alarms, and were without benefit of significant training as a unit. Each evening, one third of the reaction force assembled, was issued weapons and ammunition, then slept, fully armed and clothed, in a central location within the compound. The next night the same third was off-duty; the next night the same third manned defensive positions on the perimeter; and so on.

ing his platoon in the area of Happy Valley, not far from Da Nang. Unexpectedly, they encountered a North Vietnamese infantry battalion. In the ensuing all-night battle Lieutenant Neil's platoon was surrounded and continuously engaged in fierce fighting and hand-to-hand combat. All of his squad leaders were either killed or wounded. At dawn a relief column finally reached Lieutenant Neil's position, and as the combat continued, a medevac helicopter managed to land briefly and evacuate the most seriously wounded.

One of Lieutenant Neil's squad leaders, Corporal Larry E. Smedley, was posthumously awarded the Medal of Honor for his part in the battle. Lieutenant Neil received the Navy Cross for his heroism that night. His citation reads, in part:

> Disregarding the intense enemy fire, he led his men across 1,300 meters of thickly forested terrain . . . with complete disregard for his own safety, [he] exposed himself to the devastating fire to hurl hand grenades and direct his men's fire . . . . Shouting words of encouragement to his men, he boldly moved through the hail of enemy fire, leading an assault against the enemy positions . . . . Throwing hand grenades as he advanced, he destroyed a machine-gun emplacement and mortally wounded several enemy with his pistol.[93]

Two other platoon members were awarded Bronze Star Medals and the pilot of the medevac helicopter received the Silver Star Medal. The platoon, as a whole, was awarded a Meritorious Unit Commendation, the only infantry platoon in the Vietnam war to be so honored.*

Later, Lieutenant Neil became an air observer and eventually left Vietnam with the Navy Cross, Purple Heart, and six Air Medals. He then became a defense counsel at the Marine Corps Recruit Depot, San Diego.[94] Lieutenant Neil's combat record remains unique among Marine Corps lawyers.**

The First Lawyer General Officer: No Immediate Change

In World War II James F. Lawrence, Jr., commanded an infantry platoon and then a company on Guadalcanal and New Britain, and received the Bronze

---

*Only three other platoon-sized units in Vietnam received the MUC: a combined action platoon, an explosive ordnance disposal platoon, and a graves registration platoon. (RefSec, MCHC).

**After completing his obligated service, Neil continued to serve in reserve units—as an infantry officer and tracked vehicle officer. In 1988 he was selected for advancement to the grade of brigadier general in the Marine Corps Reserves.

Photo courtesy of BGen Michael I. Neil, USMCR
1stLt Michael I. Neil, right, seen on Hill 41 with an artillery forward observer and a Vietnamese scout in December 1967. A year after attaining a law degree 1stLt Neil led a platoon against an estimated 100-man enemy force, for which he received the Navy Cross.

Star Medal and the Purple Heart. In the Korean War he commanded the 2d Battalion, 7th Marines, during the 1st Marine Division's withdrawal from the Chosin Reservoir and received the Navy Cross and a second Bronze Star. Upon returning to the United States, he attended law school, then served in a variety of legal and nonlegal billets. Through assignments at Headquarters Marine Corps he became closely associated with Marine Corps legislative affairs. In May 1967 he was promoted to the grade of brigadier general, the first Marine Corps officer selected for flag rank specifically considered "qualified for legal duty," in the words of the selection board's precept. Notably, he was not serving in a lawyer's billet when he was selected for general. At that time Colonel Charles B. Sevier was still the head of Discipline Branch at Headquarters. "Actually," General Lawrence said, "my legal experience, as far as court-martial work was concerned . . . was quite limited."[95] Upon learning of Colonel Lawrence's selection for promotion, Colonel Sevier and the rest of the Marine Corps legal community anticipated Discipline Branch becoming a separate, new division, Judge Advocate Division, with General Lawrence at its head.[96] Brigadier General Lawrence anticipated much the same thing, recalling that "[I] had been selected, initially, to be the head of the Discipline Branch at Headquarters."[97] Instead, he was assigned to be Deputy Assistant to the Secretary of Defense for Legislative Affairs, a billet in which he had great experience and expertise. General Earl E. Anderson, a former Assistant Commandant of the Marine Corps, recalled: "Marine Corps Headquarters made a concerted effort to have General Lawrence returned to head Judge Advocate Division, but the Office of the Secretary of Defense refused to release him."[98] Brigadier General Lawrence served in the Office of the Secretary of Defense until his retirement from the Marine Corps in November 1968. Then he was recalled to active duty to fill the same billet, which he did until 1972.

Colonel Sevier, who had served much of his Marine Corps career in law billets, continued to shepherd Discipline Branch's evolution into a separate division within Headquarters Marine Corps. Because he was too junior to be selected for promotion to brigadier general, Colonel Sevier was unconcerned that General Lawrence had been considered as his replacement at a higher grade.[99] Nor were other senior Marine law-

The first Marine Corps general officer advanced to that grade specifically for duty as a lawyer was BGen James F. Lawrence, Jr. He was awarded the Navy Cross for heroism at the Chosin Reservoir in the Korean War.
Department of Defense Photo (USMC) A413996

yers concerned that General Lawrence achieved promotion as a lawyer, despite a lack of significant time in military justice billets. As Brigadier General Faw later noted, after his having been the Director of the Judge Advocate Division, "he made his star that way [as a legislative affairs expert]. But anybody that got selected at that time would have had to make their star some other way than law. I'm convinced that I made mine some other way than law."[100] Still, for the first time a lawyer, James Lawrence, had been promoted to the grade of brigadier general as a lawyer. Though the star was worn by General Lawrence in a nonlegal assignment, the legal community knew that eventually he would either be reassigned to head a new legal division at Headquarters, or retire, making the brigadier general's grade available to another Marine Corps lawyer.

Perspective

One hundred and sixty-eight Marine lawyers were on active duty in 1965, 223 in 1966, and 277 in 1967.[101] That represented an increase of 64 percent, all lieutenants and captains, in two years.* The number of general and special courts-martial, Marine Corps-wide, had increased from 4,824 to 7,091, or 47 percent, during the same period.[102] Most of the increase was in special courts, usually tried by nonlawyers at the battalion and group level. The kinds of cases that were being tried at the general court-martial level, and at the special court-martial level with lawyer counsel, were now more serious than the cases encountered prior to 1965. Murder, rape, and aggravated assault were not unusual, particularly in Vietnam, and required more lawyers, more legal support personnel, and more man-hours than anticipated in 1965.

Given the rapid growth in the lawyers' ranks and the steep increase in case numbers that was experienced, it was not surprising that the military justice system did not always operate with ideal smoothness. Captain Williams, whose infantry company had accompanied a party of lawyers into an unsecured area, thought that the legal process worked "in strange ways." He recalled that sometimes seven or eight courts would be pending, with no action taken for weeks and,

---

*This number does not include five officers who then had law degrees, but did not practice law in the Marine Corps: Major General Avery R. Kier; Brigadier General Earl E. Anderson; Brigadier General George C. Axtell, Jr.; Colonel Herbert L. Beckington; and Colonel James T. Kisgen. (Brigadier General Anderson and Colonel Kisgen both, until shortly before the Vietnam War, served in legal billets, but no longer did so.)

sometimes, months. Meanwhile, the accused Marines remained in his company, with charges unresolved. Frustrated by the lack of action, Captain Williams urged the battalion commander to resolve the cases through nonjudicial punishment rather than wait any longer. Yet, in other instances, the system acted with a swiftness that amazed him, as when one of his squad leaders purposely shot and killed a Vietnamese farmer's water buffalo. Almost immediately, the Marine was pulled from the company, tried, and convicted. Captain Williams said that he "never figured rhyme or reason for the difference."[103]

The need for additional Marine lawyers became an increasingly higher priority. In May 1967 the Secretary of the Navy chartered a committee, chaired by a Navy lawyer, Rear Admiral George R. Muse, to determine the requirements of both the Navy and the Marine Corps for uniformed lawyers. Colonel Sevier was the Marine Corps representative to the committee. The possibility of discontinuing all Marine lawyer billets and replacing them with Navy law specialists was discussed but ultimately rejected.[104] Instead, the Muse Committee recommended that 67 additional lawyer billets be authorized for the Marine Corps and that new lawyer procurement programs be initiated.[105]

Elsewhere in the naval service on 8 December 1967, after efforts spanning several years, legislation was passed that created a Navy Judge Advocate General's Corps. Henceforth Navy law specialists would be designated "judge advocates."

Anticipating the Marine Corps lawyer shortage, the Excess Leave Program (Law) was initiated in June

The Commandant of the Marine Corps visited Vietnam in August 1967. General Wallace M. Greene, Jr., toured I Corps headquarters with Vietnamese LtGen Lam. III MAF Commanding General, LtGen Robert E. Cushman, Jr., is in the background. Gen Greene decided many of the issues that affected Marine Corps lawyers during the Vietnam War.

Department of Defense Photo (USMC) A189011

Photo courtesy of Capt Dennis R. Zoerb, USMC (Ret.)

Capt Michael E. Rich, left, a future director of the Judge Advocate Division, was an infantry company commander at Gio Linh in 1967. He and platoon leader 2dLt Dennis R. Zoerb hold the flak jacket and helmet of a Marine killed by an artillery round.

Among the first of the Marine Corps' "legal admin" officers, pictured before their promotions, are, from left, GySgt William S. Kirkpatrick, GySgt Kenneth W. Jones, unidentified nonlegal NCO, and MSgt Len E. Pierce, on Okinawa prior to their departure for Vietnam.

Photo courtesy of Capt William S. Kirkpatrick, USMC (Ret.)

1967: TRYING TIMES

1967.[106] Officers already on active duty for a minimum of two years and a maximum of six years were allowed to apply for excess leave without pay to attend law school, with an obligation to serve an additional three years active duty as a lawyer upon graduation. This was viewed as a way to attract line officers to the legal field at little cost, while also encouraging them to remain on active duty as career officers.[107] Six officers entered the program in its first year and nine more followed in 1968.*[108]

After a long gestation period constructive service credit for lawyers was authorized in December 1967.[109] Although not used until 1968, the original commissioning date of lawyers could now be revised, retroactively, for a period equalling the years spent in law school before becoming a Marine officer. The effect was to give lawyers that additional time in their current grade. Because eligibility for promotion was by lineal list seniority, this "leg up" on the promotion ladder made a Marine Corps commission more attractive to newly graduated civilian lawyers. It also put the Marines on an equal footing with the other Services, which had similar policies for their lawyers.[110] Until 1968, however, constructive service credit was available only to those lawyers who contracted to serve on active duty for four years. Those opting for only three years' service did not receive constructive service and might not be promoted to captain until their period of active service was about to end. Admiral Joseph B. McDevitt, the Judge Advocate General of the Navy, questioned whether the requirement to volunteer for four years was a correct interpretation of the law, nevertheless, until 1968 that was how the law was applied.[111] Until then constructive service was a great inducement to "sign up" for four, rather than three years' service.

The Platoon Leaders' Class (Law) continued to be the principal source of newly commissioned lawyers. As PLC (Law) graduate, Captain H. Edward Moore, Jr., noted:

> Most of the individuals who were in the PLC (Law) program did exceedingly well in the PLC program and in Basic School. For instance, at my graduation from PLC there were two of us in my company who were our platoon's honor men. The fact that . . . lawyers had to undergo the strenuous and demanding training required of all Marine Corps officers did, without doubt, contribute to our being much better lawyers . . . . It has always been somewhat surprising to me that, in light of the fact that all . . . lawyers had to undergo a total of nine months of infantry training, that the Marine Corps did attract individuals with strong academic backgrounds . . . . I found that the typical reserve lawyer was far above average in all respects.[112]

To relieve Marine lawyers from some of the burdensome administrative tasks that legal clerks were not qualified to carry out, a legal administrative officer pilot program was initiated at Camp Pendleton, California.[113] Chief Warrant Officer 4 Maynard K. "Sonny" Baird was the first such officer. He, and Chief Warrant Officer 4 Len E. Pierce, the first two "legal admin" officers, demonstrated the value of experienced nonlawyer officers in smoothing the administrative intricacies of the court-martial process. Their skills, and those of Marine Corps lawyers, would be severely tested in the next few years.

---

*One of the nine was Captain Michael E. Rich, who commanded Company F, 2d Battalion, 9th Marines, while in Vietnam (and who took his LSAT examination in Da Nang). He received the Bronze Star Medal and the Purple Heart. After law school, among other assignments, he was the Staff Judge Advocate of the Marine Corps Logistics Base, Barstow, the 1st and 3d Marine Divisions, and III MAF. Later he was a Distinguished Graduate of the Naval War College. In September 1988 he was promoted to the grade of brigadier general and became the 11th Director of the Judge Advocate Division.

CHAPTER 5
1968: High Tide

*1st Marine Division: Lawyers in the Storm's Eye — 3d Marine Division: Every Marine a Rifleman
1st Marine Aircraft Wing/Force Logistic Command: Doing Time at Da Nang — From a Lawyer's Case File:
Civilian Court-martial — Drugs: 'High' Tide — Trying Cases — Trial Under Fire: Khe Sanh Court
Legal Assistance, Claims, Reviews: Someone Has To Do It — Fragging: Friendly Fire With Malice
Homicide on Patrol: Nothing Hidden — III MAF Brig Riot: Prisoner's Kangaroo Courts — Perspective*

In January 1968 III MAF numbered over 100,000 Marines, sailors, and soldiers. Besides the 1st and 3d Marine Divisions, the 1st Marine Aircraft Wing, and Force Logistic Command (FLC), III MAF now included portions of the 5th Marine Division, the Army's 23d Infantry (Americal) Division, and nearly 3,000 Marines of the Seventh Fleet's two special landing forces.[1]

North Vietnamese Army large-unit operations, which had increased in late 1967, continued into 1968. To meet them, III MAF had shifted Marine forces northward, the resulting gaps being filled by U.S. Army troops. Construction of the strongpoint obstacle system, the "McNamara Wall," continued along the Demilitarized Zone (DMZ), despite strong enemy opposition and a shortage of men and materiel.

Operation Checkers, designed to relieve the 3d Marine Division from covering the approaches to Hue, was essentially completed by mid-January. The entire 3d Marine Division was deployed either along the DMZ or at Khe Sanh. In turn, the 1st Marine Division shifted one regiment northward to Phu Bai to cover the western approaches to Hue.

In late 1967 and in early 1968 the North Vietnamese launched a series of company-size attacks on Marine positions near the DMZ. Further south the 1st Marine Division engaged strong enemy forces throughout the southern portion of its tactical area of responsibility. Many signs indicated a major enemy offensive was imminent.[2] General William C. Westmoreland, Commander, U.S. Military Assistance Command, Vietnam (ComUS), wrote:

> Quite apart from the assault on Khe Sanh and the presence there of two North Vietnamese divisions, the enemy threat in the north [in I Corps] was real and disturbing: another North Vietnamese division was in the DMZ north of the Rock Pile . . . . Another was just outside the gates of the vital Da Nang airfield; the equivalent of a reinforced division was at Hue; and two more were within the DMZ or just south of it near the coast — all together seven enemy divisions.[3]

The 1968 Tet Offensive began on 30 January when the Da Nang Airbase, Marble Mountain Air Facility, and Chu Lai were all heavily rocketed. All provincial capitals had been marked for attack, but the main efforts were reserved for Hue and Da Nang. For 12 days heavy fighting raged throughout South Vietnam. As Marine Corps historian, Brigadier General Edwin H. Simmons later wrote:

> The enemy's ambitions for the Tet offensive had been large. He had told his troops and his political cadre that the time had come for a general offensive and a popular uprising . . . . He did achieve considerable surprise. He did tear up lines of communication and cause widespread destruction and temporary chaos in the populated areas. But by the middle of February, he was through. He had not gained the popular support he expected. The American presence was unshaken.[4]

Task Force X-Ray, deactivated at Chu Lai in 1967, was reformed on 13 January 1968 at Phu Bai and assumed responsibility for the surrounding tactical area

Col John L. Ostby was Task Force X-Ray's Chief of Staff and the former Staff Legal Officer, 1st Marine Division.
Department of Defense Photo (USMC) A419003

The senior lawyers of the 1st Marine Division during 1967-68, greet Fleet Marine Force, Pacific's Staff Legal Officer in August 1967. LtCol William T. Westmoreland, Jr., right, is about to be relieved by Col John L. Ostby, second from left. Four months later Col Ostby became Task Force X-Ray's chief of staff and LtCol Clyde R. Mann, left, became SLO. They join Col Robert C. "Curly" Lehnert, second from right, FMFPac's SLO, on Hill 327.

of responsibility. It quickly became engaged in the Tet Offensive. During the clearing of Hue, the brigade-sized unit was involved in some of the heaviest sustained combat of the war. From its reforming until its second deactivation on 16 August 1968, Task Force X-Ray's chief of staff was Colonel John L. Ostby, formerly the staff legal officer (SLO) of the 1st Marine Division.[5] By virtue of his World War II combat record as an infantry officer, Colonel Ostby was well-qualified for the post. He later received the Legion of Merit for his performance with TF X-Ray.[6]

During the Tet Offensive Captain Bernard A. Allen, Jr., a defense counsel with the 1st Marine Division, was dispatched to Hue to investigate reports of looting by Marines who had retaken the imperial citadel.[7] The reports were not substantiated, but Captain Allen was the sole lawyer involved in the offensive in a legal capacity.[8]

1st Marine Division: Lawyers in the Storm's Eye

It was relatively quiet for the 1st Marine Division as the year began. Rather than defend Da Nang from the heavily patrolled "rocket belt," extending in a semi-circle around the city, Major General Donn J. Robert-son, the division's commanding general, decided to fan out in deeper-reaching operations which would keep enemy forces at arm's length.[9]

On 13 January Colonel Clyde R. Mann assumed the duties of the Division SLO when Colonel Ostby was transferred to Task Force X-Ray. In 1950 then-First Lieutenant Mann was the assistant operations officer of the 2d Marine Division, when he was selected for assignment to law school. Later, as a lieutenant colonel, he was assigned to Vietnam as the deputy SLO and had since been promoted to the grade of colonel.*

By now the SLO's offices were well-established on the north slope of Hill 327: two Quonset huts for offices, one 80 feet long, the other somewhat shorter; and a plywood, tin-roofed, windowless, air-conditioned courtroom. When power was lost, a still-frequent occurrence, the courtroom was completely

---

*A former infantry officer and air observer, Colonel Mann was awarded the Legion of Merit following his duty in Vietnam. He went on to serve as SJA of MCRD, Parris Island, South Carolina, and then graduated with honors from the Naval War College. On 20 August 1971, he was promoted to the grade of brigadier general and became the fourth Director of the Judge Advocate Division.

darkened and had to be evacuated until power was restored. Although the Quonset huts occasionally slipped from their moorings, creating alarming inclines until repaired, conditions were adequate. The officers' quarters were further up the hillside in other SEAhuts, usually four to six men to a hut, with Vietnamese "hoochmaids" to clean, do laundry, and polish boots. The enlisted legal personnel lived in identical huts, five or six men to a hut. Like the officers' quarters, most of the enlisted hooches had both a small refrigerator and a small black and white television set.[10] Cold water showers were available.[11] Unlike 1st Marine Aircraft Wing legal personnel who enjoyed flush toilets, the head facilities were of the four- or six-hole variety.[12]

Sixteen lawyers were assigned to the division, an adequate number.[13] Among the 16 were five trial counsels, six defense counsels, and one review officer.[14] Each lawyer's caseload remained low, but included serious general court-martial offenses such as murder and negligent homicide.[15] Trial teams were frequently sent to outlying units. Eighteen enlisted men were assigned to the office. Once again, enlisted court reporters' lack of adequate training was often a source of problems. Some came to Vietnam directly from boot camp with inadequate schooling. Of five newly assigned reporters Colonel Mann said: "They couldn't even type their names! I used one of them as a driver, and one as a coffee maker. I tried to get their MOSs changed."[16] The FLC reporter schools, which had eased the reporter problem in 1966 and 1967, had been forgotten.

One of several exceptions to the inadequate reporter syndrome was Sergeant R. Thomas Seymour, a 1967 Harvard law school graduate, who had been an unsuccessful Marine Corps officer candidate. "In addition to being an excellent court reporter, he was a platoon sergeant in my reaction company," recalled Captain W. Hays Parks, chief trial counsel for the division. "I shall always remember this Marine of slight build, weighed down with all of his equipment, hustling around his platoon, a blue streak of invective worthy of the saltiest gunnery sergeant streaming from his mouth, but grammatically perfect . . . . I had great respect for him."[17]

For the first (and only) time, accused Marines who were assigned to distant division units were being

By 1968 the 1st Marine Division SLO's offices and quarters were well-established on the north slope of Hill 327. Shown is the hooch of the deputy SLO, LtCol Daniel F. McConnell.

Photo courtesy of Col Daniel F. McConnell, USMC (Ret.)

transferred to Headquarters Battalion on Hill 327.[18] In this way they were easily available to their defense counsels and the trial process, problems of travel and communication were avoided, and their operational commands were relieved of an administrative burden. It was an ideal solution to the lawyers' recurring difficulties, so long as the number of accused individuals brought in from the field remained low, their offenses were such that they could remain at liberty within the Headquarters Battalion area, and numerous accompanying witnesses were not required. Unfortunately, those circumstances often did not prevail, and the practice of transferring accused Marines to Headquarters Battalion did not continue for long.

The lawyer's lot was not all work. Marines could check out basketballs and volleyballs from division special services.[19] Even skin-diving equipment was available. Several legal clerks dived regularly at the U.S. Navy Seal Base beach, beyond the Tien Sha deep water pier.[20]

3d Marine Division: Every Marine a Rifleman

The tempo of combat operations had increased in the 3d Marine Division as well as in the 1st. On 10 January 1968 elements of the 3d Division Headquarters moved north from Phu Bai to Dong Ha. On 7 March Colonel Eugene B. "Doc" Fallon's legal personnel moved to Quang Tri, which was a few miles short of the Division's forward elements at Dong Ha. For the next four days, without lights, communications, or power, the attorneys and legal clerks dug fighting holes and bunkers.[21] The 20 lawyers and other staff officers drew M16 rifles and ammunition and were assigned defensive positions. Colonel Fallon had responsibility for coordinating the defense of a section of the perimeter while camp construction continued. Office huts had first priority, so officers and men again were billeted in tents until SEAhuts were raised. Throughout this period courts-martial continued to be tried despite occasional enemy rocket and mortar fire and, sometimes, friendly fire. Captain Richard D. Lane's diary entry for 27 April read: "At 1100 I was sitting in the courtroom observing a trial when we took incoming . . . . It was [friendly] RVN troops. They erred."[22] There were no casualties.

The deputy SLO, Lieutenant Colonel Paul F. Hen-

Vietnamese "hoochmaids" did laundry and cleaning for officers and enlisted Marines. These women worked in the lawyer's tents at Camp Books, Red Beach, near Da Nang.

Photo courtesy of Col Charles R. Larouche, USMC (Ret.)

The 3d Marine Division SLO's trial counsel office was at Quang Tri in September 1968. "We didn't have the luxury of sending people back to sit in a brig for a month or two."

derson, Jr., recalled, "[When] there was incoming while a court-martial was in session . . . you can believe there was no formal declaration of a recess as everyone exited and made for the nearest hole."[23] During one shelling a mortar fragment killed a court member as he lay on the courtroom floor.[24]

Coincidentally, Captain Jerome R. Klukas, a 3d Marine Division lawyer, was assigned to the Division Inspector's office as the friendly fire investigator. Whenever there was an injury resulting from friendly fire, Captain Klukas investigated the incident. Sadly, it was a full-time job.[25]

Throughout 1968 the caseload in the 3d Marine Division tended to be higher than that of the 1st Division, probably because there were more personnel in the 3d than in the 1st. In June, for example, 3d Division lawyers tried only three general courts-martial, though six trial teams visited subordinate units, and tried numerous special courts with each visit. Thus, a lawyer could try 104 cases, 97 of them specials, in a 13-month tour, as Captain Clarke C. Barnes did.[26] Legal assistance continued to be heavily employed, as well, with 85 cases handled in a typical month.[27]

In 3d Marine Division cases a court-martial sentence to confinement often was not carried out. "Unless a guy really got convicted of something serious . . . they stayed at the firebase, because we didn't have the luxury of sending people back to sit in a brig for a month or two," the division chief of staff recalled.[28] A full 13 months of "good time" was required, before one was eligible for a return to the United States. Time spent in the brig was "bad time" and was deducted from the prisoner's time in country.

In the 3d Marine Division a shortage of junior officers had developed. Infantry platoon commanders, particularly, were needed. The shortfall was addressed by a lawyer, Colonel Joseph R. Motelewski. Colonel Motelewski already had a law degree when he enlisted in the Marine Corps in May 1942. Commissioned a second lieutenant five months after enlisting, he saw combat on Guadalcanal and Peleliu as an infantry officer. In Korea he had been a legal officer in the early part of his tour and, later, was executive officer and, briefly, commander of the 1st Battalion, 7th Marines.

Colonel Motelewski arrived at 3d Marine Division Headquarters at Dong Ha, anticipating assignment as the Division SLO. Instead, on 7 September, the commanding general, Major General Raymond G. Davis, designated him the division's chief of staff. No lawyer had been chief of staff of a division in combat before. When asked why he was selected, Colonel Motelewski replied:

1968: HIGH TIDE

Capt Philip S. Keith is shown preparing for trial at Quang Tri in 1968. Military reporter volumes are at right and a "short-timer's calendar" is just above Capt Keith's head.

I don't know. I know there were a lot of colonels whose butts were burned—who felt really upset about that. Of course, when I went to General Davis I told him, in Korea I had primarily been in legal work . . . . I wanted him to understand what he was getting. He told me, "Don't worry about it." He said he knew enough about me that he "was confident."[29]

During Colonel Motelewski's tenure as chief of staff, Lieutenant Colonel Rollin Q. Blakeslee was the division's deputy SLO, having succeeded Colonel Fallon. Colonel Blakeslee was away on other tasks much of the time, however, "So," as Colonel Motelewski recalled, "[Captain David J.] Cassady handled the legal shop and he did an outstanding job."[30]

To relieve the shortage of infantry lieutenants Colonel Motelewski, with General Davis' approval, authorized volunteers from the division staff sections to become platoon leaders on a temporary basis. Lawyer lieutenants, Reserve officers all, leaped at the opportunity. The lawyers' workload was manageable enough that one officer's cases could be shifted to the other lawyers remaining in the legal office. While lawyers had not previously been regularly employed as platoon commanders in Vietnam, there was no reason why they could not be. As Commandants had insisted since the 1950 Uniform Code of Military Justice became effective, all Marine Corps officers, including

The Chief of Staff of the 3d Marine Division, Col Joseph R. Motelewski, shown here in a 1965 photograph, was originally slated to be the Division SLO.

Quang Tri had no hoochmaids. These were a 3d Marine Division lawyer's quarters in September 1968. A sandbagged bunker may be seen outside the tent's rolled-up sidewall.

lawyers, were unrestricted in the assignments they could assume, commensurate with their grade. Regarding the call for volunteer platoon leaders, Colonel Motelewski explained:

> And from that we grew into, "Well, let's assign [all lieutenants] up there for two or three months." . . . Once we assigned a lawyer up there, particularly when they just came in-country, they wanted to stay up there! They wanted to get at it, even though they knew they were lawyers [and weren't required to] . . . . Their battalion commanders or company commanders would go to bat for them . . . . Nobody's arm was twisted, and it wasn't held against anybody if he didn't go . . . . It was the greatest thing in the world, because when these guys came back and subsequently went out to firebases [on trial teams], they knew what the hell they were talking about.[31]

So, what began as a call for volunteers from the division headquarters evolved into an unwritten practice of assigning all willing lieutenants, including lawyers, to be infantry platoon commanders for three months. On several occasions, captain-lawyers were appointed company commanders. The practice continued for roughly the next six months.

During that period lawyer First Lieutenant David G. Moore earned the Bronze Star Medal and Vietnamese Cross of Gallantry while a platoon leader in the 3d Battalion, 9th Marines. On a search and destroy operation his platoon came under heavy automatic weapons and mortar fire and one of his wounded men fell in a position exposed to enemy fire. Lieutenant Moore crawled to the wounded man, stood, threw him across his shoulders and, in the words of his citation, "fearlessly maneuvered through the intense hostile fire" to a place of safety. Lieutenant Moore later received the Navy Commendation Medal for his service as a defense counsel.[32]

Lawyer First Lieutenant William T. Allison II did not volunteer for infantry duty, but nevertheless he found himself in the infantry.[33] As executive officer of Company I, 3d Battalion, 3d Marines he earned the Bronze Star Medal. While wounded Marines from his company were being evacuated, he led a team against North Vietnamese positions that had taken the medevac landing zone under fire. His daring assault accounted for numerous enemy dead. Later, he became commanding officer of the company and was awarded the Vietnamese Cross of Gallantry with silver star.[34]

On Mutter's Ridge, while commanding Headquarters and Service Company, 1st Battalion, 3d Marines, lawyer Captain William L. Fly was wounded in action. He also was awarded the Vietnamese Cross of Gallantry with silver star.[35]

Captain William H. McAdam, Jr., while commanding officer of Company M, 3d Battalion, 3d Marines, earned the Bronze Star Medal for a night-long defense of his position, followed by an assault on North Vietnamese Army strongpoints which resulted in 36 enemy dead. As a trial counsel he, too, later earned the Navy Commendation Medal.[36]

Other lawyers who acted as platoon and company commanders were similarly recognized for their accomplishments and bravery under fire. A number of them also received decorations for their performance of duty as lawyers, after having served as infantry commanders.

In the 3d Division the Marine Corps demonstrated that every Marine, including lawyers, was indeed a rifleman. In no other service did a judge advocate or

3d Marine Division legal personnel line up in front of the legal office at Quang Tri in mid-1968. Front, from left, Maj Ronald J. Kaye, 1stLt Boyd L. George, 1stLt Jeffery W. Maurer, Capt Harry L. Shorstein. Center, Capt Richard D. Lane, Capt Mahlon C. Schneider, Capt Sandy S. McMath, 1stLt P. Keith Keller, 1stLt M. Kevin Phalin, 1stLt Robert M. Lee. Rear, unidentified captain, Capt Charles E. Patterson, and Capt Philip S. Keith.

Photo courtesy of Mr. Jeffery W. Maurer

3d Marine Division lawyers pose at a Quang Tri Christmas party in 1968. Kneeling, from left, Capt Michael D. Schrunk and Capt David G. Moore. Rear, Capt Stanley L. Smith, Jr.; 1stLt Jerald D. Crow; Capt William L. Fly; Capt Clark A. Halderson; Capt W. Tommy Allison II; and Capt Clarke C. Barnes. Later, several acted as infantry commanders.

law specialist without special training assume command or leadership of a combat unit.

1st Marine Aircraft Wing/Force Logistic Command: Doing Time at Da Nang

Colonel Robert C. "Curly" Lehnert and Major William H. J. Tiernan, who began the year with 10 lawyers under their leadership, continued as the SLO and deputy at the Da Nang Airbase.[37] The wing was under strength in legal clerks and reporters, but each lawyer's caseload was only four or five cases, which eased the shortage of enlisted men. As Captain Charles H. Mitchell noted: "We didn't have any work, to speak of . . . so you sort of looked around for the war. You'd take Rough Riders [armed truck convoys] and stuff like that, and find out what the war was like."[38] As in most Marine Corps legal offices in Vietnam, lawyers volunteered to lead the perimeter guard and reaction units. Colonel Lehnert recalled that during the Tet Offensive most of the 1st Marine Aircraft Wing reaction units were led by lawyers.[39]

Force Logistic Command (FLC) remained at Red Beach, eight miles northwest of Da Nang. Lieutenant Colonel Verne L. "Bubs" Oliver continued as SLO. Early in the year his deputy, Lieutenant Colonel Richard E. Wray, was replaced by Major Michael Patrick Murray. They were supported by four trial and three defense counsels and a legal assistance lawyer. Although authorized six lawyers and 10 enlisted le-

1968: HIGH TIDE

Photo courtesy of Col Rufus C. Young IV, USMC (Ret.)

The lawyers of the 1st Marine Aircraft Wing, seen at Da Nang Airbase in January 1968. From left, Capt Charles H. Mitchell; 1stLt Michael I. Walling; Capt Rufus C. Young; 2dLt Macauley Carter, Jr.; Capt William F. Whiting; Deputy SLO, Maj William H. J. Tiernan; Capt Donald R. Pritchard; the SLO, Col Robert C. "Curly" Lehnert; Capt David B. King; Capt Walter A. Stewart, Jr.; Lt Jared O. Bauch, USN; and Capt John N. Post.

Home is where you hang it. Capt Robert W. Wachsmuth sits on his rack in a SEAhut in 1968. His wash basin is at left while his flak jacket and helmet hang nearby.

Photo courtesy of Mr. Robert W. Wachsmuth

By 1968 FLC's legal offices had expanded well beyond the original former pig sty.

gal clerks, FLC sought an increase to 16 attorneys. As it was, FLC lawyers provided support to two subordinate commands, Force Logistic Support Group (FLSG) A, at Phu Bai, and FLSG B, at Dong Ha and Quang Tri, as well as trying cases arising at III MAF Headquarters, all of I Corps' Combined Action Groups, and two U.S. Army detachments of the 1st Air Cavalry Division located near Red Beach. Having tried 83 cases in the last year, FLC's was the busiest legal office in Vietnam.[40] In 1968 the number of cases tried rose every month, escalating from 32 in January to a high of 67 in December. Roughly half the cases involved use or possession of hard drugs or marijuana.[41]

Working spaces and air-conditioned living quarters in the cement buildings of the 1st Marine Aircraft Wing were comfortable, although enemy sappers and rocket attacks were threats. The rocket attacks, although frequent, were often ineffective. An air support control officer who worked near the Da Nang Airbase, Second Lieutenant James A. Cathcart, said of the rocket attacks, that "there seemed something vaguely un-Marine-like about sitting in front of your tent in the squadron area, watching rockets come up out of the valley and impact around the airfield, while you sipped a beer and people acted as if it was a fireworks display."[42] (Lieutenant Cathcart later gained his law degree and attained the grade of colonel, having spent most of his Marine Corps career as a judge advocate.) Monsoon rains, hardly lethal but always memorable, were particularly heavy in 1968. On 14 October 10 inches fell at Da Nang, and on the 15th and 16th, another 15 inches fell.[43]

FLC, which lacked the more substantial structures of the wing, was even more discomforted by the rains and more endangered by rocket attacks. On 14 June a legal clerk, Lance Corporal G. E. Korson, was killed and several others wounded by an enemy rocket.[44]

Whenever the opportunity presented itself, FLC personnel took steps to improve the comfort and habitability of their camp. As Captain Robert W. Wachsmuth, an FLC counsel, recalled:

> When units of the [Army] Air Cav Division began to arrive in force in I Corps . . . they bivouacked at Red Beach. The Marines were amazed and resentful of the abundance of new equipment furnished [them]. I specifically remember the Air Cav leaving behind hundreds of brand new cots when they pulled out on operations. Of course, we very resourcefully appropriated all of the equipment we could "salvage."[45]

Weather permitting, many lawyers undertook exercise programs. "I will wager," Captain Wachsmuth noted, "we were in better physical condition than any other lawyers in Vietnam. I attribute this to Major Mike Murray [deputy SLO], who insisted that we join him in his pursuit of physical fitness. At FLC we had a complete weight room and regularly ran three miles during the lunch hour.... I have never been in better physical condition."⁴⁶

In mid-year Lieutenant Colonel Frederick M. Haden relieved Lieutenant Colonel Oliver as FLC's staff legal officer, and in August, Lieutenant Colonel Max G. Halliday replaced Colonel Lehnert as 1st Marine Aircraft Wing SLO.* Lieutenant Colonel Halliday, who had been company commander in World War II, was of a category of officer frequently encountered in Vietnam: a reservist voluntarily returning to active duty for a specified period—five years, in Colonel Halliday's case.⁴⁷

On 1 November President Lyndon B. Johnson halted all air, naval, and artillery bombardment of North Vietnam. On 3 November the Vietnamese Communists announced that they were ready to participate in peace talks.⁴⁸ But for Marine Corps lawyers, the war continued as before.

From a Lawyer's Case File: Civilian Court-martial

In August of 1967 Mr. James H. Latney, a six-foot, four-inch, 46-year-old Bermudian able seaman off the SS *Amtank*, was drinking in "Mamasan's," a Vietnamese bar at My Khe Beach, Da Nang. The *Amtank* was a Military Sea Transportation Service contract ship carrying petroleum among Japan, the Philippines, Thailand, and Vietnam. Byethe A. Trimm was a shipmate of Latney's.⁴⁹ Reportedly a former Marine who had received a bad conduct discharge, Trimm was described as a disagreeable individual with a history of goading Latney. As the two drank, they argued. Trimm threw a chair at Latney, who thereupon stabbed Trimm with a large pocket knife, killing him. The commotion brought Marine MPs from the nearby III MAF compound. They apprehended Latney and transported him to the only place available for safekeeping prisoners, the III MAF brig.⁵⁰

Shortly, Colonel Duane L. Faw, III MAF assistant chief of staff and Headquarters SLO, received a telephone call from the American Embassy in Saigon. Colonel Faw recalled the conversation. "Look," the Ambassador's representative said, "the last thing we want to do is have the Vietnamese prosecute [another] American.... Politically it's unacceptable. There's

---

*In May 1972, after serving as the Deputy Director of the Judge Advocate Division, Colonel Halliday became the first Marine in recent times to be appointed Assistant Judge Advocate General of the Navy for Military Law. In July 1975, upon his retirement, he was advanced to the grade of brigadier general, the only Marine Corps Reserve judge advocate to achieve that grade.

Photo courtesy of Mr. Victor J. Haydel
Merchant Seaman James H. Latney was a civilian confined in Da Nang's III MAF brig. Charged with murder, he was one of only four U.S. civilians who were tried by court-martial during the Vietnam War.

got to be some solution to this. What do you recommend?"⁵¹

Sixteen years after the Pentalateral Agreement settled the question of jurisdiction over American military forces in Vietnam, the unresolved issue of American non-diplomatic civilians now required immediate resolution. The choices were to leave Mr. Latney's trial to South Vietnamese courts, which had primary criminal jurisdiction, try him by U.S. court-martial, or remove him to a U.S. court outside Vietnam, where jurisdiction would be questionable. At that time two American civilian contractor employees were about to be tried by the Government of Vietnam for negligent homicide and aggravated assault, and a third American civilian was pending Vietnamese trial.⁵² If Latney, too, were tried by the Vietnamese, it could become standard practice for American civilians who committed crimes to face Vietnamese courts. The U.S. Army had consistently opposed any attempt to court-martial civilians. Colonel George S. Prugh, the MACV Staff Judge Advocate through June 1966, later wrote:

> It was our understanding of the U.S. law that we were without UCMJ jurisdiction under the circumstances. I recall briefing Ambassador Taylor and later Ambassador Lodge on this issue. Although each wanted the civilian offenders tried by court-martial, each... deferred to our recommenda-

Photo courtesy of Mr. Victor J. Haydel
Latney trial counsels Capts Victor J. Haydel and Charles J. Kall hold broom they referred to as "Norris." Latney's defense counsel was Col Norris C. Broome.

tion that the most effective remedy, if trial was essential, was to be in a Vietnamese court.[53]

But in 1968, the Latney case was to break new ground. Among the American Embassy, the Office of the Secretary of Defense, the State Department, the Army MACV SJA, and Colonel Faw, they decided to recommend to the III MAF commander, Lieutenant General Cushman, that Latney be considered a person accompanying the Armed Forces in the field in time of war and within the jurisdictional scope of Article 2 of the Uniform Code of Military Justice (UCMJ). General Cushman adopted their recommendation. Latney's case would be handled by court-martial, as would any other homicide within Marine Corps jurisdiction.[54] MACV headquarters in Saigon, which had cognizance over such matters, sought a waiver of jurisdiction from the South Vietnamese Ministry of Justice that was granted.[55] In a confidential message to the Commandant, Lieutenant General Cushman accurately noted that "we can anticipate a great hue and cry about civilians being tried by military courts."[56]

FLC was selected as the command that would try the case, over the objections of the SLO, Colonel Oliver, who observed:

> Our command could care less about two merchant seamen in a fight where one ended knifing the other in some bar 15 miles from our command.... We were in the midst of an ever-increasing caseload and a case of this magnitude would break our backs.... If Latney were to be tried in Vietnam, he should be tried by the Naval Supply Command, as the ship the accused was on was under contract to them .... Colonel Faw came up with the theory of "territorial jurisdiction." Since the M.P.s that apprehended Latney were from ... FLC, FLC should try the case.[57]

As incumbent of the senior Marine Corps legal billet in Vietnam, Colonel Faw's decision that FLC try Latney prevailed. He also promised to provide FLC with additional manpower.

Lieutenant Colonel Norris C. Broome and Major Brian B. Kent were loaned to FLC from the 3d Marine Division and III MAF, respectively, to defend Mr. Latney. Lieutenant Colonel Broome had been one of the early Marine Corps lawyers assigned as an instructor at the Navy's Naval Justice School in Newport, Rhode Island.* His employment in the case, and that of Major Kent, two experienced lawyers, would ease the workload on FLC's few attorneys and preclude any suggestion that Latney had been defended by inexperienced counsel. Until Lieutenant Colonel Broome and Major Kent were appointed, Captain George Tozi, Jr., had represented Latney. Captains Charles J. Kall and Victor J. Haydel were the trial counsels. The law officer was Lieutenant Colonel Donald E. Holben, whose reputation as a demanding jurist was well-known.

At trial the issue would not be guilt or innocence, because several people witnessed the killing. The questions, per Article 2, were whether Latney was "serving with or accompanying the Armed Forces," whether he was "in the field," and whether it was "time of war." Actually, the application of Article 2 of the UCMJ to Latney was on trial, and the resolution of pretrial jurisdictional motions would effectively decide the case.

---

*He was the sixth. In March 1947, First Lieutenant Robert C. Lehnert, although not then a lawyer, was the first Marine Corps instructor at the U.S. Naval School (Naval Justice), at Port Hueneme, California. In April 1948 he was followed by Major William A. Murphy, a lawyer. Next, the first Marine Corps instructor at the redesignated Naval Justice School in its new location at Newport, was Major John L. Ostby, followed by Captain Arthur R. Petersen, Major Thomas B. Casey, and Major Broome. (Col Casey ltr to BGen Edwin H. Simmons, dtd 30Jan89, and Col Robert C. Lehnert ltr to author, dtd 1Feb89, both ltrs in Comment folder, Marines and Military Law in Vietnam, MCHC).

Photo courtesy of LtCol Brian B. Kent, USMC (Ret.)
One of Latney's two defense counsels was Maj Brian B. Kent, assigned to III MAF's legal office. He was loaned to FLC to participate in the trial of the Latney court-martial.

In preparation, Lieutenant Colonel Holben travelled to Saigon and Japan to carry out legal research. Although he had already tried two other civilians in Vietnam for relatively minor offenses, those cases had not raised the issues that the Latney case did. "Latney was probably the poorest case, as far as jurisdiction was concerned," Lieutenant Colonel Holben recalled.[58] Unlike most civilians living in Vietnam and entitled to PX and officers' club privileges, military medical care, and free mail privileges, Latney was essentially just passing through.

Prosecutors Kall and Haydel went to Saigon to investigate how the decision was made to court-martial Latney. Captain Kall recalled: "[We] were concerned that there might be some bad news in the files of MAC-V, e.g., 'This is a test case; even if there is no jurisdiction, get the Marines to prosecute him anyway;' that sort of thing .... Everything we found was neutral or quite appropriate." After five days in Saigon they went to Japan, accompanied by assistant defense counsel Captain Tozi, to take the depositions of crewmen of the *Amtank*, then docked in Yokohama.[59] Mamasan, owner of the bar that was the crime scene, insisted that her deposition be taken at her place of business and refused to suspend business while the deposition was in progress.[60]

By now Captain Kall's 13-month tour of duty was completed and he returned to Camp Pendleton, California. But having been involved in the case for four months, his intimate knowledge of all that had transpired was missed. In January 1968 he voluntarily returned to Vietnam to see the case to completion.

Defense counsel Lieutenant Colonel Broome, accompanied by the returned trial counsel, Captain Kall, travelled to Washington, D.C., to take the deposition of Senator Herman E. Talmadge, "to plumb the depths of the constitutional underpinnings, or lack thereof, of the war in Vietnam," Captain Kall said. In the senator's office, with a court reporter at the ready, just as Colonel Broome's questioning was to begin, the trial counsel interrupted to *voir dire* — examine the witness as to his competence to give evidence on the subject.

Photo courtesy of Mr. Charles J. Kall
The owner of Mamasan's bar refused to close her establishment. The prosecution took her statement in the bar, between customers. Capts Victor J. Haydel and Robert W. Wachsmuth, with paper, listen to translator.

It quickly became apparent that the senator was not expert in constitutional law. Nevertheless, the deposition was taken and ultimately considered by the law officer for whatever weight it merited. Also considered at trial was a written jurisdictional opinion by Senator Sam J. Ervin, Jr.

In Vietnam, the night before the jurisdictional motion was to be heard by Lieutenant Colonel Holben, Captains Kall and Haydel were in a SEAhut near the courtroom formulating their arguments, when the sound of incoming enemy rockets was heard. They ran for the nearest bunker, but Captain Kall stopped to secure the classified documents they had been studying, "one of the least sensible acts I have ever performed," he later noted. As he fled the hut, an enemy rocket exploded 20 feet from Captain Kall, who was caught in the open. Amazingly, he was uninjured. A SEAhut near the courtroom and next door to the SJA's office was destroyed by a second rocket. The courtroom itself sustained heavy shrapnel damage, including decapitation of the carved wooden figure of Justice With Scales, with which Major Ziemann had decorated the law officer's bench two years before.

This Quonset hut near FLC's courtroom, was destroyed the night before the Latney trial. Although 20 feet from an exploding rocket, Capt Charles J. Kall escaped injury.
Photo courtesy of Col Charles R. Larouche, USMC (Ret.)

FLC's staff legal officer, Lieutenant Colonel Oliver, decided that Captain Kall had done enough for one whose tour of duty had been completed months before, and returned him to Camp Pendleton. Captain H. Edward Moore replaced him just as the trial began.

The next morning, with the adjacent hut leveled and still smoldering, and shrapnel damage to the courtroom unrepaired, the law officer accepted the government's argument that they were in the field in time of war. The court decided it had jurisdiction to try Seaman Latney.

The critical pretrial motions having been decided in the government's favor, the trial itself was anticlimactic. On 25 February 1968, Latney, who had been charged with premeditated murder, was convicted of the lesser included offense of unpremeditated murder and sentenced to confinement at hard labor for 15 years.[61] The law officer, Lieutenant Colonel Holben, remembered:

> After the trial, the president [senior member] was reported to have said something to the effect that they [the members] couldn't fully comprehend all of the instructions . . . but they knew he was guilty of something, so they settled on the lesser included offense . . . . Substantial justice was accomplished at the trial level, all any sensible lawyer can hope to achieve.[62]

Administratively the case remained difficult, even after its completion. The record of trial was about 700 pages long, not counting roughly 250 exhibits. As Colonel Oliver recalled, "everyone and his brother wanted a copy of the record, . . . some 26 copies."[63] Before xerography was common, copies, each with four carbons, were manually typed—a staggering task in this instance. However, Colonel Oliver encountered a stroke of luck. Returning from a conference in Hawaii, Colonel Oliver had a day's layover on Okinawa. "In the officers' club . . . I struck up a conversation with a civilian who turned out to be . . . in charge of the Government Printing Office on Okinawa. I did not realize we had such an office there."[64] Back in Vietnam, printing of the record at the Okinawa Government Printing Office was authorized and funding was approved. FLC reporters typed one original record of trial and one copy. Twenty-five additional printed copies were available in three weeks.

As Latney sat in the III MAF brig awaiting transportation to a federal facility in the United States, the lawyers involved in his case anticipated the appeal that was sure to follow. The Latney case was not over, and the precedent it established, that courts-martial had

Department of Defense Photo (USMC) A413166
"They were tried, convicted, and heaved out . . . ."
MajGen Raymond G. Davis, Commanding General, 3d Marine Division, took a tough stand on marijuana.

jurisdiction to try civilians in a combat zone, was only temporary.*

Drugs: 'High' Tide

By 1968 the use of marijuana by Marines in rear areas was becoming epidemic. Vietnamese sellers did not have to be sought out, they had to be fended off. The price was cheap, even on a private's pay. Sometimes marijuana was literally given away. Vietnamese authorities had little interest in interdicting the trade, and U.S. authorities had little success in doing so. Colonel Peter J. Mulroney, commanding officer of the 12th Marines, remembered:

> Its use is more widespread than anyone would care to admit. Every one of my battalions had investigations going all the time. It is almost impossible to keep somebody that wants to get marijuana from getting it. [It's] sold at every road-

---

*A total of four U.S. civilians were tried by military courts-martial during the Vietnam war. (Prugh, *Law At War*, pp. 109-110). *Latney v. Ignatius*, the appeal that resulted from Latney's conviction, and *United States v. Averette*, the later Vietnam court-martial involving a civilian accused that settled the jurisdictional question, are detailed in Chapter 8.

side ville, peddled by all the civilians . . . . You would have to have an officer or staff NCO on every vehicle to keep them from getting it . . . . The other point to make is misplaced loyalty. Some of the young officers and even some of the staff NCOs that have a man that does a good job in the daytime—after hours, if there is such a thing in Vietnam, he isn't going to pay attention to what that man does, or isn't going to place him on report. That is misplaced loyalty.[65]

In 1968 marijuana was usually confined to areas where there was seldom enemy contact. The 3d Marine Division's commander, Major General Raymond G. Davis, pointed out that "there is no drug problem out in the hinterlands, because there was a self-policing by the troops themselves. Their life depended on a clear head, and they would just not permit anybody to smoke a marijuana cigarette, or consume drugs."[66] Commenting on the disciplinary action taken upon discovery of drugs, General Davis continued:

At that time, anyone caught with as much as a half-inch of marijuana cigarette in their pocket was given a discharge from the Marine Corps. They were tried, convicted, and heaved out . . . . During my review of trials, where there was no other evidence except this very small piece of a cigarette, I let the conviction stand, but [directed] a year's probation.[67]

While General Davis' description of the court-martial process took a few intermediate in-court steps for granted, it correctly reflected the serious disciplinary approach being taken in attempting to reverse the rising tide of marijuana use. Lieutenant Colonel Jaeck, in his 1967 fact-finding report on drug abuse had noted that FLC referred all marijuana cases to a general court-martial as a matter of course. Other commands determined appropriate action "by the attitude of the commander."[68] By 1968 most commanders were in agreement with the need for serious steps, and that made the marijuana problem a legal problem. Fortunately, although hard drugs were available, their use in Marine units was still rare.[69]

Military personnel were being arrested in R & R ports for importation of marijuana.[70] Not even the Da Nang brig was free from the problem. Colonel James W. Shank, the III MAF Inspector noted that "the boys out of the brig, when they're travelling back and forth to where ever they're working, why, the civilians will throw marijuana into the truck for the boys, so the problem of keeping marijuana out of the brig has been a big one."[71] It was not always solved successfully. Captain Wachsmuth recalled one of his cases:

Members of brig working parties would obtain marijuana seeds [which were] planted in rows of dirt above the shower stalls which were opened to the outside by the gap between the tin roof and the wall . . . . Spray from the prisoners' showers would water the plants. When the plants reached a sufficient size, plastic . . . would be placed between the shower spray and the plant, causing the plant to die. The plants would then be crushed and rolled in toilet paper to make joints. We were never able to identify any individual prisoner being directly involved.[72]

Occasionally, marijuana was turned to a positive end, if one were detailed to transport it to Japan for analysis. In 1968, at Long Binh, the Army opened the only crime laboratory in Vietnam available to U.S. Armed Forces.[73] If the Long Binh laboratory was backlogged, or if a case had to be tried quickly to avoid end-of-tour rotation dates, a Marine Corps lawyer or enlisted clerk would travel to the crime lab at Camp Zama, Japan, to secure the documentation necessary for in-court use.* Upon arriving, the Marine's first question usually was how long the analysis would take. The reply often was, "How long do you want it to take?"[74]

Trying Cases

Special courts-martial often were still tried by non-lawyers at the battalion and group level, although visiting trial teams commonly tried any pending cases. Since the major commands all had detachments in locations separate from their headquarters, each command had adopted the trial team concept by 1968. A trial team usually consisted of two lawyers: a trial and a defense counsel. If a complex or unusual case was anticipated, a third lawyer might join the team to act as the senior member. Court reporters were still assigned to individual battalions or squadrons, as well as to the various legal offices. Captain Clarke C. Barnes, a 3d Marine Division lawyer, recalled: "Courts were held in the field in bunkers, tents, S-1 hooches at the battalion rear, et cetera . . . . The practice was to go to the field where the witnesses were, to investigate and develop a case, or see a convening authority, causing the least amount of operational interference possible."[75]

Travel between commands remained haphazard and dependent on the persistence and ingenuity of the lawyers involved. Only rarely were vehicles assigned to legal offices and lawyers often took to the road, usually hitchhiking.[76] Inadvertent trips down enemy controlled roads and helicopters forced down by mechanical failure remained unremarkable occurrences.[77]

---

*Simple tests to confirm a substance to be marijuana took up to 60 days at the Long Binh laboratory. If sent by mail, the Camp Zama lab could take as long as three months. (Mann intvw).

Photo courtesy of Col Rufus C. Young IV, USMC (Ret.)
1st Marine Aircraft Wing trial teams frequently brought legal services to the field. Capts Donald R. Pritchard, left, and Rufus C. Young, at CAP unit F-4 in January 1968.

Equipment problems persisted, too. In the 3d Marine Division the year began with three out of 10 portable Grey Keynoters working. At mid-year, two of 10 were functioning. The only effective method of repair required hand-carrying the units to Okinawa or Japan.[78] The 1st Marine Division had adhered to usual repair practice and turned in their inoperative Keynoters to 1st Force Service Regiment for repair. Now eight of those machines were missing and never recovered.[79] In self-defense three court reporters were sent to Japan to attend a Grey maintenance and repair course.[80]

Colonel John R. DeBarr, a law officer, noted that cases were being lost because of equipment that malfunctioned in the course of trial.[81] Typically, that occurred when an appellate defense counsel in Washington saw a reporter's notation in a record of trial that the testimony was "reconstructed," because the recorder quit working in the midst of a witnesses' testimony. If the appellate court considered the missing verbatim testimony substantial and critical to the defense, it was obliged to reverse the guilty verdict.

Rotation tour dates (RTDs), the scheduled dates that Marines returned to the United States, always concerned lawyers, convening authorities, and witnesses, but no cases are known to have suffered because of RTD-induced memory lapses. Commonly however, participants in pending trials asked, "My RTD's coming up. Can't you just take my statement and use it in court?" Captain Barnes recalled:

> The more senior the witness, the greater the flap . . . . On occasion Colonel Mo [J. R. Motelewski, the 3d Marine Division chief of staff] would counsel convening authorities who expected the trial counsel or defense counsel to waive the right to confrontation, but for the most part everyone cooperated. After all, everyone in the [legal] office wanted to rotate on time, also. So everyone worked hard to bring to trial quickly, cases where witnesses were on legal hold.[82]

Law officers, required for all general courts-martial, had worked out of Yokosuka, Japan, since before the Marines landed in Vietnam in 1965. A Marine Corps colonel and a Navy captain were normally assigned there. In 1968 the Yokosuka law officers were Colonel Alexander M. "Sandy" Hearn and Captain Wyman Jackson, JAGC, USN. Besides covering Japan and Vietnam, they heard cases at Subic Bay in the Philippines, on Okinawa, and, occasionally, on Guam. When in Vietnam they sat at the 1st Marine Division's Headquarters in Da Nang, FLC's Red Beach facility, and, for Navy cases, the Naval Support Activity at Tien Sha, near Da Nang. The law officers seldom knew what cases or issues they would encounter in Vietnam, but they were experienced enough to deal with most con-

Photo courtesy of Col William R. Eleazer, USMC (Ret.)
A gas attack drill at FLC's Camp Books interrupted United States v. Montovon, *a general court-martial involving the charge of murder. The testimony of a civilian defense witness, psychiatrist Dr. Pearman, masked man at right, continued after the drill's conclusion.*

tingencies. As Colonel Hearn noted, "Research materials were not a problem. At first, I tried to carry some materials, but soon abandoned that idea. As a practical matter, complicated legal issues seldom arose."[83] In late 1966 a Navy-Marine Corps Judicial Activity branch office opened at III MAF Headquarters in Da Nang to respond to in-country needs and ease the burden on the Yokosuka law officers, who spent a great deal of time travelling. Lieutenant Colonel William W. Wander, Jr., was the first law officer assigned to the new office, followed, a year later, by Lieutenant Colonel Donald E. Holben.[84] In May 1968 Colonel Holben turned over his duties to Colonel John R. De-Barr.* The law officers found it to be a demanding billet, with trials virtually every day, and always with members as was required in general courts-martial of that period. They considered their infrequent trips to Yokosuka and the Philippines to try cases almost as R & R.[85] One place not visited by a law officer, however, was Khe Sanh.

Trial Under Fire: Khe Sanh Court

At the beginning of 1968, three infantry battalions defended Khe Sanh. From January through March the base relied upon massive supporting arms fire to keep the enemy at bay. This included tactical aircraft sorties at the rate of nearly one every five minutes. B-52 bombers dropped over 75,000 tons of bombs around the base. U.S. Army and Marine Corps artillery fired nearly 1,500 rounds a day.[86] Yet the enemy still regularly placed heavy and accurate artillery, mortar, and rocket fire on Marine positions there.**

---

*The fifth Director of the Judge Advocate Division, Col DeBarr was promoted to the grade of brigadier general on 10 April 1974. In World War II he was an infantry platoon commander on Iwo Jima. In 1953-55 he served on the U.N. Truce Supervision Commission in Palestine, and later served as an appellate counsel, law officer, and military judge. In Vietnam, he tried 195 general courts-martial, including more than a dozen murders, in 12 months. In 1971 he advised President Nixon regarding the case of the United States v. Lt. William Calley, U.S. Army. (DeBarr 1986 intvw and Biographical Files, RefSec, MCHC)

**The commanding officer of Khe Sanh combat base (and 26th Marines) was Colonel David E. Lownds. In April 1968 he relinquished command to Colonel Bruce F. Meyers, who had previously earned a law degree while stationed in Washington, D.C. Colonel Meyers said of his law degree, "I kept it off my record until just prior to retirement (I was an 03 [infantryman] and wished no part of the JAG bit). Had I taken a bar, it would have precluded my having [command of] . . . Special Landing Force Alpha, the 26th Marines, and The Basic School!" (Col B. F. Meyers ltr to BGen E. H. Simmons, dtd 7Dec87, Correspondence folder, Marines and Military Law in Vietnam file, MCHC).

A special court-martial was tried in an underground Khe Sanh bunker in February 1968. After being convicted of sleeping on post the Marine was kept at Khe Sanh rather than being allowed to serve his sentence in the safer confines of Da Nang's III MAF brig.

Department of Defense Photo (USMC) A190685

An Air Force C-130, similar to the ones that delivered the court-martial counsels, sits on the runway at Khe Sanh with its cargo ramp lowered. Enemy artillery rounds land in the background and, moments after the photograph was taken, destroyed this aircraft.

Photo courtesy of LtCol David Douglas Duncan, USMCR (Ret.)

"During the lulls we all filled sandbags and reinforced our positions." Capt Harry L. Shorstein, a 3rd Marine Division lawyer, was the prosecutor in a Khe Sanh special court-martial. He returned to Khe Sanh two months later as counsel in a formal investigation.

Despite the constant and intense volume of fire, a Marine sentry, suspected of being in possession of marijuana, was found asleep at his post. In mid-February a special court-martial was convened by the commanding officer of the 1st Battalion, 26th Marines to try both charges. The counsels were Captain Harry L. Shorstein, a 3d Marine Division lawyer, and Captain Robert W. Wachsmuth of FLC.

The C-130 in which Captain Shorstein was a passenger landed at Khe Sanh under heavy artillery, rocket, and mortar fire. Captain Wachsmuth arrived a short time later, the only passenger on another C-130. Captain Wachsmuth said "the crew warned me that when they touched down, we would immediately receive incoming mortar fire. I was instructed to run down the [rear facing] ramp after all the cargo had been offloaded, as the aircraft would only be [making a] touch-and-go, i.e., a 'rolling stop.'"

After several days of investigation and court preparation, the trial was conducted in the underground command bunker of the 26th Marines. The lawyers did not anticipate a bad conduct discharge, and they made no effort to make a verbatim record of the trial.

The court acquitted the accused of marijuana possession but convicted him of sleeping on post. The members sentenced him to a reduction in grade and forfeitures. "The sentence was appropriate," thought Captain Wachsmuth. "The accused was not sent back to the brig or otherwise allowed to escape the confines of Khe Sanh."

After the court-martial, Captain Wachsmuth departed as he had arrived, by leaping aboard the lowered ramp of a moving C-130, while incoming enemy fire rained down. Captain Shorstein remained at Khe Sanh for several more days. "I stayed because . . . fixed-wing aircraft were not coming in and the choppers were full of medevacs . . . . During the lulls [in shelling] we all filled sandbags and reinforced our positions." During his stay he provided legal assistance to the Khe Sanh Marines. (On 23 February, he also witnessed the worst shelling of the entire siege of Khe Sanh: 1,307 incoming rounds in an eight-hour period, during which 10 Marines were killed and 51 wounded.)[87] When the runway reopened, Captain Shorstein left Khe Sanh on an Air Force C-123. "[It] landed, troops exited without its stopping and I, and others, jumped on while it taxied."[88] Four months later the Marines abandoned the base.[89]

Captain Shorstein received the Bronze Star Medal and the Vietnamese Cross of Gallantry, in part for his actions at Khe Sanh.* While numerous trials took place under sporadic enemy fire, few were as dramatic as the Khe Sanh court-martial.

Legal Assistance, Claims, Reviews: Someone Has To Do It

Marines were discovering that Marine Corps lawyers did more than try courts-martial. Legal assistance was for all Marines, and statistics reflected the growing appreciation of that fact. Marine Corps-wide, from 1965 through 1968, the legal assistance workload grew from 51,602 to 73,735 cases. In 1968 alone the major Marine Corps commands in Vietnam handled 4,561 legal assistance cases.

Requests to marry Vietnamese women became so common that legal assistance lawyers served on marriage counselling boards that were established by their commands.[90] Typically, a young Marine would fall in love while on R & R and propose marriage to his Vietnamese, Thai, Japanese, or Chinese girlfriend. Even if they were to marry, the bride might not be allowed to immigrate to the United States. If a background check revealed her to be a prostitute, immigration was certainly precluded and delicate and complex legal issues would likely follow. Captain W. Hays Parks noted other potential problems:

> If the Marine did marry . . . once he got back to the United States he might decide that she didn't look as good to him as she did before, and simply walk away from her . . . . She would call her nation's embassy [and] we would have a mini-diplomatic incident on our hands. Alternatively, the Marine would bring this woman home, and the Commandant of the Marine Corps would incur the wrath of some senator or congressman because a constituent (the Marine's parents) had called, asking why the Marine Corps had permitted their eighteen or nineteen year old son, whom they had entrusted to the Marine Corps, to marry.[91]

Division Order 1752.1 was the 1st Marine Division's effort to anticipate such problems. It required the commanding general's written permission before a Marine outside the United States could marry. Counselling by the division chaplain and a judge advocate and documentation of the prospective bride's background were required before that permission was given. "In Vietnam," Captain Parks recalled, "we simply had an agreement with local authorities that they were not authorized to grant any marriage licenses to Marines without the commanding general's written permission—which, of course, he would not give." Captain Parks continued:

> Practically speaking, a Marine would have to meet his prospective bride six months to a year before he ever came to Vietnam in order to wade through this intricate labyrinth during his tour. To my knowledge, only one Marine was successful in doing so. He was a major who had met and dated a Japanese woman . . . during the three-year tour at Yokosuka that preceded his Vietnam tour.[92]

The wide range of other legal assistance subject matter (wills, powers of attorney, adoptions, taxation, avoidance of civil action, citizenship, landlord-tenant, to name some of the more common topics) required skilled lawyers with a broad range of expertise.[93]

Vietnamese claims against the United States increased, as well. The ingenuity exhibited in devising fraudulent claims was impressive. For example, Captain C. Clarke Barnes, a 3d Marine Division lawyer, was once searching for a ride out of Da Nang. He walked down the road, keeping watch over his shoulder for a Marine Corps vehicle. As a Vietnamese three-wheeled bus approached him, a motorcyclist darted around the bus and into his path. Captain Barnes recalled:

> I had just enough time to step out of the way . . . but his forehead hit . . . my right arm, extended with my val-pac in it. The little man was peeled off the motorcycle like he had been clotheslined . . . . He lay there momentarily and looked dead, then moaned and struggled to his feet . . . . About a week later I encountered the area foreign claims officer (Army). As I was relating my experience, the Army officer began laughing . . . . They had received a claim from a Vietnamese that a tank had collided with him, he had received a head injury, and his motorcycle was destroyed.

---

*Two months later, Captain Shorstein was again associated with events involving the Khe Sanh garrison. On 16 April 1968 a patrol of two platoons was engaged by the enemy near Khe Sanh. A fierce engagement ensued, eventually involving three companies. The Marines finally withdrew, leaving behind what turned out to be two wounded and 13 dead. Over the next two days attempts to rescue the wounded and recover the dead tragically failed. One of the wounded, Corporal Hubert H. Hunnicutt, was finally recovered and later received the Navy Cross. At Cam Lo, on 22 April, a formal investigation inquired into the debacle. Captain Shorstein was counsel to the commander of the battalion involved. Colonel Norris C. Broome, Assistant SLO of the 3d Marine Division, was counsel to the investigation. As Captain Shorstein said, "heads rolled, from the Task Force X-Ray commander on down." The battalion commander was relieved for cause, and the regimental and task force commanders were given substandard fitness reports. (Col Walter H. Cuenin ltr to CG, 3d MarDiv, Subj: Informal investigation into circumstances of a night operation conducted by the 1st Bn., 9th Marines, in the vicinity of Khe Sanh, on the night of 16-17 April 1968 (MCHC); and Harry L. Shorstein ltr to author, dtd 30Jan89, Comment folder, Marines and Military Law in Vietnam file, MCHC).

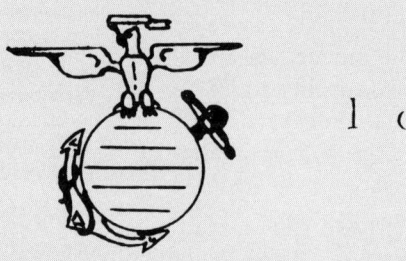

THE BEARER OF THIS PASS IS AN AUTHORIZED FOREIGN CLAIMS INVESTIGATOR FOR III MARINE AMPHIBIOUS FORCE IT IS HIS DUTY PROMPTLY AND FAIRLY TO INVESTIGATE CLAIMS IN THE III MAF AREA OF RESPONSIBILITY, TO FACILITATE THE EARLIEST POSSIBLE SETTLEMENT OF WORTHY CLAIMS AND TO PROMOTE FRIENDLY RELATIONSHIPS WITH THE VIETNAMESE PEOPLE. ALL WHO SEE THIS PASS ARE URGED TO GIVE THE BEARER ALL REASONABLE ASSISTANCE IN THE ACCOMPLISHMENT OF THIS MISSION

CHIEF OF STAFF

Courtesy of Col Daniel F. McConnell, USMC (Ret.)

The foreign claims investigator's pass issued to lawyers of the 1st Marine Division.

The [claims] office had received no reports from Army or Marine tank units admitting to such an accident, and he said, "It's obvious, you're it, you're the tank!" The veracity of that claim was the same as every claim for restitution for water buffalos killed in the field: they are always female and always pregnant.[94]

Another function of the staff legal offices was to review courts-martial and one-officer investigations (the latter referred to as "JAG Manual" investigations after the Navy legal manual that contained investigation guidelines). The Navy law specialists, attached to each office, still had to review summary courts-martial and some special courts and attest to their legal correctness. JAG Manual investigations, usually conducted to resolve losses of government property or fix responsibility for accidents, could be reviewed by any lawyer. These administrative tasks, while not as exciting as others in the legal offices, were as necessary and important as those requiring courtroom appearance.

Fragging: Friendly Fire With Malice

The Vietnam war produced a form of felony that, although a part of all wars, had never been so widespread, so callously carried out, or so frequently committed: the attack with intent to murder one's own officers and noncommissioned officers, most often by fragmentation hand grenade. The charge for the completed offense was premeditated murder. The cowardly act was commonly referred to as "fragging."

Such incidents, although hard to document, are part of the ugly lore of every conflict. The first verified incident involving the murder of a commander by his own troops occurred on 1 January 1781, when Pennsylvania soldiers of the Continental Army killed one of their captains.[95] In Vietnam fraggings were carried out for a variety of "reasons," including imagined wrongs, punishment for perceived over-zealousness in the performance of duty, for racial reasons, and simply to intimidate. Although there reportedly were such assaults as early as 1966, only in 1968 were they recognized as more than isolated occurrences. The Marine Corps did not keep fragging statistics until late in the war and then not in all commands. Official figures reflecting the number of these murders, or attempts to commit murder, and the number of deaths or woundings that resulted, are incomplete. The Marine Corps' total, based upon those incomplete statistics,

1968: HIGH TIDE

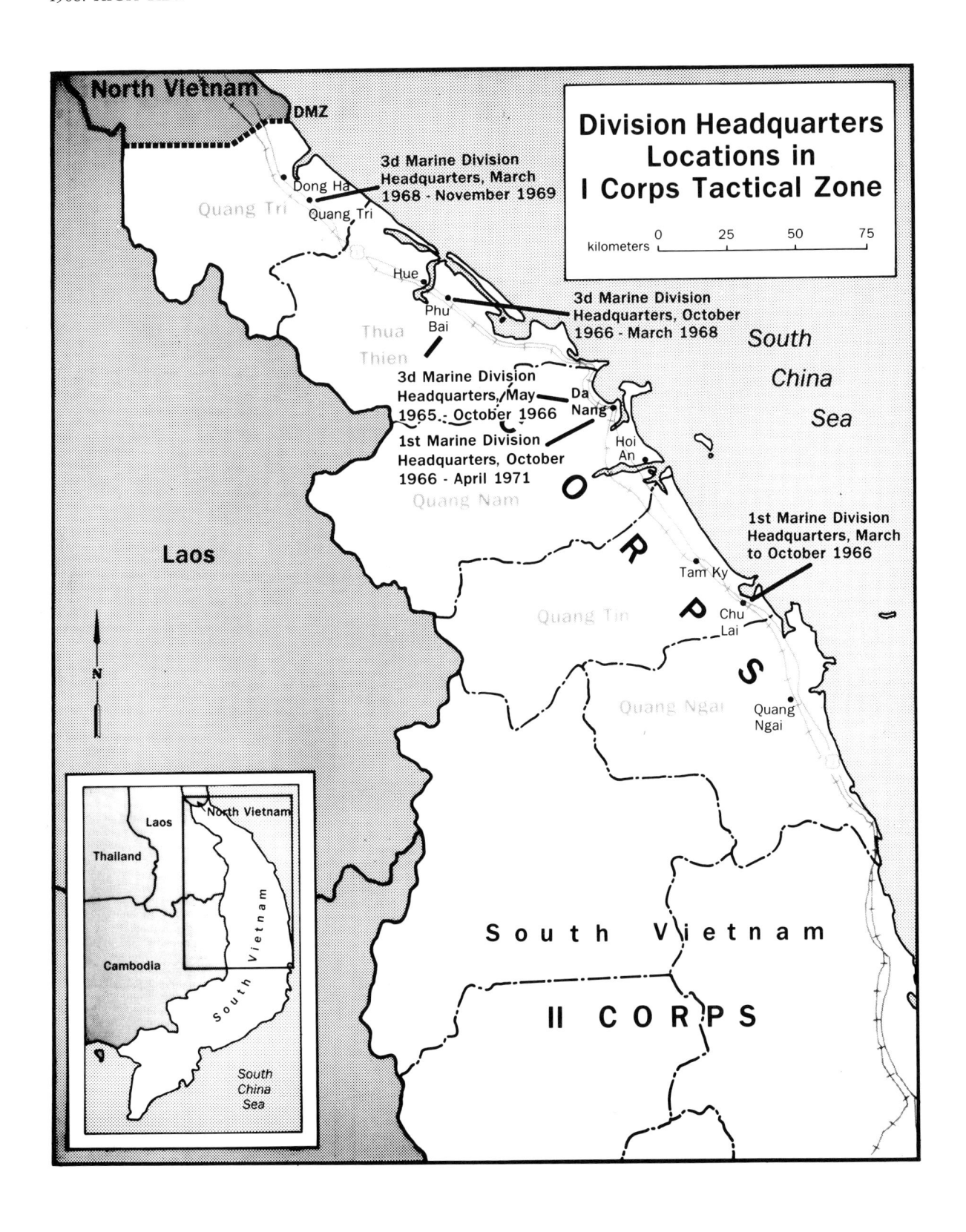

prisoners burned what they could of the cinder block cell block, destroying it. As Colonel Gambardella recalled:

> We would have to use the force necessary, but at a time and place of our choosing. We could then minimize the contact between the brig personnel and the prisoners so there would be no physical injuries.... The safety of the prisoners and my own men.... This was of prime importance .... If you force them up against the wall, there is no place for them to run except towards you. If we did that we are going to get in a hell of a lot more trouble than we already had.

Throughout Saturday the prisoners remained in control of the brig, although there was no attempt to escape. "They would have been shot, had they tried," said an MP officer, First Lieutenant Jimmie W. Glenn. But while no prisoner escaped, brig authorities learned that several prisoners had been attacked by other prisoners during the night. Chief Warrant Officer Steven J. Mihalak, the Corrections Officer, said that "each one of the [eight] injured prisoners stated that they were subject to a kangaroo court. We had to bring Prisoner Rezzoffi out on a stretcher."

Prisoner Nunnery, a black Marine, underwent one of the "courts-martial." He later testified:

> Prisoner Gardner . . . said, "I am the judge." He also said that as far as he was concerned, everyone knew what the verdict was. He walked up to the side of my rack and took a swing at me.... I knew what the rest of them were going to do.... The guy that was my defense counsel, I didn't know him, tripped me, and the rest of them jumped on me. There were six [of them].

Prisoner Berry added, "They started beating on him .... I suggested throwing him in the ditch and burying him alive with sand bags. The guys were going to do this, but then somebody threw him [Nunnery] through the window and he ran away."

Berry described another Saturday afternoon "court:"

> [Seven prisoners] came in my hut and talked about a kangaroo court they had just held because he didn't participate and he was a dime-dropper. I don't know his name .... He had a jury, prosecution, defense counsel, and a judge, just like a regular court-martial, and had sentenced him to be beaten, which they all said they participated. They talked about the one they had pulled on Prisoner Zotts the night before (Friday) and had beaten him as their sentence.

At least 11 "courts-martial" were carried out by the prisoners.

Lieutenant Colonel Gambardella contacted Lieutenant Colonel Frederick M. Haden, FLC's Staff Legal Officer, and asked that he come to the brig to "get a firsthand feel of it." Major Donald E. Malone, the III MAF Assistant Provost Marshal, testified that "all of a sudden, a bunch of lawyers appeared." The prisoners were told of their arrival and availability for consultation. The lawyers' presence, however, failed to alter the standoff.

The prisoners remained in control of the brig's interior compound throughout Saturday and into Sunday. After the usual III MAF Sunday morning staff briefing, Lieutenant Colonel Gambardella explained the situation to the commanding general. "General Cushman asked me if I had control. I told him that I was going back and get it."

That afternoon he returned to the brig and announced to the prisoners that he would give them 15 minutes to surrender, or the compound would be taken by force, to include the use of tear gas. The prisoners, armed with clubs, sharpened screwdrivers, gasoline-soaked rags, and a gasoline-filled fire extinguisher employed as a makeshift flamethrower, responded by setting another fire and again challenging Lieutenant Colonel Gambardella.

Military Police First Lieutenant Glenn selected 12 Marines from the Headquarters Battalion reaction force, most of whom were sergeants with combat experience. He armed 10 of the men with baseball bats and two with shotguns. "Some of them," Lieutenant Glenn reported, "didn't like the idea that it was going to be 12 against 300." Lieutenant Glenn told the 12 that, if a prisoner attempted to attack them, they were to use the baseball bats. "I also told the men with the shotguns that if I pointed at a man, I wanted that man to be dropped right on the spot .... If they had time, to first fire a warning shot, and then shoot at the legs."

At 1530 Lieutenant Glenn formed his men in a wedge and approached the entrance to the sallyport, beyond which the prisoners waited.[115] Lieutenant Colonel Gambardella had posted a judge advocate and a photographer at each guard tower. "I was using them as witnesses . . . to prevent false accusations about the force we would use."[116] After donning gas masks, Lieutenant Glenn's detail tossed tear gas grenades into the compound.

The riot was over within minutes. "There was only one prisoner hit with a bat," Lieutenant Glenn recalled. The prisoner refused to enter a truck, so "he

The first tear gas grenade detonates as it is thrown into the III MAF brig's sallyport. 1stLt Jimmie W. Glenn leans on a baseball bat. All 12 men of the detail wear gas masks.

The first prisoner surrenders as the tear gas is blown throughout the brig compound.

Tear gas permeates the III MAF brig, forcing rebellious confinees to surrender. As they abandon the compound they are herded to a holding area outside the brig fence line.

The takeover ended, 76 prisoners are held outside the compound. Prisoners used wet towels in an attempt to escape the tear gas. 1stLt Glenn is at lower center, without cover.

was smacked across the back of the legs . . . . It only hurt his pride."*

While FLC lawyers formulated charges and III MAF engineers rebuilt the burned cell block, 31 suspected ringleaders were held on diminished rations in open dog cages in what had previously been the military police dog kennel. III MAF authorities did not consider the brig's SEAhuts, to which the other prisoners returned, secure enough to hold the ringleaders. As soon as transportation could be arranged, about 10 days later, all 31 were moved from the dog cages to brigs at Subic Bay and Sangley Point, in the Philippines, and Camp Butler, Okinawa.[117] Normally, FLC lawyers tried offenses occurring in the III MAF brig, but because of the large number of prisoners charged, responsibility for trial reverted to the prisoners' parent units.[118] The four principal ringleaders in the riot and subsequent kangaroo courts were Privates Michael A. Roberts, Stephen F. Brice, Calvin L. White, and Talmadge D. Berry. At the time of the riot all four had been serving sentences that included bad conduct discharges.[119] They now faced charges of mutiny, riot, conspiracy to assault other prisoners, and multiple assaults.[120] The command charged the other 27 principal actors with varying lesser offenses; most were to be tried by general courts-martial. First Lieutenant Curtis K. Oberhansly was the trial counsel in many of those cases.

The lawyers involved in prosecuting and defending the 31 accused Marines began a tedious series of trips back and forth among Vietnam, the Philippines, and Okinawa, although any case requiring a trip out of Vietnam had its advantages. ("And don't come back to the 'Nam without . . . a pair of size 11 and a pair of size 13 tennis shoes and a couple of pairs of medium handball gloves for yours truly," one Da Nang defense counsel wrote another.)[121]

In early 1969 Colonel John R. DeBarr tried the four main actors in the riot, Roberts, White, Brice, and Berry at Subic Bay Naval Station. Captain Michael J. Hoblock, Jr., who had never tried a contested case before, represented all four at their request. Co-defense counsel on the four cases was Navy judge advocate Lieutenant Jerry D. Rucker, on loan from Subic Bay's Navy Legal Service Office, where he was the chief defense counsel. Captain Hoblock and Lieutenant Rucker negotiated a package pretrial agreement with the convening authority that promised guilty pleas by White, Brice, and Berry to all charges except mutiny, in return for a limit on each accused's punishment of one year's confinement and a dishonorable discharge.[122]

Of the 31 accused, only Private Roberts pleaded not guilty to the Da Nang brig charges, and to new charges of mutiny and assault that arose from what Lieutenant Rucker called a "latenight hoorah" in the Subic Bay brig. Robert's case, like those of White, Brice, and Berry, was tried at Subic Bay.[123] Defended by his requested defense counsel, Lieutenant Rucker, and his assigned defense counsel, Captain Hoblock, the prosecutor was again Lieutenant Oberhansly.** Having already prosecuted guilty pleas to essentially the same events several times before, he proved Roberts' guilt only after a hard fought, seven-day trial in which defense motions resulted in half the charges being dismissed by the military judge. On 23 February 1969 the court sentenced Roberts to 15 years confinement at hard labor and a dishonorable discharge.*** All 31 ringleaders were convicted, most with pretrial agreements that insured their quick departure from Vietnam and a dishonorable discharge from the Marine Corps.[124]

Perspective

In the first half of 1968 the war's heaviest combat activity occurred, with the enemy's main effort centered on the two northern provinces. III MAF forces and the South Vietnamese repelled the enemy's incursions across the DMZ, ejected them from Hue, and defeated his attempts to take Khe Sanh. In May the enemy shifted his main attack southward against Da Nang and again met defeat. In the last half of the year the enemy pulled his major units back beyond the borders of Vietnam and reverted to small-unit tactics and harassment.[125]

Line officers in increasing numbers completed their Vietnam duty and began law school, to return later to active duty as lawyers. Major James P. McHenry was the operations officer of the 1st Battalion, 1st Marines.

---

*Two weeks later, at the U.S. Army's Long Binh brig, a violent and protracted riot occurred. A few of the 719 prisoners controlled a portion of that brig for more than a month. Sixty prisoners and five guards were injured and six black prisoners were charged with conspiring and beating a white prisoner to death with a shovel. One murder conviction resulted. (*New York Times*, 1Oct68, p. 3, and 8Jan69, p. 12; David Cortright, *Soldiers in Revolt* [Garden City: Anchor Press/Doubleday, 1975], p. 40-41).

**During the trial, Lieutenant Oberhansly met, and six months later married, the daughter of Captain Robert H. Nicholson, the Naval Base Staff Judge Advocate. Lieutenant Oberhansly's best man was his courtroom opponent, Lieutenant Rucker.

***Roberts was released in February 1973, having served just under four years post-trial confinement.

He received the Bronze Star Medal and returned to the United States and law school through the excess leave program. He then continued his career as a judge advocate and attained the grade of colonel.[126] Captain Ronald C. Rachow provided ground defense for the Da Nang Airbase as a member of the 1st Military Police Battalion before becoming a judge advocate and, eventually, a lieutenant colonel and general court-martial military judge.[127] Captain Harry K. Jowers was an Army officer in Vietnam. In one remarkable year of combat he earned three Silver Star Medals, two Bronze Star Medals, four Purple Hearts, five Air Medals, and two Army Commendation Medals. After completing nine years in the Army and attending law school, he joined the Marine Corps as its most highly decorated judge advocate.[128] The value of such tested and experienced officers was proven in their leadership and direction of judge advocates and the legal community long after the war was over.

Judge Advocate Division came into being on 17 April 1968. In a reorganization of Headquarters Marine Corps effective that date, Discipline Branch (Code DK) was redesignated as the new division (with the correspondence code AI). Colonel Charles Sevier had led Discipline Branch since July 1966 and he continued as the first Director, Judge Advocate Division until August 1968. The new division was comprised of 15 officers, 10 enlisted men, and 14 civilians. It had four functional branches: Military Law; Research and Plans; Legal Assistance; and General Law, Regulations, and Reference. Colonel Sevier's official title was Director, Judge Advocate Division; Staff Judge Advocate for the Commandant of the Marine Corps. That title recognized the fact that there was only one Judge Advocate General in the Naval Service, the JAG of the Navy.[129]

At year's end an even 300 Marine Corps lawyers were on active duty. Brigadier General James Lawrence retired in November, but was immediately recalled to active duty to continue serving as Deputy Assistant to the Secretary of Defense (Legislative Affairs).[130] While he had remained unretired and on active duty, no other lawyer colonel would be selected for promotion to his grade, because Brigadier General Lawrence

Capt Ronald C. Rachow of the 1st Military Police Battalion takes a break outside Da Nang. He completed his Marine Corps career as a general court-martial military judge.

Photo courtesy of LtCol Ronald C. Rachow, USMC (Ret.)

Capt Harry K. Jowers, U.S. Army, second from right, was awarded one of his three Silver Star Medals by Adm John S. McCain, Jr., Commander-in-Chief, Pacific, on 17 September 1968. Capt Jowers later was a Marine Corps colonel and judge advocate. Marine Maj-Gen Hugh M. Elwood, Assistant Chief of Staff (J-3), CinCPac, stands with hand on hip.

held the sole "qualified for legal duty" general's slot that had been authorized. Even after he retired and was recalled, it was two years before the annual brigadier general selection board was authorized to again select for promotion a colonel lawyer "qualified for legal duty."

Also on active duty were 21 lawyer colonels, 31 lieutenant colonels, a mere 18 majors, and 206 captains. (Captain Patricia A. Murphy was still the sole woman Marine Corps lawyer on active duty.*) Finally, 11 first lieutenants and 12 second lieutenants were on active

---

*Captain Murphy became the first Marine Corps woman lawyer in Vietnam when, on 30 November 1968, she arrived from Okinawa, where she was assigned, to attend an I Corps Bar Association meeting held at the U.S. Air Force's Gunfighter's Officers Club, in Da Nang. Departing on 1 December, she was eligible for two months combat pay. (Parks 28Dec88 ltr., p. 11; and Halliday intvw.)

duty.[131] The number of these officers who were serving in Vietnam at any given time varied, but was roughly between 60 and 70.

For the moment, the number of lawyers exceeded the number of billets requiring lawyers. This surplus resulted from several initiatives that came to fruition in 1968. The excess leave program, by which regular officers were granted up to three and a half years excess leave (without pay or allowances) to obtain a law degree, placed 15 officers in law school, nine of whom would soon return to active duty rolls. Another program had already returned six experienced lawyer reservists to active duty. Their seniority helped ease the continuing shortage of majors. In addition, the Platoon Leaders Class (PLC), Law was successfully recruiting newly graduated lawyers.

A Department of Defense Lawyer Working Group

Senior lawyers attended the Pacific Legal Conference at FMFPac Headquarters, Hawaii, in 1968. Front row, from left, Col Donald E. Holben; Col Paul W. Seabaugh; Col Marion G. Truesdale; Col Jack E. Hanthorn; Col Joseph R. Motelewski; Col Robert C. Lehnert; Col Charles B. Sevier; Col Verne L. Oliver. Second row, Maj Curtis W. Olson; LtCol William C. Jaeck; LtCol Frederick M. Haden; Col Arthur R. Petersen; Col John R. DeBarr; LtCol Max G. Halliday; LtCol Rollin Q. Blakeslee; Maj Joseph A. Mallery, Jr. Back row, Maj William H. J. Tiernan; Maj Lawrence G. Bohlin; and nonlawyer Capt Frederick B. Steves, FMFPac staff.

Photo courtesy of Col Curtis W. Olsen, USMC (Ret.)

recommended lawyer incentive pay and bonuses for those lawyers who volunteered to extend their initial service obligation. The Group believed this would enhance retention. The recommendation, however, became mired in bureaucratic discussion and was not put into effect.[132] The next year, however, both the U.S. Senate and House would introduce bills providing for special pay and reenlistment bonuses for military lawyers.[133]

In 1968, for the first time, the Judge Advocate General of the Navy kept statistics on courts-martial tried in Vietnam: 148 general courts; 1,284 specials (the bulk of them tried by lawyers, though not required by the UCMJ); and 1,406 summary courts (virtually none of which involved lawyers) were tried.[134]

Since the beginning of the war, the number of courts-martial throughout the Corps had grown commensurate with the increase in manpower: a 62 percent rise in trials and a 65 percent increase in personnel. Significantly, however, the number of general courts-martial rose by 209 percent.[135] This reflected the lesser quality of recruit and the more serious offenses being committed. (Three percent of Marine Corps strength was now of the lowest intelligence group, Mental Category Group IV—"Cat four"—with projections of six percent and seven percent for the next two years.)[136]

In Vietnam, Marine Corps troop strength continued its steady climb, reaching a peak of 85,520 in September 1968. The departure of Regimental Landing Team 27 reversed that trend. By year's end about 81,000 Marines and sailors were in III MAF.[137]

Captain Donald Higginbotham of the 1st Marine Division's legal office wrote: "As ridiculous as it may sound to some, if I had one year of my life to live over, it would be the time I spent in Vietnam. Everything in my life since that time has seemed anticlimactic."[138]

PART III
WINDING DOWN

CHAPTER 6
1969 Preamble: Discipline in Disarray

The Military Justice Act of 1968: Evolutionary Fine-Tuning — Marijuana: Persons of Ill Repute — Racial Conflict: Black, White, and Green — Administrative Discharge: The Right Fix — Fragging: Killers In Our Midst — From A Lawyer's Case File: Murder of a Company Commander — Real or Imagined: The 'Mere Gook' Rule — Perspective

---

Disciplinary problems foreshadowed in preceding years rose to troubling levels in 1969. While most Marines quietly carried out their duties without fanfare or disciplinary involvement, more and more of them were becoming enmeshed in the military justice system. Marijuana use, which increased dramatically in 1968, was virtually out of control in 1969. "Fraggings" were no longer unusual. Marine Corps draftees with antagonistic attitudes were more frequently encountered. Disciplinary incidents were no longer uncommon in combat elements and were alarmingly frequent in combat support units. Racial conflicts were becoming violent and more frequent. Tensions in American society were being reflected in America's military society.

Retired Marine Colonel Robert D. Heinl, Jr., expressed a disturbing view when he wrote: "The morale, discipline and battleworthiness of the U.S. Armed Forces are, with a few salient exceptions, lower and worse than at any time in this century and possibly in the history of the United States."[1] Marine Corps lawyers, reviewing burgeoning court dockets, would have agreed.

The Marine Corps was shocked by a July race riot at a Camp Lejeune, North Carolina, enlisted man's club. It resulted in the death of one Marine and the injury of 14 others.[2] A riot at the Camp Pendleton, California, brig in September further alarmed Marine Corps leaders.[3]

Gunnery Sergeant Joseph Lopez, an infantryman who returned to Vietnam for a third tour of duty in February 1969, said:

> At first I noticed the discipline of the troops was very lax . . . . Tell a man to square his cover away, tell him he was out of uniform, the man look at you like he was gonna kill you . . . . Never did I ever see anybody give a superior NCO the looks that these young men give us nowadays . . . . Once they was brought up on charges that should have warranted a court-martial and brig time, well, they didn't get no brig time or court-martial . . . . We're dealing with a different type of Marine, here . . . . We need more discipline in this Marine Corps, or we're going to lose out.[4]

"Where do we get these individuals—these young criminals in Marine uniform?" asked Colonel John R. DeBarr, a general court-martial military judge.[5]

In 1969 slightly more than 18,600 Mental Category IV enlistees were wearing Marine green—six percent of Marine Corps active duty strength. Although not all disciplinary problems were their fault, Project 100,000 individuals had a boot camp dropout rate more than twice that of other recruits and continued to have a higher disciplinary rate than other Marines.[6]

Marines now arrived in Vietnam for 12-, rather than 13-month tours of duty.[7] The 12-month tours brought the Marine Corps in line with the Army, which had always assigned one-year tours. But the continuous personnel turbulence meant that each rotation's lawyers tended to face the same problems as their predecessors; each year they rediscovered the same solutions.

Marine Corps attorneys were now assigned the 4400 legal MOS (Military Occupational Specialty) designator as a matter of course.[8] Besides entering an arena filled with legal challenges, new 4400s found that the military justice system itself was on the brink of a major change for the better.

The Military Justice Act of 1968: Evolutionary Fine-Tuning

Since the first court-martial guide, *Manual for Courts-Martial, U.S. Army* (1920), three other Army manuals had been in use.* A fourth came into use on 1 August 1969, when the Military Justice Act of 1968 became effective.[9] *Naval Courts and Boards*, the legal manual employed by the Navy and Marine Corps prior to the Uniform Code of Military Justice, first appeared in 1910. Revised editions were issued in 1917, 1923, and 1937. In 1969 the old "Red Book," the 1951 *Manual for Courts-Martial*, was to be replaced by a larger, loose-leaf volume.

In 1963 Senator Sam J. Ervin, Jr., introduced legislation to, as he put it, "perfect the administration of justice in the Armed Forces."[10] After lengthy hearings and delays the legislation became law. The Uniform

---

*Manual for Courts-Martial, U.S. Army (1928) and (1949) (the short-lived *Manual for Courts-Martial, U.S. Air Force* [1949] was virtually identical to the Army manual), and the *Manual for Courts-Martial* (1951). A draft proposal for a 1964 revision of the 1951 manual was completed but not adopted.

Code of Military Justice (UCMJ) of 1950 had been a landmark improvement in military law, but the years since its implementation had revealed flaws and gaps that the Military Justice Act of 1968, with its revised UCMJ, was designed to cure.

Among the changes, the act provided that an accused could not be tried by a summary court-martial (in which there was no right to a defense counsel or an independent judge or jury) over the accused's objection. Now, the accused could refuse a summary court and opt for a special court, where those rights would automatically be available.

Military trial procedures were brought more into line with federal court practice. The act added pre- and post-trial sessions involving the military judge, the accused, and both lawyers, but without the members.[11] At such sessions motions and procedural issues could be decided.

The designation "law officer" was changed to "military judge," and military judges were given authority roughly equivalent to that of federal district court judges. The act provided that a military judge was mandatory in any case in which a bad conduct discharge might be imposed. Effectively then, military judges would be required in virtually all special courts and, certainly, in all general courts-martial (where law officers had always been mandated). That provision was a compromise resulting from Congress' desire to see military judges in all special courts and the Armed Services' opposition to judges in any special court. Military judges were required to be certified for such duty. Special court-martial military judges remained in the normal chain of command. General court-martial judges, however, would be responsible only to their Service's Judge Advocate General (JAG). Because the Marine Corps had no JAG, it would look to the Navy's JAG for certification. This removed general court judges from the local chain of command and fitness report chain, and ensured their independence and freedom from local command influence. For the first time an accused was allowed to opt for trial by military judge alone. This corresponded to the civilian bench trial.

The most significant change in the 1968 act required that a lawyer represent every accused at special courts-martial, whether or not a bad conduct discharge was a possibility (unless lawyers were unavailable because of military conditions, an unlikely situation). Senator Ervin said of prior provisions allowing nonlawyer defense counsels, "it is sheer fantasy, in my view, to contend that a veterinary officer or a transportation officer who has read a few pages of the Uniform Code . . . can adequately represent a defendant in [a court-martial]." Constitutional and criminal law had changed dramatically since adoption of the 1950 UCMJ. Landmark opinions such as *Miranda v. Arizona*, *Mapp v. Ohio*, and *Gideon v. Wainwright*, had been issued, and all of those decisions were binding on military courts as well as civilian.* Given the rights now available to suspects, evidentiary limitations, and the increasingly complex nature of a special court-martial, the Senator's view was not unreasonable. Nevertheless, the Navy resisted the counsel provision of the act, citing the difficulty of securing lawyers in sufficient numbers and problems in convening courts at sea. The Air Force held that it was already capable of providing lawyers in every special court-martial, and the Army, by regulation, did not then permit special courts to impose bad conduct discharges.[12]

Finally, the new amendments to the UCMJ provided that Marine Corps lawyers could be designated "judge advocates" and allowed designation of the senior lawyer of a command as "staff judge advocate," rather than staff legal officer.[13] Authorized by a Marine Corps order, both changes in designation became the practice as soon as the act was passed and before it became effective.[14]

With the act, instead of a battalion commander telling one of his officers acting as trial counsel that he, the commander, expected a certain case to be tried within a certain period, the commander had a judge advocate defense counsel to work with (or contend with). On the other hand, he also had a judge advocate trial counsel assigned to prosecute his cases. But neither defense nor trial counsels were in the battalion commander's chain of command. Years later, General Paul X. Kelley, 28th Commandant of the Marine Corps, said of the Military Justice Act:

> Under the old system there's a great psychology in having the commander say, "I award you a special court-martial," and for that individual to know that the commander is going to follow that special court-martial through . . . . This was a great change, and a culture shock for [commanders], because no longer were you the man in charge.[15]

From the judge advocate's perspective, his skills were

---

*The warning of rights required by Miranda (384 U.S.436; 86 S.Ct.1602 [1966]) are well known. Mapp (367 U.S.643; 81 S.Ct.1684 [1961]) forbade admission of improperly seized evidence. Gideon (372 U.S.335; 83 S.Ct.792 [1963]) settled the right of indigents to appointed counsel in noncapital cases.

simply extended into new arenas. As Captain John S. Papa, a Force Logistic Command (FLC) lawyer, noted:

> A battalion commander sees a lawyer come in and say, "Sir, this is a good pretrial agreement, because this is all I can get from a court," and in fact that's all he does get; or he comes in and says, "This is a bad search and seizure," and . . . in fact the court dismisses the charge. Slowly, a confidence is built up. The lawyer begins to be respected for what he can do for the command.[16]

Captain Papa added that "we lawyers had a growing experience, also, when we began working at the battalion level. We're beginning to learn a little bit more about our bastard system . . . being a disciplinary as well as a legal system."[17]

A critic, after reviewing the Military Justice Act of 1968, conceded that "it extended substantially new due process rights to servicemen, some of them more favorable than were then provided in civilian courts, and its changes in court-martial procedures, especially the general court-martial, considerably replaced the old disciplinary flavor with a judicial one."[18] President Lyndon B. Johnson, upon signing the act into law, noted: "We have always prided ourselves on giving our men and women in uniform excellent medical service, superb training, the best equipment. Now, with this, we're going to give them first-class legal service as well."[19] All of the act's improvements were needed to cope with the disciplinary crisis building in the Armed Forces and in Vietnam.

Contrary to the Navy JAG's fears, there were enough judge advocates to meet the expanded requirement for lawyers. Marine Brigadier General Duane L. Faw recalled that "my problems were with retention . . . not with getting bodies. The [new act] didn't make that much difference."[20]

When the act went into effect on 1 August, law officers—those senior Marine Corps lawyers assigned to Navy and Marine Corps Judicial Activity offices—changed titles and became general court-martial military judges. FLC conducted seminars on the new act for both judge advocates and commanders.[21] The newly mandated special court-martial military judges were drawn from the more experienced trial and defense counsels in each staff judge advocate's (SJA) office. Of necessity, they were predominantly captains and almost exclusively Reserve officers who were on their first tours of duty as lawyers and Marines. III MAF sent as many of them as possible to Subic Bay Naval Base in the Philippines for a Navy-conducted, 10-day military judges' course.[22] The requirement for special court-martial military judges strained legal office manpower, because the newly created posts were filled from the complement of judge advocates then present without compensating replacement lawyers.[23]

At 0730 on 1 August 1969 five 1st Marine Division judge advocates were sworn in by the division's commanding general as special court-martial military judges. Because of time zone differences, it was still 31 July in the United States. Promptly at 0800, Vietnam time, as planned by the division's lawyers, Lieutenant Colonel William R. Eleazer opened the first court-martial anywhere to employ the 1968 act's new military judge provision.[24]

Marijuana: Persons of Ill Repute

Nearly half the cases tried in Vietnam in 1969 involved possession or use of marijuana. MACV's 1969 Command History reported:

> Marijuana was sold by taxi drivers, prostitutes, street urchins, and other persons of ill repute. The enforcement effort directed toward the elimination of the source of marijuana was hampered by the lack of . . . interest by Government of Vietnam authorities.[25]

Marijuana cost ten cents a stick at virtually any store or traffic light.[26] (A "stick" of marijuana, as the name implied, was a slim wooden stick, around which were wound strands of the marijuana leaf.) In a postwar interview, Army General William C. Westmoreland was asked about accounts of Vietnam drug use and fraggings. He replied: "I was aghast when they had soldiers killing other soldiers, smoking pot in their bunker. It didn't happen . . . . If it happened, it was very exceptional."[27] But judge advocates knew that those offenses were all too unexceptional.

In 1969 Marine Corps leaders faced an epidemic of marijuana use and the breakdown of authority that accompanied it. Major Ives W. Neely, commanding officer of Maintenance Company, Force Logistic Supply Group-Bravo, said with resignation:

> In the company at least 70 to 80 percent—a very high number of people—were using marijuana . . . . People who were pushing the marijuana had put fear into the personnel not using it, to the point that no one down in the troops' area, from private through sergeant, would put a man on report, even when he knew he was smoking marijuana, because of the strong union of marijuana smokers.

Reflecting the pernicious effect that marijuana had on overall discipline, Major Neely continued:

> They would catch a new man as he reported into the unit and tell him that if he was going to buy marijuana he would

At 0730 on 1 August 1969, the day the Military Justice Act became effective, newly appointed special court-martial military judges took their oaths at the 1st Marine Division Headquarters in Da Nang from Assistant Division Commander, BGen Samuel Jaskilka. The new judges were, from left, Capt Martin G. McGuinn, Jr.; Capt George G. Bashian, Jr.; LtCol James P. King; LtCol William R. Eleazer; and Capt Arthur W. Tifford.

buy it from them, and if anyone told, turned in any of their names, there were ways to do these people in. Usually it was with the threat of a hand grenade.[28]

Marijuana detecting dogs first appeared in III MAF in 1968. Kept by the Military Police Battalion Dog Platoon near the III MAF brig, they were invaluable in detecting concealed marijuana. They were especially effective in stemming entry of the substance into Vietnam by Marines returning from R & R ports. Colonel Duane Faw, formerly the III MAF assistant chief of staff and headquarters staff legal officer, recalled:

> Before disembarking the [aircraft], passengers were told that the provost marshal was beyond the end of the ramp with a marijuana sniffing dog, and anyone detected with marijuana . . . would be prosecuted. They could avoid punishment only one way: at the end of the ramp was an "amnesty barrel." . . . A substantial number of returning service personnel placed something in the amnesty barrel.[29]

A new Marine drug rehabilitation center located at Cua Viet was available to drug users from nearby infantry battalions.[30] Still, marijuana use increased. Its burden on the military justice system was reflected in the changing approach to penalties. In 1968, FLC sent cases involving use of marijuana to general courts-martial; by 1969 such cases were tried at special courts and, for first offenders, at summary courts.[31] Only dealers and those involved with hard drugs faced general courts-martial.*[32] Nor was drug abuse any longer restricted to rear area units.

As Lieutenant Colonel Carl E. Buchmann, FLC's deputy SJA, observed: "I don't know what the solution is. It's a problem that's going to be with us for a long time, the way the climate back in the States appears at the moment . . . . I don't know what the hell we're going to do."[33]

Racial Conflict: Black, White, and Green

"Tensions of Black Power Reach Troops in Vietnam," a *New York Times* headline read. "There is no longer any doubt that the black-power issue and its tensions have come to the United States troops in Vietnam . . . . The racial problem appears to be caused mainly by a hard core of militants of both races, estimated at 1 percent or less."[34]

Approximately 41,000 black Marines served in Viet-

---

*A not-unusual case was *U.S. v Pvt Lester E. Allison*, of 1st Force Service Regiment. On 25 October 1969 he was convicted by general court-martial of possession of 1,400 marijuana cigarettes. He was sentenced to a bad conduct discharge, confinement at hard labor for 18 months, and forfeiture of all pay and allowances. (III MAF results of trial by general court-martial ltr, dtd 3Nov69. Federal Records Center folder, Marines and Military Law in Vietnam file, MCHC.)

nam, many in demanding combat leadership roles. But a significant number, victims of prejudice in civilian life and suspicious of the military system, were quick to find or infer discrimination in the Marine Corps.³⁵

The first black Marine was not enlisted until 1942, and then only in compliance with an Executive Order directing an end to racial discrimination in the Armed Forces. Initially, blacks were restricted to all-black units commanded by white officers. The Korean War finally brought integration to the services. At the end of that conflict 15,000 blacks were in Marine Corps ranks in every military occupational specialty. (Not until March 1954, however, did Marine Corps enlistments for "Steward Duty Only" end.) By the 1950s official policy required an end to segregation in the Marine Corps. But the actions and attitudes of a few white Marines who were products of a lifetime of segregation, the hardcore one percent, ran counter to that policy and often created situations ending in disciplinary proceedings.³⁶

In Vietnam in mid-1969 the commanding general of the 3d Marine Division, Major General William K. Jones, distributed a letter to his commanders, addressed, "Confidential, Addressee Eyes Only":

> In view of the apparent lack of awareness of some officers and staff non-commissioned officers of the basic human rights of all Marines, I will amplify that point . . . . Every Marine, regardless of race, color, creed, or rank has certain basic human rights. These are the right to fair and equal treatment and the right to respect for his individual dignity. [Those rights] deserve more than lip-service; [they] must be vigorously observed.³⁷

In rear areas blacks and whites mingled on the job but usually re-segregated themselves when off duty. Many liberty areas near Marine Corps bases had *de facto* white and black sections, which members of the other race entered at their peril.³⁸

In April 1969 Second Lieutenant James H. Webb, Jr., future Secretary of the Navy, commanded a rifle platoon in the 1st Battalion, 5th Marines. While his company was in the regimental rear at An Hoa, one of his men reported the theft of his .45 caliber pistol and his belief that it was concealed in the "Black Shack." Lieutenant Webb confirmed that the pistol had indeed been stolen by the occupants of the Black Shack, apparently so it could be sold. As Webb recounted: "There were four individuals, all of them out of the inner city, who were awaiting courts-martial for violent acts, who literally would just as soon slit your throat as look at you. They had forcibly taken over half

Department of Defense Photo (USMC) 122-1092-01-73
LtCol Carl E. Buchmann was FLC's Deputy SJA in 1969-70. He is shown in a 1973 photograph as a colonel. He said of marijuana use in Vietnam: "It's a problem that's going to be with us for a long time."

of a tent, a space normally reserved for a dozen Marines." Lieutenant Webb confirmed that the four had the pistol and were going to try to sell it. Webb continued:

> I walked over to the black shack. There was a sign up above the door—I'm going to quote it exactly: "Chuck dudes, stay the f--- out—this means you!" . . . I walked into the tent. [A poster of] Bobby Seale was staring at me from one wall. A sign, "Kill the Beast," was up on another wall. This is inside a Marine compound in Vietnam.

Although Lieutenant Webb faced down the four and ordered them to empty their packs and other equipment onto their cots he did not locate the pistol.³⁹ The incident illustrates the tenor of race relations in the combat units during the period.

Bernard C. Nalty, in his history of blacks in the Armed Forces, notes:

> Like the Army, the Marine Corps had been experiencing occasional racial clashes since 1965, the year of the Watts riot and the Americanization of the Vietnam War . . . . Senior Marine Corps officers saw no emerging pattern and treated the incidents as unrelated lapses in discipline. There are no black Marines and no white Marines, only green Ma-

rines (a reference to the color of the uniform), ran the slogan of the mid 1960s.[40]

Nalty went on to note that by 1969 some blacks were "streetwise advocates of black power who would take offense at injustices, real or imagined, and lash out violently."[41]

"Dapping," passing power, afros, and black power symbols all took on special significance. Dapping was the stylized ritual some black servicemen employed upon meeting, involving a series of mirrored, uniform motions beginning with a variation of a handshake. Dapping was akin to a secret fraternity grip raised to a new level, representing a form of cultural identification and a solidarity—a kind of racial salute. "Passing power" was essentially dapping with an intent to represent racial assertiveness and aggressiveness. Afros, the haircuts favored by some young blacks, were rarely in compliance with Marine Corps grooming regulations. Many white NCOs and officers viewed Afros, dapping, and passing power as threats to authority and challenges to leadership. Confrontations over these things often resulted in court-martial charges of disobedience, disrespect, assault, and resisting apprehen-

2dLt James H. Webb, Jr., was a platoon commander in Company D, 1st Battalion, 5th Marines. He was awarded the Navy Cross, the Silver Star, and two Bronze Star Medals, as well as two Purple Hearts. In 1987 he became Secretary of the Navy. While in An Hoa, Vietnam, he had to deal with racial problems.
Marine Corps Historical Collection

sion, the almost visible progression of offenses discernable from a charge sheet. Judge advocates referred to that progression as the bursting radius of a hot Marine.

On 2 September the Commandant of the Marine Corps, General Leonard F. Chapman, Jr., issued a directive to all Marines (called an ALMAR) regarding race relations and racial violence. He directed commanders to make "positive efforts to eradicate every trace of discrimination, whether intentional or not." He further instructed them to permit "Afro/Natural" haircuts, provided they conformed with haircut regulations. He declared that "individual signs between groups and individuals will be accepted for what they are—gestures of recognition and unity," but, he continued, "they are grounds for disciplinary action if executed . . . in a manner suggesting direct defiance of duly constituted authority."[42] While the Commandant's intent was clear, imprecise wording of the directive provided grist for many a defense counsel's argument.

In a letter to Headquarters Marine Corps, the SJA of the 1st Marine Division, Colonel Robert M. Lucy, noted the looseness of the directive's language, saying:

> We have found it to be in need of clarification. The "Afro haircut" is not well understood . . . . Our Division Sergeant Major says the NCOs do not know how to enforce it. Often when admonished to get a haircut, Negro Marines will pull out a battered copy of the ALMAR and wave it at the NCO involved.[43]

In a remarkable message, the commanding general of III MAF, Lieutenant General Herman Nickerson, Jr., told the commanding general of FMFPac, Lieutenant General Henry W. Buse, Jr., that "blacks whom I am dealing with out here feel that the Commandant owes them an explanation concerning ALMAR 65. Part of this explanation would be a description of what actually is allowable for an Afro-American haircut."[44] But other than courtroom interpretations, clarification was not to be had.

Colonel Lucy advised the division commanding general, "militancy among Negro Marines is definitely on the increase. It cuts across almost every unit in the Division."[45] Indeed, racial concerns were becoming a major command preoccupation. A system of I Corps Tactical Zone Watch Committees was established to "monitor and recommend appropriate action on racial tensions and incidents." The Watch Committees' reports recapitulated courts-martial and disciplinary actions resulting from racial incidents.[46] Weekly Subversive Activity Reports included "assessment of the

Department of Defense Photo (USMC) A193460

LtGen Herman Nickerson, Jr., III MAF commanding general, right, wanted the Commandant, Gen Leonard F. Chapman, Jr., center, to explain his message on racial matters. In this 1970 picture the Commandant presents LtGen Hoang Xuan Lam the Legion of Merit.

current threat to the command from subversive/racial standpoint."[47] Still, serious racial incidents increased in number. Between April and June 1969 there was an average of one "large scale riot," per month, according to the Watch Committee's report. Racially motivated fraggings, armed confrontations, and even intramural small-arms firefights were cases on the dockets of III MAF judge advocates.[48]

Only three black Marine Corps judge advocates were assigned to Vietnam during the war. All three arrived in Da Nang in 1969. Captain Jacob R. Henderson, Jr., was assigned to FLC. Captains Cecil R. "Butch" Forster, Jr., and Robert C. Williams were both 1st Marine Division judge advocates.

Captain Williams proved an abrasive but effective defense counsel, and was often requested by black defendants who may have heard of the Malcolm X and black power posters in his quarters. Brigadier General James P. King, a former Director of the Judge Advocate Division, recalled that "Williams had quite a few rough edges . . . . He was not the easiest to get along with."[49] Among the other 1st Division attorneys, he was referred to as "X," or "Brother X," an appellation intended, and accepted, in good nature. Many lawyers actually thought that his middle initial was "X," it was so commonly applied. Captain Stephen C. Berg recalled that Captain Williams was effectively unorthodox in the courtroom and always ready for a legal battle.[50]

Colonel Robert M. Lucy had requested that Captain Forster be assigned to his 1st Marine Division office, saying "[he] would be very helpful, I believe, with any future racial problems."[51] Captain Forster did prove to be an exceptionally able counsel, defending 128 Marines in nine months.[52] He was articulate, well-liked, and often referred to by Captain Williams as "Oreo"—black on the outside, white on the inside. The two were not close.[53]

Major Charles A. Cushman recalled of Captain Henderson, the third black judge advocate:

1969 PREAMBLE: DISCIPLINE IN DISARRAY

Jake Henderson was an ethical and competent judge advocate who never compromised his professional ethics or principles for the benefit of a black accused. You must also bear in mind that the NAACP and other civil rights groups were distressed by the small number of black attorneys in uniform and with the lack of confidence young blacks had in the military justice system.[54]

The 1969 general officers' symposium at Headquarters Marine Corps concluded that "we do have a dissent/racial problem in the Marine Corps. We should not overreact to this problem, and the Corps should rely on fair, impartial leadership" to resolve it.[55] The commanding general of the 1st Marine Division, Major General Ormond R. Simpson, in the combat zone, agreed that racial conflict was the 1st Division's number one problem.[56] While there were only green Marines in the eyes of some, Marine Corps judge advocates knew better.

Administrative Discharge: The Right Fix

As the phrase implies, an administrative discharge is the mechanism by which a Service member is discharged by administrative process. An administrative discharge cannot be given by a court-martial. Also, an administrative discharge may be issued only after due process—notice, representation by counsel, an opportunity to be heard, and cross-examination of witnesses. An "admin" discharge hearing, conducted before a board of at least three officers, could result in a discharge characterized as undesirable, unsuitable, general, or honorable, or could result in retention, although that was seldom the outcome. If the Marine under consideration requested, he was provided judge advocate representation. The government might or might not be represented by a lawyer. The board heard evidence, deliberated, and made a recommendation to be acted upon by the commanding general, who had authority to administratively discharge individuals. If he disagreed with the board's recommendation, he could upgrade the discharge, that is, elevate it to a more desirable type, or even retain the Marine. He could not downgrade the discharge recommended.

From the Marine Corps' viewpoint the significant advantage to an admin discharge was that, unlike a court-martial, an admin could be processed in a matter of one or two weeks—days, if walked through the administrative processing stages. Unlike a court, however, no punishment other than a discharge of bad character could be imposed by an admin board; it was

Three black Marine Corps lawyers served in Vietnam. Capt Robert C. Williams, fourth from right, received his certification as a special court-martial military judge from the commanding general of the 1st Marine Division in February 1970, at Da Nang. From left, Col Robert M. Lucy, the Division SJA, observing; LtCol James P. King, who had taken his judge's oath five months before; Capt Mark L. Haiman; Capt Daniel H. LeGear, Jr.; Williams; Capt Adrian R. King; Capt Gary E. Bushell; and MajGen Edwin B. Wheeler.

Photo courtesy of Col Robert J. Blum, USMC (Ret.)

a simple question of the board reviewing the case and deciding whether the individual should be retained in the Corps, or discharged. If discharged, the additional question was the type of discharge. Those were the only issues. Usually, an act that could result in a court-martial could be the basis for an administrative discharge proceeding. Frequent involvement with authorities, character and behavior disorder (emotional unsuitability), and conviction of a felony by civilian courts were some of the other grounds for admin discharge.

Through his court-martial counsel, an accused Marine could request an admin discharge in lieu of trial, as well. If granted, the accused would avoid court-martial and its prospect of conviction and confinement. This was often referred to as a "good of the service" discharge, or "G.O.S.," after its description in the *Administrative Discharge Manual*. The price for an admin discharge in lieu of trial, a "GOS," was admission of culpability for the offense charged, and an undesirable discharge was automatic. If the request for discharge was denied, no reference to the accused's admission of guilt could be made in a subsequent court-martial.

The military justice system was becoming so overburdened that the initial decision in many pending special courts was whether a Marine should go to an admin board or to a court. Was the goal simply to be rid of the man as expeditiously as possible, without concern for punishment? Of course, a board recommendation for retention was always a possibility. That required the command to take the man back.

The commanding general's considerations regarding approval or disapproval of a board-recommended discharge included Marine Corps-wide personnel policies. Admin discharges had a cumulative effect on Marine Corps strength—on the number of Marines on active duty. That, in turn, was tied to the Corps' budget; when strength dropped below certain levels, Congressionally imposed budget restrictions took effect. So, depending on Corps-wide manpower levels, commanding generals could be constrained to disapprove a recommendation for discharge for reasons unrelated to the conduct of the Marine involved.

Previously, administrative discharges had been sparingly employed. But rising caseloads and the tide of marijuana were combining to compel consideration of administrative discharges as a safety valve allowing quick separation of problem Marines. In late 1968, and even more so in 1969, admin discharges were liberally employed. As Captain John Papa noted: "The Marine Corps has to cut out, [in] the least expensive way . . . those persons who are non-rehabilitatable, and those persons who just can't hack it, and the right route is the administrative route."[57] The 3d Marine Division's assistant division commander, Brigadier General Regan Fuller, was more direct when he remarked that "we're getting rid of these bums who shouldn't have been in the Marine Corps in the first place!"[58] General Fuller went on to detail the "jump summary"—a quick summary court-martial conducted in the field, that primed the record of a habitual offender for an undesirable discharge, once he came before an administrative discharge board. In 1969 few commanders were inclined to question the ethical issue of the jump summary's fairness.

An example of the admin discharge process, although hardly typical, was the case of Corporal Leo O. Testman, Force Reconnaissance Company, 3d Marine Division.[59] Corporal Testman, with 10 months in Vietnam, had been meritoriously promoted to his grade and had been wounded in action. He was highly regarded in his unit as a Marine and a combat leader. He was also a deserter from the U.S. Air Force, with a prior general court-martial conviction. A routine FBI record check uncovered his past. Upon being notified, his unit had no choice but to forward the fraudulent enlistment charge to an admin discharge board, although Force Reconnaissance Company made it known that it would like Testman back. His platoon commander, First Lieutenant Ronald W. McLean, visited the office of the Division SJA and provided a statement to Corporal Testman's counsel, Captain Clarke C. Barnes.

Sadly, by the date of the hearing, late July 1969, Lieutenant McLean, the stepson of actor Jimmy Stewart, and Testman's most persuasive witness, had been killed in action. Still, despite Corporal Testman's Air Force record, the board recommended Testman's retention in the Marine Corps. The commanding general differed with the board's recommendation and advised the Commandant of the Marine Corps of the case. The Commandant disagreed with the division commander. In a message to the Air Force, the Commandant noted Testman's wounding and two promotions while in Vietnam. He concluded: "Based on the above, it is recommended Testman be discharged from the Air Force and allowed to continue serving his country in the Marine Corps."[60] The Air Force acquiesced. Corporal Testman was retained in the Marine Corps, returned to his unit, and went on to be awarded the Navy Achievement Medal for combat valor.[61]

Few administrative discharge cases involved Marines like Corporal Testman or outcomes similar to his. During the last six months of 1968, 2,535 enlisted Marines and 14 officers were administratively discharged from the Marine Corps worldwide.[62] During 1969 in the 1st Marine Division alone 121 undesirable and unsuitable administrative discharges were ordered.[63] Worse was to come in following years.

Fragging: Killers In Our Midst

Even without official statistics to establish the number of Marine Corps fragging incidents in Vietnam, they clearly increased sharply in 1969.* In the U.S. Army, fraggings escalated from 126 incidents in 1969, to 271 in 1970, and 333 in 1971.[64]

Major Charles A. Cushman, an FLC judge advocate, said about this type of assault: "They may or may not have known the victim or even had a grudge against him. Their only thought was to 'Get the lifer and blow him away.' "[65] Colonel John R. DeBarr, general court-martial military judge, said: "It's just a way for them to lash out against authority . . . . These boys are real criminals, and there's no way you can protect yourself against that individual . . . . It has to be stamped out!" Indiscriminate assaults were becoming frequent, but evidence admissible at court-martial was difficult to obtain. Colonel DeBarr, in a debriefing following completion of his tour of duty, said of the homicide cases awaiting trial in Vietnam: "Most of them are fragging cases . . . and don't be disappointed in the results. I'll be surprised if you get convictions. These are difficult cases . . . . To prepare such a case takes a lot of effort, a lot of time, and a lot of money." He went on to note that usually there were witnesses to fragging assaults, or those who knew who had committed them, but they were intimidated into silence. He urged that those witnesses had to be assured of protection and suggested they be removed from Vietnam until they testified, and then, after testifying, be transferred to a command in the United States.[66]

---

*Department of Defense figures specify that no Marine in Vietnam died of a nonhostile gunshot, grenade, fragmentation wound, or "misadventure." Twenty-two Marines are said to have died of "intentional homicide." Those figures are clearly, and unaccountably, incomplete. It is possible that deaths by fragging are considered in that category, although that would reflect a remarkably low number of deaths and would have to ignore the more logical categories under which such deaths should be listed. (DOD, *U.S. Casualties in Southeast Asia: Statistics as of April 30, 1985* [Washington: 1985], p. 5.)

Department of Defense Photo (USMC) A413516
MajGen William K. Jones was commanding general of the 3d Marine Division from April 1969 to April 1970. He took aggressive and imaginative action to meet the fragging scourge. "It is deemed of paramount importance to find and punish those responsible."

The 3d Marine Division, commanded by Major General William K. Jones, suffered 15 fragging assaults in the first six months of 1969. A suspect was apprehended in only one case. Moreover, the usual minimizing statement—that problems were confined to rear-echelon units, and that combat-committed Marines were too busy fighting the enemy to engage in such acts—was no longer true. Only five of the 15 3d Division incidents were committed in rear areas.

General Jones took energetic and imaginative steps to end fraggings in his division, saying: "It is deemed of paramount importance to find and punish those responsible for these senseless acts of violence, not only for the crimes already committed, but because continued undetection will almost certainly lead to continued frequency." He directed that access to hand grenades be restricted where feasible, that informants be relied upon, and that they be protected by transfers to other commands or to units in the United

States. He directed his commanders to be alert to groups of malcontents and to disperse them by transfers to other units. Administrative discharge of "hardcore troublemakers" was emphasized, even if it meant giving them honorable discharges. General Jones emphasized that "commanding officers must abandon the concept that the only way a 'bad' Marine should leave the service is with a bad discharge," because the lag time involved in processing courts-martial or undesirable discharges only allowed the troublemaker opportunity to contaminate others. An administrative honorable or general discharge, on the other hand, could be processed quickly and easily and without appeal. All 3d Division clubs were ordered closed at 2130 and a 2200 curfew was instituted in rear areas. Military Police Company sought volunteers from Marines who had clean records and who had already served six months in an infantry battalion. MP Company was carried overstrength. An extensive division intramural athletic program was instituted, as well.

While aggressively taking action directed towards malcontents, General Jones reminded his commanders:

> In any dispersal of a group or association, particularly where the membership of that group is based upon race, the utmost degree of common sense, tact, and discretion is required. Under the First Amendment . . . every man is guaranteed the right of peaceful assembly and freedom of speech. While these rights are not absolute, they are still to be held in the highest respect.[67]

Finally, by division order, General Jones outlined procedures to be followed after any act of violence, such as a racial incident or fragging assault: The area where the act occurred was immediately isolated by MP teams who controlled movement into or out of the area. Next, a roll call was held to determine who was missing and who was present who should not be. Concurrently, all transient movement (R & R departures, temporary additional duty departures, even permanent change of station departures to the United States) was suspended for the period of the investigation. All sergeants and below were ordered to their tents or SEAhuts for as long as the investigation lasted. Sandwiches were delivered from the mess hall to the men's quarters, as no movement was permitted until the investigation concluded. After consultation with the SJA, quarters of all suspects were searched by a team headed by an officer. Each Marine in the area of isolation was escorted, one-at-a-time, to an interrogation site for questioning and was reminded of the policy to protect those providing information. After questioning, suspects were isolated and not returned to their quarters.[68]

Fragging assaults in the 3d Marine Division declined, but did not end. Recognizing the value of aggressive action in such cases, other commands adopted the 3d Marine Division's blueprint for the apprehension of suspects. Nevertheless, fragging assaults continued as long as Marines were in Vietnam.

From a Lawyer's Case File: Murder of a Company Commander

The commanding general of the 3d Marine Division, Major General Raymond G. Davis, remembered First Lieutenant Robert T. "Tim" Rohweller: "[He was] a very fine lieutenant—in fact, at one time he was my son's company commander—who was killed by a couple of Marines . . . Marines who were avoiding their duty and had been caught at it."[69]

First Lieutenant Tim Rohweller commanded Company K, 3d Battalion, 9th Marines. He was a "mustang," an officer with prior enlisted service, and had completed a previous Vietnam tour of duty as a sergeant in a reconnaissance battalion. Now, according to his battalion commander, Lieutenant Colonel Elliott R. Laine, Jr., he was one of the best company commanders in the battalion and was widely recognized as a superior leader.[70]

On 20 April 1969, shortly after the conclusion of Operation Dewey Canyon, Lieutenant Rohweller left his company's forward position for Quang Tri Combat Base to take care of company matters and to check on the "sick, lame, and lazy" in the rear. In the course of the day he confronted several Marines who thought to remain in Quang Tri, until forcefully told otherwise by Lieutenant Rohweller. The rear area Marines included Privates Reginald F. Smith and Jimmie Dudley, and Privates First Class Donald R. Egan and David Napier. All four were billeted in the transient hooch, a few yards from the company office. Throughout the day and into the evening the four, Smith particularly, nursed imagined wrongs. Their anger gradually escalated into a determination that the focus of their discontent, Lieutenant Rohweller, was responsible not only for their problems, but for the imagined unnecessary death of other Marines during combat operations, as well. Smith formed a plan to murder the lieutenant.[71]

Lieutenant Rohweller was aware of the danger. The company administrative chief later testified that in the early evening the lieutenant entered the company office and retrieved his pistol, chambered a round, and

MajGen Raymond G. Davis, right, was Commanding General, 3d Marine Division. Here, assisted by Col Robert H. Barrow, 9th Marines commander, he promotes his son, Miles Davis, to first lieutenant. Lt Davis was assigned to 1stLt Robert T. Rohweller's company.

stuck the .45 automatic, cocked and locked, into the waistband of his utility trousers. Later at the officers' club several officers noticed the pistol, but said nothing.

Late that night, Smith, Napier, Egan, and Dudley, joined by Private First Class Bobby R. Greenwood and Lance Corporal Hercules E. Brooker, sat before the transient hooch smoking marijuana and discussed Smith's plan. According to Brooker's later trial testimony, Smith said, "Lieutenant Rohweller and Lieutenant Newsome are in the rear, and when those m----------s go to the field, they're taking every-f---ing-body with them." Smith said of Lieutenant Rohweller that he, Smith, was "going to 'do' that m---------- as soon as he crashes" and discussed his plan to frag the lieutenant. Dudley told Smith that he was crazy and left the group.

At 0210 on 21 April those in the transient hooch were awakened by an explosion. An M26 fragmentation grenade had detonated in the neighboring company office directly under the cot upon which Lieutenant Rohweller slept and inflicted shrapnel wounds of the head, chest, and abdomen. As the battalion surgeon worked over the lieutenant, the first sergeant quickly held a company formation and determined that one man, Egan, was unaccounted for. Suspicion immediately centered on him and his companions.

While standing in the formation, Smith held his hand up to Dudley. Dudley testified that on Smith's index finger was a metal ring, the pin from a hand grenade. "I did that m--------- ," Smith confided. "He won't f--- with nobody else no more."

Transported to the hospital ship *Repose*, Lieutenant Rohweller died at 1120 that morning. Back at Quang Tri members of Company K were still being questioned. When word was passed that the lieutenant had died, Lance Corporal Hercules Brooker made a quick decision. As he testified in Napier's trial, "I grabbed my tape recorder and went into the company office and saw a lieutenant and just started blurting out names. I told him Smith threw the frag and that Napier held the door; also about Egan and Dudley."

Given the strong case against him, Private Smith and his counsel concluded that a guilty plea was unavoidable. Before Smith went to trial, however, his alleged accessory to murder, Napier, was first tried for having held the door open while Smith rolled the grenade into the hooch. The evidence against Napier appeared as overwhelming as that against Smith.

The general court-martial of Private First Class Napier convened on 11 August. He was 19 years old, a ninth grade dropout. Charged with conspiracy to commit murder and premeditated murder, he pleaded not guilty. His defense counsel was Captain Clark A. Halderson. The trial counsel and assistant trial counsel were Lieutenant Robert D. Zsalman, JAGC, U.S. Navy, and Captain Edward L. Murphy, respectively. The military judge was Lieutenant Colonel Henry "Hank" Hoppe.

The government's principal evidence against Napier was the testimony of Lance Corporal Brooker. He swore that immediately after the blast he had seen Smith and Napier run back into the transient hooch, and that later Napier had told him he had held the door open while Smith rolled the grenade into the office hooch.

Napier testified in his own behalf, swearing he had been asleep when the lieutenant had been assaulted. The defense vigorously attacked the credibility of Brooker. Brooker's platoon commander testified that Brooker "tends to fabricate fantasies" and he would believe Napier over Brooker. His platoon sergeant swore, "Brooker has the worst character for truth and veracity I have ever known." Another lance corporal testified: "I wouldn't trust him as far as I could throw him." In another vein, a corporal testified that, when the grenade went off, he had leapt from his rack and stepped on the accused, who, rather than holding any doors open, was asleep on the floor of the transient hooch. Another witness, Lance Corporal Wilkinson, testified almost in passing that Private First Class Greenwood had told him that he, Greenwood, had assisted in the killing.

In retrospect, spotlighting snippets of testimony and ignoring days of conflicting evidence, Napier's inno-

1stLt Robert T. "Tim" Rohweller, kneeling right, shown two weeks before his murder by fragging. The officers of the 3d Battalion, 9th Marines pose outside the officers' mess at Vandegrift Combat Base on 5 April 1969. The occasion was a farewell dinner for the regimental commander, Col Robert H. Barrow, standing second from right. 1stLt Rohweller's battalion commander was LtCol Elliott R. Laine, standing third from right. Others are Capt Thomas F. Hinkle, standing far right, and Capt Joe A. Arroyo, kneeling left.

Photo courtesy of Col Elliott R. Laine, USMC (Ret.)

cence seemed apparent. But at the moment of decision, after lengthy contradictory testimony, unresolved discrepancies, and emotional arguments, the members found Napier guilty of conspiracy to commit murder but not guilty of the murder itself. They sentenced him to reduction to private, loss of all pay and allowances, confinement at hard labor for 20 years, and a dishonorable discharge.

After Napier's conviction, but before Smith's trial, events took an unusual turn. Dudley, who was originally charged with the murder but not tried because of his withdrawal from the conspiracy, revealed that,

Lt Robert D. Zsalman, JAGC, USN, was a 3d Marine Division trial counsel. After learning of new evidence he joined the defense in seeking to overturn Napier's conviction of the murder of 1stLt Tim Rohweller.
Photo courtesy of Col Clarke C. Barnes, USMCR

while he had been in pretrial confinement with Smith, Smith repeatedly told him that it was Greenwood, not Napier, who had held the door open when he tossed the grenade under the lieutenant's cot.

Wilkinson, the witness from the Napier court, reaffirmed that Greenwood had admitted to him that he, Greenwood, had assisted Smith in the killing. Although awaiting trial himself, Smith made a sworn statement that Napier had nothing to do with the murder, and that it was Greenwood who had held the door for him. A polygraph examination indicated that Napier was not deceptive in his denial of guilt.

At his separate trial Private Smith pleaded guilty to premeditated murder and conspiracy to murder. With a record of two prior nonjudicial punishments in Vietnam for avoiding service in the field, Smith was sentenced to life imprisonment, later reduced to 40 years confinement.* Because he pleaded guilty, there is no detailed testimony or courtroom record of the details of the killing, although Smith repeated that it was Greenwood, not Napier, who had held the door open for him when he rolled the grenade into the hooch.

Before it was known that Smith would plead guilty, Egan had been granted immunity in return for his testimony in the Smith court-martial. But before Smith's trial, Egan was diagnosed as a schizoid personality and he was administratively discharged from the Marine Corps.[72]

What of Brooker's damning testimony against Napier? Under post-trial questioning he admitted he had been "guessing" when he identified Napier, because he had figured that Napier was guilty, and he thought that was what the government wanted him to say. Captain Clarke C. Barnes, a 3d Marine Division defense counsel, later wrote that "Brooker was a first class prevaricator—his lies kept him embroiled in the investigation and out of 'the bush.' I'm convinced that was his primary motivation."[73] After Napier's trial Brooker returned to the hospital where he was recovering from a self-administered injection of saliva into his knee, which rendered him unfit for combat duty. He received a medical discharge.

Upon learning of Greenwood's involvement, Napi-

---

*In May 1971, Smith was transferred from the Naval Disciplinary Command, Portsmouth, New Hampshire, to a federal prison. He died on 25 July 1982, while still in confinement, after having served almost 13 years. No record has been located that shows the cause of death. (NC & PB ltr to author, dtd 31Aug88; and Reginald F. Smith service record; both in war crimes folder, Marines and Military Law in Vietnam file, MCHC.)

er's counsel made a motion for a new trial based upon newly discovered evidence. After investigation of the allegations contained in the motion, the findings of guilty and the sentence of Napier's court were disapproved, and the charges against him were dismissed. He was released after having served two and a half months in confinement, returned to his former grade, given back pay and honorably discharged, because his enlistment had expired.

A year and three months after Lieutenant Rohweller's murder, Lance Corporal Bobby R. Greenwood's general court-martial convened at Camp Pendleton on 17 July 1970. Represented by civilian, as well as military counsel, he pleaded not guilty to conspiracy, murder, and perjury. The case was long and hard-fought, with an extraordinary number of defense motions to dismiss charges and for mistrial.

Private Smith was brought from confinement to testify that Greenwood had held the door for him. Wilkinson repeated Greenwood's admissions that he had been involved in the murder. Napier was called but, strangely, invoked his right to not incriminate himself and answered no questions.

Greenwood testified effectively in his own defense. He had an unblemished record with excellent conduct marks and was quite intelligent. The written testimony of 27 defense character witnesses was read to the members. That testimony was from, among others, Greenwood's high school principal, four teachers, two ministers, and a hometown police lieutenant.

The members were faced with the conflicting testimony of several questionable defense and government witnesses and the stipulated testimony of numerous citizens who had long familiarity with Greenwood. The members took 64 minutes to find Greenwood not guilty of all charges.

Real or Imagined: The 'Mere Gook' Rule

Three 3d Division Marines were charged with assault and rape. The evidence proved that while on patrol the three had entered a Vietnamese hut in which they found three women: grandmother, mother, and daughter. The grandmother and daughter fled when the criminal intentions of the three Marines became apparent. The mother was held at rifle point, while each raped her. The three were quickly found out and charged with assault with a deadly weapon and rape. The trial counsel, Captain David J. Cassady, elected to first try the Marine against whom the evidence was strongest. The accused did not deny intercourse, but raised consent as his defense. The members, in findings difficult to reconcile, found him guilty of assault, but not guilty of rape.

Based upon the results of the first court-martial, the charges against the two co-accuseds were dropped. If the strongest case of the three produced so negligible a result, the cost and effort involved in prosecuting the two weaker cases was not justified. Captain Cassady later spoke to the colonel who had been the senior member of the court-martial. Captain Cassady recalled the colonel saying: "Well, there's not much doubt what happened there, but we're not going to ruin the lives of these young Marines for some 'Vietnamese.'" That wasn't the word he used, Captain Cassady noted, "but that's essentially what he said. This became referred to—and there were other cases similar to that . . . . the mere gook theory. I've never forgotten that case."[74]

The term "gook" originally referred not to Vietnamese or orientals, but to Nicaraguans, its first use noted during the U.S. intervention in Nicaragua in 1912.[75] The term was a common one in Vietnam. In his book on the Vietnam war, Professor Guenter Lewy wrote: "Callousness toward the Vietnamese was . . . caused by the writings and pronouncements of many American journalists and politicians who . . . for years exaggerated the faults of the South Vietnamese . . . and gradually created an image of people not worth defending, if not altogether worthless."[76] Still, soldiers of all nations in every modern war, and probably in ancient conflicts as well, have ascribed base racial or cultural characteristics to peoples and cultures they don't understand, particularly when the enemy people or culture was of a differing race or color.

Professor Lewy continued: "acceptance of the 'mere-gook' rule has probably been exaggerated. For each misdeed and instance of mistrust and hostility, unbiased observers in Vietnam could see examples of friendship and generosity."[77] As far as courts-martial were concerned, the record demonstrates that Professor Lewy is correct: acceptance of the "mere gook" rule has been exaggerated.

Marine Corps judge advocates were aware of the asserted existence of the "mere gook" rule, and if it might aid the defense of their client, were not above considering its effect. An FLC defense counsel recalled a 1969 murder case in which the accused had purposely thrown a heavy pipe from the rear of a moving truck at a column of South Vietnamese soldiers. He killed the soldier he hit. At the outset of the Marine's court-martial the defense counsel requested that enlisted men be included on the panel of members, admitting:

> My theory was that enlisted Marines (knowing I would get E-9's [master gunnery sergeants and sergeants major] and above) who had fought in the Pacific during World War II, Korea and now, Vietnam, would not be particularly disturbed about the death of another "gook." In interviewing members of the court following the trial, my hypothesis proved correct.

The accused was convicted only of a lesser offense and sentenced to six months confinement, later reduced to a shorter period after the enlisted members of the court and one of the officers joined in a petition for clemency.[78]

Individual anomalies like the foregoing case can always be found, but did the usual case exhibit a callousness toward the Vietnamese victim?* During the war, 27 Marines were convicted by courts-martial of murdering South Vietnamese non-combatants.**[79] In several of those cases there were multiple victims or associated crimes, such as rape. Twenty-five of the 27 received, among other punishments, dishonorable discharges; the other two received bad conduct discharges. In 15 of the 27 convictions, the sentence imposed by the trial court included confinement at hard labor for life; three other cases included confinement for 20, 30, and 50 years. Only in seven of the cases was the imposed confinement less than 10 years.[80] Case comparisons are suspect, but the range of sentences meted out by courts-martial was comparable, at least, with those that might be anticipated in a civilian jurisdiction. At the trial level, Captain Cassady's case notwithstanding, Marine Corps court members apparently did not consider the Vietnamese to be beneath justice.

Acquittals can be as revealing as sentences imposed, because acquittals may indicate the reluctance of a court to convict, let alone sentence an accused. Sixteen Marines, or 37 percent of those tried for the murder of Vietnamese noncombatants, were acquitted or had their charges judicially dismissed.[81] In United States District Courts in 1969, 33 percent of the homicide cases that went to trial resulted in acquittal or dismissal, a rate essentially the same as that found in Marine Corps courts.[82]

As in civilian jurisdictions, however, significant reductions in the confinement portions of sentences resulted from appellate review and parole and clemency action. How did the 27 Marines convicted of murdering Vietnamese noncombatants fare? After completion of clemency action only two of the 27 court-martial sentences remained in excess of 10 years: 12 and 19 years.*** Seventeen of the other sentences were reduced to less than five years confinement. Charges were dismissed in two instances.[83] The average time served by the 27 convicted murders was less than four years.[84]

The "mere gook" rule may have existed in isolated instances at the trial level, employed in either the findings or sentencing phases of courts-martial, but statistical evidence refutes any assertion that such a racist, reprehensible mind-set had any recurring effect in homicide cases. Similar statistics are available for other major felonies and reflect a like conclusion. But notable reductions in sentences were seen at the appellate level, followed by further abatement as a result of clemency and/or parole action.**** Professor Lewy suggests that those reductions, too, were consistent with civilian experience:

> It is well known that civilian parole boards often act as much in response to political pressures and the currents of public opinion as on the basis of the severity of the crime or the conduct of the prisoners, and the situation was probably no different in the case of servicemen convicted of atrocities or war crimes in Vietnam. In short, in order to account for light sentences and early release on parole for such men there is no need for the "mere-gook" hypothesis.[85]

As in any codal or statutory scheme, the UCMJ raised such safeguards as were possible against courtroom injustices, but there is no litmus test to uncover hidden ignorance and bigotry.

---

*In *U.S. v. PltSgt Roy E. Bumgarner*, U.S. Army (43 CMR 559, ACMR, 1970), the accused, charged with premeditated murder, admitted killing three Vietnamese male noncombatants. He argued the killings were justifiable as having been committed in the performance of duty during a combat mission. Found guilty of the lesser included offense of unpremeditated murder in all three instances, the members sentenced him to reduction in rank to private, and forfeitures of $97 per month for 24 months. No confinement was imposed. At the appellate level error was found and the sentence was reduced to reduction to private and forfeiture of $97 dollars per month for six months. Pvt Bumgarner was then reenlisted.

**Ninety-five Army personnel were similarly convicted. (Lewy, *America in Vietnam*, p. 325.)

***"Good time," the credit received for good behavior while in confinement, potentially reduced longer sentences by as much as a third. If a prisoner was confined at the United States Disciplinary Barracks, Fort Leavenworth, Kansas, or the Disciplinary Command, Portsmouth, New Hampshire, "extra abatement" was sometimes available, in addition to good time. So, although the Corrections Manual indicated the maximum "good time" applicable in sentences of 10 years or more was 10 days per month, in fact, if an extra abatement waiver was in effect, a prisoner could receive up to 17 days credit per month beyond time actually served, effectively reducing a sentence by 57 percent even before clemency or parole action was considered. The decision to issue an extra abatement waiver for a certain period of time rested with the Commandants of the Disciplinary Barracks and Disciplinary Command.

****See Appendices E and F.

On the morning of 1 March 1969 an eight-man Marine ambush was discovered by three Vietnamese girls, aged about 13, 17, and 19, and a Vietnamese boy, about 11. The four shouted their discovery to those in the nearby village who were being observed by the ambush. Seized by the Marines, the four were bound, gagged, and led away by Corporal Ronald J. Reese and Lance Corporal Stephen D. Crider.[86] Minutes later, the four Vietnamese were seen, apparently dead, in a small bunker. The Marines tossed a fragmentation grenade into the bunker, which then collapsed the damaged structure atop the bodies. Those responsible were apprehended and tried. Reese was convicted of four specifications of murder. His sentence included confinement at hard labor for life and a dishonorable discharge.

Crider, too, was convicted of four specifications of murder and received a like sentence, except that no discharge was imposed. Moreover, all eight of the members of Crider's court, including two colonels, joined in a petition for clemency. In it they told the convening authority that, given the military judge's instructions, they felt compelled to impose confinement for life, but they urged that all confinement in excess of three years be disapproved. A telling phrase in the petition read that "the fact of his apprehension, confinement, and trial are sufficient in themselves to satisfy the requirements of the Vietnamese society."

The military judge again was Lieutenant Colonel Hank Hoppe. He received the members' petition with its recommendation of three years confinement and, because the sentence included no discharge, a return to duty. Incredulous, he asked the members, on the record, if they had considered imposition of a discharge? He was assured they had, but they felt that Crider should be returned to duty as a Marine after serving his confinement for the murder of four children. Colonel Hoppe described what followed:

> I adjourned the court, the court reporter shut off his machine, at which time I told the members of the court that they had, in my opinion, just prostituted 190-odd years of Marine Corps history . . . . The next day [I] was advised that the commanding general [the convening authority in the case] wanted to see me. You are aware, of course, that commanding generals have no control over the judges . . . . The general inquired if I had indeed made those remarks to officers who were my seniors? I assured him that I had, and he said, "Thank you very much. Now I don't have to do so."[87]

At the appellate level Crider's confinement was reduced to three years. Because his co-actor's confine-

General court-martial military judge, Col Henry Hoppe III, seen returned from Vietnam. "I told the members of the court that they had, in my opinion, just prostituted 190-odd years of Marine Corps history."

ment was cut, Reese's confinement for life also was reduced to three years.

Perspective

Not only was the 1969 court-martial rate higher than ever before, but the nature of the offenses had changed. Currency manipulation, black marketeering, destruction of government property, even negligent homicide, although still frequent enough, were no longer the daily fare of the Marine Corps judge advocate. Now the lawyers were coping with a major breakdown in discipline and a disrespect for authority in general, as evidenced by the most serious kinds of offenses: murders and aggravated assaults in numbers that only three years previously would have been considered incredible. The sale and use of marijuana was so prevalent that it overloaded the general court-martial process and often did not even result in a special court-martial. The brig was so filled with hardened individuals that, even when a court-martial ended in a sentence to confinement, commanders declined to send first-time offenders to its confines. Racial incidents, which had been a frequent occurrence, now sometimes evolved into deadly encounters in which the participants armed themselves with weapons intended for combat with the enemy. At FLC, to prevent further fraggings, the Maintenance Battalion enlisted men's club was lit by high-powered search lights and armed sentries patrolled its perimeter.[88]

With all this, however, it should not be forgotten that the far greater number of Marines served honorably and bravely. Relatively few became involved in the military justice process. Nevertheless, Marine Corps judge advocates who dealt with the criminals on a daily basis might have agreed with Colonel Robert D. Heinl when he wrote:

> By every conceivable indicator, our army that now remains in Vietnam is in a state approaching collapse . . . . Murdering their officers and noncommissioned officers, drug-ridden, and dispirited . . . buffeted from without and within by social turbulence . . . race war . . . and common crime . . . . Often reviled by the public, the uniformed services today are places of agony for the loyal, silent professionals who doggedly hang on and try to keep the ship afloat.[89]

Discipline had fallen into disarray, and it would be a long time recovering. During this period some Marine judge advocates assumed from their experience that 1969 was representative of caseloads and case complexion. They did not realize that they were struggling through the Marine Corps' disciplinary nadir.

CHAPTER 7
1969: Military Justice Tested

III MAF: No Longer Two Hats — 1st Marine Division: The Law Center Concept
3d Marine Division: More Combat, Fewer Courts — From a Lawyer's Case File: Murder on Stage
1st Marine Aircraft Wing: Looking For Action — Force Logistic Command: Approaching Breakdown
Trying Cases — Exits: Marine Corps Draw Downs — Perspective

At the outset of 1969 III MAF estimated there were 90,000 enemy troops in the I Corps tactical area of responsibility or poised on its borders. Along the DMZ the 3d Marine Division enjoyed a combat lull, until it began Operation Dewey Canyon, south of Khe Sanh. By the time that operation ended in mid-March, more than 1,600 of the enemy had been killed and 1,461 weapons captured. The 1st Marine Division guarded the approaches to Da Nang, while its Operation Taylor Common continued. The 1st Marine Aircraft Wing was preparing to redeploy several squadrons to Iwakuni, Japan, and to Okinawa.[1]

By 1969 the assignment of junior lawyers to Vietnam, lieutenants and captains, was controlled by the Staff Legal Officer (SLO) of Headquarters, Fleet Marine Force, Pacific (FMFPac), in Hawaii. In 1969 the SLO was Colonel Robert C. "Curly" Lehnert, who was assisted by his deputy, Major William H. J. Tiernan. Both officers had led the 1st Marine Aircraft Wing's Da Nang legal office in 1968. Headquarters Marine Corps forwarded to FMFPac the names of captain and lieutenant lawyers to be transferred to Vietnam, Okinawa, and Japan. At FMFPac, the SJA allocated the lawyers, by name, to the various commands.[2] Assignment of attorney majors, lieutenant colonels, and colonels continued to be controlled by Headquarters Marine Corps. About 90 Marine Corps judge advocates were in Vietnam at any given time in 1969. By comparison, the U.S. Army had 135 lawyers in Vietnam during the same period.[3]

III MAF: No Longer Two Hats

On 26 March 1969 Lieutenant General Herman Nickerson, Jr., succeeded Lieutenant General Cushman as Commanding General, III MAF.[4] Colonel Duane L. Faw, who had been double-hatted as III MAF Deputy Chief of Staff and MAF Headquarters Staff Legal Officer, had been succeeded by Colonel Paul W. Seabaugh in August 1968. Colonel Seabaugh, holder of the Bronze Star Medal for service in Korea, was assisted by Captain G. Ward Beaudry, followed by Captain Stanton M. Cole, and later Captain Emilic V. Belluomini, Jr. Although there were few court-martial cases in the Headquarters—never more than two at a time during this period—Colonel Seabaugh acted solely as the SLO/SJA.[5] III MAF still did not have the authority to convene courts-martial, and as in the early months of the war military justice activity in the legal office was slow. But the SLO/SJA billet was a busy one. Hundreds of "JAG Manual" personal property loss investigations were processed by III MAF "legal," for example. Each time a supply dump or depot was rocketed or burned, Marines who lost personal gear to damage caused by the enemy shelling submitted claims for reimbursement for their lost belongings. Legal assistance matters arising in the Headquarters were continually dealt with, as well. To keep the III MAF brig population manageable, the SLO/SJA coordinated shipment of prisoners out of Vietnam to other brigs.[6] There was more than enough work to keep III MAF Headquarters lawyers occupied.

On 27 April Ammunition Supply Point No. 1, not far from III MAF Headquarters, caught fire when burning trash started a grass fire which, in turn, ignited stored munitions. The resulting explosions destroyed 38,000 tons of ammunition and 20,000 drums of fuel. The fire damaged the nearby III MAF brig to the extent that the prisoners were moved to temporary locations at Camp Books, Red Beach, and the Naval Supply Activity Hospital prison ward.[7]

In August 1969 Colonel Marion G. Truesdale, previously Colonel Charles B. Sevier's successor as Director of the Judge Advocate Division at Headquarters Marine Corps, relieved Colonel Seabaugh. In World War II Colonel Truesdale had been an infantryman, commanding a machine gun platoon on Peleliu under Lieutenant Colonel Lewis B. "Chesty" Puller. Colonel Truesdale had also been in combat on Okinawa. At III MAF Headquarters, in addition to his duties as SJA, he acted as Chief of Staff whenever the actual Chief was absent.[8]

1st Marine Division: The Law Center Concept

The enemy's 1969 Tet Offensive, although only a shadow of the prior year's offensive, struck Da Nang

1969: MILITARY JUSTICE TESTED

Photo courtesy of Col Marion G. Truesdale, USMC (Ret.)

In August 1969 Col Marion G. Truesdale, left, being sworn as a military judge, relieved Col Paul W. Seabaugh, right, as SJA of Headquarters, III MAF.

on 23 February. The enemy suffered heavy losses when his sapper attacks on the 1st Marine Division's command post on Hill 327 were beaten back, largely by reaction companies and elements of the 7th Marines.[9] One of the reaction companies was commanded by a judge advocate, Captain Francis J. Kaveney. The executive officer (second in command) of another heavily engaged reaction company was Captain W. Hays Parks, chief trial counsel for the 1st Division. Several other judge advocates were involved in the defense of the command post as commanders of reaction platoons, as well.

In August 1968 Colonel Jack E. Hanthorn replaced Colonel Clyde Mann as Division SJA. Colonel Hanthorn was in combat on Roi-Namur, Saipan, Tinian, and Iwo Jima in World War II and fought in Korea. Several times he had commanded infantry companies and briefly in 1965 had commanded the 1st Marine Brigade.[10] In mid-year Lieutenant Colonel Robert M. Lucy, who would be promoted to colonel two months after his arrival in Vietnam, succeeded Colonel Hanthorn. While virtually all of the senior legal officers early in the Vietnam conflict had been in combat in World War II, now the in-coming SJAs, like Colonel Lucy, had not. Colonel Lucy, a 1947 graduate of the U.S. Naval Academy, had been an infantry officer in the Korean War and participated in the Inchon landing as a weapons company commander, and was awarded the Bronze Star Medal.[11]

Living conditions at 1st Marine Division Headquarters remained comfortable. The SJA shared his SEAhut with one other colonel and dined in the commanding general's mess each evening. He enjoyed luxury unsuspected by less senior Marines.[12] Captains and lieutenants were billeted six to a SEAhut, but their hooches were larger than the colonel's and usually included a television set and a small, two-cubic-foot refrigerator, which passed from occupant to occupant, as tours of duty were completed. The enlisted legal Marines had quarters identical to the officers, usually including refrigerators and television sets. Like Marines at the Da Nang Airbase, lawyers on Hill 327 had learned to live with the rocket attacks on Da Nang.

Personnel of the Office of the SJA, 1st Marine Division, shown on Hill 327 in 1969. Seated officers are, from left, Capt Allen E. Falk; Capt George G. Bashian, Jr.; Capt Martin G. McGuinn, Jr.; LtCol William R. Eleazer; SJA Col Robert M. Lucy; Deputy SJA LtCol James P. King; Capt Arthur W. Tifford; legal admin officer, CWO4 Maynard K. Baird; Capt Franz P. Jevne; and Capt John D. Moats. The legal chief, MSgt Atkins, stands at right.

Photo courtesy of Col William R. Eleazer, USMC (Ret.)

The III MAF brig, shown in 1969. The brig buildings, right center, adjoin the POW compound, which still housed 19 North Vietnamese sailors, the compound's only occupants during the war. Many buildings show the effects of the explosion of Ammunition Supply Point 1 shortly before this photograph was taken. The top of one guard tower is destroyed.

Captain Daniel H. LeGear, Jr., a 1st Marine Division defense counsel recalled: "We did have sandbag bunkers for such attacks, but after the first few attacks they were rarely used. We would either sleep through them or awake and watch the action down around the airfield."[13]

The 1st Division SJA's manning level was 23 judge advocates, 1 legal administration officer, and 38 enlisted men.[14] During 1969 the actual number of lawyers varied from 18 to 33, with the average being somewhere between 20 and 25. The quality of the officer lawyers was termed "excellent" by the SJA, although three out of four arriving lawyers came straight from Naval Justice School (now expanded from 7 to 10 weeks in length) and had never tried a case before.[15] "That's a very bad policy," Colonel Lucy said. "We're in the big leagues, now." The return to Vietnam of seasoned officers such as Lieutenant Colonel James P. King, on his second Vietnam tour, was an important addition to office effectiveness.

One of those assigned to the 1st Marine Division's SJA office was 1st Lieutenant James M. Schermerhorn, a law school graduate who had not yet passed a bar examination. Because he was not a member of any state's bar, he could not be designated a judge advocate and could not be a defense counsel. He could be employed as a nonlawyer trial counsel (prosecutor). Any mistake he might make would affect the government rather than the accused. For six months before joining the SJA's office, Lieutenant Schermerhorn had been a platoon commander with the 7th Marines, where he served with distinction and was awarded the Silver Star and Navy Commendation Medals for combat bravery.[16]

The caseload in the 1st Division remained low, although its nature had changed. Each judge advocate carried about one general court-martial and eight to 10 specials.[17] The overall decline in discipline was bringing more significant cases. "Sixty percent of all our crimes are crimes of violence—and they're serious," Colonel Lucy reported.[18] The trial of several murder cases in a single month was no longer unusual. During 1969 1st Division personnel were charged with 13 murders, 32 aggravated assaults, 41 simple assaults, 2 rapes, and 490 marijuana/narcotics offenses.[19]

By 1969 those convicted and sent to the brig were usually such poor quality personnel that commanders hesitated to allow any but their worst men to be incarcerated there. They believed that conditions in the brig offered no hope of rehabilitation. As First Lieutenant Warren S. Mathey, FLSG-A's group legal officer, reported:

> Any time we have a man that goes before a special court that we feel is a good man and has learned his lesson from a court alone, we do not confine him at the brig .... Borderline cases that received six months from a court, six

months confinement, we've kept them out of the brig .... If they went to the brig it'd have a much greater ill-effect on them.[20]

Lieutenant Mathey also noted that the brig was not even considered for pretrial confinement of accused Marines. Instead, they were held for up to 10 days in CONEX boxes—metal storage containers about eight feet by ten feet and about six feet tall. Not as harsh as their description implies, CONEX boxes were often partially buried and sandbagged, making them fairly secure from enemy fire and insulated, to a degree, from weather extremes.[21]

The same inadequacies that plagued the legal effort in the past remained problems. Colonel Lucy called the recording equipment "still a miserable situation," noting that, even though IBM equipment had largely replaced the Grey recorders, repairs were available only in Saigon. That required an officer or NCO to escort the gear there and back to ensure it was not lost or forgotten. Mail, Colonel Lucy said, just took too long. The remaining Greys still had to go to Japan for repair, which took three to four months if sent by mail. Finally, the colonel authorized purchase of four Sony tape recorders from the PX for the use of court reporters.

Equally vexing was court reporter proficiency. Colonel Lucy noted that, while there were enough of them, "the quality of court reporters that we've been getting has been terrible." Most required on-the-job training, risking the loss of a case because of a significant error in recording or transcribing the record of trial.[22] Each year since the beginning of the war SLOs and now SJAs had discovered anew the same reporter inadequacies. Each had passed word of those inadequacies to higher authority, yet the deficiency continued unresolved. Without priority in assignment of MOS, the legal community was too often left with enlisted personnel who had been shunted from infantry training because of a lack of aptitude or ability in that nontechnical field. While many junior legal clerks were stellar Marines and impressive workers, too often they were forced to carry the workload for their less able peers.

Second lieutenant John R. "Rusty" Taylor, Jr., and his wife Priscilla were married shortly before he departed for Vietnam and the office of the 1st Marine Divi-

Rather than send Marines to the III MAF brig, pretrial confinement was sometimes served in CONEX boxes like the one at left. This CONEX box was part of a mail facility.
Photo courtesy of LtCol David Douglas Duncan, USMCR (Ret.)

sion's SJA. Priscilla obtained a 90-day visa allowing her to enter Vietnam on the strength of promised employment in Saigon with an American doctor who was a family friend. Three weeks after her husband's departure Priscilla flew to Saigon where she and Rusty had assumed he would be stationed. Lieutenant Taylor had managed to get word to her prospective employer of his actual location and Priscilla took an Air Vietnam commercial flight to Da Nang. Unaware of Priscilla's arrival, Lieutenant Taylor did not meet her at the airbase, which also serviced the country's few civilian aircraft. An American civilian worker took Priscilla in tow and delivered her to the 1st Marine Division compound and her husband's office.

Lieutenant Taylor had arranged for Priscilla to be quartered in Da Nang in the back room of the office of an American Catholic priest. She found employment at the Da Nang USO as a counter girl with a grand salary of 50 cents per day. Although Lieutenant Taylor was required to be "inside the wire" each night, he and Priscilla met in Da Nang with some regularity over the next month and a half. Inevitably the SJA, Colonel Lucy, learned of her presence. When he did he ordered Lieutenant Taylor to immediately see to her departure, upon pain of his being sent to the farthest of the division's outposts. Already concerned for her safety in the frequent rocket attacks on Da Nang, Lieutenant Taylor bid Priscilla goodbye and she returned to the United States without having been paid by the USO. All concerned heaved a sigh of relief, including the Catholic priest who found it difficult to explain to his flock his relationship with the woman who slept in the back of his office.[23]

With implementation of the Military Justice Act of 1968, the law center concept became a practical alternative to prior methods of managing and processing cases. All legal assets and personnel were consolidated in the various SJAs' offices. No longer were reporters assigned to the separate infantry battalions and aircraft groups. Line officers were no longer trial and defense counsels, and charge sheets were no longer drafted by infantry administrative clerks. The staff judge advocate's office embraced the entire process. Now, a field command sent an offense report to the SJA's office, where charges were drafted, counsels assigned, and a tentative trial date set. At trial a legal clerk assigned to the SJA's office recorded the trial and afterward made a typed copy of the record. An initial review was prepared in the review "shop" of the SJA's office and forwarded to the convening authority for approval. Once approved, the case continued up the appellate chain, if appropriate. For the first time the SJA's office had the capacity to act as a full-service legal center.

The Navy had been first to employ the law center approach in 1966.* Initially calling it the County Courthouse System, Colonel Lucy found the law center concept an efficient method which relieved field commanders of a heavy burden. As he pointed out, "if we can do it in combat, we can do it anywhere."[24]

Law centers required a knowledgeable manager to ensure their smooth functioning; someone, akin to a civilian office manager, not concerned with trial preparation, who could track case progress and ensure proper documentation, format, and timeliness from original complaint to conviction or release. Those managers were the Marine Corps' legal administrative officers. In 1967 a one-year pilot program had been initiated at Camp Pendleton to test the practicality of "legal admin" officers, and it proved a major success. As a result such officers were assigned to all Marine Corps legal offices. Legal admin officers were usually former enlisted legal clerks or reporters, appointed as warrant officers and given a general administrative officer's MOS. Later, they would have a separate MOS designating them as legal administration specialists. Colonel Lucy wrote to Brigadier General Faw, then the Director of the Judge Advocate Division at Headquarters Marine Corps that "I think this warrant officer billet of administrative officer is absolutely essential . . . . Chief Warrant Officer Baird [the 1st Marine Division's incumbent] is an outstanding addition to this office."[25]

Chief Warrant Officer 4 Maynard K. "Sonny" Baird, the first Marine to be designated a legal admin officer by military occupational specialty (MOS), was also the first to arrive in Vietnam. ("Gunner" Baird had briefly been in Soc Trang, Vietnam, in 1962 with Shufly personnel.** He had been the station adjutant and legal officer at the Marine Corps Air Station, Fute-

---

*In 1965 a Secretary of the Navy task force recommended formation of Navy legal services offices. The pilot office was established at Norfolk, Virginia, in 1966. When that proved successful a second was formed in San Diego, California, with others soon following. By 1970 the Navy had 30 operational law centers worldwide. (U.S. Court of Military Appeals, *Annual Report of the U.S. Court of Military Appeals & the Judge Advocates General of the Armed Forces & the General Counsel of the Department of the Treasury, For the Period January 1–December 31, 1966*; and [same title] *For the Period January 1–December 31, 1969* [Washington: GPO, 1966 and 1969, respectively], pp. 26 and 28, respectively.)

**See Chapter 1.

At Quang Tri, 3d Marine Division legal personnel take time out. Capt Clarke C. Barnes, center, spikes the ball past Cpl J. R. Hartman. Capt David J. Cassady, left, looks on.

ma, Okinawa, at the time.)[26] He was invaluable in establishing and refining the law center concept to which Marine Corps SJAs were moving, while also serving as the 1st Marine Division's claims officer and review officer. For his work in Vietnam he later received the Bronze Star Medal.[27] The law center concept became the model employed throughout the Corps for the rest of the war and afterward.

3d Marine Division: More Combat, Fewer Courts

Operations Kentucky, Dewey Canyon, and Virginia Ridge, three of the division's most costly but successful 1969 operations, continued through February, March, and July, respectively.[28] The office of the 3d Marine Division's SJA remained at Quang Tri Combat Base with the division headquarters (rear). After four months as the division chief of staff, Colonel Joseph R. "Mo" Motelewski returned to legal duty as the division SJA. The number of judge advocates in the 3d Division varied throughout the year from 20 to 30.[29]

Construction of an air conditioned courtroom was completed in April. Styrofoam, used in packing artillery fuses, was seldom encountered in volume but Lieutenant Colonel Rollin Q. Blakeslee, the deputy SJA, managed to have an entire planeload of it delivered to the SJA's office. No one was sure what to do with it but eventually the lawyers decided that it would make great insulation for the courtroom, which is how it was finally employed.[30]

In September Lieutenant Colonel Benjamin B. Ferrell became the division SJA, succeeding Colonel Motelewski, who later received the Legion of Merit for his performance of duty as chief of staff and SJA. Lieutenant Colonel Ferrell would later oversee the 3d Marine Division lawyers as they withdrew from Vietnam, together with the rest of the division and would, himself, receive the Legion of Merit. But for the two months his office was in Vietnam, his difficulties as SJA were no different than his predecessors': transportation, court reporters, and equipment. As Lieutenant Colonel Ferrell noted: "The most frustrating aspect . . . was the continual breakdown of recording equipment. No system we tried could be relied on to function for long in the dusty or rainy weather of Vietnam."[31]

The most heavily engaged division in III MAF, the 3d Marine Division also had the fewest court-martial offenses.[32] Although more cases were awaiting trial than ever before, the division was still relatively untouched by the breakdown of discipline, which affected most rear area units. At any given time a 3d Marine Division judge advocate's caseload was around two or three general courts-martial, 20 to 30 specials, and five or six admin discharge cases.[33] While the numbers were as high as in the 1st Marine Division, the offenses tended to be less serious.

Interestingly, infantry officers and air observers who had completed roughly 10 months of their 12-month tours in Vietnam with good combat records were sometimes assigned to be standing court-martial members until their tours of duty ended. Those officers, captains and lieutenants, were temporarily quartered in the judge advocate's SEAhuts. The lawyers enjoyed the company of the combat veterans, and the visiting officers enjoyed the more relaxed assignment at Quang Tri.[34] The periodic rocket attacks were minor matters to them. As Captain Clarke C. Barnes, a 3d Marine Division attorney, recalled, "a rocket attack was considered no big deal. It was just another inconvenience that would pass."[35] The question of court members fraternizing with and actually living with the lawyers who tried the cases in which they sat as members, never arose.

From a Lawyer's Case File: Murder on Stage

On 20 July 1969 a USO show was in progress in the Staff and Officers' Club at the 1st Force Reconnaissance Company's base camp. Miss Catherine Anne Warnes, singer for the Australian musical group, "Sweethearts on Parade," stepped back from the microphone after singing the show's final song, just as there was a muffled shot. The 20-year old Australian fell to the floor, dead.[36]

A month before, during the night of 21-22 June,

Department of Defense Photo (USMC) 016248573
LtCol Benjamin B. Ferrell, shown as a colonel, was SJA of the 3d Marine Division. Under his leadership the division's judge advocates left Quang Tri for Okinawa.

The 3d Marine Division courtroom at Quang Tri, Vietnam, center, was a styrofoam insulated SEAhut. It stands among other structures housing division headquarters elements.
Photo courtesy of Col Paul F. Henderson, USMC (Ret.)

Miss Catherine Ann Warnes was a USO performer in Vietnam. She was shot and killed as she sang in the 1st Reconnaissance Battalion's staff and officers' club.

a .22-caliber Hi-Standard semiautomatic pistol had been stolen from the desk of the 1st Force Reconnaissance Company operations office. The pistol had a silencer permanently affixed to its muzzle. According to later testimony, on the afternoon of Miss Warnes' murder Corporal Robert E. Stockham and Lance Corporal Ronald B. Prohaska were examining a handgun said to belong to Stockham. They fired a round into the deck of their hooch to test the pistol's functioning. The handgun was a discolored, rust pitted, .22-caliber Hi-Standard semiautomatic, without a magazine or grips. It had a nonremovable silencer. Because the slide return spring was broken, each round had to be individually inserted into the chamber, and the slide manually pushed forward into the locked position. Sergeant James W. Killen, a 28-year-old reconnaissance scout and the battalion operations NCO, entered Stockham's and Prohaska's hooch.* Sergeant Killen, often referred to as "Pappy" because of his relatively older age, held the Purple Heart and the Viet-

---

*1st Force Reconnaissance Company, of which Killen was a member, was attached to the 1st Reconnaissance Battalion, thus he could be assigned to the battalion staff although not a member of the battalion.

namese Cross of Gallantry and had been on numerous combat operations. At his request he was loaned the pistol and several rounds of ammunition before he left. Killen later testified that he took it to shoot feral dogs that were in the area, and finding none, he claimed he returned the weapon within a few minutes. Before he left, Killen, Stockham, and Prohaska discussed how a person could kill without discovery by using a silenced weapon.

By 2100 the Staff and Officers' Club was filled with Marines anxious to hear the band and the attractive singer in the pink miniskirt. The 1st Force Reconnaissance Company commander, Major Roger E. Simmons, sat about eight feet from the stage. At the nearby Enlisted Mens' Club Sergeant Killen drank 11 to 12 beers and then left at around 2120. Later investigation revealed that the killer had fired one .22-caliber round from behind a jeep that was parked 35 yards from the Staff and Officers' club. The bullet cut through the club's screen wall, entered Miss Warnes' left side, pierced her aorta, and exited her right side, killing her almost instantly.

Was Major Simmons the intended target? Newspapers speculated that Miss Warnes had stepped into the line of fire ("Was Girl's Killer Gunning for Maj?" read one headline), but Major Simmons thought not.[37] It was not an issue at trial, although a straight line could be drawn from the major's position to Miss Warnes to the jeep from behind which the fatal round was fired.

At Sergeant Killen's court-martial, Lance Corporal Prohaska testified that Killen had entered his, Prohaska's, hooch just after the incident, while the camp was still searching for the presumed enemy sniper. Suspicious, Prohaska, according to his testimony, asked Killen, "Why in the hell did you do something like that for?" Killen replied, "She was just winged." Asked where the gun was, Killen replied it was "taken care of." Those statements were the only evidence linking Killen to the murder. The pistol, later found in a ditch, revealed no fingerprints and there were no witnesses.

The trial counsel, Captain John D. Moats, and assistant counsel, Captain John A. Milici, used the testimony of Stockham and Prohaska to prove Killen's possession of the murder weapon near the time of the killing. They also used his incriminating statements shortly after the event. Defense counsels Captains Daniel H. LeGear and Theodore J. Padden were unable to shake their accounts. Sergeant Killen testified

The 1st Reconnaissance Battalion's thatch-roofed staff and officers' club was located near Da Nang, Vietnam. Miss Catherine Warnes was standing in the center of the cleared area when she was killed by a .22-caliber bullet that passed through the screening at left.

A .22-caliber Hi Standard semiautomatic pistol with a silencer permanently affixed. Although rusted and without grips, on 20 July 1969 this weapon killed Miss Warnes.

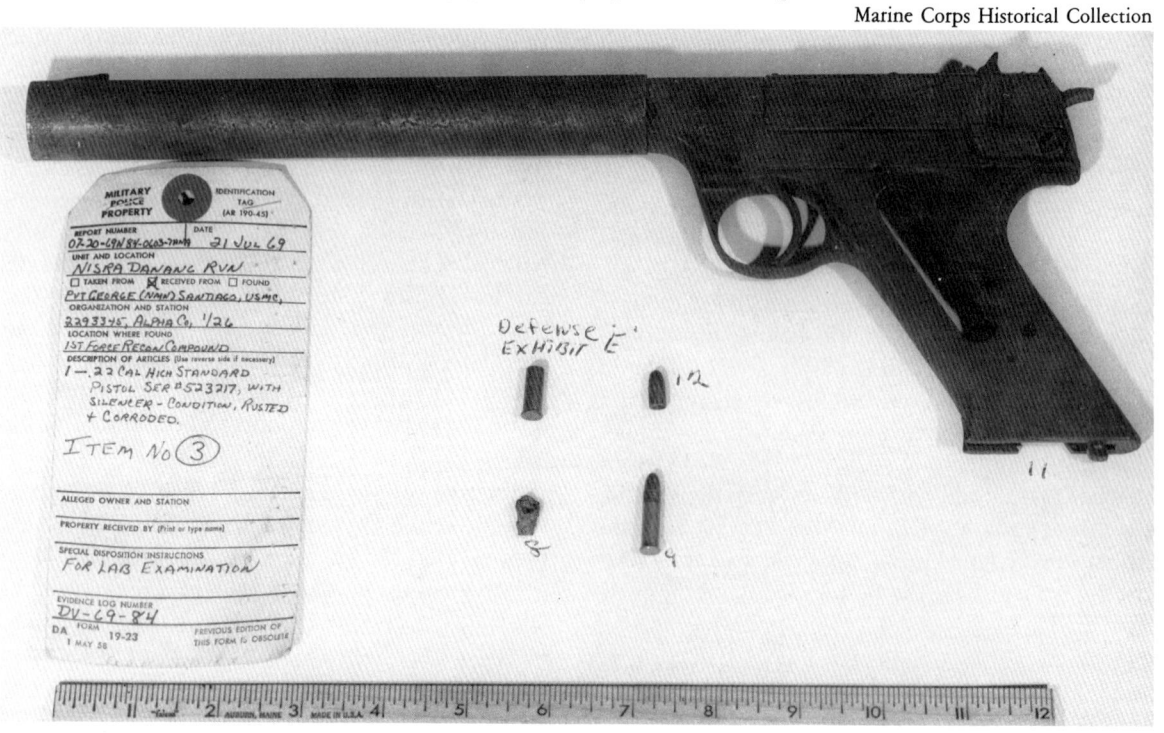

The headline read: "Was Girl's Killer Gunning for Maj?" Maj Roger E. Simmons, Sgt James W. Killen's company commander, points to the hole in the screening made by the bullet that killed Miss Warnes.

in his own defense that he had handled the murder weapon earlier on the day of the murder, that he had been intoxicated, and that he had left the Enlisted Club at about the time of the murder. He denied any knowledge of the killing itself. A motive for the killing was never established.

On 29 October 1969 the court members found Sergeant Killen guilty of unpremeditated murder and sentenced him to 20 years confinement at hard labor, loss of all pay and allowances, reduction to private, and a dishonorable discharge.

The day after the court-martial, the trial counsel mentioned to Captain LeGear, the defense counsel, that Stockham and Prohaska had at one point been offered grants of immunity in return for their testimony, but that ultimately, the immunity grants had not been required. That was the first the defense had heard of an immunity offer, and Captains Dan LeGear and Ted Padden immediately recognized an issue of importance to the defense. (If a witness testifies under a grant of immunity, the members must be advised of that fact so they may evaluate the credibility of the testimony in light of the immunization.) In this case, because Stockham and Prohaska, the closest of friends, had themselves been initial suspects and because the two admitted they had lied in their initial sworn statements to investigators to avoid incriminating themselves or each other, immunity took on an even greater import. According to affidavits submitted later, Stockham and Prohaska had been told that immunity was "available." Prohaska was shown a copy of a letter from the SJA to the Naval Investigative Service assuring the latter that immunity would be granted, "if necessary." The trial counsel also orally assured Prohaska that immunity was obtainable. Shortly thereafter, Stockham and Prohaska both revised their original statements and implicated Killen, in the mistaken belief that they enjoyed full immunity. The case proceeded to trial on the basis of the revised statements.

A year and a half later, the Navy Court of Military Review, in a unanimous opinion, held that "unquestionably, the testimony of Stockham and Prohaska was induced, in part at least, by the offers of immunity. To what extent their testimony might have been rendered less believable by this inducement is a question for the [members]."[38] Significantly, the court added, "the evidence of record, if believed, supports a finding beyond a reasonable doubt that the accused [Killen] shot her." Nevertheless, the court members were required to evaluate Stockham's and Prohaska's testimony, knowing that it was given after the two thought they were immune from possible prosecution. Killen's findings of guilty and his sentence were set aside.

A rehearing—another trial—was authorized. In mid-1971, after the 1st Marine Division had returned to Camp Pendleton the SJA advised the commanding general: "Because it has been nearly two years since the death of Miss Warnes any rehearing would be time consuming and expensive . . . . Physical evidence and vital witnesses are scattered across the United States . . . however, due to the serious nature of the charges I respectfully recommend that you order a rehearing."[39] Killen was retried on the same charges on 4 and 5 August 1971. He was found not guilty and immediately released from confinement. His enlistment having expired in August 1969, he was released from active duty. He served only two years and nine days confinement for his initial conviction of the murder of a 20-year-old woman.

1st Marine Aircraft Wing: Looking For Action

The 1st Marine Aircraft Wing had as many as 26 squadrons in Vietnam. At the end of 1969, because one fighter and two helicopter squadrons had departed for Okinawa and Iwakuni, Japan, a new wing legal office was established in Japan.[40] But for the time being, Colonel Max G. Halliday continued as wing SJA at the Da Nang Airbase. Throughout the year the number of lawyers on board varied from 12 to 16, and enlisted personnel from 10 to 19.[41]

Late in 1969 Colonel Halliday traded the SJA's office spaces in the old French compound for a larger, air conditioned building outside the compound near the Golden Gate USO. The new building had recently been vacated by the 1st Light AntiAircraft Missile Battalion, which had returned to Okinawa in August. Although not as centrally located, the new building's air conditioning allowed for greater comfort and productivity.[42]

Colonel Halliday and his deputy, Major David M. Brahms, had the same complaints legal officers always had in III MAF: equipment durability, a lack of transportation, and untrained court reporters.* As in the other legal offices, IBM equipment was gradually replacing the Grey and Dictaphone recorders, but problems persisted throughout most of 1969. Each brand was repaired in a different location, Saigon, Okinawa, or Japan, and each required someone to accompany it through the otherwise interminable repair process. Even new gear had to be jury-rigged to accommodate the closed-microphone mask reporting technique. Major Brahms recalled the difficulty:

> There were no masks that came with any of this equipment. It was an IBM machine with an open microphone. So we simply took the closed-microphone mask, cut a hole in it, and put the microphone from the IBM machine into the closed microphone mask. We also had to jury-rig the plug because none of the plugs were appropriate to the receptacles we had. Despite the warnings from the IBM folks that our warranties would be invalidated, we whacked the plugs off and put on our own. Screw it! It got the job done.[43]

To meet the critical need for competent preparation of records of trial, Colonel Halliday took novel measures. He hired five female Vietnamese typists to assume some of the burden. The young ladies spoke little English. However, two other Vietnamese civilian secretaries, "Sally" and "Lee," who had been working for the SJA for some time, relayed instructions to the new typists each morning. Marine Corps court reporters worked through the night preparing rough records of trial from tapes of courts-martial. The roughs were reviewed and corrected by the counsel involved in the case. The corrected roughs were then turned over to the Vietnamese typists who copied whatever was on the pages in the smooth, understanding little of what they were typing. Major Brahms recalled "it didn't work very well . . . . The guys would work all night and spend all day chasing after all the pretty, young Vietnamese, so they weren't getting much sleep. The equipment was breaking down because it was being used 24-hours a day . . . . We finally said, 'That ain't gonna work.' " The experiment was abandoned after a month's trial.[44]

A new legal chief, Master Sergeant Cecil Reitz, found a solution to the backlog of untyped records by instituting team reporting. He formed several teams around a few competent reporters and initiated a competition between the teams to see which could produce the most error-free pages the quickest.

Among the more capable reporters were two enlisted Marines with law degrees. They were draftees who had been sent to court reporter school because of their backgrounds. Not sure how to best utilize enlisted Marines with such unusual credentials, the two were used sometimes as reporters and sometimes as legal assistance attorneys.[45]

Difficulties with translators remained unresolved. The case of *United States v Hodge* illustrated the problems encountered when local Vietnamese acted as translators. All of the witnesses in that murder trial were Vietnamese. The trial counsel was Captain Richard A. Muench. Wary of the interpreter's reliability, he conferred with him before trial. As he later recalled:

> I totally lost confidence in him when he asked me, "What do you want the witnesses to say?" . . . The last thing I needed was a double credibility problem created by an interpreter of questionable integrity. (It was tough enough to get a conviction where Vietnamese witnesses were involved.) I got real lucky. I went to the Army's Americal Division in Chu Lai and found a Spec-5 interrogator/translator . . . . Fortunately the Army made him available. He did a fantastic job, and we got our murder conviction.[46]

Caseloads were not heavy in wing legal. The few cases allowed, for example, Captain Michael G. McCollum to spend successive weeks with friends at Fire Support Base Vandegrift; 1st Battalion, 5th Marines in "the Arizona;" and 3d Combined Action Group, south of

---

*As a first lieutenant Major Brahms was deputy SLO of Marine Corps forces during the 1965 Dominican Crisis. Just before his duty in Vietnam he was the distinguished graduate of the Army Judge Advocate General's School career course. After Vietnam, he was the SJA at Albany, Georgia, then Head, Research & Policy Branch of the Judge Advocate Division. After receiving a master of laws degree with highest honors from George Washington University, he again was Head, Research & Policy Branch, then SJA of the 3d Marine Division, and Head, Research & Policy Branch a third time. As a colonel he was Deputy Director of the Judge Advocate Division, followed by duty as Chief of Staff of Camp Pendleton, California. On 25 July 1985 he was promoted to the grade of brigadier general and a month later became the tenth Director of the Judge Advocate Division.

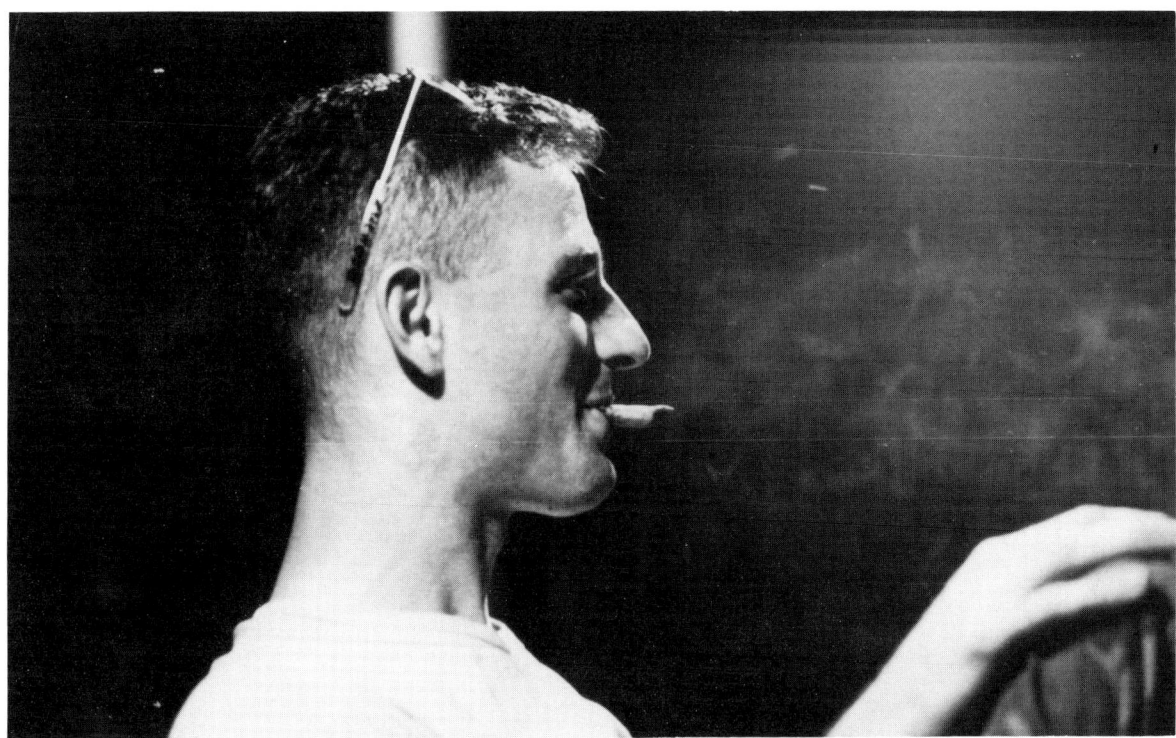

Photo courtesy of BGen David M. Brahms, USMC (Ret.)

Maj David M. Brahms was Deputy SJA of the 1st Marine Aircraft Wing during 1969. He and the SJA, Col Halliday, hired five female Vietnamese to type records of trial.

Personnel of the Staff Judge Advocate's office, 1st Marine Aircraft Wing, pose at Da Nang in 1969. Front, from left, Capt Michael J. Hoblock, Jr.; Capt Richard A. Muench; Capt G. David Carlock III; and Capt Carey H. Johnson. Rear, Lt Frank A. Wohl, JAGC, USN; Capt John C. Reynolds; legal administrative officer, CWO 2 Len E. Pierce; Maj David M. Brahms; MSgt Ronald L. Green; Capt Thomas J. Glenn, Jr.; and Capt James D. Stokes.

Marine Corps Historical Collection

Photo courtesy of Mr. Nathaniel F. Emmons

A special court-martial is shown in progress at the 1st Marine Aircraft Wing. The court reporter, right, talks into a closed microphone recording mask. The accused, left, sits beside his counsel, Capt Michael M. Anello. Trial counsel is Capt Anthony L. Hodge.

Photo courtesy of Mr. Nathaniel F. Emmons

Maj David M. Brahms gave Christmas presents to the legal office's Vietnamese employees.

Sunday brunch in the 1st Marine Aircraft Wing messhall was always enjoyable. From left, Lt John G. Niles, JAGC, USN; Capt G. David Carlock III; and Capt Nathaniel F. Emmons finish dessert and coffee. Uniformed Vietnamese waitresses stand in the background.

Photo courtesy of Col Michael G. McCollum, USMCR

Capt Nathaniel F. Emmons at work in the office of the Staff Judge Advocate, 1st Marine Aircraft Wing. The arrow on the map reads, "Shea stadium 8,975 miles."

Photo courtesy of Mr. Nathaniel F. Emmons

Phu Bai.[47] Similarly, Major Brahms, in conversation at the officers' club with a Navy pilot, learned of long delays in trying cases on board the pilot's ship, the aircraft carrier *Ranger* (CV-61). Navy trial teams, rather than making the trip from Subic Bay to ships underway off the coast of Vietnam, usually waited for the ship to return to Subic Bay before trying her courts-martial. Major Brahms offered to solve the *Ranger's* military justice problems on the spot. Within two days a Marine Corps trial team was at sea disposing of cases, to the delight of the aircraft carrier's captain and the Marine Corps lawyers, who rarely had an opportunity to go on board ship.[48]

When wing cases were to be tried, the lawyers were equally aggressive. One trial team, headed by Major Brahms, tried seven special courts in two days. The team hitched helicopter rides from wing headquarters, where they tried the first three cases, to Quang Tri Combat Base, where they tried two more cases, then to Phu Bai for the final two trials. Customarily, on such trial teams the lawyers would alternate, acting first as trial counsel then as defense counsel.[49] Only the military judge's role remained constant, because he was required to be certified to act in that capacity. If more than one trial team member was certified, the judge's role, too, would rotate.

Like the 1st Marine Division, the 1st Marine Aircraft Wing had its indispensable legal administrative officer to act as office manager. Chief Warrant Officer 2 Len E. Pierce had been a master sergeant when selected for commissioning in 1966. Little went on in the office of the SJA that escaped his scrutiny. The Gunner's room in the BOQ area, unaccountably known as "The Beaver Den," was a popular gathering place.[50]

The legal chief, Master Sergeant Noah Green, was accomplished in locating supplies and material for the legal section's operation. Warrant Officer Pierce recalled that "his uncanny ability . . . was a large boost to morale and efficiency of the law center . . . . His favorite saying was, 'How can I tell you what I need until I see what you've got?'"[51]

As in the 1st Marine Division, the wing considered the III MAF brig so filled with dangerous individuals that it was used only for prisoners sentenced to more than two months confinement, and an unsuspended bad conduct discharge. No Marine from the wing went to the brig for pretrial confinement unless awaiting court-martial for a crime of violence.[52] The other Da Nang-based command, Force Logistic Command (FLC), took a similar approach. The SJA of FLC, Lieutenant Colonel Frederick M. Haden, noted that "the worst bunch of people I've ever seen are in that brig," and he urged that no FLC personnel be held there, unless sentenced to confinement for more than two months.[53]

In July 1969, shortly before the Military Justice Act made it unnecessary that lawyers be appointed to the position, Captain Nathaniel F. Emmons was the senior

CWO 2 Len E. Pierce was the legal administrative officer of the 1st Marine Aircraft Wing. He is shown at a farewell party for a departing judge advocate.

Photo courtesy of BGen David M. Brahms, USMC (Ret.)

member at the special court-martial of Private First Class Willie Harrison. Captain Emmons was usually a 1st Wing defense counsel. He recalled that at Chu Lai, at 2200 on an evening a month or two earlier, Harrison and four friends were wending their way back to their unit when they were passed by a jeep from the U.S. Army's nearby Americal Division. The jeep skidded to a stop. One of its three Army officer occupants barked, "You soldiers better square away!" One of the Marines replied, "We ain't soldiers, m----------, we're Marines!" The Army lieutenants dismounted for further discussion of the matter. The ensuing fight ended only after one of the officers pulled his pistol and fired a round into the air. Two of the officers were briefly hospitalized. The third, First Lieutenant William L. Calley, was merely beaten up. The four Marines pleaded guilty at special courts-martial, in each of which it was stipulated they had not known the soldiers had been officers. Captain Emmons' panel reduced Harrison to the grade of private and imposed forfeitures. Harrison's accuser, Lieutenant Calley, was himself tried a year and a half later for the murder of 107 Vietnamese noncombatants at My Lai.[54]

Captain Mike McCollum, a defense counsel in the wing legal office, joined the Platoon Leader's Class (Law) program in 1966, while in law school. After obtaining his law degree he came on active duty, hoping to be an infantry officer. Instead he was assigned a legal MOS. He arrived at the 1st Marine Aircraft Wing's legal office in Da Nang in June 1969, a second lieutenant hoping to avoid receiving constructive service credit for his time in law school. He knew that with constructive service he would immediately be promoted to the grade of captain, which would preclude a later transfer to an infantry unit as a platoon commander, which was his goal. But, unable to affect inexorable administrative process, he was promoted to captain anyway. As his Vietnam tour of duty neared its end, Captain McCollum submitted a request to Headquarters Marine Corps. He asked to revert to the grade of first lieutenant (although he had never been one), remain in Vietnam, and be assigned to an infantry command or, failing that, to attend the air observer's (AO) school near Marble Mountain and remain in Vietnam as an AO. Instead, with a newly awarded Navy Commendation Medal, he was transferred to Camp Lejeune, North Carolina, as a reluctant legal assistance officer. With the blessing of former 3d Marine Division chief of staff and SJA, Colonel Motelewski, who was by then the Camp Lejeune SJA, Captain McCollum attended AO school

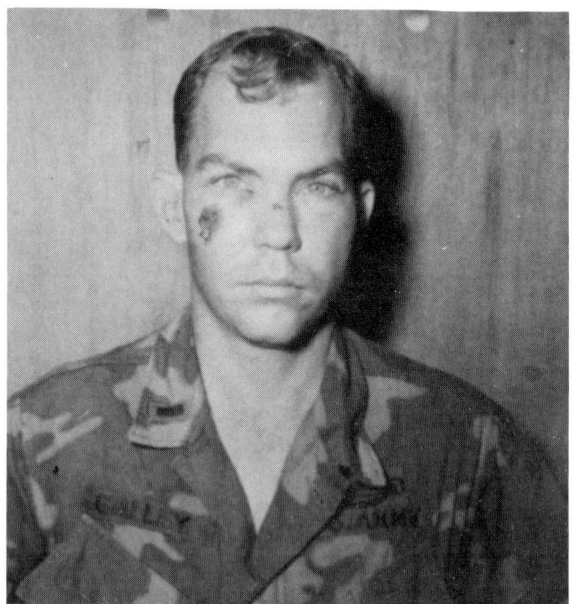

Photo courtesy of Capt G. H. O'Kelley, USMCR
Army 1stLt William L. Calley as he appeared the day after an encounter with several Marines. This photograph was admitted into evidence in the court-martial of PFC Willie Harrison to show Calley's injuries.

at Camp Lejeune and wrangled an extraordinarily quick transfer to Okinawa. Once there, through a series of probably unenforceable promises, he managed an assignment trade and six months after he had left, was again in Vietnam. Over the next half year Mike McCollum became the chief air observer of the 1st Marine Division, flew 217 missions and earned the Bronze Star Medal and 19 Air Medals.[55]

Colonel Nalton M. Bennett replaced Colonel Halliday as the wing SJA on 7 September, and in November Rear Admiral Joseph B. McDevitt was the first Judge Advocate General of the Navy to come to Vietnam. He visited Marine Corps and Navy legal offices in the Da Nang area, where he had informal discussions with many of the younger Marine judge advocates.[56]

Force Logistic Command: Approaching Breakdown

The year began with Lieutenant Colonel Frederick M. Haden continuing as SJA. His relief, in May, was Lieutenant Colonel William M. "Ace" Cummings, who was followed only three months later by Lieutenant Colonel Arthur R. Petersen. Throughout the year FLC's lawyer strength hovered around 15: the SJA, deputy SJA, five trial counsels, six defense counsels, and two review officers. A legal clerk, Lance Corporal Thomas

Capt Michael G. McCollum flew 217 missions as an air observer after his tour as a judge advocate was completed. He stands, left, with other Marines in his air observer unit.

"As solid a bunch as I've ever seen in a shop," the command staff judge advocate said. Personnel of FLC's defense section are shown, from left, kneeling, Capt Jack C. Provine, LtCol Carl E. Buchmann, PFC Wong, Capt Richard D. Lane, Capt John J. Reilly. Standing, Capt Rex L. Jones III, unidentified, GySgt Jones, unidentified, Vietnamese interpreter, Maj Charles A. Cushman, MSgt Bruno B. Bucknas, and unidentified.

McGrath, was also a law school graduate, and he served as a legal assistance officer as well as a clerk.[57]

Legal assistance was a secondary duty shared by Lance Corporal McGrath and all the other attorneys. It had become a widely employed service. In March, for example, 119 legal assistance cases were handled, with other monthly legal assistance totals ranging from 52 to 105 cases.

Lieutenant Colonel Cummings described his FLC lawyers: "As solid a bunch as I've ever seen in a shop. No wise asses, no obstructionists, all candid, responsible and honorable advocates."[58] The FLC lawyers were trying more cases than ever before, despite having no more, and sometimes fewer, judge advocates to meet the caseload. And they were falling behind. In February, they tried nine general courts-martial and 22 specials. In April, 15 generals and 53 specials were disposed of. In June, six and 44 were tried.[59] The disciplinary breakdown was being felt with full force at Camp Books, and it was badly straining FLC legal facilities at the same time the 1st Marine Aircraft Wing lawyers were experiencing slack periods.

Upon his arrival, Colonel Petersen was greatly concerned with the situation that greeted him. "I found one hell of a mess."[60] "I immediately became aware of a then-current posture of the staff judge advocate's office of complete helplessness to cope with disciplinary problems of any magnitude . . . . No one had any real hope of ever catching up."[61] The problem had arisen in part, because of the unusually high number of Marines, roughly 18,000, in the 16 different commands that FLC's legal office serviced. Additionally, the rear echelon Marines tended to have a higher disciplinary rate than the combat troops who made up the bulk of the 1st and 3d Marine Divisions. When the Military Justice Act took effect in 1969, the requirement for a greater number of lawyers to try all special courts-martial began to overburden the Red Beach SJA's office. Case backlogs quickly reached a serious, then a critical, level.[62]

A growing number of court-wise accuseds only added to the difficulty. Every accused had the right to retain civilian counsel to represent him at trial, even in Vietnam. Prosecution evidence often consisted of the testimony of Marines who were subject to transfer from Vietnam. In 1969 canny defendants were more often exercising their right to civilian representation simply as a tactic to postpone the trial date. They hoped that the convening authority, who might be unwilling to keep witnesses on legal hold for the possible conviction of a single wrongdoer, would release the

Marine Corps Historical Collection

LtCol Arthur R. Petersen, shown as a colonel, was FLC's SJA from July 1969 to June 1970. He inherited a nearly unmanageable backlog of untranscribed cases.

witnesses and drop the case. Trial counsels and military judges soon realized that some requests for civilian lawyers were often no more than a ruse to be raised on the day of trial for purposes of delay. Major Charles A. Cushman recalled how the accused would stand and tell the court:

> [He] recently had mailed a letter requesting representation to a civilian attorney in the States but had not received a reply. The issue for the military judge was whether to grant a continuance knowing that the witnesses may or may not be available at a later date, or note the objection on the record and proceed with the trial of the case. More often than not the objections were noted and the trial continued.[63]

Legitimate requests for civilian counsel, initiated a reasonable time prior to the date of trial, were always sufficient cause for a continuance, witness problems or not.

With the centralization of legal assets in SJA offices, courts-martial, other than summary courts, were tried at the headquarters location, rather than throughout the command. An unanticipated bonus was that the need for lawyer travel was greatly reduced. Now trial participants came to the lawyers, rather than vice versa. Pretrial interviews and convening authority conferences still required the judge advocate to go on the road, however. Fortunate FLC lawyers hardly traveled at all, because their command was largely self-

Mai worked in FLC's civil affairs section. Marine Corps legal offices in the Da Nang and Red Beach areas were often able to hire Vietnamese to act as interpreters.

contained at Red Beach. Conditions for the trial of courts-martial were poor at FLC, though the courtroom and office spaces were standard SEAhuts with screened sides and tin roofs and were subject to the noise and the dust clouds raised by constantly passing trucks. In an effort to keep up, cases were tried in those SEAhuts seven days a week, from seven in the morning, often until nine at night, with an hour and a half off for lunch and for dinner. During the hottest months, August and September, courtroom and office temperatures usually exceeded 100 degrees and often rose as high as 117 degrees.[64] Finally, in the fall of 1969, the courtroom was moved to FLC's former computer building, a windowless, air conditioned, dust-free structure across the road from the camp's donut shop (referred to by one officer as "The War-Is-Hell Donut Shop"). Conditions there were ideal for courts-martial, and, as Major Cushman recalled, "that is when we started getting good records of trial."[65]* The lawyers' offices remained in SEAhuts.

Although located in the largest and busiest supply depot in the I Corps area, the SJA's office was burdened with a shortage of the most mundane supply items. Lieutenant Colonel Carl E. Buchmann, the deputy SJA, noted with irritation:

> Recording belts, typewriter ribbons, paper, pencils, a great number of just plain ol' office supplies! And the only real feasible solution we came up with was to have people from the States send us some of theirs. I never experienced a supply system . . . as bad as it appears to be over here. So we used to write away for CARE packages from friends of ours in other legal offices.[66]

He went on to detail FLC's version of the familiar unavailable-repair refrain:

> We bought a number of IBM machines and . . . there was to be a service contract with this. We bought a great number of them—reproducers and typewriters. Well, they never did finish getting that service contract negotiated. [IBM] said it was too expensive to have a guy in Da Nang. Now they have a man in Saigon, but the cost of having that repairman come here is confiscatory. He charges $27 an hour, portal to portal, so you pay him for flying up here, sleeping, flying back, et cetera.[67]

Nor was FLC immune from the problem of inadequately trained reporters. Lieutenant Colonel Buchmann noted: "We have been plagued with this . . . . We're not getting any assistance from Headquarters Marine Corps or FMFPac . . . . It can't be solved here at this level."[68]

Even with manpower and equipment difficulties, FLC remained the most active trial activity in III MAF in 1969. Still, case loads steadily rose as the number of personnel available to meet the load diminished. A shortage of court reporters, when they were most needed, contributed to the mounting backlog of untranscribed cases, leading FLC into the next year with serious handicaps.

Trying Cases

"The Marines," wrote author Richard Gabriel, "seem to have maintained . . . a rapid and efficient prosecutorial system for containing and dealing with disciplinary problems."[69] Perhaps so, but Marine Corps lawyers in Vietnam in 1969 were unaware of their institutional superiority. They found it to be plain, hard, often frustrating, work. Travel was as difficult as it had been in previous years. Captain Daniel H. LeGear recalled: "It seems as though I was always getting on a helicopter to go to one unit or the other to interview witnesses and clients."[70] FLC's Lieutenant Colonel Buchmann said: "We were losing a lot of lawyer time by travelling to the far reaches of I Corps." Captain Mike McCollum, of the 1st Marine Aircraft Wing,

---

*After Vietnam, Major Cushman was SJA of the 1st Marine Aircraft Wing (Rear), then the 1st Marine Brigade, the 1st Marine Aircraft Wing, and the Marine Corps Development & Education Command. He also was a branch head in HQMC's Judge Advocate Division, and graduated from the Naval War College. In 1984 he became Assistant JAG of the Navy for Military Law and Officer in Charge of the Navy and Marine Corps Appellate Review Activity. On 1 July 1987 he was advanced to the grade of brigadier general and retired from active duty.

remembered a brig prisoner whom he had signed for and taken to a distant medical facility for psychiatric evaluation. Unable to locate a ride when the evaluation concluded, Captain McCollum and his client began hitchhiking back. Jaded brig personnel took little notice when the lawyer arrived at the gate, briefcase in hand, prisoner in tow, riding the front bumper of a 50-ton Bay City crane![71]

Early in 1969 the general court-martial military judge for all of III MAF and the naval commands was Colonel John R. DeBarr, who in 12 months presided in 195 cases, including 15 murder trials.[72] In mid-year Colonel DeBarr was succeeded by Lieutenant Colonels Henry "Hank" Hoppe III, then Lieutenant Colonel Paul A. A. St.Amour. Lieutenant Colonel Hoppe recalled one of his first Vietnam trials, which began around 0930 in the 1st Marine Aircraft Wing courtroom. Shortly thereafter, "there was a tremendous detonation, the building rattled, and I, having been in-country only a few days, recessed the court on my way to the bunker. About 4 or 5 steps out, I realized nobody else was moving and [the counsels and members] were just cracking up laughing." At that point the judge learned that at precisely 1000 each morning the South Vietnamese were authorized to detonate their damaged ammunition stockpiles in a quarry just outside the airbase. "Shamefacedly," Colonel Hoppe recalled, "I returned to the bench and we resumed the trial."[73]

In December Colonel DeBarr returned to Da Nang from Camp Pendleton to attempt to salvage several Vietnam records of trials at which he had presided. Undiscovered equipment failures had rendered the records so deficient that they could not pass appellate muster, unless they could be reconstructed.[74]

In order to implement the provisions of the Military Justice Act that required military judges in special courts-martial, the Judge Advocate General of the Navy certified approximately 500 Navy and Marine Corps judge advocates as special court-martial judges. The number of Navy and Marine Corps general court-martial military judges was also expanded from 12 to 23.[75]

The judges found no lack of cases in Vietnam. "It is fair to say that blackmarketing and currency violations literally went out of control," wrote Major General George S. Prugh, former Judge Advocate General of the Army. "By 1969 [they] were beyond the capabilities of the law enforcement agencies until the drawdown of troops changed the situation."[76]

"It seems as though I was always getting on a helicopter to go to one unit or another to interview witnesses and clients." A CH-46 of HMM-161 about to lift off from a 3d Marine Division landing zone while several Marines wait for the next available helicopter.

Marine Corps Historical Collection

Col John R. DeBarr was a general court-martial military judge assigned to III MAF in 1969. He tried 185 courts-martial, including 15 murders, in one year.

A case of currency violation that was not beyond the capabilities of law enforcement was that of Private Jimmie Dunbar, tried by general court-martial on 5 January 1969. He and two other Marines had deserted from Khe Sanh. While hiding out in Da Nang, they sold stolen items on the black market and, with cash in hand, typed bogus orders that allowed them to fly to Saigon. Once there they joined a ring of 47 U.S. Army deserters in a postal money order scheme. Using bad checks, the ring purchased numerous money orders at various military post offices. They often bribed postal clerks to leave the payee line blank, which was in violation of regulations then in effect. Each day the money orders were sold at a premium on the Vietnamese black market, sometimes to a single buyer. The proceeds of the sales were used to cover that day's checks, which had financed the money orders, and the sales profits were split among those involved. By such apparently modest means, the group garnered hundreds of thousands of dollars each month, which allowed them to rent Saigon apartments, pay cash for American automobiles to be delivered in the United States, and bribe military police for advance word of random raids.

Eventually, military authorities apprehended the members of the ring. Dunbar and the ring's two other Marines were escorted from Saigon to the III MAF brig by Captains W. Hays Parks and Patrick H. Mathews, and Navy Lieutenant William J. Cosgriff, the 1st Marine Division lawyers who were to try the apprehended Marines. Captain Parks signed for $990 in military payment certificates and $2,800 in U.S. postal money orders that had been in Private Dunbar's pockets when he was apprehended. "As I had no handcuffs," Captain Parks recounted, "I made each Marine remove his boot laces and belt, and loosen his trousers to the point that they would fall down unless he held them up." For the trip back to Da Nang Captain Parks emphasized his seriousness with a loaded shotgun.[77]

Dunbar pleaded guilty to desertion, currency violations, and possession of marijuana, and was sentenced to confinement at hard labor for 10 years, forfeiture of all pay, and a dishonorable discharge. In accordance with a pretrial agreement, his confinement was reduced to two years. The fate of the others is unremembered.

While few courts-martial had the visibility of the Dunbar case, the sad, the bizarre, and the uplifting were often encountered at trial. In the latter category was the case of the *United States v Private First Class Eugene R. Hofstetler*. Captain Clarke C. Barnes defended Hofstetler, who was charged with sleeping on post twice in one week. The charge sheet did not indicate that during that week, his first in Vietnam, Hofstetler had been engaged in Operation Dewey Canyon and constant patrolling. After the operation ended and by the time of trial Hofstetler had become a mainstay of his platoon. Although his platoon commander now urged that the charges be dropped, the convening authority, the battalion commander, believed them too serious to disregard. He did, however, refer the case to a special, rather than a general court-martial. At trial Captain Barnes introduced the brief, handwritten statements of 12 Marines from Hofstetler's platoon. Although some were barely legible and some not particularly articulate, their sincerity was unquestionable: "He has lots of guts and he does his share," wrote one Marine. Another wrote, "During Operation Dewey Canyon . . . Huff was equal in everything including the risk of death. He fast thinking and action saved the lives of his buddies and mine." A fellow private first class simply wrote: "In the bush, I would trust my back to him." Hofstetler pleaded guilty to the charges. The maximum permissible punishment was the jurisdictional maximum of a special court, which included six months confinement at hard labor and a bad conduct discharge. Instead, the members

162   MARINES AND MILITARY LAW IN VIETNAM

Marine Corps Historical Collection

Col Max G. Halliday, 1st Marine Aircraft Wing SJA, in a 1972 photograph. After the war he became Assistant Judge Advocate General of the Navy for Military Law.

sentenced him to 45 days hard labor without confinement. Hofstetler happily returned to his platoon, where every day was hard labor without confinement.[78]

Another court-martial, tried at Cua Viet, had a more serious outcome. On the night of 10 April 1969 a staff sergeant walked out of his hooch and froze, staring at the hand grenade taped beside the doorway inches away from him. Dangling from the string that he had just pulled by opening the door was the pin from the grenade. But there was no explosion. Instead, the now-assembled hooch occupants read a typewritten note tucked behind the deactivated grenade: "Dear Lifers, I'm tired of this peddy bullshit. If it keeps up, I'm sorry to say that I'll have to do you a *JOB*. This little frag is just a warning . . . . Maybe I won't get all of yous, but *who* will I get? You, you, or you." It was signed "Your Friendly famthom frager." The staff noncommissioned officers were not amused.

At his special court-martial the "famthom frager," Lance Corporal Richard E. Eicholtz, pleaded guilty to assault and was sentenced to a bad conduct discharge, reduction to private, and confinement at hard labor for four months.[79] No one took such cases lightly.

Exits: Marine Corps Draw Downs

On 8 June 1969 President Nixon announced his decision to withdraw U.S. troops from South Vietnam. Redeployments were to take place in increments; a total of 45,000 troops, including 18,483 Marines were scheduled to leave South Vietnam by year's end. The 3d Marine Division was to redeploy to Okinawa and Camp Pendleton, California, and portions of the 1st Marine Aircraft Wing to Iwakuni, Japan.[80]

The Commanding General, 3d Marine Division, left for Okinawa on 7 November, having been preceded two days earlier by Colonel Ben Ferrell and his legal staff of 21 officers and 25 enlisted Marines.[81] Colonel Ferrell said of the redeployment:

> Leaving Vietnam was the most difficult job I had in the Marine Corps. [The commanding general] ordered me to have all cases tried before leaving country. We did our best and did get nearly every case tried . . . . What kept us from completing all cases was the fact that we had to pack and crate all equipment and move it to the dock about 10 days before we left . . . . We packed our [gear] in wooden boxes and banded them. They were all crated and in rows outside the legal office and then it poured rain for about five days and nights. That did not make much difference, however. Before the crates were loaded aboard ship, high-pressure hoses were turned on them to kill bugs, etc. When we got back to Okinawa everything, including books, were water soaked.[82]

The lawyers boarded Navy landing craft and followed the Cua Viet river to the sea, where they embarked on board the LPD-8, *Dubuque*, for the trip to Okinawa.[83]

Shortly before the Marines of the 3d Marine Divi-

Col Max G. Halliday seen at his June 1969 wetting-down party upon promotion to colonel. His escorts are Maj David M. Brahms, left, and CWO 2 Len E. Pierce.
Photo courtesy of BGen Max G. Halliday, USMCR (Ret.)

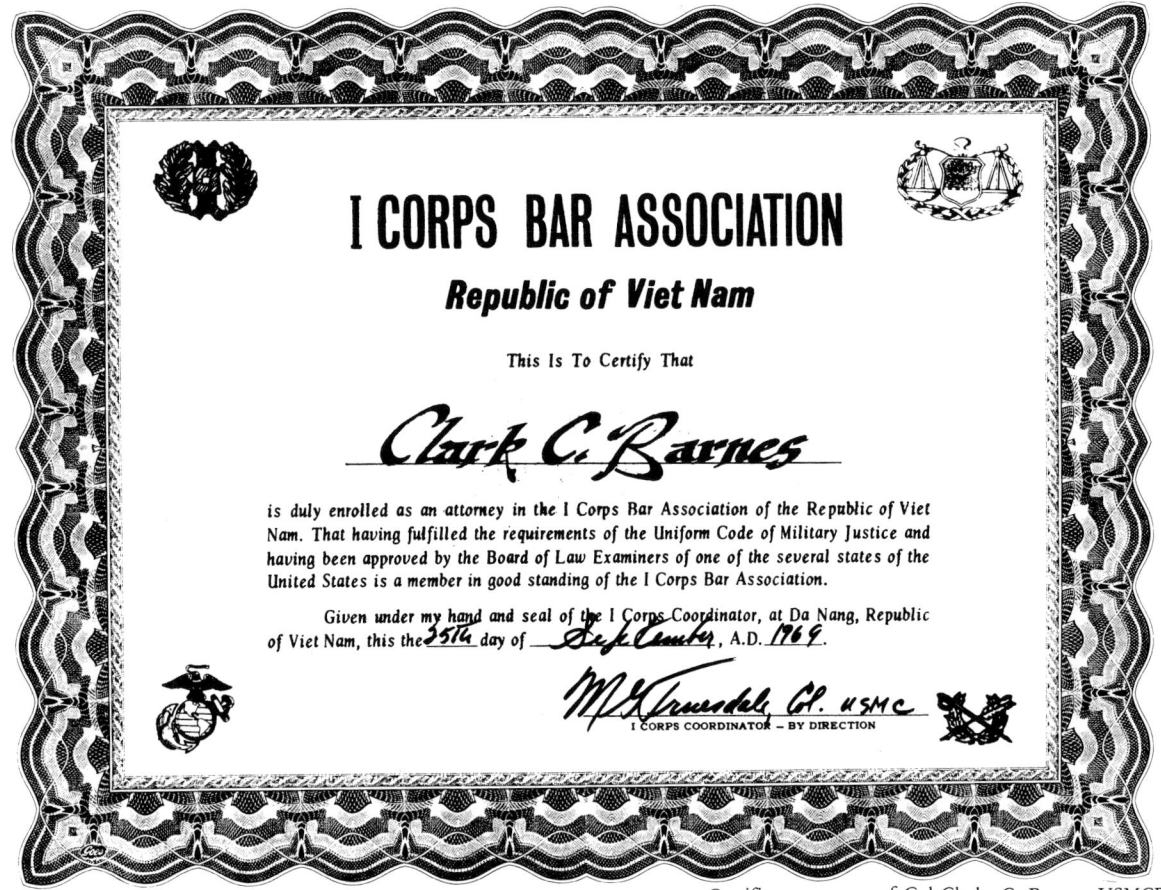

The I Corps Bar Association flourished throughout the war. The certificates were designed and printed by the mother of a Vietnam-stationed Marine Corps judge advocate.

sion embarked for Okinawa, Major General William K. Jones, the commanding general, asked his SJA if he could order all troop baggage searched for weapons. Lieutenant Colonel Ferrell replied: "General, before I answer that question let me ask you, do you want weapons, or do you want convictions?" General Jones wanted to ensure weapons were not smuggled to Okinawa, so blanket searches were conducted knowing that, lacking probable cause, convictions could not follow.[84]

Lieutenant Colonel Max Halliday, SJA of the 1st Marine Aircraft Wing, was promoted to colonel in July. Two months later, Colonel Nalton M. Bennett relieved him. Before departing, Colonel Halliday designated three judge advocates to move to Iwakuni to establish a legal office at the wing's rear headquarters.[85] Captain Alan R. Wolfert was the first (Acting) SJA (Rear). He opened shop on 10 November. On 24 November Lieutenant Colonel Joseph A. Mallery succeeded him.[86] Elements of the wing withdrew from Vietnam from August through the end of the year (going to Iwakuni, Futema, Okinawa, and MCAS El Toro, California), but most of Colonel Bennett's judge advocates remained at Da Nang.

The principal wing unit leaving Vietnam for Iwakuni was Marine Aircraft Group (MAG) 12. At Iwakuni the wing headquarters (rear) and Colonel Mallery's few lawyers were in for a surprise. As Major Brahms recalled: "We loaded up MAG-12 with every bandit we could find, on the theory that we would make the combat zone less of a problem and they could probably deal with these things a lot better in Iwakuni. MAG-12 became a very big group."[87]

If the wing sent its disciplinary problems to Iwakuni, there was a measure of justice in the wing SJA becoming responsible for most of the 3d Marine Division's small units that were left in Vietnam. "We took over all the cat and dog outfits, up and down I Corps," recalled Major Brahms. These included the 3d Reconnaissance Battalion, four Combined Action Platoon units, an engineer battalion, and a bridge company, among others.*⁸⁸ What units the wing did not take over, the 1st Marine Division fell heir to, as it too prepared to leave Vietnam.

The 1st Marine Division and Force Logistic Command continued to march. The year began with 79,844 Marines, 3,378 sailors, and 59,403 soldiers in III MAF. It ended with 54,541 Marines, 2,144 sailors, and 61,792 soldiers.⁸⁹

Perspective

On 7 August 1969 at Headquarters Marine Corps, Colonel Duane L. Faw was promoted to the grade of brigadier general and assumed the directorship of the Judge Advocate Division, the first general officer to hold the billet.⁹⁰ He succeeded Colonel Truesdale, who had previously replaced Colonel Sevier.

General Faw immediately set to work to cure several ills affecting the Marine Corps' legal community. In a letter to Colonel Bob Lucy, the 1st Marine Division SJA, he wrote: "Turning first to the lawyer problem: it is worse than I imagined . . . . My top priority project is to *obtain* and *retain* qualified lawyer assistance for you . . . . Our poor lawyer retention record in the past is really the result of many factors," and he specified uncaring personnel assignment policies and lack of professional recognition. He detailed his efforts at Headquarters to cure those situations: More attention would be given to the wishes and needs of lawyers when assignments were considered; at the Congressional level he was seeking approval for lawyer "incentive retention pay;" and he assigned Lieutenant Colonel Charles E. "Chuck" Spence responsibility for procurement of legal personnel. Lieutenant Colonel Spence's efforts soon produced excellent results.⁹¹

General Faw was also concerned that senior officers have the career incentive that a frequently available brigadier general's billet would provide. Because there was only one general's billet for lawyers, that of Director, Judge Advocate Division, he obtained the Commandant's approval for selection of a new director every two years. "It is my intention," General Faw wrote, "to set the pace by taking whatever measures are necessary to precipitate the selection of a Marine Corps lawyer as a brigadier general at a rate of one every two years."⁹² In other words, after two years in office he would either retire or move to a billet outside the Judge Advocate Division (as Brigadier General Lawrence did) to make the general's star available to another lawyer. That was a significant and selfless decision because, by statute, General Faw could remain on active duty in the director's billet for several years. He chose not to, recognizing that otherwise no colonel would have further promotion opportunity. Lacking that incentive, many senior judge advocates would retire as quickly as they became eligible to do so. That "gentleman's agreement," as it was often referred to, whereby the director retired after two years in office continued to be honored by the next four directors.

General Faw closed his letter to Colonel Lucy by saying: "We have a hard job ahead of us to make the career of a Marine Corps judge advocate sufficiently attractive to retain the number and quality of lawyers needed. I am convinced the career is actually more rewarding than it appears to junior officers."⁹³ At that time 359 Marine Corps judge advocates were on active duty, a 20 percent increase in one year.**⁹⁴ Compared to their authorized strength the Marines were still short 95 field grade lawyers—majors and above—and short 14 lawyers overall. As General Faw noted, the retention rate for first-term judge advocates was bad. In Vietnam Lieutenant Colonel Carl Buchmann highlighted the retention issue when he said:

> Of the 22 lawyers on the Office of the Staff Judge Advocate at FLC right at the moment, there are three regulars [regular officers, as opposed to reservists]: a colonel, a lieutenant colonel, and a major. Now, none of the remaining 19 . . . have any intention of staying in the Marine Corps. What is hurting us is the fact that we have no depth in the legal office . . . . You have some senior people who've been around anywhere from 12 to 28 years, and then you have the next group down, in the service less than a year.⁹⁵

Colonel John R. DeBarr said of the one-term judge advocate: "He's dedicated, he's professional, he's eager, he works—he's working hard! But he goes home."⁹⁶ At the 1969 General Officers Symposium, held at Headquarters Marine Corps, the assembled generals heard Brigadier General Homer S. Hill, Assistant Commanding General, 1st Marine Aircraft Wing, say: "We cannot afford to lose our Marine lawyer capability. All-out efforts in retention and procurement must now be made."⁹⁷

General Hill's view was in keeping with a major internal study, completed only a few days before his statement.⁹⁸ The Commandant had directed the study

---

*Combined Action Platoons were small units based in Vietnamese villages that, along with Vietnamese forces, provided security for the area.

**Besides General Faw and General Lawrence, who continued in his legislative billet in a retired, but on-active-duty status, there were 25 colonels, 26 lieutenant colonels, 17 majors, 257 captains, and 32 first and second lieutenants.

to recommend "the most practicable procedures for providing future legal services to the Marine Corps." Chaired by the Director of Personnel, Lieutenant General Louis B. Robertshaw, and without judge advocate membership, the panel also examined whether it was practical to even compete for lawyer entrants into the Marine Corps or whether it would be preferable to simply go to "blue suiters," that is, to ask the Navy to fill Marine Corps legal needs. In its wide-ranging report the panel made several suggestions that were to shape the Judge Advocate Division for many years to come.

Among its 18 recommendations the panel concluded that the system then in place best answered Marine Corps needs. ("Marine commanders will be better able to accomplish [their function with] advice from Marine lawyers who think, are trained, have experienced field hardships . . . the same as their Commanders.") The panel also recommended that nonlawyers, such as legal administrative officers, take a greater role in the legal process; that more women Marines be employed as judge advocates; that, because over 10 percent of Marine Corps judge advocate strength was assigned to Navy JAG billets, the Secretary of the Navy be asked to assign a Marine Corps lawyer on a continuing basis as Deputy Judge Advocate General of the Navy (another brigadier general's billet); and that judge advocates be allowed to attend graduate legal school at Marine Corps expense. The panel essentially threw up its hands over the retention issue, reporting that "this problem has not been satisfactorily resolved during the past 18 years by the Marine Corps (or any of the Armed Services)." They did, however, predict that with the end of the war in Vietnam and its associated unaccompanied tours, sufficient lawyers would become available to meet Marine Corps needs. Finally, the panel noted: "Judge Advocates who choose the Marine Corps for a career definitely want to be recognized as Marine officers and part of the Marine Corps team; not as a group of specialists outside the regular officer corps."

The Commandant, General Leonard F. Chapman, Jr., penned on the panel's report: "This is one of the best staff studies I have ever read. It has removed all my doubts, and I now unequivocally, without reservation, endorse and support our present system, with noted improvements. Let's go all-out to effect those approved improvements."[99]

The next issue of *The Reserve Marine*, the newsletter sent to all inactive reservists, was headlined: "Services of Experienced Lawyer Officers Needed," followed by a story detailing the situation ("There is an urgent need . . . ") with instructions as to how inactive reserve Marines could volunteer to return to active duty.[100] Recruitment of law students was intensified, and soon PLC (Law) programs for law students graduating in 1971 and 1972 were over-subscribed by 50 percent.[101]

Colonel James H. Granger, a reservist infantry officer who had gone to law school following active duty, was one of those who returned:

> I was practicing law in Austin, Texas, in 1969 when the Marine Corps initiated its full-court press to recall experienced lawyers. Brigadier General Faw, himself, had called me, as well as Lieutenant Colonel [Rollin Q.] Blakeslee, and as enticement to returning to active duty, I was given my first two preferences [for duty and location].[102]

A closely watched and much discussed aspect of lawyer retention was commonly referred to by judge advocates as "pro pay." The Department of Defense proposed to Congress that the lawyer retention issue could be solved by paying attorneys a monthly premium and a bonus upon extending their period of obligated service. Higher ranking lawyers would receive a higher monthly premium, to encourage majors, lieutenant colonels, and colonels to remain on active duty. The lump sum paid for continuing one's initial period of active duty would encourage captains to remain. These bonuses in recognition of professional training—pro pay—would be similar to those long paid to doctors, dentists, and veterinarians in the Army, Navy, and Air Force. On 12 December 1969 Senator Daniel K. Inouye addressed the Senate on the subject of a bill he had introduced on 22 July:

> The problem of keeping competent, experienced judge advocates has become acute . . . . The number of experienced lawyers relative to the total on board will be as follows: Army, 29 percent; Navy, 36 percent; Marine Corps, 16 percent; and Air Force, 42 percent . . . . This is not a safe balance between experienced and inexperienced lawyers . . . . S. 2674 will meet this problem of retention by providing increased compensation for military lawyers. First, there will be special pay each month, ranging from $50 for a second lieutenant to captain to $200 for colonels and above. Second, the judge advocate who agrees to extend for at least 3 years will receive continuation pay at a rate equal to 2 months' basic pay per additional year he agrees to remain on active duty . . . . The time has come to recognize the critical dimensions of the problem.[103]

A similar bill had already passed the House of Representatives, and service lawyers anticipated a significant raise in pay. Instead, the legislative session ended without the Inouye bill coming to a vote. Reintroduced the next year, the bill again failed to come

Capt Clarke C. Barnes, left, poses with Capt Michael J. Levin outside a 3d Marine Division legal office at Phu Bai. Capt Barnes said: "The professional experience was fantastic. But even more important was the urgency of it all, the team work, the camaraderie."

to a vote. That pattern continued for several years, until finally, pro pay expired along with the crisis in discipline. Military lawyers receive no special pay and never have.

In Vietnam, largely unaware of the events in Washington, Marine Corps judge advocates continued to try cases: 123 general and 1,023 special courts-martial in 1969, declines from the preceding year of 18 and 20 percent, respectively. (Troop strength, late in the year, had dropped 32 percent.)[104]

In Vietnam, the I Corps Bar Association held a "ball." With the commanding general's permission the III MAF officers' club was reserved and excess quarters were acquired for attendees who were not billeted in Da Nang. Musically trained Marines were hired as a band. Colonel Truesdale recalled: "We sent out invitations to all members . . . . All Army, Navy, and Air Force nurses in the area received invitations. The ball was held on a Sunday evening [14 September 1969] and was a great success."[105] Nurses from the German hospital ship, the *Helgoland*, were also invited.

While Marine Corps judge advocates may have sponsored a dance, that was an anomaly; creative whimsy near the field of battle. Close by, the war continued. Captain Clarke C. Barnes reminisced: "The professional experience was fantastic. But even more important was the urgency of it all, the team work, the camaraderie . . . . My experience in the combat zone was invaluable."[106]

CHAPTER 8
1970-71 Preamble: Discipline in Disarray

Civilians at Courts-martial: Latney Reversed — Fragging: Killers in Our Midst
From a Lawyer's Case File: Criminal-Criminologist — Drugs: Marijuana and More — Racial Conflict: High Tension
Administrative Discharge: The Marines Clean House — From a Lawyer's Case File: Homicide on Patrol

---

In July 1970 General Leonard F. Chapman, Jr., Commandant of the Marine Corps, opened the annual General Officers Symposium. In remarks to the assembled generals he said: "In preparing for this talk this morning, I looked back over the notes I've used for last year and the year before, and I was impressed with the fact that so many of the problems I spoke about are still with us."[1] Elsewhere, Major General William K. Jones, ending his tour as commanding general of the 3d Marine Division in Vietnam, recalled: "I was absolutely astounded and horrified by the breakdown of discipline that I witnessed."[2]

In 1970 the Armed Forces continued to confront a deterioration of discipline. The unrest reflected the divisions within American society as a whole and their effects on the Services, which were engaged in a long and unpopular conflict. The prospect of redeployment actually weakened discipline, as servicemen found it difficult to maintain a sense of purpose in a war that was ending without decisive results.[3] Rapid manpower turnover, a decline in training standards and personnel quality, and boredom as combat action diminished, added to the undermining of discipline and morale. All of the Armed Services were affected. In July 1970 there was a major riot in the Marine Corps brig at Iwakuni, Japan.[4] The superintendent of the U.S. Military Academy, Lieutenant General David Palmer, later recalled: "The Army was hollow at the gut. It nearly disintegrated."[5] In May the Navy's *Richard B. Anderson* (DD 786), on her way to a western Pacific deployment, was the first reported victim of Vietnam-era ship sabotage and was forced to return to port with major engine damage.[6] For four days in May the Air Force suffered large-scale riots at Travis Air Force Base, California, a primary Vietnam air embarkation point.[7] Colonel Paul X. Kelley, on his second Vietnam tour of duty in 1970, commanded the 1st Marines. Years later, after retiring as Commandant of the Marine Corps, he said of that period:

> We had a new Marine Corps.... By 1970 ... we had basically "fillers," people who hadn't come over [to Vietnam] with units.... The average age of a squad leader in the 1st Marines was 18 and a half [and] we had all the cultural problems of the United States.... There was a very dramatic difference in the Marine Corps between the time we went in, in '65, and the time we went out in '71. A very, very dramatic difference in the Corps.... When I arrived on the scene [in 1970] I was somewhat appalled.[8]

The difficulties of preceding years had not lessened, and solutions were yet to be found.

Civilians at Courts-martial: Latney Reversed

James Latney, the civilian seaman convicted of murder in a 1968 general court-martial, set the precedent that military courts had jurisdiction over civilians who committed crimes in the combat zone. Latney had appealed. Sixteen months after his court-martial the Court of Appeals for the District of Columbia overturned his conviction. The appellate court held that the UCMJ could not reach a civilian seaman who lived on his ship, and who had not assimilated with mili-

Department of Defense Photo (USMC) A419099
Gen Leonard F. Chapman, Jr., was Commandant of the Marine Corps as the Vietnam War neared end. He told a gathering of generals: "I was impressed with the fact that so many of the problems . . . are still with us."

167

tary personnel in terms of living quarters or conditions.[9]

The Marine Corps considered urging an appeal of the appellate court's decision, but Brigadier General Faw, Director of the Judge Advocate Division, explained: "This [opinion] wasn't binding on even another Federal District Court . . . . If we sent it up . . . we might get a loser, so let him go, because . . . our disciplinary needs are met when he's convicted."[10] Nine months later, even this limited victory of conviction was negated by the Court of Military Appeals' decision in another case, *United States v. Averette*.

In Vietnam civilians continued to commit crimes, most often black marketeering and currency violations. The State Department considered administrative measures, such as withdrawal of military privileges and loss of employment, to be sufficient punishment. Courts-martial should be reserved for only the most serious cases. MACV, on the other hand, urged courts-martial in all cases. While that disagreement continued, only 16 civilian cases entered the military justice system through 1968. No military charges were brought in 10 of those cases, two more were dropped after charges were preferred, and four civilians were tried by courts-martial.[11] One of the four was Latney. Another was Mr. Raymond G. Averette.

Averette, a civilian employee of an Army contractor, was convicted by an Army general court-martial of conspiracy to commit larceny and attempted larceny of 36,000 batteries. He appealed his conviction and sentence to confinement at hard labor for one year and a $500 fine. In April 1970 the Court of Military Appeals reversed the conviction and dismissed the case. The Court noted that, unlike Latney, Averette was assigned to an Army post in Vietnam and enjoyed full military privileges. Moreover, his offenses could be tried in a United States District Court. The rationale of the decision, however, was that the article of the UCMJ upon which jurisdiction was based required that the civilian's offense be committed in time of war. "We conclude," the Court wrote, "that the words 'in time of war' mean . . . a war formally declared by Congress." Because there was never a declaration of war against North Vietnam, the UCMJ could not apply to civilians accompanying U.S. Armed Forces in the field, or so the military appellate court reasoned. (In the same opinion the court held that the lack of a declaration of war was not a bar to invoking the "in time of war" provision of the unauthorized absence article.)[12] The question of criminal jurisdiction over American civilians in Vietnam, not addressed by the 1950 Pentalateral Agreement, was resolved. As a matter of law, civilians in Vietnam could not be court-martialed.

The Averette decision created a significant problem. The South Vietnamese Government routinely declined to exercise jurisdiction in cases involving Americans who committed crimes against other Americans or American law. Moreover, American civilian laws against most criminal acts, including murder, manslaughter, assault, blackmarketing and currency violations, had no extraterritorial application and could not be tried by any Federal District Court. As a result, in a later case involving a civilian and a soldier in a bribery-blackmarket scheme, the soldier was convicted by court-martial and the civilian was set free. The Averette case created a group of U.S. civilians, contractor employees, that was not subject to prosecution for crimes committed in Vietnam.[13]

After the Averette decision, administrative debarment was the sanction applied in most cases of civilian wrongdoing. That involved a bar to the wrongdoer's employment by any U.S. contractor in Vietnam and the firing of the wrongdoer. As an indication of the level of civilian misconduct in Vietnam, by the end of the war 943 contractor employees had been debarred.[14]

Fragging: Killers in our Midst

The Marine Corps did not record the number of fraggings that occurred during the war. In 1970, however, the principal infantry command remaining in Vietnam, the 1st Marine Division, did: One Marine was killed and 43 were wounded in 47 fragging incidents.*[15] As experience was gained in dealing with fragging incidents, apprehension of those responsible became more frequent. That was largely attributable to "Operation Freeze," a III MAF Order based on Major General William K. Jones' similar 3d Marine Division order of the preceding year. Operation Freeze provided for swift isolation of any unit in which an act of violence occurred, followed by immediate investigation. Additionally, an order directing the pro-

---

*In comparison, the U.S. Army, which during the same period had eight times as many men in Vietnam (an average of 274,100 soldiers to the Marines' 32,500), suffered six times as many (271) fragging incidents. Thirty-four soldiers were killed. (Guenter Lewy, *America In Vietnam* [New York: Oxford University Press, 1978], p. 156; and DOD, Selected Manpower Statistics, Fiscal Year 1982 [Washington, 1982], p. 129).

The bunker in which Sgt Richard L. Tate died. Fragging, the murder of one Marine by another with a fragmentation hand grenade, occurred throughout the Vietnam War.

tection of informants resulted in greater cooperation from those with knowledge of the incidents. Still, only 22 of the 1st Division's 47 fraggings resulted in apprehensions. Of the 37 Marines apprehended, 21 were court-martialed and five received administrative discharges. The remaining cases were dropped for lack of evidence.[16] No fraggings occurred in Marine Corps units in 1971, the year in which all remaining Marine combat units redeployed from Vietnam.[17]

From a Lawyer's Case File: Criminal-Criminologist

On 23 October 1970 the 1st Marine Division's only death by fragging occurred on Hill 190, west of Da Nang. That evening, Private Gary A. Hendricks of Company L, 3d Battalion, 1st Marines, was one of two Marines found sleeping on post by their platoon sergeant, Sergeant Richard L. Tate. Tate reprimanded the two in strong words, but took no further action. At 0110 the next morning Private Hendricks dropped a fragmentation grenade down the air vent of the bunker in which Sergeant Tate and two others were sleeping. The grenade landed on Sergeant Tate's stomach. Reflexively, the sergeant brought his legs up to his chest, cradling the grenade in his lap, where it exploded. His legs torn from his body, Sergeant Tate died several minutes later. He had been due to return to the United States and his wife and child in three weeks. The explosion also wounded the other two sergeants occupying the bunker.[18]

Hendricks' regimental commander was Colonel Paul X. Kelley, who clearly recalled the case years later. "Why would a kid like that, a farm boy from Ohio, brought up very decently, why would [he] frag and murder a very fine noncommissioned officer?"[18]

Captain Philip C. Tower was assigned to defend Hendricks, who was charged with aggravated assault and premeditated murder, which carried a possible sentence of death. Hendricks, who was apprehended after admitting his act to other Marines, said he hoped he "had gotten one [sergeant], at least." Besides his admissions and physical evidence placing him at the scene, Hendricks had signed a written confession. With few avenues available to the defense, Captain Tower sought psychiatric evaluations in Vietnam and on Okinawa, neither of which raised a basis for an insanity defense. Captain Tower remembered:

> It was clear to me that the command did not wish to negotiate in this case, and that they very much wanted to see the defendant receive the death penalty. I was informed that no one had been executed in the naval services for almost a century, but I was extremely concerned that this case might end up being the first one. At trial I had very little to present in the way of a defense.

Hendricks was convicted and sentenced to death. The convening authority, however, mitigated the sentence to confinement at hard labor for life and a dishonorable discharge. While in military confinement Hendricks pursued an unsuccessful appeal in the U.S. Court of Claims, based upon an asserted inadequacy of counsel.* He was paroled from the Federal Corrections Institute at Ashland, Kentucky, in November 1980, having served eight years and nine months confinement. He went on to obtain college and postgraduate degrees. His major was criminology.

Drugs: Marijuana and More

"The Vietnam drug situation is extremely serious," read the *New York Times*.[20] Drug abuse had reached "crisis proportions." Major General Alan J. Armstrong, 1st Marine Aircraft Wing commander, told an audience at Hawaii's FMFPac Headquarters in 1971: "Those of you that think you know a lot about the drug problem, if you were not out there in the last year, you need to reappraise your thoughts."[21] Drug abuse in Vietnam reflected the drug problem in American society, except drugs were cheaper and more easily available in Vietnam. According to the Security Company commander at Force Logistic Command's (FLC) Camp Books, "The kids would come up and toss the marijuana over the wire to sentries, day and night."[22] Marines in rear areas who sent their utility uniforms to Vietnamese laundries often found several marijuana "joints" in their shirt pockets upon return of the uniforms — a form of business solicitation. The abundance of cheap, pure quality drugs, coupled with lax Vietnamese enforcement of its own narcotics control laws, made it easy for Marines with drug habits to continue and facilitated experimentation by the uninitiated. "We found," Lieutenant General William K. Jones said, "that 48 percent, or nearly half of the Marines, indicated a use of drugs at one time or another."[23]

Heroin was rare until late 1970, when cheap and plentiful quantities of the narcotic, long available further south, reached northern I Corps.[24] Major General Armstrong noted that "[drugs] really began to take their toll on our Marine population in Vietnam at about the 1970-71 period, and particularly in 1971, when the tempo of operations had slacked down."[25] The increase in drug use was reflected in the number of apprehensions for drug abuse. MACV, which included all American troops in Vietnam, reported that in 1965 there had been 47 apprehensions; there were 344 in 1966; 1,722 in the next year; 4,352 in 1968; and 8,446 in 1969. In 1970 the number was 11,058, despite rapidly dropping troop strength. MACV's command history noted that "it became apparent apprehensions were not an accurate measure of the magnitude of the problem."[26] Department of Defense and Congressional drug and narcotics committees which came to Vietnam for firsthand views of the issue were told that drug use was even greater than the numbers indicated.[27] In 1970, in the 1st Marine Division alone, there were 142 courts-martial for drug abuse and 211 drug-related administrative discharges.[28]

The Army also used administrative discharges for drug abuse as a relief valve. As Major General George S. Prugh, Judge Advocate General of the Army, wrote:

> It became increasingly clear that trial by court-martial was an awkward, ineffective, and expensive means of attempting to cope with a large-scale [drug] problem . . . . Soldiers whose behavior indicated that they lacked the desire or ability to rehabilitate themselves were eliminated through administrative channels.[29]

FLC, like other Marine Corps and Army commands, employed admin discharges to clear the decks of drug users and marijuana smokers. As Lieutenant Colonel Carl Buchmann, FLC's Deputy SJA, said:

> We had used administrative discharges for marijuana smokers, extensively . . . . When I arrived [in 1969] we had something like 85 or 95 general courts that . . . hadn't been tried yet. So we let it be known [to defense counsel] that we [the commanding general, with the SJA's advice] would entertain some admin discharges to avoid trial, and in one period, I remember giving out 25 in a very short period of time; approving them after they requested — for pot . . . . Some we did, some we didn't give admins to. So, if you say a solution has been arrived at, no, it hasn't. We're still guessing.[30]

The flow of drugs was unabated. Retired Marine Colonel Robert D. Heinl reported in a magazine article that: "In March [1971], Navy Secretary John H. Chafee . . . said bluntly that drug abuse in both the Navy and Marines is out of control."[31] Lieutenant General Leo J. Dulacki recalled that "just about the time the last Marines were leaving, the countryside suddenly appeared flooded with hard drugs, available anywhere and everywhere."[32] In January 1971 Brigadier General Edwin H. Simmons, Assistant Division Commander of the 1st Marine Division, pointed out that "you can go down to Freedom Hill recreation area and you can find a mama-san who will sell you a cap of pure heroin for from three to five dollars. It's a bargain! The same cap would cost you

---

*An appeal of a court-martial conviction via the Court of Claims is very unusual. Presumably the appeal was collateral to a claim for back pay.

50 dollars in [the U.S.]."[33] Major General Armstrong reported that one air group "had a heroin problem that I viewed as an operational problem, no longer an administrative problem."[34]

The Marine Corps took action to fight marijuana and drugs in Vietnam, which relied heavily on troop education. A platoon leaders' antidrug pamphlet was issued. Special drug education teams were employed, and drug abuse councils were formed.[35] Finally, lawyers of the various SJA offices tried abusers, or processed their administrative discharges. Throughout that period the Marine Corps took an adamant stand against amnesty programs. As the Commandant said: "The Marine Corps cannot tolerate drug use within its ranks. Those who experiment with drugs can expect to be punished. Those who become addicted will be separated."[36] Until the Department of Defense required all Armed Services to initiate amnesty programs, the Marine Corps maintained its resistance to them.[37] Meanwhile, drug use increased.

The lawyers' involvement with drug users was not always a matter of charge sheets and analysis. Captain Tommy W. Jarrett, an FLC defense counsel, was interviewing a client when he became suspicious of his state of sobriety. Captain Jarrett paused in his questioning and asked the young Marine: "Tell me something. Just between you and me, have you had a little pot today?" His client replied: "Sir, just between you and me, I have a little pot every day."[38]

Racial Conflict: High Tension

According to MACV's 1971 Command History for Vietnam:

> Many black soldiers in RVN, increasingly more articulate, better educated, and more impatient than their predecessors, continued to view the military establishment as a racist institution, within which little redress was possible. To many of them, the war in Vietnam was viewed, rightly or wrongly, as a white man's war in which they had no vested interest.[39]

Major General Edwin B. Wheeler, Headquarters Marine Corps' G-1, noted:

> There can be little doubt . . . that the most insidious obstacle to manpower readiness is that of racial unrest and violence. It strikes at the heart of two essential principles upon which our Corps is built: good order and discipline . . . . And it is especially unsettling when it results in Marines killing each other."[40]

Another Marine Corps general, questioned by newsmen after a racial incident, reportedly said: "We're not having a racial problem; we're having a criminal problem."[41] That hard line was mixed with Marine Corps efforts to ease racial friction and to take action against those who participated in racially inspired offenses, regardless of their race. During this period blacks constituted about 13 percent of Marine Corps strength, but were the accused in an estimated 50 percent of Vietnam courts-martial.[42] In FLC monthly Subversive Activities Reports, actually racial disturbance reports, were a continuing requirement for all subordinate commands.[43] In the 1st Marine Division leadership councils ("just a euphemism for race relations," admitted Brigadier General Simmons, the assistant division commander) were conducted at company, battalion, regimental, and division levels each month.[44] Keeping in mind that, as General Simmons noted, "the aggravation doesn't always come from the black side, it's very often prompted by the white side," human relations seminars, workshops, and black studies programs were efforts made to improve relations between races.[45]

The "Green Marine" approach (there are no black Marines or white Marines, only green Marines) was being recognized as ineffective. Not every problem was solvable through traditional leadership methods. Lieutenant General Jones, Commanding General of the 3d Marine Division in early 1970, and then Commanding General of the Fleet Marine Force, Pacific, said: "I think that 'all Marines are green' is an oversimplification of the very basic psychological quivers that are going through our society. And I think that it is wrong."[46] In 1970, despite changing attitudes and the Marine Corps' best efforts, 1,060 violent racial incidents occurred throughout the Corps, resulting in 79 Marines being seriously injured and two killed.[47] As redeployments from Vietnam continued into 1970, far fewer such incidents occurred in the war zone, and in 1971 there were none.[48]

Administrative Discharge: The Marines Clean House

The Marine Corps was having serious disciplinary problems among its junior personnel. III MAF's sergeant major in 1971 was Sergeant Major Edgar R. Huff. He noted:

> There is an element of men in the Corps today who have gotten past the recruiters . . . . This element has managed to fool, momentarily, the leadership of our Corps, just enough to get by for the time being . . . bent on ruining the proud record of the Corps. This element seems to make up less than one percent of the Corps' strength . . . . An element of hate, discontent, and even subversion, aimed at terrorizing . . . . They must be found out, punished, and expelled from our Corps.[49]

Besides malcontents, the Marines were troubled by

Department of Defense Photo (USMC) A419515

SgtMaj Edgar R. Huff was III MAF's sergeant major in 1971. He was troubled by the poor quality of Marine recruits that he saw in Vietnam. "They must be found out, punished, and expelled from our Corps."

the highest desertion rate in modern Marine Corps history—twice the rate of the Korean War's peak and nearly four times that of World War II.[50] The U.S. Army's desertion rate was even higher than that of the Marine Corps.[51] Often both soldiers and Marines deserted while on R & R in the country they were visiting.* Another 2,500 military men deserted and remained in hiding in Vietnam, most of them in Saigon.[52]

---

*In a variation on this theme, Marine PFC Douglas Beane deserted on 28 February 1970 while awaiting a general court-martial for black marketeering and threatening a witness. He made his way to Australia, a popular R & R spot, and remained there until he voluntarily returned to the United States in June 1987 and was apprehended by the Marine Corps. Newspaper reports quoted Beane as saying, "I went AWOL after one year of fighting in Vietnam, because I had enough of the war." He had been a cook, assigned to the 1st Force Service Regiment in Da Nang. In a controversial decision, the Marine Corps gave Beane an other-than-honorable administrative discharge, and dropped all charges against him. (*Navy Times*, 22Jun87, and 6Jul87, p. 11; *Washington Post*, 18Dec86, p. A59.).

Administrative discharge was the quick fix for dealing with malcontents, returned deserters, and drug abusers, all of whom, by their sheer number, threatened to overwhelm the military justice system. Colonel Robert M. Lucy, 1st Marine Division SJA, reflected: "If he appears to be a troublemaker . . . we just can't afford to keep him around. We just need to go ahead and get him out [through administrative discharge] because it's too dangerous, in a combat area, to keep that individual around."[53] Lieutenant General Jones spoke to the Commandant, General Chapman, about the need to act:

> I used the administrative discharge before Chappy said do it. I told him I was doing it, and I said, "I know Senator Ervin's given us hell for 20 years on it, but," I said, "we've got to do it. I'm administratively getting rid of these bums!" and Chappy said, "Go ahead."[54]

As the Marines left Southeast Asia, General Chapman anticipated post-Vietnam manpower reductions and initiated a "house cleaning" to separate those who didn't measure up. "Instead of moving in the direction of what is the mood of society in relaxing discipline," General Chapman told his generals, "what we must do is move in the other direction and tighten it up."[55] In Vietnam, commanders took full advantage of that policy. The 1st Marine Division, for example, ordered only 121 admin discharges in 1969, but issued over 800 in 1970.[56] In the first six months of 1970 III MAF issued 199 admin discharges for drug abuse alone.[57] As Brigadier General Simmons noted: "The greatest boon to our efforts at solving the marginal Marine problem has been the liberalized use of administrative discharges."[58]

Brigadier General William H. J. Tiernan, a former Director of the Judge Advocate Division, recalled the role that the administrative discharge (to escape trial by court-martial, a specific type of admin discharge) played, particularly in major U.S. commands: "It's amazing that we survived that era," he said, "and I think the reason we did survive it was because we developed the discharge . . . in lieu of court-martial."[59] Often referred to as a "good of the service" discharge, or "GOS," this variety of administrative discharge required only that the defense counsel prepare a statement in which his client admitted his desertion, for example, and requested an administrative undesirable discharge in lieu of court-martial. Almost always approved by the commanders involved, by 1971 the process took only a day or two to complete. It allowed both the Marine Corps and the accused Marine to close the books on offenses without a costly court-martial,

The 1970 FMFPac meeting of senior judge advocates took place at Camp Smith, Hawaii. Present were, front, from left, Col Robert M. Lucy; Col Donald E. Holben; Col Verne L. Oliver; Col Robert C. Lehnert; BGen Duane L. Faw; Col Marion G. Truesdale; Col Nalton M. Bennett; Col Arthur R. Petersen. Rear, LtCol William H. J. Tiernan; unidentified; LtCol Brian B. Kent; LtCol Robert J. Chadwick; Col Charles E. Spence, Jr.; Col Benjamin B. Ferrell; LtCol Henry Hoppe III; LtCol Joseph A. Mallery, Jr.; and Maj Curtis W. Olson.

on the Marine Corps' part, or a sentence to the brig, on the accused's part. Few deserters were concerned that the discharge was characterized as undesirable. "While the discharge to escape trial definitely did play a role in . . . Vietnam," Brigadier General Tiernan continued, "its use was insignificant in comparison with its use [in the U.S.] as the war wound down."[60] "We were, frankly, going under, and we could not have survived if we hadn't come up with the . . . discharge to escape trial. . . . It was a difficult and very painful evolution because it was contrary to all previous Marine Corps disciplinary standards."[61] While commanders only reluctantly authorized admin discharges in lieu of court-martial for absentees, many of whom had deserted to avoid service in Vietnam, they had little choice. As Brigadier General Tiernan recalled:

> The base legal office [in the U.S.] could not have processed this group of malingerers if trial . . . was required in every case . . . . It would take literally years to complete the process, even with the maximum utilization of assets, i.e., trying cases both nights and weekends . . . . On any given day during this period, members of this group [of unauthorized absen-

tees] could be seen arriving on foot at the gate, some with lengthy beards, headbands, ponytails, earrings, etc . . . . When it was recognized that extraordinary methods were required to process these unauthorized absentees, the "GOS" provided a solution.[62]

Each administrative discharge was processed by lawyers, whether in the U.S. or in Vietnam. Besides assigning a judge advocate to represent the individual, the SJA prepared a recommendation for the commanding general's consideration. In Vietnam in late 1970 Major James H. Granger was a lawyer in the 1st Division's SJA office. He recalled that "administrative discharges peaked in December [1970] when we processed 69 new cases, although we had another big month in March, as the Division prepared to withdraw."[63]

Upon learning of the increased number of admin discharges, then-retired Lieutenant General Victor H. Krulak said: "I applaud them, because it's wise . . . . They're culling out the Project 100,000s, and the dissidents, and recalcitrants . . . the guys who don't belong in the Marine Corps."[64]

From a Lawyer's Case File: Homicide on Patrol

"This is an initial report of possible serious incident involving . . . Vietnamese civilians of Thang Tay (1) hamlet," read the message to the commanding general of III MAF. It continued:

> Civilians allege U.S. Marine unit entered hamlet on 19 Feb 1970 and killed women and children. Patrol sent to check allegation found the bodies of approximately 16 women and children recently slain . . . . M-16 and .45 cal cartridge cases were noted in the immediate area. Earlier a patrol . . . reported a contact . . . in the same area with an estimated 25 VC resulting in 6 enemy kills. There are some indications that this report is inaccurate. Full scale inquiry commencing immediately.[65]

The hamlet designated Thang Tay (1) on American maps and the events that transpired there were soon known to Marine Corps lawyers by the hamlet's Vietnamese name: Son Thang (4).

Later, during his debriefing at FMFPac Headquarters in Hawaii, Colonel Robert M. Lucy, recently the SJA of the 1st Marine Division, noted:

> The fella who really gets out there and meets the [Vietnamese] civilians so frequently is a 19-year-old lance corporal who has very little maturity. It's a tremendous amount of responsibility. He's got all that firepower, and it's not a great surprise that every once in a while one out of many goes astray . . . . It's really, really serious business . . . . The great majority of them are doing a great job . . . . They're bearing such a tremendous burden and load in the war. Still . . . .[66]

Colonel Robert C. Lehnert, the SJA for Headquarters, FMFPac, agreed, saying that "the 19-year-old lance corporal is the same one that couldn't be driving the family car, at home, yet is placed in a position of tremendous pressure and responsibility . . . . It's a wonder that he functions as well as he does, under the circumstances that we place him in."[67]

Of the hundreds of thousands of Marine patrols conducted in Vietnam, only a very few resulted in improper or illegal acts. The Son Thang (4) case was one of those few. It remains a sad and tragic illustration of misused authority.

The 1st Battalion, 7th Marines operated from Landing Zone (LZ) Ross in southern Quang Nam Province. Lieutenant Colonel Charles G. Cooper, the battalion commander, described the area as "mostly uncultivated rice paddies, tree lines and . . . ruined villages, thinly populated, now. This area is honeycombed with bunkers, trench lines, spider holes, a million and one places a unit could be ambushed."[68]

Complicating the commander's execution of tactical responsibilities in that hostile environment was the impact of "Mixmaster." In September 1965 the Marine Corps ended its peacetime intertheater battalion rotation between the Eastern Pacific and Western Pacific and moved to an individual replacement system, codenamed Operation Mixmaster.[69] Lieutenant Colonel Cooper noted that Mixmaster involved not only replacements from the United States, but transfers of Marines within Vietnam, where the tactical situation in the south of III MAF's area of operations differed dramatically from that in the north, along the demilitarized zone (DMZ). "The DMZ was like World War I," Lieutenant Colonel Cooper said. "If it moved, blow it away."[70] In the more heavily populated south, however, greater restraint was required in combat operations, to preclude or at least minimize civilian casualties. Lieutenant Colonel Cooper recalled the effort to educate new arrivals to the southern portion of the III MAF battle area:

> Our approach to the constant influx of new people, both experienced and newly arrived, was to put them through a three- to four-day orientation period, and specific instructions on the rules of engagement . . . . It concerned me no end that the mystery of identifying who the enemy was, never was resolved, nor could it have been. Basically you responded to fire, and often that was too late.[71]

Despite training in the local rules of engagement, Lieutenant Colonel Cooper contended that "the trooper rightly never understood why we could order an air strike on a village that was the source of [enemy] fire, but a more definitive rule of conduct applied to the man with the rifle."[72] Cooper believed that Mixmaster played an unnoted but important role in the Son Thang (4) incident.

On 19 February 1970 Company B, 1st Battalion, 7th Marines, commanded by First Lieutenant Lewis R. Ambort, an experienced combat leader, was in a night defensive perimeter on Hill 50, southwest of LZ Ross. The company had been in heavy combat over the past few months and had suffered 14 Marines killed in action and 85 wounded since November. Two weeks before, while pursuing several suspicious Vietnamese women later determined to be enemy nurses, a Company B patrol was led into a booby trap which wounded several Marines.*[73] A week before a patrol had encountered three Vietnamese boys, estimated to be

---

*Lieutenant Colonel Cooper's recollection is that the patrol was led into an ambush that resulted in heavy casualties and a two-day battalion-level engagement. (LtGen C. G. Cooper ltr to author, dtd 23Jan89, Comment folder, Marines and Military Law in Vietnam file, MCHC.)

9 to 12 years old, carrying automatic weapons. In the ensuing firefight, one of the youths was killed.

That same day, on 19 February, before occupying their night defensive position on Hill 50, Company B had observed five or six Vietnamese boys, between 9 and 13 years old, in a nearby treeline, just before the company was taken under heavy automatic weapons fire. In yet another incident that day a member of the company had been shot and killed in an ambush. Company B had learned that the enemy could be a woman as well as a man and that youth did not preclude a deadly intent.

Late that afternoon the battalion operations officer, Major Richard E. Theer, had radioed Lieutenant Ambort and asked what patrols he planned for the night. "He told me his company was pretty well bushed. . . . He only intended to send out local security and one short patrol."[74] As dusk fell, Lieutenant Ambort ordered a "killer team" formed. At a later court-martial a corporal from Company B (who had not been involved in the events being tried) described a killer team's purpose: "A killer team is to go out and rove around and try to catch the enemy off guard, trying to hit quick and fast and try to get out of the area as quickly as possible without getting any casualties . . . . Any movement after dark was considered fair game, because they're [the Vietnamese] supposed to be in their hooches sleeping."*[75]

Usually such teams were led by noncommissioned officers, but that night Lance Corporal Randell D. "Randy" Herrod, recently transferred from the 3d Marine Division in the northern part of the III MAF, was in charge. Lieutenant Colonel Cooper recalled that Herrod "was considered bush wise and more mature that most of his comrades."[76] He was also a proficient map reader, a valuable skill on night missions beyond friendly lines. Further, Herrod was awaiting presentation of the Silver Star Medal, having been recommended for the award by his previous platoon commander, First Lieutenant Oliver L. North.[77]

Herrod had been convicted of unauthorized absence at a recent special court-martial. As a result he would be reduced to the grade of private within a few days, when the sentence of the court was approved. On the evening of 19 November he was still a lance corporal.

All of the members of the killer team were volunteers. Herrod was armed with a .45-caliber pistol and an M79 grenade launcher with buckshot rounds. There were four others in the killer team: Lance Corporal Michael S. Krichten, Private First Class Thomas R. Boyd, Private First Class Samuel G. Green, Jr. (on his first patrol, having arrived in Vietnam only 12 days before), and Private Michael A. Schwarz (transferred to the unit from the 1st Reconnaissance Battalion in the northern portion of III MAF just six days before). Lieutenant Colonel Cooper noted that during that period, "this type of small unit jury-rigging was unfortunately not unusual, and the high level of personnel turbulence added to the reduced professionalism."[78]

Shortly before the killer team departed, Lieutenant Ambort spoke to them:

> I gave them a pep talk . . . . I was talking to Herrod. I told him . . . I didn't want any casualties . . . . I emphasized the fact to him not to take any chances, to shoot first and ask questions later. I reminded him of the nine people that we had killed on the twelfth of February, and I reminded him of Whitmore, who had died that day. I said, "Don't let them get us any more. I want you to pay these little bastards back!" That's about it.[79]

At the Article 32 investigation the platoon sergeant, Sergeant Harvey E. Meyers, testified:

> I heard this rumor that the killer team was supposed to kill anything that moved, so I asked Private Herrod about it; exactly what he was told to do. And he said that the skipper [the company commander] told him to kill anything that moves. And I told him not to do it. I said, "Don't do anything stupid. Just go out and do your job and get some."**[80]

Asked what the term "get some" meant, Sergeant Meyers replied, "It means going and getting as many kills as possible; make contact with VC or NVA; kill as many as possible."[81]

---

*The same corporal was asked to describe a killer team mission he had been on: "Answer: Yes, sir. Like, let's see . . . . There were five of us and we went into a ville area. There was some movement and talking in this one hooch . . . . This man from another bunker starts hollering . . . . He's got a rifle, or something, so I went over and fragged him. Then, when I did that, all of the women started to run for the hootch—went around back. So my men opened up on the three mamasans. And, the next morning we came back, we found one man and one mamasan dead.

"Trial counsel [to military judge]: Colonel, the government requests that this witness be warned of his rights under Article 31 [against self-incrimination].

"Military judge: It's a bit late in the day, isn't it, Captain?"

**An Article 32 investigation is a pretrial investigation, required before a general court-martial may be convened. It is conducted by an impartial officer, usually a senior lawyer in the SJA's office, to determine if there is reason to believe an offense has been committed, and that the individual charged is the one who committed it. It is similar to a civilian preliminary hearing. The accused's counsel rights are fully applicable at an Article 32, but the rules of evidence are relaxed. Often, evidence comes to light that will not be admissible in a subsequent court-martial, with its more stringent application of evidentiary rules.

Department of Defense Photo (USMC) A371757

"I don't know who shot first, but I think it was a '79 that went off first and then Herrod said to kill them all." Here a Marine fires an M79 grenade launcher.

As darkness fell the killer team moved out. There was a bright moon as they approached the hamlet of Son Thang (4), only 500 yards from Company B's position on Hill 50, but a considerable distance in the area's harsh terrain.[82] Approaching a Vietnamese hooch, Herrod directed Schwarz to enter and inspect its interior. The six Vietnamese occupants were gathered at the front of the hooch on what was subsequently referred to as the "patio."

Later, testifying under a grant of immunity, Krichten recalled the sudden and unexpected events of the next few minutes:

> Herrod gave the order to kill the . . . people, and I told him not to do it . . . . Then he says, "Well, I have orders to do this by the company commander, and I want it done," and he said it again, "I want these people killed!" And I turned to PFC Boyd, and I said to PFC Boyd, "Is he crazy, or what?" And Boyd said, "I don't know, he must be." . . . And then everybody started opening up on the people.[83]

The range was estimated to be 10 to 15 feet. Schwarz, testifying in his own court-martial, said:

> A. . . . . All of a sudden, Herrod started yelling, "Shoot them, shoot them all, kill them."
> Q. What was in your mind at that time?
> A. To "get some" . . . . I grabbed my rifle, started firing, got with them in the direction they were firing and fired the same way . . . .
> Q. And what was in your mind at this minute?
> A. That we had some gooks in the bushes firing at us.
> Q. What about the people [on the patio]?
> A. I didn't even see the people. I didn't even remember. I had forgotten completely about the people.
> Q. And how did the firing stop?
> A. Someone yelled, "Cease fire," . . . . Then it dawned on me that these people, a bunch of people were lying there in front of me.[84]

According to later trial testimony, the killer team then formed in a column and, without discussion, walked towards another hooch. They left behind a Vietnamese woman of 20, three boys aged 13, 8, and 6, and two 13-year-old girls, all dead.

At the second hooch, much the same events occurred. As Krichten testified: "Schwarz was just coming out of the hooch, and Boyd and myself were just coming up on line, when Private Herrod gave the order to kill them all. And everybody hesitated. Then again he hollered at us, and said, 'I want these people killed immediately!' And then everybody started firing."[85]

Schwarz testified concerning the same event:

> A. Herrod yelled, "Open up, shoot them, kill them all."
> Q. What was in your mind at that time?
> A. The gooks had come back; we had more gooks . . . . Then I was firing and it dawned on me the women and people were right there in front of me . . . .[86]

Again, according to trial testimony, the team turned and, with no discussion, moved on toward a nearby tree line. This time they left behind two women (one of them blind), and two girls, aged eight and six, all dead in front of their thatched-roof dwelling.

At a third hooch the scene was repeated. Schwarz entered to ensure the hooch was empty. Outside, Herrod yelled: "There's a mamasan reaching for something!" and as Krichten later testified:

> I don't know who shot first, but I think it was a '79 [M79 grenade launcher] that went off first, and then Herrod said to kill them all, and everybody hesitated again, and he hollered at us again, "I told you that I want these people killed, and I mean it!" By that time everybody started opening up on the people.[87]

Schwarz testified:

> Herrod said, "Open up, kill them all, kill all of them!" . . . He fired his '79, then he reloaded, and all this time he was reloading he was yelling, "Shoot them, kill them all, kill all of them bitches!"
> Q: Did you ever fire your .45?
> A. Yes, sir, I did . . . . All of a sudden I started catching these flashes . . . so I started firing through there . . . . I thought they were muzzle flashes . . . .
> Q. What about these people [in front of the hooch]? Did you shoot at these people?
> A. I shot towards the people, but I didn't shoot at the people.
> Q. You shot between them?
> A. Yes, sir. I was trying to put my rounds between them, sir. . . . Then someone yelled, "Cease fire," sir.
> Q. What happened after that?
> A. I was standing there. I heard a baby cry and Herrod said, "[Schwarz], go shoot the baby and shut it up. . . ."

This was investigative exhibit number 23 from the Article 32 investigation of events that occurred in Son Thang (4). Huts 1, 2, and 3 mark where the Vietnamese victims died.

I put my .45 down and fired two rounds over the right shoulder [of the baby].

Q. You didn't hit anybody?

A. No, sir. I know definitely I didn't hit anyone.[88]

Krichten then testified: "I heard Private Herrod, I heard Private Herrod tell Private Schwarz to go shoot the baby that was crying, but I don't know if he did. I don't know if he did. All I heard was a .45 go off."[89] (At the Article 32 investigation, the officer who first viewed the bodies the next day reported that a dead woman at the third hooch was clutching a baby, "about 5 or 6 years old, at the most," who was also dead. "Its head had just been blown apart, and its grey matter was laying on the ground," he testified.)[90] At the third hooch the killer team left four females, aged 40, 35, 13, and 8, and two boys, 10 and 6, all dead.

Back at Hill 50 the firing was heard, raising concern for the killer team. The platoon sergeant testified: "We called them in and told them to return immediately to the pos [position], and then they told me that they had six confirms [confirmed enemy killed]."[91] Private Herrod and Lieutenant Ambort conferred to formulate the required spot report. Herrod told the lieutenant that there could have been as many as 12 to 16 enemy confirmed killed. Lieutenant Ambort called for an enemy rifle that had been captured several days before. He directed that it now be sent to battalion headquarters with the Son Thang (4) spot report, to add veracity to the claim of six enemy killed.

The report was logged in the battalion operations journal at 1950 that evening: "Spotted 15-20 VC, some carrying arms, with no packs, moving southwest along

Photo courtesy of LtCol Richard E. Theer, USMC (Ret.)
Maj Richard E. Theer, operations officer of 1st Battalion, 7th Marines, shown as a captain during a previous tour of duty in Vietnam. He conducted the initial investigation of the events of 19 February 1970.

trail. Set up hasty ambush, killed 6 NVA and 1 female. Patrol withdrew to Co. CP with 1 SKS."[92] The next morning, the battalion intelligence officer led a patrol in the vicinity of Son Thang (4) to check motion sensors that had been planted in the area. He was approached by a Vietnamese woman who indicated that the night before Marines had killed inhabitants of her hamlet. He radioed that information to the battalion command post, where it was received by Major Theer. Theer recalled that "I had switched the radio off the squawk box in the combat operations center to receive [his] message, because he indicated he did not want anyone to hear our conversation."[93] Directed by Major Theer, the lieutenant detoured to investigate and discovered the bodies of 16 women and children laying before three different hooches, along with a number of spent M16, .45-caliber, and M79 cartridge casings. He radioed his discovery to the battalion command post.

The report was again received by the operations officer, Major Theer. Theer, on his third tour of duty in Vietnam, was a highly experienced combat veteran who had operated in the same area as a company commander in 1965-66.[94] He knew there had been an enemy contact reported in that location the night before by a patrol from Company B and suspected that something was amiss. After approval by the battalion commander, Lieutenant Colonel Cooper, Major Theer recalled all of Company B to the battalion headquarters at LZ Ross to determine what might have happened. Later in court, Major Theer was asked:

> Q. When he mentioned that 16 women and children [were dead], this raised no suspicion in your mind?
> A. No, because it was in the hamlet where they had a contact on the nineteenth, and I had no reason to doubt that those people might have died as a result of fire between the Marines and the enemy, in that contact. That happens, you know, in war.
> Q. Did you find it unusual that there were no men mentioned?
> A. Not at all. That area, there are very few men out there. The men that you see out there are usually past the age of 70 or below the age of 10.

To determine if there had been any Marine involvement in the deaths, Lieutenant Colonel Cooper immediately ordered Major Theer to conduct an investigation.* The major interviewed the company commander, Lieutenant Ambort, who admitted that his spot report was false, and that the enemy rifle had not been recovered by the previous night's patrol. Next, the major interviewed each member of the patrol after warning them, in writing, of their rights to counsel and against self-incrimination. Each of the

---

*After the war, Lieutenant Colonel Cooper remembered the events somewhat differently. His recollection is that the first report of the incident was overheard on a battalion tactical radio net by himself, sometime after midnight. He recalls that soon afterward he asked for more information and upon learning that only one enemy weapon had been recovered, "I began to smell a rat." The next morning he recollects flying to Company B's position by helicopter, and thinking, "something just didn't add up." He recalls that he then sent the patrol to Son Thang (4) to investigate his suspicions. He further recollects that before Major Theer later interviewed the patrol, he, Lieutenant Colonel Cooper, had first warned them of their rights and interviewed them, only to stop them when they began to admit the truth. (LtGen Charles G. Cooper intvw, 14Aug, Session 10, Oral HistColl, MCHC; and Cooper ltr to author, dtd 12Sep88). Major Theer, on the other hand, recalls that he and Lieutenant Colonel Cooper had agreed that only he, Major Theer, should question Lieutenant Ambort and the patrol members because of Lieutenant Colonel Cooper's potential conflicting role as a court-martial convening authority. (Maj Theer ltr to author, dtd 24Feb89, Theer folder, Marines and Military Law in Vietnam file, MCHC.)

1970-71 PREAMBLE: DISCIPLINE IN DISARRAY

five readily agreed to an interview, and each declined legal counsel. All five gave written, sworn statements similar to the oral reports they had given Lieutenant Ambort upon their return from Son Thang (4) the night before: As they approached the hamlet they heard men's voices from a large group gathered on a patio. Thinking they had stumbled onto a meeting of VC, they stealthily approached, only to find the males gone. As they were detaining the remaining women and children they received enemy small arms fire. They returned the fire. Then, hearing noises in a previously cleared hooch, they returned to it and forced the occupants outside, whereupon the patrol was again taken under fire. Again, they returned fire. Implicit in their recitations describing the two instances was that the women and children had been caught in a crossfire. At the Article 32 investigation, Major Theer testified: "In each case their statements were almost identical, with a few discrepancies. And . . . I know that no five people could see the same thing."[95]

The next morning, accompanied by a patrol, an interpreter, and a scout dog, Major Theer made his own examination of Son Thang (4). He later testified:

> I went to each of these places that the men had described that they had taken fire from, and I put myself where I would have believed a sniper would have been hidden, or enemy soldier, or soldiers . . . and in every case it was impossible for me to see the patio in front of each house where these people were located.

Additionally, Major Theer looked for signs of the enemy:

> There were numerous freshly expended M79, M-16, and .45 caliber casings lying on the patio . . . . The patrol probed the entire scene in a 180 degree fan . . . without finding any expended enemy brass . . . or any sign of blood, drag marks, footprints, or broken vegetation . . . . At that point I seriously began to doubt the statements the patrol had given me.[96]

Upon returning to LZ Ross the major learned that after Company B had been called back to the battalion headquarters, and before he had conducted his interviews, Lieutenant Ambort apparently had second thoughts about the patrol report. Ambort had gathered the patrol members and told them that events were taking a very serious turn, that it would be best to simply tell the truth, and that he intended to do so himself, starting with revealing his own false spot report.

Major Theer was concerned that the statements he had taken might have been subtly coerced without his having known so. He testified:

> I felt that perhaps each of these men might have been under some duress, and I could recall the Colonel [Cooper, the battalion commander] had told me that we must insure that each man's rights were preserved . . . . Having been a company commander myself once before, you have a family relationship, the company commander being the father. The platoon commander, the platoon sergeants are the brothers, and all the men are the teenagers of the family . . . . There are very tight bonds. If the commanding officer said something, I'm sure that the men would feel like that might be what—they would take it as authoritative. Like your father speaking to you.[97]

Major Theer approached Lieutenant Colonel Cooper and told him that he needed legal advice. He suggested that division legal be consulted and Lieutenant Colonel Cooper immediately contacted division headquarters.

That evening Colonel Bob Lucy, the 1st Marine Division SJA, arrived by helicopter at LZ Ross. For two hours Lieutenant Colonel Cooper, Major Theer, and he discussed the cases in general terms, because it appeared that Colonel Lucy would soon be involved in the processing of the cases. Major Theer asked Colonel Lucy if he should keep, or disregard as improperly obtained, the statements he already had. "He said that was my decision, since I was the investigating officer."[98]

After Colonel Lucy's departure Major Theer decided to again interview each of the patrol members. This time he advised each of them in a typewritten preamble on a blank page: "I should not be influenced into making a statement merely because my commanding officer, First Lieutenant Ambort, told me to tell the truth and tell the whole story." Additionally, "I do desire/do not desire to withdraw my statement which was made on 21 February," was added to the written advice. Each of the five were to be given the option of withdrawing their previous statement, and would have to line out and initial his choice on the new form Major Theer would give each of them. One by one, he called the patrol members to his hooch for a second interview.

Lance Corporal Herrod said he would stand by the statement he had already given. Next, Private First Class Green, after being advised that he could withdraw his first statement and that, if he did so, it could not be used against him, said he too would stand by his original statement, but that he would orally respond to new questions. As Major Theer later testified:

> I asked Green to go over the circumstances again . . . and he began to tell me this in his narrative, and then he mentioned sniper fire. When he said that I said, "Now wait a

A member of the patrol from 1st Battalion, 7th Marines which investigated allegations of murder in Son Thang (4). He stands on the "patio" where six women and children died.

This photograph was Article 32 investigative exhibit 15. Marine investigators examine the Son Thang (4) hut where four Vietnamese women and children were murdered.

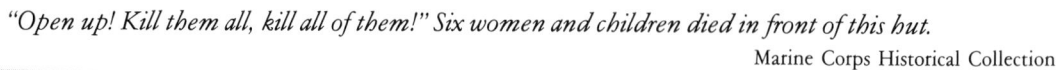

"Open up! Kill them all, kill all of them!" Six women and children died in front of this hut.

Maj Robert J. Blum conducted the joint Article 32 investigation that resulted in charges of murder against the Son Thang (4) "killer team" members. In later years he became one of the Marine Corps' most experienced general court-martial military judges.

minute, Sam. You know and I know that there wasn't any sniper fire." And he became very hostile at that point and turned towards me with fire in his eyes, and said, "What do I care about a gook woman or child? It's them or me! If they get in my way, that's too bad!" And then I asked him to go on, and mentioned, he mentioned the next house, and also taking sniper fire from it. And I told him, I said, "I've been out there. The area that you are describing was impossible for anyone to see where you were, if you were standing on the patio." And, with that, he turned around and said that he wasn't going to answer any more questions . . . that he had been in jail for some 23 months prior to coming in the Marine Corps, and that he wasn't going back. And I said, "Okay, Sam. The interview is terminated. You may return to your post."[99]

Next, Private Schwarz entered and, like the others, was again advised of his right against self-incrimination, to have legal counsel present, to decline a further interview, and to retract his statement of the day before. As Major Theer recalled:

> When Schwarz came into my quarters that night, he had a very bold approach. Very confident air about him . . . . While we were going over this narrative . . . he became nervous, and continued to smoke cigarettes one after another, and I, I felt that he was under some pressure. And I asked him . . . if what he had been telling me was the truth? And he indicated that it had not been the truth . . . . I asked if he was willing to make another written statement, or modify the one that he had already presented me. He said that he would . . . . I gave him a pad and a pen. He went in to the desk and commenced writing another statement . . . . During the course of the time he was writing this statement I could hear him sobbing in there, crying in the office.[100]

Schwarz was a 21-year-old ninth grade dropout. (He had scored a notably low 79 on the Armed Forces General Classification Test—GCT—a test akin to the civilian IQ test.) In his seven-page, handwritten statement he wrote: "When I relised what was happening I got scard and sick but was orderd to shot the people and knew if I did not obey the order I could get court mariald. From the time we started shotting I regetted ever going with this team . . . . The patrol resicved no sniper fire."[101]

Within four days of the incident, despite the patrol members' attempt to conceal their crime, it had been discovered, investigated, and revealed by the command. The five suspects were placed in pretrial confinement. The commanding general of the division, who had been kept informed of the progress of Major Theer's investigation, initiated daily message reports to the Commandant of the Marine Corps, as was usual in any major event. The press was advised of the case, and two helicopters flew 11 reporters to LZ Ross, where they were briefed for an hour by Lieutenant Colonel Cooper.[102] Newspaper reports quoted him: "You've got to realize the tremendous mental pressure these men are under . . . . Just because they are charged doesn't

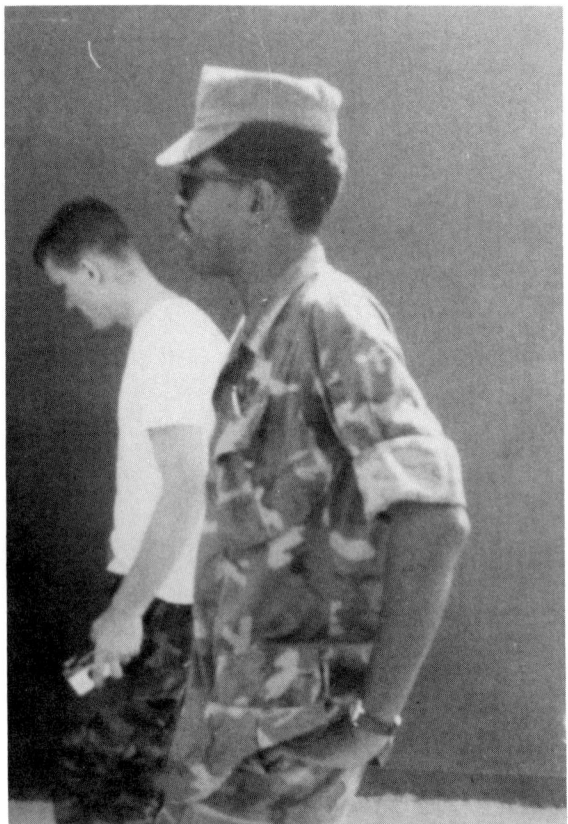

Capt Robert C. Williams was Pvt Randell D. Herrod's military defense counsel. His statements to the media resulted in a warning letter from the SJA.

at all mean they are guilty."[103] On 4 March the division SJA, Colonel Lucy, briefed seven newsmen regarding the legal events in progress. Afterwards he reported:

> We've been hit with more reporters than Carter has pills . . . . We've tried to give the press as much information as possible on these investigations, and on the trials. Of course, we've had [civilian] reporters attend all of our trials . . . . Our biggest problem has been how much information to give them in the investigative stage . . . . So far we haven't had . . . any real conflicts that couldn't be resolved . . . . At the general's direction [I] try to cut them in, informally, on what is going on in the case.[104]

Additionally, newsmen were permitted to accompany patrols that passed through or near Son Thang (4).[105] No aspect of the case was hidden.

Press reports of the charges provoked numerous letters to Headquarters Marine Corps objecting to what some perceived as the prosecution of young men for doing the killing they had been trained for. Many of the letters stressed the emotional toll of counterguerrilla operations as a mitigating factor. In replying to such letters on the Commandant's behalf, the Judge Advocate Division avoided comment on the pending cases, but noted:

> There is no denying that the ordeal of combat puts extreme pressures on the Marines fighting in Vietnam. However, the Marine Corps is fighting in Vietnam in the name of a nation which requires certain standards of civilized conduct to be maintained even under the trying circumstances of combat. Those standards do not permit the intentional killing of persons, such as civilians or prisoners of war, who are not actually participating in combat. When there is an allegation that such an event has occurred appropriate action must be taken in accordance with the law.[106]

Seventeen days after Schwarz' admissions a joint Article 32 investigation, at which the government had to present its evidence against all five accuseds, was convened. The investigating officer, Major Robert J. Blum, found it a demanding task to control the inquiry, with its five accuseds and five lawyers. Captain Robert C. Williams, defending newly demoted Private Herrod, was particularly aggressive in his representation: "Sir, are you aware of the fact that I was ordered into this courtroom, today?" He repeatedly moved to have Captain Cecil Forster allowed to join in defending Herrod, despite repeated denials of that request. He questioned the investigating officer's activities outside the hearing and his conversations with the SJA when the investigation was not in session: "During the course of the recess, Mr. Investigating Officer, where did you go? . . . Did you have a conversation with the Staff Judge Advocate?" Captain Williams correctly pointed out that the investigating officer was the same Major Blum who had presided at Private Herrod's special court-martial a few months before. Although Herrod had pleaded guilty then, and Major Blum had recommended clemency by reviewing authorities, Captain Williams made repeated, unsuccessful demands that Major Blum not be allowed to conduct the investigation of Herrod's involvement: "On the start along the long row of motions I have here today, it's requested, first, that a separate Article 32 investigation be held for Private Herrod. . . ."

After eleven days the Article 32 investigation was completed. Acting on Major Blum's recommendations, the commanding general referred Herrod and Schwarz to general courts-martial, in which they were charged with 16 specifications (counts) of premeditated murder. Both cases were referred to trial with instructions that they were to be tried as noncapital. Boyd and Green were referred to general courts, in which they were charged with 16 specifications of unpremeditated murder. Krichten's unrebutted testimony had been that he never fired at any of the civilians. Lieutenant Colonel Cooper recommended that he not be charged at all.[107] Krichten was granted immunity in return for his promise to testify in the trials of the other four.

First Lieutenant Ambort, the company commander, was defended by Captain Frank G. Roux, Jr., at his separate Article 32 investigation. The investigating officer, Lieutenant Colonel James P. King, the 1st Marine Division deputy SJA, ultimately recommended that Lieutenant Ambort receive nonjudicial punishment. At that proceeding, held by the 1st Marine Division's commanding general, Major General Charles F. Widdecke, Lieutenant Ambort received a letter of reprimand and forfeitures of $250 per month for two months for having made a false report. That was the maximum punishment imposable.[108]

Shortly before the first of the courts-martial began, Herrod's military lawyer, Captain Williams, was quoted in the *Pacific Stars and Stripes*:

> [Captain Williams] said the case was "political" in nature and controlled by headquarters to make sure that "the Marine Corps is not going to get caught up like the Army did, covering up at My Lai . . . . Everybody [is] scared . . . . The Marine Corps just wants to wash its dirty linen in public."

Finally, Captain Williams argued that, "evidence presented against the men at a pretrial hearing was not sufficient to warrant a court-martial, but that one was ordered by 'authorities higher than the 1st Marine Division.'"[109] His remarks were also carried on Armed Forces Vietnam radio. Five days later the SJA, Colonel Lucy, gave Captain Williams a letter citing Canon 7 of the American Bar Association's Code of Professional Responsibility. The letter read, in part:

> Disciplinary Rule 7-107 . . . cautions all lawyers in a criminal matter against expressing publicly opinions "as to the guilt or innocence of the accused, the evidence or the merits of the case." I do not intend to take any further action in relation to the statement attributed to you . . . . however . . . any further public communications of this type will be closely examined and may require the trial counsel to request official consideration of them prior to trial, by the . . . military judge.[110]

Private Herrod arranged for civilian counsel shortly after this, and Captain Williams played a minor role at trial.

Private Schwarz' court-martial began on 15 June 1970. The military judge was Lieutenant Colonel Paul A. A. St.Amour. Captains Franz P. Jevne and Charles E. Brown represented the United States. Captain Daniel H. LeGear, Jr., who had represented Schwarz from the outset, was defense counsel. Seven officer members heard the case, which lasted six days.* During the trial the defense counsel emphasized the danger of the area in which the 1st Battalion, 7th Marines operated. On cross-examination the defense counsel asked the lieutenant who discovered the bodies, "Would you consider the areas surrounding that ville to be 'indian country?'" The lieutenant replied: "I'd say it definitely wasn't pacified, sir."[111] Lieutenant Colonel Cooper, in a newspaper interview conducted about the time of the trial, said: "That's a big fort, out there," and described the area as one fighting trench and bunker after another. He went on to detail the many instances where Vietnamese children and women had proven to be the enemy.[112] (Major Blum later wrote of Lieutenant Colonel Cooper: "He could never quite accept as true that his Marines could commit murder.")[113] Confirming the hostile nature of the area's inhabitants, the Vietnamese district chief reported that the husbands of three of the dead women were confirmed to be Viet Cong, and that the inhabitants of Son Thang (4) had refused resettlement.[114]

Much of the court-martial was spent in an unsuccessful defense effort to keep Schwarz' damning written statement from being admitted into evidence. When defense motions and objections were overruled, and it was admitted and shown to the members, the defense shifted to an attempt to demonstrate that Schwarz had only acted in obedience to the direct orders of Herrod to shoot the victims.

In the end, Private Schwarz was convicted of 12 of the 16 specifications of premeditated murder. The members apparently accepted Schwarz' testimony that, at the hooch where four victims had been killed, he fired only when he thought he was himself being fired upon by an enemy. They found him not guilty of those four murders. The military judge's lengthy instructions to the members included: "I repeat, the accused committed no crime unless he knew that the enemy forces were not attacking him and his teammates at the time the alleged victims were allegedly shot."[115] The later

---

*There is no prescribed maximum number for a court-martial panel. The minimum number for general courts is five, and three for special courts. Any number above the minimum may be initially appointed, often 8 to 12 for general courts. That number may be reduced by an unlimited number of challenges for cause available to both sides. Each side also has one preemptory challenge. As long as the minimum number remains on the panel after challenges are exercised, the trial proceeds. If challenges reduce the membership below quorum, the court is recessed for as long as it takes to appoint new members and secure their attendance.

Pvt Michael A. Schwarz with his lawyer, Capt Daniel H. LeGear, Jr., in the second day of Schwarz' trial. In his fourth court-martial, Schwarz was sentenced to confinement at hard labor for life for the premeditated murder of 12 Vietnamese women and children.

appellate opinion in Schwarz' case held that "by their conviction of the accused, the court members necessarily found as a matter of fact that the accused could not have honestly and reasonably believed that Herrod's order to kill the apparently unarmed women and children was legal."[116] Outside the courtroom, Boyd heard of the verdict and cried: "They're a bunch of pigs, man. A bunch of . . . pigs."[117]

After determining Schwarz' guilt, the members were required to determine an appropriate sentence. During that phase of the trial they learned that, in just over three years, Schwarz had compiled a disciplinary record of five nonjudicial punishments, a prior summary court-martial, two special court-martial convictions, and now a general court-martial conviction. The members sentenced him to be confined at hard labor for life, to forfeit all pay and allowances, and to be dishonorably discharged from the Marine Corps.

The day after Schwarz was convicted, the court-martial of Private First Class Boyd, who already had one special court-martial conviction, was convened. As in the Schwarz case, Lieutenant Colonel St.Amour was the military judge. Captain Charlie Brown was trial counsel. In addition to his military defense counsel, Captain Michael P. Merrill, Boyd was defended by Mr. Howard P. Trockman of Evansville, Indiana. Mr. Trockman was reportedly paid through donations from the citizens of Evansville, Boyd's home town.[118] The 19-year-old Boyd and his lawyers opted to be tried by the military judge alone, perhaps out of concern for the heavy sentence the members had imposed in the Schwarz case. Even though Boyd would have had an entirely new panel of members, Boyd and his lawyers went "judge alone." It could not be any worse and it might be better.

Lance Corporal Krichten, again testifying for the government, swore that Boyd "fired well over their [the victims'] heads when they were already on the deck . . . . He was aiming over the people by about five feet and was the last to fire in all three shootings."[119] Krichten had not mentioned those facts in Schwarz' trial, but that testimony from the principal prosecution witness made Boyd's defense considerably easier. (Krichten's grant of immunity required him only to

Photo courtesy of Col Robert J. Blum, USMC (Ret.)

Capt Franz P. Jevne, left, prosecuted two of the four Son Thang (4) cases. Capt Daniel H. LeGear, right, defended one. They sit outside the 1st Marine Division Officers' Club on Hill 327 with Capt Theodore J. Padden after the courts-martial had ended.

PFC Thomas R. Boyd, right, and his defense counsel, Capt Michael P. Merrill, on their way to court on 22 June 1970. PFC Boyd was acquitted of all charges against him.

Associated Press

testify truthfully in the trials of the other four; it could not require that he testify "against" the other four.) Boyd was found not guilty a few hours later.

Private First Class Samuel G. Green, Jr.'s trial began shortly thereafter. Again, the military judge was Lieutenant Colonel St. Amour. Again, the trial counsels were Captains Jevne and Brown. Captain John J. Hargrove defended the 18-year-old Green. The case was heard by three officer and two enlisted members. Several pretrial motions had been denied, including a change of venue motion. Once more, the government's principal witness was Krichten, who testified that Green had fired his weapon in each instance where the victims had been killed, but that he did not see Green personally shoot any one of the 16. The government, however, did not proceed on the theory that Green had personally killed anyone. Rather, it urged that he was guilty as a principal to the murders, for having aided and abetted those who actually shot the victims—Herrod and Schwarz.

As in the Schwarz trial, the defense argued that whatever Green had done was only in obedience to Herrod's orders and stressed Herrod's command of the patrol and his combat experience, as opposed to Green's youth, his 12 days in Vietnam, and five and a half months total Marine Corps service. After the close of evidence, and arguments by counsels, the military judge's instructions to the members included:

> If you find beyond a reasonable doubt that the accused, under circumstances of his age, and military experience, could not have honestly believed the orders issued by his team leader to be legal under the law and usages of war, then the killing of the alleged victims was without justification. A Marine is a reasoning agent who is under a duty to exercise judgement in obeying orders.[120]

As in Schwarz' case, the members apparently believed that Green could not have honestly and reasonably believed an order to kill unarmed women and children was legal. He was convicted of 15 specifications of unpremeditated murder. He was acquitted of one specification in which testimony indicated Herrod alone had shot one woman, and Schwarz had followed Herrod's order to finish her off. Apparently giving Green the benefit of his youth and inexperience, the members sentenced him to confinement at hard labor for five years, reduction to private, forfeiture of all pay and allowances, and a dishonorable discharge.

A week after Green's conviction, 21-year-old Private Randell D. Herrod went to trial.[121] The military judge was Commander Keith B. Lawrence, JAGC, USN. Trial counsels were Captains Charlie Brown, Gary E. Bushell, and J. Len Skiles. Defending Herrod were Mr. Gene Stipe, assisted by Mr. Denzil D. Garrison, both Oklahoma state senators who had agreed to defend one of their constituents. They were assisted by civilian attorneys Richard Miller and Harry Palmer and military counsel, Captain Williams. As in the Boyd case, reports arose that Herrod's defense costs were paid through donations from the citizens of Oklahoma. In fact, State Senators Stipe and Garrison received no payment for their services and incurred considerable out-of-pocket expenses as a result of their representation of Herrod. "We did not ask for a fee, nor did we expect one," Senator Garrison later wrote.[122] Captain Williams' services, of course, were free. One hundred and sixty thousand Oklahomans did sign a petition to the Commandant of the Marine Corps urging the release of the five "unjustly confined" men.[123] All civilian defense counsels were flown to Vietnam at Marine Corps expense.[124]

The courtroom was small and filled by the various counsels and media representatives. Although all of the judge advocates assigned to the defense section had become part of the defense effort, there was little room for them to view the proceedings.[125]

The defense's pretrial motions were numerous and aggressively presented, supported by witnesses and legal authority. The government vigorously met each defense gambit with its own witnesses and citations. The defense raised motions for a new Article 32 in-

Capt John J. Hargrove defended PFC Samuel G. Green, Jr. Green was convicted of the unpremeditated murder of 15 Vietnamese women and children.
Photo courtesy of Col Robert J. Blum, USMC (Ret.)

The 1st Marine Division courtroom where the Son Thang (4) defendants were tried. The members' box spans the far side of the room. The witness stand is to the left. The reporter's table is partially visible at right. The military judge's bench is out of the photo to the right.

vestigation (denied), a change of venue (denied), production of the service records and billeting assignments of everyone involved in the case (records denied/billeting granted), all messages mentioning the case, including classified message traffic (granted), suppression of photographs of the dead victims (granted—a significant defense victory), release of Herrod from confinement (denied), autopsies of the victims (withdrawn), "relief from all of the other oppressive procedures of the UCMJ" (denied), for the Marine Corps to pay for the hire and attendance of a civilian psychiatrist (granted), for an entirely enlisted members panel (denied), and numerous other motions, as well. Disposing of motions took five days.

The maximum penalty for premeditated murder was death, but the commanding general had directed that Herrod's case be considered noncapital. Six months after the Son Thang (4) incident, the presentation of evidence in the court-martial of the team leader began. (The government now referred to the patrol as a "mobile night ambush," rather than a "killer team.") The prosecution took less than eight hours to present its case. The defense took less than three days, including presentation of testimony from Lieutenant Colonel Cooper, who returned to Vietnam for the sole purpose of testifying on Herrod's behalf. He returned only four days after reaching the United States, following his own Vietnam tour.[126] In addition, Senators Stipe and Garrison presented evidence of an American M60 machine gun that had been captured in the vicinity of Son Thang (4) shortly after the incident. That supported other testimony that a machine gun was heard by Company B personnel, firing while the killer team was in Son Thang (4), and buttressed the contention that the team had been returning fire when the victims were killed. Senator Garrison noted: "In my judgement, this was a very important facet of evidence. Schwarz and Green did not have that testimony to corroborate their story."[127]

Major Theer's tour of duty was also completed before the courts-martial began. He twice returned to Vietnam to testify, first against Schwarz, then Herrod. He later wrote that he had been "very disturbed" upon learning that Lieutenant Colonel Cooper had testified for the defense.[128] Additionally, although Major Theer was a government witness in the Herrod trial, he had been unaware of the testimony regarding the captured machine gun. Years later, when he learned of it Major Theer wrote:

> I very clearly recall that M-60 capture. I frequently spoke by radio with the S-3 [operations officer] of 3d Battalion, 21st Infantry, 196th [U.S. Army] Brigade . . . . I remember him telling me about one of his units capturing an M-60 machine gun after an engagement with a VC unit south and west of Hiep Duc. That location was over 15 miles southwest of Son Thang (4) . . . . Further, there was never any mention of a machine gun being fired by any of the patrol members in the alleged enemy contact on the evening of 19 February.[129]

As the trial continued, Herrod's platoon commander, Second Lieutenant Robert B. Carney, also testified in his behalf, as did his past platoon commander, First Lieutenant Oliver L. North. Through Lieutenant North's testimony the members learned of Herrod's pending Silver Star Medal, direct evidence of which had been ruled inadmissible. A distinguished Oklahoma psychiatrist, Dr. Hayden Donahue, testified as to the conditioned response that Marine training ingrained in infantrymen like Herrod. Finally, Herrod took the stand in his own defense and repeated that the victims had been killed in cross-

The Herrod defense team poses with some of the defense witnesses. From left: State Senator Gene Stipe, partially hidden; attorney Mr. Richard Miller; Capt Robert C. Williams; Pvt Randell D. Herrod; 1stLt Lloyd S. Grant; 1stLt Oliver L. North; attorney Mr. Harry Palmer; 1stLt Lewis Ronald Ambort; and State Senator Denzil D. Garrison.

Photo courtesy of Mr. Denzil D. Garrison

fires between his team and enemy forces. He told the members: "I do not now, and I did not then, feel that I had killed anyone it wasn't necessary to kill."[130]

Before resting, the defense made several motions for a mistrial based upon purported misconduct by government counsels. All were denied. After resting, there were further defense motions for mistrial, renewal of motions previously denied, motions to dismiss, and motions for a finding of not guilty, one based on Herrod's asserted lack of mental responsibility. All were denied.

After 12 days in court, the members were instructed, and retired to deliberate. They returned with their verdict after three hours. The members found Herrod not guilty of all charges and specifications. "We walked the patrol leader," defense counsel Garrison later said, seemingly still amazed.[131]

Captain Paul J. Laveroni, a 1st Marine Division defense counsel, recalled that the outcome "raised all the usual questions in the minds of laymen, who couldn't understand how Herrod had walked, when two of his subordinates ended in the slammer."[132] They were not unreasonable questions.

Private Herrod was released from confinement. Soon thereafter, the deputy SJA, Lieutenant Colonel Peter N. Kress, escorted him to division headquarters, where he received the Silver Star Medal for his combat actions before Son Thang (4). It was a muted award presentation, conducted by the division personnel officer, Colonel Hugh S. Aitken.[133] Within days, Private Herrod returned to the United States and was discharged, having served his enlistment.[134]

The commanding general of the 1st Marine Division reduced Private Schwarz' confinement from life to one year. His dishonorable discharge was left undisturbed. With credit for "good time" and for pretrial confinement, Schwarz was eligible for release in January 1971, less than a year after the murders of which he stood convicted.

On appeal, Schwarz' lawyers argued that the acquittal of Herrod required disapproval of Schwarz' conviction. The appellate court did not dispute Herrod's role. ("The record . . . shows beyond any doubt that Herrod's orders to kill the unarmed women and children were patently illegal.") It noted, however, that Schwarz' conviction was based upon the theory that he either did the actual killing, or aided and abetted the actual killing. Under the latter theory, the court held that, "the acquittal of the principal [Herrod]

Photo courtesy of Mr. Denzil D. Garrison

The accused and witnesses for the defense await the trial's outcome. Pvt Herrod is flanked by his company commander, 1stLt Lewis R. Ambort, left, and his former platoon commander, 1stLt Oliver L. North, who had recommended Herrod for the Silver Star Medal.

presents no impediment to the trial and conviction of a person charged with aiding and abetting the commission of the crime. This is because one who aids or abets . . . is guilty as a principal of a substantive, independent offense." The appellate court denied Schwarz' appeal.[135]

Private Green's five years confinement was similarly reduced by the commanding general to one year. His dishonorable discharge, too, remained undisturbed. On appeal, his argument that Herrod's acquittal required disapproval of his own conviction met the same result as Schwarz' similar argument.[136]

Future Secretary of the Navy James H. Webb served as a Marine Corps platoon commander and company commander in the Son Thang (4) area.* He found unfairness in the conviction of Private Green and later wrote a law review article urging that "justice was not served."[137] He suggested several bases upon which the

---

*Webb earned the Navy Cross, Silver Star Medal, two Bronze Star Medals, and two Purple Hearts. In 1972 he was medically retired from the Marine Corps as a captain, and in 1975 attained a law degree.

conviction should be set aside, including Green's belief that Herrod's orders to kill the civilians were justified, and that Green had a duty to obey the orders of his team leader. Captain Webb, an infantry officer, also pointed out that none of the members who heard Green's case had infantry backgrounds. While still in law school, Webb aided a civilian attorney, Mr. James Chiera, in an unsuccessful attempt to have the courts of Ohio, which had jurisdiction over then-civilian Green, set aside the court-martial conviction. Although the civilian judge dismissed the collateral attack on the military conviction he was sufficiently impressed with Green's case to himself write the Secretary of the Navy urging clemency. The Secretary declined to act.[138]

In 1977, at Webb's urging, Green's dishonorable discharge was upgraded to a general discharge.[139] But in July 1975, before Webb's intervention, former Private Green had shot and killed himself.

While awaiting a general court-martial for his part in the coverup of the My Lai incident, Army Colonel Oran K. Henderson charged that every large American combat unit in Vietnam had its own My Lai.[140] If there was anything positive in the Son Thang (4) cases, it was that no thought was ever given to a My Lai-type coverup at any point, at any level.

CHAPTER 9

1970-1971: Redeployment

*Force Logistic Command: Playing Catch-Up—From a Lawyer's Case File: The Defense Wins Four
1st Marine Aircraft Wing: Prepared for Takeoff—1st Marine Division: New Broom—Trying Cases
Last Call for Combat—Closing Cases Versus Best Defense—The Last Marine Lawyer Out—Perspective*

By early 1970 the timetable for Marine Corps withdrawal from Vietnam had taken form. U.S. Army units in the I Corps area were assuming Marine Corps tactical responsibilities. During March, in an exchange of roles, the Army's XXIV Corps took command of all remaining United States forces in the I Corps area. The reduced III MAF Headquarters, now under Army operational control, continued to command the 1st Marine Division, squadrons of the 1st Marine Aircraft Wing, and elements of Force Logistic Command. The Army's XXIV Corps took over the III MAF compound east of Da Nang. The Marine headquarters moved to Camp Haskins, Red Beach, near FLC's cantonment at Camp Books. By 9 March, the date of the official change of command, III MAF Headquarters was reduced in strength to 105 Marine Corps and six Navy officers. Under it were 40,000 Marines, down 15,000 from just two months before.[1]

Colonel Marion G. Truesdale continued as III MAF Headquarters staff judge advocate (SJA) until the end of February 1970. Upon his departure, III MAF SJA responsibilities were assumed by the SJA of FLC, Colonel Arthur R. Petersen, who had been promoted to that grade in October 1969.[2] Three Marine Corps SJA offices remained in Vietnam: those of the 1st Marine Division, 1st Marine Aircraft Wing, and FLC/III MAF Headquarters.

Force Logistic Command: Playing Catch-up

In July 1969 when Colonel Petersen first became FLC's staff judge advocate, he found an "appalling" backlog of untranscribed cases, a shortage of both judge advocates and court reporters, and equipment deficiencies.[3] "It was in a hell of a mess," recalled Captain W. Mark Wood, one of his trial counsels.[4] The tapes of 34 general courts-martial awaited transcription, an alarmingly high number, and there was no accurate count of the special courts awaiting typing.[5] If a court-martial is not tried within a reasonable period, or if a conviction is not reviewed for legal sufficiency and correctness in timely fashion a conviction may be set aside and the charges are subject to dismissal. FLC's backlog was affecting the review of cases at the appellate level.

FLC's SJA office was a very active trial shop. In 1969, with roughly 23 percent of the Marines in Vietnam assigned to it, its 12 judge advocates (the average number in 1969) tried 55 percent of all general courts-martial and 46 percent of all special courts tried by Marines in Vietnam.*

The assignment of lawyers to Vietnam did not recognize FLC's disproportionate case load. As 1970 began, 17 judge advocates were assigned to FLC, 26 to the 1st Marine Division, and 14 to the 1st Marine Aircraft Wing. That distribution was consonant with the number of Marines assigned those commands. However, it did not take into account that aircraft wings historically had fewer courts-martial than other similarly sized commands. Additionally, units engaged in combat operations also had a lower disciplinary rate when compared to rear-echelon units like FLC.

Headquarters Marine Corps and FMFPac responded to Colonel Petersen's urgent requests and the number of judge advocates assigned to FLC began to increase from 13 in September 1969 to 15 in November, then 17 in January, and eventually a peak of 22 in late 1970. Throughout 1970 the number averaged an adequate 15.[6]

When lawyer strength was still low, Colonel Petersen, his deputy, Lieutenant Colonel Carl E. Buchmann, and the legal administrative officer, Chief Warrant Officer 2 Len E. Pierce, redoubled their efforts to reduce the transcription backlog. Captain Wood recalled, "Those guys worked themselves from morning till night, and everybody else, too."[7] Reporters and typists were assigned to shifts and the typing of backlogged court-martial tapes progressed around the clock. One judge advocate was assigned to do nothing but write reviews of those records—seven days a week. Trips to Da Nang were curtailed, liberty runs to China Beach were cancelled, and leave was delayed.

---

*In January 1970, FLC personnel totalled approximately 11,550; the 1st Marine Division, 24,000; the 1st Marine Aircraft Wing, 12,050; Headquarters III MAF, 3,050 (Cosmas and Murray, *Vietnamization and Redeployment*, App. F, pp. 457-461). In 1969, FLC tried 68 of 123 GCMs and 472 of 1023 specials (Navy JAG, Code 64.2; and FLC ComdC, Jan-Dec69, MCHC.)

Photo courtesy of Capt G. H. O'Kelley, USMCR

Judge advocates seen at Camp Books. Kneeling, Capt Reynold L. Caleen, Jr. Standing, from left, Capt Richard L. Franks; Capt Stephen H. Vengrow; Capt Tommy W. Jarrett; Capt John S. Papa; Capt W. Mark Wood; Capt Jacob R. Henderson, Jr. (raised fist); Capt Richard S. Towers; Capt Terrance B. Rodsky; and Lt Kenneth Rothmeier, Medical Corps, USN.

Reducing the backlog overrode all considerations except prosecuting current cases.

Since the movement of the courtroom to the air conditioned, former computer building in late 1969, courts-martial proceeded smoothly. But more court reporters and typists were needed to attack the backlog and to maintain the flow of current trials. Because typists were not arriving from stateside schools or commands, Colonel Petersen sought them from local FLC personnel officers. Unlike the response to the reporter shortage in 1966, commanders were unwilling to give up personnel for an in-house reporter school since the trial and processing of courts-martial was now solely the SJA's responsibility. As Colonel Petersen noted, "No general officer who is already understrength in personnel . . . wants to surrender even more billets to bring up to [strength] the office . . . that deals exclusively with his 5 to 10 percent 'bad asses.' "[8] But recognizing the reluctance to meet the problem did not ease it. "My patience with personnel types is growing thin," Colonel Petersen wrote, "poor planning, or guessing, as to an adequate [SJA office] table of organization initially, and ever-increasing requirements under the law, have placed FLC in the position it presently finds itself."[9]

The enlisted tide began to turn when Brigadier General Mauro J. Paladino, FLC's new commanding general, ignored manning levels and tables of organization and ordered 10 clerk-typists transferred from various other FLC units to the SJA's office for training as legal clerks. Gunnery Sergeant John Casey, the reporter chief, soon had them typing excellent records of trial. By mid-1970 the accumulation of untyped trial records was shrinking and lawyer assignments were increasing.[10]

During 1970 the number of special court-martial convening authorities dropped from 16 to 11 as units departed Vietnam.[11] That, too, helped the lawyers reduce backlogs. In the months remaining before FLC was itself deactivated, the caseload wound down with the decreasing number of personnel—only 3,800 by year's end.[12] From July 1970 through March 1971 eight general and 144 special courts-martial were tried. It was a large but manageable caseload.[13]

Colonel Petersen was relieved by Colonel Daniel F.

McConnell on 1 July 1970. Colonel McConnell had enlisted in the Marine Corps during World War II and served in the Marshall Islands and on Okinawa. After the war he was a first sergeant when selected for commissioning. He commanded a Marine aircraft group headquarters squadron in Korea during that conflict and obtained his law degree in 1954. Now on his second tour in Vietnam, he inherited 44 previously tried cases that remained to be cleared. Although there were sufficient captain judge advocates, Colonel McConnell was essentially without a deputy and not a single major was assigned to his office. FLC's personnel situation, so recently corrected, was again skewed in anticipation of deactivation and withdrawal from Vietnam. Colonel McConnell recalled that working hours for legal personnel were from 0700 to 2100. "Fortunately, I had some fine captains," he said.[14] Nevertheless, FLC's last two years in Vietnam were difficult ones.

From a Lawyer's Case File: The Defense Wins Four

On 5 February 1970 The Chiffons, a three-girl Australian singing group backed by a three-man combo,

The new SJA of FLC, Col Daniel F. McConnell, found many backlogged cases, as had his predecessor.
Photo courtesy of Col Daniel F. McConnell, USMC (Ret.)

was performing at "Andy's Pub," the Maintenance Battalion enlisted men's club at FLC's Camp Books. Initially the USO group had been asked to cancel their show because of simmering racial discontent among the battalion's Marines, but recognizing that cancellation could cause more problems than it might avoid, the show went on. About 400 Marines crowded into the 50-by-30-yard patio outside the club, which was surrounded by a seven-foot-high wooden fence.

At 2045, as the girls sang one of their last numbers, a band member saw an object tossed over the fence. A few seconds later, a second object was thrown over. The first hand grenade had failed to detonate. The second exploded.[15] "Suddenly there was an explosion," a band member later said, "and sand, stones, and bits of wood, and metal from tables and chairs came flying up on the stage."[16] Corporal Ronald A. Pate, who had been standing by the patio fence watching the show, was killed. Sixty-two other Marines were injured, 52 of them requiring hospitalization.[17]

A few hours before the explosion, there had been a gathering of 20 to 30 black Marines assigned to Maintenance Battalion. In the past, many similar meetings took place on the battalion basketball court. Grievances were aired and responses discussed. The most frequent complaints were seemingly minor issues—haircut regulations and the lack of soul music in the enlisted club's jukebox. The battalion commander later testified he had been aware of the meetings for five months, but had taken no action either to address the men's concerns or to end the gatherings.[18] At the meeting on 5 February Lance Corporal Joseph L. Jones told the assembly, "we're going to 'do' some beasts [white Marines] tonight," and those present were warned not to go to the enlisted men's club.

In a written statement he later provided investigators, Corporal Ronald E. Gales admitted breaking into an ammunition storage locker, assisted by Lance Corporals Jones and James B. Addison. They stole 12 M26 fragmentation hand grenades and placed them in an empty sandbag.[19] The three were then joined by Lance Corporal Andrew M. Harris, Jr. All four had been at the earlier meeting on the basketball court.[20] Asked if the only motivation for the attack had been racial, trial counsel Captain Mark Wood opined: "Definitely . . . This was a deliberate, carefully thought out attempt to kill a hell of a lot of people . . . strictly because of racial problems. That was the only motivation."

In the early evening darkness Gales, Harris, Jones,

The scene in "Andy's Pub" shortly after an M26 fragmentation hand grenade was detonated near the fence, at right. One Marine was killed and 62 others were injured.

and Addison walked to the enlisted men's club where The Chiffons were performing. Jones entered to warn blacks inside to leave, but because of the crowd, reached only a few. Those he did reach left without question. According to Gales, when Jones rejoined the other three outside the club, Harris exclaimed, "I'm going to fire a whole bunch of these beasts up!" and lobbed a grenade over the fence. According to Gales, Harris had pulled the grenade's pin, but neglected to remove the tape that secured the spoon to the striker, preventing detonation. When it failed to detonate, again according to Gales, Harris tossed the second grenade over the fence.* Blacks and whites alike were wounded in the explosion that followed.[21]

Sirens blared as reaction platoons rushed to their assigned areas, assuming that enemy infiltrators were inside the wire. Minutes later, when the first, unexploded grenade was found in the debris, investigators realized what had happened. After several days of intense investigation Jones was identified as the Marine who had warned blacks to leave the club. He was apprehended, and the other three were soon identified. Harris, two days from his discharge, was returned from Camp Pendleton to Vietnam to stand trial.

The trial counsel for all four cases was Captain Wood, who was assisted by Captain John A. Bergen. Although investigators had been able to identify the accuseds by piecing together numerous statements, there were no witnesses to the act who could provide testimony against the four, other than the conspirators themselves. The investigators did, however, have the detailed written, sworn statement of Gales, which appeared sufficient to convict him, at least. He might then be used as a witness against the other three. Still, when Gales' defense counsel, Captain Stephen H. Vengrow, offered his client's testimony in the other three cases in return for immunity, the command, for reasons not recorded, accepted the offer. Captain Wood

---

*Other evidence indicated that Gales threw the grenade that had not detonated, and that Harris threw the one that did detonate. It was never proven who threw which grenade, however.

was not consulted, although defense counsel Captain George H. O'Kelley recalled that "the government was sucking wind for any strong proof, without Gales." Later events demonstrated that Gales was not the government's best choice for immunity.

Gales was transferred to the brig at Iwakuni, Japan, out of fear for his safety in the III MAF brig, where anyone testifying for the government faced physical harm by other prisoners. Several other Maintenance Battalion personnel who provided statements incriminating the four accuseds were transferred to Okinawa "for their own safety. It was feared that reprisals would be taken against them by unknown persons."[22]

On 1 June 1970 Lance Corporal Andrew M. Harris went on trial before Lieutenant Colonel Paul A. A. St.Amour and a panel of officer members, charged with premeditated murder, conspiracy to commit murder, and 62 specifications of assault with intent to commit murder. He was defended by a seasoned civilian counsel, Mr. Reuben A. Garland of Atlanta, Georgia, and by his military defense counsel, Captain O'Kelley. Later, Captain Wood ruefully said: "I can tell you, I learned a lot about the practice of law from that civilian counsel."[23]

Testifying under his grant of immunity, Gales described the events of 5 February and identified Harris as having thrown both grenades. Taking the stand in his own defense, Harris swore it was Gales who threw both grenades. In this "swearing contest," the prosecution had the problem of employing one "bad guy" to point the finger at another. Unfortunately, the prosecution's "bad guy" had a poor disciplinary record, while the accused had a clean record. That fact was spotlighted for the court by Mr. Garland.

This was prosecution exhibit 4 from U.S. v Harris. *The enlisted men's club is at right. The messhall where the accused conspirators worked is bottom center. The area between the barracks where they gathered before walking to the enlisted men's club is upper center.*

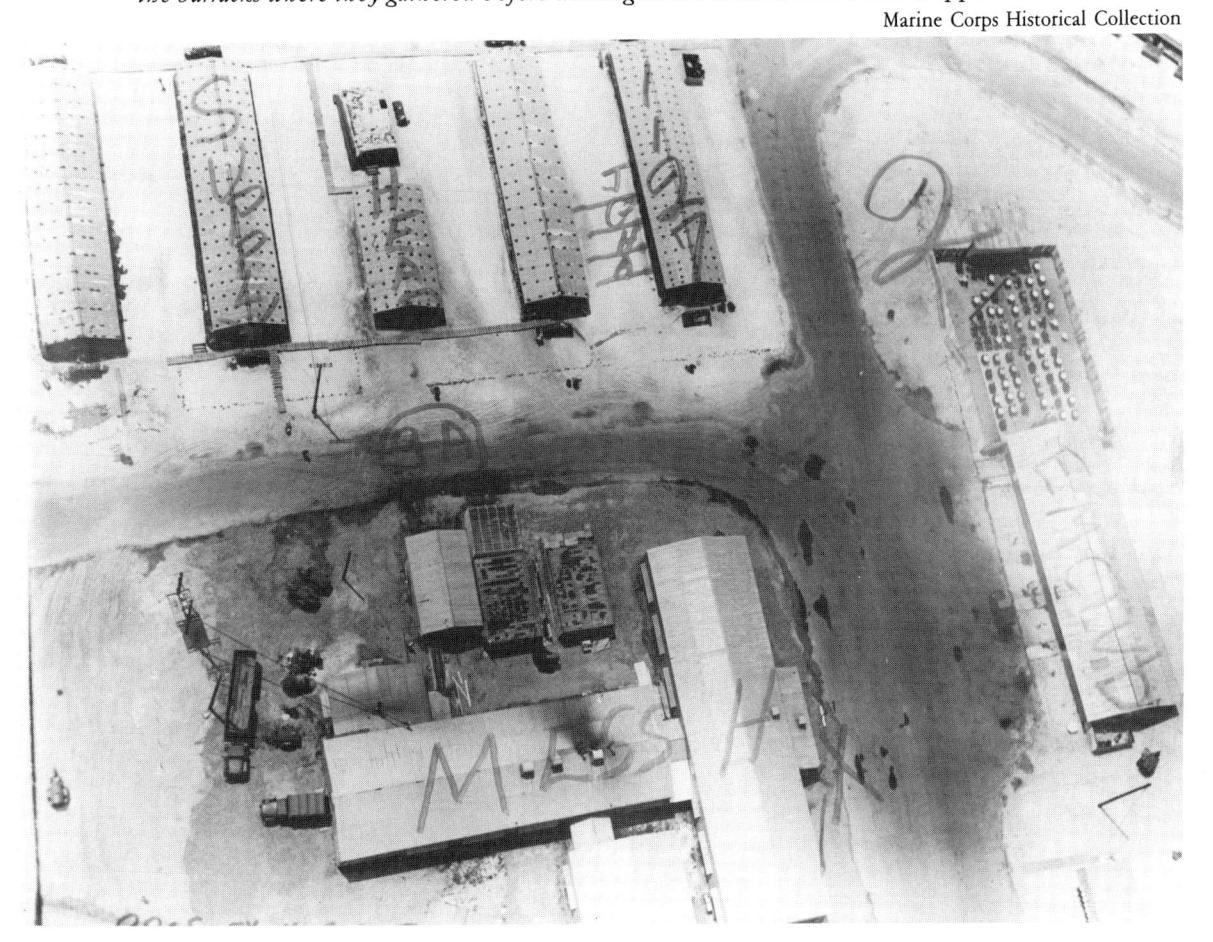

Marine Corps Historical Collection

Marine Corps Historical Collection

This was the first fragmentation hand grenade that was tossed over the fence of the enlisted men's club. The conspirators pulled the pin but neglected to remove the tape that allowed the striker to operate.

After a six-day trial, the members found Lance Corporal Harris not guilty of all charges. His enlistment having been served, he was honorably discharged.

Next to be tried was Lance Corporal James B. Addison. All parties agreed that he had not thrown the grenades, but he was to be tried as a principal to the act. Defended by Captains William A. Price and Reynold L. Caleen, Jr., Addison's case, too, was heard by Lieutenant Colonel St.Amour and a second panel of officer members. After Gales testified against him, Addison swore that on 5 February he had turned and ran when he realized what was about to happen. Choosing, as in the first trial, to believe the accused and to disbelieve the government's witness, Gales, the members found Addison not guilty of all charges.

The Marine Corps was unwilling to meet the expense and effort of another trial in what appeared to be a losing cause. Rather than try Jones, the remaining accused, he was administratively discharged for unrelated drug involvement which predated the murder-assault charges.

Although the overwhelming percentage of courts-martial that go to trial end in conviction, in the cases of Harris, Addison and Jones, no one was convicted of the murder and 62 assaults. Later, Captain Wood pondered what might have happened if the four had been tried in a different order, or if someone other than Gales had been granted immunity. If tried first, Captain Wood wondered, how would Jones have explained his entry into the club to warn away black patrons, other than as a prelude to the fatal attack? If convicted, would he have been willing to testify against the others in return for sentence reduction?[24] Like all post-trial second guessing, Captain Wood knew they were questions without answers.

1st Marine Aircraft Wing: Prepared for Takeoff

In 1969 two fixed-wing and two helicopter squadrons together with support personnel left Vietnam. In March 1970 the 1st Marine Aircraft Wing's strength in Vietnam was down to 10,243. In August and September additional squadrons of the wing redeployed to Hawaii and El Toro, California. By the end of 1970 the wing, with 6,100 Marines remaining in Vietnam, was working out final standdown and redeployment schedules.[25]

In September 1970 Colonel Nalton M. Bennett, SJA since September 1969, was succeeded by Major Curtis W. Olson, a former helicopter pilot and the deputy SJA for the preceding three months. Having completed a previous tour in the office of the SJA of the 1st Marine Division, Major Curt Olson served slightly more than two years in Vietnam, longer than any other Marine Corps judge advocate in the Vietnam war.* Of his two tours he recalled:

> There was a considerable difference between my two tours in Vietnam. In my first tour I do not recall any drug cases . . . nor do I recall any black market or currency exchange cases. Upon my return . . . those types of cases were a large share of the case load . . . . My second tour also covered racial incidents and murderous assaults on officers and NCOs, both categories of which were absent on my first tour. On the brighter side, living conditions were vastly improved. We had better food, the amenities such as clubs, movies, television . . . floor shows, the USO, libraries . . . and large, well-stocked PXs.[26]

Major Olson recalled of his eight-month tenure as the wing's last SJA in Vietnam: "Not much of interest happened . . . . The wing never did have much military justice action, and by that time, things had begun to wind down. Except for the big increase in drug activity . . . there just wasn't much remarkable."[27]

1st Marine Division: New Broom

In early 1970 the 1st Marine Division's four infantry regiments were deployed in concentric belts around Da Nang in defense of the city.[28] Picking up many of the small units left behind when the 3d Marine Division left Vietnam the year before, the division strength

---

*Second Lieutenant, later Captain, Edward F. Kelly served in the office of the 1st Marine Division SJA from 30 September 1967 to 7 June 1969 — over 20 months — the longest continuous period served in Vietnam by a Marine Corps judge advocate.

Photo courtesy of Col Robert J. Blum, USMC (Ret.)
The 1st Marine Division SJA buildings were located near the eastern base of Hill 327. Maj Robert J. Blum sent this captioned photograph to show his wife where he worked.

grew to 24,000 personnel. Before, Colonel Robert M. Lucy, division SJA, believed that the 33 judge advocates called for by the division table of organization were about seven too many. Now, however, the 25 judge advocates he actually had were pressed to keep up with the increase in cases. Moreover, division "legal" had only 27 of the 43 legal clerks it rated. Like FLC, Colonel Lucy had acquired unschooled typists from other division units and was training them to be legal clerks. That took time.[29] Lieutenant Colonel James P. King, deputy SJA, recalled "six and-a-half-day workweeks, and working at night were routine . . . . We handled a tremendous volume of cases."[30] Colonel Lucy, noting the number of general courts-martial scheduled for trial, wrote a friend, "Our work load is out of this world, and rising every day, it seems."[31] During the first four months of 1970, 30 general and 225 special courts-martial were tried in the division, a notable total, even for 25 judge advocates. In June the division's offense reports reflected three new murders and 52 new drug offenses.[32] Captain James H. Granger remembered:

> Business was booming, and the work load was staggering. "Case load" is a poor measurement of work load in a combat environment, in any event, because the administrative and logistical problems thoroughly distort case time. And, of course, ours was a seven-day-per-week job, although Sunday usually began late, ended early, and was used for catching up on paperwork and research, with occasional forays to China Beach.[33]

While most 1st Marine Division courts-martial were conducted at the division headquarters, trial teams were still frequently dispatched to outlying units. Unlike FLC, whose constituent commands were either located at the Red Beach cantonment or nearby, division units were distributed throughout a large area. "But when there were several cases from the same unit," Captain Granger noted, "all those involved were required to leave their positions and report to division headquarters for trial, and the unit practically shut down. A commander in that situation must wonder if military justice is worth it."[34]

"Arranging trials so as to accommodate the command," Captain Granger noted, "is quite simply, sound management, ensuring that the military justice tail does not wag the dog."[35] Former Judge Advocate General of the Army, Major General George S. Prugh, agreed that military operations and courts-martial did not always mix smoothly:

> Many commanders found the procedures less than satisfactory because of the difficulties in performing their operational tasks and at the same time meeting the time restrictions imposed by the military justice system. Many deserving cases simply were not referred to trial, with consequences on discipline impossible to calculate but obviously deleterious . . . . Statistics do not reflect these serious problems.[36]

During this period Captains Franz P. Jevne and Charles E. Brown, prosecutors in the Son Thang (4) cases, were awarded the Navy Achievement Medal and the Navy Commendation Medal, respectively. On the defense side, Captains Daniel H. LeGear, Jr., and John J. Hargrove received Navy Commendation Medals, while Captain Michael P. Merrill was awarded the Navy Achievement Medal. The awards were only in part based on the Son Thang (4) trials.[37]

The deputy SJA of the 1st Marine Division was LtCol James P. King. On his second tour of duty in Vietnam, he recalled six-and-a-half-day workweeks.
Photo courtesy of BGen James P. King, USMC (Ret.)

Department of Defense Photo (USMC) A705288
Col Donald E. Holben became the SJA of the 1st Marine Division in July 1970. Under his direction the 1st Division left Vietnam with virtually no cases pending.

In mid-year Colonel Lucy was succeeded by Colonel Donald E. Holben, a 1945 Naval Academy graduate with two years prior service as an enlisted Marine. Colonel Holben had served as a company commander in North China under Colonel Samuel B. Griffith II, a renowned World War II combat leader, and was later assigned to the light cruiser *Worcester* (CL 144). After graduating from law school in 1954, Colonel Holben commanded a company at Parris Island's Recruit Training Battalion. Following that he served as an instructor at Quantico's Junior School, a Marine Corps career officer's school. By 1967, when he became the second law officer (military judge) assigned to the Navy-Marine Corps Judiciary Activity office in Da Nang, he had served in a wide variety of legal billets. As the only in-country law officer from mid-1967 to mid-1968, he heard over 160 general courts-martial and established a reputation as a demanding jurist. Judge advocates appearing before him soon learned that his gruff exterior actually was bone deep.

On 22 June Colonel Holben assumed the duties of staff judge advocate of the division. Lieutenant Colonel Pete Kress was his deputy, relieving Lieutenant

Cpl Mario A. Gomez was an experienced court reporter. 1st Marine Division reporters transcribed cases virtually until the day they left Vietnam. Their role was a critical one.

Colonel Jim King.* Five years before, then-Major King had relieved then-Captain Kress as legal officer of 9th MEB/III MAF. By the date of Colonel Holben's arrival the Grey Audiograph recording machines were replaced by IBM equipment and the division was flush with lawyers. Colonel Holben was unimpressed: "There was a backlog of cases to be tried and a backlog of cases to get off the tapes and on to paper . . . . Not as bad as FLC. The problems in FLC were a result of bad management. [They] didn't know how to run a legal office." Colonel Holben vowed "that was the problem at FLC that I wasn't going to let develop in the 1st Division."[38] He believed that it was counterproductive to attempt to try every case that was referred to trial. If a reasonable plea bargain could be reached, all parties gained, and he was willing to recommend that the convening authority accept the agreement between the accused and the lawyers assigned to the case. He also knew that the Marines would soon be leaving Vietnam. He did not intend to have cases left untried when that date arrived, and he took steps to ensure there were none:

> As soon as I got there and my predecessor had left, I got [the chief defense counsel] in and I said, "We're going to do it differently, now. You're well aware of what the 'Fleet Of Foot Doctrine' is; and that's if you have some defense counsel that want to come in and talk about pleading guilty and getting a good deal, get 'em in here fast, because the longer you hang on, the less likely I'm going to recommend something that's advantageous to you and to the general [the court-martial convening authority]." As a result, we cleared up the backlog of cases fairly early.[39]

The reporters were key personnel in moving cases through the system. "There was always a shortage of good court reporters," Colonel Holben noted. "and the conditions under which they worked in the 1st Division were atrocious . . . . The office spaces they had, had bad lighting."[40] In 1970, Corporal Mario A. Gomez was one of the 1st Division general court-martial court reporters. He recalled the manual typewriters as the most frustrating aspect of his job. The lack of copying machines forced the use of the manifold system—

---

*Lieutenant Colonel King was commissioned in 1952. He twice served as a weapons platoon leader, then an infantry company executive officer. After obtaining a law degree in 1959 he was honor student at the Army's Civil Affairs School and later, chief trial counsel, 3d Marine Division, then division Civil Affairs Officer in Vietnam. He later was SJA of Marine Corps Air Station, Cherry Point, North Carolina, senior Marine Corps instructor at the Naval Justice School, and, again in Vietnam, deputy SJA, 1st Marine Division. Following that he was SJA FMFPac, then earned an LL.M degree with highest honors. After serving as Deputy Director of the Judge Advocate Division he was advanced to the grade of brigadier general on 27 February 1978, becoming seventh Director of the Division.

an original page bonded to a series of multi-hued flimsies with carbon paper between each page. Corrections were a lengthy process of separate erasures on each page. "Sometimes we'd run out of a simple thing like ribbon, typewriter ribbon, and we'd have to use the cloth-type ribbon that you had to replace frequently in order to have legible copies," Corporal Gomez commented. "As far as the equipment we used—I wouldn't wish that on anybody. But I can't say that it didn't get the job done. It did."[41]

To reduce the backlog of untyped cases, 1st Division reporters, like those at FLC, went to day and night shifts to wring maximum use from the available equipment. When Brigadier General Duane L. Faw, Director of the Judge Advocate Division, made the first of his two 1970 visits to Vietnam, he asked Colonel Holben if he needed anything. "I said, 'Yes!'" Holben recalled. "Send me 10 court reporters."[42] Shortly, 10 court reporters, assembled from legal offices on Okinawa and in the United States, arrived with six-week temporary duty orders to assist in reducing the accumulation of untyped cases. "We ended up with about four or five good ones," Colonel Holben noted. "The rest we terminated their orders and returned them to the United States as soon as we found out who was capable and who wasn't."[43]

Colonel Holben saw to the air conditioning of the reporters' work space, and he did not object when they moved into the office permanently. He reported:

> Production went up, to the point where we would get a judge from the Philippines and [the reporters] would hand him the record of trial for correction before he left Vietnam. They prided themselves on doing that. Staff Sergeant [William L.] Rose was our chief reporter at that time. So any time they got off, I would have a truck take them to the beach, and just gave them a break from their work. And it paid off.[44]

Upon arrival at Da Nang Colonel Holben also assessed the lawyers assigned to the office:

> If there was anything I didn't need, it was more lawyers! I had more lawyers than I needed. Some quality was lacking in some of them, but we assigned them to jobs that were appropriate to their skills. One . . . was the "property officer." I always found that was an adequate job for him. And when he left, I assigned another officer . . . to handling typewriters. The proper assignment of officers was probably more important than the numbers we had . . . . We ended up, after a few moves and a few transfers, with a very capable staff.[45]

Colonel Holben's concern with the operation of the military justice system extended to all facets of the court-martial process. When a sentence imposed by a military judge was conspicuously less than he considered appropriate, Colonel Holben, himself a former judge, summoned the military judge to his office to

The court reporters of the 1st Marine Division SJA's office relaxing at China Beach, near Da Nang. Afternoons off resulted in improved morale and greater office productivity.
Photo courtesy of Maj Mario A. Gomez, USMC

air his opinion of the judge's sentence. " 'If we want sentences like that, we'll keep these cases at office hours!' is a line I particularly recall," said Captain Stephen C. Berg, remembering the incident.[46] The military judge involved, Navy Commander Keith B. Lawrence, noted that he was extensively questioned by the counsels involved in his next few courts-martial. Having learned of his conversation with Colonel Holben, they were concerned that Commander Lawrence might be influenced, one way or another, in his disposition of their cases. He assured them that he would not be, and later wrote that "the defense counsel were reasonable and professional lawyers and after about three trials . . . the matter was dropped."[47]

Colonel Holben instilled in his legal personnel that their mission was to serve, and not impair, the command. Not to the prejudice of fairness or ethical conduct, but to the limits that their roles in the military justice system allowed. If some 1st Division lawyers viewed being urged to serve the command as only a step from overbearing influence on their professional discretion, no one could dispute the results the SJA's office produced. 1st Marine Division cases moved, and as in any civilian jurisdiction, "deals" were available to the accuseds who sought them. Those who contested their cases had a prompt day in court.

The perspective of most Reserve captain-lawyers differed from that of the SJA and the few career judge advocates. These reservists were the backbone of the Marine Corps' legal effort in Vietnam. One such was Captain Philip C. Tower, who served four years' active duty. As he recalled:

> While in law school I was aware that I was facing the possibility of being drafted once my student deferment ran out at the end of law school . . . . To be perfectly frank, my main reason for joining the Marine Corps was that, by that time, I was rather tired of school, and was not looking forward to proceeding on to work in a Phoenix law firm. In short, I was looking for something different.[48]

He came on active duty, attended The Basic School, then Naval Justice School, and was ordered to Vietnam. "I had no desire to go to Vietnam . . . . Arriving was, for me, a truly overwhelming experience, because it was something that I felt would never actually happen to me. I certainly had concerns for my personal safety, and was not particularly happy," he admitted. "Moreover, as I began my work, my main revelation was realizing how inadequate I felt to handle real cases. However, as time went on, the overall experience of Vietnam expanded into one of the most incredible experiences of my life." Continuing, he recalled:

> While we were certainly part of the war, and while I made it a practice to get out in the field as much as I could . . . and while our office hootch was right above a medical landing port where the body bags of the dead were brought in each evening, there was still a true sense of unreality to the position we occupied. While our accommodations were rustic at best, they were nothing compared to the adverse conditions under which most Marines in the field lived . . . While there were a number of occasions when I felt that my life might be in some danger, I did not have to live with the constant threat of death, day after day, day in and day out, as most Marines in Vietnam did.[49]

In addition to their legal work, Captain Tower and Captain Tone N. Grant, another defense counsel, taught English to local Vietnamese school children. At the conclusion of his Vietnam tour Captain Tower was awarded the Navy Commendation Medal for his work as a defense counsel.

Additionally, the lawyers were allowed the opportunity to temporarily escape Da Nang entirely. Following a particularly heavy rocket attack on the Da Nang Airbase, the 1st Marine Aircraft Wing decided to fly its multi-million dollar C-130 cargo aircraft to Ubon, Thailand, each night, since enemy attacks were almost always in darkness. Flight time to Ubon was barely an hour. Colonel Holben received permission to send legal section personnel to Thailand on board the otherwise empty flights and he allowed them to stay for up to three days. The flights were "for anybody that wanted to go, anybody that could get away," Colonel Holben said. "And we used them!"[50] Similarly, he routinely allowed the officers and enlisted men to catch the weekly flight to the Philippines for informal R & R. China Beach, a broad beach with white sand and no women, remained popular and more readily available a few miles from division headquarters. Colonel Holben regularly sent lawyers and clerks alike to China Beach. Morale improved in the SJA's office.

The monsoon season was particularly harsh in 1970. Four typhoons passed through I Corps in October. The last two brought more than 17 inches of rain in eight days and halted virtually all military activity.[51] Trials, however, continued uninterrupted. Major James H. Granger, a special court-martial judge during that time, recalled that no day was necessarily a free day:

> Holidays were business as usual, and I sat as military judge on two cases [on Christmas] day. Defense counsels Jack Lynch and Phil Tower requested the unusual trial date, no doubt hoping that the occasion might stir some vestigial trace of beneficence in the judge. The trial counsel, [James W.]

The monsoon rains were particularly harsh and heavy in 1970. A Force Logistic Command bulldozer clears a drainage path to allow accumulated rainwater to drain.

"Killer" Carroll, took perverse delight in the idea of Christmas trials, savoring the expectation that the two accuseds' first meal in the brig would be Christmas dinner . . . [and] both accused did dine in confinement.[52]

Colonel Holben added: "I *insisted* that all accused tried on Sunday be given the opportunity to attend the church service of their choice."[53]

As 1970 drew to a rainy close, Jim Granger, promoted to the grade of major a short time before, planned a wetting down party, to celebrate his advancement.* The event was to be held in the lawyers' hooch ("a majestic structure"), which reportedly had originally housed the Seabees who constructed the encampment. That rumor was fueled by the fact that the unique, double-sized SEAhut contained, along with several individual rooms and a bar, two smaller rooms that harbored the cantonment's only flush toilets outside the commanding general's quarters. Major Granger decided that nurses from the hospital ship *Sanctuary* (AH 17) would add to the celebration. Indeed, the wet-

ting down was later described by the Deputy SJA, Lieutenant Colonel Kress, as "truly one of the highlights of the Vietnam legal experience."[54] But as Major Granger recalled:

> It was not an easy thing to get approval . . . . Colonel Holben, his gruff manner hardly concealing his enthusiasm for the idea, gave me permission to approach the division chief of staff, Colonel [Don H.] "Doc" Blanchard. The chief of staff was gravely concerned that women in the cantonment was a recipe for catastrophe, and agreed to permit such an event only if the function was chaperoned by stern, high-ranking, mature leaders. He reckoned as how he fit that bill, and he was promptly invited. Then it looked doubtful that helicopters could be diverted from their combat roles to transport the nurses to and from the hospital ship, but after invitations were extended to the operations officer and an aviator or two, the mission was approved. The motor transport officer graciously accepted my invitation and promptly approved my request for ground transportation. Thus it was that a brave contingent of greatly outnumbered nurses was entertained by the lawyers of the 1st Marine Division. It was a splendid affair.[55]

Trying Cases

Tactically, American units no longer conducted operations on their own, but supported and assisted South Vietnamese forces in their operations. For the

---

*The term "wetting down" originated in the British Army with the now forgotten custom of the promoted person placing his new grade insignia at the bottom of a large glass filled with beer, then drinking it dry without stopping.

judge advocates of the 1st Marine Division, circumstances were changing as well. For the first time in several years case loads were declining as Marines continued to leave Vietnam. In January 1971, 48 cases were tried; in February, 43; and in March, 27.[56]

Although the number of cases dwindled, the bleak disciplinary picture that continued into 1971 was not brightened by the large number of Mental Category IVs still mandated by Project 100,000. In 1970 seven percent of Marine Corps enlisted strength were Cat IVs. A comparison of their service with that of other Marines showed their recruit attrition rates and desertion rates were twice as high, their promotion rates significantly lower, and their nonjudicial disciplinary rate significantly higher. Surprisingly, though, the Cat IV's court-martial rate remained less than that of other Marines.[57] The Commandant of the Marine Corps, General Leonard F. Chapman, Jr., declared:

> We're going to fight to the highest levels of government projects like Project 100,000 . . . . They've got a lot of merit in the social sense, but they don't contribute a single thing to the readiness of the Marine Corps, to the combat capability of the Marine Corps . . . . We're going to do everything possible to get rid of them.[58]

The Military Justice Act of 1968 took effect in August 1969. By 1970 it was already clear that its implementation had brought about significant improvement in the court-martial system. Lawyers were now involved in the trial of special courts-martial, as well as general courts, and the process was centralized in SJA offices. Lieutenant Colonel Carl E. Buchmann, FLC's deputy SJA, noted that "errors in the records of trial were less severe . . . and we had less errors in drafting charges that, in the past, had been left up to the local legal offices in the battalions . . . . And we speeded up the process all the way around."[59] A 1st Marine Division study found that 37 percent of the cases in which bad conduct discharges were adjudged were disapproved due to legal error before the act was implemented. After it became effective, only five percent "bounced."[60]

Worldwide the number of general court-martial military judges in the Navy-Marine Corps Trial Judiciary decreased by two in 1970 to 21, even though

Officers' call was sometimes held in the double-sized lawyers' hooch. 1st Division lawyers present were, from left, Capt William J. O'Byrne (hidden); Capt Lawrence W. Secrest (partially hidden); 1stLt Roland K. Iverson, Jr. (glasses); Lt Allen C. Rudy, Jr., JAGC, USN; 1stLt Joel Levine (sunglasses); Maj James H. Granger (seated); legal administrative officer, 1stLt Armand H. Desjardin (glasses); unidentified nonlawyer; Col Donald E. Holben; Capt Dirk T. Metzger; Capt Otis F. Cochran (hat); and Capt E. Randall Ricketts.

Photo courtesy of Col James H. Granger, USMC

Photo courtesy of LtCol Richard A. Muench, USMCR

Capt James D. Stokes, left, Capt Richard A. Muench, center, and Lt Richard Blume, JAGC, USN, shown on a river patrol boat (RPB). Captains Stokes and Muench assisted Lt Blume in investigating Cambodia's capture of a RPB that had strayed into Cambodian waters.

general courts-martial increased 42 percent that year; in 1971 there was a further decrease of one, while the number of general courts-martial declined roughly 25 percent.[61] The 1970 decrease in judges, in the face of a rising workload, may have anticipated post-Vietnam manpower reductions.

In Vietnam those figures translated, for example, to 160 general courts-martial tried by Lieutenant Colonel Henry Hoppe during one year in Vietnam, a very heavy docket, and no different from that of the other general court judges in Vietnam. The good news for military judges was that, since implementation of the Military Justice Act, the number of members courts—jury trials—had declined dramatically.* A members court-martial is complicated and lengthy, compared to a "judge alone" trial. A members trial requires selection of panel members (voir dire), opening instruction of the members, instructions on findings (guilt or innocence), followed by sentencing instructions if the accused is found guilty. In a "judge alone" case those phases are dispensed with. Moreover, there tends to be less repetition by the trial and defense counsels, because there are no members to impress and the military judge usually recognizes and recalls critical evidence without having to be reminded. Thus, a "judge alone" case is tried much more quickly. As Lieutenant Colonel Buchmann recalled, "instead of two cases in a day's time . . . we could try four or five with 'judge alone.' Much quicker, same safeguards, but you didn't have all this business of going back and forth with the members . . . . Ninety-nine percent of our special courts are now 'judge alone.' We are not enjoying this same rate at general courts."[62] General courts-martial, at which the more serious offenses were tried, still tended to "go members," sometimes because the matter at issue was thought too weighty to ask one person, the military judge, to decide; sometimes in the defense counsel's hope that he could convince members of that which a military judge would not accept. Also, a military judge tends to know what a case is worth. That is, after long courtroom experience a judge knows the range of punishments that an offense merits. Members, on the other hand, having found an accused guilty, have no bench

---

*Either the accused or the government may request trial by members, rather than by judge alone. In practice the option is exercised by the accused in virtually all cases where members are requested.

mark by which to fashion an appropriate sentence.

A number of general court-martial military judges heard cases in Vietnam in 1970 and 1971. Besides those stationed in the Da Nang office of the Trial Judiciary Activity, other senior Navy and Marine Corps judge advocates from Okinawa, Japan, the Philippines, and, on occasion, from Washington, D.C., heard cases.

To ensure their independence and freedom from command pressure, all general court-martial military judges were assigned to the Navy-Marine Corps Trial Judiciary Activity, based in Washington, D.C. Their fitness reports were completed by the Chief Judge of that organization and they were exempt from local watch duties, or additional duty assignments. In the rare case of a general court-martial judge's substandard performance, either in personal conduct or in court, there was nothing to be done in the field, other than to notify the Chief Judge in Washington, either directly or through one's superiors, and await a response. Similarly, meritorious service could not be locally recognized.

In 1970 Colonel Petersen, SJA of FLC, became concerned at what he considered the continuing deficient performance of a particular general court-martial judge. He twice advised Brigadier General Faw, Director of the Judge Advocate Division, of the officer's conduct on the bench, once attaching the verbatim record of the murder trial concerned. In his initial letter to General Faw, Colonel Petersen noted that "he has antagonized the court, counsel, and witnesses with displays of impatience, omnipotence and almost contempt." In a subsequent letter Colonel Petersen pointed out that the judge had "refused" to instruct the members on an essential matter, despite the trial counsel's request, which refusal all but mandated a not guilty finding. Colonel Petersen continued, "It is another instance of what is likely to occur when judicial inexperience, compounded with an abrasive personality becomes the third-party litigant . . . . I would like [him] advised of my observations in this matter, for his own benefit and for the fact that we have officially expressed concern."[63] Eventually, the military judge was transferred to other duties outside the courtroom.

Another general court-martial judge had an ill-concealed drinking problem. In response to discreet inquiry from the Chief Judge of the Judiciary Activity, Colonel Lucy, then-SJA of the 1st Marine Division replied, "We all know that he drinks too much. This is obvious even to those who meet him for the first time."[64] Colonel Petersen, not one to equivocate, responded to the chief judge about the same officer: "So long as I am here, I will not permit [him] to be appointed to a general court-martial convened by this command . . . . His alcoholic intake was such as to be a matter of note by the commanding general, the chief of staff, and all counsel practicing before him."[65] (Colonel Holben, referring to the same military judge, later remarked that "he was a better judge drunk than some of the others I could mention.")[66]

In an era before "alcohol abuse" was a fashionable phrase, a number of officers in rear echelons of the combat zone over-indulged occasionally, some with regularity. Judge advocates were among them. In all but a few cases, however, military judges, staff judge advocates, and judge advocates remained above reproach.

Major General Charles F. Widdecke, Commanding General of the 1st Marine Division for most of 1970, wrote to the Judge Advocate General of the Navy concerning general court-martial military judge Lieutenant Colonel Henry Hoppe:

> [He] has been the military judge in over 63 1st Marine Division general courts-martial . . . . I would like to report to you on the high esteem in which he is held . . . . The many difficulties of presiding over courts-martial in a combat environment, such as the numerous unavoidable trial delays, frequent losses of electrical power . . . interruption of court proceedings by enemy fire . . . have not deterred him from maintaining a dignified, judicial atmosphere in his court . . . . I have refrained from conveying any comment on Lieutenant Colonel Hoppe's performance of duty until the end of his tour to avoid any hint of influence on his decisions. It seems appropriate at this time, however, to inform you of his unusually fine record of service.[67]

Lieutenant Colonel Hoppe was awarded the Legion of Merit for his Vietnam service.[68]

Special courts-martial were usually heard by "ad hoc" military judges. Since few senior, experienced judge advocates were designated military judges, they were employed almost exclusively in general courts-martial. For the more numerous special courts, captains and majors with courtroom experience were designated by the Judge Advocate General of the Navy, ad hoc, to be special courts-martial military judges. Their designation was based upon the recommendation of the Director of the Judge Advocate Division.* "Ad hoc" judges were a makeshift response to the staggering caseload that confronted the few military judges of the period. The "ad hoc" judges could

---

*A separate Marine Corps Special Court-Martial Judiciary was established in 1974.

sit only in special courts. Unlike the general court-martial judges, they were not selected and interviewed by the Judge Advocate General of the Navy, nor did they always receive special schooling as judges before assuming their judging duties. Often they were lawyers still on their initial period of commissioned service who had shown skill and promise as courtroom advocates. Their workload in Vietnam was high. Major Robert J. Blum, for example, tried 210 special courts-martial in one year.[69] Worldwide, in both the Navy and Marine Corps, approximately 500 "ad hoc" special court-martial military judges were appointed in 1969, and 673 more in 1970. General court-martial military judges, on the other hand, never numbered more than 23.[70]

In 1970 a common special court-martial offense was sleeping on post. As Captain George H. O'Kelley, an FLC defense counsel, recalled:

> It was so common that the standard sentence was two months brig time. It was also the practice that anyone that got two months or less did not go to the brig. The sentence was automatically suspended. If the person got in more trouble, then the suspension was revoked and he served the two months and also faced any other sentence from the new . . . charges.*[71]

Although a common offense, obtaining a conviction for sleeping on post was not an easy matter. Captain W. Hays Parks recalled that "at night, in the dark, it is very hard to catch a Marine in such a way that you can convince a court beyond a reasonable doubt (in the face of denials) that he was sleeping on post."[72]

Petty black marketeering offenses were also in vogue. The profits were tempting: A box of laundry soap that cost 40 cents in the PX was worth $1.75 on the black market. A $3 bottle of whiskey brought between $10 and $14 from unauthorized Vietnamese purchasers. In October 1970 the legal rate of exchange was 118 piasters to one U.S. dollar, while on the currency black market the rate was 220 to 1.[73] Unless the charges involved significant figures, however, few convicted Marines were jailed for black marketeering, either.

After he left Vietnam, Colonel Lucy reported that "the III MAF brig is not adequate. It never has been . . . . It should not be used other than just as a detention facility. We've been recommending this for some time, but it stays at capacity, at over capacity."[74] Colonel John R. DeBarr, concluding a year as a general court-martial military judge, agreed: "I suggest we get the brig out of there just as fast as we possibly can—out of country."[75] Colonel Petersen urged that there was no place in a combat zone for "honest to goodness criminals," and he would "strongly recommend serious rethinking of our solution to that problem."[76] The brig passed to U.S. Army control in 1970, and was finally closed in June 1971.[77]

As far as case preparation was concerned, transportation remained a sometimes thing for Marine Corps lawyers, as Captain Paul J. Laveroni, a 1st Marine Division defense counsel, recalled:

> There were a lot of ways to get around Vietnam, and during the course of our tour we used them all . . . . The preferred mode of travel was by helicopter . . . . Most of my helicopter jaunts were in Mission 10 birds, the daily milk run . . . . The typical aircraft used was the CH-46, usually in pairs, but sometimes a CH-53 was used . . . . To catch Mission 10 you had to be at the helipad [below the division's legal offices] about 0730-0800 . . . . Recon teams, loaded up and heavily camouflaged, waited for their lift, along with dog handlers and their dogs, troops who had come to the rear on some boondoggle or other, lawyers trying to get somewhere.[78]

One always had to confirm the helicopter's destination with the crew chief, as itineraries frequently changed and one had to be prepared to leap from the helicopter at the spot closest to one's destination. Captain Laveroni continued:

> Mission 10 wasn't very glamorous nor usually very exciting, but it was a tremendous asset for us . . . . We sent one of our sergeants to Hill 10 to bring back a Vietnamese woman who was going to be a witness. He got her and himself on board a '46 . . . . Someone must have miscalculated the lift because the '46 barely cleared the ground, then slowly tipped to one side and rolled down the hill. Miraculously, no one was killed, but the experience so unnerved our sergeant that . . . he would never step on board a chopper again. That's the problem with mass transit. You just can't please everyone.[79]

On a professional level, lawyers in Vietnam continued to attend meetings of the Federal Bar Association, the I Corps Bar Association, and even continuing legal education (CLE) classes for which various state bar associations granted credit. The classes and meetings were often held in Saigon.[80]

A three-man civilian law office, funded by the Lawyers' Military Defense Committee, of Cambridge, Massachusetts, was also located in Saigon. The antimilitary attorneys provided free civilian legal services to servicemen—Army personnel, almost exclusively—facing courts-martial.[81]

In October 1970 Captain Eileen M. Albertson be-

---

*First Marine Division prisoners sentenced to more than two months confinement were transferred to the brig at Camp Pendleton as soon as possible. (Cmd Information Notebook, 1st MarDiv, RVN, 10Apr71, p. 9.)

Photo courtesy of Col Eileen M. Albertson, USMC
Capt Eileen M. Albertson poses at Camp Tien Sha, NSA. She was the only woman Marine Corps lawyer to reach Vietnam in relation to a court-martial.

came the second woman Marine Corps judge advocate to reach Vietnam and the only one to do so in connection with a court-martial. (Captain Patricia A. Murphy attended a Da Nang legal conference in September 1969.) Captain Albertson was a trial counsel assigned to the joint law center on Okinawa. In the prosecution of a three-month unauthorized absence case defense witnesses and documents supporting the accused's claim of innocence were located in Da Nang, where the absence had begun. With the exception of a small number assigned to the joint-service staff of MACV in Saigon, woman Marines were not normally permitted to enter Vietnam.* With the approval of her SJA and the convening authority, Captain Albertson received area clearance from FMFPac, and her name was added to the manifest of a Vietnam flight. The Camp Butler, Okinawa, G-1, Colonel Valeria F. Hilgart, a woman Marine, ensured that neither the area clearance request nor the flight manifest included the "W" that normally preceded women Marines' service numbers. On the flight to Vietnam, Captain Albertson was listed merely as "E. M. Albertson," in the usual manner of manifest lists. Accompanied by defense counsel, Captain Robert A. Preate, Captain Albertson arrived at Camp Tien Sha, the Naval Support Activity camp in east Da Nang. Because woman Marines did not wear the utility uniform in that era, she wore the smallest men's utilities she could borrow, and size 8 1/2 combat boots worn with multiple pairs of socks.

Just after her arrival all hands were restricted to base for five days because of Vietnamese presidential elections. Captain Albertson was billeted in the Tien Sha BOQ with special hours arranged for the head and shower facilities. During the restriction to base she accepted an invitation to accompany a night patrol of Da Nang Bay on a U.S. Navy Swift boat.

After restrictions were lifted, five day's investigation confirmed the accused's innocence and Captain Albertson returned to Okinawa. Having been in Vietnam for 10 days, the last few days of October and the first few of November, she received two months combat pay at $65 per month.[82]

Occasionally in the trial of courts-martial, judge advocates encountered cases more notable for their actors than for their facts. Captain George H. O'Kelley was an FLC defense counsel who represented Private Curtis Crawford, originally charged with sleeping on post. Against the advice of Captain Tommy Jarrett, his initial defense counsel, Crawford went to trial and was found guilty and received the usual two months confinement from the court and the usual suspended sentence from his commander. Three nights later Crawford was again found asleep on post in the 3d MP Battalion guard tower. He swore to the officer of the day who had discovered his offense that it would never happen again. But as Captain O'Kelley recounted:

> About two hours later, the O.D. made the rounds. Curtis had moved his sleeping area on top of the trap door [into the guard tower enclosure] so no one could catch him sleeping. The O.D. couldn't arouse him, so he stepped down and fired his .45. Curtis jumped up and yelled, "Halt! Who goes there?" He went to the brig, this time.[83]

His previously suspended sentence was vacated and Crawford was jailed. He became ill while in the brig and was given a mild narcotic medicine. Later, when the Navy doctor declined to continue the narcotic treatment, Crawford badly beat the doctor. "Curtis was placed in solitary confinement, awaiting disposition. I was appointed to represent Curtis, this time," Captain O'Kelley recalled. "He faced 37 years as a possi-

---

*Throughout the war, only 36 women Marines were stationed in Vietnam. (Col Mary V. Stremlow, USMCR, *A History of the Women Marines, 1946-1977* [Washington: Hist&MusDiv, HQMC, 1986, p. 82.])

ble sentence on all charges. I was then approached by the SJA, Colonel Petersen, about Curtis getting an admin discharge. Well, I jumped on that." Crawford, meanwhile, was seen by FLC's commanding general at request mast, with a complaint of mistreatment in the brig. The commanding general, too, decided that an administrative discharge would best serve the interests of all parties. In light of Crawford's past disciplinary record an undesirable discharge (U.D.) would be administratively imposed. As Captain O'Kelley recalled:

> I took the U.D. package . . . to the brig and saw Crawford in his cell. I explained the U.D. to him. He said, "Wait a minute, lawyer. The general said I was gonna get an administrative discharge." And so you are, I explained to him. I couldn't make him understand that a U.D. was the type of admin he was getting. The tops of the cells at the III MAF brig were covered with bars, so other prisoners in solitary confinement could hear us. Other prisoners started yelling, "Don't sign it, Doodle!" "That lawyer's lying, Doodle!" "Generals don't make mistakes, man!"

The commanding general made a special trip to the brig to assure "Doodle" that the discharge he was getting was, in fact, the one they had agreed upon. That was not the end of the case. Curtis Crawford was released from the brig and ordered to the Da Nang Airbase to board his flight to the United States, and discharge. Captain O'Kelley reported what followed:

> Some MPs spotted Curtis going towards his plane with a large brown box under his arm. They knew Curtis, of course, because he had been in their outfit. "What's in the box, Curtis?" . . . They took the box. It was full of marijuana, a little going away present from Curtis to himself. These two young MPs would have made sergeant major, if they stayed in the Corps. They exercised remarkable initiative. They confiscated the marijuana, snatched Curtis up by the scruff of the neck and showed him to his seat aboard the plane. They saved the government a sack full of money in legal problems.

Last Call For Combat

Throughout the war Marine Corps judge advocates took every opportunity to assume command billets in combat units. Except in the 3d Marine Division in 1968, when all incoming officers were assigned to infantry units for three months, the infantry billet usually available to lawyers was that of reaction platoon or reaction company commander. Lawyers sought that additional duty and excelled. Although the war was coming to a close for the Marine Corps and enemy activity grew less frequent, judge advocates still sought assignment to infantry commands.* While he was the 1st Marine Division SJA, Colonel Bob Lucy, in a letter to the assistant division commander noted, "A lawyer from this office has consistently been C.O. of the Bravo Reaction Company . . . . I have always had more volunteers for this type of duty than I could fill. I might also add that every officer who has filled this billet has been commended highly."[84]

During the 1969 Tet offensive, as executive officer (second in command) of a provisional rifle company, Captain W. Hays Parks, 1st Marine Division chief trial counsel, led two rifle platoons in the defense of the division command post, an action resulting in seven enemy dead. He received the Navy Commendation Medal.[85] Captain Robert M. MacConnell received the same award in recognition of his service as Sub-Team Commander, 13th Interrogation-Translation Team.[86] Captain Raymond T. Bonner was awarded the Navy Achievement Medal for his performance of duty as the regimental S-5 (Civil Affairs Officer) for the 5th Marines.[87] Numerous other Marine Corps lawyers were recognized for their performance outside the legal field, as well, demonstrating the utility of maintaining lawyers' status as unrestricted officers.

Closing Cases Versus Best Defense

In 1977 Major Stephen C. Berg, a former 1st Marine Division judge advocate, wrote: "Any official history will, I expect, place Marine military justice in a most favorable light because, superficially, the system ran smoothly . . . . But, from an insider's point of view, no history will be complete unless the impact of personality on the system, and those executing the system, is discussed."[88] As a captain, Berg had served under Colonel Donald E. Holben, certainly a strong personality, during the trial of the Aragon/Anderson cases.

Sergeant Adrian Aragon was a 60mm mortar squad leader in Company M, 3d Battalion, 7th Marines. His assistant squad leader was Corporal Joseph W. "Thumper" Anderson, Jr., who was particularly noted for his skill as a mortar gunner. The squad, as a whole, was respected within the company for its ability and performance in combat. At 1425 on 17 August 1970, as Company M prepared to return to LZ Ross, the company commander directed his mortar squad to fire 20 rounds on a distant tree line from which sniper fire

---

*In 1969 the Marine Corps suffered 2,258 battle deaths, compared to 529 in 1970. In 1971 only 20 Marines were killed in action. (Casualty file, RefSec, MCHC)

Photo courtesy of Mr. Philip C. Tower

Capts Tone N. Grant, left, and Stephen C. Berg in the field during an investigation. Capt Grant was a reaction force company commander, in addition to being a defense counsel.

had earlier been received. Witnesses later testified that from nine to 12 rounds impacted in the tree line. According to the investigation, the remaining eight to 11 mortar rounds landed at the base of the hill occupied by Company M and inexorably marched back up the hill into Company M's own position. Three Marines and a female Vietnamese prisoner were killed while 30 Marines were wounded, including the acting company commander. One of the injured Marines died of his wounds a few days later.[89] Mortar fin assemblies of detonated rounds found in Company M's position carried lot numbers that were traced to rounds issued to an unrecorded unit at LZ Ross, Company M's base. In a message to the commanding general, FMFPac, the commanding general of the 1st Marine Division reported that "cursory examination indicates an extremely high angle of impact," suggesting that the mortar rounds had been fired straight up and fallen back into the company's own position.[90] The mortar squad, concluded the initial investigation, had fired more rounds than necessary in order to avoid having to carry them back to LZ Ross and had simply been careless in the control of its fire. A later message from the division commander to the commanding general, FMFPac, reported that there was "abundant supporting evidence that the incident was caused by misapplication of friendly fire."[91]

Sergeant Aragon and Corporal Anderson were charged with five specifications of negligent homicide. Aragon was also charged with negligence in instructing and supervising his mortar squad.[92] The second gunner was initially charged, as well, but he accepted immunity in return for his testimony in the other two cases. Captain Tone N. Grant represented Aragon and Captain Paul J. Laveroni was Anderson's counsel. The trial counsel in both cases was Captain Edwin W. Welch, assisted by Captain James W. Carroll.

Captain Grant had already been a reaction force company commander for several months and, to the degree that his defense counsel duties allowed, sought other opportunities to participate in combat action. His and Captain Laveroni's extensive trial preparation included several days in the field with Company M, during which they located Marine witnesses who thought the fatal mortar rounds were actually fired by Vietnamese mortars. Reportedly, the enemy occasionally retrieved lost or dropped American mortar rounds and, under cover of U.S. artillery or mortar fire, would fire them at American positions from their own 61mm mortar tubes. The noise of the U.S. fire masked that of the enemy rounds, preventing counter-fire. (Earlier, in yet another message, the commanding general of the division noted that such an occurrence could only be the "result of a series of highly improbable coincident actions.")[93] The defense counsels also found physical evidence indicating that most, if not all, of the 20 rounds may have impacted in the target tree line. Additionally, numerous members of Company M were willing to testify to the exceptional expertise of Sergeant Aragon and his mortar squad. As the trial date approached, messages began to arrive at 1st Marine Division Headquarters reflecting Congressional interest in the case.

Believing they had an effective defense to the charges, Captains Laveroni and Grant conferred with the SJA, Colonel Holben, in an attempt to persuade him that the cases should not go to trial. Captain Laveroni recalled that "as we described how expensive these trials would be and how many witnesses, including civilians, we would seek from the U.S., he blew up . . . . He decided in his own mind that we were 'threatening' him with huge costs if the command persisted in going ahead. He said he would not recommend dismissal."[94] Nor was that the first time a disagreement regarding witness requests had arisen between Colonel Holben and Captain Laveroni. Of this case Colonel Holben recalled:

> We knew we were going to come back to the States; we didn't know when, and we had to get the work done. You cannot have these trials dragged out forever by requests for numerous witnesses from the United States. And they were all in mitigation and extenuation. We offered to stipulate [to their testimony]. We offered everything we could to mitigate this process. He [Captain Laveroni] was adamant. I was willing, on occasion, and did on occasion, bring over two or three key witnesses in mitigation. So . . . I didn't say no in every event. But I did say no, this time.[95]

The question of which witnesses the government will secure for the defense (at government expense, of course) may be informally decided between the defense counsel and the government prior to trial. Lacking such agreement, it is an issue argued in open court, on the record, and decided by the military judge. The government must comply with the judge's decision or the judge may ultimately dismiss the charges. As Major General George S. Prugh, former Judge Advocate General of the Army, wrote:

> The opportunity to delay proceedings pending the location of a departed witness was and remains substantial. The expense, delay, and difficulty of returning witnesses to the theater could dissuade a convening authority from pursuing the prosecution any further. And where the witness was no longer in the service the power to require the witness to appear was severely circumscribed.[96]

In this case the military judge later ordered production of some, but not all of the witnesses requested

Capt Paul J. Laveroni, left, congratulates Cpl Joseph W. Anderson, Jr., shortly after Cpl Anderson's general court-martial for negligent homicide had ended in acquittal.

Photo courtesy of Philip C. Tower

PRISONERS OF WAR, AND OTHERS

Three enlisted Marines were charged with misconduct while prisoners of the North Vietnamese. Two of them, SSgt Alfonso R. Riate, left, and Pvt Frederick L. Elbert, Jr., are shown after returning to the United States.

The two officers, Marine Corps Lieutenant Colonel Edison W. Miller and Navy Captain Walter E. "Gene" Wilbur were charged with mutiny, failure to obey orders by accepting special favors from the enemy, making propaganda statements, informing on fellow prisoners, attempting to persuade others to disobey orders, wrongfully communicating the activities of fellow prisoners to the enemy, and attempting to promote mutiny, disloyalty, and insubordination among fellow POWs. Their accuser was Rear Admiral James B. Stockdale, who was awarded the Medal of Honor for his conduct during the seven and a half years he was a prisoner. Admiral Stockdale later said of his having to initiate the legal proceedings, "Let us hope that the U.S. government feels a little more sense of responsibility for seeing that justice is done after the next prisoner return, and files its own charges."[8] Major General George S. Prugh, the Army's Judge Advocate General, agreed, saying:

> It would have been useful for the Navy, Marine Corps, and the Air Force to have supplied senior prosecutor types to advise and assist the senior PWs in the drafting of charges, especially where the issue involved command in the PW compound by the senior officer present. That concept had not been tested in law . . . . Certainly Admiral Stockdale

. . . is justified in being disappointed that the PW command structure was not ultimately sustained.[9]*

At a 1 June 1973 meeting with the Secretary of the Navy, representatives of the Army, Navy, and Marine Corps discussed their views of the charges to assure a generally similar approach.[10] After that meeting "we sorted through the enlisted cases, first," Major Brahms recalled. "The Army decided, fairly early on, that they did not want the problem . . . and the Secretary of the Navy pretty much decided the same thing."[11]

On 22 June 1973 the Acting Judge Advocate General of the Navy, Rear Admiral Horace B. Robertson, Jr., forwarded a lengthy memorandum to the Secretary, reviewing the charges against the three enlisted Marines, discussing the legal issues, and recommending possible courses of action. The admiral pointed out that many of the charges were subject to the Department of Defense policy against prosecuting propaganda statements made in captivity, and that other charges technically failed to state an offense. He noted that the cases would be long and drawn out and accompanied by great publicity, that the possibility of conviction was marginal, and that former POWs would be called as witnesses and "would certainly be subjected to the most rigorous and searching cross-examination as to their own conduct and motives."[12] Even in the event of conviction, he noted, the likelihood of a substantial sentence was small. In light of those facts, Admiral Robertson recommended the charges be dropped. On 3 July, the Secretary of the Navy determined that further proceedings against the enlisted Marines would be inappropriate. Six days before, Sergeant Able Kavanaugh had shot and killed himself. The two remaining enlisted accuseds were given honorable discharges.[13]

The cases of Marine Corps Lieutenant Colonel Miller and Navy Captain Wilbur were addressed next. Lieutenant Colonel Miller was shot down over North Vietnam and captured on 13 October 1967. He was held captive for the next five years and four months. Captain Wilbur was a prisoner for four years and eight months. Among the charges still pending against the

---

*In discussing the prisoner's command structure while in enemy hands, Vice Admiral Stockdale wrote, "You would be doing most of us ex-prisoners of Hanoi a favor (in discussing the creation of prisoner of war law) if you would just omit that term '4th Allied POW Wing.' . . . . To most of us, references to this so-called '4th Allied Wing' make us [sick] . . . . I would just refer to it as the prisoner underground organization." (VAdm James B. Stockdale ltr to author, dtd 28Jan89. Comment folder, Marines and Military Law in Vietnam file, MCHC.)

two were soliciting fellow prisoners to mutiny, refusing to obey lawful orders, accepting special favors from the enemy, and informing against fellow prisoners.

Lieutenant Colonel Miller's assigned defense counsel was Captain John L. Euler, senior defense counsel at Camp Pendleton and formerly a defense counsel at Force Logistic Command in Vietnam.[14] Miller later retained civilian counsel. Secretary of the Navy John Warner assumed personal control of the two officer cases. He sought the recommendation of the Commandant of the Marine Corps in Miller's case. As Major Brahms recalled:

> The Marine Corps initially thought that prosecuting Miller was probably the right way to go. I was called in one Saturday morning by my boss [Brigadier General John R. DeBarr, Director of the Judge Advocate Division] and told, "The Commandant [General Robert E. Cushman, Jr.] wants a letter to the Secretary of the Navy on his position regarding prosecuting Miller." . . . I went through all the evidence again and wrote a couple of pages that concluded that prosecution was not called for . . . and [the Commandant] signed it, without change . . . . It obviously was not my decision; it was General Cushman's decision . . . and ultimately, of course, the Secretary's.[15]

In the Commandant's office on the second deck of the Navy Annex, Secretary Warner conferred with the Commandant, the Assistant Commandant, General Earl E. Anderson, and Brigadier General DeBarr. The decision was not a simple one, General Anderson later noted.[16] As Brigadier General DeBarr remembered: "The evidence and the circumstances of the case were reviewed. It was the position of the Marine Corps to try the case, but it was evident . . . that the case could not be successfully prosecuted. It was then that General Cushman signed the letter prepared by Major Brahms."[17] General Anderson recalled that "it was a very difficult decision for General Cushman to make, but he realized the constraints placed on him and reluctantly took his final position."[18]

Secretary Warner considered the advice of the Commandant and the Judge Advocate General of the Navy, and personally interviewed 19 former POWs before

Sgt Larry A. Kavanaugh is greeted at Clark Air Force Base soon after his release. Kavanaugh committed suicide six days before it was announced that he would not be court-martialed.

Department of Defense Photo (USAF)

The only Marine Corps officer charged with misconduct while a prisoner of the Vietnamese was LtCol Edison W. Miller, left. Here he is greeted by LtGen Louis H. Wilson, Commanding General, FMFPac, on 16 February 1973, as he first arrives in the United States.

Department of Defense Photo (USMC) A26909

deciding to dismiss the charges against Miller and Wilbur. He did issue both of them administrative letters of censure. Captain Wilbur accepted his letter and retired from the Navy. Lieutenant Colonel Miller's letter of censure read, in part:

> I have reached the judgement that your conduct . . . failed to meet those high standards which are required of an officer . . . . You placed your personal comfort and welfare above that of your fellow prisoners of war. But of greater seriousness, your conduct, at times and for extended periods, was severely detrimental to both the welfare and morale of your fellow prisoners.[19]

Prior to his repatriation, Miller had been selected for promotion to the grade of colonel. Although the Headquarters Marine Corps POW screening board had been aware of Miller's conduct while a prisoner, they had not reported it to the promotion board, not wanting to interfere with the regular administrative promotion process before Miller had an opportunity to respond to the allegations against him.[20]

Freed of court-martial charges, Miller was promoted to colonel and retired for physical disability. He immediately applied to the Board for Correction of Naval Records (BCNR) for removal of the letter of censure from his record. After two hearings and an amazing seven years' consideration, BCNR recommended on administrative grounds that the censure be removed. In 1982, the Assistant Secretary of the Navy for Manpower and Reserve Affairs, John S. Harrington, under whose purview such matters fell, rejected BCNR's recommendation. Miller sued the Secretary of the Navy in United States District Court, seeking removal of the censure. In 1985 the district court agreed with BCNR and ordered the censure removed.[21] That decision was appealed by the Navy, resulting in reversal of the district court's order by the District of Columbia Court of Appeals. The Court of Appeals did, however, order BCNR to decide whether or not Miller's conduct as a POW merited the letter of censure given 12 years before.[22] In a later cover memo on a letter to Vice Admiral Stockdale, apprising him of the status of the case, David Brahms, by then a brigadier general and Director of the Judge Advocate Division, wrote, "Fourteen years and we are still wrestling with Miller. Unbelievable!"[23]

Finally, on 17 May 1988 BCNR determined that there were indeed grounds for a letter of censure. It remains in Colonel Miller's permanent military record.[24]

"The bottom line," General Brahms later said, "is that we decided to let everybody off." He continued:

> I think I would [today] recommend we try those people . . . . It's probably necessary to get . . . the definitive judgement, and in this country the only way to do that is in court . . . . If I had to do it all over again, and had any input, I would feel strongly enough to take them to court-martial.[25]

After deciding against trying the returned POWs, the last echo of the Asian war still had not been heard.

From a Lawyer's Case File: Wartime Acts, Post-War Trial

Marine Corps judge advocates addressed the aftermath of the Vietnam war for years after the peace accords were signed. Even before the war ended, Marine Corps lawyers who had not served in the combat zone were trying cases that had their genesis in Vietnam. One such case was the *United States v. Sergeant Jon M. Sweeney*. Sweeney joined Company M, 3d Battalion, 9th Marines in January 1969 as a private first class, and quickly earned a poor reputation. His battalion commander, Lieutenant Colonel Elliott R. Laine, Jr., remembered that "about all he'd do was feed himself."[26] Two weeks after his arrival, during Operation Dewey Canyon, Sweeney's company was heavily engaged. In the midst of the action Captain Thomas F. Hinkle, the company commander, was repeatedly advised by radio that Sweeney, or "Sierra," as he was referred to on the radio, could not keep up with his

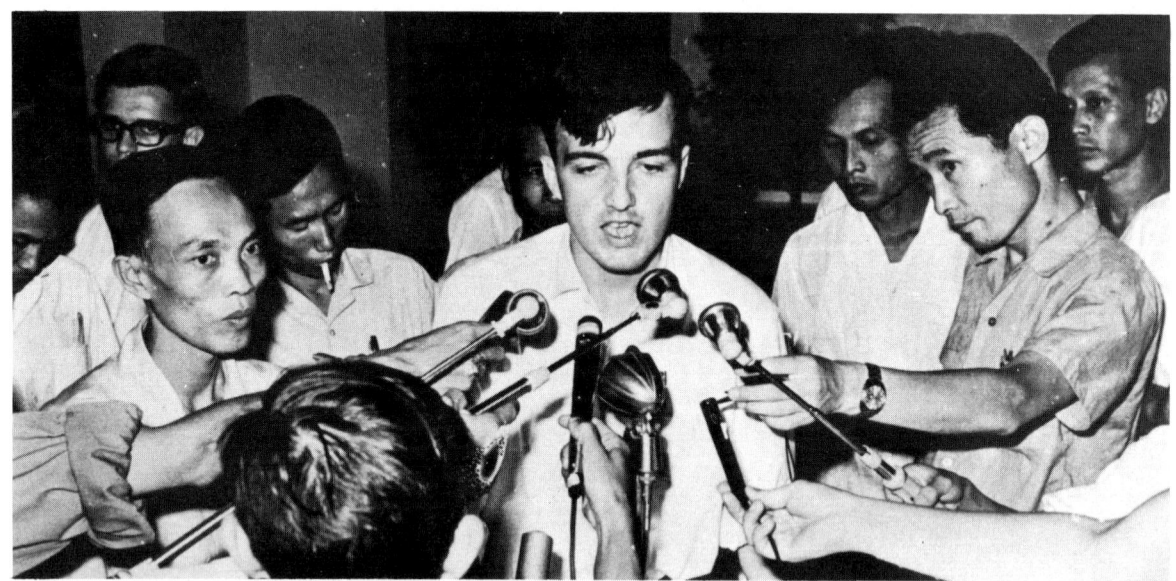

Sgt Jon M. Sweeney in Hanoi shortly after his release by the North Vietnamese. He was later tried for misconduct while a prisoner. His general court-martial ended in acquittal.

unit and had fallen behind.[27] Sweeney's company was the battalion's point company, which was fighting to wrest high ground from the enemy. Captain Hinkle later testified, "My point commander informed me that he was having difficulties with the character 'Sierra' . . . . I told him to leave him in his position and I would be up there with the senior corpsman, and we'd take a look at him." Captain Hinkle found Sweeney lying on the ground. His squad had already shouldered all his gear except his rifle and ammunition. According to Captain Hinkle, "The senior corpsman looked at him . . . . He said there was nothing wrong with him, physically. And I told him to move out and rejoin his people, and he said he couldn't make it." Disgusted, Captain Hinkle told Sweeney to wait for the rear guard which would be passing by within a few minutes, then left to rejoin the engaged lead element of his company. When the rear guard arrived they could not locate Sweeney. He had disappeared. When the firefight waned, a search was conducted. Only Sweeney's weapon and ammunition were found.

Nine months later a North Vietnamese broadcast, beamed to U.S. forces in Vietnam, was monitored by the Foreign Broadcasting Information Service.* A transcript of the broadcast read, in part: "Stage a strike against the war . . . . Refuse to obey any orders which would endanger your life . . . . Stage mass demonstrations . . . . I came to Vietnam in February '69 and I crossed over to the side of the Vietnamese people two weeks later." The speaker signed off, "Jon M. Sweeney, USMC, deserter." Fifteen other broadcasts followed in the next five months. Some urged racially oriented disobedience: "Black brothers, you must unite . . . . Your fight is in the streets and cities of the United States . . . . Refuse to serve as cannon fodder for the white oppressors." Others praised the enemy: "I am grateful to the Vietnamese people for letting me take part in their noble cause." Still others counselled desertion: "I'll inform you of the different ways to leave while on R & R, and then I will . . . tell you how to desert in Vietnam." As long as the circumstances of the broadcasts remained unknown, however, Sweeney was continued in a POW status and, in accordance with Marine Corps policy, promoted at the same rate as his nonprisoner contemporaries. That eventually proved difficult to explain to the military judge in Sweeney's prosecution for collaboration.

In a debriefing conducted soon after his release, Sweeney alleged that he had originally been captured when he wandered from where he was left by his company commander and, three days later, he was taken prisoner. Over the next month, according to Sweeney, he twice unsuccessfully attempted escape. After that,

---

*Lieutenant Colonel Laine, Sweeney's battalion commander, recalls that Sweeney, using a false name but his correct service number, made broadcasts within two weeks of his disappearance while Operation Dewey Canyon was still in progress. Those broadcasts were not offered as evidence in Sweeney's subsequent court-martial.

he said he was held in Hanoi for a year and a half, although not with any other prisoners. On 25 August 1970, for reasons not explained by the North Vietnamese, Sweeney was released. Holding a North Vietnamese passport, he was escorted to Sweden with intermediate stops in Peking and Moscow. At a Stockholm press conference Sweeney admitted that he had stayed with the enemy to engage in propaganda activities against American troops. He added, "The reason why I do not want to return to the U.S. is not only because punishment is waiting for me there. I have changed sides."[28]

An interview of Sweeney by Mr. Mike Wallace was shown on the CBS Evening News on 27 November 1970. Sweeney acknowledged making anti-American propaganda broadcasts for the enemy. The interview was later entered in evidence at Sweeney's court-martial, as was a Communist television news clip aired in Vietnam just after Sweeney's release, in which he made further incriminating statements.

Sweeney did return to the United States, and upon his arrival was placed under military apprehension (arrest). A Marine Corps intelligence debriefer noted that Sweeney's activities while a captive were not explored: "The nature of that of which he was suspected—collaboration with the enemy—and the fact he had an appointed military lawyer [Captain Carter LaPrade] to represent him during the conduct of the debriefing precluded thorough exploitation."[29]

Sweeney, a sergeant by the time he was released, was charged with deserting his unit in combat, running from the enemy, and communicating with the enemy by broadcasting disloyal statements. (The Department of Defense policy against trying former POWs for statements made in captivity had not yet been formulated.) Sweeney's general court-martial convened at Quantico, Virginia, on 15 June 1971. He was represented by Captain James R. O'Connell and Mr. Gerald Alch of Massachusetts. The trial counsels were Captains William D. Palmer and Clyde R. Christofferson. The military judge, hearing the case without members, was Captain "B" Raymond Perkins, JAGC, USN.

Brigadier General Clyde R. Mann, then Director of the Judge Advocate Division, wrote of the 10-day trial:

> We had trouble convincing the [military judge] that he had voluntarily aided the enemy, as the evidence indicated. After the Government had made a *prima facie* case . . . . Sweeney raised an affirmative defense . . . admitting that he did do certain things . . . but claimed that he did them because someone held a gun to his head. In the absence of a rebuttal witness, and in view of our lack of response during his captivity and during the time . . . he was operating on behalf of the enemy, the Court apparently was persuaded to accept his allegation that he did all of this under some type of duress.[30]

Admiral Stockdale, who later derided "our courts, spring-loaded to excuse any action to which the general term coercion is attached," might have predicted the trial's outcome.[31] On 11 August the military judge found the accused not guilty of all charges. Colonel Benjamin B. Ferrell, Quantico's Staff Judge Advocate, called the case "the greatest miscarriage of justice that I witnessed in the Marine Corps."[32] Sweeney was honorably discharged as a sergeant.

Deserters in the Hands of the Enemy

On 8 November 1967 Private Earl C. Weatherman escaped from the III MAF brig in a truck that had been filled with sandbags. He had been convicted of several relatively minor offenses at a 22 September 1967 special court-martial and sentenced to five months confinement and a bad conduct discharge. After his escape, while en route to see a girl friend in a village near Chu Lai, he was captured by the enemy. He subsequently defected to the Viet Cong and assisted in their propaganda effort by making propaganda broadcasts and signing a propaganda leaflet. The Marine Corps listed him as a deserter in the hands of the enemy.[33] Despite his actions, some American prisoners who were held in the same camp as Weatherman believed that he never really accepted the propaganda he was himself spreading. That view may be correct, for he later was again considered by the VC to be a prisoner, and on 1 April 1968 he was shot and killed while attempting to escape.[34] The only other Marine in the Vietnam war to be listed as a deserter in the hands of the enemy was Private First Class Robert R. Garwood, who reportedly had convinced Weatherman to go over to the enemy.

White VC?: Robert R. Garwood

The longest court-martial in Marine Corps history, tried long after the war's end by judge advocates who had not been to Vietnam, was also grounded in events that occurred in the combat zone. On the evening of 28 September 1965, Private Robert R. Garwood, a driver assigned to the 3d Marine Division motor pool, left on what he said was an official run within the division headquarters area.[35] Instead, he drove to Da Nang, passed the Marine checkpoint near the beach, and continued toward the village of Cam Hai, where several VC attacked and captured him. The jeep was partially dismantled then burned. For the next year and eight months Garwood was a prisoner of war, held in the regional detention camp, Camp Khu, northwest of Da Nang, along with two U.S. Army prisoners.

On 17 December 1965, three months after Garwood's disappearance, the 3d Marine Division recommended to Headquarters Marine Corps that his status be changed from missing to presumed captured. The recommendation was based on an anti-American broadcast and on propaganda leaflets, all written and signed by Garwood. Despite the broadcast and leaflets, his duplicity was not considered confirmed and as in Sweeney's case the Marine Corps promoted him, although missing, to the grade of private first class.

Neil Sheehan, a civilian war correspondent during the Vietnam war, later wrote:

> Those whom the Viet Cong thought they could convert to their cause . . . [they] "reeducated" . . . at clandestine prison camps in remote areas with indoctrination courses that consisted of work, lectures, political study, and primitive diet. The average confinement was three to six months, after which the prisoners were released.[36]

In May 1967, after repeated indoctrination sessions, Garwood, like Sweeney and several other Americans before him, was offered his release. He was given, and for the remainder of his time in Vietnam carried, an undated "Order of Release."* It was written in English, apparently so Garwood would recognize its importance, and it bore the seal and authorizing signature of the "Central Trung Bo National Liberation Front Committee," apparently so any Vietnamese would similarly appreciate its significance. It read, in part:

> Carrying out the lenient and humanitarian policy of the South Vietnam National Front for Liberation toward prisoner of war . . . . Basing on the improvement of the prisoner. The Central Trung Bo National Front for Liberation decides The prisoner: Bobby R. Garwood . . . . Captured on: September 28, 1965 at: Cam Hai village, Quangnam province be released. From now on Bobby can enjoy freedom and is not allowed to take arms or do anything against the South Vietnamese people.[37]

Unlike those who had been offered release before him, Garwood declined and instead asked to join the

---

*After the conclusion of Garwood's general court-martial, his defense counsel inadvertently delivered the Order of Release. among a sheaf of other material, to Major Werner Hellmer, Garwood's prosecutor. Hellmer wrote, "I noticed that a piece of paper . . . was protruding slightly from one of the binders. When I first opened up the sheet it looked like the standard release order given other prisoners of war who were released [and returned to U.S. control] during the 1968-69 time frame. Upon closer examination I noticed Garwood's name, age and other information!" Here was proof that Garwood had been freed by his captors. (LtCol Werner Hellmer ltr to author, dtd 2Mar89, Garwood folder, Marines and Military Law in Vietnam file, MCHC.)

Marine Corps Historical Collection
The accused in the longest court-martial in Marine Corps history was Pvt Robert R. Garwood. His boot camp photograph was taken in October 1963.

National Liberation Front. He adopted the Vietnamese name Nguyen Chien Dau and joined the enemy. As a member of the Military Proselytizing Section of Military Region 5, he taped and wrote propaganda messages, made loudspeaker broadcasts near Marine Corps positions, and assisted in guarding and indoctrinating U.S. prisoners in the MR-5 POW camp located in the village of Tra Khe, Tra Bong District, Quang Ngai Province. Garwood lived with the camp guards outside the compound and, when not in the camp, was armed with a rifle or pistol. He dressed as the guards did and had freedom of movement both within and outside the camp. He frequently questioned U.S. prisoners and, as with Weatherman, continually urged them to "cross over," as he had. In a surprisingly short period Garwood became fluent in Vietnamese and often acted as an interpreter for the North Vietnamese when they interrogated American prisoners.

In July 1968 Garwood was given officer status in the National Liberation Front and promoted to a grade equivalent to second lieutenant.[38] About a year later, Garwood had a conversation with POW Bernhard Diehl, a German nurse who, along with four other German nurses, three of whom were female, had been captured by the North Vietnamese in April 1969. Diehl later related that he asked Garwood how he

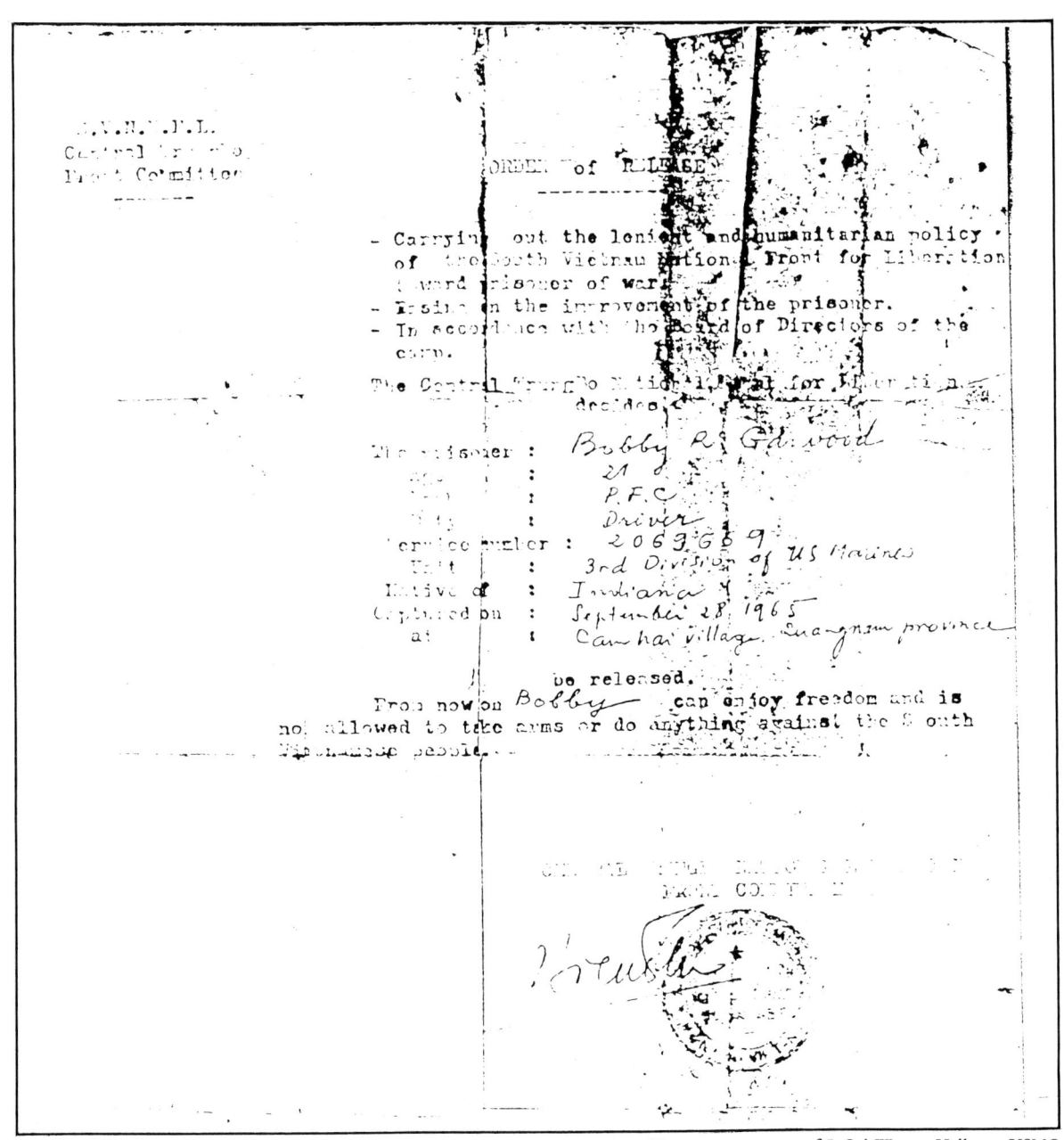

Document courtesy of LtCol Werner Hellmer, USMC

Worn, faded, and folded after years of having been carried, Garwood's release order was evidence that he had been released in May 1967 and voluntarily remained with the enemy.

came to work for the Viet Cong, and Garwood responded, "I don't think the Americans have suffered any great loss because I chose to fight on the other side. In any case, so many Americans are fighting with the South Vietnamese; why shouldn't there be a few fighting with the North?"[39] Author John Hubbell wrote in his history of the Vietnam POW experience: "Bobby Garwood was hard to believe, but he was real, a living breathing traitor who had taken up arms on behalf of the enemy and had no compunction about helping to hold American troops in vile captivity."[40]

Treason is an offense not addressed by the Uniform Code of Military Justice. Aiding the enemy and misconduct as a prisoner, Articles 104 and 105, are military offenses, each punishable by confinement at hard labor for life.

Throughout the war reports were heard of "white VC," American turncoats engaged in combat on the side of the enemy. Several Americans were suspected of such activity, and Garwood was repeatedly mentioned in intelligence reports as possibly fighting for the VC.[41] When guarding POWs, Garwood made no secret of his participation in combat against American forces.[42] Army Sergeant First Class Robert Lewis, a prisoner for six years, recounted in a sworn statement: "Garwood told me on a couple of occasions that he was shot at by the U.S. forces he was talking to, and that he came very close to being captured by U.S. forces. Garwood often bragged about close calls he had."[43]

On 15 July 1968 a 1st Force Reconnaissance Company patrol reported contact with a 20- to 25-man enemy force. At a range of 20 meters the Marines opened fire. Four patrol members identified one of the enemy as Caucasian, and they all heard him cry, "Help me!" as he fell, wounded. The patrol broke contact to escape the larger enemy force and reported that they had killed a Caucasian.[44] Based upon the patrol's report the 1st Battalion, 5th Marines searched the area of the contact for the body or a grave. "Suspect white male to be American reported in several other actions with NVA units," the battalion's orders read.[45] But neither body nor grave were found. The reconnaissance patrol's 10 members were shown photographs of captured and missing persons. Four believed that Garwood was the man they had shot. A message from III MAF to Saigon, substantiated by a later counterintelligence investigation, read, "it is considered probable that the Caucasian is in fact Garwood."[46] Army Private First Class James A. Strickland, a prisoner sometimes guarded by Garwood, said, after his release: "No, Bob Garwood wasn't killed by the Marine patrol. He left our camp in July . . . . He went to the hospital during this time [but] there was nothing to indicate Garwood had been wounded."[47] However, later medical examination of Garwood revealed, besides a preservice gunshot wound to his right upper arm, a gunshot wound in his right lower arm, as well as shrapnel wounds of the back, neck, and arm. Also, Garwood told examining doctors of having received blood transfusions after being wounded.[48]

In September or October 1969, a year after the reconnaissance patrol's encounter with the white VC, Captain Martin L. Brandtner commanded Company D, 1st Battalion, 5th Marines in an operation in "Arizona Territory." During a firefight he saw a Caucasian who appeared to be pointing out targets for the enemy. Even though the Marines fired at him the Caucasian did not appear to be hit. Captain (later brigadier general) Brandtner was aware of reports that Garwood was suspected to be in that area and believed the man he saw with the enemy was indeed Garwood.[49]

After 1969 Garwood was not seen in the POW camps. A Headquarters Marine Corps POW screening board (a member of which was judge advocate Lieutenant Colonel Michael Patrick Murray) suggested in 1972 that he had "gone to Moscow for training," and concluded that "PFC Garwood is still alive and probably still aiding the VC/NVA in SVN."[50]

In early 1979, in Hanoi, Garwood passed a note to a Finnish businessman associated with the United Nations: "I am American in Viet Nam. Are you interested? Robert Russell Garwood, 2069669 USMC."[51] On 22 March, 13 years and 6 months after he was captured, Garwood flew from Hanoi to Bangkok and was met by a contingent of diplomatic, press, and military officials. Among them was Captain Joseph Composto, the Marine Corps defense counsel assigned to represent Garwood.

Robert R. Garwood, born in April 1946, had completed two years of high school with two arrests for minor offenses as a juvenile, before joining the Marine Corps.[52] He had been on active duty for 23 months when he was captured. Before arriving in Vietnam, he had several psychiatric consultations and had been diagnosed as a "passive-aggressive personality with manipulative interpersonal relationships."[53] He also received nonjudicial punishment five times for minor infractions, usually involving brief unauthorized absences. Because his activities in the enemy camp had been known and corroborated by numerous intelligence sources, Garwood, unlike POWs, had not been promoted beyond the grade of private first class while in a missing status.

His return from Vietnam was carefully planned. Captain Composto noted that, "Planning and guidance came directly from CMC by classified message and secure voice transmission . . . . My job was to stand by and advise Garwood, should he desire it."[54] In Washington, at Headquarters Marine Corps' Judge Advocate Division, Lieutenant Colonel Brahms was detailed to coordinate legal aspects of Garwood's return, assisted by Captains William T. Anderson and James E. L. Seay, who addressed military justice and administrative law issues, respectively.[55] The Commandant, General Louis H. Wilson, Jr., wanted to ensure that Garwood was treated no differently than any other Marine returning from a lengthy unauthorized ab-

Just after his release, Garwood and his appointed military counsel, Capt Joseph Composto, talk over the roar of a C-130's engines on the flight from Bangkok, Thailand, to Okinawa.

sence. General Wilson took pains to ensure that if court-martial charges were brought against Garwood the case would not be complicated by failure to promptly advise him of his rights, including those to counsel and against self-incrimination. In a letter to the Deputy Assistant Secretary of State coordinating Garwood's return, General Wilson wrote: "I must insist that the following sequence of events take place to insure that full legal rights of PFC Garwood are protected," and he detailed the scenario he required, "Immediately, repeat immediately, advise Garwood of his full legal rights. This advice must be the first words spoken to Garwood.... The warning must be witnessed by a third party.... A tape recording of the foregoing events will be made."[56] The Commandant went on to specify the precise wording of the warnings to be given, essentially those given prior to questioning any suspect. General Wilson's instructions were carried out, witnessed in writing by the American Consul in Bangkok.[57]

Garwood's biographers, in an otherwise negative assessment of the military, describe his court-martial saying: "There was a certain correctness in everything the Marine Corps did, an air of playing fair. Hard but fair."[58] Garwood's court convened at Camp Lejeune, North Carolina, on 11 March 1980. Garwood, then a 33-year-old private first class, pleaded not guilty to desertion, soliciting American forces to refuse to fight and to defect, maltreatment of two American prisoners he was guarding, and communicating with the enemy by wearing their uniform, carrying their arms, and accepting a position as interrogator/indoctrinator in the enemy's forces. The maximum punishment for the combined offenses was death, but the base commanding general, the convening authority, referred the case to trial as noncapital.

Pretrial motions and unforeseen delays pushed the actual trial back more than eight months.[59] The military judge was Colonel Robert E. Switzer. Initially, Garwood was defended by Mr. Dermot G. Foley of New York City. Defense counsel Captain Composto was released by Garwood, as was a second appointed defense counsel, Captain Dale W. Miller, both of whom had tactical differences with Mr. Foley. A month after the trial opened, Captain Lewis R. Olshin was appointed as military defense counsel. Still later, but well before the first witness appeared, Mr. John Lowe of Charlottesville, Virginia, a former Army judge advocate, joined the defense team as lead counsel. Two weeks later he was joined by his associate, Mr. Vaughn

Garwood's military counsel during his general court-martial was Capt Lewis R. Olshin. The last of three military lawyers who represented Garwood, Capt Olshin was appointed a month after the court convened.

E. Taylor. Reflecting dissension in the defense camp, Mr. Foley left the case shortly after the arrival of Lowe and Taylor, taking with him many critical defense files. Mr. Taylor, newly discharged from the Army, had recently been an instructor at the Judge Advocate General's school, where he had a large part in drafting the mental responsibility instructions included in the military judges' handbook. The crux of the defense case was to be Garwood's mental responsibility.

Trial counsel was Captain Werner Hellmer (recently selected for promotion to the grade of major), assisted by Captain Teresa J. Wright. Ironically, Marine Captain Hellmer had attended the Army's JAG school where one of his instructors had been then-Captain Taylor. Captain Hellmer came late to the prosecution, after the trial counsel who had conducted the Article 32 investigation returned to civilian life. Adding to Captain Hellmer's considerable burden, the Garwood trial was the first general court-martial he had ever participated in.

The case was tried before five officer members. Over 11 days the government presented its case-in-chief through 14 witnesses, nine of whom were former POWs. The month-long defense case was primarily psychiatric testimony urging that Garwood's initial captivity had been so brutal as to cause him to act as he later did without the mental responsibility necessary to make his acts punishable.

Throughout the Vietnam War and its aftermath civilian defense lawyers often prevailed in courts-martial of heightened visibility and public interest. On 5 February 1981 it was the Marine Corps' and Major Hellmer's turn. Eleven months after convening, after 92 trial days, more than 60 defense motions, 3,833 pages of transcript, and two days of deliberation by the members, Garwood was convicted of communicating with the enemy and assaulting a POW. He was sentenced to reduction to private, loss of all pay and allowances, and a dishonorable discharge. No confinement was imposed and Garwood was immediately discharged from the Marine Corps.

Like Edison Miller's case, Robert Garwood's inched through military appellate forums and civilian courts for several more years. While his case was still under appellate review, Garwood sought immunity for any

PFC Garwood's civilian defense team, shown during trial. Garwood stands beside former Army judge advocate Vaughn E. Taylor, center, and John Lowe.

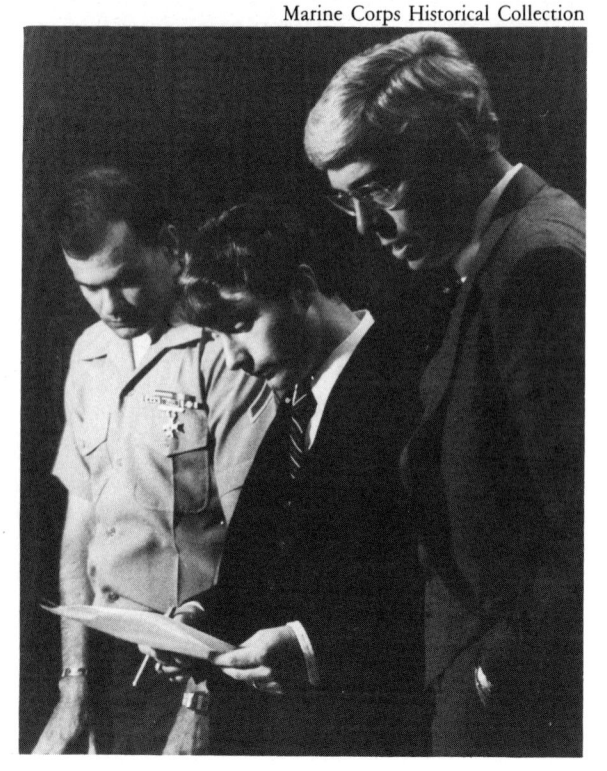

Trial counsels in the Garwood court-martial were Capts Werner Hellmer and Teresa J. Wright. The conduct of the military judge created potentially serious appellate issues.

offenses he might be charged with having committed between 1970 and 1980—the years when charges of collaboration were still a possibility if new evidence arose—in return for information he claimed to have regarding American POWs still in enemy hands. But there was "a real possibility that the Court [of Military Appeals] may reverse the court-martial conviction," wrote the General Counsel of the Navy.[60] In a handwritten addendum to his memorandum to Secretary of the Navy John Lehman, the General Counsel added: "This guy will cause lots of grief irrespective of what is done. He's no good and I wouldn't believe him."[61] General Paul X. Kelley, Commandant of the Marine Corps, agreed, saying: "I find this whole business to be repugnant. How do we explain a grant of immunity to the families of the 50 thousand KIAs in RVN?"[62] Immunity was not granted and no information was offered by Garwood.

The principal issue on appeal and the basis for the General Counsel's fear that the case might be overturned, was the conduct of the military judge, Colonel Switzer, during trial. While the court-martial was in progress, and in violation of his own instructions, he had granted several interviews to reporters, and had been interviewed on the CBS Evening News and the ABC program, "Nightline." In those interviews he voiced his opinions of the defense trial tactics, credibility of a defense witness, and the relevance of certain evidence. In a decision eventually concurred in by the United States Court of Military Appeals, Marine Corps Colonel James S. May, an appellate judge on the Court of Military Review, wrote: "We find inexcusable the decision by the trial judge here to involve himself in the clearly predictable media interest in this case . . . . There is very simply, no justification or excuse."[63] But the court went on to note that the judge's indiscretions were not shared by or with the members who had decided Garwood's guilt or innocence, and that the military judge had maintained an unbiased in-court decorum throughout the trial. Garwood's conviction was affirmed by the Court of Military Review and, later, the Court of Military Appeals. His later appeal to the United States Supreme Court was denied.[64]

Although Garwood was not promoted beyond private first class while he was classified as missing, the lesson of the Sweeney case had been forgotten, for neither had he been declared a deserter.[65]* Neverthe-

---

*In 1977, a Headquarters Marine Corps POW screening board had recommended that Garwood's status be changed from prisoner of war to deserter. At the time of his return to U.S. control that administrative action had not been completed, though his conduct was documented and well-known. (HQMC, Judge Advocate Division comment on Review Board Report RLP;caw of 28Sep77, dtd 29Aug78. Garwood folder, Marines and Military Law in Vietnam file, MCHC.)

PFC Robert R. Garwood was the only Marine convicted of misconduct while in the hands of the enemy. Here he appears to be wearing a POW bracelet.

less, upon his return from Vietnam his application for almost 14 years' back pay was refused by a Marine Corps disbursing officer. Deserters may not be paid for the period of their desertion, and the disbursing officer, supported by Headquarters Marine Corps, considered Garwood to have been a deserter from the date of his initial capture, despite the lack of official classification as such. Several months before his court-martial convened, Garwood filed suit in the U.S. Court of Claims for $146,749.24 in back pay and allowances, as well as for promotions that were, he alleged, wrongfully denied him. The Court of Claims case was stayed until the court-martial proceedings were concluded. On 6 September 1984, three and a half years after his court-martial conviction, the U.S. Claims Court (formerly the U.S. Court of Claims) granted the government's motion for summary judgement, thereby denying Garwood's claim to back pay and promotions.[66]

The longest and most expensive court-martial in Marine Corps history was over. Colonel Joseph R. Motelewski, who had been the chief of staff of the 3d Marine Division in Vietnam, was the convening authority's staff judge advocate during Garwood's pretrial maneuvering. He noted:

> I recommended, initially . . . that we should never try the Garwood case; that we should give him an administrative discharge . . . . Give him a kick in the ass and send him out, and it wouldn't have cost us a penny . . . . Every witness that we had to call back, primarily, was a former prisoner of war, and if anybody knows anything about prisoners of war, those guys went through hell. They all had to come back and . . . admit to the public those things which they had done under horrible conditions . . . . I worried about the Garwood case.[67]

But, as Admiral Stockdale suggested in alluding to Garwood's psychiatric defense, other considerations were involved in bringing Garwood to justice:

> I . . . hope that America will salvage from the tragic case of PFC Robert R. Garwood . . . a clear definition of the standard of conduct to be demanded of any future POWs . . . . To try to claim "brainwashing" or "breaking" would never do. It just doesn't happen that way . . . . Prisoner misconduct charges . . . do not pertain to pain thresholds, depression of isolation, interrupted consciousness, discontinuities of judgement patterns or temporary factors of any sort. The charges are about character . . . . Garwood's case is a particularly sad case, but to conclude from it that one's responsibility for long-term actions can be absolved by some sort of hypnotic "whammy" . . . would be dead wrong.[68]

Why was Garwood tried, while others, including a Marine Corps lieutenant colonel, were not? That question, too, was an appellate issue addressed by the Court of Military Review. The court wrote: "the specific circumstances of this case are an appropriate reference point to determine the extent, if any, of arbitrariness."[69] They found, as did the court of Military Appeals, that Garwood was in a category by himself: "We have some doubt whether he even makes a colorable claim that there were others similarly situated against whom his treatment can be measured."[70]

Garwood was the only former prisoner of war of any Armed Service convicted of acts committed while with the enemy—not for acts committed while a prisoner, for his prisoner status ended the day he refused release and asked to remain with the enemy. Robert R. Garwood *was* the enemy.

CHAPTER 11
Mopping Up

Drugs, Race, Dissent: Same Problems, New Venues—Vietnam Finale: Bien Hoa and the Rose Garden Perspective—The Uniform Code of Military Justice: Did It Work in Vietnam?—Summation

---

American forces continued to redeploy from Vietnam after the last combat unit left Da Nang and while the prisoner of war cases were progressing toward resolution. Meanwhile, on Marine Corps bases throughout the world, issues and problems that arose during the war continued to affect not only lawyer's caseloads, but morale and readiness as well. Drug use remained endemic. Racial conflict continued to divide the ranks. Dissent and disobedience still plagued commanders. Judge advocates remained overburdened with cases, some of which had arisen in Vietnam to be tried elsewhere. Marines of every occupational specialty continued to deal with the aftermath and echoes of the war long after the last round was fired.

Drugs, Race, Dissent: Same Problems, New Venues

A month after the Marines left Vietnam, Lieutenant General William K. Jones, Commanding General, Fleet Marine Force, Pacific, in addressing a symposium of general officers at Headquarters Marine Corps, said:

> Drug abuse, racial incidents, permissiveness fallout. This triple challenge is not an easy one to grasp and it is going to be even more difficult to solve.... We can issue directives and these will have the same general effect as the old "There will be no more V.D." orders. Yet, there must be solutions and we must find them, quickly.[1]

General Leonard F. Chapman, Jr., Commandant of the Marine Corps, added, "There are organizations like the Movement for a Democratic Military that advocate eliminating discipline in the Armed Forces. They advocate such things as electing officers ... eliminating the Uniform Code of Military Justice, and the like."[2] Civilian labor unions attempted unionization of the Armed Forces. Later, General Robert E. Cushman, Jr., General Chapman's successor as Commandant, recalled with frustration:

> Vietnam was over, yet we were still being told to take ... so many Group IVs.... We just had a hell of a time with quality.... I was always massaging the numbers and trying to get the mental Group IVs down to the lowest possible level and the high school graduates up as far as we could.... You had to lower your standards somewhat to keep the number of people up to near the authorized strength.[3]

To maintain Congressionally ordered manpower levels without accepting an excessive number of marginal recruits, or discharging large numbers of substandard Marines, the flow of administrative discharges was curtailed in 1972. Brigadier General William H. J. Tiernan, a former Director of the Judge Advocate Division, noted that "the situation was a classic 'Catch 22.' On the one hand, we were bogged down with thousands of substandard individuals who never could be productive Marines, and on the other hand we were imposing quotas on the number we could dispose of out of fear of a declining end strength."[4] Nevertheless, Major General Edwin B. Wheeler, the Marine Corps' manpower chief, told commanders that "in the past, our approach has been, 'If they don't measure up, kick 'em out.' Our course now, in order to preserve our numbers is: 'If they don't measure up, work with them until they do.'"[5] The tilt towards numbers as opposed to quality was supposed to be overcome by traditional Marine Corps leadership skills, but that hope was not fulfilled. Discipline suffered and court-martial rates increased. Desertions rose until, in 1975, the desertion rate was the highest it had ever been. General Louis H. Wilson, Jr., who succeeded General Cushman as Commandant in 1975, wrote in a report to the Senate Armed Services Committee:

> Recent criticism of the quality of Marine Corps personnel is largely founded in such categories as unauthorized absence, desertion, drug abuse, and enlistment of non-high school graduates. These problems stem almost entirely from past acceptance of excessive numbers of substandard applicants.... The Marine Corps ... enlisted a significant number of persons who simply did not meet existing quality standards, a fact reflected in subsequent disciplinary statistics.[6]

The Commandant continued:

> Marine Corps court-martial rates have tended to be higher than those of the other services. This condition can be explained in part by the fact that the Corps has a much higher percentage (55 percent in FY 75) of personnel under 22 years of age than the average for all the military services (34 percent in FY 75). A second factor has been the fact that Marine Corps commanders have consistently adhered to high standards ... and disciplinary processes have resulted in punishments that reflect this.[7]

Upon becoming Commandant, General Wilson directed a return to higher disciplinary standards without regard to maintaining numbers. "If we can't find enough fine young men who want to bear the title 'Marine,' then we're simply going down in strength."[8] He ordered the early discharge of over 4,000 marginal and unsuitable Marines and initiated new recruiting standards that emphasized high school graduation as a prerequisite to enlistment.[9] It took time for those initiatives to have effect in the field. Meanwhile, through the mid-1970s judge advocates mopped up the disciplinary aftermath of the war. Brigadier General John R. DeBarr, Director of the Judge Advocate Division from 1973 to 1976, recalled: "Those were tough years." He noted that at one time, besides the usual courts-martial, 20 cases were pending in various Federal District courts in which the Marine Corps was the defendant. Most of those suits were brought by disgruntled Marines over such things as haircut regulations.[10]

Low quality enlistees continued to join the Marine Corps through the early 1970s, but slowly the results of higher enlistment standards began to show. Enlistment of high school graduates rose from a 1973 low of 46 percent to 74 percent in 1976.[11]* The enlistments of previously recruited "Cat IVs" were completed. Others who did not meet disciplinary standards were administratively discharged.

In 1971, 634 general and 5,835 special courts-martial were tried throughout the Marine Corps. In 1972, although Marine Corps strength dropped seven percent, general courts-martial rose slightly, and special courts lessened only minimally. In 1974, when low quality Marines who had enlisted in 1973 joined their units, 521 general and 7,690 special courts were tried, an increase of 17 percent over the preceding year's totals despite a four percent drop in strength. But in 1975, when manpower increased four percent, courts-martial dropped 17 percent, to 395 generals and 6,413 specials. That year, 1975, was the beginning of a long upward trend in the quality of recruits and a long downward trend in disciplinary cases.[12]

Another long-standing problem area, racial conflict, was attacked on a broad front. A human relations training program was initiated by Headquarters Marine Corps in 1972, and 113 instructors were assigned exclusively to human relations duties at major Marine Corps commands. The program required 20 hours of guided instruction for all Marines, officer and enlisted, in racial issues. The Marine Corps Human Relations Institute at San Diego, California, was designated a formal Marine Corps School. The Advisory Committee for Minority Affairs, composed of prominent minority civilians, advised the Commandant on equal opportunity matters.[13] Bernard C. Nalty, author of a history of black Americans in the military wrote: "These efforts seemed to be paying off . . . . Compared with the draftees inducted during the latter stages of the Vietnam War, the black volunteers [of the mid-1970s] were less likely to be streetwise advocates of black power who would take offense at injustices, real or imagined, and lash out violently."[14]

From 1970 to 1975 reenlistment rates rose and desertion rates fell.[15] Drug use remained high, but showed signs of abating.** By 1975 the problems that had plagued all of the Armed Forces continued, but they were easing significantly.

A poll of 7,000 Marines of all grades, released in 1972, indicated confidence in the military justice system. Asked if they would prefer trial by civilian or military court, if charged with an offense, sixty percent of the anonymous respondents indicated they believed a military court-martial was as fair or fairer than civilian courts. That result was constant regardless of race. The same confidence was not expressed in military lawyers, however. By a margin of almost two to one, the Marines polled preferred a civilian lawyer over a judge advocate. The poll ascribed no reasons for the lack of confidence in Marine Corps lawyers, but the younger the respondent and the more junior in grade, the greater the preference for civilian counsel.[16]

Vietnam Finale: Bien Hoa and the Rose Garden

In Vietnam the war continued after the Marines withdrew. In May 1972, responding to a determined enemy offensive and a request by the South Vietnamese government, portions of the 1st Marine Aircraft Wing revisited Vietnam. Marine Aircraft Group (MAG)-15, returned to Da Nang, and MAG-12 transplaced to Bien Hoa, just north of Saigon. In June

---

*Ten years later, in 1988, 98 percent of all enlistees would be high school graduates. Category IV (Cat IV) enlistees for the years 1986, 87, and 88 would total less than one hundred, less than 0.2 percent of all enlistees. (*Navy Times*, 6Mar89, p. 6.)

**In a 1971 survey of 6,669 anonymous Marines, conducted by FMFPac's Operations and Analysis Branch and Human Affairs Division, 48 percent of the respondents indicated they had used drugs at one time or another, 44 percent of that group indicating first use in the Marine Corps, 59 percent indicating use of LSD at least once, and 20 percent indicating use of heroin. (Analysis, FMFPac Human Affairs Poll folder, Marines and Military Law in Vietnam file, MCHC.)

MOPPING UP 233

Marine Corps Historical Collection

The Commandant of the Marine Corps, Gen Leonard F. Chapman, Jr., poses with the Advisory Committee for Minority Affairs. The 12 civilians advised the Commandant on equal opportunity issues and ways to ease racial tensions within the Marine Corps.

MAG-15 moved westward from Da Nang to a remote Royal Thai Air Force Base at Nam Phong, Thailand, and was redesignated Task Force Delta.[17] Combat air sorties would be flown over Vietnam by U.S. aircraft based at both Nam Phong and Bien Hoa. Nam Phong was shared with Royal Thai Air Force personnel, including 200 Thai security guards. The threat from Communist forces was minimal, although in September and October 1972 several U.S. Air Force bases in Thailand were attacked. During the Marine Corps' tenure, however, there was no ground combat at Nam Phong.

Because of its remoteness and inhospitableness, Nam Phong was facetiously referred to as "The Rose Garden," a nickname adopted from a Marine Corps recruiting slogan of the day, taken in turn from a then-popular song, "I Never Promised You A Rose Garden." The nearest town, Khon Kaen, was 15 miles away.

Advance elements of Task Force Delta arrived at the Rose Garden on 24 May 1972 when Seabees began base construction and erection of tents and the familiar SEAhuts. Lieutenant Colonel Raymond W. "Wes" Edwards became the SJA of the 1st Marine Aircraft Wing a few days later.

First commissioned in 1953, Lieutenant Colonel Edwards had been an artillery officer for 16 years and obtained his law degree during off-duty hours.[18] From Iwakuni, Japan, he directed the wing's lawyers throughout the Nam Phong-Bien Hoa deployments. He recalled that "the delivery of legal services during this period was amazing. The 1st Wing had units in mainland Japan, Okinawa, . . . the Philippines, Republic of South Vietnam (2 locations) and in Thailand, as well as units afloat . . . . Logistically it was a nightmare."[19] Shortly after his arrival at Iwakuni Lieutenant Colonel Edwards accompanied the wing commander on a week-long trip to Nam Phong to determine how his judge advocates could best serve the task force. He had been to Nam Phong before. In 1966, as the Plans Officer of 9th MAB/Task Force 79, he had surveyed Northern Thailand to locate potential contingency air fields. He had selected Nam Phong.[20]

Initially, legal service for the Rose Garden was provided from Bien Hoa, Vietnam. Because of the lawyer's low air travel priority, that was impracticable and legal personnel were moved to the Rose Garden, itself. Lawyers and clerks at both Bien Hoa and the Rose Garden would be rotated to and from Iwakuni every

30 days. That, too, proved impracticable. Rose Garden deployments were lengthened, generally, to six months, although deployments from Iwakuni remained flexible and responsive to individual circumstances.

In June 1972 the branch law office at the Rose Garden was opened and was initially manned by Captains Michael C. Warlow, the officer-in-charge of legal personnel, and William D. Blunk. Master Sergeant William C. Davis, the legal chief, and a court reporter/legal clerk, rounded out the four-man legal section. They had no office and worked wherever they could find space. In October Captains Warlow and Blunk were relieved by Captains Richard L. Prosise, the new officer-in-charge, and Daniel Parker, Jr. Captain Vincent J. Bartolotta, Jr., arrived in December 1972 and remained until the base was turned over to the host nation 10 months later. Several other judge advocates, including Captains Keith E. Rounsaville, Robert E. Hilton, Van E. Eden, and Stephen C. Eastham, rotated through the Rose Garden during the legal office's 15-month tenure there.[21]

Living and working conditions were Spartan. Task Force Delta's 3,200 officers and men originally anticipated remaining in Thailand no longer than 90 days, but the deployment was repeatedly extended.[22] As a result, facilities improvements were delayed in antici-

Marine Corps Historical Collection

The Staff Judge Advocate of the 1st Marine Aircraft Wing in 1972 was LtCol Raymond W. Edwards. Shown in a 1975 photograph as a colonel, he directed the judge advocates at the Rose Garden and at Bien Hoa.

Nam Phong, Thailand, "The Rose Garden," shown after the base was well-established. The legal office is center, under the trees to the right of three trailers in the shape of an "H."

Marine Corps Historical Collection

Photo courtesy of Mr. Vincent J. Bartolotta, Jr.

Recreational opportunities at the Rose Garden were few. Capt Vincent J. Bartolotta, Jr., left, plays liar's poker with an unidentified PFC, and a Navy doctor, dentist and chaplain.

Shortly after the Rose Garden was established, the enlisted legal clerks lived in this shabby hardback tent. Within a few months they moved to a more comfortable SEAhut.

Photo courtesy of Col A. F. J. Mielczarski, USMC

pation of a continually receding withdrawal date. Tents, cots, and water in five-gallon cans were the rule. The first court-martial was tried in the chapel. When a SEAhut was eventually provided the legal section, cases were tried there. The billeting spaces of the lawyers and clerks were at one end of the hooch, and field desks and office gear at the other end. Before court was convened, the lawyers would just rearrange the desks. Eventually, the enlisted reporter/clerks were provided separate living spaces.

Large rats infested the Rose Garden and the Marine SEAhuts. When Task Force Delta's aviator commanding general loaned Captain Prosise some rat traps, Captain Prosise noticed the general's prominent office wall display of spray-painted rat silhouettes, commemorating the general's numerous kills.[23]

Courts-martial were difficult to conduct so close to the flight line. The parties to the trial paused in midsentence, while aircraft took off on afterburner. The closed mask reporting system required the reporter to speak into a microphone encased in an oxygen mask-like device held directly to his face. The discomfort the mask caused in the heat of the Thai summer led to open-microphone recording of courts on cassette recorders. The microphone was simply passed back and forth between the reporter and the person speaking.[24]

The Bob Hope USO Christmas show played at the Rose Garden on 23 December 1972. An unexpected result was easier trial of courts-martial. An air conditioned trailer van, one of several employed at the Rose Garden as aircraft ready-crew sleeping vans, was cleared and set aside as a dressing room for the troupe's female members. Immediately after the show and before the van could be returned to its proper location, defense counsel Captain Bartolotta, borrowed the trailer and had it moved to another portion of the camp, where a makeshift bench was quickly installed. "Thereafter, we convinced the chief of staff that the command needed some sort of decorum for their legal proceedings, and we got to keep our 'courtroom' until we closed the base," he recalled.[25] After having perfected their claim to it, legal personnel frequently slept in the courtroom trailer when trials were not in progress.

The Bob Hope Christmas show played at the Rose Garden in December 1972. The show led to an unexpected bonus for the branch legal office: an air conditioned van.

Photo courtesy of Mr. Richard L. Prosise

Photo courtesy of Mr. Vincent J. Bartolotta, Jr.

The Rose Garden's temporary detention facility was crude but effective. Marine Corps defense counsels preferred to visit their clients at the U.S. Army's brig at Pattaya Beach.

An "ad hoc" special court-martial military judge from Iwakuni, initially Captain Richard D. Sullivan, spent several days each month at the Rose Garden.[26] During that time the judge would try the cases that had been readied since his last visit. Later military judges were Captains Michael C. Vesey, Charles R. Oleszycki and Franklin D. Holder, and Major Anthony F. Mielczarski. The judges found that flights from Iwakuni to the Rose Garden were long and circuitous. Additionally, they were often bumped from their aircraft en route to Nam Phong. To make their flights more certain, if not shorter, Lieutenant Colonel Edwards arranged for military judges to be designated as couriers, which gave them a transportation priority that precluded their being bumped.

In January 1973 a rudimentary temporary detention facility was constructed to hold prisoners awaiting transportation to the brig at Iwakuni or on Okinawa. The U.S. Army brig near Pattaya Beach, south of Bangkok, was usually used for pretrial confinement, however. Recalling the beauty of Pattaya Beach, Captain Bartolotta said that "once we realized that the counsel for these defendants would have to go to this brig to interview his clients prior to trial [defense counsel] became a much sought-after assignment."[27]

The caseload hovered around four or five special courts-martial per lawyer. Only four general courts-martial arose during the Marine Corps' stay at the Rose Garden. Three of them were transferred to Iwakuni for trial. The fourth, an attempted murder case prosecuted by Captain Rick Prosise and defended by Captain Daniel Parker, was tried in the Rose Garden messhall. The ubiquitous Colonel Donald E. Holben, once again a general court-martial military judge, came from Yokosuka, Japan, to hear the case. Corporal Clifford K. Somerville, who shot and wounded a staff sergeant with a .38 caliber revolver after having been put on report, was tried over the course of five days in February 1973. The wounded staff sergeant testified to Somerville's good character and prior good record, following his conviction. Somerville was sentenced to confinement at hard labor for two years, reduction to private, loss of pay and allowances, and a dishonorable discharge.[28]

Many courts involved Marines sent from the 3d Marine Division on Okinawa to assist the Thai police in camp security. Lieutenant Colonel Michael Patrick

Photo courtesy of Mr. Vincent J. Bartolotta, Jr.

The Rose Garden's courtroom trailer, center, was a former aircraft crew sleeping van. The spectator's section of the makeshift courtroom was deep, but narrow.

Murray, who relieved Lieutenant Colonel Edwards as SJA, said of those Marines, "[the Rose Garden] did not get the cream of the crop. They got the shitbirds and troublemakers, and with them came many of the problems, particularly racial."[29] In July 1973 there was a cross-burning incident involving white Marines, followed by a racially instigated riot in the messhall in which eight Marines were injured.

There was no status-of-forces agreement (SOFA) with the Thai government, which sometimes resulted in jurisdictional disputes with Thai police. That situation was made more difficult by the lack of availability of Thai lawyers to assist in representing Marines in Thai criminal proceedings, or in disputes with Thai nationals. In such cases the Rose Garden judge advocates telephoned U.S. Air Force lawyers at Udorn for advice and assistance. A Thai attorney employed by the Air Force grudgingly assisted Marines in legal difficulty, most of which resulted from drug involvement. As Lieutenant Colonel Edwards noted, "Beer, soft drinks, PX supplies, liberty, etc. were in limited supply, but drugs weren't."[30]

Drug use was the most common offense at the Rose Garden, despite an aggressive drug abuse prevention program. If anything, drugs and marijuana were more readily available in Thailand than in Vietnam. Early on Thai nationals began aggressively marketing marijuana to the troops. Marijuana cigarettes, often laced with heroin, came in packs of 20 for less than a dollar. Thai stick, marijuana soaked in water and dried into a cigar-like shape, was frequently encountered. Heroin was widely available and, alarmingly, was more frequently the basis for charges than was marijuana. Incoming mail was examined by drug detection dogs and outgoing mail by U.S. customs personnel. Marine passengers on buses to and from liberty spots were routinely searched at the camp gate. In Au-

In 1972, when 1st Marine Aircraft Wing lawyers were assigned to the Rose Garden, this SEAhut was both quarters and courtroom. Here, Capt Robert E. Hilton enjoys the view.

Photo courtesy of Mr. Vincent J. Bartolotta, Jr.

In the new Rose Garden legal office, Capt Richard L. Prosise anticipates opening a package from home. As in the old office, the lawyers' quarters are just behind the partition.

gust 1972 random urinalysis testing began, and within a few months an average of 1,900 such tests were conducted monthly.

After the Vietnam cease-fire took effect on 27 January 1973, Rose Garden combat flights were redirected against Laotian and Cambodian targets. When bombing throughout Indochina was halted on 15 August 1973, Task Force Delta began to redeploy to Iwakuni and Okinawa.

On 10 July 1973 Lieutenant Colonel Murray relieved Lieutenant Colonel Edwards as the Wing SJA and later directed the withdrawal of legal personnel from the Rose Garden, assisted by his deputy, Major Joseph J. Hahn, Jr. On 6 September the Nam Phong facility was turned over to the Government of Thailand. The last Marine departed on 21 September.

While the Rose Garden grew, other judge advocates from Lieutenant Colonel Edwards' 10-lawyer office in Iwakuni were deployed to Bien Hoa Airbase, a long-established Vietnamese airfield several miles north of Saigon, where the lawyers served their temporary duty in a more comfortable setting. Marine Corps aircraft from MAG-12 were based there from May 1972 until the March 1973 cease-fire.[31] The first judge advocate to arrive at Bien Hoa was Captain John T. John, accompanied by a court reporter/legal clerk. While two attorneys usually manned the Rose Garden, Bien Hoa rarely had more than one. When a court-martial was pending, another judge advocate and a military judge would fly in from Iwakuni. They enjoyed air conditioned quarters and an air conditioned trailer in which to work. The few courts-martial were tried in a courtroom on board the base. Captain Rick Prosise, one of the Rose Garden judge advocates who often flew to Bien Hoa for cases, noted, "Bien Hoa . . . was not what I expected it to be. It had an air conditioned theater, air conditioned quarters, a nice-sized PX, an officers' club with good food and frequent bands, a bank," several tennis courts and even a swimming pool."[32] Bien Hoa was also subject to frequent enemy rocket attacks, and the lawyers' office trailer was later damaged by rocket fire but, as Captain Prosise recalled, "the only casualty at Bien Hoa during the last months of the war was a dog on the Vietnamese side of the base . . . . I had come too late to find the war."[33]

There was one attempted fragging at Bien Hoa, in which the evidence was too inconclusive to bring the suspect to trial.[34] For the most part, disciplinary problems were few, and near the end of 1972 Lieutenant Colonel Edwards withdrew his clerks and lawyers to Japan.* All Marine Corps personnel returned from Bien Hoa to Iwakuni by 3 February 1973.[35] For the few weeks between the Bien Hoa legal office's closing and the return of MAG-12 to Japan trial teams

---

*Following duty as SJA of the 1st Marine Aircraft Wing, Colonel Edwards went on to be SJA of the Marine Corps Development and Education Command, then an appellate judge on the Navy-Marine Corps Court of Military Review, and Assistant Judge Advocate General of the Navy for Military Law. In July 1984, he retired with the grade of brigadier general.

Photo courtesy of Mr. Richard L. Prosise

At Bien Hoa, Vietnam, in 1973, the 1st Marine Aircraft Wing branch legal office shared space with the public information office. The signs on the door read: "MAG 12 Law Center," and "Press Center, PIO."

from Iwakuni were available. Captain Rick Prosise, the final 1st Marine Aircraft Wing judge advocate assigned temporary duty at Bien Hoa was probably the last Marine Corps lawyer to have been in Vietnam.

Perspective

After the war, a number of rehearings—retrials—were held in military courtrooms in the United States. The rehearings were cases originally tried in the combat zone in which the result had been set aside upon appellate review. They were usually the most serious of cases. Problems of proof inherent in retrying offenses long past, committed at scenes far away, often led to "not guilty" findings.[36] The courtroom echoes of Vietnam were a long time dying.

At war's end other issues faced Marine Corps judge advocates. Still alarmed by the lawyer retention issue, Brigadier General Duane L. Faw, Director of the Judge Advocate Division, conferred with the Commandant. General Faw recalled the meeting:

> He said, "We're having deep trouble with our lawyers now, and your job is to retain them." I said, "General Chapman, I know what to do to retain lawyers, if you will give me the authority to do it . . . . One of the problems, of course, is our personnel assignment problem. I would like to handle all of these through the Judge Advocate Division." He said, "Fine. You have it." Just like that![37]

General Faw had been granted a unique authority. Thereafter, the Judge Advocate Division, with the cooperation and approval of the Personnel Division, orchestrated the assignment and transfer of the relatively small legal community. General Faw recalled: "I felt that we needed to offer some stability to in-

dividuals . . . . When they finished an overseas tour I would offer them a stabilized tour that would hold them as high as six years at the same post or station, if they wanted it, so their wives could get a job, their kids could go to one high school." The Assistant Commandant, General Earl E. Anderson, noted that the artillery community, for example, would like a deal such as the lawyers had. General Faw had a response: "I told him that I had to retain lawyers, and that a 'cannon cocker' couldn't go out there and get a job cocking cannons at 10 times the pay, like my lawyers could . . . and if I'm going to have the job of retaining them, I've got to know what it takes to keep them, and I've got to do it."[38]*

General Faw's concern for first-term lawyer retention was well-founded, and his efforts quickly showed results. The pre-Vietnam requirement for 168 lawyers had grown by the war's end to a wartime requirement of 375 and a peacetime requirement of 273 judge advocates. A peacetime procurement goal was established at 60 lawyers per year.[39] The authority for the Judge Advocate Division, with the Personnel Division's assistance, to assure lawyers of certain assignments was an important tool in keeping lawyer-officers in the Corps and countering civilian recruiting efforts.

Additionally, the return of six majors completing the law school excess leave program in 1971 eased the severe shortage in mid-level supervisory billets.[40] A valuable source of experienced officers, the excess leave program returned 38 majors to the legal community in 1972, and a high of 54 more in 1973. The goal was for the excess leave program to level out with the annual return of 14 new lawyers with former line experience.[41]

The difficulty in retaining first term judge advocates lasted for the entire war. Overlaying the retention issue was the opinion of many senior judge advocates that career-oriented Marine Corps lawyers should have experience as line officers. General Faw said, "I feel very strongly that every Marine lawyer ought to be a line officer [for some period] . . . . No lawyer can do his job properly until he knows the problems of a commander."[42] Colonel Joseph R. Motelewski, formerly chief of staff, then SJA of the 3d Marine Division, agreed: "If you don't have some

---

*General Anderson, however, Marine Corps Director of Personnel at that time, recalls that assignment procedures and policies for judge advocates remained unchanged except in isolated cases. (Gen Anderson ltr to author, dtd 22Feb89, Anderson folder, Marines and Military Law in Vietnam file, MCHC.)

line officer's mark on you . . . you've got a real long row to hoe."[43] Colonel Robert B. Neville, former Discipline Branch head and deputy chief of staff of III MAF, added, "I don't think any lawyer can effectively represent his client, unless he can understand the society . . . in which his client lives."[44]

General Faw and Colonels Motelewski and Neville, with their own exceptional backgrounds in infantry and aviation commands, experienced early careers in which lawyers were not only expected to aspire to line experience, but could expect careers to wither without it. By the time the Vietnam War began, Marine Corps policy had expressly freed senior lawyers from the *de facto* requirement to command or forego promotion. As the war progressed, and to a greater degree after the war, legal services assumed an ever more prominent role. That militated against intermittent assignments to line billets, while encouraging expertise and specialization acquired through continuous application of legal skills. Still, the judge advocate's suspicion, that without line experience, he was not a "real" Marine in the line commander's view, died hard. General Paul X. Kelley, former Commandant of the Marine Corps, believed that "the great strength of our judge advocates was the fact that an awful lot of them had served as combat . . . officers, and had actually led troops . . . . I was concerned that if the trend [to judge advocates without line experience] continued, we could end up literally with a civilian judiciary in uniform."[45] Vietnam demonstrated that Marine Corps lawyers, having received the same basic training as every infantry officer, willingly and capably commanded line units, given the opportunity.

The Uniform Code of Military Justice: Did It Work in Vietnam?

In 1949 the House Armed Services Committee Report on the newly enacted Uniform Code of Military Justice (UCMJ) read: "The law which we are now writing will be as applicable and as workable in time of war as in time of peace and . . . we must avoid the enactment of provisions which will unduly restrict those who are responsible for the conduct of our military operations."[46]

The Code became law in May 1950, a month before the outbreak of the Korean War. Most courts-martial tried in that conflict were conducted in Japan, not the combat zone. Colonel Robert M. Lucy, former SJA of the 1st Marine Division, noted that "Vietnam posed a peculiar set of disciplinary problems which may not be repeated . . . . I was a company commander in Korea . . . and I don't recall having many disciplinary problems—certainly none of a violent nature which was so common in Vietnam."[47] The Vietnam War was the first real application and test of the Code under combat conditions, although "combat conditions" was an elastic term when examining the circumstances in which judge advocates worked.

Brigadier General Edwin H. Simmons, assistant division commander of the 1st Marine Division in the final year of the war, wrote of conditions in the late stage of the war:

> Neither the 3d nor the 1st Marine Division headquarters ever really operated "in the field" in Vietnam . . . . There were air-conditioned work spaces, good billeting, first-class messing, adequate recreational facilities, good clubs . . . . Probably a whole generation of Marines thinks that is the way a Division command post in a combat zone should look and operate. (I have heard far more senior officers say that our experience in Vietnam "proves" that . . . the present cumbersome system of military justice will "work" in a combat environment.) . . . . We must find ways of keeping the extraneous administrative functions in the rear out of the objective area.[48]

Colonel John R. DeBarr, after having been a general court-martial judge in Vietnam, noted that the judicial process could no longer easily be moved to a secure area like Okinawa or Japan. He pointed out that the trial should be held where the crime was committed, because witnesses and evidence were there, and the commander will want to keep apprised of the administration of military justice, a function of command.[49]

More important than the place of trial is the question of the workability of the system itself. Did the UCMJ work in Vietnam? Clearly, it worked in the sense that thousands of courts-martial were tried.

Many senior judge advocates thought the system had worked quite well. Throughout the war lawyers worked hard and prosecuted thousands of cases through to conviction. But opinion was divided. Brigadier General Faw, Director of the Judge Advocate Division during the war, bluntly stated:

> I'm one of the people that thinks that the Uniform Code of Military Justice failed in Vietnam, and it'll be a greater failure in succeeding wars, if we get into one like World War II . . . . There were too many people who were guilty of very, very serious crimes who were never brought to trial because of the difficulties of getting witnesses, keeping witnesses [in country], and so forth . . . . Justice isn't just unless it also convicts those who are guilty.[50]

Another former Director, Brigadier General Tiernan, agreed:

> [The military justice system] was far less than satisfactory, far less than ideal.... A lot of cases, I know for a fact, were just not prosecuted.... Resources were so limited [that minor cases] were, necessarily, ignored. We had to concentrate on the more serious crimes.... What we considered to be a special court-martial misdemeanor, military-type offense was not being prosecuted, simply because of a lack of resources. We couldn't do it, period.[51]

A seminal law journal article examining the Code's effectiveness in Vietnam was written by Major General George S. Prugh, former Judge Advocate General of the Army, and General William C. Westmoreland, former commander of MACV and Chief of Staff of the Army. They wrote:

> It is our conclusion that the Uniform Code of Military Justice is not capable of performing its intended role in times of military stress.... It is presently too slow, too cumbersome, too uncertain, indecisive, and lacking in the power to reinforce accomplishment of the military mission, to deter misconduct, or even to rehabilitate."[52]

Professor Guenter Lewy, in his analysis of the war, wrote: "Many commanders felt that the system of military justice was too permissive and over-zealous in guarding the rights of individuals, and thus was more of an antagonist than an ally of their efforts to control the deterioration of discipline."[53] Colonel Arthur R. Petersen, while still an SJA in Vietnam, wrote: "The Code does not work in combat and does not accomplish its only legitimate objective of promoting discipline.... Changes must be made."[54]

Colonel Donald E. Holben had more practical experience with the Code in Vietnam than any other Marine Corps judge advocate. He said:

> The system does not work, from a military viewpoint.... Under no circumstances will it work in an all-out war, as it is now organized.... Under the phoney circumstances of Vietnam we were sitting there in barracks, in essence, in Da Nang and Chu Lai and Quang Tri... it permitted us to operate the system.... It did not adequately support command, and accomplishment of its mission. Proceedings are too long and drawn out, too far removed from reality. I think even now [1986], with the new changes, with the defense "command structure," it would be ridiculous to think that the system would work.[55]

Major Curt Olson, the 1st Marine Aircraft Wing's last SJA in Vietnam, agreed that post-war changes to the Code made its future application in combat even more difficult. "I do not think that we could have made it under those conditions with our present rules."[56] Major Olson was also concerned about defense tactics that affect case disposition:

> Defense requests for numerous character witnesses from the U.S.; requests for psychiatric examinations in the U.S.;

Photo courtesy of MGen George S. Prugh, JAGC, USA, (Ret.)
MajGen George S. Prugh was the Judge Advocate General of the Army from 1971 to 1975. He said: "The Uniform Code of Military Justice is not capable of performing its intended role in times of military stress."

> requests for expert witnesses from the U.S.; requests for delay while the accused attempted to obtain civilian counsel in the U.S.; requests for individual military counsel who just happened to be across the world from Vietnam. All of these combined with the witness problems... made the trial of a serious or complex case very difficult to get off the ground.... The system survived in Vietnam not so much because it was a superior system, there were serious flaws, but because... a lot of people worked very hard to make it work.[57]

General Tiernan, as well, believed that changes in military law since the Vietnam War had critical impact:

> It's totally unworkable in a combat environment. The state of case law has grown ever more complex, and the role of the defense counsel... has expanded many times over.... You could come up with a dozen things the defense counsel can legitimately request in order to assist the defense of his client that were not even considered in 1970.... I see no way that the UCMJ could function today, even in a Vietnam-type situation.[58]

What solutions present themselves? Senior lawyers with long Vietnam experience recommend major change in the military justice system. Colonel Holben suggested the system "should be done away with. Not be revised, cosmetically. I mean the whole system should be done away with and a different system imposed."[59] Colonel Motelewski, SJA of the 3d Marine Division in Vietnam, essentially agreed: "We should get some realists to revise the Uniform Code of Military Justice.... In wartime you've got to operate on a different basis.... I hesitate to even say it: have two different systems for wartime and peacetime."[60] According to Brigadier General Tiernan, "We've got to... give serious thought to going to another set of rules [in combat]—summary-type procedures that would function, perhaps in a limited jurisdiction."[61]

In a law review article predating the Vietnam War, Army Colonel Archibald King suggested: "If it is impossible, impracticable, or undesirable to... follow in time of peace a procedure which will work in time of war, then the law should provide in advance for an automatic change on the outbreak of war from the peacetime procedure to that of wartime."[62] Major General Prugh concurred, saying: "A much more significant overhaul is necessary, and the time to do this is when we are at relative peace and can study and experiment without wartime risks. Furthermore, the study must encompass experienced line commanders, not judges of the U.S. Court of Military Appeals."[63] Along the lines suggested by Colonel King, Generals Westmoreland and Prugh, offering a draft amendment to the UCMJ, said: "One possible way of dealing with the inadequacies of the Code in its wartime or military stress operation is to enact a special codal provision which would take effect only in time of war or other military exigency."[64]

Colonel Charles H. Mitchell, Assistant Judge Advocate General of the Navy for Military Law and former Vietnam trial counsel, suggested that "it's probably time to rethink the entire process from the ground up. We have to have something that's a whole lot more summary than we now have in dealing with relatively minor offenses, and maybe even all disciplinary offenses."[65]

Colonel Mitchell also raised a theme that goes to the fears of civilian critics of military justice when he noted, "we're disciplining an Armed Force, not providing the panoply of Constitutional safeguards to individual citizens.... We need to have a system which balances the realities against what the lawyers perceive to be necessary to due process."[66] Colonel Neville wrote: "The drive to make military justice identical to that found in civilian life [is] one of the greatest dangers.... If we cannot educate our people to the *essential* differences, we may as well disband our Armed Forces."[67] No one would suggest employing the Punishment Battalions of the Nazi *Wehrmacht*, where conviction resulted in dangerous battlefield assignments, but neither should one confuse the ends of military justice and civilian justice.[68]

In 1983 the Judge Advocate General of the Army appointed a Wartime Legislation Team (WALT) of Army lawyers to evaluate the system and recommend wartime improvements.[69] The WALT report noted that after the UCMJ was first promulgated:

> The United States Court of Military Appeals quickly established a new doctrine called "military due process of law," a powerful concept whereby the Court applies legal protections derived from principles applicable in civilian criminal proceedings, but not provided for by the UCMJ.[70]

Court decisions, the report continued, combined with statutory enactments, led to "judicialization" of military discipline. "American society has come to expect a high level of 'due process' to be built into its punitive systems. In military law... too many shortcuts in the system will lead to perceptions of unfairness."[71] Nevertheless, the WALT committee urged limiting or suspending the right to representation by counsel of the accused's choice, including civilian counsel, in areas of hostilities.[72] Generals Westmoreland and Prugh agreed, saying the right to competent counsel "does not require that the counsel be a civilian attorney transported halfway around the world."[73]

A major concern of the WALT committee was the lack of court-martial jurisdiction over civilian employees who, during wartime, might desert their posts in the combat zone. Civilians, such as technical representatives of civilian defense firms ("tech reps"), and civilian combat service support personnel, provide critical skills needed by military forces. Indeed, civilian employees of the military services constitute virtually the entire logistic personnel base in Europe. Currently, the only penalty a civilian would suffer for deserting his post is monetary loss and a possible breach of contract action, both of which would apply after the fact and far from the combat zone.[74]

In addressing the application of military law to the combat serviceman, the WALT report quoted an Army Judge Advocate General Corps (JAGC) brigadier general who urged, "Revive the use of depositions. In wartime, they will be indispensable."[75] In their article Generals Westmoreland and Prugh also urged such a step.[76]

An Army JAGC major general urged in the WALT report, "Travel of witnesses to areas of hostilities should be virtually eliminated." Another JAGC major general addressed Article 32 investigations as well as trials, saying, "After the experiences we all went through in Vietnam, I believe it is obvious that in future wartime conditions... we must eliminate the requirement for personal appearance of witnesses before both bodies."[77] Generals Westmoreland and Prugh suggested the substitution of depositions or videotape for witnesses who were no longer in the combat zone.[78]

The WALT report concluded that "although the current system will work with reasonable efficiency during a short, low intensity conflict, several changes are necessary in order to be confident that the system will operate effectively during a general war."[79] The WALT report was submitted, but no changes resulted.

Colonel Robert M. Lucy, who left Vietnam and later became legal advisor and legislative assistant to the Joint Chiefs of Staff, suggested that "relatively simple changes could make [the system] much more workable, such as removing the option to refuse trial by a military judge sitting alone, and restricting the requirement to produce certain witnesses from outside the combat zone."[80]

In 1984 the Secretary of Defense appointed a nine-member commission to report to the Armed Services Committees on aspects of the 1983 Military Justice Act, which had already been passed. Two members of the committee were Colonel Mitchell and Captain Edward M. Byrne, JAGC, USN, who joined in a trenchant separate report to the full committee report. Besides noting the wholesale inapplicability of civilian law to the Armed Forces, they proposed a "field court," akin to a nonjudicial punishment hearing, which would be authorized to try petty crimes and all disciplinary offenses and empowered to impose up to six months confinement, but no punitive separation.[81] No changes resulted from the commission's report.

In their article, Generals Westmoreland and Prugh emphasized:

> Probably the most worrisome aspect of this situation [is] that nowhere does there seem to be any recognition of the special need for the military justice system to work in times of military stress. Certainly there has been no effort to evaluate how it has worked and might work in the future. The emphasis has all been in the direction of civilianization. The one certainty is that it is not at all likely to do the job of requiring obedience . . . in time of hostilities.[82]

The final word may be that of Brigadier General Charles A. Cushman, former Assistant Judge Advocate General of the Navy for Military Law. He was asked if the military justice system would work in a future war. His answer strikes a familiar chord with any Marine: "Would it work? Of course it would work. It would work with major flaws and major difficulties and major delays, but . . . you would make it work."[83]

Summation

The last major operation in Vietnam involving U.S. ground forces, Operation Jefferson Glenn, ended in October 1971. U.S. forces continued to support the South Vietnamese with advisers and air support. On 27 January 1973 cease-fire agreements were signed in Paris. On 29 March the last American troops, other than defense attaché personnel and Marine Corps embassy guards, left South Vietnam. On 30 April 1975 Marine Corps and Air Force helicopters evacuated the last Americans from Saigon. For the United States the Vietnam War was over.

Over 448,000 Marines served in Vietnam. Approximately 400 Marine Corps lawyers served in the combat zone, 13 of them for two tours. No lawyer was killed and only two, Captain William L. Fly and First Lieutenant Michael I. Neil, were wounded, both while serving as infantry officers.

For most Marine Corps lawyers who practiced in Vietnam, particularly those in the Da Nang area after the first year or two of operations, the circumstances of everyday living were not particularly harsh and certainly less onerous than those of the Marine infantryman. But, as for all combat support Marines, the possibility of violent death was a constant. The threat of rocket attack, enemy sappers, misdirected friendly fire, and death or wounding while in the field with a trial team, forever separated the Marine Corps lawyer from those who had not undergone their experience. As British novelist John LeCarre wrote, "Nothing ever bridged the gulf between the man who went and the man who stayed behind."[84]

Notes

PART I
From Genesis to Vietnam

CHAPTER 1
ORIGINS OF MILITARY LAW AND MARINE CORPS LAWYERS

1. Jack Shulimson and Maj Charles M. Johnson, *U.S. Marines in Vietnam: The Landing and the Buildup, 1965*: (Washington: Hist&MusDiv, HQMC, 1978), pp. 6-15, hereafter Shulimson and Johnson, *Landing and Buildup, 1965*.
2. Edward J. Marolda and Oscar P. Fitzgerald, *From Military Assistance to Combat: The United States Navy and the Vietnam Conflict, Vol II* (Washington: Navy Historical Center, 1986), p. 526.
3. Col Peter N. Kress intvw, 5Dec86, Tape 6469 (Oral HistColl, MCHC), hereafter Kress intvw; and Col Kress ltr to author, dtd 25Nov86 (Kress folder, Marines and Military Law in Vietnam file, MCHC).
4. Col Hamilton M. Hoyler, "Legal Status of the Marine Corps," *Marine Corps Gazette*, Nov50, pp. 6-12. This article is a detailed examination of the legal basis of the Marine Corps and its relationship with the Navy, originally written for the Armed Services unification hearings that followed World War II.
5. Capt Edward M. Byrne, JAGC, USN, *Military Law* (Annapolis: Naval Institute Press, 3d ed., 1981), pp. 1-8.
6. Act of 2 March 1865 (13 Stat. 468), 22 June 1870 (16 Stat. 162), and Act of 19 June 1878 (20 Stat. 205).

Beginnings: Army Courts, Naval Boards

7. Act of 8 June 1880 (21 Stat. 164).
8. *Naval Courts and Boards* (Washington: Government Printing Office, 1917), hereafter *Naval Courts and Boards*; and, *A Manual For Courts-Martial, Courts of Inquiry, And of Other Procedure Under Military Law* (Washington: Government Printing Office, 1916).
9. William T. Generous, Jr., *Swords and Scales: The Development of the Uniform Code of Military Justice* (New York: Kennikat Press, 1973) pp. 12-13, hereafter Generous, *Swords and Scales*. This excellent volume provides a detailed history of the development of the UCMJ from World War I to the Military Justice Act of 1968.
10. Ibid, p. 8.
11. Edmund M. Morgan, "The Background of the Uniform Code of Military Justice," 6 *Vanderbilt Law Review*, 1952-1953, p. 172.
12. 10 U.S.C., sec. 5148 (1950).
13. *Naval Courts and Boards*, Ch.IX, Pt.I., sec. 379, pp. 363, 364.

World War II and Beyond: Military Justice is to Justice as Military Music is to Music

14. RAdm Robert J. White, ChC, USN (Ret), "The Background and the Problem," 35 *St. John's Law Review*, 1961, p. 200.

15. Edward F. Sherman, *With Justice For Some: An Indictment of the Law by Young Advocates*, B. Wasserstein and M. J. Green, eds., (Boston: Beacon Press, 1970), pp. 69-70.
16. LtCol Frank O. Hough, Maj Verle E. Ludwig, and Henry I. Shaw, Jr., *History of Marine Corps Operations in World War II, Vol I: Pearl Harbor To Guadalcanal* (Washington: Historical Branch, G-3 Division, HQMC, 1958), p. 48; and Col Robert D. Heinl, Jr., *Soldiers of the Sea: The United States Marine Corps, 1775-1962* (Annapolis: U.S. Naval Institute, 1962), p. 508.
17. Table of Organization D-95: Special Staff Sections, Division Headquarters; Headquarters Company, Headquarters Battalion, Marine Division, approved Jul42 (MCHC).
18. BGen Duane L. Faw intvw, 8Oct86, Tape 6470 (Oral HistColl, MCHC), hereafter Faw intvw; and Col Olin W. Jones ltr to BGen Edwin H. Simmons, n.d. (Comment folder, Marines and Military Law in Vietnam file, MCHC), hereafter Jones ltr. Gen Faw recalls that the Marine Corps bulletin was in effect in 1943. Col Jones' recollection is that it was not in force until 1945.
19. Col Robert M. Lucy ltr to BGen Simmons, dtd 16Jan89 (Comment folder, Marines and Military Law in Vietnam file, MCHC).
20. In Tokyo, Japan, after World War II an international military tribunal tried 28 Japanese officers for war crimes. Field Marshal Shunroku Hata was defended by Marine 1stLt Aristides G. Lazarus, a Marine Corps Reserve lawyer. (U.S. Department of State, *Trial of Japanese War Criminals*, Publication 2613, Far Eastern Series 12 [Washington, 1946], p. 45; and Aristides G. Lazarus ltr to author, dtd 1Sep87, [Lazarus folder, Marines and Military Law in Vietnam file, MCHC]).
21. Act of 17Jul1862 (Sec. 5, 12 Stat. 598).

The Uniform Code of Military Justice, 1950: Old Ills Readressed

Except where otherwise noted, this section is based on Generous, *Sword and Scales*, pp. 34-53.

22. A. C. Cole, A. Goldberg, S. A. Tucker, and R. A. Winnacker, eds., *The Department of Defense: Documents on Establishment and Organization, 1944-1978* (Washington: Office of the Secretary of Defense Historical Office, 1979), pp. 33, 87. Originally referred to in the National Security Act of 1947 as the "National Military Establishment," it was denominated the Department of Defense in a 1949 amendment to that act.
23. James V. Forrestal memorandum to UCMJ Committee, "Precept and Terms of Reference," quoted in Generous, *Sword and Scales*, p. 34.
24. Col Hamilton M. Hoyler, "Caveat: The Manual for Courts-Martial," *U.S. Naval Institute Proceedings*, Jan60, p. 59.
25. Uniform Code of Military Justice (Act of May 5, 1950), Article 98b, knowingly and intentionally failing to enforce or comply with the provisions of the Code; and nonpunitive Article 37, unlawfully influencing action of the court.
26. Gen William C. Westmoreland, USA, and MajGen George S.

245

Prugh, USA, "Judges in Command: The Judicialized Uniform Code of Military Justice in Combat," *3 Harvard Journal of Law and Public Policy*, 1-94 (1980), at 12.

27. U.S. Court of Military Appeals, *Annual Report of the United States Court of Military Appeals and the Judge Advocates General of the Armed Forces and the General Counsel of the Department of the Treasury, For the Period January 1, 1960, to December 31, 1960* (Washington: Government Printing Office, 1961), p. 5.

28. PL 506, 81st Congress, c 169, sec. 1, 64 Stat. 108, 50 USC (chap.22) secs. 551-736.

29. Executive Order No. 10,214, 16 *Federal Register* 1,303 (1951).

30. *Manual for Courts-Martial, United States, 1951*, par. 6b; and Uniform Code of Military Justice (Act of 5 May 1950), Article 6.(a).

Continuing Tension: Justice Versus Discipline

31. Hearings on H.R. 2575, Committee on Armed Services, House of Representatives, 1947, p. 2161, quoting from the *Chicago Tribune*, 8Jun45.

32. Hearings on H.R. 2498, before a special subcommittee of the House Committee on Armed Services, 81st Cong., 1st Sess. 780 (1949).

33. Jones ltr.

34. F. Lee Bailey, with Harvey Aronson, *The Defense Never Rests* (New York: Stein and Day, 1971), p. 259.

The Death Penalty in the Armed Forces: Yes But No

35. James E. Valle, *Rocks & Shoals — Order and Discipline in the Old Navy, 1800-1861* (Annapolis: Naval Institute Press, 1980), pp. 8-9, 103-110. This excellent book provides a highly readable coverage of discipline in the Navy's age of sail.

36. LCdr Mark Dawson, JAGC, USN, "Is the Death Penalty in the Military Cruel and Unusual?," *31 JAGJ 53* (Summer, 1980), at 54; and *Navy Times*, 25Jul88, p. 10.

37. Col W. Hays Parks, USMCR, Chief, International Law Branch, International Affairs Division, Office of the JAG, Dept of the Army, memorandum for the record, Subj: Executions of U.S. Military Personnel in World Wars I and II, dtd 30Oct81 (Articles folder, Marines and Military Law in Vietnam file, MCHC); and *Navy Times*, 25Jul88, p. 10.

Marine Corps Lawyers: From the Line to Discipline Branch

38. *Naval Courts and Boards*, sec. 266, p. 192.

39. Col Hamilton M. Hoyler ltr to author, dtd 30May88 (Hoyler folder, Marines and Military Law in Vietnam file, MCHC).

40. 1stLt St.Julien R. Marshall, for example, was selected to attend Harvard's School of Law in February 1931. LtCol Hamilton M. Hoyler, was another Harvard law graduate.

41. Col Marion G. Truesdale intvw, 7Oct86, Tape 6471 (Oral Hist-Coll, MCHC); BGen James F. Lawrence, Jr., transcript of intvw by Oral History Unit, Hist&MusDiv, HQMC, dtd 22Aug78, p. 80 (Oral HistColl, MCHC); Gen Earl E. Anderson ltr to author, dtd 22Feb89 (Anderson folder, Marines and Military Law in Vietnam file, MCHC); and Col Donald E. Holben intvw, 7Oct86, Tape 6472 (Oral Hist-Coll, MCHC).

42. Gen Anderson ltr to author, dtd 22Feb89 (Anderson folder, Marines and Military Law in Vietnam file, MCHC), hereafter Anderson ltr.

43. CMC Gen Randolph McC. Pate memo to Secretary of the Navy, Subj: Proposed administrative solution to the Marine Corps lawyer shortage, dtd 23Apr59. (4400 MOS folder, Marines and Military Law in Vietnam file, MCHC).

44. MCO 1120.10 dtd 1Oct59, Subj: Regulations for the Platoon Leaders Class (Law) Program. MCHC, Washington.

45. MCBul 1040 dtd 9Aug61, Subj: Marine Corps Lawyers, policy concerning; and MCO 1040.21 dtd 26Dec62, Subj: Marine Corps Lawyers, policy concerning. MCHC, Washington.

46. Navy Chief of Legislative Affairs, Office of Legislative Liaison, memo for Assistant Secretary of the Navy (P&RF), Subj: Proposed legislation to establish a Judge Advocate General's Corps in the Navy; request for resolution of differences concerning, dtd 30Sep59. (4400 MOS folder, Marines and Military Law in Vietnam file, MCHC), hereafter Navy Chief of Legislative Affairs memo.

47. U.S. Court of Military Appeals, Report of the JAG of the Navy, *Annual Report of the United States Court of Military Appeals and the Judge Advocates General of the Armed Forces and the General Counsel of the Department of the Treasury, For the Period January 1, 1967 to December 31, 1967* (Washington: Government Printing Office, 1968), p. 26.

In Support: Navy Lawyers

48. Col Daniel F. McConnell ltr to author, dtd 25Jan89 (Comment folder, Marines and Military Law in Vietnam file, MCHC).

49. Navy Chief of Legislative Affairs memo, pp. 10-11.

50. Col Matthew A. Clary, Jr., intvw, 14Apr87, Tape 6473 (Oral Hist-Coll, MCHC); Navy Chief of Legislative Affairs memo, p. 1; CMC memo to Chief of Legislative Affairs, DON, Subj: S. 2002-2015, S. 2017-2019, amendments to the UCMJ, dtd 22Aug63, encl.(15); and DepChief of Legislative Affairs memo to SecNav, Subj: S. 2016, a bill "To further insure due process in the administration of military justice in the Department of the Navy by establishing a Judge Advocate General's Corps in such department," dtd 23Oct63 (memos in 4400 MOS folder, Marines and Military Law in Vietnam file, MCHC).

51. AJAG for Military Justice memo to Navy JAG, Subj: Marine Corps objection to Navy JAG Corps, dtd 4Oct63 (4400 MOS folder, Marines and Military Law in Vietnam file, MCHC).

52. HQMC Staff Study: Marine Corps Legal Services Study Rpt, dtd 6Jun69, pp.15-16: summary of C/S Project 13-68 (Legal Services Study Report folder, Marines and Military Law in Vietnam file, MCHC), hereafter Marine Corps Legal Services Study.

In Support: Headquarters Marine Corps

Except where otherwise noted, the material in this section is from Marine Corps Legal Services Study, pp. 3-10.

53. Col Robert J. Chadwick, "Judge Advocates of the Marine Corps," *The Judge Advocate Journal*, 1964, pp. 50-51; biographical files (RefSec, MCHC); Sevier intvw; and Truesdale intvw.

54. MCO 1040.24 dtd 10Dec64, Subj: Marine Corps Policies and Programs Relating to Officer Lawyers, pertaining to assignment of captains and lieutenants; and MCO 1040.21 dtd 26Dec62, Subj: Marine Corps Lawyers; policy concerning. The latter order remained in effect until 12Nov71 and pertained to assignments vis-a-vis MOS. (4400 MOS folder, Marines and Military Law in Vietnam file, MCHC).

55. Ibid.

NOTES

56. Col W. Hays Parks ltr to author, dtd 22Dec88 (Parks folder, Marines and Military Law in Vietnam file, MCHC).
57. Bernard C. Nalty and LtCol Ralph F. Moody, USMC, *A Brief History of U.S. Marine Corps Officer Procurement, 1775-1969* (Washington: HistDiv, HQMC, 1958, revised 1970), pp.20-21.

The Pentalateral Agreement: Diplomatic Riflemen

58. Wilson v. Girard, 354 US 524,529; 77 SCt 1409 (1957).
59. MajGen George S. Prugh, USA, *Vietnam Studies, Law At War: Vietnam, 1964-1973*, (Washington: Dept of the Army, 1975), p. 118; hereafter Prugh, *Law At War.*
60. Ibid., pp. 88-90.

Military Law Comes to Vietnam

61. Capt Robert H. Whitlow, USMCR, *U.S. Marines in Vietnam, The Advisory & Combat Assistance Era, 1954-1964* (Washington: Hist&MusDiv, HQMC, 1977), pp. 15-16, hereafter Whitlow, *Advisory & Combat Assistance Era.*
62. Prugh, *Law At War*, p. 118.
63. Whitlow, *Advisory & Combat Assistance Era*, pp. 39, 60, 74-75, 175.
64. Col Robert J. Blum ltr to Maj W. Hays Parks, dtd 24Jan77 (Blum folder, Marines and Military Law In Vietnam File, MCHC).
65. Anderson ltr; and RefSec, MCHC.
66. LtCol Brian B. Kent ltrs to author, dtd 29Apr87 and 28Feb89 (Kent folder, Marines and Military Law In Vietnam File, MCHC).
67. Col Paul F. Henderson, Jr., ltr to author, dtd 14Oct86, (Henderson folder, Marines and Military Law In Vietnam File, MCHC).
68. Jones ltr.
69. RAdm Hugh D. Campbell, JAGC, USN, intvw, 26Nov86, Tape 6475 (Oral HistColl, MCHC).

CHAPTER 2
1965: 3D MARINE DIVISION
AND 9TH MEB OPEN SHOP

1. Col Peter N. Kress ltr to author, dtd 24Jan89 (Comment folder, Marines and Military Law in Vietnam file, MCHC), hereafter Kress letter.
2. Donald W. Harris intvw, 23Jul87, Tape 6480 (Oral HistColl, MCHC), hereafter Harris intvw; and Harris ltr to author, dtd 12May87 (Harris folder, Marines and Military Law in Vietnam file, MCHC).
3. 1st Lt Donald W. Harris Navy Achievement Medal citation, n.d. (Harris folder, Marines and Military Law in Vietnam file, MCHC).
4. Col Peter N. Kress ltr to author, dtd 25Nov86 (Kress folder, Marines and Military Law in Vietnam file, MCHC).
5. MajGen George S. Prugh, USA (Ret), ltr to BGen Edwin H. Simmons, dtd 29Dec88 (Comment folder, Marines and Military Law in Vietnam file, MCHC).
6. Col Charles B. Sevier intvw, 9Oct86, Tape 6474 (Oral HistColl, MCHC), hereafter Sevier intvw; and Kress ltr.
7. Shulimson and Johnson, *Landing and Buildup, 1965*, pp. 24-49, 120, 228.
8. SSgt Matthew C. McKeon court-martial notebooks, part 2 (RefSec, MCHC).

9. BGen James P. King intvw, 5Nov86, Tape 6478 (Oral HistColl, MCHC), hereafter King intvw.
10. Sevier intvw.
11. Shulimson and Johnson, *Landing and Buildup, 1965*, p. 44.
12. 3d Marine Division (Fwd) general court-martial appointing order Ser: 1-65 (i.e., 3d MarDiv [Fwd]'s first appointing order in 1965) directs that the court convene at 0900, 14 July 1965 at Da Nang (Harris folder, Marines and Military Law in Vietnam file, MCHC).
13. Sevier intvw.
14. LtCol Fred Grabowski questionnaire to Maj W. Hays Parks, n.d.; John E. Gillmor, Jr., ltr to author, dtd 23Jan87; and Col Robert A. Godwin, USMCR, ltr to author, dtd 9May87 (Grabowski, Gillmor, and Godwin folders, Marines and Military Law in Vietnam file, MCHC), hereafter Gillmor ltr and Godwin ltr.
15. RAdm Hugh D. Campbell intvw, 26Nov86, Tape 6475 (Oral HistColl, MCHC), hereafter Campbell intvw.
16. Campbell intvw; Gillmor ltr.
17. Gillmor ltr.
18. *Manual for Courts-Martial, United States, 1951*, par. 79.d.(1); and Uniform Code of Military Justice (Act of 5 May 1950), Article 20.
19. Col Robert A. Godwin, USMCR, ltr to BGen Edwin H. Simmons, dtd 30Jan89 (Comment folder, Marines and Military Law in Vietnam file).
20. Col Daniel F. McConnell ltr to author, dtd 25Jan89 (Comment folder, Marines and Military Law in Vietnam file, MCHC).
21. Uniform Code of Military Justice (Act of 5 May 1950), Article 26.(a).
22. Campbell intvw; Gillmor ltr.
23. Godwin ltr.

From a Lawyer's Case File:
One Homicide, Two Victims

24. Throughout, the text cases are referred to as they are titled in the court-martial record of trial, a public record. The Navy court-martial (NCM) number, where available, is included.
25. Record of trial, United States v. PFC Kenneth W. Wheeler, NCM 66 0376; and service record book of Kenneth W. Wheeler. Pertinent portions of the record of trial are in Godwin folder (Marines and Military Law in Vietnam file, MCHC).

Trying Cases

26. Col Harry S. Popper, Jr., ltr to Maj Charles W. Collier, dtd 5Oct65 (Popper folder, Marines and Military Law in Vietnam file, MCHC).
27. Ibid.; Campbell intvw.
28. LCdr John F. Erickson questionnaire to Maj W. Hays Parks, dtd 1Nov77 (Erickson folder, Marines and Military Law in Vietnam file, MCHC).
29. Campbell intvw.
30. Gillmor ltr. In 1965 Gillmor was the third-oldest second lieutenant in the Marine Corps, other than officers commissioned from the enlisted ranks.
31. LtCol William B. Draper, Jr., questionnaire to Maj W. Hays Parks, dtd 12Dec76 (Draper folder, Marines and Military Law in Vietnam file, MCHC).
32. Sevier intvw.
33. Ibid.
34. 3d MarDiv ComdC, Nov65, encl. (1), p. 27 (Unit Command Chronology File, MCHC).
35. Godwin ltr.

III MAF: Headquarters Without Lawyers

36. Shulimson and Johnson, *Landing and Buildup, 1965*, p. 188; and 3d MarDiv ComdC, Nov65, encl. (1), p. 11 (Unit Command Chronology file, MCHC).
37. Col Harry S. Popper, Jr., ltr to Col Earl W. Johnson, dtd 26Oct65 (Popper folder, Marines and Military Law in Vietnam file, MCHC).
38. Sevier intvw.
39. Col Vernon A. Peltzer intvw, 7Oct86, Tape 6479 (Oral HistColl, MCHC), hereafter Peltzer intvw.
40. III MAF ComdC, Jul, Aug65 (Unit Command Chronology File, MCHC); and Jones ltr.
41. Biographical files (RefSec, MCHC); and Shulimson and Johnson, *Landing and Buildup, 1965*, pp. 47, 142-144.
42. Capt William T. Warren III intvw, n.d., Tape 18 (Oral HistColl, MCHC).
43. Maj Benjamin B. Ferrell Bronze Star Medal citation, n.d. (Ferrell folder, Marines and Military Law in Vietnam file, MCHC).

1st Marine Aircraft Wing: Touching Down

44. Shulimson and Johnson, *Landing and Buildup, 1965*, pp. 25, 229.
45. Col Harry S. Popper, Jr., ltr to author, dtd 15Sep86 (Popper folder, Marines and Military Law in Vietnam file, MCHC).
46. Col Popper ltr to RAdm Wilfred Hearn, dtd 28Oct65 (Popper folder, Marines and Military Law in Vietnam file, MCHC).

Legal Duty in a Combat Zone: Problems

47. Col Clyde B. Mann intvw, 8Aug68, Tape 2980 (Oral HistColl, MCHC).
48. Col Verne L. Oliver ltr to BGen Edwin H. Simmons, dtd 2Feb89 (Comment folder, Marines and Military Law in Vietnam file, MCHC).
49. MGySgt Gene E. White ltr to author, dtd 18Mar87 (White folder, Marines and Military Law in Vietnam file, MCHC).
50. Campbell intvw.
51. Record of trial, United States v. PFC Gary O. Harrison, NCM 65 2160.
52. Col Popper ltr to Col Robert B. Neville, dtd 14Oct65 (Popper folder, Marines and Military Law in Vietnam file, MCHC).
53. Campbell intvw.
54. Sevier intvw.
55. Ibid.
56. Peltzer intvw.
57. Prugh, *Law at War*, pp. 104-106.
58. Ibid., p. 103.
59. Robert W. Wachsmuth ltr to author, dtd 13Nov87 (Wachsmuth folder, Marines and Military Law in Vietnam file, MCHC).

From a Lawyer's Case File: First Marine War Crime Conviction in Vietnam

60. Department of the Army, *The Law of Land Warfare, FM 27-10* (Washington, 1956), p. 178.
61. HQ, USMACV Dir No. 20-4, dtd 10Jul70 (War Crimes folder, Marines and Military Law in Vietnam file, MCHC).
62. Prugh, *Law At War*, p.102.
63. Director, Judge Advocate Division ltr to Professor Guenter Lewy, dtd 9Mar76 (War Crimes folder, Marines and Military Law in Vietnam file, MCHC).
64. Guenter Lewy, *America in Vietnam* (New York: Oxford University Press, 1978), p. 325.
65. Record of trial, United States v. LCpl Marion McGhee, NCM 66 0484 (1966); pet. den. 16 USCMA 663 (19,701).
66. Naval Clemency & Parole Board ltr to author, dtd 31Aug88 (War crimes folder, Marines and Military Law in Vietnam file, MCHC).

Perspective

67. U.S. Court of Military Appeals, Report of the JAG of the Navy, *Annual Report of the United States Court of Military Appeals and the Judge Advocates General of the Armed Forces and the General Counsel of the Department of the Treasury, For the Period January 1, 1966 to December 31, 1966* (Washington: Government Printing Office, 1967) p. 51. There are records that reflect the total number of courts-martial tried, but they do not reflect the places where they were tried.
68. CG FMFPac msg to CG III MAF, dtd 28Sep65 (POW folder, Marines and Military Law in Vietnam file, MCHC).
69. CG FMFPac msg to CG III MAF, dtd 6Nov65 (POW folder, Marines and Military Law in Vietnam file, MCHC).
70. LtCol John L. Zorack intvw, 14Sep87, Tape 6483 (Oral HistColl, MCHC).
71. Marine Corps Legal Services Study, p. 31.
72. Kenneth W. Condit, Maj John H. Johnstone, USMC, and Ella W. Nargele, *A Brief History of Headquarters Marine Corps Staff Organization* (Washington: HistDiv, HQMC, 1963, revised 1970), p. 34.
73. Bernard C. Nalty and LtCol Ralph F. Moody, *History of Marine Corps Officer Procurement* (Washington: HistDiv, HQMC, 1958, rev. 1970), p. 21.
74. BGen Raymond G. Davis, Personnel: G-1 Presentation, HQMC, General Officers Symposium, 1965, tab V.A.1., p. 5.

CHAPTER 3
1966: BUILDING ON SAND

1. Jack Shulimson, *U.S. Marines in Vietnam: An Expanding War, 1966* (Washington: Hist&Mus Div, 1982,) pp. 3-6, 9-10, 75, hereafter Shulimson, *An Expanding War*.

Trying Cases: Using 'The Red Book'

2. Col John T. Fischbach, USMCR, questionnaire to author, n.d. (Fischbach folder, Marines and Military Law in Vietnam file, MCHC).
3. Gen Paul X. Kelley intvw, 30Sep87. Tape 6477 (Oral HistColl, MCHC).
4. Col Kenneth T. Taylor ltr to author, n.d. (K. T. Taylor folder, Marines and Military Law in Vietnam file, MCHC).
5. Maj Philip A. Seymour ltr to author, dtd 6Oct86; and Sgt Seymour Navy Commendation Medal citation, n.d. (Seymour folder, Marines and Military Law in Vietnam file, MCHC).
6. 1stLt Anthony P. Tokarz Silver Star citation, n.d. (Tokarz folder, Marines and Military Law in Vietnam file, MCHC).
7. Col James S. May ltr to author, dtd 29Mar87 (May folder, Marines and Military Law in Vietnam file MCHC).
8. The missions for which the award was made were classified and for years there was no notation of the award in Col Campbell's officer

NOTES

qualification record. Fortunately, there was a photograph of the Commandant awarding the medal to then-Capt Campbell. For years that was his primary substantiation for the award he wore.

9. 1stMarDiv ComdC, Jul66 (Unit Command Chronology file, MCHC).

From a Lawyer's Case File: Pilot to Copilot to Brig

10. Record of trial, United States v. PFC Lucien J. Gonzales II, NCM 65 2090 (1965). Pertinent portions of the record of trial are in Harris folder (Marines and Military Justice in Vietnam file, MCHC).

The Other Prisoners: North Vietnamese POWs

11. United States Military Assistance Command, Vietnam, Command History, 1966 (MACV Cmd Histories folder, Marines and Military Law in Vietnam file, MCHC), pp. 689-693.
12. United States Military Assistance Command, Vietnam, Command History, 1970, Vol II (MACV Cmd Histories folder, Marines and Military Law in Vietnam file, MCHC), p. X-51.
13. MajGen George S. Prugh, USA, *Vietnam Studies, Law At War: Vietnam, 1964-1973* (Washington: Dept. of the Army, 1975), p. 67-72.

The 1st Marine Division Arrives: More Lawyers, More Cases

14. Col George P. Blackburn, Jr., questionnaire to author, dtd 4Dec86 (Blackburn folder, Marines and Military Law in Vietnam file, MCHC), hereafter Blackburn questionnaire.
15. Col Thomas P. Casey ltr to author, dtd 9Oct86 (Casey folder, Marines and Military Law in Vietnam file, MCHC).
16. Ibid.
17. Blackburn questionnaire.
18. 1st MarDiv ComdC, Sep66 (Unit Command Chronology file, MCHC).
19. USMC, 1stMarDiv SLO ltr to CO, 7th Marines, Subj: Recommendation for commendation for meritorious service; case of 2ndLt William S. Kirkpatrick, dtd 6Aug66 (Granger folder, Marines and Military Justice in Vietnam file, MCHC). Lt Kirkpatrick received the Navy Commendation Medal for his performance of duty, and received a second Navy Commendation Medal for a second tour of duty in Vietnam.
20. Capt William S. Kirkpatrick ltr to author dtd 10Aug87 (Kirkpatrick folder, Marines and Military Law in Vietnam file, MCHC).
21. LtCol Kenneth W. Jones ltr to BGen Edwin H. Simmons, dtd 29Dec88 (Comment folder, Marines and Military Law in Vietnam file, MCHC), hereafter Jones ltr.
22. Shulimson, *An Expanding War*, p. 223.
23. LtCol John L. Zorack ltr to author, dtd 9Feb89 (Comment folder, Marines and Military Law in Vietnam file, MCHC).

Force Logistic Command: New Guy on the Block

24. MajGen Avery R. Kier, FMFPac Presentation, HQMC, General Officers Symposium, 1966, tab II.A, Statistics and Supplementary Data, p. 38, hereafter, MajGen Kier presentation.
25. Ibid., pp. 287-289.
26. Col Charles R. Larouche ltr to author, dtd 8Dec86 (Larouche folder, Marines and Military Law in Vietnam file, MCHC), hereafter Larouche ltr.
27. Ibid.
28. FLC ComdC, Aug66 (Unit Command Chronology file, MCHC).
29. Col Charles A. Cushman intvw, 4Dec86. Tape 6481 (Oral Hist-Coll, MCHC), hereafter Cushman intvw.
30. III MAF Provost Marshal ltr to CG, FLC, Subj: CID Physical Security Survey of FLC, dtd 28Sep67 (Federal Records Center folder, Marines and Military Justice in Vietnam file, MCHC).
31. LtCol James R. Ziemann questionnaire to Maj W. Hays Parks, n.d. (Ziemann folder, Marines and Military Law in Vietnam file, MCHC), hereafter Ziemann questionnaire.
32. FLC ComdC, Sep, Oct 1966; Apr, Jun 1967 (Unit Command Chronology file, MCHC).
33. LtCol Fred Grabowsky questionnaire to author, dtd 2Sep86 (Grabowsky folder, Marines and Military Law in Vietnam file, MCHC).
34. Col Robert B. Neville ltr to Maj Parks, dtd 12Jun77, (Neville folder, Marines and Military Law in Vietnam, MCHC) p.8, hereafter Neville ltr.
35. Larouche ltr, p. 11.

Trying Cases

36. CG, FMFPac ltr to CGs, III MAF, 1st MarDiv, 1st MAW, 3d MAW, 3d MarDiv, Force Troops, and COs, 1st MarBrig, Camp Butler, Subj: Staff Legal Officers Conference, dtd 3Jan66 (Popper folder, Marines and Military Law in Vietnam file, MCHC).
37. LtCol William B. Draper, Jr., ltr to Maj Parks, dtd 5Jan77 (Draper folder, Marines and Military Law in Vietnam file, MCHC), hereafter Draper ltr.
38. Col Daniel F. McConnell ltr to author, dtd 25Jan89 (Comment folder, Marines and Military Law in Vietnam file, MCHC).
39. Larouche ltr, p. 9.
40. Lt John F. Erickson Navy Achievement Medal citation, n.d. (Erickson folder, Marines and Military Law in Vietnam file, MCHC).
41. Maj Truong Tan Thuc ltr to the people of Clay County, Kansas, U.S.A., dtd 4Apr67 (Erickson folder, Marines and Military Law in Vietnam file, MCHC).
42. LtCol William B. Draper, Jr., intvw, 13Oct86. Tape 6482 (Oral HistColl, MCHC), hereafter Draper intvw; and Draper ltr.
43. CG III MAF msg to CMC, 20Dec66 (Federal Records Center folder, Marines and Military Law in Vietnam file, MCHC).
44. CMC msg to CG III MAF, 27Dec 66 (Federal Records Center folder, Marines and Military Law in Vietnam file, MCHC).
45. Capt Francis T. Coleman, USMCR, "Lawyers In Vietnam," *Res Ipsa Loquitur; Georgetown Review of Law and Public Interest*, Vol. 17, No. 1, Fall, 1966, p. 14.
46. Ibid.
47. Col Curtis W. Olson ltr to author, dtd 23Jan87 (Olson folder, Marines and Military Law in Vietnam file, MCHC).
48. Col Charles H. Beale ltr to Maj W. Hays Parks, dtd 31Dec76, (Beale folder, Marines and Military Law in Vietnam file, MCHC), hereafter Beale ltr.
49. Kress intvw.
50. Larouche ltr, pp. 12-14; and Col Charles R. Larouche ltr to author, dtd 16Sep86 (Larouche folder, Marines and Military Law in Vietnam file, MCHC).
51. Col Curtis W. Olson questionnaire to author, dtd 27Oct86, (Olson folder, Marines and Military Law in Vietnam file, MCHC), hereafter Olson questionnaire.

52. Jones ltr.
53. MajGen Kier presentation, p. 16.
54. Col Daniel F. McConnell questionnaire to author, dtd 16Sep86 (McConnell folder, Marines and Military Law in Vietnam file, MCHC).
55. Col Benjamin B. Ferrell unpublished study, "Critique of U.S. Courts-Martial Proceedings Against War Criminals in the Vietnam War: A Case Study," (Ferrell folder, Marines and Military Law in Vietnam file, MCHC), p. 17.

Courtroom Personnel: Just Passin' Through

56. Biographical files (RefSec, MCHC).
57. Neville ltr, pp. 10-11.
58. Draper intvw.
59. Campbell intvw.
60. Lt John F. Erickson questionnaire to Maj W. Hays Parks, dtd 1Nov77 (Erickson folder, Marines and Military Law in Vietnam file, MCHC).
61. Campbell intvw.
62. Beale ltr.
63. U.S. Court of Military Appeals, Report of the JAG of the Navy, *Annual Report of the United States Court of Military Appeals and the Judge Advocates General of the Armed Forces and the General Counsel of the Department of the Treasury, For the Period January 1, 1966 to December 31, 1966* (Washington: Government Printing Office, 1967), p. 53.
64. Draper questionnaire.
65. Beale ltr., pp. 5-6.
66. Col Charles R. Larouche questionnaire to author, dtd 8Dec86 (Larouche folder, Marines and Military Law in Vietnam file, MCHC).
67. Col Ralph K. Culver questionnaire to author, dtd 20Oct86 (Culver folder, Marines and Military Law in Vietnam file, MCHC).

Homicide on Patrol: Men, Women, and Children

68. LtGen Leo J. Dulacki intvw, 24Oct74, pp. 111-112 (Oral Hist-Coll, MCHC, Washington, D.C.), hereafter Dulacki intvw.
69. Record of trial, United States v. PFC John D. Potter, Jr., NCM 67 1348, 39 CMR 791 (1967). Unless otherwise attributed, all quotes relating to this case are from the record of PFC Potter's trial. The records of trial of the companion cases, Vogel and Boyd, as many other records from the Vietnam era, have been lost.
70. United States v. Sergeant Ronald L. Vogel, NCM 67 1347, 18 USCMA 160, 39 CMR 160 (1967).
71. Naval Clemency Board action, serial no. F006A-71, dtd 10Jun71; and Naval Clemency & Parole Board ltr to author, dtd 31Aug88 (War crimes folder, Marines and Military Law in Vietnam file, MCHC), hereafter NC & PB ltr.
72. Ibid.
73. Navy JAG memorandum for SecNav, dtd 6Sep68 (CMR opinions folder, Marines and Military Law in Vietnam file, MCHC).
74. SLO, 1st MarDiv ltr to CG, FMFPac, Subj: Recommendation for Navy Commendation Medal, case of Capt James P. Shannon, n.d. (Granger folder, Marines and Military Law in Vietnam file, MCHC).
75. LtCol William B. Draper, Jr. questionnaire to Maj W. Hays Parks, dtd 12Dec76 (Draper folder, Marines and Military Law in Vietnam file, MCHC).

3d Marine Division: On the Road Again

76. Shulimson, *An Expanding War*, pp. 75, 223, 342-344.
77. Beale ltr.
78. Ibid.

III MAF: Double-Hatting the Lawyer

79. III MAF ComdC, Jun66 (Unit Command Chronology file, MCHC).
80. Neville ltr.
81. CG III MAF msgs to CG FMFPac, 29Jul66 and 11Sep66; and CG FMFPac msg to CG III MAF, 8Aug66 (Neville folder, Marines and Military Law in Vietnam file, MCHC).
82. CG FMFPac msg to CG III MAF, 16Sep66 (Neville folder, Marines and Military Law in Vietnam file, MCHC).

Perspective

83. HQMC, Code DK, Directory of Marine Officer Lawyers, dtd Feb66 (Directories folder, Marines and Military Law in Vietnam file, MCHC).
84. Marine Corps Legal Services Study, p. 31.
85. Col Robert B. Neville Navy Commendation Medal citation, n.d. (Neville folder, Marines and Military Law in Vietnam file, MCHC).

PART II
Build Up and Consolidation

CHAPTER 4
1967: TRYING TIMES

1. Maj Gary L. Telfer, LtCol Lane Rogers, and V. Keith Fleming, Jr., *U.S. Marines In Vietnam: Fighting the North Vietnamese, 1967* (Washington: Hist&MusDiv, HQMC, 1984), pp. 4-5, hereafter, Telfer, Rogers, and Fleming, *Fighting the North Vietnamese, 1967*.
2. Ibid., pp. 6-10.
3. CMC Bulletin 5370 to all commanding officers, Subj: Personal Conduct of Marines in the Republic of Vietnam, dtd 28Nov66 (Parks folder, Marines and Military Law in Vietnam file, MCHC).
4. FMFPacO 1610.2 dtd 28Nov66, Subj: Individual Responsibility, para. 2 (War Crimes folder, Marines and Military Law in Vietnam file, MCHC).
5. Col Eugene B. Fallon intvw, 11Jul68, Tape 2979 (Oral HistColl, MCHC), hereafter Fallon intvw.
6. Ibid.
7. United States Military Assistance Command, Vietnam, Command History, 1967, Vol II, p. 932 (MACV Cmd Histories folder, Marines and Military Law in Vietnam file, MCHC).
8. LtCol William T. Westmoreland, Jr., ltr to Maj W. Hays Parks, dtd 23Mar77 (Westmoreland folder, Marines and Military Law in Vietnam file, MCHC), hereafter Westmoreland ltr.
9. Col Mary V. Stremlow, *A History of the Woman Marines, 1946-1977* (Washington: Hist&MusDiv, HQMC, 1986), p. 83.

III MAF: Double-Hatted Twice

10. Telfer, Rogers, and Fleming, *Fighting the North Vietnamese, 1967*, pp. 273, 293.

NOTES

11. LtCol G. Ward Beaudry questionnaire to Maj Parks, dtd 4Feb77 (Beaudry folder, Marines and Military Law in Vietnam file, MCHC).
12. Faw intvw.
13. Col Marion G. Truesdale intvw, 7Oct86, Tape 6471 (Oral Hist-Coll, MCHC); and Faw intvw.

1st Marine Division: Rising Caseloads, More Lawyers

14. LtCol William T. Westmoreland, Jr., questionnaire to Maj Parks, dtd 23Mar77 (Westmoreland folder, Marines and Military Law in Vietnam file, MCHC), hereafter Westmoreland questionnaire.
15. Col Curtis W. Olson ltr to Maj Parks, dtd Dec76 (Olson folder, Marines and Military Law in Vietnam file, MCHC), hereafter Olson ltr.
16. TF X-Ray ComdC, Jun67 (Unit Command Chronology file, MCHC); LtCol John L. Zorack ltr to author, dtd 9Feb89; and LtCol Zorack Bronze Star Medal citation, n.d. (Comment and Zorack folders, respectively, Marines and Military Law in Vietnam file, MCHC).
17. Maj Donald Higginbotham, USMCR, questionnaire to Maj Parks, dtd 15Jan77 (Higginbotham folder, Marines and Military Justice in Vietnam file, MCHC), hereafter Higginbotham questionnaire.
18. Telfer, Rogers, and Fleming, *Fighting the North Vietnamese, 1967*, pp. 52, 74, 139, 141.

3d Marine Division: More Combat, Fewer Courts

19. Ibid., pp. 86-92.
20. Col Charles H. Beale, Jr., questionnaire to Maj Parks, dtd 31Dec76 (Beale folder, Marines and Military Law in Vietnam file, MCHC), hereafter Beale questionnaire.
21. Col Paul F. Henderson, Jr., ltr to author, dtd 3Oct86 (Henderson folder, Marines and Military Law in Vietnam file, MCHC), hereafter Henderson ltr.
22. Capt Charles E. Patterson intvw, 13Dec68, Tape 3497 (Oral HistColl, MCHC).
23. Capt Francis T. Coleman, "Lawyers in Vietnam," *Res Ipsa Loquitur; Georgetown Review of Law and Public Interest*, Vol. 17, No. 1, Fall, 1966, p. 13.
24. Personnel, telephone, and brig problems: Fallon intvw.
25. Ibid.; and Col Eugene B. Fallon questionnaire to Maj Parks, n.d. (Fallon folder, Marines and Military Law in Vietnam file, MCHC).
26. Fallon intvw.
27. Henderson ltr.
28. MajGen Rathvon McC. Tompkins. Transcript of intvw by Oral History Unit, HistDiv, HQMC, dtd 13Apr73 (Oral HistColl, MCHC), p. 9, hereafter Tompkins intvw.

Force Logistic Command: Continue to March

29. Telfer, Rogers, and Fleming, *Fighting the North Vietnamese, 1967*, pp. 224-225, 277.
30. FLC ComdC, Mar67 (Unit Command Chronology file, MCHC).
31. United States Military Assistance Command, Vietnam, Command History, 1967, Volume II, pp. 953, 954 (MACV Cmd Histories folder, Marines and Military Law in Vietnam file, MCHC).
32. FLC ComdC, Jun67 (Unit Command Chronology file, MCHC).
33. Col Rufus C. Young intvw, 12Oct86, Tape 6485 (Oral Hist-Coll, MCHC), hereafter Young intvw.

34. Col Verne L. Oliver ltr to BGen Edwin H. Simmons, dtd 2Feb89 (Comment folder, Marines and Military Law in Vietnam file, MCHC).

1st Marine Aircraft Wing: Much Like Home

35. Telfer, Rogers, and Fleming, *Fighting the North Vietnamese, 1967*, pp. 278-281.
36. Col Charles H. Mitchell intvw, 28Oct86, Tape 6486 (Oral Hist-Coll, MCHC), hereafter Mitchell intvw.
37. Faw intvw.
38. MCHC RefSec; and Col Robert C. Lehnert ltr to author, dtd 1Feb89 (Comment folder, Marines and Military Law in Vietnam file, MCHC), hereafter Lehnert ltr.
39. BGen William H. J. Tiernan intvw, 14Oct86, Tape 6484 (Oral HistColl, MCHC), hereafter Tiernan intvw.
40. Mitchell intvw.
41. Young intvw.
42. Tiernan intvw.
43. Lehnert ltr.
44. Young intvw.
45. Lehnert ltr.

From a Lawyer's Case File: Psychiatry and Appellate Review

46. United States v. PFC Edward P. Boltik, NCM 68 0552 (1968) (CMR Opinions folder, Marines and Military Law in Vietnam file, MCHC).

Project 100,000: Prelude to Problems

47. James William Gibson, *The Perfect War; Technowar in Vietnam* (Boston/New York: The Atlantic Monthly Press, 1986), p. 216.
48. Ibid., p. 215.
49. BGen Jonas M. Platt, Manpower, G-1 Presentation, HQMC, General Officers Symposium, 1967, tab II-E-1, p. 9.
50. Tompkins intvw, pp. 93-94.
51. Maj W. Hays Parks, "Crimes in Hostilities," part 2, *Marine Corps Gazette*, Sep76, p. 35.
52. Laura Palmer, "The General, At Ease: An Interview with Westmoreland," *MHQ, The Quarterly Journal of Military History*, Autumn 1988, p. 34.
53. Gen Bruce Palmer, Jr., Army Vice Chief of Staff, hearings before House Committee on Appropriations, Subcommittee on Department of Defense, DOD Appropriations for 1972, 92nd Cong., 1st sess., pt. 9 at 578-582 (1971), cited in Lewy, *America in Vietnam* (New York, Oxford University Press, 1978), p. 160.

Drugs: Recognizing the Problem

54. CG III MAF msg to CG FMFPac, 10Sep67 (Command concerns folder, Marines and Military Law in Vietnam file, MCHC).
55. MajGen George S. Prugh, USA, *Vietnam Studies, Law At War: Vietnam, 1964-1973* (Washington: Dept of the Army, 1975), p. 106.
56. United States Military Assistance Command, Vietnam Command History, 1967, Volume II, p. 957 (MACV Cmd Histories folder, Marines and Military Law in Vietnam file, MCHC).
57. CG III MAF msg to ComUS MACV, 3Oct67 (Command Concerns folder, Marines and Military Law in Vietnam file, MCHC).

58. CG FMFPac msg to CG III MAF, 23Nov67 (Command Concerns folder, Marines and Military Law in Vietnam file, MCHC).
59. LtCol William C. Jaeck ltr to author, dtd 1Feb87 (Jaeck Folder, Marines and Military Law in Vietnam file, MCHC).
60. LtCol William C. Jaeck TAD Trip Report to CG, FMFPac, dtd 9Dec67 (Jaeck folder, Marines and Military Law in Vietnam file, MCHC).

Transportation: Hitchhiking to Court

61. Maj Donald Higginbotham ltr to Maj W. Hays Parks, dtd 15Jan77 (Higginbotham folder, Marines and Military Law in Vietnam file, MCHC), hereafter Higginbotham ltr.
62. Maj Eugene A. Steffen questionnaire to Maj Parks, dtd 26Jan77 (Steffen folder, Marines and Military Law in Vietnam file, MCHC), hereafter Steffen questionnaire.
63. Godwin ltr.
64. Michael G. McCollum tapes appended to ltr to author, dtd 15Oct86 (McCollum folder, Marines and Military Law in Vietnam file; and Tapes 6495, Oral HistColl, MCHC).
65. Col Daniel F. McConnell questionnaire to author, dtd 16Sep86 (McConnell folder, Marines and Military Law in Vietnam file, MCHC).
66. Col Mark L. Haiman questionnaire to author, n.d. (Haiman folder, Marines and Military Law in Vietnam file, MCHC).

Trying Cases

67. Beale ltr, p. 6.
68. Higginbotham ltr.
69. Campbell intvw.
70. Record of trial, United States v. Cpl Richard M. Ford, NCM 66 0269 (1965), Art. 32 Investigating Officer's report, pp. 3, 6. Pertinent portions of the record of trial, including the Art. 32 report. (CMR Opinions folder, Marines and Military Law in Vietnam file, MCHC).
71. Col James L. Williams summary of intvw to author, dtd 5Nov86 (Williams folder, Marines and Military Law in Vietnam file, MCHC), hereafter Williams intvw.
72. Fallon intvw; Westmoreland questionnaire.
73. Fallon intvw.
74. Col Earl W. Johnson ltr to author, dtd 4Sep86 (Johnson folder, Marines and Military Law in Vietnam file, MCHC).
75. Tiernan intvw.
76. Mitchell intvw.
77. Col Michael Patrick Murray questionnaire to author, dtd 8Dec86 (Murray folder, Marines and Military Law in Vietnam file, MCHC).
78. *Manual for Courts-Martial, United States, 1951*, par. 34c, 48a, and 102.c.
79. LtCol William T. Westmoreland, Jr., questionnaire to Maj W. Hays Parks, dtd 23Mar77 (Westmoreland folder, Marines and Military Law in Vietnam file, MCHC).
80. United States v. PFC Charles W. Keenan, NCM 67 0913; 18 USCMA 108, 39 CMR 108 (1969), and the companion case, United States v Cpl Stanley J. Luczko, NCM 67 0952, 18 USCMA 638 (1969).
81. Westmoreland questionnaire.
82. Col Thomas P. Casey ltr to author, dtd 9Oct86 (Casey folder, Marines and Military Law in Vietnam file, MCHC).
83. CG III MAF msg to CMC, 21Jan67 (Casey folder, Marines and Military Law in Vietnam file, MCHC).
84. CG III MAF msg to CMC, 23Jan67 (Casey folder, Marines and Military Law in Vietnam file, MCHC).
85. Representative John M. Slack ltr to Honorable Clark M. Clifford, dtd 14Jun68 (Zorack folder, Marines and Military Law in Vietnam file, MCHC), hereafter Slack ltr.
86. Slack ltr.
87. SecDef Clark M. Clifford ltr to Representative John M. Slack, dtd 21Jun68 (Zorack folder, Marines and Military Law in Vietnam file, MCHC).
88. Draper questionnaire.
89. Record of trial, United States v. LCpl Douglas R. Collard, NCM 67 2117 (1967). Pertinent portions of the record of trial included. (Draper folder, Marines and Military Law in Vietnam file, MCHC).
90. Steffen questionnaire.

Marine Corps Lawyers in Combat: They Also Serve

91. Higginbotham ltr; and Capt Donald Higginbotham Legion of Merit citation, n.d. (Higginbotham folder, Marines and Military Law in Vietnam file, MCHC).
92. Marine Corps Legal Services Study, p. 55.
93. 1stLt Michael I. Neil Navy Cross citation, n.d. (Neil folder, Marines and Military Law in Vietnam file, MCHC).
94. Col Michael I. Neil, USMCR, intvw, 15Oct86, Tape 6487 (Oral HistColl, MCHC).

The First Lawyer General Officer: No Immediate Change

95. BGen James F. Lawrence, Jr., Transcript of intvw by Oral History Unit, Hist& MusDiv, HQMC, dtd 29Aug78 (Oral HistColl, MCHC) p. 138, hereafter Lawrence intvw.
96. Faw intvw.
97. Lawrence intvw, pp. 128-129.
98. Gen Earl E. Anderson ltr to author, dtd 22Feb89 (Anderson folder, Marines and Military Law in Vietnam file, MCHC).
99. Sevier intvw.
100. Faw intvw.

Perpective

101. HQMC, Code DK, Directory of Marine Officer Lawyers, dtd Aug67 (Directories folder, Marines and Military Law in Vietnam file, MCHC).
102. Legal Services Study, p. 31.
103. Williams intvw.
104. Sevier intvw.
105. Legal Services Study, pp. 11-12.
106. MCO 1050.14 dtd 6Jun67, Subj: Excess Leave Program (Law).
107. Supplement to Symposium Book, HQMC, General Officers Symposium, 1966, pp. A-5, A-6.
108. Legal Services Study, p. 46.
109. 10 U.S.C. sec. 801 (1967), Pub. L. No. 90-179 (1967). The U.S. Code does not reflect the language relating to constructive service. That is in sec. 5587a.(a) of the public law upon which the code section is based. The same public law establishes the Navy JAG Corps and amends a prior law to provide that a Marine Corps major general may be detailed as JAG of the Navy and a Marine Corps brigadier general may be Assistant JAG. Finally, the law added language to assure annual promotion of judge advocates in a proportion at least equal to that of line officers. This latter provision was repealed by Public Law 96-513, Title 3, section 333, 12Dec80, 94 Stat.2897.

NOTES

110. Legal Services Study, p. 3.
111. Col Robert M. Lucy ltr to BGen Duane L. Faw, dtd 22Nov69 (Lucy folder, Marines and Military Law in Vietnam file, MCHC).
112. H. Edward Moore ltr to author, dtd 26Mar87 (Moore folder, Marines and Military Law in Vietnam file, MCHC).
113. CWO 4 Maynard K. Baird intvw, 10Oct86, Tape 6488 (Oral HistColl, MCHC).

CHAPTER 5
1968: HIGH TIDE

1. Jack Shulimson ms, "U.S. Marines in Vietnam: January to May, 1968" (MCHC, 1987), pp. 1-42.
2. Ibid.
3. Gen William C. Westmoreland, USA, *A Soldier Reports* (New York: Doubleday & Co., Inc., 1976), p. 342.
4. BGen Edwin H. Simmons, "Marine Corps Operations in Vietnam, 1968," *The Marines in Vietnam, 1954-1973, An Anthology and Annotated Bibliography*, 2nd ed. (Washington: Hist&MusDiv, HQMC, 1985) p. 111, hereafter, *Marines in Vietnam Anthology*, Simmons, "Marine Corps Operations in Vietnam, 1968."
5. TF X-Ray ComdCs, Jan-Aug68 (Unit Command Chronology file, MCHC).
6. FMFPac Awards Alpha Roster, dtd Aug77 (MCHC), n.p.
7. CG III MAF msg to COMUSMACV, 28Feb68; and Gen Creighton W. Abrams, USA, msg to Gen William C. Westmoreland, USA, 2Mar68 (Abrams EOs, Abrams Collection, Center of Military History, Washington, D.C.), (Federal Records Center folder, Marines and Military Law in Vietnam file, MCHC).
8. Gen Abrams, USA, msg to Gen Westmoreland, USA, 2Mar68 (Federal Records Center folder, Marines and Military Law in Vietnam file, MCHC).

1st Marine Division: Lawyers in the Storm's Eye

9. *Marines in Vietnam Anthology*, Simmons, "Marine Corps Operations in Vietnam, 1968," p. 115.
10. GySgt Richard A. Bailey, Cpl Gerald L. McCall, and LCpl George J. Leahey combined intvw, 20Feb68, Tape 2476 (Oral HistColl, MCHC), hereafter Bailey-McCall-Leahey intvw.
11. Col Jack E. Hanthorn questionnaire to Maj W. Hays Parks, dtd 8Jan77 (Hanthorn folder, Marines and Military Law in Vietnam file, MCHC).
12. LtCol Ronald C. Rachow ltr to author, dtd 8Nov87 (Rachow folder, Marines and Military Law in Vietnam file, MCHC), hereafter Rachow ltr.
13. Col Clyde R. Mann intvw, 8Aug68, Tape 2980 (Oral HistColl, MCHC), hereafter Mann intvw.
14. Bailey-McCall-Leahey intvw.
15. Lt William J. Cosgriff, JAGC, USN, ltr to Maj W. Hays Parks, dtd 28Dec76; and Col Parks, ltr to author, dtd 22Dec88 (Cosgriff and Parks folders, Marines and Military Law in Vietnam file, MCHC), hereafter Parks ltr.
16. Mann intvw.
17. Parks ltr.
18. Ibid.
19. Daniel H. LeGear, Jr., ltr to author, dtd 6May87 (LeGear folder, Marines and Military Law in Vietnam file, MCHC).
20. Bailey-McCall-Leahey intvw.

3d Marine Division: Every Marine a Rifleman

21. Col Eugene B. Fallon intvw, 11Jul68, Tape 2979 (Oral HistColl, MCHC), hereafter Fallon intvw.
22. Richard D. Lane ltr to author, dtd 18Aug88 (Lane folder, Marines and Military Law in Vietnam file, MCHC).
23. Col Paul F. Henderson, Jr., ltr to author, dtd 14Oct86, (Henderson folder, Marines and Military Law in Vietnam file, MCHC).
24. BGen John R. DeBarr intvw, 2Oct86, Tape 6491 (Oral HistColl, MCHC), hereafter DeBarr 1986 intvw.
25. LtCol Kenneth W. Jones ltr to BGen Edwin H. Simmons, dtd 29Dec88 (Comment folder, Marines and Military Law in Vietnam file, MCHC).
26. Col Barnes, ltr to author, dtd 10Dec86 (Barnes folder, Marines and Military Law in Vietnam file, MCHC), hereafter Barnes Dec. ltr.
27. 3d MarDiv ComdC, Jun68 (Unit Command Chronology File, MCHC).
28. Col Joseph R. Motelewski intvw, 24Feb87, Tape 6489 (Oral HistColl, MCHC).
29. Ibid.
30. Ibid.
31. Ibid.
32. Captain David G. Moore Bronze Star and Navy Commendation Medal citations, both n.d. (Citations folder, Marines and Military Law in Vietnam file, MCHC).
33. Capt William T. Allison II questionnaire to Maj W. Hays Parks, dtd 13Dec76 (Allison folder, Marines and Military Law in Vietnam file, MCHC).
34. 1st Lt William T. Allison Bronze Star citation, n.d. (Citations folder, Marines and Military Law in Vietnam file, MCHC).
35. Capt William L. Fly Navy Commendation Medal citation, n.d. (Fly folder, Marines and Military Law in Vietnam file, MCHC).
36. Capt William H. McAdam, Jr., Bronze Star and Navy Commendation Medal citations, both n.d. (Citations folder, Marines and Military Law in Vietnam file, MCHC).

1st Marine Aircraft Wing/Force Logistic Command: Doing Time at Da Nang

37. 1st MAW ComdC, Dec67 (Unit Command Chronology File, MCHC).
38. Col Charles H. Mitchell intvw, 28Oct86, Tape 6486 (Oral HistColl, MCHC).
39. Col Robert C. Lehnert ltr to author, dtd 1Feb89 (Comment folder, Marines and Military Law in Vietnam file, MCHC), hereafter Lehnert ltr.
40. FLC ComdC, Feb-Dec68 (Unit Command Chronology File, MCHC); and Maj Michael Patrick Murray intvw, dtd 22Jun68, Tape 2849 (Oral HistColl, MCHC), hereafter Murray intvw.
41. Victor J. Haydel III questionnaire to author, dtd 16Sep87 (Haydel folder, Marines and Military Law in Vietnam file, MCHC).
42. Col James A. Cathcart ltr to author, dtd 23Nov87 (Cathcart folder, Marines and Military Law in Vietnam file, MCHC), hereafter Cathcart ltr.
43. *Marines in Vietnam Anthology*, Simmons, "Marine Corps Operations in Vietnam, 1968," p. 125.
44. Murray intvw; and FLC ComdC, Jun68 (Unit Command Chronology File, MCHC).
45. Robert W. Wachsmuth ltr to author, dtd 13Nov87 (Wachsmuth

folder, Marines and Military Law in Vietnam file, MCHC), hereafter Wachsmuth ltr.
46. Ibid.
47. BGen Max G. Halliday intvw, 13Oct86, Tape 6490 (Oral Hist-Coll, MCHC), hereafter Halliday intvw.
48. *Marines in Vietnam Anthology*, Simmons, "Marine Corps Operations in Vietnam, 1968," p. 126.

From A Lawyer's Case File: Civilian Court-Martial

49. Jurisdictional brief for accused, at 1-2, United States v. Latney, NCM 68 1965. Like many records of trial of the Vietnam era the Latney record has been lost. A copy of the defense brief re jurisdiction was retained by defense counsel, LtCol Kent. (Kent folder, Marines and Military Law in Vietnam file, MCHC).
50. Victor J. Haydel III ltr to author, dtd 10Feb87 (Haydel folder, Marines and Military Law in Vietnam file, MCHC), hereafter Haydel Feb ltr.
51. Faw intvw.
52. United States Military Assistance Command, Vietnam, Command History, 1967, Volume II, p. 953 (MACV Cmd Histories folder, Marines and Military Law in Vietnam file, MCHC), hereafter MACV History.
53. MajGen George S. Prugh, USA, ltr to BGen Edwin H. Simmons, dtd 29Dec88 (Comment folder, Marines and Military Law in Vietnam file, MCHC).
54. Faw intvw; and MACV History, 1967, Vol II, pp. 949, 953.
55. MACV History, 1967, Volume II, p. 953; and MajGen George S. Prugh, USA, *Vietnam Studies, Law At War: Vietnam, 1964-1973*, (Washington: Dept of the Army, 1975), p. 10, 109, hereafter, Prugh, *Law At War*.
56. CG III MAF msg to CMC, 15Aug67 (Federal Records Center folder, Marines and Military Law in Vietnam file, MCHC).
57. Col Verne L. Oliver ltr to BGen Edwin H. Simmons, dtd 2Feb89 (Comment folder, Marines and Military Law in Vietnam file, MCHC), hereafter Oliver ltr.
58. Col Donald E. Holben intvw, dtd 13Oct86, Tape 6472 (Oral HistColl, MCHC), hereafter Holben intvw.
59. Capt Victor J. Haydel intvw, 16Sep68, Tape 3243 (Oral Hist-Coll, MCHC).
60. Robert W. Wachsmuth ltr to author, dtd 13Nov87 (Wachsmuth folder, Marines and Military Law in Vietnam file, MCHC).
61. Latney v. Ignatius, 416 F.2d 821 (1969).
62. Pretrial and posttrial descriptions and quotations, unless otherwise attributed: Haydel Feb ltr; Col Donald E. Holben ltr to author, dtd 27Feb87, Holben folder; LtCol Brian B. Kent ltr to author, dtd 3Mar87, Kent folder; Charles J. Kall attachment to ltr to author, dtd 8May87, Kall folder; H. Edward Moore, Jr. ltr to author, dtd 26Mar87, Moore folder (Marines and Military Law in Vietnam file, MCHC).
63. Oliver ltr.
64. Ibid.

Drugs: 'High' Tide

65. Col Peter J. Mulroney intvw, 17Jul69, Tape 4384 (Oral Hist-Coll, MCHC).
66. Gen Raymond G. Davis, Transcript of intvw by Oral History Unit, Hist & MusDiv, HQMC, dtd 2Feb77 (OralHistColl, MCHC), p. 250.
67. Ibid., pp. 251-252.

68. LtCol William C. Jaeck TAD Trip Report to CG FMFPac, dtd 9Dec67 (Jaeck folder, Marines and Military Law in Vietnam file, MCHC), pp. 2-3.
69. LtCol W. Hays Parks, "Statistics Versus Actuality in Vietnam," *Air University Review*, May-Jun 1981, pp. 84, 86.
70. United States Military Assistance Command, Vietnam Command History, 1968, Volume II, p.811 details the arrest of three soldiers in Sydney, and the concern of the Sydney Special Federal Court over the rising number of similar cases (MACV Cmd Histories folder, Marines and Military Law in Vietnam file, MCHC).
71. Col James W. Shank intvw, 19May69, Tape 4268 (Oral Hist-Coll, MCHC).
72. Wachsmuth ltr.
73. Fallon intvw.
74. Wachsmuth ltr.

Trying Cases

75. Col Clarke C. Barnes ltr to author, dtd 10Dec86 (Barnes folder, Marines and Military Law in Vietnam file, MCHC).
76. 1st Lt Jeffery W. Maurer intvw, 12Dec68, Tape 3498 (Oral Hist-Coll, MCHC).
77. Col Clarke C. Barnes ltr to author, dtd 5Feb87 (Barnes folder, Marines and Military Law in Vietnam file, MCHC), hereafter Barnes Feb. ltr.; and Wachsmuth ltr.
78. Col Eugene B. Fallon intvw, 11Jul68, Tape 2979 (Oral HistColl, MCHC).
79. Mann intvw.
80. Col Jack E. Hanthorn, "The Charge of the First Legal Division," *Harvard Law School Bulletin*, Mar-Apr69 (Parks folder, Marines and Military Law in Vietnam file, MCHC), p. 11.
81. DeBarr 1986 intvw.
82. Barnes Dec. ltr.
83. Colonel Alexander M. Hearn ltr to author, dtd 27Feb87 (Hearn folder, Marines and Military Law in Vietnam file, MCHC).
84. Holben intvw.; and Col Donald E. Holben ltr to BGen Edwin H. Simmons, dtd 16Feb89 (Comment folder, Marines and Military Law in Vietnam file, MCHC).
85. Ibid.; and BGen John R. DeBarr ltr to author, dtd 25Jan89 (Comment folder, Marines and Military Law in Vietnam file, MCHC).

Trial Under Fire: Khe Sanh Court

86. *Marines in Vietnam Anthology*, Simmons, "Marine Corps Operations in Vietnam, 1968," pp. 106, 113.
87. Capt Moyers S. Shore II, *The Battle For Khe Sanh* (Washington, D.C.: Historical Branch, G-3 Division, Headquarters, U.S. Marine Corps, 1969), p. 122.
88. Unless otherwise noted, descriptions and quotations are from: Robert W. Wachsmuth ltr to author, dtd 13Nov87, Wachsmuth folder; and Harry L. Shorstein ltrs to author, dtd 8Oct86 and 4Dec86, Shorstein folder (Marines and Military Law in Vietnam file, MCHC).
89. *Marines in Vietnam Anthology*, Simmons, "Marine Corps Operations in Vietnam, 1986," p. 120.

Legal Assistance, Claims, Reviews: Someone Has to Do It

90. LtCdr Larry R. Rowe ltr to Capt W. Hays Parks, dtd 10Feb77 (Rowe folder, Marines and Military Law in Vietnam file, MCHC).

91. Parks ltr.
92. Ibid.
93. Legal Services Study, p. 32, and Annex E.
94. Barnes Dec ltr.

Fragging: Friendly Fire With Malice

95. Col Robert D. Heinl, Jr., "The Collapse of the Armed Forces," *Armed Forces Journal*, 7Jun71, p. 31.
96. See, e.g., Richard A. Gabriel and Paul L. Savage, *Crisis in Command—Mismanagement in the Army* (New York: Hill and Wang, 1978), table 3, p. 183; James William Gibson, *The Perfect War; Technowar in Vietnam* (Boston/New York: The Atlantic Monthly Press, 1986), p. 211; and David Cortright, *Soldiers in Revolt; The American Military Today* (Garden City, N.Y.: Doubleday, 1975), p. 44.
97. United States v. LCpl John W. Thomas, 41 CMR 828 (NCMR 1970), rev'd 43 CMR 89, 20 USCMA 249 (1971), involved a rear-echelon Marine who murdered another Marine through use of a hand grenade to escape a $1,000 poker debt. Both were junior enlisted Marines and the case is not considered a fragging.
98. Col James W. Shank intvw, 19May69, Tape 4268 (Oral Hist-Coll, MCHC).
99. Dr. Thomas C. Bond, "Fragging: A Study," *Army*, Apr77, pp. 45-47, citing his own study in *The American Journal of Psychiatry*, Vol. 133, 1976, pp. 1328-1331.
100. LtGen Victor H. Krulak. Transcript of intvw by Oral History Unit, HistDiv, HQMC, dtd 1973, intvw dtd 20Jun70 (Oral Hist-Coll, MCHC), pp. 132-133.

Homicide on Patrol: Nothing Hidden

101. LtCol W. Hays Parks, "The Law of War Adviser," 31 *The JAG Journal* 44-47 (Summer, 1980).
102. United States v. LCpl Denzil R. Allen, NCM 68 3152, pet. den. 19 USCMA 604 (1970); 436 F.2d 625; cert. den. 402 U.S. 1008. (Allen was represented by Calley defense counsel and former Court of Military Appeals judge, George W. Latimer. Government counsel was LtCol Charles J. Keever, last seen in Saigon, attached to the Office of Civil Operations. In 1971 he was head of the government section, Navy Appellate Review Activity, Washington, D.C.)
103. NC & PB ltr.
104. Ibid.
105. Ibid.
106. United States v. LCpl James A. Maushart, NCM 68 3388, pet. den. 18 USCMA 636 (1970); United States v. LCpl John D. Belknap, NCM 68 3657, pet. den. 18 USCMA 636 (1970); and United States v. LCpl Anthony Licciardo, Jr., NCM 69 0205; pet. den. 18 USCMA 643 (1970).
107. Col Jack E. Hanthorn ltr to Maj W. Hays Parks, dtd 3Jan77 (Hanthorn folder, Marines and Military Law in Vietnam file, MCHC).
108. Parks, op. cit., p. 47.
109. Parks ltr.
110. Ibid.

III MAF Brig Riot: Prisoner's Kangaroo Courts

111. All riot events and quotations, unless otherwise noted, are from the record of Article 32 investigation, an incomplete copy of which (with a mis-matched Article 32 appointing letter incorrectly attached as cover sheet) is included. (Reynolds folder, Marines and Military Law in Vietnam file, MCHC).
112. LtCol William C. Jaeck TAD Trip Report to CG FMFPac dtd 9Dec67 (Jaeck folder, Marines and Military Law in Vietnam file, MCHC).
113. Col Joseph J. N. Gambardella ltr to author, dtd 10Feb89 (Comment folder, Marines and Military Law in Vietnam file, MCHC), hereafter Gambardella ltr.
114. Ibid.
115. "2d Riot Quelled at Vietnam Brig," New York Times, 19Aug68, p. 5. (The Times considered the events of Friday night and Sunday afternoon to constitute separate riots.)
116. Gambardella ltr.
117. Michael J. Hoblock, Jr, intvw, 2Mar87, Tape 6493 (Oral Hist-Coll, MCHC), hereafter Hoblock intvw.
118. CO, Marine Wing HQ Group One ltr to CG 1st MAW, dtd 24Nov68 (Hoblock folder, Marines and Military Law in Vietnam file, MCHC).
119. Hoblock intvw.
120. DD Form 458 (Charge Sheet), case of Pvt Stephen F. Brice, dtd 26Sep68 (Hoblock folder, Marines and Military Law in Vietnam file, MCHC).
121. 1st Lt Curtis K. Oberhansly ltr to Lt Jerry D. Rucker, JAGC, USN, dtd 4Dec68 (Rucker folder, Marines and Military Law in Vietnam file, MCHC).
122. Hoblock intvw.; and Cdr Jerry D. Rucker ltr to author, dtd 16Jan89 (Comment folder, Marines and Military Law in Vietnam file, MCHC), hereafter Rucker ltr.
123. United States v Pvt Michael A. Roberts, NCM 70 0021.
124. Rucker ltr; and Hoblock intvw. Petitions for grants of review in both of Pvt Roberts' cases, the first of which had resulted in a bad conduct discharge, were eventually denied by the Court of Military Appeals (18 COMA 629 [Feb69], and 21 COMA 628 [Mar72]).

Perspective

125. *Marines in Vietnam Anthology*, Simmons, "Marine Corps Operations in Vietnam, 1968," p. 128.
126. Col James P. McHenry questionnaire to author, dtd 1Oct86 (McHenry folder, Marines and Military Law in Vietnam file, MCHC).
127. LtCol Ronald C. Rachow ltr to author, dtd 8Nov87 (Rachow folder, Marines and Military Law in Vietnam file, MCHC).
128. Col Harry K. Jowers questionnaire to author, dtd 11Apr86 (Jowers folder, Marines and Military Law in Vietnam file, MCHC).
129. Col Robert J. Chadwick, "Judge Advocate of the Marine Corps," *The Judge Advocate Journal*, Bicentennial Issue, 4Jul76, pp. 50-54; and Legal Services Study, p. 6.
130. Biographical Files (RefSec, MCHC).
131. *Combined Lineal List of Officers on Active Duty in the Marine Corps*, 1 January 1969.
132. Legal Services Study, pp. 4, 13, 46, 57.
133. S. Res. 2674; H.R. 4296 and H.R. 9567, 91st Cong., 1st sess. See Chapter 6 for the fruitless outcome of those resolutions.
134. Office of the Judge Advocate General of the Navy, Code 64.2 (Case Stats folder, Marines and Military Law in Vietnam file, MCHC).
135. Legal Services Study, p. ii.
136. MajGen Jonas M. Platt, Manpower, G-1 Presentation, HQMC, General Officers Symposium, 1969, tab E, pp. 18-19.
137. *Marines in Vietnam Anthology*, Simmons, "Marine Corps Operations in Vietnam, 1968," p. 128.

138. Col Donald Higginbotham questionnaire to Maj W. Hays Parks, dtd 15Jan77 (Higginbotham folder, Marines and Military Law in Vietnam file, MCHC).

PART III
Winding Down

CHAPTER 6
1969 PREAMBLE: DISCIPLINE IN DISARRAY

1. Col Robert D. Heinl, Jr., "The Collapse of the Armed Forces," *Armed Forces Journal*, 7Jun71, pp. 30-38, hereafter Heinl, "The Collapse of the Armed Forces."
2. Henry I. Shaw, Jr., and Ralph W. Donnelly, *Blacks in the Marine Corps* (Washington: Hist&MusDiv, HQMC, 1975), pp. 72-73, hereafter Shaw and Donnelly, *Blacks in the Marine Corps*; and *New York Times*, 15Aug69, p. 1, p. 23.
3. *New York Times*, 16Sep69, p. 95.
4. GySgt Joseph Lopez intvw, 21Feb70, Tape 4749 (Oral HistColl, MCHC).
5. Col John R. DeBarr debriefing at FMFPac, dtd 9Jun69, Tape 4254 (Oral HistColl, MCHC), hereafter Col DeBarr intvw.
6. MajGen Jonas M. Platt, Manpower, G-1 Presentation, HQMC, General Officers Symposium, 1969, Tab E, p. 19.
7. BGen James P. King intvw, 5Nov86, Tape 6478 (Oral HistColl, MCHC), hereafter King intvw.
8. Col David J. Cassady intvw, 4Nov86, Tape 6493 (Oral HistColl, MCHC).

The Military Justice Act of 1968:
Evolutionary Fine-Tuning

9. Pub.L. No. 90-632, 82 Stat. 1335 (1968).
10. Senator Sam J. Ervin, Jr., "The Military Justice Act of 1968," 45 *Military Law Review* 76, 79 (Jul 1969).
11. U.S. Court of Military Appeals, Joint Report of the U.S. C.O.M.A. and the JAGs of the Armed Forces and the General Counsel of the Dept. of Transportation, p. 2, *Annual Report of the United States Court of Military Appeals and the Judge Advocate Generals of the Armed Forces and the General Counsel of the Department of Transportation, For the Period January 1, 1968 to December 31, 1968* (Washington: Government Printing Office, 1969).
12. Ervin, op. cit., p. 80-94.
13. Uniform Code of Military Justice, as amended by the Act of 24 Oct 1968, Articles 1.(13), and 6.(b).
14. MCO 5800.7 dtd 28Oct68, Subj: Marine Corps Judge Advocates; Designation as and Granting of Service Credit to.
15. General Paul X. Kelley intvw, 30Sep87, Tape 6477 (Oral HistColl, MCHC).
16. Capt John S. Papa intvw, 24Feb70 Tape 4750 (Oral HistColl) MCHC), hereafter Papa intvw.
17. Ibid.
18. Edward F. Sherman, *With Justice For Some: An Indictment of the Law by Young Advocates*, B. Wasserstein and M. J. Green, eds. (Boston: Beacon Press, 1970), p. 77.
19. Ibid., cited at p. 83.
20. BGen Duane L. Faw intvw, 8Oct86, Tape 6470 (Oral HistColl, MCHC).
21. BGen Charles A. Cushman intvw, 4Dec86, Tape 6481 (Oral HistColl, MCHC), hereafter Cushman intvw.
22. Daniel H. LeGear, Jr., ltr to author, dtd 6May87 (LeGear folder, Marines and Military Law in Vietnam file, MCHC), hereafter LeGear ltr.
23. King intvw.
24. Col William R. Eleazer ltr to Maj W. Hays Parks, dtd 11Nov77 (Eleazer folder, Marines and Military Law in Vietnam file, MCHC).

Marijuana: Persons of Ill Repute

25. United States Military Assistance Command, Vietnam, Command History, 1969, Vol III, p.XIV-4 (MACV Cmd Histories folder, Marines and Military Law in Vietnam file, MCHC).
26. LtCol Frederick M. Haden intvw, 12May69, Tape 4258 (Oral HistColl, MCHC), hereafter Haden intvw.
27. Laura Palmer, "The General At Ease: An Interview with Westmoreland," *MHQ, The Quarterly Journal of Military History*, Autumn 1988, p. 34.
28. Maj Ives W. Neely, Jr., intvw, 21Feb70, Tape 4748 (Oral HistColl, MCHC).
29. BGen Duane L. Faw ltr to author, dtd 15Jun88 (Faw folder, Marines and Military Law in Vietnam file, MCHC).
30. Commandant of the Marine Corps WestPac Visit, 4-12Aug69, Briefing Book 3, Tab S, p. 3 (Command Concerns folder, Marines and Military Law in Vietnam file, MCHC), hereafter CMC WestPac Visit Briefing Book.
31. Haden intvw.
32. Cushman intvw.
33. LtCol Carl E. Buchmann intvw, 26Feb70 (Oral HistColl, MCHC).

Racial Conflict: Black, White, and Green

34. *New York Times*, 13Apr69, p. 1.
35. Shaw and Donnelly, *Blacks in the Marine Corps*, pp. 78, 81-82.
36. Ibid., pp. 1-3, 15, 47, 54, 66.
37. CG 3d MarDiv ltr to commanders, dtd 19Jun69, CMC WestPac Visit Briefing Book 3, Tab 5, enclosure (5). The letter, signed by MajGen W. K. Jones, was written by his SJA, Col Rollin Q. Blakeslee, according to the originator's code. (Command Concerns folder, Marines and Military Law in Vietnam file, MCHC).
38. Graham A. Cosmas and LtCol Terrence P. Murray, *U.S. Marines in Vietnam: Vietnamization and Redeployment, 1970-1971* (Washington: Hist&MusDiv, HQMC, 1986), p. 354.
39. Hon. James H. Webb, Jr., ltr to author, dtd 22Dec88 (Webb folder, Marines and Military Law in Vietnam file, MCHC); and Col John C. Scharfen, "An Exclusive Interview With James H. Webb, Jr., Secretary of the Navy," *Amphibious Warfare Review*, Summer 1987, pp. 25-28. A fictionalized version of this encounter appears in James H. Webb, *Fields of Fire* (Englewood Cliffs, N.J.: Prentice Hall, Inc., 1978) pp. 162-165.
40. Nalty, *Strength for the Fight*, p. 306.
41. Ibid., p. 339.
42. CMC msg to ALMAR, dtd 2Sep69 (Negro Marines, ALMAR-65 Subject File, RefSec, MCHC).
43. Col Robert M. Lucy ltr to BGen Duane L. Faw, dtd 22Nov69 (Lucy folder, Marines and Military Law in Vietnam file, MCHC).
44. LtGen H. Nickerson, Jr., msg to LtGen H. W. Buse, Jr., dtd 16Dec69 (Command Concerns folder, Marines and Military Law in Vietnam file, MCHC).
45. Col Robert M. Lucy memo to MajGen Ormond R. Simpson, Subj: Asst. Secretary of Defense (Civil Rights) Visit, dtd 6Nov69 (Lucy folder, Marines and Military Law in Vietnam file, MCHC).

46. III MAF Fact Sheet, Subj: I Corps Tactical Zone Watch Committee, dtd 7Aug69 (Command Concerns folder, Marines and Military Law in Vietnam file, MCHC), hereafter III MAF Fact Sheet.
47. CG III MAF msg to CGs, 1st and 3d MarDivs, 1st MAW, and FLC, dtd 25Aug69 (Command Concerns folder, Marines and Military Law in Vietnam file, MCHC).
48. III MAF Fact Sheet.
49. King intvw.
50. LtCol Stephen C. Berg ltr to author, dtd 29Oct86 (Berg folder, Marines and Military Law in Vietnam file, MCHC), hereafter Berg ltr.
51. Col Robert M. Lucy ltr to Col Robert C. Lehnert, n.d. (Lucy folder, Marines and Military Law in Vietnam file, MCHC).
52. Capt Cecil R. Forster, Jr., Navy Achievement Medal recommendation, n.d. (Granger folder, Marines and Military Law in Vietnam file, MCHC).
53. Berg ltr.
54. BGen Charles A. Cushman ltr to author, dtd 17Jan89 (Comment folder, Marines and Military Law in Vietnam file, MCHC), hereafter Cushman ltr.
55. MajGen Jonas M. Platt, Manpower, G-1 Presentation, HQMC, General Officers Symposium, 1969, tab E, p. xx.
56. Col Lucy ltr to BGen Faw, dtd 22Nov69 (Lucy folder, Marines and Military Law in Vietnam file, MCHC).

Administrative Discharge: The Right Fix

57. Papa intvw.
58. BGen Regan Fuller intvw, 17Nov69, Tape 4689 (Oral HistColl, MCHC).
59. United States v. Leo O. Testman, aka Andre Orville Testman, administrative discharge hearing, 24Jul69, 1st MarDiv, Quang Tri, RVN, (Barnes folder, Marines and Military Law in Vietnam file, MCHC).
60. CMC msg to USAFMPC, Randolph AFB, Texas, dtd 16Aug69 (Barnes folder, Marines and Military Law in Vietnam file, MCHC).
61. FMFPac Awards Alpha Roster, dtd 24Aug77, Book 4 of 4, n.p. (MCHC).
62. Legal Services Study, p. 32.
63. Command Information Notebook, 1st MarDiv, FMF, Republic of Vietnam, dtd 10Apr71, n.p. (Command Info Notebook folder, Marines and Military Law in Vietnam file, MCHC).

Fragging: Killers in our Midst

64. U.S. House, Committee on Appropriations, Subcommittee on Dept of Defense, *DOD Appropriations for 1972, Hearings*, 92nd Congress, 1st sess., part 9, 17 May-23 Sep 1971, p. 585; as cited in: Guenter Lewy, *America in Vietnam* (New York: Oxford University Press, 1978), p. 156.
65. Cushman ltr.
66. Col John R. DeBarr debriefing at FMFPac, 9Jun69. Tape 4254 (Oral HistColl, MCHC).
67. Descriptions of 3d Division actions to counter violent acts, and quotations, are from: CMC WestPac Visit Briefing Book 3, Tab 5, enclosure (5) (Command Concerns folder, Marines and Military Law in Vietnam file, MCHC).
68. 3d MarDivO 5370.4, dtd 4Jul69, Subj: SOP for Apprehension of Individuals Involved in Acts of Violence Towards Members of This Command, a copy of which is in CMC WestPac Visit Briefing Book 3, Tab 5 (Command Concerns folder, Marines and Military Law in Vietnam file, MCHC).

From a Lawyer's Case File: Murder of a Company Commander

69. Gen Raymond G. Davis, Transcript of intvw by Oral History Unit, Hist&MusDiv, HQMC, dtd 2Feb77 (Oral HistColl, MCHC), pp. 250-251.
70. Col Elliott R. Laine, Jr., summary of intvw to author, dtd 16Mar87 (Laine folder, Marines and Military Law in Vietnam file, MCHC).
71. The description of events and all quotations, except where otherwise indicated, are from the records of trial, United States v PFC David Napier, NCM 70 1453, and United States v LCpl Bobby R. Greenwood, NCM 70 3843.
72. Col Clarke C. Barnes ltr to author, dtd 10Dec86 (Barnes folder, Marines and Military Law in Vietnam file, MCHC).
73. Col Clarke C. Barnes ltr to author, dtd 6Feb89 (Comment folder, Marines and Military Law in Vietnam file, MCHC).

Real or Imagined: The 'Mere Gook' Rule

74. Col David J. Cassady intvw, 4Nov86, Tape 6493 (Oral HistColl, MCHC).
75. Col John R. Elting, USA, SgtMaj Dan Craig, USA, SFC Ernest Deal, USA, *A Dictionary of Soldier Talk* (NY: Charles Scribner's Sons, 1984), p. 135.
76. Guenter Lewy, *America in Vietnam* (New York: Oxford University Press, 1978), p. 310, hereafter Lewy, *America in Vietnam*. This outstanding work provides an excellent analysis of the treatment of servicemen of both the Army and the Marine Corps who were accused of crimes in Vietnam.
77. Ibid.
78. Robert W. Wachsmuth ltr to author, dtd 13Nov87 (Wachsmuth folder, Marines and Military Law in Vietnam file, MCHC).
79. Maj W. Hays Parks, "Crimes in Hostilities," *Marine Corps Gazette*, Aug76, p. 14.
80. BGen J. R. DeBarr, Dir JA Div, ltr to Prof G. Lewy, dtd 9Mar76 (War Crimes folder, Marines and Military Law in Vietnam file, MCHC), encl. 9, hereafter DirJAD ltr.
81. DirJAD ltr, encl. 8
82. U.S. Department of Commerce, *Statistical Abstract of the United States 1970* (Washington: 1970), table no. 236, p. 153.
83. Lewy, *America In Vietnam*, table 10-5, p. 458.
84. NC & PB ltr.
85. Lewy, *America in Vietnam*, p. 371.
86. Appellate opinions, United States v. Cpl Ronald J. Reese, NCM 70 0855, and United States v. LCpl Stephen D. Crider, NCM 69 4114. (CMC Opinions folder, Marines and Military Law in Vietnam file, MCHC).
87. Hoppe ltr.

Perspective

88. Cushman ltr.
89. Heinl, "The Collapse of the Armed Forces."

CHAPTER 7
1969: MILITARY JUSTICE TESTED

1. *Marines in Vietnam Anthology*, Simmons, "Marine Corps Operations in Vietnam, 1969-1972."
2. BGen William H. J. Tiernan intvw, 14Oct86, Tape 6484 (Oral

HistColl, MCHC); and Office of the Force SJA memo to Force Personnel Office, Subj: Assignment of incoming judge advocates to WestPac, dtd 11Sep69 (Lucy folder, Marines and Military Law in Vietnam file, MCHC).
3. Prugh, Law At War, p. 100.

III MAF: No Longer Two Hats

4. *Marines in Vietnam Anthology*, Simmons, Marine Corps Operations in Vietnam, 1969-1972," p. 135.
5. Maj George Ward Beaudry questionnaire to Maj W. Hays Parks, dtd 4Feb77 (Beaudry folder, Marines and Military Law in Vietnam file, MCHC).
6. Col Marion G. Truesdale ltr to BGen Edwin H. Simmons, n.d. (Comment folder, Marines and Military Law in Vietnam file, MCHC).
7. III MAF ComdC, Apr69 (Unit Command Chronology File, MCHC); and *Marines in Vietnam Anthology*, Simmons, "Marine Corps Operations in Vietnam, 1969-1972," p. 137.
8. Col Marion G. Truesdale intvw, 7Oct86, Tape 6471 (Oral HistColl, MCHC); hereafter Truesdale intvw.

1st Marine Division: The Law Center Concept

9. *Marines in Vietnam Anthology*, Simmons, "Marine Corps Operations in Vietnam, 1969-1972," p. 133-134.
10. Col Jack E. Hanthorn questionnaire to Maj Parks, dtd 8Jan77 (Hanthorn folder, Marines and Military Law in Vietnam file, MCHC).
11. Col Robert M. Lucy questionnaire to author, dtd 29Oct86 (Lucy folder, Marines and Military Law in Vietnam file, MCHC).
12. Col Jack E. Hanthorn ltr to Maj Parks, dtd 3Jan77 (Hanthorn folder, Marines and Military Law in Vietnam file, MCHC).
13. Daniel H. LeGear, Jr., ltr to author, dtd 6May87 (LeGear folder, Marines and Military Law in Vietnam file, MCHC); hereafter LeGear ltr.
14. Col Robert M. Lucy debriefing at FMFPac, 24Jun70, Tape 4814 (Oral HistColl, MCHC); hereafter Lucy intvw.
15. U.S. Court of Military Appeals, *Annual Report of the United States Court of Military Appeals and the Judge Advocates General of the Armed Forces and the General Counsel of the Department of Transportation, For the Period January 1, to December 31, 1969* (Washington: Government Printing Office, 1970), p. 29.
16. 1stLt James M. Schermerhorn Silver Star and Navy Commendation Medal citations, both n.d. (Citations folder, Marines and Military Law in Vietnam file, MCHC).
17. Lt William J. Cosgriff, JAGC, USN, ltr to Maj Parks, dtd 28Dec76 (Cosgriff folder, Marines and Military Law in Vietnam file, MCHC); and LeGear ltr.
18. Lucy intvw.
19. 1stMarDiv ComdCs, Jan-Dec69 (Unit Command Chronology file, MCHC).
20. 1stLt Warren S. Mathey intvw, 11Jun69, Tape 4283 (Oral HistColl, MCHC).
21. Ibid.
22. Ibid.
23. John R. Taylor, Jr., summary of intvw to author, dtd 31Jan87 (J. R. Taylor folder, Marines and Military Law in Vietnam file, MCHC).
24. Lucy intvw.

25. Col Lucy ltr to BGen D. L. Faw, dtd 22Nov69 (Lucy folder, Marines and Military Law in Vietnam file, MCHC).
26. CWO 4 Maynard K. Baird intvw, dtd 10Oct86, Tape 6488 (Oral HistColl, MCHC).
27. CWO-4 Baird Bronze Star Medal recommendation, dtd 20Apr70 (Granger folder, Marines and Military Law in Vietnam file, MCHC); and FMFPac Awards Alpha Roster, vol I, dtd Aug77, MCHC, n.p.

3d Marine Division: More Combat, Fewer Courts

28. *Marines in Vietnam Anthology*, Simmons, "Marine Corps Operations in Vietnam, 1969-1972," pp. 133-136.
29. Col Benjamin B. Ferrell and Maj David J. Cassady questionnaires to Maj Parks, n.d. and 22Dec76, respectively (Ferrell and Cassady folders, Marines and Military Law in Vietnam file, MCHC).
30. Col David J. Cassady intvw, 4Nov86, Tape 6493 (Oral HistColl, MCHC).
31. Col Benjamin B. Ferrell, "Critique of U.S. Courts-Martial Proceedings Against War Criminals in the Vietnam War," p. 17. Case study, The School of the Judge Advocate General of the Army, n.d. (Ferrell folder, Marines and Military Law in Vietnam file, MCHC).
32. Col John R. DeBarr debriefing at FMFPac, 9Jun69, Tape 4254 (Oral HistColl, MCHC).
33. Col Clarke C. Barnes questionnaire to author, dtd 10Dec86 (Barnes folder, Marines and Military Law in Vietnam file, MCHC), hereafter Barnes questionnaire.
34. Capt Christopher Q. Britton summary of intvw to author, dtd 14Apr88 (Britton folder, Marines and Military Law in Vietnam file, MCHC).
35. Barnes questionnaire.

From a Lawyer's Case File: Murder on Stage

36. Record of trial, United States v. Sgt James W. Killen, NCM 70 1100. Unless otherwise attributed, all quotes relating to this case are from the record of trial (U.S. v. Killen folder, Marines and Military Law in Vietnam file, MCHC).
37. *The Overseas Weekly – Pacific Edition*, 13Sep69 (LeGear folder, Marines and Military Law in Vietnam file, MCHC), p. 1.
38. U.S. v. James W. Killen, NCM 70 1100, 43 CMR 865 (NCMR, 1971).
39. SJA ltr to CG 1st MarDiv, Subj: SJA's advice on recommendation for trial by GCM, case of James W. Killen, n.d. (U.S. v. Killen folder, Marines and Military Law in Vietnam file, MCHC).

1st Marine Aircraft Wing: Looking For Action

40. *Marines in Vietnam Anthology*, Simmons, "Marine Corps Operation in Vietnam, 1969-1972," pp. 136, 137.
41. 1st MAW ComdCs, Jan-Dec69 (Unit Command Chronology file, MCHC).
42. BGen Max Halliday intvw, 13Oct86, Tape 6490; and BGen David M. Brahms intvw, 2Dec86, Tape 6494 (Oral HistColl, MCHC), hereafter, Halliday intvw and Brahms intvw, respectively.
43. Brahms intvw.
44. Brahms and Halliday intvws.
45. Brahms intvw.
46. LtCol Richard A. Muench ltr to author, dtd 3Sep86 (Muench folder, Marines and Military Law in Vietnam file, MCHC).

NOTES

47. Col Michael G. McCollum intvw, 17Feb87, Tapes 6495 (Oral HistColl, MCHC), hereafter McCollum intvw; and Col McCollum ltr to author, dtd 21Dec88 (Comment folder, Marines and Military Law in Vietnam file, MCHC), hereafter McCollum ltr.
48. Brahms intvw; McCollum intvw.
49. Ibid.
50. Brahms intvw.
51. CWO 4 Len E. Pierce ltr to BGen Edwin H. Simmons, dtd 7Jan89 (Comment folder, Marines and Military Law in Vietnam file, MCHC).
52. Ibid.
53. LtCol Frederick M. Haden intvw, 12May69, Tape 4258 (Oral HistColl, MCHC).
54. Nathaniel F. Emmons ltr to author, dtd 19May88; Capt George H. O'Kelley, Jr., ltr to author, dtd 16May88; and Emmons ltr to BGen Edwin H. Simmons, dtd 24Feb89 (Emmons, O'Kelley, and Comment folders, respectively, Marines and Military Law in Vietnam file, MCHC).
55. McCollum intvw; McCollum ltr; and FMFPac Awards Alpha Roster, dtd Aug77, MCHC, Vol 3, n.p.
56. 1st MAW ComdC, Nov69 (Unit Command Chronology file, MCHC); and Col Arthur R. Petersen ltr to BGen Duane L. Faw, dtd 25Nov69 (Petersen folder, Marines and Military Law in Vietnam file, MCHC).

Force Logistic Command: Approaching Breakdown

57. Col W. Hays Parks ltr to author, dtd 22Dec88 (Parks folder, Marines and Military Law in Vietnam file, MCHC), hereafter Parks ltr.
58. Col William M. Cummings ltr to Col Arthur R. Petersen, dtd 26Apr69 (Petersen folder, Marines and Military Law in Vietnam file, MCHC).
59. FLC ComdCs, Jan-Dec69 (Unit Command Chronology file, MCHC).
60. Col Arthur R. Petersen ltr to author, dtd 11Jul88 (Petersen folder, Marines and Military Law in Vietnam file, MCHC).
61. Col Arthur R. Petersen, affidavit, dtd 4Apr70 (Petersen folder, Marines and Military Law in Vietnam file, MCHC), hereafter Petersen affidavit.
62. Ibid.
63. BGen Charles A. Cushman ltr to author, dtd 17Jan89 (Comment folder, Marines and Military Law in Vietnam file, MCHC).
64. Petersen affidavit.
65. Ibid.
66. LtCol Carl E. Buchmann intvw, 26Feb70, Tape 4751 (Oral HistColl, MCHC), hereafter Buchmann intvw.
67. Ibid.
68. Ibid.

Trying Cases

69. Maj Richard A. Gabriel, USAR, "Professionalism Versus Managerialism in Vietnam," *Air University Review*, Jan-Feb81, pp. 77-85.
70. Capt Daniel H. LeGear ltr to author, dtd 6May87 (LeGear folder, Marines and Military Law in Vietnam file, MCHC), hereafter LeGear ltr.
71. McCollum intvw.
72. BGen John R. DeBarr intvw, 2Oct86, Tape 6491 (Oral HistColl, MCHC), hereafter DeBarr intvw II.
73. Col Henry Hoppe III ltr to author, dtd 27Mar87 (Hoppe folder, Marines and Military Law in Vietnam file, MCHC), hereafter Hoppe ltr.
74. DeBarr intvw II.
75. U.S. Court of Military Appeals, *Annual Report of the United States Court of Military Appeals and the Judge Advocates General of the Armed Forces and the General Counsel of the Department of the Transportation, For the Period January 1, 1969, to December 31, 1969* (Washington: Government Printing Office, 1970), p. 28.
76. Gen William C. Westmoreland, USA, and MajGen George S. Prugh, USA, *Judges in Command: The Judicialized Uniform Code of Military Justice in Combat*, 3 Harvard *Journal of Law and Public Policy* 4 (1980), 1-93, at 60.
77. Parks ltr; and Court-Martial Order, case of U.S. v. Pvt. Jimmie Dunbar, dtd 31Jan69 (Parks folder, Marines and Military Law in Vietnam file, MCHC).
78. Barnes ltr, with copies of 12 written statements.
79. Trial counsel ltr to CO 3d Shore Party Bn, 3d MarDiv; Subj: SpCM, case of LCpl Richard E. Eicholtz—result of trial (Barnes folder, Marines and Military Law in Vietnam file, MCHC).

Exits: Marine Corps Draws Downs

80. *Marines in Vietnam Anthology*, Simmons, "Marine Corps Operations in Vietnam, 1969-1972," p. 140; and LtGen Henry W. Buse, Jr., Pacific Operations Presentation, HQMC, General Officer's Symposium, 1969, tab M, p. 7.
81. 3d MarDiv ComdCs, Oct-Dec69 (Unit Command Chronology file, MCHC).
82. Col Benjamin B. Ferrell ltr to author, dtd 2Jan87 (Ferrell folder, Marines and Military Law in Vietnam file, MCHC).
83. LtCol Michael J. Levin ltr to author, dtd 17Mar89 (Comment folder, Marines and Military Law in Vietnam file, MCHC).
84. Ibid.
85. BGen Max G. Halliday intvw, 13Oct86, Tape 6490 (Oral HistColl, MCHC).
86. 1st Marine Aircraft Wing (Rear) History (Unit Command Chronology file, MCHC).
87. Brahms intvw.
88. Ibid.
89. *Marines in Vietnam Anthology*, Simmons, "Marine Corps Operations in Vietnam, 1969-1972," p. 142.

Perspective

90. Biographical files (RefSec, MCHC).
91. BGen Duane L. Faw ltr to author, dtd 15Jun88 (Faw folder, Marines and Military Law in Vietnam file, MCHC).
92. BGen Faw ltr to Col Robert M. Lucy, dtd 22Sep69 (Lucy folder, Marines and Military Law in Vietnam file, MCHC).
93. Ibid.
94. *Combined Lineal List of Officers on Active Duty in the Marine Corps*, 1 January 1970.
95. Buchmann intvw.
96. DeBarr intvw I.
97. BGen Homer S. Hill, General Officers' Comments, p. 2, General Officers Symposium, 1969.
98. Legal Services Study Rpt, p. 1.
99. Ibid., at CMC Decision page, appended to final page of report.
100. *The Reserve Marine*, Nov69, p. 1.
101. Legal Services Study Rpt, p. 45.

102. Col James M. Granger ltr to author, dtd 1Jun88 (Granger folder, Marines and Military Law in Vietnam file, MCHC).
103. U.S. Senate, 12 December 1969, *Congressional Record* S16572.
104. Office of Navy JAG, Code 64.2 (Case Stats folder, Marines and Military Law in Vietnam file, MCHC).
105. Truesdale intvw.
106. Barnes questionnaire.

CHAPTER 8
1970-71 PREAMBLE: DISCIPLINE IN DISARRAY

1. Gen Leonard F. Chapman, Jr., Opening address, HQMC General Officer's Symposium, 1970, p. 1.
2. LtGen William K. Jones. Transcript of intvw by Oral History Unit, Hist&MusDiv, HQMC, dtd 13Apr73 (Oral HistColl, MCHC), p. 40, hereafter Jones intvw.
3. Graham A. Cosmas and LtCol Terrence P. Murray, USMC, *U.S. Marines in Vietnam: Vietnamization and Redeployment, 1970-1971* (Washington: Hist&MusDiv, 1986), pp. 352-353, hereafter Cosmas and Murray, *Vietnamization and Redeployment.*
4. Clark Smith, "Marine Doves and the Baffled Brass," *The Nation*, Sep70, p. 201.
5. Michael Satchell, "The Military's New Stars," *U.S. News and World Report*, 18Apr88, p. 34.
6. NHD, NavDept, *Dictionary of American Naval Fighting Ships*, vol VI (Washington, 1976), p. 95; and David Cortright, *Soldiers in Revolt* (New York: Anchor Press/Doubleday, 1975), p. 123, hereafter Cortright, *Soldiers in Revolt.*
7. Facts On File, Inc., *Facts On File Yearbook, 1971* (New York, 1972), p. 388; and Cortright, *Soldiers in Revolt*, p. 130.
8. Gen Paul X. Kelley intvw, 30Sep87, Tape 6477 (Oral HistColl, MCHC), hereafter Kelley intvw.

Civilians at Courts-Martial: Latney Reversed

9. Latney v. Ignatius, 416 F2d 821 (CA DC Cir, 1969).
10. Faw intvw.
11. Prugh, *Law At War*, p. 109, where Averette's first name is mistakenly noted as William.
12. United States v. Averette, 19 USCMA 363, 41 CMR 363 (1970).
13. *United States Military Assistance Command, Vietnam, Command History, 1970, Vol II* (MACV Cmd Histories folder, Marines and Military Law in Vietnam file, MCHC), p. XII-17.
14. Prugh, *Law At War*, p. 110-111.

Fragging: Killers in Our Midst

15. BGen Edwin H. Simmons, Vietnam service debriefing to CG FMFPac, dtd 24May71; and Command Information Notebook, 1st MarDiv, FMF, Republic of Vietnam, dtd 10Apr71 (Command Info Notebook folder, Marines and Military Law in Vietnam file, MCHC), p. 4 and p. 24, respectively; hereafter Simmons Vietnam Debriefing, and Command Information Notebook, respectively.
16. Command Information Notebook, p. 24. Twenty-nine of the 47 incidents occurred in or near the Da Nang/Division CP area; 18 occurred in forward areas. Nine of the 42 casualties were officers, nine were SNCOs, and 24 were sergeants or below, including 11 corporals and four PFCs. Those wounded were not always the intended victims.
17. Command Information Notebook, p. 6.

From a Lawyer's Case File: Criminal-Criminologist

18. Except where otherwise noted, all descriptions are from: CMC (JAM) first endorsement on NC&PB ltr 5800 NC&PB:401 of 23Oct86 to Exec Secretary, Naval Clemency and Parol Board, Subj: Progress Reports In Certain General Court-Martial Cases, dtd 6Nov86; Philip C. Tower questionnaire to author, dtd 18Nov86 (Tower folder, Marines and Military Law in Vietnam file, MCHC); and 1st MarDiv, BGen Edwin H. Simmons Orientation Talk, dtd 10Jan71 (Command Info Notebook folder, Marines and Military Law in Vietnam file, MCHC), p. 24-26, hereafter Simmons Orientation Talk; and Marine Corps Casualty Reports (RefSec, MCHC).
19. Kelley intvw.

Drugs: Marijuana and More

20. *New York Times*, 5Sep71, p. 36.
21. MajGen Alan J. Armstrong debriefing at FMFPac, 29Jun71, Tape 5010 (Oral HistColl, MCHC), cited in Cosmas and Murray, *Vietnamization and Redeployment*, p. 359, hereafter Armstrong debriefing.
22. Capt Jerry K. Taylor intvw, 29Mar71, Tape 4997 (Oral HistColl, MCHC).
23. LtGen William K. Jones, CG FMFPac Presentation, HQMC, General Officers Symposium, 1972, tab M, p. 23.
24. Cosmas and Murray, *Vietnamization and Redeployment*, p. 360.
25. MajGen Alan J. Armstrong. Transcript of intvw by Oral History Unit, Hist&MusDiv, HQMC, dtd 2Oct73 (Oral HistColl, MCHC), p. 48, hereafter Armstrong transcript.
26. United States Military Assistance Command, Vietnam, Command History, 1970, Vol II, p. XII-4.
27. CG III MAF msg to CG FMFPac, dtd 11Sep70 (Command Concerns folder, Marines and Military Law in Vietnam file, MCHC).
28. Simmons Orientation Talk, p. 14.
29. Prugh, *Law At War*, p. 108.
30. LtCol Carl E. Buchmann intvw, 26Feb70, Tape 4751 (Oral HistColl, MCHC).
31. Colonel Robert D. Heinl, Jr., "The Collapse of the Armed Forces," *Armed Forces Journal*, 7Jun71, p. 34.
32. LtGen Leo J. Dulacki. Transcript of intvw by Oral History Unit, Hist&MusDiv, HQMC, dtd 24Oct74 (Oral HistColl, MCHC), p. 106.
33. Simmons Orientation Talk, p. 14.
34. Armstrong debriefing, p. 360; and Armstrong transcript, p. 46.
35. Cosmas and Murray, *Vietnamization and Redeployment*, pp. 360-361.
36. Ibid., p. 361.
37. The DOD-wide amnesty program was not a successful approach, either. The Chief of Staff of XXIV Corps wrote to the Chief of Staff of USARV LBN RVN, "The amnesty program, or promise of immunity does not bring on a rush of volunteers . . . . While the response varies from unit to unit, it can be categorized as minimal." (MajGen W. E. Shedd, USA, msg to MajGen V. L. Bowers, USA, dtd 15Aug70 (Case Stats folder, Marines and Military Law in Vietnam file, MCHC), hereafter: Shedd to Bowers msg.
38. Capt George H. O'Kelley, Jr., ltr to author, dtd 12Sep86 (O'Kelley folder, Marines and Military Law in Vietnam file, MCHC).

Racial Conflict: High Tension

39. United States Military Assistance Command, Vietnam, Command History, 1971, Volume II, p. x-9.

40. MajGen Edwin B. Wheeler, Manpower, G-1 Presentation, HQMC, General Officers Symposium, 1971, tab E, p. 40, hereafter Wheeler, Manpower Presentation.
41. Capt George H. O'Kelley, Jr., ltr to author, dtd 16May88 (O'Kelley folder, Marines and Military Law in Vietnam file, MCHC).
42. Dept of Defense, "Race Relations in the U.S. Marine Corps," *Commanders Digest*, 30Nov72, p. 8; and Col Robert M. Lucy memo to 1st MarDiv chief of staff, dtd 6Nov69 (Lucy folder, Marines and Military Law in Vietnam file, MCHC). Note that court-martial statistics were not kept by race and the 50 percent figure was only Col Lucy's estimate.
43. CG FLC ltr 2/FRW/dwe 5500 of 8Oct69, referred to in Supply Bn Subversive Activities Report, dtd 16Aug70 (Command Concerns folder, Marines and Military Law in Vietnam file, MCHC).
44. Simmons Orientation Talk, p. 11.
45. Ibid., pp. 11-12.
46. Jones intvw, p. 84-85.
47. Wheeler, Manpower Presentation, p. 40.
48. Command Information Notebook, p. 6.

Administrative Discharge: The Marines Clean House

49. SgtMaj Edgar R. Huff. Transcript of intvw by Oral History Unit, HistDiv, HQMC, dtd 27Jun72 (Oral HistColl, MCHC), pp. 176-177.
50. MajGen Wheeler, Manpower Presentation, p. 29.
51. *New York Times*, 5Sep71, p. 36.
52. United States Military Assistance Command, Vietnam, Command History, 1970, Vol II, pp. XII-2 – XII-4.
53. Col Robert M. Lucy debriefing at FMFPac, 24Jun70, Tape 4814 (Oral HistColl, MCHC), hereafter Lucy debriefing.
54. Jones intvw, p. 42.
55. Gen Leonard F. Chapman, Jr., CMC's introductory remarks to HQMC, General Officers Symposium, 1970, p. 21.
56. U.S. Marine Corps, *Report on Marine Corps Manpower Quality and Force Structure*, dtd 31Dec75, pp. 18-19 (Report on Manpower folder, Marines and Military Law in Vietnam file, MCHC); and Cosmas and Murray, *Vietnamization and Redeployment*, p. 363.
57. Shedd to Bowers msg.
58. Simmons Vietnam Debriefing, p. 2.
59. Tiernan intvw.
60. BGen Tiernan ltr to author (Comment folder, Marines and Military Law in Vietnam file, MCHC), hereafter Tiernan ltr.
61. Tiernan intvw.
62. Tiernan ltr.
63. Col James M. Granger ltr to author, dtd 1Jun88 (Granger folder, Marines and Military Law in Vietnam file, MCHC), p. 5.
64. LtGen Victor H. Krulak. Transcript of intvw by Oral History Unit, HistDiv, HQMC, dtd 20Jun70 (Oral HistColl, MCHC), pp. 135-136.

From a Lawyer's Case File: Homicide on Patrol

65. CG 1st MarDiv msg to CG III MAF, dtd 20Feb70 (Son Thang [4] folder, Marines and Military Law in Vietnam file, MCHC).
66. Lucy debriefing.
67. Ibid. (Col Lehnert made his remarks in introducing Col Lucy to the debriefing audience.)
68. Record of trial, United States v. Pvt Michael A. Schwarz, NCM 71 0028; 45 CMR 852 (NCMR, 1971). Since Krichten was granted immunity and Herrod and Boyd were found not guilty the only verbatim records of trial were those of Green and Schwarz. The Green record has been lost, checked out from the government repository in December 1976 and never returned. All exhibits from the Schwarz record of trial, including his critical initial written statements and the photos of the victims taken the morning after the events, are missing from his record of trial, as are the last 32 pages of the record itself. (Copies of the missing statements are included in the record of the Article 32 investigation.)
69. Jack Shulimson, *U.S. Marines in Vietnam: An Expanding War, 1966* (Washington: Hist&Mus Div, 1982), p. 283n.
70. LtGen Charles G. Cooper ltr to author, dtd 23Jan89 (Comment folder, Marines and Military Law in Vietnam file, MCHC), hereafter Cooper Jan89 ltr.
71. Cooper Jan89 ltr.
72. Ibid.
73. LtGen Charles G. Cooper ltr to author, dtd 12Sep88 (Cooper folder, Marines and Military Law in Vietnam file, MCHC), hereafter Cooper Sep88 ltr.
74. LtCol Richard E. Theer ltr to author, dtd 24Feb89 (Theer folder, Marines and Military Law in Vietnam file, MCHC), p. 6, hereafter Theer ltr.
75. Record of trial, United States v. Pvt Michael A. Schwarz, NCM 71 0029, 45 CMR 852 (NMCR, 1971), pp. 370-371, hereafter U.S. v. Schwarz.
76. Cooper Sep88 ltr.
77. CG 1st MarDiv msg to CMC, dtd 1Mar70 (Son Thang [4] folder, Marines and Military Law in Vietnam file, MCHC, Washington); and FMFPac Awards Alpha Roster, dtd 24Aug77, Book 2 of 4, n.p. (MCHC).
78. Cooper Sep88 ltr.
79. U.S. v. Schwarz, p. 348.
80. Verbatim record of joint Article 32 investigation, cases of Pvt R. D. Herrod, PFC T. R. Boyd, PFC S. G. Green, LCpl M. S. Krichten, and Pvt M. A. Schwarz; testimony of Sgt H. E. Meyers, pp. 549-550. A partial copy of the Article 32 record is included. (Blum folder, Marines and Military Law in Vietnam file, MCHC). Except where otherwise noted, all subsequent quotes, extracts from the record, and descriptions are from this document; hereafter Son Thang (4) Article 32.
81. Ibid.
82. United States v. PFC Samuel G. Green, Jr., NCM 70 3811; 21 USCMA 609 (24,527).
83. U.S. v. Schwarz, p. 287.
84. Ibid., pp. 406-407.
85. Ibid., p. 290.
86. Ibid., pp. 408-409.
87. Ibid., p. 294.
88. Ibid., pp. 411-412.
89. Ibid., p. 295.
90. Son Thang (4) Article 32, pp. 50, 60-61; and U.S. v. Schwarz, p. 50.
91. U.S. v. Schwarz, p. 185.
92. 1/7 ComdC, Feb70 (Unit Command Chronology file, MCHC).
93. Theer ltr, p. 6.
94. An account of a 1966 patrol led by then-Captain Theer is related in a *Readers Digest* feature book condensation by Andrew Jones, "Where Do We Get Such Men?," *Readers Digest*, Sep85, pp. 216-218.
95. Son Thang (4) Article 32, p. 216.
96. Theer ltr, p. 8.
97. Son Thang (4) Article 32, p. 190.
98. Ibid., p. 190.
99. Ibid., p. 232.

100. Ibid., pp. 327-328.
101. Ibid., statement of Pvt Schwarz, dtd 23Feb70, Investigation Exhibit 47.
102. CG 1st MarDiv msg to CMC, dtd 28Feb70 (Son Thang [4] folder, Marines and Military Law in Vietnam file, MCHC).
103. Associated Press, in *Los Angeles Times*, 27Feb70; and *Washington Post*, 28Feb70.
104. CG 1st MarDiv msg to CMC, dtd 4Mar70 (Son Thang [4] folder, Marines and Military Law in Vietnam file, MCHC); and Lucy debriefing.
105. CG 1st MarDiv msg to CMC, dtd 6Mar70 (Son Thang [4] folder, Marines and Military Law in Vietnam file, MCHC).
106. Col Max G. Halliday, Head, Military Law Branch, JAD, ltr to Mrs. Kenneth D. Coffin, dtd 19Mar70, cited in Cosmas and Murray, *Vietnamization and Redeployment*, p. 347.
107. CG 1st MarDiv msg to CMC, dtd 20May70 (Son Thang [4] folder, Marines and Military Law in Vietnam file, MCHC).
108. CG 1st MarDiv msgs to CMC, dtd 31Mar70, 8Apr70, 19Apr70, and 15May70 (Son Thang [4] folder, Marines and Military Law in Vietnam file, MCHC).
109. UPI in *Pacific Stars and Stripes*, 21May70, p. 6.
110. CG 1st MarDiv msg to CMC, dtd 26May70 (Son Thang [4] folder, Marines and Military Law in Vietnam file, MCHC).
111. Son Thang (4) Article 32, p. 142.
112. *Pacific Stars and Stripes*, 1Mar70, p. 6.
113. Col Robert J. Blum ltr to author, dtd 2Mar89 (Blum folder, Marines and Military Law in Vietnam file, MCHC).
114. *Pacific Stars and Stripes*, 2Mar70.
115. United States v. Pvt Michael A. Schwarz, 45 CMR 852 (NCMR, 1971).
116. Ibid.
117. *Los Angeles Times*, 22Jun70.
118. James H. Webb, "The Sad Conviction Of Sam Green: The Case for the Reasonable and Honest War Criminal," *Res Ipsa Loquitur; Georgetown Review of Law and Public Interest*, Vol. 26, No. 1, Winter, 1974, p. 11, hereafter Webb, "The Sad Conviction of Sam Green."
119. *Pacific Stars and Stripes*, 24Jun70.
120. United States v. PFC Samuel G. Green, Jr., NCM 70 3811, 21 USCMA 609 (#24,527).
121. Record of trial, United States v. Pvt Randell D. Herrod, NCM 70 2970.
122. Denzil D. Garrison ltr to author, dtd 22Aug88 (Garrison folder, Marines and Military Law in Vietnam file, MCHC), hereafter Garrison ltr.
123. Lewy, *America in Vietnam*, p. 356; and Webb, "The Sad Conviction of Sam Green," p. 12.
124. CG 1stMarDiv msg to CMC, dtd 7Mar70 (Son Thang [4] folder, Marines and Military Law in Vietnam file, MCHC).
125. LtCol Paul J. Laveroni ltr to author, dtd 1Oct87 (Laveroni folder, Marines and Military Law in Vietnam file, MCHC), hereafter Laveroni ltr.
126. Cooper Sep88 ltr.
127. Garrison ltr.
128. Theer ltr, p. 9.
129. Theer ltr, p. 12.
130. Ben Bradlee, Jr., *Guts and Glory: The Rise and Fall of Oliver North* (New York: Donald I. Fine, Inc., 1988), p. 92.
131. Quoted in Robert Timberg, "The Private War of Ollie and Jim," *Esquire*, Mar88, p. 144, at 152, hereafter Timberg, "The Private War of Ollie and Jim."
132. Laveroni ltr.
133. Col Peter N. Kress ltr to author, dtd 24Jan89 (Comment folder, Marines and Military Law in Vietnam file, MCHC).
134. *Washington Post*, 23Dec86, p. D1.
135. United States v. Pvt Michael A. Schwarz, 45 CMR 852 (NCMR, 1971).
136. United States v. PFC Samuel G. Green, Jr., unpublished NCMR opinion, decided 19May71; 21 USCMA 609 (#24,527).
137. Webb, "The Sad Conviction of Sam Green," p. 13.
138. Hon. James H. Webb, Jr., telephone conversation with author, 3Jan89 (Memorandum for the record, General Correspondence folder, Marines and Military Law in Vietnam file, MCHC).
139. Timberg, "The Private War of Ollie and Jim," p. 152.
140. *New York Times*, 25May71, p. 13.

CHAPTER 9
1970-71: REDEPLOYMENT

1. Cosmas and Murray, *Vietnamization and Redeployment*, pp. 15-20, 88.
2. III MAF and FLC ComdC, Jan-Mar70 (Unit Command Chronology File, MCHC).

Force Logistic Command: Playing Catch-up

3. Col Arthur R. Petersen ltr to Col Robert C. Lehnert, SJA, FMFPac, dtd 3Jun70 (Petersen folder, Marines and Military Law in Vietnam folder, MCHC), hereafter Petersen-Lehnert ltr.
4. W. Mark Wood intvw, 27Jul88, Tape 6496 (Oral HistColl, MCHC); hereafter Wood intvw.
5. Col Arthur R. Petersen affidavit, dtd 4Apr70 (Petersen folder, Marines and Military Law in Vietnam file, MCHC), hereafter Petersen affidavit. This unusual and revealing document was prepared to explain the circumstances prevailing in FLC upon Col Petersen's arrival as SJA. It appears to have been prompted by complaints of appellate counsel concerning delays in FLC's processing of cases. Such delays were legitimate grounds for appellate defense attack.
6. FLC ComdC, Sep69-Dec70 (Unit Command Chronology file, MCHC).
7. Wood intvw.
8. Petersen-Lehnert ltr.
9. Ibid.
10. Ibid.
11. Petersen affidavit.
12. Cosmas and Murray, *Vietnamization and Redeployment*, p. 192.
13. FLC ComdC, Jul70-Mar71 (Unit Command Chronology file, MCHC).
14. Col Daniel F. McConnell ltr to author, dtd 25Jan89 (Comment folder, Marines and Military Law in Vietnam file, MCHC).

From a Lawyer's Case File: The Defense Wins Four

15. *New York Times*, 8Feb70, p. 2, and 9Feb70, p. 12; *Pacific Stars and Stripes*, 25May70; and Capt George H. O'Kelley ltr to author, dtd 12Sep86 (O'Kelley folder, Marines and Military Law in Vietnam file, MCHC).
16. *New York Times*, 9Feb70, p. 12.
17. *Pacific Stars and Stripes*, 25May70.
18. Verbatim record of joint Article 32 investigation; cases of Cpl Ronald E. Gales, LCpl Joseph L. Jones III, LCpl James B. Addison, and LCpl Andrew M. Harris, Jr., hereafter Joint Article 32.

NOTES

19. Ibid.
20. Joint Article 32; Capt George H. O'Kelley ltrs to author, dtd 12Sep86, 16May88, and 9Jun88 (O'Kelley folder, Marines and Military Law in Vietnam file, MCHC); and Wood intvw.
21. Record of trial, United States v. LCpl James B. Addison, NCM 70 2433.
22. Ibid., appellate exhibit 5.
23. Wood intvw.
24. Ibid.

1st Marine Aircraft Wing: Prepared For Takeoff

25. Cosmas and Murray, *Vietnamization and Redeployment*, pp. 11, 15, 95, 192.
26. Col Curtis W. Olson questionnaire to Maj W. Hays Parks, dtd Dec76 (Olson folder, Marines and Military Law in Vietnam file, MCHC).
27. Col Olson questionnaire to author, dtd 27Oct86 (Olson folder, Marines and Military Law in Vietnam file, MCHC).

1st Marine Division: New Broom

28. Cosmas and Murray, *Vietnamization and Redeployment*, p. 27.
29. Col Robert M. Lucy ltr to Col Robert C. Lehnert, dtd 23Dec69 (Lucy folder, Marines and Military Law in Vietnam file, MCHC).
30. BGen James P. King intvw, 5Nov86, Tape 6478 (Oral HistColl, MCHC).
31. Col Lucy ltr to Col John R. DeBarr, n.d. (Lucy folder, Marines and Military Law in Vietnam file, MCHC).
32. 1st MarDiv ComdC, Jun70 (Unit Command Chronology file, MCHC).
33. Col James M. Granger ltr to author, dtd 1Jun88 (Granger folder, Marines and Military Law in Vietnam file, MCHC), hereafter Granger ltr.
34. Ibid.
35. Col James M. Granger ltr to BGen Edwin H. Simmons, dtd 24Jan89 (Comment folder, Marines and Military Law in Vietnam file, MCHC).
36. Gen William C. Westmoreland, USA, and MajGen George S. Prugh, USA, *Judges in Command: The Judicialized Uniform Code of Military Justice in Combat*, 3 Harvard *Journal of Law and Public Policy* 4 (1980), 1-93, at 60; hereafter Westmoreland and Prugh, *Judges in Command*.
37. FMFPac Awards Alpha Roster, dtd 24Aug77, Books 1, 2, and 3 of 4, n.p., MCHC.
38. Col Donald E. Holben intvw, 13Oct86, Tape 6472 (Oral HistColl, MCHC), hereafter Holben intvw.
39. Ibid.
40. Ibid.
41. Capt Mario A. Gomez intvw, 10Oct86, Tape 6488 (Oral HistColl, MCHC), hereafter Gomez intvw.
42. Holben intvw.
43. Ibid.; and Kress intvw.
44. Holben intvw.
45. Ibid.
46. Maj Stephen C. Berg questionnaire to Maj W. Hays Parks, dtd 5Jan77 (Berg folder, Marines and Military Law in Vietnam file, MCHC), hereafter Berg questionnaire.
47. Capt Keith D. Lawrence, JAGC, USN, ltr to author, dtd 16Feb89 (Lawrence folder, Marines and Military Law in Vietnam file, MCHC).
48. Tower ltr.
49. Ibid.
50. Holben intvw.
51. Cosmas and Murray, *Vietnamization and Redeployment*, pp. 108-109.
52. Granger ltr.
53. Col Donald E. Holben ltr to BGen Edwin H. Simmons, dtd 16Feb89 (Comment folder, Marines and Military Law in Vietnam file, MCHC), hereafter Holben ltr.
54. Col Peter N. Kress ltr to author, dtd 24Jan89 (Comment folder, Marines and Military Law in Vietnam file, MCHC), hereafter Kress ltr.
55. Granger ltr.

Trying Cases

56. Ibid.
57. MajGen Jonas M. Platt, Manpower, G-1 Presentation, HQMC, General Officers Symposium, 1969, Tab E, p. 19.
58. Gen Leonard F. Chapman, Jr., opening remarks, HQMC, General Officers Symposium, 1970, p. 20.
59. LtCol Carl E. Buchmann intvw, 26Feb70, Tape 4751 (Oral HistColl, MCHC), hereafter Buchmann intvw.
60. Col Lucy ltr to BGen Duane L. Faw, dtd 22Nov69 (Lucy folder, Marines and Military Law in Vietnam file, MCHC).
61. U.S. Court of Military Appeals, *Annual Report of the United States Court of Military Appeals and the Judge Advocates General of the Armed Forces and the General Counsel of the Department of Transportation, For the Period January 1, to December 31, 1971*, and, (same title) . . . , *For the Period January 1, to December 31, 1972* (Washington: Government Printing Office, 1972 and 1973), pp. 27 and 29, respectively.
62. Buchmann intvw.
63. Col Petersen ltrs to BGen Faw, dtd 15 and 25Jun70 (Petersen folder, Marines and Military Law in Vietnam file, MCHC).
64. Col Lucy ltr to Capt B. R. Perkins, JAGC, USN, dtd 9Jun70 (Lucy folder, Marines and Military Law in Vietnam file, MCHC).
65. Col Petersen ltr to Capt Perkins, dtd 14Jun70 (Petersen folder, Marines and Military Law in Vietnam file, MCHC).
66. Holben ltr.
67. CG 1st MarDiv ltr to Navy JAG, Subj: Performance of duty as Military Judge of Lieutenant Colonel Henry Hoppe III, dtd 14May70 (Granger folder, Marines and Military Law in Vietnam file, MCHC).
68. FMFPac Awards Alpha Roster, dtd 24Aug77, Book 2 of 4, n.p., MCHC.
69. Col Robert J. Blum questionnaire to Maj W. Hays Parks, dtd 24Jan77 (Blum folder, Marines and Military Law in Vietnam file, MCHC).
70. U.S. Court of Military Appeals, *Annual Report of the United States Court of Military Appeals and the Judge Advocates General of the Armed Forces and the General Counsel of the Department of Transportation, For the Period January 1, to December 31, 1969*, and (same title) . . . , *For the Period January 1, to December 31, 1970*, pp. 28 and 27, respectively.
71. O'Kelley ltr.
72. Col W. Hays Parks, USMCR, ltr to author, dtd 22Dec88 (Parks folder, Marines and Military Law in Vietnam file, MCHC).
73. United States Military Assistance Command, Vietnam, Command History, 1970, Vol II, p. XII-1.
74. Col Lucy debriefing at FMFPac, 24Jun70, Tape 4814 (Oral HistColl, MCHC).
75. Col John R. DeBarr debriefing at FMFPac, 9Jun69, Tape 4254 (Oral HistColl, MCHC).

76. Col Petersen ltr to author, dtd 11Jul88 (Petersen folder, Marines and Military Law in Vietnam file, MCHC).
77. Holben intvw.; and Cosmas and Murray, *Vietnamization and Redeployment*, p. 250.
78. LtCol Paul J. Laveroni ltr to author, dtd 2Oct87 (Laveroni folder, Marines and Military Law in Vietnam file, MCHC), hereafter Laveroni ltr.
79. Ibid.
80. Col Edwin W. Welch questionnaire to author, dtd 18Sep86 (Welch folder, Marines and Military Law in Vietnam file, MCHC); and O'Kelley ltr.
81. Col Robert D. Heinl, Jr., "The Collapse of The Armed Forces," *Armed Forces Journal*, 7Jun71, p. 32.
82. Col Eileen M. Albertson intvw, 2Dec86, Tape 6498 (Oral HistColl, MCHC).
83. O'Kelley ltr.

Last Call For Combat

84. Col Lucy ltr to ADC, 1st MarDiv, dtd 26Apr70 (Lucy folder, Marines and Military Law in Vietnam file, MCHC).
85. Capt W. Hays Parks Navy Commendation Medal citation, n.d. (Granger folder, Marines and Military Law in Vietnam file, MCHC).
86. Capt Robert M. MacConnell Navy Commendation Medal citation, n.d. (Granger folder, Marines and Military Law in Vietnam file, MCHC).
87. Capt Raymond T. Bonner Navy Achievement Medal citation, n.d. (Granger folder, Marines and Military Law in Vietnam file, MCHC).

Closing Cases Versus Best Defense

88. Maj Stephen C. Berg questionnaire to Maj Parks, dtd 5Jan77 (Berg folder, Marines and Military Law in Vietnam file, MCHC).
89. 3/7 ComdC, Aug70 (Unit Command Chronology file, MCHC); and Cosmas and Murray, *Vietnamization and Redeployment*, p. 350.
90. CG 1st MarDiv msg to CG FMFPac, dtd 18Aug70 (1st MarDiv msg files, MCHC).
91. CG 1st MarDiv msg to CG FMFPac, dtd 29Aug70 (1st MarDiv msg files, MCHC).
92. DD Form 458, Charge Sheet; case of Sgt Adrian Aragon. Sgt Aragon's and Cpl Anderson's records of trial have both been lost. A copy of Sgt Aragon's charge sheet is available (Grant folder, Marines and Military Law in Vietnam file, MCHC).
93. CG 1st MarDiv msg to CG FMFPac, dtd 19Aug70 (1st MarDiv msg files, MCHC).
94. The description of events surrounding the cases and the events that followed, except where otherwise indicated, are from: LtCol Paul J. Laveroni ltr to author, dtd 1Oct87; Tone N. Grant, ltrs to author, dtd 11May88 and 22Jul88; and Col Edwin W. Welch ltr to author, dtd 16Feb87 (Laveroni, Grant, and Welch folders, respectively, Marines and Military Law in Vietnam file, MCHC); and Holben intvw.
95. Holben intvw.
96. Westmoreland and Prugh, *Judges in Command*, p. 34.
97. BGen James P. King intvw, 5Nov86, Tape 6478 (Oral HistColl, MCHC).
98. Holben ltr.
99. SJA ltr to Asst Chief of Staff, G-4, 1st MarDiv, Subj: Letter of continuity, case of Capt Tone N. Grant, dtd 23Feb71 (Grant folder, Marines and Military Law in Vietnam file, MCHC).

100. LtCol Paul J. Laveroni ltr to author, dtd 1Oct87 (Laveroni folder, Marines and Military Law in Vietnam file, MCHC).
101. Holben ltr.
102. LtCol Paul J. Laveroni ltr to author, dtd 30Jan89 (Comment folder); and Maj Berg questionnaire to Maj Parks, dtd 5Jan77 (Berg folder) (Both Comment and Berg folders in Marines and Military Law in Vietnam file, MCHC).

The Last Marine Lawyer Out

103. Office of the Judge Advocate General of the Navy, Code 64.2 (Case Stats folder, Marines and Military Law in Vietnam file, MCHC).
104. Cosmas and Murray, *Vietnamization and Redeployment*, pp. 211-213.
105. Kress ltr.
106. Ibid., pp. 190, 235, 238.
107. Col Curtis W. Olson ltr to author, dtd 9Jan87 (Olson folder, Marines and Military Law in Vietnam file, MCHC); and 3d MAB's "Final ComdC of 1st MAW," dtd 25May71 (Unit Command Chronology file, MCHC).
108. Granger ltr; and Kress intvw.
109. MajGen Alan J. Armstrong. Transcript of intvw by Oral History Unit, Hist&MusDiv, HQMC, dtd 25Sep73 (Oral HistColl, MCHC), pp. 8-9.
110. Col Daniel F. McConnell questionnaire to author, dtd 16Sep86 (McConnell folder, Marines and Military Law in Vietnam file, MCHC).
111. Cosmas and Murray, *Vietnamization and Redeployment*, p. 246.
112. Ibid., p. 240-241, 243.
113. Ibid., p. 236; and 1st MarDiv ComdC, 14Apr-30Jun71 (Unit Command Chronology file, MCHC).
114. Holben intvw.
115. Kress intvw; and Kress ltr.
116. Granger ltr.
117. Kress intvw.
118. Granger ltr.
119. Ibid.
120. Holben intvw; and Holben ltr.
121. Gomez intvw.
122. Cosmas and Murray, *Vietnamization and Redeployment*, pp. 246, 369.
123. Ibid
124. Cosmas and Murry, *Vietnamization and Redeployment*, pp. 246, 369.
125. Guenter Lewy, *America in Vietnam* (New York: Oxford University Press, 1978), p. 159.
126. Tower ltr.

Perspective

127. *Combined Lineal List of Officers on Active Duty in the Marine Corps*, 1 January 1971.
128. BGen Harvey E. Spielman, Education and Transition Presentation, HQMC, General Officers Symposium, 1972, tab V, pp. 4-5.
129. U.S. Court of Military Appeals, Joint Report of the U.S. C.O.M.A. and the JAGs of the Armed Forces and the General Counsel of the Dept. of Transportation, *Annual Report of the United States Court of Military Appeals and the Judge Advocate Generals of the Armed Forces and the General Counsel of the Department of Transportation, For the Period January 1, 1972 to December 31,*

NOTES

1972 (Washington: Government Printing Office, 1973), p. 3.
130. Kelley intvw.

PART IV
Aftermath and Echoes

CHAPTER 10
PRISONERS OF WAR, AND OTHERS

1. Director, OSD Historical Office ltr to BGen Edwin H. Simmons, dtd 29Dec88 (Comment folder, Marines and Military Law in Vietnam file, MCHC).
2. USAF, *13th Air Force Joint Homecoming Reception Center (JHRC) After Action Report* (POW folder, Marines and Military Law in Vietnam file, MCHC).
3. BGen David M. Brahms intvw, 2Dec86, Tape 6494 (Oral Hist-Coll, MCHC), hereafter Brahms intvw.
4. DOD, "Prisoner of War Return Underway," *Commanders Digest*, March 1, 1973, p. 2.
5. Col Richard G. Moore Certificate of Commendation, dtd 2Dec75 (POW folder, Marines and Military Law in Vietnam file, MCHC).
6. CG III MAF, "Homecoming Marine, Phase II After Action Report, 13 Dec 1972-6 Apr 1973," dtd 5Apr73 (POW folder, Marines and Military Law in Vietnam file, MCHC).
7. Brahms intvw.

Prisoner Misconduct: Charges

8. *The Washington Post*, 9Feb81, p. A13.
9. MajGen George S. Prugh, USA, ltr to BGen Edwin H. Simmons, dtd 29Dec88 (Comment folder, Marines and Military Law in Vietnam file, MCHC).
10. Office of the Judge Advocate General of the Navy. Memorandum for the Record, dtd 4Jun73 (POW folder, Marines and Military Law in Vietnam file, MCHC). Maj Brahms was not present at this particular meeting. Those present were: Secretary of the Navy Warner; Secretary of the Army Callaway; Acting General Counsel, DoD, Leonard Niederlehner; Asst General Counsel, DOD, Frank Bartimo; General Counsel, Dept of the Army, Robert Berry; Asst JAG of the Army, MajGen Parker; Dep JAG of the Navy, RAdm Robertson; Acting DirJAD, Col John R. DeBarr, USMC; Col Charles Keever, USMC; and Special Counsel to SecNav, Cmdr Lynch, JAGC, USN.
11. Brahms intvw.
12. Office of the Judge Advocate General of the Navy. Memorandum for the Secretary of the Navy, Subj: Court-martial charges against three enlisted Marine ex-POWs, dtd 22Jun73 (POW folder, Marines and Military Law in Vietnam file, MCHC).
12. Director, Judge Advocate Division memo to Acting Commandant of the Marine Corps, Subj: POW Discipline Cases, dtd 5Jul73 (POW folder, Marines and Military Law in Vietnam file, MCHC).
14. Affidavit of Capt Thomas P. Coffey at 3, Miller v Lehman (U.S. Ct. of Appeals, D.C., No. 85-5328)(POW folder, Marines and Military Law in Vietnam file, MCHC).
15. Brahms intvw.
16. Gen Earl E. Anderson ltr to author, dtd 22Feb89 (Anderson folder, Marines and Military Law in Vietnam file, MCHC); hereafter Anderson ltr.
17. BGen John R. DeBarr ltr to author, dtd 25Jan89 (Comment folder, Marines and Military Law in Vietnam file, MCHC).

18. Anderson ltr.
19. Cited at 3, Miller v. Lehman, No. 85-5328 (U.S. Ct of Appeals for D.C., 19Sep86).
20. Brahms intvw.
21. Miller v. Lehman, 603 F. Supp. 164 (D.C. Cir. 1985).
22. Miller v. Lehman, 801 F.2d 492 (D.C. Cir. 1986).
23. HQMC routing sheet on Navy JAG ltr to VAdm James B. Stockdale, dtd 27Aug87 (POW folder, Marines and Military Law in Vietnam file, MCHC).
24. Draft Dep Asst Navy JAG memo to "Distribution List," Subj: File Materials on Colonel Edison W. Miller, n.d. (POW folder, Marines and Military Law in Vietnam file, MCHC).
25. Brahms intvw.

From a Lawyer's Case File: Wartime Acts, Post-War Trial

26. Col Elliott R. Laine, Jr., summary of intvw to author, dtd 16Mar87 (Laine folder, Marines and Military Law in Vietnam file, MCHC).
27. Record of trial, United States v. Sgt Jon M. Sweeney, NCM 71 2662.
28. United States Military Assistance Command, Vietnam, Command History, 1970, Vol II, p. X-35.
29. DepDir of Personnel route sheet to Asst Chief of Staff, G-1, Subj: Briefing of father of Sgt J. M. Sweeney, dtd 26Aug70 (Sweeney folder, Marines and Military Law in Vietnam file, MCHC).
30. JAD (Code AI) Comments dtd 4Nov71 to Screening Bd Recommendation; case of PFC Garwood, dtd 6Jan72 (Sweeney folder, Marines and Military Law in Vietnam file, MCHC).
31. VAdm James B. Stockdale, USN, *A Vietnam Experience: Ten Years of Reflection* (Stanford: Hoover Institution, 1984), p. 124.
32. Col Benjamin B. Ferrell ltr to BGen Edwin H. Simmons, dtd 21Feb89 (Comment folder, Marines and Military Law in Vietnam file, MCHC).

Deserters in the Hands of the Enemy

33. Rpt of Disposition Bd. to review the case of Pvt Earl C. Weatherman, dtd 3Jul79; JAR memo to SecNav, Subj: Pvt Earl C. Weatherman; contemplated action with respect to, n.d. (Weatherman folder, Marines and Military Law in Vietnam file, MCHC); CMC Reference Notebook-1972, Book III, tab 3-H-7, encl. (3); and U.S. Marine Corps Prisoner of War and Missing in Action Roster, HQMC (Code MP), dtd 17Oct72 (POW folder, Marines and Military Law in Vietnam file, MCHC).
34. HQMC Marine Liaison ltr to AO2A, Subj: Summary No. 27 . . . Operation HOMECOMING Intelligence Debriefs, dtd 14Mar73; and Headquarters Marine Corps (Code INT) briefing, "Experience of POWs", n.d., with transparency labeled: "Died in Captivity" (POW folder, Marines and Military Law in Vietnam file, MCHC).

White VC?: Robert R. Garwood

35. Unless otherwise noted the material relating to the capture and activities of PFC Garwood is derived from an amalgam of intelligence, administrative, and litigation sources: HQMC, "Biographic Site Rpt as of 20 Mar 1979," n.p., n.d.; "US Troops Held By VC," n.d., n.p.; 11th CI Team "Camp Location Study," dtd 22Sep71, n.p., all in JAD Garwood file; and CO, HQ Bn, 3dMarDiv msg to CMC, dtd 17Dec65; USDAU msg to JCS/DIA, dtd 12May73; Draft, Navy JAG ltr to Civil Div, Dept of Justice, n.d.; Defense Information

Report Evaluations (Bright Light rpts), dtd 2Jun71, 22Sep77; and NIS rpt of intvw of SFC Robert Lewis III, USA, dtd 2May79; copies of all of which are on file. (Garwood folder, Marines and Military Law in Vietnam file, MCHC).

36. Neil Sheehan, *A Bright Shining Lie: John Paul Vann and America in Vietnam* (New York: Random House, 1988), p. 115.

37. Enclosure to LtCol Werner Hellmer ltr to author, dtd 2Mar89 (Garwood folder, Marines and Military Law in Vietnam file, MCHC).

38. Defense Information Report Evaluation (Bright Light rpt), dtd 19Sep73; NIS rpt of intvw of SFC Robert Lewis III, USA, dtd 2May79; and USMC, Headquarters, "Biographic Site Rpt as of 20 Mar 1979," JAD Garwood file, n.p.; copies of all of which are available (Garwood folder, Marines and Military Law in Vietnam file, MCHC).

39. Monika Schwinn and Bernhard Diehl, *We Came To Help* (New York: Harcourt Brace Jovanovich, Inc., 1976), p. 86.

40. John G. Hubbell, *P.O.W.* (New York: Reader's Digest Press, 1976), p. 401.

41. E.g., Department of Defense interrogation report, dtd 14Nov68 (Garwood folder, Marines and Military Law in Vietnam file, MCHC).

42. Navy JAG draft ltr to Civil Div, Dept of Justice, n.d. (Garwood folder, Marines and Military Law in Vietnam file, MCHC).

43. NIS rpt of intvw of SFC Robert Lewis III, USA, dtd 3May79 (Garwood folder, Marines and Military Law in Vietnam file, MCHC).

44. Operation Order 305-68, Operation Houston; Patrol: Dublin City; Patrol Report dtd 15Jul68, in 1st Force Reconnaissance Co. ComdC, Jul68 (Unit Command Chronology file, MCHC).

45. 5th Mar FragO 66-68 to FragO 65-68 in 5th Mar ComdC, Jul68 (Unit Command Chronology file, MCHC).

46. 1st CIT Investigation Rpt 024-9K-68, dtd 24Jul68; and CG III MAF msg to ComUSMACV, dtd 17Jul68 (Garwood folder, Marines and Military Law in Vietnam file, MCHC).

47. Zalin Grant, *Survivors* (New York: W.W. Norton & Co., Inc., 1975), p. 149.

48. Rpt of Medical Examination, USNRMC Okinawa, dtd 25Mar79 (Garwood folder, Marines and Military Law in Vietnam file, MCHC); hereafter Medical Examination.

49. Col Martin L. Brandtner summary of intvw, dtd 5Apr88 (Brandtner folder, Marines and Military Law in Vietnam file, MCHC).

50. USMC Headquarters, Screening Bd Recommendation; Case of PFC Garwood, dtd 30Mar72 (Garwood folder, Marines and Military Law in Vietnam file, MCHC).

51. Plaintiff's Brief for Summary Judgement at 1, Garwood v. U.S., U.S. Ct. Cl. (No. 551-79C) (Garwood folder, Marines and Military Law in Vietnam file, MCHC); and HQMC, JAD Garwood file.

52. NIS rpt of police records review, Indianapolis, Indiana Police Dept., dtd 17Apr79 (Garwood folder, Marines and Military Law in Vietnam file).

53. Medical Examination.

54. Maj Joseph Composto ltr to author, dtd 25Nov86 (Garwood folder, Marines and Military Law in Vietnam file, MCHC).

55. LtCol William T. Anderson ltr to BGen Edwin H. Simmons, dtd 26Jan89 (Comment folder, Marines and Military Law in Vietnam file, MCHC).

56. CMC memo to Dep Asst Secretary of State and Coordinator for POW/MIA Matters, Subj: Return of PFC Robert R. Garwood USMC from Vietnam, dtd 7Mar79 (Garwood folder, Marines and Military Law in Vietnam file, MCHC).

57. Certification of U.S. Counsel, Bangkok, Thailand, dtd 22Mar79 (Garwood folder, Marines and Military Law in Vietnam).

58. Winston Groom and Duncan Spencer, *Conversations with the Enemy* (New York: G. P. Putnam's Sons, 1983), p. 342, hereafter *Conversations with the Enemy*.

59. Unless otherwise noted, material relating to the court-martial is from appellate opinions, U.S. v. PFC Robert R. Garwood, 16 M.J. 863 (NMCMR 1983); U.S. v. PFC Robert R. Garwood, 20 M.J. 148 (CMA 1985); and JPAO AAR for GCM of PFC Robert R. Garwood, dtd 5Mar81 (Garwood folder, Marines and Military Law in Vietnam file, MCHC); and *Conversations with the Enemy*, pp. 333-394.

60. Walter T. Skallerup, Jr., memo to Secretary of the Navy, Subj: Grant of Immunity For PFC Garwood, USMC, dtd 25Feb85 (Garwood folder, Marines and Military Law in Vietnam file, MCHC).

61. Ibid.

62. CMC comment on Routing Sheet, dtd 13Feb85, covering Navy JAG memo to DoD General Counsel, Subj: Grant of Immunity In Case of PFC Robert R. Garwood (Garwood folder, Marines and Military Law in Vietnam file, MCHC).

63. U.S. v. PFC Robert R. Garwood, 16 M.J. 863, 869 (NMCMR 1983).

64. cert. den., 474 U.S. 1005; 106 SCt. 524.

65. Navy JAG draft ltr to Civil Division, Dept of Justice, n.d. (Garwood folder, Marines and Military Law in Vietnam file, MCHC).

66. HQMC, Memorandum, Subj: PFC Robert R. Garwood, USMC, n.d., in JAD Garwood file (Garwood folder, Marines and Military Law in Vietnam file, MCHC).

67. Col Joseph R. Motelewski intvw, 24Feb87, Tape 6489 (Oral HistColl, MCHC).

68. *The Washington Post*, 9Feb81, p. A13.

69. U.S. v. Garwood, 16 M.J. 863 (NMCMR 1983), at 873.

70. U.S. v. Garwood, 20 M.J. 148 (CMA 1985), at 154.

CHAPTER 11
MOPPING UP

Drugs, Race, Dissent: Same Problems, New Venues

1. LtGen William K. Jones, CG FMFPac presentation, HQMC, General Officers Symposium, 1971, tab J, p. 13.

2. Gen Leonard F. Chapman, Jr., opening address, HQMC, General Officer's Symposium, 1970, p. 21.

3. Gen Robert E. Cushman, Jr. Transcript of intvw by Oral History Unit, Hist&MusDiv, HQMC, dtd 5NOv82 (Oral HistColl, MCHC), pp. 344, 361-2.

4. BGen William H. J. Tiernan ltr to author, dtd 6Feb89 (Comment folder, Marines and Military Law in Vietnam file, MCHC).

5. MajGen Edwin B. Wheeler, Manpower, G-1 Presentation, HQMC, General Officers Symposium, 1972, tab H, p. 18.

6. USMC, *Report on Marine Corps Manpower Quality and Force Structure*, dtd 31Dec75 (MCHC), pp. 1-2 of Executive Summary; p. 7, hereafter *Report on Marine Corps Manpower*.

7. Ibid., p. 9-10.

8. *The Camp Lejeune Globe* (MCB Camp Lejeune, N.C.), 14Aug75, p. 1.

9. *Report on Marine Corps Manpower*, p. 2 of cover ltr.

10. DeBarr intvw.

11. *Report on Marine Corps Manpower*, p. 6.

12. Office of Navy JAG, Code 40.12 (Case Stats folder, Marines and Military Law in Vietnam file, MCHC); and Directorate for Information, Operations and Reports, The Pentagon, *Department of Defense, Selected Manpower Statistics, Fiscal Year 1982*, p. 77.

13. "Race Relations in the U.S. Marine Corps," *Commanders Digest*, 30Nov72, pp. 8-9.

NOTES

14. Bernard C. Nalty, *Strength For the Fight* (New York: The Free Press, 1986) pp. 338-339.
15. *Report on Marine Corps Manpower*, pp. 8, 12.
16. USMC, *Analysis of FMFPac Human Affairs Poll; July 1972* (FMFPac Human Affairs Poll folder, Marines and Military Law in Vietnam file, MCHC), pp. 2-1—2-4.

Vietnam Finale: Bien Hoa and the Rose Garden

17. Except where otherwise noted all material in this section is derived from: Hq, 1st Marine Aircraft Wing, "The Rose Garden Story," n.d. (The Rose Garden folder, Marines and Military Law in Vietnam folder, MCHC).
18. Bio File, (RefSec, MCHC).
19. BGen Raymond W. Edwards ltr to author, dtd 9Dec86 (Edwards folder, Marines and Military Law in Vietnam file, MCHC).
20. BGen Raymond W. Edwards ltr to BGen Edwin H. Simmons, dtd 26Jan89 (Comment folder, Marines and Military Law in Vietnam file, MCHC), hereafter Edwards 1989 ltr.
21. Edwards 1989 ltr; and Vincent J. Bartolotta ltr to Col Michael Patrick Murray, dtd 2Feb87 (Comment folder and Bartolotta folder, both in Marines and Military Law in Vietnam file, MCHC); hereafter Bartolotta ltr.
22. HqFMFPac, Narrative Summary of Significant Activities: "Operations of U.S. Marine Forces in Southeast Asia, 1 July 1971 Thru 31 March 1973," n.d., p. 3-17; hereafter HqFMFPac Narrative Summary.
23. Richard L. Prosise ltr to author, dtd 9Mar89 (Comment folder, Marines and Military Law in Vietnam file, MCHC); hereafter Prosise ltr.
24. Ibid.
25. Bartolotta ltr.
26. BGen Raymond W. Edwards ltr to author, dtd 9Mar88 (Edwards folder, Marines and Military Law in Vietnam file, MCHC).
27. Bartolotta ltr.
28. Prosise ltr.
29. Col Michael Patrick Murray ltr to author, dtd 10Feb87 (Murray folder, Marines and Military Law in Vietnam file, MCHC).
30. Edwards 1989 ltr.
31. HqFMFPac Narrative Summary, p. 2-22.
32. Prosise ltr.
33. Ibid.
34. Ibid.
35. HqFMFPac Narrative Summary, p. 6-6.

Perspective

36. One notable rehearing, however, resulted in a second conviction and spanned five years from the offense (murder of a first lieutenant in Vietnam) to a second conviction at Quantico, Virginia, illustrating the Marine Corps' willingness to pursue a case about which it felt strongly. See United States v. Cpl Charlie Eason, III, NCM 70 2612, 45 CMR 109 (COMA, 1972); 49 CMR 845 (NMCMR, 1974).
37. Faw intvw.
38. Ibid.
39. Legal Services Study, pp. 42-43.
40. Ibid., p. iii.
41. BGen Harvey E. Spielman, Personnel Presentation, HQMC, General Officers Symposium, 1972, tab V, pp. 4-6.
42. Faw intvw.

43. Col Joseph R. Motelewski intvw, 24Feb87, Tape 6489 (Oral HistColl, MCHC), hereafter Motelewski intvw.
44. Col Robert B. Neville ltr to Maj W. Hays Parks, dtd 12Jun77 (Neville folder, Marines and Military Law in Vietnam file, MCHC), hereafter Neville ltr.
45. Gen Paul X. Kelley intvw, 30Sep87, Tape 6477 (Oral HistColl, MCHC), hereafter Kelley intvw.

The Uniform Code of Military Justice: Did It Work in Vietnam?

46. House Report, to accompany HR 4080, No. 491, Hearing before the House Armed Services Committee, 81st Con., 1st Sess., p. 8 (1949).
47. Col Robert M. Lucy ltr to BGen Edwin H. Simmons, dtd 16Jan89 (Comment folder, Marines and Military Law in Vietnam file, MCHC), hereafter Lucy ltr.
48. BGen Edwin H. Simmons, Vietnam service debriefing to CG FMFPac, dtd 24May71 (Command Info Notebook folder, Marines and Military Law in Vietnam file, MCHC), p. 10.
49. Col John R. DeBarr debriefing at FMFPac, 9Jun69, Tape 4254 (Oral HistColl, MCHC).
50. Faw intvw.
51. Tiernan intvw.
52. Gen William C. Westmoreland and MajGen George S. Prugh, *Judges in Command: The Judicialized Uniform Code of Military Justice in Combat*, 3 Harvard Journal of Law and Public Policy 4 and 53, 1-93; hereafter Westmoreland and Prugh, *Judges in Command*. This is an outstanding and comprehensive review of the problems of codal application in combat.
53. Guenter Lewy, *America in Vietnam* (New York: Oxford University Press, 1978), p. 160.
54. Col Arthur R. Petersen ltr to BGen Duane L. Faw, dtd 9Mar70 (Cushman folder, Marines and Military Law in Vietnam file, MCHC).
55. Holben intvw.
56. LtCol Curtis W. Olson questionnaire to Maj W. Hays Parks, dtd Dec76 (Olson folder, Marines and Military Law in Vietnam file, MCHC).
57. Col Olson questionnaire to author, dtd 27Oct86 (Olson folder, Marines and Military Law in Vietnam file, MCHC).
58. Tiernan intvw.
59. Holben intvw.
60. Motelewski intvw.
61. Tiernan intvw.
62. Col Archibald King, JAGC, USA (Ret), *Changes in the Uniform Code of Military Justice Necessary To Make It Workable In Time of War*, 22 Fed. Bar J. 49, 49-59 (Winter 1962).
63. MajGen George S. Prugh, USA, ltr to BGen Edwin H. Simmons, dtd 29Dec88 (Comment folder, Marines and Military Law in Vietnam file, MCHC).
64. Gen William C. Westmoreland and MajGen George S. Prugh, *Judges in Command: The Judicialized Uniform Code of Military Justice in Combat (A Draft Code Amendment)*, 4 Harvard Journal of Law and Public Policy 199. This is an addendum to their article of the same name, op. cit.
65. Mitchell intvw.
66. Ibid.
67. Neville ltr.
68. "Ein Menschenleben gilt fur nix" (A Human Life Is of No Account), *Der Spiegel*, 28Oct87 (Articles folder, Marines and Military Law in Vietnam file, MCHC), p.112. This brief article recounts how many of the 1.3 million German soldiers convicted by courts-

martial after December 1940 were assigned to *Strafbataillons* (punishment battalions), tasked with the most dangerous battlefield duties. Alternatively, they were assigned to *Disziplinieren und Kleinkriegen* (field punishment groups), to dig trenches, erect obstacles, and bury the dead, on a subsistence diet, subject to execution for failure or refusal to work.

69. USA, Report to the Judge Advocate General by the Wartime Legislation Team, dtd Sep83 (UCMJ in Combat folder, Marines and Military Law in Vietnam file, MCHC), p. 3.
70. Ibid., p.1.
71. Ibid., p. 6.
72. Ibid., p. 28-31.
73. Westmoreland and Prugh, *Judges in Command*, p. 83.
74. Ibid., pp. 13-17; App. F, pp. F-5–F-9.
75. Ibid.
76. Westmoreland and Prugh, *Judges in Command*, pp. 37 and 83.
77. Ibid., App. D, p. D-19.
78. Ibid., p. 37.
79. Ibid., p. 51.
80. Lucy ltr.
81. DoD, *The Military Justice Act of 1983: Advisory Commission Report*, Vol I, Commission Recommendations and Position Papers; Transcript of Commission Hearings (Washington: 1984), pp. 54-67. A copy of the Mitchell-Byrne minority rpt is included. (Mitchell folder, Marines and Military Law in Vietnam file, MCHC).
82. Westmoreland and Prugh, *Judges in Command*, p. 55.
83. BGen Charles A. Cushman intvw, 4Dec86, Tape 6481 (Oral Hist-Coll, MCHC).

Summation

84. John LeCarre, *The Looking Glass War* (New York: Coward-McCann, Inc., 1965), p. 266.

Appendix A

Marine Corps Lawyers, Navy Law Specialists, and Naval Service Judge Advocates Who Served as Lawyers in Vietnam

No official record of those lawyers who served in Vietnam was kept, either by the officer assignment branch of Headquarters Marine Corps, or by the Judge Advocate Division. Later in the war some Vietnam units, such as Force Logistic Command, listed individual lawyers in their command chronology. Other units, such as the 3d Marine Division, never did so. The following listing was compiled by the author from command chronologies, convening orders, records of trial, telephone directories, photos, and letters. Regrettably, errors and a few omissions are inevitable.

1965

Col George P. Blackburn . . . . 1st MarDiv
Col Olin W. Jones, Jr. . . . . III MAF
Capt James E. Keys, USN* . . . . Law Officer, Yokosuka
Col Vernon A. "Vap" Peltzer . . . . III MAF
Col Harry S. Popper, Jr. . . . . 1st MAW
Col Charles B. Sevier . . . . 3d MarDiv/III MAF

LtCol Frederick H. Campbell . . . . 1st MAW
LtCol Fred Grabowski . . . . 3d MarDiv
LtCol Verne L. "Bubs" Oliver . . . . Law Officer, Yokosuka
LtCol Thomas B. Sparkman . . . . 3d MarDiv

Maj Robert J. Chadwick . . . . 3d MarDiv
Maj John E. Crandall . . . . 1st MarDiv
Maj Benjamin B. Ferrell . . . . III MAF (civil affairs)
Maj Charles J. Keever . . . . III MAF/MACV, Saigon
Maj James P. King . . . . 9th MEB/III MAF
Maj Joseph A. Mallery . . . . 3d MarDiv
Maj Paul A. A. St.Amour . . . . 1st MAW

Lt Edward A. Arianna, USN . . . . 1st MAW
Capt Robert J. Blum . . . . 3d MarDiv
Lt Hugh D. Campbell, USN . . . . 3d MarDiv/III MAF
Capt Fred R. "Buck" Files, Jr. . . . . 3d MarDiv
Capt Robert A. Godwin . . . . 3d MarDiv
Capt Peter N. Kress . . . . 9th MEB/3d MarDiv
Capt J. Kent Riegel . . . . 3d MarDiv
Capt Philip D. Sharp, Jr. . . . . 1st MAW
Capt James W. Spindler . . . . 3d MarDiv
Lt Norman D. Wolff, USN . . . . III MAF

1stLt William J. Carroll . . . . 3d MarDiv
1stLt John W. Clark . . . . 1st MAW

*The designation, "JAGC," did not follow Navy lawyers' names until their Judge Advocate General's Corps was formed on 8 December 1967.

1stLt Roger G. Darley . . . . 3d MarDiv
1stLt Larry B. Funderburk . . . . 9th MEB/Chu Lai
1stLt Donald W. Harris . . . . 9th MEB/3d MarDiv
1stLt Theodore J. Hodan, Jr. . . . . 1st MAW
1stLt Bruce A. Hoffman . . . . 1st MAW
Lt (jg) Keith G. O'Brian, USN . . . . 3d MarDiv
1stLt James K. Rader . . . . 3d MarDiv
1stLt David M. Skeels . . . . 1st MAW
1stLt William T. Warren III . . . . 3d MarDiv
1stLt Frederick C. Woodruff . . . . 3d MarDiv

2dLt John E. Gillmor, Jr. . . . . 3d MarDiv
2dLt Lonnie O. Grigsby . . . . 3d MarDiv
2dLt William H. Hampton . . . . 3d MarDiv

1966

Col Charles H. Beale, Jr. . . . . 3d MarDiv
Col Ralph K. Culver . . . . 1st MAW
Capt Wyman N. Jackson, USN . . . . Law Officer, Yokosuka
Col Earl W. Johnson . . . . TAD, FMFPac
Col Robert B. Neville (and Asst CofS) . . . . III MAF

LtCol Thomas P. Casey . . . . 1st MarDiv
Cdr William E. Clemmons, USN . . . . . . 1st MarDiv/Law Officer
LtCol Donald E. Holben . . . . Law Officer, Da Nang
LtCol Charles R. Larouche . . . . FLC
LtCol Daniel F. McConnell . . . . 3d MarDiv
LtCol Charles E. Spence, Jr. 1st MAW
LtCol William W. Wander, Jr. . . . . Law Officer, Da Nang
LtCol John L. Zorack . . . . 1st MarDiv (TF X-Ray)

Maj George L. Bailey . . . . 1st MarDiv
Maj Frederick D. Clements . . . . 3d MarDiv
Maj Charles W. Collier . . . . 1st MAW
Maj William B. Draper, Jr. 1st MarDiv
Maj Curtis W. Olson . . . . 1st MarDiv
Maj Robert E. Switzer . . . . 1st MarDiv
Maj Winn M. Thurman . . . . 1st MarDiv
Maj James R. Ziemann . . . . FLC

Capt George B. Bancroft, Jr. . . . . 1st MarDiv
Capt Ronald D. Bonnett . . . . 1st MarDiv
Capt Francis T. Coleman . . . . 1st MarDiv (TF X-Ray)
Capt Paul R. Constantino . . . . 1st MarDiv (TF X-Ray)
Capt James R. DeMarco . . . . 3d MarDiv
Lt John F. Erickson, USN . . . . FLC
Capt Peter D. Fitzgerald . . . . 1st MarDiv
Capt Edward F. Fogarty . . . . 3d MarDiv
Capt Mark F. Geary . . . . 1st MarDiv
Capt Franklin P. "Skip" Glenn . . . . FLC
Capt Daniel M. Hanlon . . . . 1st MarDiv (TF X-Ray)
Capt Harry R. Hull, Jr. . . . . 3d MarDiv

Lt Walter J. Landon, USN............1st MarDiv
Capt Robert L. Luce...................1st MarDiv

Capt Robert J. Madigan................1st MarDiv
Capt Robert W. Mann...................1st MAW
Lt Brian P. Murphy, USN...............3d MarDiv
Capt Joseph C. Olson..................1st MarDiv
Capt Kurt M. Penn.....................3d MarDiv
Capt Clifford E. Roberson.............1st MAW
Capt Harry D. Sabine..................1st MarDiv
Capt Allen R. Saxe....................3d MarDiv
Capt James P. Shannon.................1st MarDiv
Capt Sheldon K. Stock.................3d MarDiv
Lt John S. Szymanski, USN.............1st MAW
Capt Paul S. Zonderman................3d MarDiv

1stLt Bernie S. Allen.................1st MarDiv
1stLt James E. Barnett................1st MarDiv
1stLt James Ehlers....................1st MarDiv
1stLt Michael J. Naughton.......Force Logistic Cmd
Lt (jg) Larry D. Schlue, USN..........3d MarDiv
1stLt Richard N. Stuckey..............3d MarDiv
1stLt Donald E. Wittig................1st MarDiv

1967

Capt Benjamin H. Berry, USN......Law Officer, Yokosuka
Col Norris C. Broome..................3d MarDiv
Col Eugene B. "Doc" Fallon............3d MarDiv
Col Duane L. Faw (and Asst CofS)......III MAF
Col Alexander M. "Sandy" Hearn....Law Officer, Yokosuka
Col Robert C. "Curly" Lehnert.........1st MAW
Col John L. Ostby.....................1st MarDiv

LtCol Paul F. Henderson...........9th MEB/3d MarDiv
LtCol Richard D. Humphreys.........1st and 3d MarDivs
LtCol William C. Jaeck................TAD, FMFPac
LtCol Clyde R. Mann...................1st MarDiv
LtCol William F. Morely...............Not specified
LtCol Verne L. "Bubs" Oliver..........FLC
LtCol William T. Westmoreland, Jr.....1st MarDiv
LtCol Richard E. Wray.................FLC

Maj Max C. Fischer....................3d MarDiv
Maj Ronald J. Kaye...............III MAF/3d MarDiv
Maj Brian B. Kent.....................III MAF
Maj Michael Patrick Murray............FLC
Maj H. Terry Reiniche.................9th MAB
Maj William H. J. Tiernan.............1st MAW

Capt Bernard A. Allen, Jr.............1st MarDiv
Capt G. Ward Beaudry..................III MAF
Lt Jared O. Bauch, USN................1st MAW
Capt Michal B. Cotten.................1st MAW
Capt Vincent J. Erichs, Jr............1st MarDiv
Capt Harvey G. Gleason................FLC
Capt Mark L. Haiman...................3d MarDiv
Capt Victor J. Haydel.................FLC
Capt Donald Higginbotham..............1st MarDiv
Capt Bruce R. Hoffman.................1st MAW
Capt Tristam T. Hyde..................3d MarDiv

Capt James W. Jones...................3d MarDiv
Capt Charles J. Kall..................FLC
Capt Philip S. Keith..................3d MarDiv
Capt David B. King....................1st MAW
Capt Richard D. Lane..............9th MAB/3d MarDiv
Lt Robert L. Locke, USN...............3d MarDiv
Capt Vincent P. Maroney...............FLC
Lt John J. Martens, USN...............1st MarDiv
Capt Michael C. McCarey...............1st MarDiv
Capt Michael J. McHale................1st MAW
Capt Larry J. Miner...................FLC
Capt Charles H. Mitchell..............1st MAW
Capt H. Edward Moore, Jr..............FLC
Capt Jerrold Oldani...................1st MarDiv
Capt Charles E. Patterson.............3d MarDiv
Capt William E. Peacock...............1st MAW
Capt John N. Post.....................1st MAW
Capt Donald R. Pritchard..............1st MAW
Capt Jay D. Reynolds..................1st MarDiv
Capt Ross T. Roberts..................1st MarDiv
Capt John E. Russell..................1st MarDiv
Capt Gary A. Sargent..................1st MarDiv
Capt Mahlon C. Schneider..............3d MarDiv
Capt Harry L. Shorstein...........3d MarDiv/9th MAB
Capt Dennis H. Siems..................FLC
Capt Eugene A. Steffen................1st MarDiv
Capt Walter A. Stewart, Jr............1st MAW
Capt George Tosi, Jr..................3d MarDiv
Capt Robert W. Wachsmuth..............FLC
Capt William F. Whiting...............1st MAW
Capt John P. Williams.............1/9, 3d MarDiv
Capt Richard M. Williams..............3d MarDiv
Capt Peter B. Work....................3d MarDiv
Capt Rufus C. Young IV................1st MAW

1stLt Morrill Dunn III................1st MarDiv
1stLt Boyd L. George..................3d MarDiv
1stLt Robert M. Lee...................3d MarDiv
1stLt Jeffery W. Maurer...............3d MarDiv
1stLt Michael K. Phalin...............3d MarDiv
1stLt Michael I. Walling..............1st MAW

2dLt Macauley Carter, Jr..............1st MAW
2dLt Jerry G. Cunningham..............FLC
2dLt William E. Eaken.................1st MarDiv
2dLt James G. Ehlers..................1st MarDiv
2dLt Thomas M. Flournoy, Jr...........Not specified
2dLt Edward F. Kelly..................1st MarDiv

1968

Col Jack E. Hanthorn..................1st MarDiv
Col Joseph R. Motelewski (and CofS)...3d MarDiv
Col Paul W. Seabaugh..................III MAF

LtCol Rollin Q. Blakeslee.............3d MarDiv
LtCol William M. "Ace" Cummings.......1st MarDiv/FLC
LtCol John R. DeBarr..............Law Officer, Da Nang
LtCol William R. Eleazer..............1st MarDiv
LtCol Frederick M. Haden..............FLC
LtCol Max G. Halliday.................1st MAW

THOSE WHO SERVED AS LAWYERS IN VIETNAM

Maj Lawrence G. Bolin..................9th MAB/3d MarDiv
Maj Richard G. Moore........................FLC

Capt W. Tommy Allison II....................3d MarDiv
Capt Charles W. Babcock, Jr...................FLC
Capt Robert B. Baker........................1st MAW
Capt Clarke C. Barnes........................3d MarDiv
Capt Steven H. Bowytz........................3d MarDiv
Capt James B. Brookshire....................1st MarDiv
Capt David J. Cassady........................3d MarDiv
Capt Charles W. Cherry.........................FLC
Capt Stanton M. Cole..........................III MAF
Capt Martin E. Conway, Jr....................3d MarDiv
Capt William J. Cook........................1st MAW
Lt William J. Cosgriff, JAGC, USN.............1st MarDiv
Capt Chapman B. Cox........................9th MAB
Capt Jerald D. Crow........................3d MarDiv
Capt James H. Cummings....................1st MarDiv
Capt Robert R. Davis, Jr....................1st MarDiv
Capt Richard J. Dove........................1st MAW
Capt Donald W. Doyle, Jr....................1st MarDiv
Capt William L. Fly........................3d MarDiv
Capt Clark A. Halderson....................3d MarDiv
Capt Michael J. Hoblock, Jr..................1st MAW
Capt Carey H. Johnson......................1st MAW
Capt Edward F. Kelly (back-to-back tours)........1st MarDiv
Capt Jerome R. Klukas......................3d MarDiv
Capt Edward J. Lopata......................9th MAB
Capt Peter J. Mastaglio........................FLC
Capt Patrick H. Mathews....................1st MarDiv
Capt William H. McAdam, Jr..................1st MarDiv
Capt Martin G. McGuinn, Jr..................1st MarDiv
Capt Sandy S. McMath..........3d MarDiv/FLC/9th MAB
Capt Jack R. Mennis.....................Not specified
Capt John D. Moats........................1st MarDiv
Capt David G. Moore........................3d MarDiv
Capt Stephen P. Oggel......................1st MAW
Capt W. Hays Parks........................1st MarDiv
Capt William G. Proctor, Jr..................1st MAW
Capt Jack C. Provine..........................FLC
Capt John C. Reynolds......................1st MarDiv
Lt Lawrence R. Rowe, JAGC, USN..............1st MAW
Lt Jerry D. Rucker, JAGC, USN.....TAD, NavBase, Subic Bay
Capt Michael D. Schrunk....................3d MarDiv
Capt Thomas A. Schwindt.....................FLC
Capt Robert L. Sikma........................1st MAW
Capt Stanley L. Smith, Jr....................3d MarDiv
Capt Arthur W. Tifford......................1st MarDiv
Capt Ronald W. Williamson....................FLC
Lt Robert D. Zsalman, JAGC, USN.............3d MarDiv

1stLt Thomas A. Bergstrom..................1st MarDiv
1stLt Marshall W. Dooley....................1st MAW
1stLt Donald W. Griffis........................FLC
1stLt Robert A. Jones........................9th MAB
1stLt Francis J. Kaveney....................1st MarDiv
1stLt P. Keith Keller........................3d MarDiv
1stLt Thomas A. King........................1st MarDiv
1stLt Harry N. Lembeck......................9th MAB
1stLt William G. Nash......................1st MarDiv
1stLt Curtis K. Oberhansly..................1st MAW

1stLt John J. Reilly..........................FLC

2dLt George G. Bashian, Jr..................1st MarDiv
2dLt Barry M. Gallagher............III MAF/ 1st MarDiv

1969

Col Nalton M. Bennett........................1st MAW
Col Robert M. Lucy........................1st MarDiv
Col Arthur R. Petersen.........................FLC
Col Marion G. Truesdale......................III MAF

LtCol Carl E. Buchmann.........................FLC
LtCol Benjamin B. Ferrell (2d tour)............3d MarDiv
LtCol Fred Grabowski (2d tour).................FLC
LtCol Henry Hoppe III..............Mil Judge, Da Nang
LtCol James P. King (2d tour)..................1st MarDiv
LtCol Rufino R. Saez........................3d MarDiv

Maj Steve R. Balash, Jr........................FLC
Maj Robert J. Blum........................1st MarDiv
Maj David M. Brahms........................1st MAW
Maj Charles A. Cushman.........................FLC
Maj Leo K. O'Drudy........................3d MarDiv

Capt Steve A. Bamberger........................FLC
Capt Emilic V. "Bob" Belluomini, Jr............III MAF
Capt John A. Bergen..........................FLC
Capt Terry A. Bond........................3d MarDiv
Capt Raymond T. Bonner....................1st MarDiv
Capt Martin D. Boudreau....................1st MarDiv
Capt John A. Bracher......................3d MarDiv
Capt Charles E. Brown......................1st MarDiv
Capt David M. Brown......................1st MarDiv
Capt Gary E. Bushell......................1st MarDiv
Capt Reynold L. "Rip" Caleen, Jr.................FLC
Capt G. David Carlock III....................1st MAW
Capt Dallas C. Clark, Jr....................3d MarDiv
Capt Robert W. Cook........................1st MAW
Lt William T. Cranfill, Jr, JAGC, USN............1st MarDiv
Capt Thomas A. Crawford, Jr..................1st MarDiv
Capt Stephen E. Davis.........................FLC
Capt Nathaniel F. Emmons....................1st MAW
Capt Allen E. Falk........................1st MarDiv
Capt Cecil R. Forster......................1st MarDiv
Capt Fred L. Fox........................1st MarDiv
Capt Richard L. Franks........................FLC
Capt Thomas J. Glenn, Jr....................1st MAW
Lt James C. Gries, JAGC, USN.................3d MarDiv
Capt Mark L. Haiman (2d tour)................1st MarDiv
Capt Clark A. Halderson....................3d MarDiv
Capt Dennis L. Hanssen....................3d MarDiv
Capt J. Michael Hardin....................3d MarDiv
Capt John J. Hargrove......................1st MarDiv
Capt Louis J. Hellerman....................1st MAW
Capt Jacob R. Henderson, Jr.....................FLC
Capt Douglas G. Hendricks..................1st MarDiv

Capt Anthony L. Hodge...........................1st MAW
Capt William E. Iorio...............1st MarDiv/3d MarDiv
Capt Tommy W. Jarrett.................................FLC
Capt Franz P. Jevne...............................1st MarDiv
Capt Rex L. Jones III..................................FLC
Capt Edward J. Karfeld............................1st MAW
Capt Scott Keep...FLC
Capt John F. Kent, Jr............................3d MarDiv
Capt Adrian R. King.............................1st MarDiv
Capt Joseph S. King...............................3d MarDiv
Capt Richard D. Lane (2d tour)......................FLC
Capt E. Ray Lanier.....................................FLC
Capt Thomas O. Lavoy...........................1st MarDiv
Capt Daniel H. LeGear, Jr.......................1st MarDiv
Capt Michael J. Levin.......................3d MarDiv/FLC
Capt Robert M. MacConnell.....................1st MarDiv
Capt Alfred W. Mackey..........................1st MarDiv
Capt Fred C. Mather.............................3d MarDiv
Capt Michael P. Merrill..........................1st MarDiv
Capt John A. Milici..............................1st MarDiv
Capt Louis A. Moore, Jr..........................3d MarDiv
Capt Charles H. Moses III..........................1st MAW
Capt Richard A. Muench............................1st MAW
Capt Edward L. Murphy..........................3d MarDiv
Lt John G. Niles, JAGC, USN.....................1st MAW
Capt George H. O'Kelley..............................FLC
Capt Theodore J. Padden.........................1st MarDiv
Capt John S. Papa.....................................FLC
Capt Robert E. Parker.................................FLC
Capt Terrance B. Rodsky..............................FLC
Capt Peter M. Rosen..............................1st MAW
Capt Jack A. Rosenzweig..........................3d MarDiv
Capt Frank G. Roux, Jr..........................1st MarDiv
Capt Thomas A. Rulon..............................1st MAW
Capt Donald F. Shanahan..........................3d MarDiv
Capt David E. Skaggs............................1st MarDiv
Capt J. Len Skiles...............................1st MarDiv
Capt David P. Smith..................................FLC
Capt Edwin A. Snyder.................................FLC
Capt Richard F. Staley...........................3d MarDiv
Capt James D. Stokes..............................1st MAW
Capt John R. Taylor, Jr..........................3d MarDiv
Capt Richard S. Towers...............................FLC
Capt Stephen H. Vengrow..............................FLC
Capt Paul F. Wendler, Jr.............................FLC
Capt John L. Westney, Jr.............................FLC
Capt Charles E. Williams.............................FLC
Capt Robert C. Williams.........................1st MarDiv
Lt Frank A. Wohl, JAGC, USN.....................1st MAW
Capt W. Mark Wood....................................FLC
Capt John R. Woodard............................3d MarDiv
1stLt Thomas D. Horne................................FLC
1stLt James M. Schermerhorn....................1st MarDiv

2dLt Christopher Q. Britton.....................3d MarDiv
2dLt Michael G. McCollum.........................1st MAW

1970–1971

Col Donald E. Holben (2d tour)................1st MarDiv

Capt James E. Keys, JAGC, USN (2d tour).....Military Judge
Col Daniel F. McConnell (2d tour)............III MAF/FLC

LtCol John E. Crandell (2d tour).....................FLC
LtCol Peter N. Kress (2d tour)..................1st MarDiv
Cdr Keith B. Lawrence, JAGC, USN..........Military Judge
LtCol Paul A. A. St.Amour (2d tour).....MilJudge, Da Nang

Maj James H. Granger...........................1st MarDiv
Maj Curtis W. Olson (2d tour)....................1st MAW

Capt Eileen M. Albertson..................TAD, 3d MarDiv
Capt Michael M. Anello............................1st MAW
Capt James J. Barry, Jr.........................1st MarDiv
Capt Stephen C. Berg............................1st MarDiv
Capt Allen J. Borne.............................1st MarDiv
Capt Michael G. Carpenter.......................1st MarDiv
Capt James W. Carroll...........................1st MarDiv
Capt Otis F. "Butch" Cochran, Jr.....................FLC
Capt Thomas A. Crawford.........................1st MarDiv
Capt John L. Euler...................................FLC
Capt Bruce M. Frey..............................1st MarDiv
Capt Tone N. Grant..............................1st MarDiv
Capt Robert Kirkman..............................3d MarDiv
Capt Paul J. Laveroni...........................1st MarDiv
Capt John A. Lockwood............................3d MarDiv
Capt John J. Lynch..............................1st MarDiv
Capt Michael J. Mangan...............................FLC
Capt Michael G. McCollum (2d tour)........AO, 1stMarDiv
Capt Dirk T. Metzger............................1st MarDiv
Capt Carl J. Moroney.................................FLC
Capt James V. Murray III.........................3d MarDiv
Capt William J. O'Byrne.........................1st MarDiv
Capt Frank J. O'Connor..........................1st MarDiv
Capt Allan L. Paglia............................1st MarDiv
Lt Robert Pierson, JAGC, USN................Not specified
Capt William R. Porter..........................1st MarDiv
Capt Robert A. Preate...........................1st MarDiv
Capt John P. Proctor.............................3d MarDiv
Capt E. Randall Ricketts.............................FLC
Capt Alan W. Roles..............................1st MarDiv
Lt Allen C. Rudy, Jr., JAGC, USN................1st MarDiv
Capt Lawrence W. Secrest........................1st MarDiv
Capt Bruce D. Strathearn.............................FLC
Capt Reginald K. Templeton........................1st MAW
Capt James L. Thompson............................1st MAW
Capt Michael C. Vesey.............................1st MAW
Capt Edwin W. Welch.............................1st MarDiv
Capt Robert S. Wiggins, Jr......................1st MarDiv

1stLt Robert W. Detrick..............................FLC
1stLt Robert E. Dinardo...........................1st MAW
1stLt Roland K. Iverson, Jr.....................1st MarDiv
1stLt Joel Levine...............................1st MarDiv
1stLt Donald B. Myers...........................1st MarDiv
1stLt Philip C. Tower...........................1st MarDiv

2dLt William A. Price................................FLC

THOSE WHO SERVED AS LAWYERS IN VIETNAM

Marine Corps and Navy judge advocates who served with Marine Wing Headquarters Squadron 1, 1st Marine Aircraft Wing, Bien Hoa, South Vietnam, and Nam Phong ("The Rose Garden"), Thailand.

June 1972 – Sept 1973

LtCol Raymond W. Edwards (SJA) (2d tour)
LtCol Michael Patrick Murray (SJA) (2d tour)

Maj Anthony F. J. Mielczarski

Capt William J. Baker
Capt Vincent J. Bartolotta, Jr.
Capt William D. Blunk
Capt Stephen C. Eastham
Capt Van N. Eden
Capt John S. Edwards
Capt William T. Enslen
Capt Robert E. Hilton
Capt Franklin D. Holder
Capt John T. John
Capt Michael C. McDermott
Lt Jack C. Myers, JAGC, USN
Capt Charles R. Oleszycki
Capt Daniel Parker, Jr.
Capt Richard L. Prosise
Capt Keith E. Rounsaville
Capt Richard D. Sullivan
Capt Michael C. Vesey
Capt Michael C. Warlow

Appendix B
Staff Legal Officers/Staff Judge Advocates in Vietnam

III Marine Amphibious Force

8Mar65-May65 (9th MEB)	Capt Peter N. Kress
May65-Jul65	Maj James P. King
Jul65-31Jul65	LtCol Thomas B. Sparkman
1Aug65-Nov65	LtCol Charles B. Sevier
Nov65-29Jul66	Col Vernon A. Peltzer
30Jul66-29Jul67	Col Robert B. Neville (and Asst Chief of Staff)
30Jul67-4Aug68	Col Duane L. Faw (and Asst Chief of Staff)
5Aug68-31Jul69	Col Paul W. Seabaugh
1Aug69-28Feb70	Col Marion G. Truesdale
1Mar70-1Jul70	Col Arthur R. Petersen
2Jul70-14Apr71	Col Daniel F. McConnell

Originally located at the Da Nang Airfield, MAF headquarters and the SLO's office displaced on 26 Jun 1966 to Camp Horn on the east bank of the Song Han (Da Nang River), opposite east Da Nang. The office moved to Camp Haskins, Red Beach, north of Da Nang, on 9 March 1970. On 28 Feb 1970 III MAF SJA's duties were assumed by FLC's SJA.

3d Marine Division

1Aug65-Jun66	LtCol Charles B. Sevier (and III MAF SLO)
Jun66-Jun67	Col Charles H. Beale, Jr.
Jun67-30Jun67	LtCol Norris C. Broome
1Jul67-10Jul68	Col Eugene B. Fallon
11Jul68-Oct68	LtCol Rollin Q. Blakeslee
Oct68-Sep69	Col Joseph R. Motelewski
Sep69-5Nov69	LtCol Benjamin B. Ferrell

Originally located at the Da Nang Airfield, the SLO's office displaced on 11-15 Nov 1965 to Hill 327, northwest of Da Nang. In Nov 1966 the legal office moved to Phu Bai, following the division headquarters which had moved there the month before. On 7 Mar 1968 the SLO displaced to Quang Tri. On 5 Nov 1969 the SJA's office redeployed to Okinawa with the Division headquarters.

1st Marine Aircraft Wing

20May65-2Jul65	Maj Paul A. A. St.Amour
3Jul65-31May66	Col Harry S. Popper, Jr.
1Jun66-31Jul66	Maj Charles W. Collier
1Aug66-31Jul67	LtCol Ralph K. Culver
1Aug67-26Aug68	Col Robert C. Lehnert
27Aug68-6Sep69	Col Max G. Halliday
7Sep69-Sep70	Col Nalton M. Bennett
Sep70-14Apr71	Maj Curtis W. Olson

The Wing SJA's office, originally at the Da Nang Airfield, remained there until redeploying to Iwakuni, Japan, on 14 Apr 1971.

1st Marine Division

1Jul65-9Aug66	Col George P. Blackburn
10Aug66-13Feb67	LtCol Thomas P. Casey
14Feb67-6Aug67	LtCol William T. Westmoreland, Jr.
7Aug67-3Dec67	Col John L. Ostby
4Dec1967-5Aug1968	Col Clyde R. Mann
6Aug68-8Jul69	Col Jack E. Hanthorn
9Jul69-21Jun70	Col Robert M. Lucy
22Jul70-14Apr71	Col Donald E. Holben

Originally located at Chu Lai, the SLO's office displaced on 23 Nov 1966, a month after the rest of the division headquarters, to Hill 327, northwest of Da Nang. During April and May 1971 the legal office, along with the rest of the division headquarters, redeployed to Camp Pendleton, California.

Force Logistic Command

17May66-31May67	LtCol Charles R. Larouche
1Jun67-31May68	LtCol Verne L. Oliver
1Jun68-1May69	LtCol Frederick M. Haden
2May69-13Jul69	LtCol William M. Cummings
14Jul69-18Jul69	LtCol Carl E. Buchmann
19Jul69-30Jun70	LtCol Arthur R. Petersen (and III MAF SJA)
1Jul70-21Apr71	Col Daniel F. McConnell (and III MAF SJA)

The SJA's office, originally located at Camp Books, Red Beach, remained there until the office was deactivated on 21 Apr 1971.

3d Marine Amphibious Brigade

14Apr71-3Jun71	Col Donald E. Holben
4Jun71-24Jun71	Maj James H. Granger

Established at Hill 327, the SJA's office and most of the MAB headquarters remained there until deactivated on 24 June 1971.

Appendix C
U.S. Medals Awarded Marine Corps Lawyers and Judge Advocates for Vietnam Service

No official awards roster exists. This listing is extracted from the untitled record of Headquarters, Fleet Marine Force, Pacific, considered by the Decorations and Medals Branch of Headquarters Marine Corps to be the most complete and accurate record available. Nevertheless, several omissions have been noted and corrected. Other unidentified omissions may have escaped notice. The Legion of Merit, Bronze Star Medal, Navy Commendation Medal, and Navy Achievement Medal may be awarded with or without Combat V. In all but a few instances those awards to lawyers and judge advocates were with Combat V. No distinction is made here between medals awarded with Combat V and those few awarded without.

Navy Cross

1stLt Michael I. Neil

Silver Star

1stLt James M. Schermerhorn

Legion of Merit

Col Nalton M. Bennett
Col Norris C. Broome
Col John R. DeBarr
Col Eugene B. Fallon
Col Duane L. Faw
LtCol Benjamin B. Ferrell
LtCol Frederick M. Haden
LtCol Max G. Halliday
Col Jack E. Hanthorn
Capt Donald Higginbotham
Col Donald E. Holben
LtCol Henry Hoppe, III
Maj Charles J. Keever
Col Robert C. Lehnert
Col Robert M. Lucy
Col Clyde R. Mann
Col Daniel F. McConnell
Col Joseph R. Motelewski
Col Robert B. Neville
Col Verne L. Oliver
Col John L. Ostby
Col Charles B. Sevier

Distinguished Flying Cross

Col Robert C. Lehnert

Bronze Star Medal

Capt W. Tommy Allison II
Col Charles H. Beale, Jr.
LtCol Rollin Q. Blakeslee
LtCol Robert J. Blum
Maj David M. Brahms
LtCol Carl E. Buchmann
LtCol Thomas P. Casey
Capt Martin E. Conway, Jr.
LtCol William M. Cummings
Maj William B. Draper, Jr.
LtCol William R. Eleazer
Maj Benjamin B. Ferrell
Capt Fred L. Fox (2 awards)
LtCol Fred Grabowski
1stLt Donald W. Griffis
LtCol Paul F. Henderson, Jr.
LtCol James P. King
Capt Jerome R. Klukas
LtCol Peter N. Kress
Capt E. Ray Lanier
Capt William H. McAdam, Jr.
Capt Michael G. McCollum
LtCol Daniel F. McConnell
1stLt David G. Moore
Maj Richard G. Moore
Maj Curtis W. Olson (2 awards)
Capt Charles E. Patterson
Col Vernon A. Peltzer
Capt Harry L. Shorstein
Maj Winn M. Thurman
Maj William H. J. Tiernan
Col Marion G. Truesdale
LtCol William W. Wander, Jr.
LtCol John L. Zorack

Air Medal

Col Robert C. Lehnert (7 awards)
Capt Michael G. McCollum (19 awards)
1stLt Michael I. Neil (6 awards)

Purple Heart Medal

Capt William L. Fly
1stLt Michael I. Neil

Navy Commendation Medal

Capt Bernard A. Allen, Jr.
Maj George L. Bailey
1stLt George G. Bashian
Col George P. Blackburn
Capt Raymond T. Bonner
Capt Steven H. Bowytz (2 awards)
Capt James B. Brookshire
Capt Charles E. Brown
Capt Gary E. Bushell
Capt G. David Carlock III
Capt Michael G. Carpenter
Capt James W. Carroll
1stLt William J. Carroll
1stLt Macauley Carter, Jr.
Capt David J. Cassady
Capt Dallas C. Clark, Jr.
Capt Francis T. Coleman
Capt Paul R. Constantino
Col Charles W. Collier
Capt Jerald D. Crow
Col Ralph K. Culver
Capt James H. Cummings
1stLt Jerry G. Cunningham
Maj Charles A. Cushman
Col John R. DeBarr
Capt Robert E. Dinardo
1stLt Morrill Dunn III
Col Raymond W. Edwards
1stLt James G. Ehlers
Capt Nathaniel F. Emmons
Capt Vincent J. Erichs, Jr.
Capt John L. Euler
Capt William L. Fly
Capt Cecil R. Forster
Capt Mark F. Geary
1stLt Boyd L. George
Capt Harvey G. Gleason
Maj James H. Granger
Capt Tone N. Grant
Capt Mark L. Haiman
Capt Clark A. Halderson
Capt Daniel M. Hanlon
Capt John J. Hargrove
Capt Victor J. Haydel
Capt Louis J. Hellerman
Capt Douglas G. Hendricks
Capt Thomas D. Horne
Col Richard D. Humphreys
Capt Tristam T. Hyde
Capt Roland K. Iverson, Jr.
Capt Carey H. Johnson
Capt Charles J. Kall
1stLt Francis J. Kaveney (2 awards)
Maj Ronald J. Kaye
Capt Adrian R. King
Capt Jerome R. Klukas
Capt Richard D. Lane
LtCol Charles R. Larouche

Capt Paul J. Laveroni
Capt Daniel H. LeGear, Jr.
1stLt Robert M. Lee
Capt Joel Levine
Capt Edward J. Lopata
Capt John J. Lynch
Capt Robert W. Mann
1stLt Jeffery W. Maurer
Capt William H. McAdam, Jr.
Capt Michael G. McCollum
Capt Robert M. MacConnell
Capt Martin G. McGuinn, Jr.
Capt Sandy S. McMath
Capt John A. Milici
Capt Charles H. Moses III
Capt Richard A. Muench
Maj Michael Patrick Murray
Capt Donald B. Myers
1stLt William G. Nash
Maj Leo K. O'Drudy
Capt Stephen P. Oggel
Capt Jerrold Oldani
Capt Theodore J. Padden
Capt John S. Papa
Capt W. Hays Parks
1stLt Michael K. Phalin
Col Harry S. Popper
Capt Richard L. Prosise
Capt Jack C. Provine
Maj H. Terry Reiniche
Capt Ross T. Roberts
Capt Frank G. Roux, Jr.
Capt Thomas A. Rulon
Capt John E. Russell
Capt Gary A. Sargent
Capt Allen R. Saxe
1stLt James M. Schermerhorn
Capt Mahlon C. Schneider
Capt Dennis H. Siems
Capt David E. Skaggs
Capt J. Len Skiles
Capt Stanley L. Smith, Jr.
LtCol Charles E. Spence, Jr.
Capt Reginald K. Templeton
Capt Arthur W. Tifford
1stLt Philip C. Tower
Capt Robert W. Wachsmuth
LtCol William T. Westmoreland, Jr.
Capt Richard M. Williams
Capt Ronald W. Williamson
Capt W. Mark Wood
LtCol Richard E. Wray
Capt Rufus C. Young IV

Navy Achievement Medal

Capt Steve A. Bamberger
1stLt James B. Barnett
1stLt Thomas A. Bergstrom
Capt Allen J. Borne
Major Robert J. Chadwick

U.S. MEDALS AWARDED MARINE CORPS LAWYERS AND JUDGE ADVOCATES FOR VIETNAM SERVICE

Capt Otis F. Cochran, Jr.
Capt Stanton M. Cole
Capt Chapman B. Cox
Capt John L. Euler
Capt Fred R. Files, Jr.
Capt Michael J. Hoblock
Capt William E. Iorio
Capt Franz P. Jevne
Capt Rex L. Jones III
Capt Scott Keep
1stLt Edward F. Kelly
Capt Robert Kirkman
Capt Richard D. Lane
Capt Thomas O. Lavoy
Capt Michael J. Levin
Capt Alfred W. Mackey
Capt Patrick H. Mathews
Capt Michael C. McCarey
Capt Michael P. Merrill
Capt Charles H. Mitchell
Capt David G. Moore
Capt William J. O'Byrne

Capt Frank J. O'Connor
Capt Charles E. Patterson
Capt John N. Post
Capt J. Kent Riegel
Capt John J. Reilly
Capt E. Randall Ricketts
Capt Clifford E. Roberson
Capt Terrance B. Rodsky
Capt Harry D. Sabine
Capt Michael D. Schrunk
Capt Lawrence W. Secrest
Capt James P. Shannon
Capt Philip D. Sharp, Jr.
Capt Edwin A. Snyder
Capt Bruce D. Strathearn
Maj Robert E. Switzer
Capt James L. Thompson
1stLt Michael I. Walling
Capt John L. Westney, Jr.
Capt Robert S. Wiggins, Jr.
1stLt Donald E. Wittig
Maj James R. Ziemann

Appendix D
Cases Cited

Latney v. Ignatius, 416 F.2d 821 (1969)..................................n, 103; 167
U.S. v. LCpl James B. Addison, NCM 70 2433...............................193
U.S. v. LCpl Denzil R. Allen, NCM 68 3152.................................111
U.S. v. Pvt Lester E. Allison..n, 127
U.S. v. Pvt Martin R. Alvarez..112
U.S. v. Cpl Joseph W. Anderson, Jr...208
U.S. v. Sgt Adrian Aragon..208
U.S. v. Mr. Raymond G. Averette, 19 USCMA 363 (1970)................103; 168
U.S. v. PFC Douglas Beane..n, 172
U.S. v. LCpl John D. Belknap, NCM 68 3657..................................112
U.S. v. Pvt Talmadge D. Berry..119
U.S. v. PFC Edward P. Boltik, NCM 68 0552...................................70
U.S. v. PFC James H. Boyd, Jr...54
U.S. v. PFC Thomas R. Boyd...175
U.S. v. HN Jon R. Bretag..53
U.S. v. Pvt Stephen F. Brice...119
U.S. v. PFC Robert L. Bright..37
U.S. v. PltSgt Roy E. Bumgarner, U.S. Army............................n, 139
U.S. v. 1stLt William L. Calley, U.S.Army..................................111
U.S. v. LCpl Douglas R. Collard, NCM 67 2117................................81
U.S. v. Pvt Curtis Crawford..207
U.S. v. LCpl Stephen D. Crider, NCM 69 4114................................140
U.S. v. Pvt Jimmie Dunbar..161
U.S. v. Cpl Charlie Eason, III, NCM 70 2612................................240
U.S. v. LCpl Richard A. Eicholtz...162
U.S. v. Pvt Frederick L. Elbert, Jr..218
U.S. v. Cpl Richard M. Ford, NCM 66 0269....................................76
U.S. v. PFC Robert R. Garwood, NMCM 81 1892................................223
U.S. v. PFC Lucien J. Gonzales II, NCM 65 2090..............................37
U.S. v. PFC Samuel G. Green, Jr., NCM 70 3811..............................175
U.S. v. Bobby R. Greenwood, NCM 70 3843....................................135
U.S. v. LCpl Andrew M. Harris Jr...193
U.S. v. PFC Gary O. Harrison, NCM 65 2160...................................30
U.S. v. PFC Willie Harrison..156
U.S. v. Pvt Gary A. Hendricks..169
U.S. v. Pvt Randell D. Herrod, NCM 70 2970.................................175
U.S. v. PFC Eugene R. Hofstetler...161
U.S. v. Sgt Larry A. Kavanaugh...218
U.S. v. PFC Charles W. Keenan, NCM 67 0913..................................79
U.S. v. Sgt James W. Killen, NCM 70 1100...................................149
U.S. v. Mr. James H. Latney, NCM 68 1965...............................99; 167
U.S. v. LCpl Anthony Licciardo, Jr., NCM 69 0205...........................112
U.S. v. Cpl Stanley J. Luczko, NCM 67 0952..............................n, 81
U.S. v. LCpl James A. Maushart, NCM 68 3388................................112
U.S. v. LCpl Marion McGhee, NCM 66 0484.....................................32
U.S. v. LtCol Edison W. Miller...219

CASES CITED

U.S. v. PFC David Napier, NCM 70 1453.................................134
U.S. v. PFC John D. Potter, Jr., NCM 67 1348...........................53
U.S. v. Ronald J. Reese, NCM 70 0855..................................140
U.S. v. SSgt Alfonso R. Riate...218
U.S. v. Pvt Michael A. Roberts..119
U.S. v. Pvt Michael A. Schwarz, NCM 71 0028...........................175
U.S. v. Pvt Reginald F. Smith...134
U.S. v. Cpl Clifford K. Somerville....................................237
U.S. v. Sgt Jon M. Sweeney, NCM 71 2662...............................221
U.S. v. 2dLt Stephen J. Talty..53
U.S. v. LCpl John W. Thomas...111
U.S. v. PFC Robert J. Vickers...112
U.S. v. Sgt Ronald L. Vogel, NCM 67 1347...............................53
U.S. v. PFC Kenneth W. Wheeler, NCM 66 0376............................23
U.S. v. Pvt Calvin L. White...119

Appendix E

Review of Confinement Adjudged in Cases of Marines Convicted of the Murder of Vietnamese Noncombatants, 1965-71

Individual	Sentence Adjudged (in years)	Sentence Approved (in years) By CA[a]	Sentence Approved (in years) By NCMR[b]	Action by USCMA[c]	Sentence Resulting from Parole (P) or Clemency (C) Action[d] (in years)
1	10	10	7	Appeal denied	C: 6 1/12
2	Life	Life	25	Sentence affirmed	C: 6
3	5	5	5	Appeal denied	C: Denied
4	Life	Life	3	Appeal denied	
5	Life	25	5	Appeal denied	C: 2 3/4
6	4	4	4	Appeal denied	C: Denied
7	Life	Life	Life	Appeal denied	C: 12
8	50	35	10		C: 8
9	Life	35	5	Appeal denied	C: 2 5/12
10	30	30	Dismissed (insanity)		
11	10	5	5	No petition	C: 4
12	Life	30	30	Appeal denied	C: 3
13	Life	Life	Life	Appeal denied	C: 9
14	Life	20	20	Appeal denied	C: 7 1/12
15	Life	20	20	Appeal denied	C: 7
16	2	2	2	Appeal denied	C: Denied
17	2	2	2		C: Denied
18	2	2	2	Appeal denied	
19	Life	Life	3	Appeal denied	
20	Life	30	3	Appeal denied	
21	4	1 1/4	2/3	Did not petition	C: Denied
22	Life	30	15	10 years	P: 3
23	Life	40	15	Appeal denied	P: 3 3/4
24	5	1	1	Appeal denied	C: Denied
25	Life	1	1	Did not petition	C: Denied

CONFINEMENTS ADJUDGED FOR MARINES CONVICTED OF MURDER OF NONCOMBATANTS

Individual	Sentence Adjudged (in years)	Sentence Approved (in years) By CA[a]	Sentence Approved (in years) By NCMR[b]	Action by USCMA[c]	Sentence Resulting from Parole (P) or Clemency (C) Action[d] (in years)
26	20	20	Dismissed		
27	Life	25	25	Appeal dismissed	C: 19

SOURCES: Data provided by U.S. Marine Corps and Department of the Navy, Offices of the Judge Advocate General, and by Naval Clemency and Parole Board.

[a] Convening authority.
[b] Navy Court of Military Review.
[c] U.S. Court of Military Appeals.
[d] Does not take into account time off earned for good behavior.

Excerpted with permission from: Guenter Lewy, *America in Vietnam* (New York: Oxford University Press, 1978), Table 10-5, p. 458.

Appendix F

Confinement Actually Served in Selected Cases of Marines Convicted of the Murder of Vietnamese Noncombatants, 1965-71

The numbers and adjacent names correspond to the numbers in Appendix E. Only those cases listed in Appendix E and mentioned in the text are included here.

	Trial Court's Sentence	Release Date	Confinement Actually Served
1. M. McGhee	10 yrs	14 Dec 1971	6 yrs, 1 month
6. J. H. Boyd	4 yrs	23 Jan 1970	3 yrs
7. J. D. Potter (1)	Life	16 Feb 1978	12 yrs, 1 month
8. R. L. Vogel	50 yrs	? 1975	9 yrs, plus
15. D. R. Allen (2)	Life	2 Aug 1971	2 yrs, 11 months
16. J. D. Belknap	2 yrs	5 Dec 1969	1 yr, 3 months
18. J. A. Maushart	2 yrs	1 May 1970	1 yr, 8 months
19. S. D. Crider (3)	Life	2 Mar 1973	3 yrs, 9 months
20. R. J. Reese (3)	Life	8 Dec 1971	2 yrs, 4 months

(1) Convicted of five specifications of premeditated murder, rape, and attempted rape
(2) Convicted of five specifications of unpremeditated murder
(3) Convicted of four specifications of premeditated murder
(Release dates provided by Navy Clemency & Parole Board)

Appendix G
Senior Marine Corps Lawyers, 1950 to 1966

Prior to 1941, legal matters, including courts-martial, were the province of Marine Corps personnel officers. In 1941, at Washington, D.C., the Courts and Boards Division was established within the Personnel Department of Headquarters Marine Corps. Thereafter legal affairs, other than the actual trials of courts-martial, were centralized in that division. Most active-duty lawyers were reservists, supervised by a few regular officers who alternated legal and nonlegal assignments. All lawyers were assigned either to Headquarters Marine Corps or to Headquarters, Fleet Marine Force Pacific, in Hawaii, or to Headquarters, Fleet Marine Force Atlantic, in Norfolk, Virginia.* There were no billets for attorneys in the fleet or at any post or station until 1942 when a billet for a captain-lawyer was included in each Fleet Marine Force division headquarters.

During World War II the Courts and Boards Division evolved into Discipline Section, then Discipline Division, and, finally, into Discipline Branch. Although partially staffed by lawyers, Discipline Branch was headed by a nonlawyer personnel officer.

In May 1950 the Uniform Code of Military Justice became law. At the same time a lawyer was appointed head of Discipline Branch for the first time. Colonel James C. Bigler, whose father had also been a Marine Corps officer and a lawyer on active duty from 1900 to 1925, was the first lawyer Discipline Branch head. Colonel Bigler, a 1932 graduate of the U.S. Naval Academy, had been an infantry officer until 1938, when he was ordered to George Washington University's law school. After his graduation in 1941 he alternated legal and infantry assignments until ordered to Discipline Branch in late 1949. He continued as Branch head until August 1952.

Subsequent Discipline Branch heads were: Colonel St.Julien R. Marshall, from August 1952 to July 1954; Colonel Paul D. Sherman, from July 1954 to June 1956; Colonel John S. Twitchell, from June 1956 to an undetermined month in 1958; and Colonel Hamilton M. Hoyler, branch head until July 1958. Colonel Robert A. Scherr filled the billet from July 1958 to July 1964. During his tenure there were 129 lawyer billets in the Marine Corps. Colonel Robert B. Neville headed Discipline Branch from July 1964 to July 1966. When Marine Corps units landed at Da Nang in March 1965 there were 168 lawyers on active duty.

Colonel Charles B. Sevier assumed the duties of branch head in July 1966. There were 223 lawyers on active duty then, increasing to 277 in 1967. On 17 April 1968 Discipline Branch was deactivated and, in a reorganization of the Headquarters Marine Corps staff, the Judge Advocate Division was established as a separate division. All of the 15 Headquarters Marine Corps lawyers, in addition to 10 enlisted clerks and 14 civilians, were assigned to the new division which was divided into four branches: military law; research and plans; general law; and legal assistance.

Colonel Sevier continued as the first Director, Judge Advocate Division, with the additional title of Staff Judge Advocate for the Commandant of the Marine Corps, from July 1966 until August 1968.

---

*FMFPac was formed in April 1944. Before that the lawyers were assigned to FMFPac's predecessor, Headquarters V Amphibious Corps. FMFLant was formed in December 1946. Before then the lawyers were assigned to FMFLant's precursor, the 1st Special Marine Brigade.

Appendix H
Heads of Discipline Branch and Directors of the Judge Advocate Division, 1950 to 1988

Col James C. Bigler
Head of Discipline Branch
May 1950 - September 1952

Col St. Julien R. Marshall
Head of Discipline Branch
September 1952 - July 1955

Col Paul D. Sherman
Head of Discipline Branch
July 1955 - June 1956

Col John S. Twitchell
Head of Discipline Branch
July 1956 - ? 1958

Col Hamilton M. Hoyler
Head of Discipline Branch
? 1958 - June 1958

Col Robert A. Scherr
Head of Discipline Branch
July 1958 - July 1964

Col Robert B. Neville
Head of Discipline Branch
July 1964 - July 1966

Col Charles B. Sevier
Director, Judge Adovcate Division
July 1966 - July 1968

Col Marion G. Truesdale
Director, Judge Advocate Division
July 1968 - July 1969

HEADS OF DISCIPLINE BRANCH AND DIRECTORS OF JUDGE ADVOCATE DIVISION, 1950 TO 1988

BGen Duane L. Faw
Director, Judge Advocate Division
August 1969 - August 1971

BGen Clyde R. Mann
Director, Judge Advocate Division
September 1971 - July 1973

BGen John R. DeBarr
Director, Judge Advocate Division
April 1973 - July 1973 (Acting)
July 1973 - June 1976

BGen Robert J. Chadwick
Director, Judge Advocate Division
July 1976 - February 1978

BGen James P. King
Director, Judge Advocate Division
March 1978 - April 1980

BGen William H. J. Tiernan
Director, Judge Advocate Division
May 1980 - June 1983

BGen Walter J. Donovan, Jr.
Director, Judge Advocate Division
June 1983 - September 1985

BGen David M. Brahms
Director, Judge Advocate Division
September 1985 - August 1988

BGen Michael E. Rich
Director, Judge Advocate Division
September 1988 - present

Appendix I
List of Reviewers

Marines

Hon. James H. Webb, Jr.,
    Secretary of the Navy (Capt, Ret)
Gen Earl E. Anderson (Ret)
Gen Leonard F. Chapman, Jr. (Ret)
Gen Wallace M. Greene, Jr. (Ret)
Gen Louis H. Wilson, Jr. (Ret)

LtGen Charles G. Cooper (Ret)
LtGen William K. Jones (Ret)
LtGen Victor H. Krulak (Ret)

BGen Charles A. Cushman (Ret)
BGen John R. DeBarr (Ret)
BGen Walter J. Donovan (Ret)
BGen Raymond W. Edwards (Ret)
BGen Duane L. Faw (Ret)
BGen Max G. Halliday (Ret)
BGen James F. Lawrence, Jr. (Ret)
BGen Michael I. Neil
BGen Michael E. Rich
BGen William H. J. Tiernan (Ret)

Col Eileen M. Albertson
Col Clarke C. Barnes
Col Charles H. Beale, Jr. (Ret)
Col George P. Blackburn (Ret)
Col Robert J. Blum (Ret)
Col Norris C. Broome (Ret)
Col Carl E. Buchmann (Ret.)
Col Thomas P. Casey (Ret)
Col David J. Cassady
Col James A. Cathcart
Col Ralph K. Culver (Ret)
Col William R. Eleazer (Ret)
Col Benjamin B. Ferrell (Ret)
Col Joseph J. N. Gambardella (Ret)
Col Robert A. Godwin
Col James H. Granger
Col Mark L. Haiman
Col Jack E. Hanthorn (Ret)
Col Paul F. Henderson, Jr. (Ret)
Col Donald Higginbotham
Col Donald E. Holben (Ret)

Col Henry Hoppe III (Ret)
Col Hamilton M. Hoyler (Ret)
Col Olin W. Jones (Ret)
Col Peter N. Kress (Ret)
Col Elliott R. Laine, Jr. (Ret)
Col Charles R. Larouche (Ret)
Col Robert C. Lehnert (Ret)
Col Robert M. Lucy (Ret)
Col Michael G. McCollum
Col Daniel F. McConnell (Ret)
Col Joseph R. Motelewski (Ret)
Col Michael Patrick Murray (Ret)
Col Verne L. Oliver (Ret)
Col Curtis W. Olson (Ret)
Col W. Hays Parks
Col Arthur R. Petersen (Ret)
Col Harry B. Popper (Ret)
Col Charles B. Sevier (Ret)
Col Marion G. Truesdale (Ret)

LtCol William T. Anderson
LtCol Stephen C. Berg
LtCol William B. Draper (Ret)
LtCol David C. Hague
LtCol Werner Hellmer
LtCol William C. Jaeck (Ret)
LtCol Kenneth W. Jones (Ret)
LtCol Paul J. Laveroni
LtCol Richard A. Muench
LtCol Ronald C. Rachow (Ret)
LtCol Richard E. Theer (Ret)
LtCol John L. Zorack (Ret)

Capt George H. O'Kelley

CWO 4 Len E. Pierce (Ret)

MGySgt Gene E. White

Others

VAdm James B. Stockdale, USN (Ret)
RAdm Hugh D. Campbell, JAGC, USN (Ret)
MajGen George S. Prugh, JAGC, USA (Ret)
Col Ted B. Borek, JAGC, USA

LIST OF REVIEWERS

Capt Edward M. Byrne, JAGC, USN
Col Henry G. Green, USAF
Capt Keith B. Lawrence, JAGC, USN (Ret)
Cdr Jerry D. Rucker, JAGC, USN
Mr. Vincent J. Bartolotta, Jr.
Mr. Nathaniel F. Emmons
Mr. Denzil D. Garrison
Professor William T. Generous, Jr.
Mr. Tone N. Grant
Mr. Donald W. Harris
Mr. Victor J. Haydel
Judge Richard D. Lane

Mr. Daniel H. LeGear
Professor Guenter Lewy
Mr. Richard L. Prosise
Mr. Harry L. Shorstein
Mr. Robert W. Wachsmuth

Historical Office, Office of the Secretary of Defense
Historical Division, Joint Chiefs of Staff
Chief of Military History & the Center of Military History, Department of the Army
Office of Air Force History

Index

Key: **boldface type** = illustrations; *n* = footnote

"ad hoc" special court-martial judges, 205-206, 237
Adams, Sgt James W., 112-13
Addison, LCpl James B., United States v., 193, 196
Administrative discharge, 131-33, 147, 170-73, 196, 208, 213-14
Advance Base Receiving Barracks, Port Hueneme, California, 11
Agreement for Mutual Defense Assistance in Indochina. (*See also* Pentalateral Agreement)
Agreement on Ending the War and Restoring Peace in Vietnam, 218
Aitken, Col Hugh S., 189
Alberson, Capt Eileen M., 206-207, **207**
Albrink, Cdr Frederick, JAGC, USN, **12**
Alch, Gerald, 223
Allen, Capt Bernard A., Jr., 63, 89
Allen, LCpl Denzil R., United States v., 111-12
Allison, Pvt Lester E., United States v., 127*n*
Allison, 1stLt William T., II, 95; Capt, **96**
Alvarez, Pvt Martin R., United States v., 112-13
Ambort, 1stLt Lewis R., United States v., 174-75, 177-79, 183, **188**
American Legion, 5
Amtank (SS), 99, 101
Anderson, Maj Earl E., 9; Col, 16; BGen, 84*n*; Gen, 10*n*, **17**, 84, 220, 240
Anderson, Cpl Joseph W., Jr., United States v., 208-209, **210**, 211
Anderson, Capt William T., 226
Anello, Capt Michael M., **154**
Aragon, Sgt Adrian, United States v., 208-11
Arianna, Lt Edward A., USN, **30**
Armed Forces Qualification Test, 73
Armstrong, MajGen Alan J., **212**, 212-13
Army Commands and Units
    Judge Advocate General's Corps, 5, 5*n*, 11, 243
    Task Force Oregon, 63
    U.S. Military Advisory Command, Vietnam, 18, 30, 39, 60, 63
Articles for the Government of the Navy, 3-6 (*See also* "Rocks and Shoals.")
Articles of War, 2-6
Averette, Raymond G., United States v., 168
Axtell, Col George C., Jr., 47; **47**; BGen, 84*n*; LtGen, 9, 10*n*

Bailey, F. Lee, 7
Baird, CWO 4 Maynard K. "Sonny", 87, **143**, 146
Barnes, Capt Clarke C., 92, **96**, 104-105, 109, 132, 137, **147**, 148, 166, **166**
Barnett, 1stLt James E., **65**
Barrow, Col Robert H., **135**, **136**
Bartolotta, Capt Vincent J., Jr., 234, **235**, 236
Bashian, Capt George G., Jr., **127**, **143**
Bauch, Lt Jared O., JAGC, USN, **97**
Beale, Col Charles H., Jr., **47**, 49, 51, 53-54, **55**, 56, 66
Beane, PFC Douglas, United States v., 172*n*
Beaudry, Capt G. Ward, 142
Beckington, Col Herbert L., 84*n*; LtGen, 9, 10*n*

Belknap, LCpl John D., United States v., 112-13
Belli, Melvin, **61**
Belluomini, Capt Emilic V., Jr., 142
Bennett, Col Nalton M., 156, 163, **173**, 196
Berg, Capt Stephen C., 130, 201, **209**; Maj, 208
Bergen, Capt John A., 194
Berry, Pvt Talmadge D., 114, 119
Bigler, Col James C., 11
Black market activities, 32
Blackburn, Col George P., Jr., 30, 40-41, **41**, 72
Blakeslee, LtCol Rollin Q., **122**, 147
Blanchard, Col Don H. "Doc", 202
Blum, 1stLt Robert J., 15, **16**; Maj, **181**, 182-83, 206
Blume, Lt Richard, JAGC, USN, **204**
Blunk, Capt William D., 234
Board for Correction of Naval Records, 221
Bohlin, Maj Lawrence G., **122**
Boltik, PFC Edward P., United States v., 70, 72, **72**, 73
Bonner, Capt Raymond T., 208
Boyd, PFC James H., Jr., United States v., 54
Boyd, PFC Thomas R., United States v., 175, 182, 184, **185**, 186
Boyington, William, USMC, 7
Bradford, SSgt Lonnie J., 214
Brahms, Maj David M., 152, **153**, **154**, 155, **162**, 163, 218, 219-20; LtCol, 226; BGen, 221
Brandtner, Capt Martin L., 226
Bretag, HM Jon R., USN, United States v., 53-54
Brice, Pvt Stephen F., United States v., 119
Brig facilities, **145**
    in 1966, 39
    damage to, 142
    III MAF, 66, **144**, 155, 206
    increased populations, 114
    lack of, 31-32
    riots in, 114-19
Bright, PFC Robert L., United States v., 37, 39. (*See also* United States v. PFC Lucien J. Gonzales.)
Brooker, LCpl Hercules E., 134-37
Broome, LtCol Norris C. "Sweeper", 66, **66**, 100-101; Col, 109*n*
Brown, Capt Charles E., 183-84, 186, 198
Buchmann, LtCol Carl E., 127, **128**, **157**, 159, 164, 170, 191, 203-204
Bucknas, MSgt Bruno B., **157**
Bui Thi Huong, 53-54
Bumgarner, PlSgt Roy E., USA, United States v., 139*n*
Buse, LtGen Henry W., Jr., 129
Bushell, Capt Gary E., **131**, 186
Byrne, Capt Edward M., JAGC, USN, 244

Caleen, Capt Reynold L., Jr., **192**, 196
Calley, 1stLt William L., USA, 111, 156, **156**
Calvert (APA 32), 37
Cam Lo, 65

INDEX

Camp Books, Red Beach, 42, 44, **45**, 50, 59, **78**, 142, 158-59, 170, 193
Camp Carroll, 65
Camp Haskins, Red Beach, 191
Camp Zama, Japan, 74, 104
Campbell, Capt Wallace L., 37, **38**
Campbell, Lt Hugh D., JAGC, USN, 16-17, 26, **26**, 27, **31**; RAdm, 51
Campbell, LtCol Frederick H., **30**
Carlock, Capt G. David, III, **153**, 154
Carney, 2dLt Robert B., 188
Carroll, Capt James W., 201-202, 209
Carter, 2dLt Macauley, Jr., 97; 1stLt, **71**
Casey, GySgt John, 192
Casey, LtCol Thomas P., 40, **40**, 42, **47**, **56**, 59; Col, 63
Cassady, Capt David J., 93, 138, **147**
Category IV personnel, 73-74, 122, 203, 231-32
Cates, Gen Clifton B., **9**, 10*n*
Cathcart, 2dLt James A., 98
Catholic University, 9
Cavalier (APA 37), 39
Chadwick, Maj Robert J., **56**, 76; LtCol, **173**; BGen, 76*n*
Chafee, Secretary of the Navy John H., 170
Chapman, Gen Leonard F., Jr., 129, **130**, 165, 167, **167**, 172, 203, 231, **233**

Chiera, James, 190
China Beach, 21
Christofferson, Capt Clyde R., 223
Chu Lai, 26, 33-35, 40, 42, 63, 68
Chu Lai Airbase, construction of, 20
Civic action, 27-28, 47-48, 68
Civil affairs, 18
Civilian courts-martial, 99-100, 103*n*, 168
Clark, 1stLt John W., **30**
Clemmons, Cdr William E., USN, 40
Clifford, Secretary of Defense Clark M., 81
Cochran, Capt Otis F., **203**
Cole, Capt Stanton M., 142
Coleman, Capt Francis T., 42, 49, 66, **79**, **80**
Composto, Capt Joseph, 226-27
Con Thien, 65
Constantino, Capt Paul R., 42, **62**, 63
Constructive service, 87
Conway, Capt Martin E., Jr., 114
Cooper, Grant B., 81-82
Cooper, LtCol Charles G., 174-75, 178, 178*n*, 179-81, 183, 187-88
Corrections Manual, 31
Cosgriff, Lt William J., JAGC, USN, 161
Court of Military Appeals. (*See also* U.S. Court of Military Appeals)
Court of Military Review, 60*n*, 73. (*See also* Navy Board of Review)
Crandell, LtCol John E., 211
Crawford, Pvt Curtis, United States v., 207-208
Crider, LCpl Stephen D., United States v., 140
Croizat, LtCol Victor J., 15
Cronk, PFC Richard E., 23
Crow, 2dLt Jerald D., 13; 1stLt, **96**
Crow, GySgt Wesley, 40
Culver, LtCol Ralph K., **47**, 59, 69, **71**; Col, 72
Cummings, LtCol William M. "Ace," 156, 158
Cunningham, 1stLt Jerry G., **78**
Cushman, LtGen Robert E., Jr., 60, 74, **85**, 100, 142; Gen, 220, 231

Da Nang, 2, 11, 15-17, 20-23, 25-26, 29, 32, 35, 42, 50, 54, 56, 59, 65, 68, 70
Da Nang Airbase, **15**, 27-28, 34, 39, 59, 63, 69
Da Nang River. (*See also* Han River)
Dao Quang Thinh, 53
Dartmouth College, 48
Davis, 1stLt Miles, **135**
Davis, MajGen Raymond G., 92-93, 104, 134, **135**; Gen, **212**
Davis, MSgt William C., 234
DeBarr, Col John R., 104, 106, 112, 119, **122**, 124, 133, 160, **161**, 164, 206, 241; BGen, 220, 232
Deck court, 3. (*See also* Summary court-martial)
Dedic, GySgt William, 47, 53
Demilitarized Zone, 35, 59, 60, 65
Department of Defense, 6
    Lawyer Working Group, 121
    Prisoner of War Policy Committee, 218
Desjardin, 1stLt Armand H., **203**
Diehl, Bernhard, 224
Direct Commissioning Program, 216
Disciplinary Laws of the Coast Guard, 6
"Dogpatch", 42, 75-76
Donahue, Dr. Hayden, 188
Dong Ha, 44, 54, 59, 65, 68
Donovan, Maj Walter J., **66**; BGen, 65*n*
Draper, Capt William B., Jr., 26, 56-57; Maj, 47-48, **48**, 54, **62**, **65**, 81
Drug rehabilitation, 127
Drug testing facilities, 104
Drug use, 74, 103-104, 170-71, 231-32, 238. (*See also* marijuana use)
Dudley, Pvt Jimmie, United States V., 134-36
Dulacki, LtGen Leo J., 53, 170
Dunbar, Pvt Jimmie, United States v., 161
Durbin, LtCol Paul J., USA, 15, **15**

Eastham, Capt Stephen C., 234
Eden, Capt Van E., 234
Edwards, LtCol Raymond W. "Wes", 233, **234**, 237-39
Egan, PFC Donald R., United States v., 134-35, 137
Ehlers, 1stLt James, **65**
Eicholtz, LCpl Richard E., United States v., 162
Eisenhower, Gen Dwight D., USA, 5
Elbert, Pvt Frederick L., Jr., United States v., 218, **219**
Eleazer, LtCol William R., **113**, 126, **127**, 143
Elwood, MajGen Hugh M., 121
Emmons, Capt Nathaniel F., **154**, 155, **155**
Erickson, Lt John F., JAGC, USN, 47, 51
Erickson, Lt(jg) John F., JAGC, USN, 25
Ervin, Senator Sam J., Jr., 102, 124-25
Euler, Capt John L., 220
Ewing, 7-8
Excess Leave Program (Law), 85, 121, 216, 240
Executions, 8

Falk, Capt Allen E., **143**
Fallon, Col Eugene B. "Doc", 60, 66, **66**, 67, 78, 91
Faw, Maj Duane L., 8; Col, 60, 60*n*, 61, **61**, 61*n*, 63, 99-100, 127; BGen, 84, 126, 146, 164, 168, **173**, 200, 205, 211, 216, 240-41
Federal Task Force on Manpower, 73

Ferrell, Majl Benjamin B., 28; LtCol, 147, **148**; Col, 51, 162-63, **173**, 223
Fields, MajGen Lewis J., **41**
Files, Capt Fred R., **31**
Fishbach, 1stLt John T., 35-36
Fly, Capt William L., 95, **96**, 244
Foley, Dermot G., 227
Foreign claims, 68
Forrestal, Secretary of Defense James V., 6
Forster, Capt Cecil R., 130
Fragging, 34, 57, 110-11, 124, 133-34, 136n, 141, 168-69, 239 (*See also* Operation Freeze, 168)
Franks, Capt Richard L., **192**
Fuller, BGen Regan, 132

Gabriel, Richard, 159
Gales, Cpl Ronald E., 193-95
Gambardella, LtCol Joseph J. N., 114-15
Garland, Reuben A., 195
Garrison, Senator Denzil D., 186-88, **188**, 189
Garwood, PFC Robert R., 37 **224**; United States v., 223-30, 224n
General court-martial, 4, 22, 23, 69
    Article 32 investigation, 49
    requirement for lawyers in, 35, 51
general court-martial commands, 59
General Officers' Symposium, Marine Corps
    1966, 50
    1967, 73
    1969, 131
George, 1stLt Boyd L., **95**
George Washington University, 9
Georgetown University, 9
Gideon v. Wainwright, 125
Gillmor, 2dLt John E., Jr., 21, 26
Gio Linh, 65
Glasgow, Cdr Raymond W., JAGC, USN, **73**
Gleason, Capt Harvey J., **78**
Glenn, 1stLt Jimmie W., 116, **117**, 118
Glenn, Capt Franklin P., 44, 50, **67**
Glenn, Capt Thomas J., Jr., **153**
Godwin, 1stLt Robert A., 23, 23, 27; Capt, 75
Gomez, Cpl Mario A., **199**, 199-200
Gonzales, PFC Lucien J.; United States v., 37, 39. (*See also* United States v. PFC Robert L. Bright.)
Grabowski, Maj Fred, 20-21, **21**; LtCol, **55**
Granger, Capt James H., 197-98; Maj, 173, 201-202, **203**, 214; Col, 165
Grant, 1stLt Lloyd S., **188**
Grant, Capt Tone N., 201, **209**, 209-11
Green, MSgt Noah, 155
Green, MSgt Ronald L., **153**
Green, PFC Samuel G., Jr., United States v., 175, 179, 182, 186, 189-90
Greene, Gen Wallace M., Jr., 10n, 59, **85**
Greenwood, PFC Bobby R., United States v., 135-38
Gridley, LtCol Lily H., 17n, 57n
Gulf of Tonkin, 39
Guy, LtCol Theodore, USAF, 218

Haden, LtCol Frederick M., 79, 99, 116, **122**, 155-56

Hahn, Capt Joseph J., 239
Hai Van Pass, 59
Haiman, Capt Mark L., 70, 76, **76**, **131**
Halderson, Capt Clark A., **96**, 136
Halliday, LtCol Max G., 99, **122**; Col, 151-52, 156, **162**, 163
Hamilton, K. B., 72
Han River, 56, 60
Hanlon, 1stLt Daniel M., **80**; Capt, 42, **79**
Hanthorn, Col Jack E., 113, **113**, 122, 143
Hargrove, Capt John J., 186, **186**, 198
Harrington, Assistant Secretary of the Navy John S., 221
Harris, LCpl Andrew M., Jr., United States v., 193-96
Harris, 1stLt Donald W., 18, **19**, 39
Harrison, PFC Gary O., United States v., 30
Harrison, PFC Willie, United States v., 156
Harvard University School of Law, 9
Haydel, Capt Victor J., **78**, 100, **100**, 101-102, **102**
Hayes, President Rutherford B., 3
Hearn, Col Alexander M. "Sandy", 105-106
Heinl, Col Robert D., Jr., 170
Helgoland (West German hospital ship), 61, **62**, 63, 166
Hellmer, Capt Werner, 228, **229**; Maj, 224n
Henderson, Capt Jacob R., Jr., 130-31, **192**
Henderson, Col Oran K., 190
Henderson, Maj Paul F., Jr., 16; LtCol, 67, 91-92; Col, **73**
Hendricks, Pvt Gary A., United States v., 169-70
Herrod, Pvt Randell D., United States v., 175-77, 179, 182-83, 186-90, **188**, 188-89, **189**
Higginbotham, Capt Donald, 63, **63**, 65, 75-76, 82, **82**, 122
Hilgart, Col Valeria F., 207
Hill, BGen Homer S., 164
Hill 22, 53
Hill 327, 27, 28, 35, 63, 143
Hilton, Capt Robert E., 234, **238**
Hinkle, Capt Thomas F., 221-22
Hoblock, Capt Michael J., Jr., 119, **153**
Hodge, Capt Anthony L., 154
Hoffman, 1stLt Bruce A., **30**
Hofstetler, PFC Eugene R., United State v., 161-62
Holben, LtCol Donald E., **66**, 70, 101-103, 106; Col, **122**, 173, **198**, 198-200, 202, **203**, 205, 208, 210-11, 213, **213**, 214, 237, 242
Holder, Capt Franklin D., 237
Hoppe, LtCol Henry, III, 136, 140, **140**, 160, **173**, 204-205
Hoyler, Col Hamilton M., 8, 13
Hubbell, John, 225
Hue, 89
Huff, SgtMaj Edgar R., 171, **172**
Hunnicutt, Cpl Hubert H., 109n

I Corps Bar Association, 47, 63, 121n, **163**, 166, 206
Inouye, Senator Daniel K., 165
Iverson, 1stLt Roland K., Jr., **203**; Capt, 214

Jackson, Lt Wyman N., JAGC, USN, **12**; Capt, 51, 105
Jaeck, LtCol William C., 74-75, 104, 114, **122**
Jarrett, Capt Tommy W., 171, **192**, 207
Jaskilka, BGen Samuel, 127
Jevne, Capt Franz P., **143**, 183, **185**, 186, 198
John, Capt John T., 239

INDEX

Johnson, Capt Carey H., **153**
Johnson, Col Earl H., 45
Johnson, President Lyndon B., 99, 126
Jones, J. Fielding, **73**
Jones, Capt James W., 70
Jones, LCpl Joseph L., United States v., 193-94, 196
Jones, GySgt Kenneth W., 42, **86**
Jones, Col Olin W., 2, 7, 16, 18-19, 27-28
Jones, Capt Rex L. III, **157**
Jones, MajGen William K., 133, **133**, 134, 163, 167-68; LtGen, 170-72, 231
Jowers, Capt Harry K., 120, **121**
Judge advocate, 7, 125
Judge Advocate General, U.S. Navy, 3-4, 9, 11-13, 34, 51, 122, 125-26, 160, 205-206
Judge Advocate General's Corps, U.S. Army, 5, 5*n*, 11, 243
  formation of, 5
Judge Advocate General's Corps, U.S. Navy; creation of, 85
Judge Advocate General's School, U.S. Army, 60
Judge Advocate of the Army, 5*n*

Kall, Capt Charles J., **67**, 100, **100**, 101, 103
Karch, BGen Frederick J., 2, 18, **19**
Kavanaugh, Sgt Larry A., **220**; United States v., 218-19
Kaveney, Capt Francis J., 143
Kaye, Maj Ronald J., 60, **95**
Keenan, PFC Charles W., United States v., 79-81, 81*n*
Keever, Maj Charles J. "Chuck", 28, **28**; LtCol, 48
Keith, Capt Philip S., **93**, **95**
Keller, 1stLt P. Keith, **95**
Kelley, Capt Edward F., 196*n*
Kelley, LtCol Paul X., 37; Col, 167, 169; Gen, 125, 216, 229, 241
Kent, Maj Brian B., 16, 100, **101**; LtCol, **173**
Keys, Capt James E., JAGC, USN, **33**
Khe Sanh, 65, 108-109
Kier, MajGen Avery R., 9, 10*n*, 50, 84*n*
Killen, Sgt James W., United States v., 1
King, 1stLt Thomas A., 113
King, Capt Adrian R., **131**
King, Capt David B., **71**, **97**
King, Col Archibald, USA, 243
King, Maj James P., 19, **20**, 31; LtCol, **127**, **131**, **143**, 183, 197; Col, 199; BGen, 130, 211
Kirkpatrick, GySgt William S., 41, **41**, **86**; 2dLt, 42
Kisgen, Col James T., 84*n*
Klukas, Capt Jerome R., 92
Korean War, 4
Korson, LCpl G. E., 98
Kress, Capt Peter N., 2, **3**, 15-18, **19**; LtCol 189, 198-99, 202, 213, **213**, 214
Krichten, LCpl Michael S., United States v., 175-76, 183-84
Krouse, Capt Gale E., JAGC, USN, **73**
Krulak, LtGen Victor H., **20**, 34, 56, 59, 74-75, **75**, 111, 114, 173
Kyle, MajGen Wood B., 54

Laine, LtCol Elliott R., Jr., **136**, 221, 222*n*; Col, 134
Landon, Lt Walter J., JAGC, USN, **79**
Lane, Capt Richard D., 91, **95**, **157**
Laos, 35

LaPadre, Capt Carter, 223
Larkin, Asst General Counsel of DOD Felix E., 6
Larouche, LtCol Charles R., 42-43, **43**, 44, **44**, 45, 47, **47**, 59, **67**, 68
Latney, Merchant Seaman James H., United States v., 99-102, 167
Laveroni, Capt Paul J., 189, 206, 209-10, **210**, 211
Law center, 146
Law officer, 6, 51, 105-106, 125, 198
Lawrence, Maj James F., Jr., 8-9; BGen, 83-84, **84**, 120, 216
Lawrence, Cdr Keith B., JAGC, USN, 186, 201
Lawyers' Military Defense Committee, 206
Le Chi Cuong, Mayor of Da Nang, 28, 61, 74
Lee, 1stLt Robert M., **95**
Legal administrative officers, 146
Legal assistance, 15-16, 23, 44, 59, 63, 68, 92, 96, 108, 109, 158, 214, 218
Legal status of American civilians in Vietnam, 14
LeGear, Capt Daniel H., Jr., **131**, 144, 149, 151, 159, 183, **184**, **185**, 198
Lehman, Secretary of the Navy John, 229
Lehnert, 1stLt Robert C. "Curly", **12**, **70**; Col, 69-70, **73**, **89**, 96, 97, 99, **122**, 142, **173**, 174
Levin, Capt Michael J., **166**
Levine, 1stLt Joel, 203
Lewis, SFC Robert, USA, 226
Lewy, Guenter, 138-39, 215, 242
Licciardo, LCpl Anthony, Jr., United States v., 112-13
Lopez, GySgt Joseph, 124
Lowe, John, 227, **228**
Lucy, LtCol Robert M., 143, **143**; Col, 129, **131**, 144-45, 164, 172, **173**, 174, 179, 182, 197-98, 205-206, 208, 241, 244
Lynch, Capt John, 201

MAAG. (*See also* U.S. Military Advisory Assistance Group)
MacConnell, Capt Robert M., 208
Magistri Militum, 2
Mallery, Maj Joseph A., Jr., **122**; LtCol, 163, **173**, 218
Malone, Maj Donald E., 116
Mann, LtCol Clyde R., 89, **89**, 89*n*, 90; Col, 143; BGen, 223
Mapp v. Ohio, 125
Marijuana
  detecting dogs, 127
  offenses, 68
  use, 74, 124, 126, 140
    effect on discipline, 126-27
    problems in prosecution for, 74-75
    testing for, 74
Marine Corps Air Station, Futema, Okinawa, 2
Marine Corps Commands and Units
  Headquarters Marine Corps, 5, 10, 12
    Judge Advocate Division, 13, 60n, 83-84, 165
      creation of, 120
    Personnel Department/Division, Discipline Branch, 11, 13-14, 34, 57, 83-84
      disestablishment of, 120
  3d Engineer Battalion, 37
  Air
    1st Marine Aircraft Wing, 15-16, 18-20, 28-29, 35, 53, 59, 69
    3d Marine Aircraft Wing, 16
  Ground
    III Marine Amphibious Force (III MAF), 18-20, 35, 39, 59,

63, 88
  Force Logistic Command, 32, 42, 44, 50, 53, 69, 96
  Force Logistic Support Group, 42
  9th Marine Expeditionary Brigade (9th MEB), 2, 16, 18-19
  1st Marine Division, 27, 37, 40, 42, 59, 67
    Legal Office, 34, 41, 63
  3d Marine Division, 2, 15-16, 18, 27-28, 31, 35, 42, 59, 63, 65, 67-68, 70, 142, 147-48
    Legal Office, 24
  3d Marine Division (Rear), 20
  Task Force X-Ray, 20, 26, 42, 59, 63, 88
  3d Marines
    1st Battalion, 2
    3d Battalion
      Company M, 33
  4th Marines
    2d Battalion, 37
      Company H, 76
  5th Marines
    1st Battalion, 53
  7th Marines
    1st Battalion
      Company B, 174-75
      Company D, 82
  9th Marines, 2
    2d Battalion
      Company E, 23
  12th Marines
Headquarters Battalion, 29
Marine Corps Human Relations Institute, 232
Marshall, Col St.Julien R., 11
Martens, Lt John J., JAGC, USN, 63
Mathews, Capt Patrick H., 161
Mathey, 1stLt Warren S., 144-45
Maurer, 1stLt Jeffery W., **95**
Maushart, LCpl James A., United States v., 112
May, Capt James S., 37; Col, **38**, 229
McAdam, Capt William H., Jr., 95
McCain, Adm John S., Jr., USN, **121**
McCollum, Capt Michael G., 152, 156, **157**, 159-60
McConnell, LtCol Daniel F., 22, 76; Col, 192-93, **193**, 213
McDevitt, RAdm Joseph B., JAGC, USN, 87, 156
McGhee, LCpl Marion, United States v., 33-34
McGrath, LCpl Thomas, 156, 158
McGuinn, Capt Martin G., Jr., **127**, **143**
McHenry, Maj James P., 119
McLean, 1stLt Ronald W., 132
McMath, Capt Sandy S., **95**, 112
McNamara, Secretary of Defense Robert S., 65, 73
"McNamara Wall", 65, 88
"Mere gook" rule, 138-39
Merrill, Capt Michael P., 184, **185**, 198
Metzger, Capt Dirk T., **203**
Meyers, Col Bruce F., 106*n*
Meyers, Sgt Harvey E., 175
Mielczarski, Maj Anthony F., 237
Mihalak, CWO Steven J., 116
Milano, Capt Louis L., JAGC, USN, **73**
Milici, Capt John A., 149
Military judge, 125
Military Justice Act

  of 1968, 124-26, 146, 155, 158, 203
  of 1983, 244
Miller, Capt Dale W., 227
Miller, LtCol Edison W., **221**, United States v., 219-20
Miller, Richard, 186, **188**
Miner, Capt Larry J., **67**
Miranda v. Arizona, 125
Mitchell, Capt Charles H., 69, 78, 96, **97**; Col, 243-44
Moats, Capt John D., **143**, 149
Moore, 1stLt David G., 94; Capt, **96**
Moore, Capt H. Edward, Jr., **78**, 87, 103
Moore, Col Richard G., 218
Morgan, Capt Horace H., JAGC, USN, **73**
Morgan, Edward M., 6
Morgan Committee, 6
Motelewski, Maj Joseph R., 8; Col, 92, **93**, 93-94, 105, **122**, 147, 230, 240-41
Moynihan, Senator Daniel Patrick, 73
Muench, Capt Richard A., 152, **153**, **204**
Mulroney, Col Peter J., 103
Murphy, 1stLt Patricia A., 57*n*, 60*n*; Capt, 121, 121*n*, 207
Murphy, Capt Edward L., 136
Murphy, Capt William A., **12**
Murphy, Lt Bruce C., JAGC, USN, **55**
Murray, Maj Michael Patrick, 78, 96, 98; LtCol, 218, 226, 237-39
Muse, RAdm George R., JAGC, USN, 85
Muse Committee, 85
My Lai, 111, 190

Nalty, Bernard C., 128-29, 232
Napier, PFC David, United States v., 134-38
National Defense Establishment, 6
Naughton, 1stLt Michael J., **79**
Naval Courts and Boards, 3*n*, 4, 5, 70, 124
Naval Justice School, 11, **12**, 25, 43-44, 100, 144
Naval Supplement to the Manual for Courts Martial (1951), 6*n*
Navy Board of Review, 72
Navy-Marine Corps Trial Judiciary Activity, Da Nang, 51, 205
Neely, Maj Ives W., 126
Neil, 2dLt Michael I., 82-83, **83**; 1stLt, 244; BGen, 83*n*
Neville, Col Robert B., 13, 34, 44, 51, 57, **57**, 59, 60, **61**, 61*n*, 241, 243
Nguyen Chien Dau. (*See also* United States v. PFC Robert R. Garwood.)
Nickerson, LtGen Herman, Jr., 129, **130**, 142
Niles, Lt John G., JAGC, USN, **154**
North, 1stLt Oliver L., 175, 188, **188**
Nunnery, Pvt Nolan J., 114, 116

Oberhansly, 1stLt Curtis K., 119
O'Brian, Lt(jg) Keith G., JAGC, USN, 18
O'Byrne, Capt William J., **203**
O'Connell, Capt James R., 223
Office of Civil Operations, Saigon, 48
Ohman, Robert, 80
O'Kelley, Capt George H., 195, 206, 207
Okinawa, 18
Oleszycki, Capt Charles R., 237
Oliver, LtCol Verne L. "Bubs", 29, 68, 96, 99, 103; Col, 51, 100, **122**, **173**

INDEX

Olshin, Capt Lewis R., 227, **228**
Olson, Maj Curtis W., 49, **49**, 80, **80**, **122**, **173**, 196, 212, 242
Operations in Vietnam
    Checkers, 88
    Cochise, 63
    De Soto, 63
    Dewey Canyon, 134, 142, 147, 221
    Kentucky, 147
    Lafayette, 63
    Medina, 65
    Mixmaster, 174
    Praire II, 65
    Praire III, 65
    Prairie IV, 65
    Shufly, 15, 16
    Stone, 63
    Taylor Common, 142
    Union II, 65
    Virginia Ridge, 147
Ordinances of Armies (British), 2
Ostby, Col John L., 65, **73**, **88**, 89, **89**
Owens, BGen Robert C., Jr., 60

Padden, Capt Theodore J., 149, 151, **185**
Padalino, BGen Mauro J., 192
Palmer, Capt William D., 223
Palmer, Harry, 186, **188**
Palmer, LtGen David, USA, 167
Papa, Capt John S., 126, 132, **192**
Parker, Capt Daniel, Jr., 234, 237
Parks, Capt W. Hays, 13, 74, 90, 109, 113, 143, 161, 206, 208
Partyka, Cpl Michael J., 77
Pate, Cpl Ronald A., 193
Patterson, Capt Charles E., 66, 70, **95**
Peltzer, Col Vernon A. "Vap", 27, 30-31, 35, 56, **56**
Pentalateral Agreement, 14-15, 99, 168
Perkins, Capt "B" Raymond, JAGC, USN, 223
Petersen, LtCol Arthur R., 156, 158; Col, **122**, **173**, 191-92, 205-206, 208, 242
Phalin, 1stLt M. Kevin, **95**
Phoi Hoi, 50
Phu Bai, 20, 35, 42, 44, 56, 59, 65, 68
Pierce, MSgt Len E., 40, 42, **86**; CWO 2, **153**, 155, **155**, **162**, 191; CWO 4, 87
Platoon Leaders' Class (Law), 13, 34, 87, 121, 156
Platoon Leaders' Class (PLC), 13
Platt, BGen Jonas M., 73
Popper, Col Harry S., Jr., 29, **29**, 30, **30**, 35
Post, Capt John N., 97
Potter, PFC John D., Jr., United States v., 53-54
Preate, Capt Robert A., 207
Price, Capt William A., 196
Prisoners of war, 39
Pritchard, Capt Donald R., 71, **72**, **97**, **105**
Prohaska, LCpl Ronald B., 149-50
Project 100,000, 73-74, 124, 173, 203. (*See also* Category IV personnel)
Prosise, Capt Richard L., 234, 236, 237, **239**, 239-40
Prugh, Col George S., USA, 18, 99; MajGen, 14, 160, 170, 198, 210, 219, 242, **242**, 243-44

Quang Tri, 68

Rachow, Capt Ronald C., 120, **120**
Racial conflict, 34, 124, 127-31, 140-41, 171, 231, 238
    as reported in Subversive Activity Reports, 129-30, 171
    Watch Committees, 129-30
Ranger (CV-61), 155
Red Book. (*See also* Manual for Courts-Martial)
Reese, Cpl Ronald J., United States v., 140
Reilly, Capt John J., **157**
Reitz, MSgt Cecil, 152
Remey, Capt William B., 3; Col, **4**
Repose (AH 16), 135
Retention of lawyers, 240-41
Revolutionary Development, 48
Reynolds, Capt John C., **153**
Riate, SSgt Alfonso R., **219**, United States v., 218
Rich, Capt Michael E., **86**, 87*n*
Richard B. Anderson (DD 786), 167
Ricketts, Capt E. Ronald, **203**
Riser, SSgt Jerome E., 44
Roberts, Capt Ross T., **62**, 77
Roberts, Pvt Michael A., 119
Robertshaw, LtGen Louis B., 165
Robertson, MajGen Donn J., 89
Robertson, RAdm Horace B., Jr., JAGC, USN, 219
Rockpile, the, 65
"Rocks and Shoals", 3-4. (*See also* Articles for the Government of the Navy.)
Rodsky, Capt Terrance B., **192**
Rohweller, 1stLt Robert T. "Tim", 134, 134-35, **136**, 138
Rose, Sgt William L., 214; SSgt 200
Rose Garden, the, 233-34, 236-39
Rothmeier, Lt Kenneth, MC, USN, **192**
Roundtree, Maj Neal T., 218
Rounsaville, Capt Keith E., 234
Roux, Capt Frank G., Jr., 183
Rucker, Lt Jerry D., JAGC, USN, 119
Rudy, Lt Allen C., Jr., JAGC, USN, **203**, 214
Rules for the Regulation of the Navy of the United Colonies, 2-3

Sabine, Capt Harry D., **62**, **65**, 81
Saigon, 18, 19, 30
Sanctuary (AH 17), 202
Schermerhorn, 1stLt James M., 144
Scherr, Col Robert A., 13
Schneider, Capt Mahlon C., **95**
Schrunk, Capt Michael D., **96**
Schwarz, Pvt Michael A., **184**, United States v., 175-78, 181-84, 186, 189
Seabaugh, Col Paul W., **113**, **122**, 142, **143**
Seay, Capt James E. L., 226
Secrest, Capt Lawrence W., **203**, 214
Sevier, LtCol Charles B., 19-20, **22**, 24, **33**; Col, 27, 30, 35, 54, **55**, 57, 83-85, 120, **122**, 142
Seymour, Cpl Philip A., 37, **38**
Seymour, Sgt R. Thomas, 90
Shank, Col James W., 104, 111
Shannon, Capt James P., 54, **62**, **80**, 81

Sherman, Col Paul D., 11
Sherman, Gen William Tecumseh, USA, 7
Shorstein, Capt Harry L., **95**, 108, **108**, 109
Siems, Capt Dennis H., **78**
Simmons, BGen Edwin H., 88, 170, 172, **212**, 241
Simmons, Maj Roger E., 149, **150**
Simpson, MajGen Ormond R., 131
Skiles, Capt J. Len, 186
Smedley, Cpl Larry E., 83
Smith, Gen Holland M., **10**, 10n
Smith, Pvt Reginald F., United States v., 134-38
Smith, Capt Stanley L., **96**
Smith, Capt Thomas P., Jr., JAGC, USN, **73**
Snedeker, BGen James, 9, 10n
Soc Trang, 15
SOFA. (*See also* Status of Forces Agreement)
Somers, 7-8
Somerville, Cpl Clifford K., United States v., 237
Son Thang (4), 175, **177**, 178-79, **180**, 182, 187-90
Sparkman, LtCol Thomas B., 19, 20
Special court-martial, 22-23, 69, 205
    military judges for, 126
    requirement for lawyers in, 35
Spence, LtCol Charles E., Jr., 69, **71**, 164; Col, **173**
Spencer, Mdn Philip, USN, 7
Staff Legal Officers' Conference, 1966, 45
St.Amour, Maj Paul A. A., 28-29; LtCol, 160, 183-85, 195, 212
Status of Forces Agreement (SOFA), 14
Steele, Maj Orlo K., 48
Steffen, Capt Eugene A., **77**
Steves, Capt Frederick B., **122**
Stewart, Capt Walter A., Jr., **97**
Stipe, Senator Gene, 186-87, **188**
Stockdale, RAdm James B., USN, 219; VAdm, 221, 223, 230
Stockham, Cpl Robert E., 149-50
Stokes, Capt James D., 153, **204**
Strickland, PFC James A., 226
Strongpoint obstacle system, 60. (*See also* "McNamara Wall")
Sullivan, Brendan V., Jr., 211
Summary court-martial, 3, 22
    requirement for lawyers in, 35
Sweeney, Sgt Jon M., **222**, United States v., 221-23, 222n
Switzer, Col Robert E., 227, 229
Szymanski, Lt John S., JAGC, USN, **46**

Talmadge, Senator Herman E., 101
Talty, 2dLt Stephen J., 53-54
Tate, Sgt Richard L., 169, **169**
Taylor, 2dLt John R., 145-46
Taylor, Capt Kenneth T., 37, **38**
Taylor, Vaughn E., 227-28, **228**
Testman, Cpl Leo O., 132
Tet Offensive
    1968, 88-89, 96
    1969, 142
Tetrick, MSgt Harold L., 21, 53-54
Theer, Maj Richard E., 175, 178-79, 181, 188
Thong Tay (1), 174
Thurman, Maj Winn M., 62, 63, **77**
Tiernan, Maj William H. J., 69, 70, 96, **97**, **122**, 142; LtCol, **173**;
    BGen, 69n, 172-73, 231, 241-43

Tifford, Capt Arthur W., **127**, **143**
Timblin, Capt Charles, JAGC, USN, **73**
Tokarz, 1stLt Anthony P., 36-37
Tompkins, MajGen Rathvon McC., 74
Tower, Capt Philip C., 169, 201, 215, **215**
Towers, Capt Richard S., **192**
Tozi, Capt George, 100-101
Trimm, Merchant Seaman Byethe A., 99
Trockman, Howard P., 184
Truesdale, Col Marion G., **122**, 142, **143**, 166, **173**, 191
Twining, Gen Merrill B., 9, 10n
Twitchell, Col John S., 11, 13

Uniform Code of Military Justice, 5-7, 14, 35, 51, 57, 241-43
    amendment of, 12-13
    application to civilians, 100, 168
    ommission of Marine Corps lawyers in, 11-12
United States v.
    Lance Corporal James B. Addison, 193, 196
    Lance Corporal Denzil R. Allen, 111-12
    Private Lester E. Allison, 127n
    Private Martin R. Alvarez, 112-13
    First Lieutenant Lewis R. Ambort, 174-75, 177-79, 183
    Corporal Joseph W. Anderson, Jr., 208-211
    Sergeant Adrian Aragon, 208-11
    Raymond G. Averette, 168
    Private First Class Douglas Beane, 172n
    Lance Corporal John D. Belknap, 112-13
    Private First Class Thomas R. Boyd, 54, 175, 182, 184, 186
    Hospitalman Jon R. Bretag, USN, 53-54
    Private Stephen F. Brice, 119
    Private First Class Robert L. Bright, 37, 39
    Platoon Sergeant Roy E. Bumgarner, USA, 139n
    Private Curtis Crawford, 207-208
    Lance Corporal Stephen D. Crider, 140
    Private Jimmie Dudley, 134-36
    Private Jimmie Dunbar, 161
    Private First Class Donald R. Egan, 134-35, 137
    Lance Coporal Richard E. Eicholtz, 162
    Private Frederick L. Elbert, Jr., 218
    Private First Class Robert R. Garwood, 223-30, 224n
    Private First Class Lucien J. Gonzales, 37, 39
    Private First Class Samuel G. Green, Jr., 175, 179, 182, 186, 198-90
    Private First Class Bobby R. Greenwood, 134-38
    Lance Corporal Andrew M. Harris, Jr., 193-96
    Private First Class Gary O. Harrison, 30
    Private First Class Willie Harrison, 156
    Private Gary A. Hendricks, 169-70
    Private Randell D. Herrod, 175-77, 179, 182-83, 186-90, 188-89
    Private First Class Eugene R. Hofstetler, 161-62
    Lance Corporal Joseph L. Jones, 193-94, 196
    Sergeant Larry A. Kavanaugh, 218-19
    Private First Class Charles W. Keenan, 79-81, 81n
    Sergeant James W. Killen, 149-50
    Lance Corporal Michael S. Krichten, 175-76, 183-84
    Merchant Seaman James H. Latney, 99-102, 167-68
    Lance Corporal Anthony Licciardo, Jr., 112-13
    Lance Corporal James A. Maushart, 112
    Lance Corporal Marion McGrath, 33-34

INDEX

Lieutenant Colonel Edison W. Miller, 219-21
Private First Class David Napier, 134-38
Corporal Ronald J. Reese, 140
Staff Sergeant Alfonso R. Riate, 218
Private Michael A. Schwarz, 175-78, 183-84, 186, 189
Private Reginald F. Smith, 134-38
Corporal Clifford K. Somerville, 237
Sergeant Jon M. Sweeney, 221-22, 222*n*, 223
Private First Class Robert J. Vickers, 112-13
Private Calvin L. White, 119
Captain Walter E. Wilbur, USN, 219, 221
U.S. Coast Guard, 6*n*, 7
U.S. Court of Military Appeals, 6-7, 151, 168, 229, 243
U.S. Court of Military Review, 230
U.S. Military Advisory Assistance Group, 14-16

Van Ryzin, 1stLt Peter, 36
Vengrow, Capt Stephen H., **192**, 194
Vesey, Capt Michael C., 237
Vickers, PFC Robert J., United States v., 112-13
Vogel, Sgt Ronald L., United States v., 53-54

Wachsmuth, Capt Robert W., 32, **78**, **97**, 98, **102**, 108
Wallace, Mike, 223
Walling, 1stLt Michael I., **97**
Walt, MajGen Lewis W., 20, 24, 27-28, 34-35; LtGen, 48, 53-54, 56, **57**, 60, 80
Wander, LtCol William W., Jr., **47**, 106; Col, 51
War crimes, 32
Warlow, Capt Michael C., 234
Warner, Secretary of the Navy John, 220
Warnes, Catherine Anne, 148, **149**, 150
Warren, Capt William T., 28
Wartime Legislation Team (WALT), USA, 243-44
Weatherman, Pvt Earl C., 223-24

Webb, 2dLt James H., 128, **129**; Capt, 189-90
Welch, Capt Edwin W., 209
Wensinger, LtGen Walter W., 9, 10*n*
Westmoreland, Gen William C., USA, 74, 88, 126, 242-44
Westmoreland, LtCol William T., Jr., 60, **62**, 63, 65, 79-80, **89**
Wheeler, MajGen Edwin B., **131**, 231
Wheeler, PFC Kenneth, United States v., 23-24
White, LCpl Gene E., 29
White, Pvt Calvin L., United States v., 119
Whiting, Capt William E., **97**
Widdecke, MajGen Charles F., 183, 205
Wieseman, LtGen Frederick L., **3**
Wilbur, Capt Walter E., USN, United States v., 219, 221
Williams, Capt James L., 76, 78, 84
Williams, Capt Robert C., 130, **131**, 182, **182**, **188**
Wilson, LtGen Louis H., Jr., **221**; Gen, 226-27, 231
Wittig, 1stLt Donald E., **62**; Capt, **77**
Wohl, Lt Frank A., JAGC, USN, **153**
Wolfert, Capt Alan R., 163
Wood, Capt W. Mark, 191, **192**, 193-94, 196
Woodruff, 1stLt Frederick C., 18, 39
Wray, LtCol Richard E., **67**, 96
Wright, Capt Teresa J., 228, **229**

Xuan Ngoc (2), 53

Young, Capt Rufus C., **97**, **105**

Ziemann, Maj James R., 42, **44**, 45, **46**, 47
Zoerb, 2dLt Dennis R., **86**
Zonderman, Capt Paul S., 70
Zorack, LtCol John L., **25**, 26, 34, 42, 59, 63, **80**
Zsalman, Lt Robert D., JAGC, USN, 136, **137**